PATERNOSTER BIBLICAL MONOGRAPHS

Congregational Evangelism in Philippians

The Centrality of an Appeal for Gospel Proclamation to the Fabric of Philippians

PATERNOSTER BIBLICAL MONOGRAPHS

Congregational Evangelism in Philippians

The Centrality of an Appeal for Gospel Proclamation to the Fabric of Philippians

Mark J. Keown

WIPF & STOCK · Eugene, Oregon

Wipf and Stock Publishers
199 W 8th Ave, Suite 3
Eugene, OR 97401

Congregational Evangelism in Philippians
The Centrality of an Appeal for Gospel Proclamation to the Fabric of Philippians
By Keown, Mark J.

ISBN 13: 978-1-60608-475-5
Publication date 2/19/2009
Previously published by Paternoster, 2008

"This Edition Published by Wipf and Stock Publishers
by arrangement with Paternoster"

This book is dedicated to Jesus Christ my Lord and to my wonderful wife Emma and our sensational daughters Gracie, Annie and Esther. Press on to win the prize…

Series Editors

Paternoster Biblical Monographs

Series Preface

One of the major objectives of Paternoster is to serve biblical scholarship by providing a channel for the publication of theses and other monographs of high quality at affordable prices. Paternoster stands within the broad evangelical tradition of Christianity. Our authors would describe themselves as Christians who recognise the authority of the Bible, maintain the centrality of the gospel message and assent to the classical creedal statements of Christian belief. There is diversity within this constituency; advances in scholarship are possible only if there is freedom for frank debate on controversial issues and for the publication of new and sometimes provocative proposals. What is offered in this series is the best of writing by committed Christians who are concerned to develop well-founded biblical scholarship in a spirit of loyalty to the historic faith.

CONTENTS

PREFACE

This work is a revision of my doctoral thesis entitled 'the Missing Imperative: A Discussion of the Absence of a Clear Imperative to Proclaim the Gospel in the Pauline Epistles with Particular Reference to Philippians', which I completed in 2006 through the Australian College of Theology under the supervision of Dr Paul Trebilco. The intention of the study is to explore the question of how Paul envisaged his congregations being involved in evangelistic mission.

Over time the focus of the doctorate became Philippians with an in-depth exploration of texts in Philippians which bear on the question at hand. The book expresses my conviction that essential to Philippians is an appeal to the Philippians to persevere in sharing their faith through lives wholly given over to Christ in the face of resistance and in renewed unity.

It is my hope that this work will continue to stimulate interest in the proclamation of the gospel. In particular, that readers will delve more deeply into the New Testament to see what and how the first Christians shared the Christian message and then to consider how this challenging task should be continued in these perplexing times.

Without the constant encouragement and generosity of my good friend and mentor Dr Paul Trebilco this work would not have happened and for that I am truly grateful. Similarly for the patience of my wife and children, I am filled with gratitude.

Most importantly I thank our triune God for his constant encouragement and inspiration in this work. I pray that it serves to inspire some to take up the task of evangelisation as Paul's imprisonment in Philippi catalysed the Romans (Phil 1:12-14).

Acknowledgements

I want to express my gratitude to all those who helped me at some time or another in the journey of producing this book. To my Mum and Dad, thanks for teaching me to read, to analyse and to love learning. To my wife Emma and my girls Gracie, Annie and Esther, thanks for making so many sacrifices to help me complete this work; I truly love you all. Thanks to those pastors and evangelists who have been used by God to plant in me a passion for evangelism and learning including Rev Graeme Murray who led me to Christ, Sean and Gill Pawson who discipled me and taught me to share the faith; Peter Robertson, Gerald Bradley, Rev Jim Wallace and others. A special thanks to the lecturers of BCNZ who showed me the path to scholarship and exegesis; namely, Dr Chris Marshall, Rev Dr John Roxborough, Dr Bill Osborne, Rev Stuart Lange, Dr Merv Coates, Edward Sands, Dr John Hitchen and others. Thanks to my good friends Jack Zoutenbier, Rob Winthrop, Greg Fleming and Adrienne Hunt for your constant encouragement. Finally, a huge thanks to my supervisor and friend Rev Dr Paul Trebilco without whose encouragement and generosity I would not have ended this challenging journey. Shalom.

ABBREVIATIONS

AB	*Atlantic Baptist*
ABC	Anchor Bible Commentary
ABD	*Anchor Bible Dictionary*
ABR	*Australian Biblical Review*
AJBS	African Journal of Biblical Studies
ANTC	Abingdon New Testament Commentary
AnBib	Analecta Biblica
BA	*Biblical Archaeologist*
BDAG	W. Bauer, W. F. Arndt, F.W. Gingrich and F.W. Danker, *Greek-English Lexicon of the New Testament and other Early Christian literature*, 2nd ed.
BBR	*Bulletin for Biblical Research*
BECNT	Baker Exegetical Commentary on the New Testament
Bib	*Biblica*
BibRev	*Bible Review*
BJRL	*Bulletin of the John Rylands Library*
BNTC	Black's New Testament Commentaries
BSac	*Bibliotheca Sacra*
BST	The Bible Speaks Today
BT	*Bible Translator*
BTB	*Biblical Theology Bulletin*
BZ	*Biblische Zeitschrift*
CBC	The Cambridge Bible Commentary
CBQ	*Catholic Biblical Quarterly*
CBNT	*Coniectanea Biblica, New Testament Series*
CNTC	Calvin's New Testament Commentaries
CPNIVC	The College Press NIV Commentary
CV	*Communio Viatorum*
CTR	*Criswell Theological Review*
DPL	*Dictionary of Paul and his letters*
DS	*Daughters of Sarah*
EBC	Expositors Bible Commentary
EEC	Eerdmans Critical Commentary
EDNT	Exegetical Dictionary of the New Testament
EC	Epworth Commentaries
EPC	Epworth Preacher's Commentaries
EGT	Expositors Greek Testament
EQ	*Evangelical quarterly*
ExpTim	*Expository Times*
FM	*Faith and Mission*
FNT	*Filología Neotestamentaria*

FRLANT	Forschungen zur Religion und Literatur des Alten und Neuen Testaments
HBT	*Horizons in Biblical Theology*
HDB	Hastings Dictionary of the Bible
HTKNT	Herders Theologische Kommentar zum Neuen Testament
HTR	*Harvard Theological Review*
HNT	*Hanbuch zum Neuen Testament*
IB	Interpreters Bible.
IBS	*Irish Biblical Studies*
ICC	International Critical Commentary
IBC	Interpretation: a Bible Commentary for Teaching and Preaching
IVPNTCS	The IVP New Testament Commentary Series
JBC	The Jerome Bible Commentary
JBL	*Journal of Biblical Literature*
JCBRF	*Journal of the Christian Brethren Research Fellowship*
JETS	*Journal of the Evangelical Theological Society*
JFSR	*Journal of Feminist Studies in Religion*
JGWR	*Journal of Gender in World Religions*
JSNT	*Journal for the Study of the New Testament*
JSNTSS	Journal for the Study of the New Testament Supplement Series
JTS	*Journal of Theological Studies*
Jos. *Ap.*	Josephus, *Against Apion*
Jos. *Ant.*	Josephus, *Jewish Antiquities*
Jos. *War*	Josephus, *The Jewish War*
Jos. *Life*	Josephus, *The Life*
LTJ	*Lutheran Theological Journal*
M-M	J.H. Moulton and G. Milligan, *The Vocabulary of the Greek New Testament*
MNTC	Moffatt New Testament Commentary
NAC	The New American Commentary
NCBC	The New Century Bible Commentary
NIBC	New International Bible Commentary
NICNT	New International Commentary on the New Testament.
NICOT	The New International Commentary on the Old Testament
NIGTC	New International Greek Testament Commentary
NIDNTT	*The New International Dictionary of New Testament Theology*
NIVAC	The New International Version Application Commentary
NovT	*Novum Testamentum*
NovTSup	Novum Testamentum Supplement
NTC	New Testament Commentary
NTD	Das Neue Testament Deusch
NTS	*New Testament Studies*

NTM	New Testament Message Series
PG	Patrologia Graeca, ed. J.P. Migne
PNTC	Pillar New Testament Commentary
ResQ	*Restoration Quarterly*
RevExp	*Review and Expositor*
SBT	*Studies in Biblical Theology*
SBLDS	Society for Biblical Literature Dissertation Series
SNTSMS	Society for the New Testament studies monograph series
SNTW	Studies of the New Testament and its World
SPS	Sacra Pagina Series
StudRel	*Studies in Religion/Sciences Religieuses*
TDNT	*Theological Dictionary of the New Testament.*
TH	Théologie Historique
THNT	Theologischer Handkommentar zum Neuen Testament
TJT	*Toronto Journal of Theology*
TynB	*Tyndale Bulletin*
TNTC	Tyndale New Testament Commentaries
WC	Westminster Commentaries
WTJ	*Westminster Theological Journal*
WUNT	Wissenschaftliche Untersuchungen zum Neuen Testament
WZUJ	Wissenschaftliche Zeitschrift der Universität Jena
WBC	Word Bible Commentary
ZNW	*Zeitschrift für neutestamentliche Wissenschaft*

CHAPTER 1

General Introduction

It was a shock to me in my early theological study to hear that Paul gives no direct appeal for general evangelism to his congregations.[1] As I had heard innumerable sermons assuming this very thing and had preached such messages myself, this led to some serious self-questioning. Initially I felt a sense of liberation, thinking that perhaps these reticent congregations are off the hook.

My initial approach led me to take the line that Paul did not envisage his congregations being proactively evangelistic but merely supporting the specialists financially, prayerfully and in ethical and apologetic witness. During my research however, I came across W.P. Bowers' article 'Church and mission in Paul.'[2] As I read the article, I became rather disturbed, since his case did not seem to be convincing. As I examined his argument more deeply, I determined that his exegetical conclusions lacked in-depth analysis. I went back to these texts and this work was formed.

Initially, I intended to discuss all relevant texts within the Pauline corpus. However, over time I narrowed the discussion down and have limited myself to the book of Philippians, which introduces most of the issues that I believe are relevant to this discussion. My essential argument in what follows is that the notion that Paul's theology of church and mission limited the involvement of the church to finance, prayer, apologetic and ethical witness is flawed. The book is an attempt to argue that, essential to Paul's understanding of evangelistic proclamatory mission, was his desire that the church continue this work in their own towns and regions.

I believe this is clearest in Philippians although glimpses are seen throughout the Pauline epistles. In terms of Philippians, I will suggest that 'corporate general proclamatory evangelism' is essential to the fabric and rhetoric of the letter.[3] I will seek to demonstrate how this element intersects with other key themes throughout the letter.

As such this book is a discussion of the absence of an explicit imperative for members of the Pauline congregations to proclaim the gospel to unbelievers in

---

[1] Assuming authorship which is disputed, the only such direct appeal is to the individual co-worker Timothy in 2 Tim 4:1-5. For my view of authorship see later in assumptions.

[2] W.P. Bowers, 'Church and Mission in Paul', *JSNT* 44 (1991): 89-111.

[3] See below section 4 for definitions.

the Pauline Epistles. It falls within the framework of Pauline theology of mission, exploring one small but significant element of Paul's missiological theology, strategy, and praxis. That is, I am concerned to examine Paul's theology and practice of evangelism with particular reference to the role of the church. In terms of Paul's ecclesiology then, I am asking 'did Paul expect his converts and congregations to embark on their own evangelistic program?' Or again, 'did Paul confine evangelism to himself, apostles and/or co-workers?' These questions take one into the arena of pneumatology and leadership, asking how Paul's perception of charismata and leadership impact on his understanding of individual and/or corporate involvement in evangelism. My purpose is to examine to some degree or other these questions with a study focussed on Philippians whilst touching on other relevant Pauline passages.

I consider that this discussion is important for a number of reasons. First, due to the relative neglect in recent scholarship of the questions, 'who' did the evangelism in the early church and how the church was involved.[4] Secondly, I consider it to be self-evident that any discussion of Paul's mission strategy and thought should negotiate the important question of the manner in which the church was to be involved. Thirdly, if indeed there is an almost naïve assumption among many writers that the imperative exists, then it is essential that this be questioned and either rejected or a solid platform for it established.[5] Fourthly, I consider that this work will bring fresh insight and clarity to an understanding of Philippians and in particular, the importance of general evangelism and its interaction with other important themes within the letter. Finally, I hope to contribute to contemporary evangelistic theory, giving a stronger basis for suggesting evangelism lies at the heart of the mission of the church.[6]

The Current State of the Discussion

A review of the literature indicates that there are two essential schools of thought concerning the role of the church in evangelistic mission in Paul. First, there are those who argue that Paul did not envisage his congregations

[4] I.H. Marshall, 'Who Were the Evangelists?' in J. Ådna and H. Kvalbein, *The Mission of the Early Church to Jews and Gentiles*. WUNT 127 (Tübingen: Mohr [Siebeck], 2000), 252. This is currently being corrected through a number of works I will note in a review of the current state of the debate below.

[5] Similarly W.P. Bowers, *Studies in Paul's Understanding of his Mission* (unpublished Ph.D. dissertation, Cambridge, 1976), 104; 'Church': 89-90 concerning modern literature. I consider that this work falls into the category of aspects of charismatic theology that need a more extensive analysis as suggested by T. Smail, 'The Cross and the Spirit: Towards a Theology of Renewal' in T. Smail, A. Walker and N. Wright, *Charismatic Renewal* (London: SPCK, 1995), 49-52.

[6] Marshall, 'Evangelists?' 258 and Bowers, 'Church': 110 both note that this is a separate but connected question.

consciously seeking to evangelise their contexts through the proclamation of the gospel. Rather, they suggest Paul's emphasis was the creation of Christian communities that would support the Pauline mission with finance, prayer, social integration, public worship, ethical, apologetic witness and not proactive evangelism. Secondly, there are those who not only accept these lines of mission are apparent in Paul, but argue that Paul did want his congregations to proactively proclaim the gospel within their regions. I will look briefly at some of the main contributors to the discussion on each side.

Those That See the Church as Responsive in Terms of Proclamatory Evangelism

The aforementioned position is upheld by a number of scholars[7] including A.J. Hultgren,[8] W.P. Bowers,[9] D. Bosch[10] and J.P. Dickson.[11]

Arland J. Hultgren proposes an eschatological understanding to the question. He believes that Paul's imminent expectation of the *Parousia* precludes him from expecting all to hear the gospel individually.[12] He also sees Paul's congregations not as mission centres, but as the first fruits of the harvest of nations, representative of the whole.[13] He explains that Paul's desire to go to Spain is due to his goal of establishing congregations in each geographical nation.[14]

In light of this he interprets Romans 15:14-29 in geographical terms i.e. Paul has completed his ministry so that there is no room in which to proclaim from Illyricum to Jerusalem, in that he has planted a church in each nation. Hultgren does not discuss at all the possible evangelisation of the hinterlands. He argues

---

[7] R. Banks, *Paul's Idea of Community* (Exeter: Paternoster Press, 1980), 161-164; R.Y.K. Fung, 'Body of Christ', in *DPL*, 81; E. Ellis, *Pauline Theology: Ministry and Society* (Grand Rapids: Eerdmans, 1989), 14. J.C. Beker, *Paul the Apostle: the Triumph of God in Life and Thought* (Augsburg: Fortress Press, 1980), 306 suggests 'it is interesting that Paul does not give the mission of the church a more important role than the unity of the church. Although he is occasionally concerned with the effect of the church on outsiders (Gal 6:10; 1 Cor 10:32; 14:23-25), there is no conscious emphasis on public relations as, for instance, in 1 Peter (1 Pet 1:12; 3:15-17; but cf. Rom 12:17-21; 13:1-7; Phil 1:12-14);' N. Elliott, *Liberating Paul: The Justice of God and the Politics of the Apostle* (Maryknoll: Orbis, 1994), 197.

[8] A.J. Hultgren, *Paul's Gospel and Mission* (Philadelphia: Fortress Press, 1985).

[9] Bowers, *Studies*, 104-121; 'Church': 89-111. Surprisingly Bowers pays little attention to this important question in 'Mission', in *DPL*, 608-619.

[10] D. Bosch, *Transforming Mission* (New York: Orbis Books, 1992).

[11] J.P. Dickson, *Mission-Commitment in Ancient Judaism and in the Pauline Communities*. WUNT 2 (Tübingen: J.C.B. Mohr [Paul Siebeck], 2003).

[12] Hultgren, *Gospel*, 144.

[13] Hultgren, *Gospel*, 144.

[14] Hultgren, *Gospel*, 134-135.

that the only way to comprehend what Paul has written is that Paul does not think in terms of individual persons but of nations.[15]

W. Paul Bowers begins with the 'common assumption in much of the modern literature' that Paul's statement in Romans 15:19b, 'so that from Jerusalem and as far round as Illyricum I have fully preached the gospel of Christ', refers to the completion of his task of 'creating mature centres for the dissemination of the gospel land by land throughout the area.'[16] In other words Paul wanted his congregations to continue the Pauline evangelistic mission.

Bowers challenges the reliability of this assumption asking the question: 'what is the relation, in Paul's thought, of church and mission?'[17] Bowers begins by outlining under three categories the main Pauline texts which seem to indicate that Paul 'could see his churches as independent instruments of active mission such as he was engaged in', and then critiques the evidence.[18]

First, he questions the notion of 'evangelistic mission as a natural corollary of Paul's own missionary commitments.'[19] Bowers notes Paul's appeals to his congregations to imitate his own example that included 'exhortation to mission' and particularly 1 Cor 9:1-11:1. Secondly, he comments on the context of 2 Cor 5:18 in which Paul states, 'we are ambassadors for Christ.' It is set in the context of Paul's previous statement that 'we have been reconciled through Christ' and that 'for us' Christ has been made sin.[20] These together give the impression of an inclusive mission. In his evaluation however, Bowers contends that Paul's appeals for his converts to imitation (especially 1 Cor 11:1) refer, not to evangelistic outreach, but to a life of voluntary self-renunciation within the Christian church. The 'we' references of 2 Cor 5:18 are not to be understood as inclusive but, rather, set against the 'you' i.e. the Corinthian congregation.[21]

Secondly, Bowers looks at Paul's concept of a numerically increasing church. Here Bowers discusses the assumption that Paul's use of the building-metaphor (1 Cor 3:9b-15), and particularly the church as body, includes the notion of numerical growth (cf. Eph 4:16).[22] In regard to references to the church as a building Bowers responds: 'the church is the object, not the agency, of such growth.'[23] He argues: 'evangelistic activity by the church to bring about

[15] Hultgren, *Gospel*, 137.

[16] Bowers, *Studies*, 104; see also 'Church': 89-90. See note 1 for a list of works reflecting this assumption.

[17] Bowers, *Studies*, 104; see also 'Church': 90.

[18] Bowers, *Studies*, 104-19 (quote 118-119); see also 'Church': 90-101.

[19] Bowers, *Studies*, 104.

[20] Bowers, *Studies*, 104-5; see also 'Church': 91.

[21] Bowers, *Studies*, 106-110; see also 'Church': 92-5.

[22] Bowers, *Studies*, 105-6; see also 'Church': 92.

[23] Bowers, 'Church': 95. For an extensive defence of Bowers' conviction that the establishment of strong local churches and not the centrifugal mission of the church was the goal of Paul see Bowers, *Studies*, 82-103 and W.P. Bowers, 'Fulfilling the Gospel:

such growth is not suggested in this passage.'[24] In regard to the body metaphor (Eph 4:12-16; Col 2:19), Bowers contends that 'it is far from clear, however, that this growth includes the growth of enlargement (by accessions) in addition to the growth of maturation (by development).'[25] He argues that growth by evangelism is at best a mere possibility. He writes, 'it appears, then, that in the Pauline imagery of the church as building and as body there is no clearly expressed notion of that church as an active instrument of independent mission.'[26]

Thirdly, he examines examples of churches involved in missionary outreach. Here Bowers notes particularly the Thessalonian (1 Thess 1:8), Roman (Rom 1:8), Corinthian (2 Cor 3:2), Philippian (Phil 2:15, 16) and Colossian churches (Col 4:5).[27] In response, Bowers argues that the Thessalonian and Romans' references are to be interpreted passively; i.e. referring not to outward mission to the surrounding contexts, but as references to the spread of reports of these churches.[28] Further, he reads πάντων ἀνθρώπων of 2 Cor 3:2 as metaphorical and not missionary.[29] He prefers to render λόγον ζωῆς ἐπέχοντες as 'holding fast' rather than 'holding forth' in relation to 'the word of life' removing any missionary appeal from Phil 2:15, 16.[30]

Finally, he notes Paul's appeal in Col 4:5-6 to believers to conduct themselves wisely toward outsiders and making good use of opportunities. He sees the exhortation as straightforward: 'it is a ministry of attraction and responsiveness rather than one of deliberate outreach and active solicitation. If it may be put that way, it is a stationary rather than a mobile witness. But it is a witness.'[31]

Bowers suggests Paul's appeals for prayer and financial support also lend support to his contention that Paul gave no thought to churches initiating their own independent mission. Rather, the churches were to support Paul's mission.[32] Bowers also notes the inclusion of other individuals in mission did not suggest that his teams functioned as a church nor that his churches were

---

The Scope of the Pauline Mission', *JETS* 30/2 (1987): 185-198. Bowers suggests that the goal of Paul's mission was three-fold: 1) Evangelism i.e. preaching the gospel for the purpose of creating churches; 2) Church planting; 3) Nurturing Emerging Churches. He concludes that the primary goal of Paul's mission was not preaching but the establishment of new strong congregations. When he writes in Rom 15:19 suggesting that his work is fulfilled he means that viable settled churches exist in these areas.

[24] Bowers, *Studies*, 110; 'Church': 96.

[25] Bowers, *Studies*, 110; 'Church': 96.

[26] Bowers, *Studies*, 112; 'Church': 97.

[27] Bowers, *Studies*, 106; 'Church': 92.

[28] Bowers, *Studies*, 112-4; 'Church': 98-99.

[29] Bowers, *Studies*, 115; 'Church': 100.

[30] Bowers, *Studies*, 115-116; 'Church': 100-01.

[31] Bowers, *Studies*, 116-17; 'Church': 101.

[32] Bowers, 'Church': 102.

missionary work-teams, but that 'mission was for him a function of certain believers.'[33] Hence, Paul viewed positively parallel complementary evangelistic ministries (e.g. 1 Cor 3:4-9) while expressing annoyance at ministries that violated others spheres (e.g. 2 Cor 10:12-16). He contends that 'not only is evidence apparently lacking to indicate that Paul expected his churches, as churches, to engage in active evangelistic outreach ... but also, evidence of any sort is entirely absent to suggest that Paul expected his churches as churches, to duplicate the second aspect of his mission, to engage, that is in the founding of additional churches.'[34] However, Bowers suggests that 'Paul did without question expect his churches to be involved in self-nurture, in building themselves up in the faith.'[35] Bowers concludes by asserting these five points:

i. The goal of Paul's mission was the church.
ii. Paul encouraged the churches to support his own mission with prayer and finance.
iii. The church is to 'facilitate accessions to their community by an attractive behaviour and a responsiveness to inquiries.'[36]
iv. Paul's churches are to take up the role of nurturing their own to maturity.
v. They are to maintain cordial relationships with other churches created in the Pauline mission.[37]

He thus contends that Paul promoted a centripetal mission for the church rather than a centrifugal one, rooted possibly in his Jewish heritage that focussed on individuals and Israel as a living witness, a light to the nations.[38] He suggests that 'missionary activity *may* lie somewhere in the conceptual background, but it is not present, or cannot persuasively be shown to be present, in the text itself; or in the imagery or expression employed *could* have been, but in the particular texts available is not, used to this effect.'[39] He suggests that this should not be made to imply that Paul opposed churches becoming involved in mission. Rather, it is 'more accurate to say simply that a concept of the church at mission failed to take any distinct shape in Paul's thinking' due to Paul's overwhelming personal missionary self-conception.[40] Thus for Bowers, the church is the object of Paul's mission.[41]

At first appearance *David Bosch* seems to critique the assumption referred to by Bowers. Bosch writes:

---

[33] Bowers, 'Church': 103.
[34] Bowers, 'Church': 105.
[35] Bowers, 'Church': 105.
[36] Bowers, 'Church': 107.
[37] Bowers, 'Church': 106-11.
[38] Bowers, *Studies*, 119-20; see also 'Church': 109.
[39] Bowers, *Studies*, 119 (italics his).
[40] W.P. Bowers, 'Paul and Religious Propaganda', *NovT* 22, 4 (1980): 316-323 argues that Paul was unique in his intentional geographical approach to evangelisation.
[41] Bowers, *Studies*, 120-21.

> Paul thinks regionally not ethnically; he chooses cities that have a representative character. In each of these he lays the foundations for a Christian community, *clearly in the hope that, from these strategic centres the gospel will be carried into the surrounding countryside and towns.* And apparently this indeed happened, for in his very first letter written to the believers in Thessalonica less than a year after he first arrived there, he says, 'The word of the Lord [has] sounded forth from you in Macedonia and Achaia (1 Thess 1:8).'[42]

However, further examination suggests that Bosch's analysis of Paul's theology of mission takes a similar line to that of W.P. Bowers.[43] Bosch recognises the imperative of a missionary lifestyle in Paul. He suggests that 'the Christians' lifestyle should not only be exemplary, but also winsome. It should attract outsiders and invite them into the community; the believers practising a missionary lifestyle.'[44] He notes the manner in which the Pauline churches differ from the exclusivity of a sect like Qumran. Paul's communities are characterised by 'a missionary drive, which sees in the outsider a potential insider... Their "exemplary existence" is a powerful magnet that draws outsiders toward the church.'[45]

Consequently, he argues the missionary dimension remains implicit not explicit. They are to be missionary rather than missionising. Bosch notes that 'references to specific cases of direct missionary involvement are rare in the Paul's letters.'[46] He argues that for Paul, 'the primary responsibility of "ordinary" Christians is not to go out and preach, but to support the mission project through appealing conduct and by making "outsiders" feel welcome in their midst.'[47]

Bosch calls the church the 'community of those who glorify God by showing forth his nature and works and by making manifest the reconciliation and redemption God has wrought through the death, resurrection, and reign of Christ' (cf. 2 Cor 5:18-20).[48] The church's primary mission is to be the new redeemed creation, 'its very existence should be for the sake of the glory of God.' This existence will either attract or offend outsiders. 'Where it is attractive, people are drawn into the church, even if the church does not actively "go out" to evangelise them.' Bosch considers this to be the case in 1 Thess 1:8; 2 Cor 3:2; Rom 1:8 and 16:19: 'these comments probably do not suggest that the Thessalonian, Corinthian, and Roman churches are actively involved in direct missionary outreach, but rather that they are "missionary by

---

[42] Bosch, *Transforming*, 130 (italics added).

[43] Bosch, *Transforming*, 123. Unlike Green and other earlier writers he focuses exclusively on the Paul of the seven undisputed Paulines.

[44] Bosch, *Transforming*, 137.

[45] Bosch, *Transforming*, 137.

[46] Bosch, *Transforming*, 137.

[47] Bosch, *Transforming*, 138.

[48] Bosch, *Transforming*, 168.

their very nature", through their unity, mutual love, exemplary conduct, and radiant joy.'[49]

For Bosch however, this does not imply that the church is merely passive and otherworldly. It is to be involved in the world, which means that it is to be missionary: 'Christians are called to practice a messianic lifestyle within the church but also to exercise a revolutionary impact on the values of the world.'[50]

It would seem then that Bosch, like Bowers, holds the view that the ecclesiological missional dimension in Paul is primarily centripetal and attraction-orientated. He recognises the role of the specialists such as the apostles, evangelists and co-workers but sees the function of the congregation as supportive of these missionaries and orientated to winning people to Christ through the attractiveness of their Christian lifestyle and fellowship.

A writer who has recently developed Bowers' view more fully with a full-length work is *John Dickson*.[51] In the light of the views of Bowers, Ollrog, O'Brien and Ware, Dickson focuses his 'study upon the relation between Paul's *converts* to the mission rather than that of the apostle himself.'[52] He examines Paul's 'expectations in regards to mission and seeks to set the discussion 'in the socio-historical context of Judaism in Paul's era' in a detailed manner.[53] As a point of comparison Dickson examines 'the missionary commitment in the various strands of ancient Judaism.'[54] Dickson avoids the 'well-worn' track of whether there was a missionary commitment in Judaism, preferring to focus on this question: 'do Jewish writings of the Second Temple period provide evidence of a commitment, on the part of individuals or communities, to mission?'[55]

In his discussion of Judaism, Dickson notes that there are two positive signs of a mission commitment in Judaism. First, 'a conceptual framework conducive for mission was clearly present amongst some Jews of the period.'[56] This is seen in the presence of both a repudiation of pagan worship and integration with pagan society, 'precisely the attitudes one would expect of those with a mission outlook.'[57] In addition, he argues that the hope that the Gentile world would, together with Israel, in some cases through human agency, turn and serve the one true God, suggests Gentile conversion was viewed positively in

---

[49] Bosch, *Transforming*, 168. One detects here a contradiction between Bosch's earlier comments above concerning 1 Thess 1:8 which suggested more than a passive ecclesiological-missional focus.

[50] Bosch, *Transforming*, 168-169.

[51] Dickson, *Mission-Commitment*.

[52] Dickson, *Mission-Commitment*, 6 (italics his).

[53] Dickson, *Mission-Commitment*, 6.

[54] Dickson, *Mission-Commitment*, 10.

[55] Dickson, *Mission-Commitment*, 13.

[56] Dickson, *Mission-Commitment*, 49.

[57] Dickson, *Mission-Commitment*, 49.

some places.[58]

Secondly, he argues that the sporadic evidence of 'intentional missionising activity' in Jewish literature should not be devalued and suggests at the least, that, 'although an obligation explicitly to proclaim the Torah to Gentiles is absent from the relevant literature, an array of texts, from both Palestinian and Diaspora contexts, do urge their respective Jewish communities to promote the virtues of Judaism amongst pagans.[59] These dimensions include 'ethical apologetic', 'Torah-obedience', 'verbal apologetic', liturgical aspects of life which performed a missionary function so that outsiders may 'observe the true worship of God and thus learn to embrace right piety for themselves.'[60] He argues that some Jewish teachers engaged occasionally in explicit Torah-instruction of Gentiles. Similarly Jewish adherants were expected to promote the Torah in missionary partnership.[61]

Dickson then analyses Paul's use of proclamatory language and particularly εὐαγγελ- language in the letters. He notes its importance to Paul, the active sense of the noun, its importance in Paul's commission and its universal use in Paul as 'primary announcement' of thc message.[62] His discussion leads him to conclude that the language of the gospel is important to Paul in his understanding of mission, that he 'envisaged a significant number of men and women working with him to further the gospel through explicit missionary proclamation.'[63]

He then moves to discuss whether Paul's converts were preachers of the gospel. He explores what he considers the five key texts that could point in the direction of general proclamation.[64] His analysis consistently leads to the rejection of an active interpretation of 1 Thess 1:8,[65] Phil 1:27,[66] Phil 2:15-16,[67] Eph 6:15,[68] 17[69] and Phil 1:3-7.[70] He then discusses a number of other texts which indicate to him that while Paul did not envisage his converts actively engaging in proclamation of the gospel, they were to be partners in the mission.

---

58 Dickson, 49-50. For detail see 13-49.

59 Dickson, 84. For detail see 51-84.

60 Dickson, 84. For detail on 'ethical apologetic' see 51-60; on 'mission-commitment' as prayer see 60-66; 'mission-commitment as verbal apologetic' see 67-73; on 'mission-commitment as public worship' see 74-84.

61 Dickson, *Mission-Commitment*, 85.

62 Dickson, *Mission-Commitment*, 86-94.

63 Dickson, *Mission-Commitment*, 94.

64 Dickson, *Mission-Commitment*, 94-122.

65 Dickson, *Mission-Commitment*, 95-103.

66 Dickson, *Mission-Commitment*, 103-107.

67 Dickson, *Mission-Commitment*, 107-114.

68 Dickson, *Mission-Commitment*, 114-120.

69 Dickson, *Mission-Commitment*, 121-122.

70 Dickson, *Mission-Commitment*, 122-129.

He discusses here Phil 1:3-5[71] and 2 Corinthians 9:13.[72] He concludes that 'Paul usually portrayed believers as passive in relation to the preaching of the gospel.'[73] He argues then, that while Paul was concerned about the heralding the gospel through himself and his colleagues, nowhere are his converts 'portrayed as responsible for or engaged in the task of proclaiming the gospel.'[74] However, he then explains that this 'in no way diminishes the involvement of Paul's converts in mission activities other than 'gospel proclamation.'[75]

He then discusses evidence that certain believers in the Pauline congregations were 'set apart (by Paul or by the congregation itself) for the task of continuing the apostolic gospel-mission.'[76] He discusses references to other gospel workers in Paul who were active preachers of the gospel including Macedonian evangelists inclusive of the 'famous brother' (2 Cor 8:18),[77] 'the apostles of the churches' who he argues are 'Apostles' rather than mere representatives of the church (2 Cor 8:23),[78] Philippian evangelists Euodia, Syntyche, Clement and 'others' (Phil 4:2-3)[79] and evangelists in Rome (Phil 1:14). He argues that the 'brothers' here are missionaries rather than general Christians.[80] He concludes that 'certain men and women among his converts were designated the task of local evangelization with or without a continued apostolic presence.'[81]

Dickson then argues that Paul's central missionary language (εὐαγγελ-) is derived from the notion of 'gospel-heralding as an eschatological, divinely commissioned activity' and as such, is inappropriate as a description of the mission of believers in general.[82] To achieve this, he discusses this from Isaiah to Paul. First, he explores εὐαγγελ-/ בשׂר language as divinely authorised speech in regards to the Jewish biblical tradition especially in Is 40-65.[83] Secondly, he examines the notion from post-biblical Jewish traditions where the messenger of Deutero-Isaiah becomes a host of messengers heralding the reign of God (*Tg. Isa.* 40:9; 61:1; *1QH*[a] 22:10-15; 11Q13; 2Q521; *Midrash Tehillim* to Ps 147:1).[84] He notes that in 'all these traditions – from biblical

---

[71] Dickson, *Mission-Commitment*, 122-129.
[72] Dickson, *Mission-Commitment*, 129-131.
[73] Dickson, *Mission-Commitment*, 131.
[74] Dickson, *Mission-Commitment*, 131.
[75] Dickson, *Mission-Commitment*, 132.
[76] Dickson, *Mission-Commitment*, 133.
[77] Dickson, *Mission-Commitment*, 134-135.
[78] Dickson, *Mission-Commitment*, 135-141.
[79] Dickson, *Mission-Commitment*, 141-143.
[80] Dickson, *Mission-Commitment*, 144-150.
[81] Dickson, *Mission-Commitment*, 150.
[82] Dickson, *Mission-Commitment*, 151.
[83] Dickson, *Mission-Commitment*, 154-156.
[84] Dickson, *Mission-Commitment*, 156-159.

Isaiah to the Rabbis – gospel-heralding was the activity of divinely commissioned heralds of great eschatological import.'[85] Dickson then considers the use of the εὐαγγελ- in the Jesus-traditions and finds a particular importance is attached to Is 61 in Q (Matt 11:2-6/Lk 7:18-23; 4:16-21). He also notes allusions to Is 40:9 and 52:7 in Mk 1:1-3, 14-15 and the messianic commission of Lk 4:17-18. He concludes that the Isaianic herald tradition is part of the Jewish eschatological outlook at the time.[86]

He then turns to study the notion of 'gospel' as authorised speech in Paul. He finds support for the idea that the tradition was integral to Paul's understanding in Paul's use of Is 40-55 in Romans and, in particular, Is 52:7 in Rom 10:15. Similarly, he notes references and allusions to Is 52:7 in Ephesians (Eph 1:13; 2:17; 6:15) indicating that the Isaianic messenger tradition was fully integrated into the Pauline tradition by the time of the writing of Ephesians.[87] While accepting the difficulty of discerning the role of the tradition in Judaism or the Synoptics, Dickson argues then that the Isaianic messenger tradition gives the best background to Paul's εὐαγγελ- usage.[88]

He argues that this is supported first through the connection between 'gospel-heralding' and 'sending' (ἀποστέλ-) found a number of times, suggesting that those who were sent as apostles were those commissioned to herald the gospel (1 Thess 2:4; Rom 1:1; 1 Cor 1:17; Gal 1:15-17 cf. Is 40:9; 41:27; 61:1).[89] In particular, Rom 10:15 suggests to Dickson that authorised sending is essential to preaching of the gospel, connecting Paul's understanding of preaching to the Isaianic heralding tradition.[90]

He concludes by arguing Paul had a two-dimensional view of mission. 'The first dimension consisted of the eschatological announcement of the gospel and was the primary (though not mutually exclusive) duty of authorised heralds, both itinerant and local.'[91] The second dimension 'involved Paul's converts – as individuals and/or as congregations – and entailed a 'partnership' (with the authorised heralds) for the furtherance of the gospel.'[92]

This latter role he called 'partnership for the gospel' or 'the work of the Lord.'[93] He then turns to explore the nature of the congregational contributions to Paul's mission.

He then examines a number of ways in which the congregation generally

---

[85] Dickson, *Mission-Commitment*, 159.

[86] Dickson, *Mission-Commitment*, 159-165.

[87] Dickson, *Mission-Commitment*, 165-173.

[88] Dickson, *Mission-Commitment*, 173-174.

[89] Dickson, *Mission-Commitment*, 227-229.

[90] Dickson, *Mission-Commitment*, 170-173. He also notes the notion of divinely authorised proclamation is found in Greek philosophical tradition such as *Discourses of Epictetus* (see p175-176).

[91] Dickson, *Mission-Commitment*, 177.

[92] Dickson, *Mission-Commitment*, 177.

[93] Dickson, *Mission-Commitment*, 177.

contributed to Paul's mission. First, mission as financial assistance involving 'maintenance of missionaries',[94] sending[95] and occasional missionary gifts.[96] Secondly, mission-commitment as prayer noted in the missionary orientation of many of Paul's prayers (Rom 10:1; 1 Tim 2:1-10; 1 Thess 5:25; 2 Thess 3:1; Col 4:2-4; Eph 6:18-20).[97] Thirdly, mission as social integration whereby the Pauline believer sought to 'make sure their entire social conduct promoted the reputation of God and secured the salvation of Christians, Jews and Greeks alike. Social integration was to have a definite missionary edge' (1 Cor 5:9-10; 10:31-11:1).[98]

Fourthly, mission as 'ethical apologetic' (1 Thess 4:11-12; Phil 4:5; Col 4:5; Tit 2:3-10; 3:1-8) whereby believers 'were to strive for a morally "good appearance" before' the unbelieving society.[99] Fifthly, he discusses mission as public worship and verbal apologetic. In terms of worship he discusses 1 Cor 14:20-25. His analysis suggests that the presence of outsiders at worship was not unusual; the congregation was to share Paul's concern for the conversion of outsiders and the presence of the visitor contained the potential for conversion.[100] In regards to mission as verbal apologetic he argues that Col 4:5-6 suggests the believer is prepared to answer the questions of unbelievers (cf. 1 Pet 3:15; 'Abot 2:14).[101]

Dickson then concludes by agreeing with Bowers and Bosch that the role of the congregation in the proactive evangelistic mission is primarily passive.[102] However, his work gives much more content to these previous works in the following ways. First, Dickson gives a more thorough exegetical analysis of the texts in question. Secondly, he develops more fully the role of the church in mission including finance, prayer, social integration, public worship, ethical apologetic and verbal apologetic. Thirdly, he gives a cogent background to

---

[94] Dickson, *Mission-Commitment*, 179-194 after discussing 1 Thess 2:1-9; 2 Thess 3:8; 1 Cor 9:1-18 argues that this relates to the apostolic office and the Jesus-sending-tradition (1 Cor 9:14) and involved provision of the basic necessities of the missionary (and wife) and not fees.

[95] Dickson, *Mission-Commitment*, 194-201 discusses προπέμπω outside Paul and in 1 Cor 16:6, 11; 2 Cor 1:16; Rom 15:24; Tit 2:13 and argues that the term was a technical one for providing travelling expenses for the departing missionary and that Paul expected this of his congregations.

[96] Dickson, *Mission-Commitment*, 201-212 finds this exclusively with regard to the Philippians who had a unique partnership with Paul.

[97] Dickson, *Mission-Commitment*, 214-227 who also notes that 'Paul did in fact expect his converts not only to support the apostolic mission but also to promote the cause of the gospel in their local context' (p227).

[98] Dickson, *Mission-Commitment*, 228-261, quote p261.

[99] Dickson, *Mission-Commitment*, 262-292, quote p291.

[100] Dickson, *Mission-Commitment*, 293-302.

[101] Dickson, *Mission-Commitment*, 302-308.

[102] Dickson, *Mission-Commitment*, 309-313.

Paul's understanding of the evangelistic proclaimer as an authorised herald in the Isaianic herald tradition. Finally, he clearly distinguishes the roles of these heralds and the congregation according to the framework of the OT, the Synoptics and Judaism.

Those That See the Church as Proactive in Terms of Proclamatory Evangelism

This position is also well represented in contemporary scholarship. Scholars holding this view can be classified in two groups. The first are those who accepted the assumption that Paul wanted his congregations to proactively evangelise their regions including A. Harnack,[103] F. Hahn,[104] M. Green,[105] G. Bornkamm,[106] G.W. Peters,[107] H. Ridderbos,[108] W.-H. Ollrog,[109] C. Stuhlmueller - D. Senior[110] and H. Doohan.[111] Secondly, there are those more recent writers who have sought to respond to Bowers, Bosch and others including P.T. O'Brien,[112] J.P. Ware,[113] I.H. Marshall, [114] E.J. Schnabel[115] and R.L. Plummer.[116]

---

[103] A. Harnack, *The Mission and Expansion of Christianity in the First Three Centuries* (Trans. J. Moffatt. New York: Harper & Brothers, 1961), 368.

[104] F. Hahn, *Mission in the New Testament* (Trans. Frank Clarke; London: SCM Press, 1965), 95-110.

[105] M. Green, *Evangelism in the Early Church* (Crowborough: Highland Books, 1970), 200-233.

[106] G. Bornkamm, *Paul* (Trans. D.M.C. Stalker. London: Hodder and Stoughton, 1971).

[107] G.W. Peters, *A Biblical Theology of Missions* (Chicago: Moody Press, 1972).

[108] H. Ridderbos, *Paul: An Outline of his Theology* (Trans. John Richard de Witt. Grand Rapids: Eerdmans, 1975), 434.

[109] W.-H. Ollrog, *Paulus und seine Mitarbeiter: Untersuchungen zu Theorie und Praxis der paulinischen Mission* (Neukirchen-Vluyn: Neukirchener Verlag, 1979), 130f.

[110] D. Senior; C. Stuhlmueller, *The Biblical Foundations for Mission* (London: SCM, 1983), 183-185.

[111] H. Doohan, *Paul's Vision of the Church* (Wilmington: Michael Glazier, 1989), 105-125.

[112] P.T. O'Brien, *Consumed by Passion. Paul and the Dynamic of the Gospel* (Homebush West: Anzea, 1993). P.T. O'Brien, 'Church', *DPL*, 123-131 fails to refer to this very important area i.e. 'the mission of the church.'

[113] J.P. Ware, *The Mission of the Church in Paul's Letter to the Philippians in the Context of Ancient Judaism* (Leiden: Brill, 2005) and 'The Thessalonians as a Missionary Congregation: 1Thessalonians 1,5-8', *ZNW* 83 (1992): 126-131.

[114] Marshall, 'Evangelists?' 251-263. See also A.F. Glasser, 'The Apostle Paul and the Missionary Task' in R.D. Winter and S.C. Hawthorne, *Perspectives on the World Christian Movement* (Pasadena: William Carey Library, 1981, 1992), 125-133 esp.130-132.

[115] Eckhard J. Schnabel, *Early Christian Mission. Paul and the Early Church.* Vol 2 of 2 (Trans. E.J. Schnabel. Downers Grove/Apollos: IVP/Leicester, 2004).

Those from the first group tend to assume that the church's mission is a natural corollary of Paul's own passion for the spread of the gospel. So *A. Harnack* writes, 'we cannot hesitate to believe that the great mission of Christianity was in reality accomplished by means of informal missionaries.'[117] Similarly, *Ferdinand Hahn* argues that this strategy was self-evident, arising out of Paul's desire that the whole world hear the gospel.[118] He writes, 'Paul did not entertain a moment's doubt that the gospel must be preached to the whole world.'[119] For Hahn, this grew out of Paul's perception of the gospel itself and its worldwide horizon.[120] He goes on: 'for the early church it was a matter of course that the gospel had to be proclaimed, and that therefore mission was a necessity... The people who spread the gospel were in most places certainly not specially distinguished missionaries; the good news was simply carried farther and farther, spreading like wildfire and forming churches which were at first small and then grew rapidly.'[121] Of Paul's mission he says: 'a more or less systematic mission, such as that undertaken from Antioch or in Paul's own missionary work, was probably a special case. But even Paul was content on each occasion to carry the gospel to the centres of a district and to trust that the message would spread out from there.'[122]

Michael Green also takes the position of assuming the imperative is found throughout the NT without providing a substantial exegetical basis for his assumption and tending to blur the distinctive perspectives of Paul and Luke. In his treatment of the question, 'The Evangelists: Who were they?' Green recognises the evangelistic ministries of those in the 'professional ministry' including Paul.[123] He also notes the evangelistic work of those in the 'regular ministry' (Acts 20:20-28)[124] and wandering theologians and philosophers.[125]

Green argues however, that it was the informal missionary work of everyday Christians that accounted for the spread of Christianity.[126] Green asserts that since Acts 8, Christianity has always been a lay movement, spread primarily through 'informal chattering to friends and chance acquaintances, in homes and wine shops, on walks and around market stalls. They went everywhere

---

[116] Robert L. Plummer, *Paul's Understanding of the Church's Mission. Did the Apostle Paul Expect the Early Church Christian Communities to Evangelise?* (Milton Keynes: Paternoster, 2006).

[117] Harnack, *Mission*, 368.

[118] Hahn, *Mission*, 95-110, esp. 96.

[119] Hahn, *Mission*, 97.

[120] Hahn, *Mission*, 99.

[121] Hahn, *Mission*, 16.

[122] Hahn, *Mission*, 16.

[123] Green, *Evangelism*, 200-214 including *Didache* evidence.

[124] Green, *Evangelism*, 205. This is an example of the manner in which Green fuses the Paul of Acts and the Epistles.

[125] Green, *Evangelism*, 206-207.

[126] Green, *Evangelism*, 208-214.

gossiping the gospel; they did it naturally, enthusiastically, and with the conviction of those who are not paid to say that sort of thing.'[127]

He goes on to say that the mission involved ministers, laymen with no gender distinction.[128] He writes: 'it was axiomatic that every Christian was called to be a witness to Christ, not only by life but by lip.'[129] This they did through the quality of their example, their fellowship, their transformed characters, joy, endurance and power.[130]

Throughout, Green assumes that the commission to proclaim the gospel is evident in the example and life of the early Christians. Their commitment to the task and the implicit imperative to proclaim which is essential to the gospel led the lay Christian to respond by sharing the gospel naturally with those they met.

Günther Bornkamm writes that Romans 15:19 is anything but adventitious and exaggerated. Instead, it expresses the apostle's amazing confidence that the gospel needed only to be preached for it to spread automatically; starting from the various cities it would reach out to the whole country round about and pervade it. He writes, 'the presumption is that the fire will of itself spread to the right and the left of where it was kindled.'[131] Bornkamm, far from assuming the general imperative, sees it as a natural corollary of Paul's understanding of the universal scope of mission and the self-propagating power of the gospel.[132]

George W. Peters' work is typical of much English evangelical mission theology that takes a particular interpretative line with little discussion of context or authorial intent. He assumes that Paul's churches were to be vigorously engaged in continuing the Pauline mission into the surrounding areas. He finds his support from Paul's challenge to the Philippians (Phil 2:12-16), his commendation of the missions of the Roman and Thessalonian churches (Rom 1:8; 1 Thess 1:8) and his praise of the Philippian participation in his work (Phil 4: 10). Peters assumes that Paul's commands to imitate his own example meant 'to pursue the path of evangelism.'[133] He notes that there are a number of other standard missionary texts that cry out, 'supremely an exponent and propagator of the gospel, he [Paul] expected the early churches to be of like kind.'[134] On no occasion does he raise possible exegetical objections and defend his interpretation. He simply assumes a certain evangelical perspective without critical examination.

Herman N. Ridderbos argues 'there is a more direct, deliberate missionary

---

[127] Green, *Evangelism*, 208.

[128] Green, *Evangelism*, 211-214 who cites support from Rom 16; Phil 4:2-3; Acts and the early church.

[129] Green, *Evangelism*, 211.

[130] Green, *Evangelism*, 214-233.

[131] Bornkamm, *Paul*, 54 cf. Harnack, *Mission,* 73 (see further below).

[132] See the discussion in the whole chapter of Bornkamm, *Paul*, 49-59 esp. 52-55.

[133] Peters, *Missions*, 133.

[134] Peters, *Missions*, 133 arguing on the basis of Rom 10:12-18; 2 Cor 5:9-21; Eph 3:1-12; Rom 1:13-17; 1 Cor 9:16-18; Phil 2:14-16; 1 Tim 2:1-7.

calling of the church' on the basis of texts that call for imitation (1 Cor 4:6; 11:1; 1:6).[135] He suggests that 1 Cor 4:5, 6; Phil 1:27; Eph 6:15; 1 Thess 1:7ff; Rom 1:8; Phil 1:5, 12ff 'show clearly how the sound that went forth from them had a good ring to it.'[136] He writes:

> They had a warm active involvement (*koinōnia*; Phil 1:5) in the progress of the gospel. One may think that so little is expressly said on the missionary stance of the church because it was not so much necessary to stimulate it to activity, as that this be manifested in the right manner i.e., not in words only, but above all in good works. However this may be, that it was part of the existence of the church to give testimony to the gospel in word and deed, directly and indirectly, can scarcely be disputed on the ground of Paul's epistles, but finds corroboration, everywhere in them...'[137]

Wolf-Henning Ollrog discussed this issue under the heading 'The missionary conduct of the Church.'[138] Having determined that the co-workers were church missionaries with responsibility for the Pauline mission work in the Pauline missionary churches, he asks: 'What is the relationship of the rest of church to the mission, as expressed in the missionary awareness of the church as a whole?'[139]

First, 'through normal contact with the pagan environment, by the numerous encounters of everyday life and the fundamental openness to non-Christians, there was also a somewhat natural missionary effect; deliberate if not really planned or even organized.'[140] He sees this in 1 Corinthians in particular where the casual missionary openness of the churches to non-Christians in their services suggests this is the natural practice in Pauline churches (1 Cor 14:23).[141]

He also notes that whenever Paul speaks about missionary proclamation by any term it is never 'a church as a whole' that is the subject of acting. He notes that, 'always, the churches appear only as an object, as the recipient of the message.'[142] He goes on, 'they are also within the paraenesis never encouraged or then obliged to tell someone the Gospel, so to work as missionaries.' He argues that this finding is clear based on the frequency of the occurrence of proclamation terms.[143]

---

[135] Ridderbos, *Paul*, 434.
[136] Ridderbos, *Paul*, 434.
[137] Ridderbos, *Paul*, 434.
[138] Ollrog, *Paulus*, 130 (translations mine).
[139] Ollrog, *Paulus*, 129.
[140] Ollrog, *Paulus*, 130.
[141] Ollrog, *Paulus*, 130. He notes a connection here to 1 Thess 1:8.
[142] Ollrog, *Paulus*, 130.
[143] Ollrog, *Paulus*, 131.

He suggests that the subjects of missionary proclamation (apart from Paul, the other Apostles and travelling missionaries) are the co-workers only (1 Thess 3:2; 2:1-12; 1 Cor 3:5ff; 4:17; 9:5ff; 16:15f; Phil 1:14-18; 2:22, 25, 20; 4:3; Phm 13; 2 Cor 1:19; Rom 16:3, 5, 9, 12f).[144] He contends that these co-workers differed from the remaining members of their churches because they were selected and temporarily set aside for mission-work. The remainder of the church did not become missionaries in that they did not emigrate, leave work, possessions, family connections and their areas to enter mission. He suggests that while the mission was the task of the whole church, only the role of particular individuals is noted.[145]

Ollrog argues then that the lack of a request for the church to generate mission and to preach suggests that the proclamation of the gospel was not to be fulfilled equally by all church members. Nevertheless he considers that 'the churches as churches of Christ' share in the enhancing the 'global rule' of Christ and so had 'responsibility for the mission.'[146] The key to this for Ollrog, is the delegation and representation of the co-workers for their own churches. The churches then functioned as partners in Paul's mission work through the co-workers.[147]

Ollrog then argues that the church did have the responsibility to continue the evangelistic mission of Paul. His distinctive contribution is his contention that the co-workers carried this responsibility on behalf of the church rather than the 'simple' members.

Carroll Stuhlmueller and Donald Senior also give critical insight into Paul's expectations of the church in mission:[148]

> He [Paul] apparently focussed on provincial centres that had not yet been evangelised, leaving to the communities themselves and perhaps other apostolic workers the task of dealing with non-Christian neighbours. He himself pressed on with the urgent task of *preaching the gospel to those who had not yet heard.*[149]

Their position is based on Paul's desire to see both Jew and Gentile throughout the world hear the good news. They contend that, motivated both eschatologically and soteriologically, Paul was intense in his desire to cover the main centres with the gospel including Rome and onto Spain. For Senior and Stuhlmueller it is a logical extension of Paul's theological, universalistic vision

---

[144] Ollrog, *Paulus*, 131.

[145] Ollrog, *Paulus*, 131-132.

[146] Ollrog, *Paulus*, 132.

[147] Ollrog, *Paulus*, 132.

[148] I consider the criticism of Bowers, 'Church', 90 that Senior and Stuhlmuehler 'assume' the imperative an overstatement; the above comment is developed out of a well-considered if undetailed perception of Paul's overall missionary approach.

[149] Senior-Stuhlmueller, *Foundations*, 184 (italics mine).

that the churches would continue the work. They write: 'thus the scope and pace of Paul's mission matched his theological vision.'[150]

While considering that Ephesians and Colossians represent a post-Pauline development, they note that the heightened missiology of these books suggests that 'the church in these letters is not the final goal but only a means and a sign of Christ's own cosmic mission of salvation.'[151] They 'contend that the ultimate purpose of Ephesians is not to narrow the church's vision to itself but to stretch that vision to embrace the world.'[152] They note the focus on gifts in Eph 4 for the purpose of 'building up the body of Christ' not for 'absorption with the domestic needs of the church... but so that the church can be an effective sign and expression of the cosmic mission of Christ.'[153] Thus, the building up of the church, the body of Christ, is not achieved by a focus on pastoral concerns or the internal workings of the Church, but by the equipping of every member for their part in the Church's global mission.[154] They go onto say: 'thus the total apostolate of the church ... involves a missionary service of proclamation.'[155] According to Senior and Stuhlmueller, the writer of Ephesians intentionally offers Paul's missionary apostolate, as an example the church is to emulate.[156] In their conclusion, they emphasise (contra-Hahn) that 'the church's main task does not lie in its mere existence and growth into its head but in mission in the form of servanthood.'[157]

Helen Doohan similarly sees the church as having a role in evangelistic mission. In her examination of the essential components of the church in Paul, she suggests that the Spirit 'sanctifies and missions' the church.[158] She contends that the 'early church is a missionary church and believers proclaim the gospel with urgency and enthusiasm.'[159] She notes the collaboration of the church in ministry including local leaders who develop the church 'beyond the point of Paul's initial evangelisation.'[160] She suggests others including women 'go off on their own, establishing churches and extending the geographical boundaries of the Christian community.'[161] She observes that the co-workers were those

---

[150] Senior-Stuhlmueller, *Foundations*, detail 183-185, quote 184.
[151] Senior-Stuhlmueller, *Foundations*, 191.
[152] Senior-Stuhlmueller, *Foundations*, 199.
[153] Senior-Stuhlmueller, *Foundations*, 205.
[154] Senior-Stuhlmueller, *Foundations*, 205 cf. G.B. Caird, *Paul's Letters from Prison* (Oxford: Oxford University Press, 1979), 76.
[155] Senior-Stuhlmueller, *Foundations*, 206.
[156] Senior- Stuhlmueller, *Foundations*, 206-207.
[157] Cf. Hahn, *Mission*, 157. Similarly M. Barth, *Ephesians.* ABC Vol 1 (2 Vols. New York: Doubleday, 1974), 198-199.
[158] Doohan, *Church*, 105-106.
[159] Doohan, *Church*, 111-112.
[160] Doohan, *Church,* 121.
[161] Doohan, *Church*, 122.

men and women with 'specific gifts' who 'preach the gospel establish churches and provide assistance for developing communities.'[162]

The response in recent times to Bowers has been led first by *Peter T. O'Brien* who asks: 'did the apostle also expect his converts to be committed to the spread of the gospel as he was (though perhaps in different ways) so that others might be saved?'[163] 'Does his exhortation to imitate him include an admonition to evangelism and mission?'[164]

O'Brien notes how in recent times 'the notion that the apostle expected Christians in his churches to be engaged in evangelistic outreach has not been acceptable to a range of scholars for a number of reasons.'[165] He cites Bosch and Bowers as recent examples. O'Brien sets out to suggest that Paul did desire his congregations to engage in evangelistic mission not only through attraction but also through mobilised mission.

Unlike Bowers, O'Brien suggests that the appeal for imitation in 1 Corinthians 11:1 strongly asserts Paul's earnest desire that the church emulate his motivation to see people saved.[166] He writes: 'the apostle may not have expected his converts in Corinth to be engaged in missionary initiatives of the kind he was furthering: but each *in his or her own way and according to their personal gifts* was to have the same goal and ambitions as Paul himself, that is, that of seeking by all possible means to save many. They were to be consumed by passion as he was!'[167] He expected them, therefore, to be committed to evangelism just as he was.[168]

O'Brien then goes on to ask if Paul's silence concerning congregational evangelism is due to the possibility that the 'believers in Paul's churches were consistently speaking to their non-Christian friends, and therefore did not need to be urged to do so?'[169]

O'Brien is careful to present Bowers and Bosch's perspective and uses them as the basis for his argument. He seeks to establish a theological rationale for those who take the line that after Paul had established his churches, 'the apostolic mission would continue towards the goal of giving everyone the opportunity of hearing and believing the message of Jesus Christ, the crucified and risen Lord.'[170]

After summarising Bowers' view,[171] O'Brien argues that churches were in fact active in evangelism. This involvement is seen first, in the unnamed

---

[162] Doohan, *Church*, 124-125.
[163] O'Brien, *Consumed*, 89.
[164] O'Brien, *Consumed*, 90.
[165] O'Brien, *Consumed*, 90.
[166] O'Brien, *Consumed*, 105.
[167] O'Brien, *Consumed*, 106 (italics his).
[168] O'Brien, *Consumed*, 107.
[169] O'Brien, *Consumed*, 109.
[170] O'Brien, *Consumed*, 109.
[171] O'Brien, *Consumed*, 111-112.

Roman believers who were energetic in their proclamation of the gospel (Phil 1:14-18) and secondly, through the Philippian involvement in proclaiming the gospel (Phil 1:5, 27, 30; 2:16). O'Brien thus, in these texts, sees two positive examples of the advance of the gospel.[172]

O'Brien suggests that Ephesians 6:10-20 is 'the Pauline Great Commission.'[173] He analyses the passage and concludes that 'each and every believer is to stand firm against the onslaughts of the evil one by resistance and by proclamation. The primary aggressive action the Christian is called upon to take is the spreading of the gospel in the world – the good news of salvation through the death and resurrection of Christ.'[174]

The main contours of O'Brien's critique of Bowers are as follows. First, he disputes Bowers' claim that evangelism is intended as 'a ministry of attraction and responsiveness rather than one of deliberate outreach and active solicitation.' Both Phil 1:14-18 and 2:15-16 indicate there were believers committed to the spread of the gospel.[175] Secondly, he argues that Bowers does not take cognisance of the 'dynamic progress of the gospel.'[176] He argues Paul's silence is due in the main to Paul's focus on the ultimate source, namely, God's powerful saving action in the *kerygma*.[177]

Thirdly, while Paul distinguishes himself from his converts especially in regard to his role in the Gentile mission, his call to imitation includes the Pauline goal of winning others (1 Cor 11:1).[178] Fourthly, he claims that the Philippians' fellowship in the gospel (Phil 1:5) is not to be confined to financial support alone, 'significant though this was', but also to active evangelistic endeavour.[179] Fifthly, while agreeing with Bowers that the involvement of the church in outreach was not conducted as churches, he suggests that this statement is misleading if it implies that believers were not to engage in evangelistic outreach.[180] Sixthly, he contends that Bowers' argument for the absence of proactive congregational evangelism in Paul is an argument from silence which Eph 6:10-20 calls into question (cf. Acts 11:19-20). Finally, he

---

[172] O'Brien, *Consumed*, 117-119.

[173] O'Brien, *Consumed*, 109.

[174] O'Brien, *Consumed*, 125.

[175] O'Brien, *Consumed*, 126-127. Interestingly, O'Brien's view of 2:16 here contrasts with the view he expresses in his commentary that 2:16a should be rendered as 'hold fast' rather than 'hold forth'; see P.T. O'Brien, *The Epistle to the Philippians*. NIGTC (Grand Rapids: Eerdmans, 1991), 297 (his commentary from this point will be simply, O'Brien).

[176] O'Brien, *Consumed*, 127.

[177] O'Brien, *Consumed*, 128.

[178] O'Brien, *Consumed*, 128.

[179] O'Brien, *Consumed*, 129.

[180] O'Brien, *Consumed*, 130.

argues that believers are to be involved in the powerful advance of the gospel even though they do not have the same key role that Paul himself did.[181]

He asserts: 'it is wrong to assume that, because the apostle mentions Christians engaging in evangelism on only a few occasions, he had no great interest in the matter. He genuinely desired that believers should bear faithful witness to Jesus as Lord in the presence of their non-Christian friends.'[182]

Following O'Brien, I.Howard Marshall's essay is born of an attempt to find examples of local churches doing evangelism or of exhortations to churches to do so in the NT. This led him to ask the questions: 'who were the evangelists? Was evangelism the responsibility of individual congregations of believers?'[183] Marshall begins by asking 'were local congregations involved in evangelism?' In this section, after recognising the array of historical and theological study acknowledging the 'missionary character' of the early church, he notes that 'strangely the question of who did the evangelism and in particular whether and how local congregations were involved remains neglected.'[184] Marshall then discusses the views of the major contributors including Ollrog, Bowers and O'Brien.[185] He asks whether the picture given by these scholars 'that evangelism was generally the work of "foreign missionaries" and not of "home missionaries"' and that 'congregations were places of nurture for converts, not agencies for conversion', is justified.[186]

Marshall first notes that, in the Gospels[187] and Acts (Acts 8:1; 13:1; 19:10), the commission is applied more broadly than the twelve and concludes that, 'church-based missions and local evangelism are clearly envisaged in Acts and there is no conflict with the Pauline picture.'[188] He then reconsiders the Pauline evidence in ten points. First, he argues that it does not follow from Paul's self-identity as 'apostle to the Gentiles' that churches were not to do further evangelism in their vicinity. He suggests that Paul's strategy of planting churches in main centres was because 'he hoped that the gospel would be carried into the surrounding areas. This would imply an ongoing work of evangelism from these centres.'[189] Secondly he suggests that the Acts picture is confirmed in Paul in that other missionaries are active (1 Cor 15:9f cf. 9:5; 12:28f) and that the lines between individual and congregation are somewhat blurred (Phil 1:14-18).[190]

---

[181] O'Brien, *Consumed*, 131.
[182] O'Brien, *Consumed*, 131.
[183] Marshall, 'Evangelists?' 251.
[184] Marshall, 'Evangelists?' 252.
[185] Marshall, 'Evangelists?' 252-256.
[186] Marshall, 'Evangelists?' 256.
[187] Marshall, 'Evangelists?' 257, i.e. Luke, Matthew, John.
[188] Marshall, 'Evangelists?' 258.
[189] Marshall, 'Evangelists?' 259.
[190] Marshall, 'Evangelists?' 259.

Thirdly, he argues, contra-Bowers, that 1 Thess 1:8a should be understood in terms of Thessalonian mission.[191] Fourthly, he revisits Phil 2:14-17 and argues that the force of φωστήρ (cf. Dan 12:3) and ἐπέχοντες leads to his conclusion that one can make 'a reasonable case for seeing outward witness to the gospel as the reference in this passage.'[192] Fifthly, he argues it is impossible to deny that the soteriological motivation of 1 Cor 10:31-11:1 is relevant to the Christians in Corinth.[193] Sixthly, he suggests that it is not necessary to limit the first person plural of 2 Cor 5:18-6:2 to Paul and 'his missionary colleagues' for two reasons: due to Paul's use of 'the language of reconciliation', which is usually reserved for unbelievers/believers, and due to the variance of the application of 'we' between 'all' and Paul and his team (2 Cor 5:16-28).[194]

Seventhly, he then notes the 'openness in Paul's letters and elsewhere to witness by individual Christians (1 Cor 7:16; Tit 2:10 cf. 1 Pet 3:1f).'[195] Eighthly, he argues that the function of the spiritually endowed was to build up the church (Eph 4:12; 2 Tim 4:5).[196] Ninthly, Marshall then points out how difficult it is to draw a line between the work of the local church and missionaries as in the case of Paul in Rome (Rom 1:5 cf. 15:15f).[197] He then states: 'the comings and goings of the apostles and their co-workers will have led to a blurring of the distinction between the congregation and the missionaries.'[198] Finally, he notes the anachronistic danger of seeing a distinct line between believers and unbelievers in NT church meetings. Rather Paul assumes the presence of unbelievers (1 Cor 14:23-25) and so this suggests the possibility of evangelism in church meetings.[199]

He concludes this section stating: 'the cumulative effect of these points is to demonstrate that early congregations and individual believers did have an evangelistic function that appears to have developed simultaneously.'[200] He argues that Bowers' hypothesis is not complete and that 'the picture is much less tidy than he allows'[201] due to the picture in Acts and Paul. He notes 'we have seen that Paul did know and applaud examples of evangelism by the congregations which he founded.'[202]

Marshall suggests that the reason Paul's letters pay so little attention to evangelism by congregations is understandable historically, as evangelism was

---

[191] Marshall, 'Evangelists?' 259.
[192] Marshall, 'Evangelists?' 259-260.
[193] Marshall, 'Evangelists?' 260.
[194] Marshall, 'Evangelists?' 260.
[195] Marshall, 'Evangelists?' 261.
[196] Marshall, 'Evangelists?' 261.
[197] Marshall, 'Evangelists?' 261.
[198] Marshall, 'Evangelists?' 261.
[199] Marshall, 'Evangelists?' 261-262.
[200] Marshall, 'Evangelists?' 262.
[201] Marshall, 'Evangelists?' 262.
[202] Marshall, 'Evangelists?' 262.

considered primarily as the work of travelling preachers. He argues however, that even here, the expansion of the church in Acts and Paul's interaction with his congregations suggest that a problem with this modern debate is an anachronistic back reading from the distinctions of the modern church into the early church. He concludes:

> There is no doubt that the 'work' in which Paul found himself engaged as an apostle along with his co-workers was for him the fundamental means of mission. Beside this the work of evangelism by the congregations that he founded was of lesser importance. Nevertheless, such evangelism did go on, and when it happened Paul rejoiced in it. The examples of Philippi and Thessalonica must not be ignored, and the missionary task in the family was also significant. Itinerant evangelism and local evangelism were carried on side by side.[203]

Eckhard J. Schnabel too discusses 'the missionary work of the Christian communities' in his impressive work on Early Christian mission.[204] He notes the lack of exhortations to active mission and outlines five typical inadequate explanations. First, he notes those who argue that Rom 15:19-23 suggests Paul did not envisage churches being actively involved in mission due to their expectation of an imminent Parousia. He responds: 'there is no evidence that Paul's conviction that Jesus' return might be imminent influenced his missionary strategy, at least not with regard to the "speed" of his missionary initiatives.'[205] Secondly, he mentions those who argue that Paul did not need to appeal for missionary activity as 'new converts would have been motivated by their conversion and by God's Spirit to engage in missionary activity as a matter of course.'[206] He contends that this is unconvincing because Paul appeals for other aspects of Christian life despite the same argument applying.

Thirdly, he notes those who argue that the church is missionary in character and this explains the absence of appeal. He cites an example (Zwigchem) and then argues that the texts do not support the claims made nor clearly describe the nature of mission consciousness. Fourthly, he notes Bowers and others who argue for an attraction model of church mission. He responds that 'the individual believers do not and cannot have an evangelistic task would be problematic'[207] in the light of the negative responses of NT scholars such as O'Brien and Ware. He suggests Bowers brings a necessary corrective to the view that 'the pivotal impetus of the early Christian mission was the work of "normal believers" who "gossiped the gospel" in everyday life and in the context of their normal familial and professional relationships, representing a

---

[203] Marshall, 'Evangelists?' 263.
[204] Schnabel, *Mission*, 1451-1465.
[205] Schnabel, *Mission*, 1452.
[206] Schnabel, *Mission*, 1452.
[207] Schnabel, *Mission*, 1455.

"total mobilization" of the early church.'[208] Finally, he notes the view that the concept of missions 'both of Paul and early church was still developing or Paul's ecclesiology was simply focussed on the spiritual growth of the young churches.'[209]

Schnabel then argues that Paul did assume the involvement of Christians in missionary outreach at a local level and that he integrated churches into his missionary work. In support, first, he notes a number of general considerations. These include first of all the agreement between Matthew, Luke and John that, while each is formulated differently, Jesus gave his disciples a missionary commission which transcended the twelve and applied to different geographical localities.[210] In addition, he notes that in Acts 13:1-2 we have a local congregation sending missionaries to other regions and the activity of Jewish Christians from Jerusalem was not differentiated from that of Paul and co-workers.[211] Furthermore, he notes that the logic of the gospel implies a commitment to its progress (cf. Rom 1:1-17). Moreover, he notes that the argument that Paul considered church mission as superfluous fails to account for his recognition of the possibility of his own death or incarceration and that the existence of a Christian community in Rome did not stop his sense of call to preach in that city.[212] Besides which, Paul knows of other Christians involved in mission work and, even despite their false motivation, he is positive toward their proclamation (cf. 1 Cor 9:5; 12:28-29; Phil 1:14-18). Finally, he notes the difficulty of distinguishing between the local church and missionaries in the first century and that often Paul worked in these contexts with locals.[213]

Schnabel then turns to the evangelism of local communities and notes positive indications of church involvement. These include first, 1 Cor 14:23-24 which points to the Christian worshiping gatherings being open to outsiders.[214] Secondly, he argues that in 1 Thess 1:8 Paul applauds the Thessalonians for their active mission commitment.[215] Thirdly, he notes a number of points in Philippians which indicate active endeavour. In 1:5 Paul is thankful for the Philippian involvement in preaching, financial support and prayer. He notes in 1:12-18 that most of the Roman believers were preaching the gospel despite false motives.[216] He takes 2:16 as 'hold fast the word of life' but argues this

---

[208] Schnabel, *Mission*, 1455.

[209] Schnabel, *Mission*, 1455-1456.

[210] Schnabel, *Mission*, 1456.

[211] Schnabel, *Mission*, 1456-1457.

[212] Schnabel, *Mission*, 1458.

[213] Schnabel, *Mission*, 1458-1459.

[214] Schnabel, *Mission*, 1459.

[215] Schnabel, *Mission*, 1460.

[216] Schnabel, *Mission*, 1460. Unfortunately there is a tension between this statement which involves 'most of the believers in Rome' here and p1437 n507 which lists these believers as 'co-workers.'

extends beyond mere steadfastness but to proclamation.[217] He maintains that 1 Cor 11:1 should be taken as 'missionary intention.'[218] He argues that 'messengers' of the churches indicate missionary responsibility (cf. 2 Cor 8:23; Phil 2:25).[219] He observes the presence of 'evangelist' in Eph 4:11 whose role was for the planting of new communities and the building up the believers for the task.[220] He then argues that in Eph 6:15, 17 the shoes and sword of the armoury of the soldier of Christ are to be interpreted actively as evangelistic.[221] Finally, he takes account of 2 Tim 4:5 where the leader of the congregation Timothy is to preach the gospel. He concludes that:

> The leaders of the congregations are called to proclaim the gospel, evidently before people who have not yet heard the message of Jesus Christ; that is, they are encouraged to engage in missionary ministry. The congregations should not wait for travelling missionaries to pass through; rather, they should take it upon themselves to make sure that people hear the gospel. The believers who are responsible for 'evangelising' are, first of all, men who have preaching and teaching responsibilities in the church, and surely women, such as Priscilla, who can explain the gospel and the Scriptures.[222]

James Ware focuses on a comparative study of 'conversion of the Gentiles in Ancient Judaism' and then, in light of his conclusions, the mission of the church in Philippians. He argues that 'interest in gentiles and their conversion is widely evident in the Hebrew Scriptures, above all the book of Isaiah,' and especially Is 40-55 and the servant of the servant songs.[223] He also claims that there is a 'widespread and intense interest in conversion of gentiles among Jews throughout the second temple period.'[224] This was not accompanied by a mission to the gentiles or a desire to seek proselytes, but was understood in terms of 'a pilgrimage of the nations to Zion in the eschatological time of Israel's restoration.'[225] Proselytes were understood as anticipating this event at the nation's restoration.[226] He contends that the solution to the impasse concerning a Jewish mission is found in 'the expectation of a future conversion of gentiles in the impending time of the Jewish nation's eschatological restoration.'[227] While there is no evidence of a Jewish mission, the figure of the

---

[217] Schnabel, *Mission*, 1461. Again it is not clear which option Schnabel is going for. He translates the phrase 'hold fast' but then seems to take it actively with Fee and others?
[218] Schnabel, *Mission*, 1461-1462.
[219] Schnabel, *Mission*, 1462.
[220] Schnabel, *Mission*, 1463.
[221] Schnabel, *Mission*, 1463-1465.
[222] Schnabel, *Mission*, 1465.
[223] Ware, *Mission*, 157.
[224] Ware, *Mission*, 157.
[225] Ware, *Mission*, 157.
[226] Ware, *Mission*, 157.
[227] Ware, *Mission*, 158

servant and the 'light to the nations', sometimes seen as a corporate figure and in others as an individual, lies at the heart of Israel's hope. He then argues that Paul's missionary thinking is informed by this understanding.[228]

Ware then examines mission in Philippians. He discusses Phil 1:12-18a arguing that here we have an example of an attitude to gentile mission which is 'without parallel' in Jewish sources.[229] He notes the importance of 1:12-14 first in that 'it is one of the few passages in Paul's letters which present mission, in the sense of active proclamation of the gospel, as a general Christian activity. Moreover, the fearless proclamation of the word by the Roman believers functions in the letter as a model for Paul's converts at Philippi.'[230] He notes that the two groups in 1:15-18a 'function in turn within the wider letter as positive and negative models for the Philippians.'[231]

In his discussion of suffering and mission in Phil 1:18b-2:11 he suggests that 'in 1:27 Paul exhorts the Philippians to life, conduct and sufferings which will adorn the message and promote the spread of the gospel. The command to be unafraid of the opponents (1:28) functions within the letter as an exhortation fearlessly to proclaim the word despite persecution and suffering.'[232] He also argues that in 2:14-15 'Paul continues the exhortation to mission activity by drawing richly upon Jewish traditions to depict the Philippians as the eschatological Israel of God set in the midst of the nations.'[233] Ware finds that in 2:15 Paul utilises and adapts the imagery of Dan 12:3 'to express the missionary idenity of the Philippians as lights for the gentile world.'[234] He goes on to argue that Phil 2:16b should be read as 'hold forth the word of life' and as such is an exhortation to spread the gospel. He concludes that 'Paul's extraordinary interest in Philippians in the spread of the gospel through his converts, and his explicit command to the Philippians to hold forth the word of life' makes the view that 'Paul's missionary thinking had little or no place for an active mission of his churches' untenable.[235] As such, Ware argues strongly that Paul did expect active proclamatory involvement from his converts.

Robert L. Plummer has also recently devoted a whole monograph to the question. He begins with a survey of approaches broken into two sections; pre-1950 and 1950 to the present. Within each group he notes a number of authors who argue for a continuity of evangelistic mission and others who argue for a discontinuity.[236] He argues that the solution to the impasse between these two

---

[228] Ware, *Mission*, 158-159.

[229] Ware, *Mission*, 199.

[230] Ware, *Mission*, 198.

[231] Ware, *Mission*, 199.

[232] Ware, *Mission*, 234.

[233] Ware, *Mission*, 283.

[234] Ware, *Mission*, 283.

[235] Ware, *Mission*, 289.

[236] Pre 1950 scholars who argue for 'apostle-church mission continuity' include Gustav Warneck, Roland Allen, Adolf von Harnack, Carl von Weizäcker and Michael Green. Those who he notes argue for 'church mission discontinuity' include Paul

views is to 'consider the whole Pauline corpus and build our conclusions on a meticulous evaluation of the evidence.'[237] This he seeks to do in his analysis of Paul's theological framework and exegetical study.

He deals with the matter under three headings. First, he approaches the question theologically arguing that this leads to apostolic continuity. After defining concepts like 'church' and 'apostle',[238] Plummer suggests that there is little evidence of the Great Commission functioning as a motivation for Pauline mission nor of Paul connecting the impulse for mission to the Holy Spirit as does Acts. He proposes that the concept of 'the dynamic nature of the gospel' functions in Pauline thought as the catalyst for further spreading of the word.[239] He then argues that Paul 'speaks of the gospel as a dynamic force or power' on the basis of Rom 1:16-17 and 1 Corinthians 1:17-25; in continuity with the OT references to 'the word of the Lord.'[240] Plummer then notes points at which Paul explicitly links the gospel as 'power' with his own missionary work (cf. 1 Cor 14:36; 1 Thess 1:5; 1 Cor 9:12; 2 Tim 2:8-9; Col 1:5-7; 1 Cor 4:15; Rom 15:18-19).[241] He then submits that the gospel is a dynamic force at work in Paul's churches (cf. 1 Thess 2:13-16; 2 Thess 3:1; 1 Thess 1:8).[242] The latter verse he takes actively of the Thessalonian extension of the gospel mission.[243] He then postulates that this emphasis on the gospel as power correlates with Luke's concept of the Spirit as a mission-empowering agency and the Great Commission i.e. they are 'complementary elements of the same vision.'[244]

Plummer then examines texts which appear to confirm the theological portrait above and give instructions on evangelism. He takes note of commands in Philippians including 1:5, 12-18; 2:16, which he takes as pointing to proactive evangelisation.[245] He then turns to Ephesians noting that 6:15, 17 should be taken proactively.[246] He maintains that the imitation texts of 1 Corinthians (4:15; 11:1) are inclusive of evangelism and the 7:12-16 and 14:23-25 suggest the same.[247] He concludes, 'there can be no doubt that Paul instructs

---

Wernle, Ernest Renan and William Wrede. In the 1950's-present category he includes among those arguing for discontinuity Heinrich Greevan et al., W-H. Ollrog, W.P. Bowers, David Bosch, John P. Dickson and Stephen Chambers. Those who advocate continuity include Douwe van Swigchem, Peter T. O'Brien, James Patrick Ware, I. Howard Marshall, Eckhard J. Schnabel, John Piper, G.K. Beale and Norbert Schmidt.

[237] Plummer, *Understanding*, 42.

[238] Plummer, *Understanding*, 43-48.

[239] Plummer, *Understanding*, 50.

[240] See for a full analysis, Plummer, *Understanding*, 51-56.

[241] Plummer, *Understanding*, 56-59.

[242] Plummer, *Understanding*, 59-64.

[243] See his discussion, Plummer, *Understanding*, 61-64.

[244] Plummer, *Understanding*, 64-66.

[245] Plummer, *Understanding*, 72-77.

[246] Plummer, *Understanding*, 77-81.

[247] Plummer, *Understanding*, 81-96.

and approves of his churches actively proclaiming the gospel.'[248] He then observes examples indicating Paul's desire that churches witness to the gospel passively i.e. behavioural witness (cf. 2 Cor 6:3-7; 1 Thess 2:5-12; Tit 2:1-10).[249]

Finally, Plummer notes texts that give 'incidental evidence' that Paul expected the Churches to spread the gospel according to the apostolic pattern.[250] He references three in particular; first, 'miracles as confirmation of the gospel' (cf. Rom 15:18-19; 2 Cor 12:12; 1 Cor 2:4-5; 1 Thess 1:5; 1 Cor 12:9-30);[251] secondly, 'praying for missions and the church' (see especially 1 Tim 2:1-4)[252] and finally, 'teaching and "building up" the church' (cf. Rom 15:14; 1 Thess 5:12; Eph 4:11-16; 1 Cor 14:23-25).[253] In addition, he discusses the connection between mission and suffering and argues that for Paul, suffering in his own mission-experience and that of his churches 'reveals that the offensive, self-diffusive gospel was effectively progressing through the early Christians' cf. 2 Cor 4:7-15; Col 1:24-25; Phil 1:12-14; 1 Thess 2:14-16.[254] He states in response:

> Unlike some recent missiologists who have proposed that the apostolic mission is inherited by a para-church 'apostolic band,' Paul understands missions as a ecclesiastical task. The apostolic mission devolves upon each church *as a whole* – not upon any particular member or group. Each individual member within the church, then, will manifest missionary activity according to his or her particular gifting and life situation. All but the unrepeatable aspects of the apostles' mission (e.g., eyewitness testimony and initial promulgation of authoritative revelation) devolve upon the church *as a whole.*[255]

Conclusion to this Discussion

My brief overview indicates there are two essential views concerning Paul's understanding of the role of the church in evangelism. First, there are those who

---

[248] Plummer, *Understanding*, 96.

[249] Plummer, *Understanding*, 96-105.

[250] Plummer, *Understanding*, 107.

[251] Plummer, *Understanding*, 107-111; with a comparison with Acts which more explicitly links evangelism and miracles cf. Acts 1:8; 3:1-4:22, 29-30; 5:11-14; 6:7-10; 8:5-14; 14:21-22.

[252] Plummer, *Understanding*, 111-116. He argues 1 Tim 2:1-4 points to missionary prayer. On p113 he also notes three categories of prayer: 1) 'Prayers of thanksgiving for the congregations' missionary activity' (Phil 1:3-5; 1 Thess 1:2-8; cf. Rom 1:8); 2) 'Prayers for the salvation of certain persons' (Rom 10:1); 3) 'Prayers that have the churches' relationship with outsiders in view' (1 Thess 3:10; cf. Rom 15:7-13).

[253] See Plummer, *Understanding*, 117-121.

[254] Plummer, *Understanding*, 137.

[255] Plummer, *Understanding*, 144 (italics his).

contend that Paul's vision of evangelistic mission was centred on himself, his co-workers, other apostles and evangelists and *not the local church.* Not that the local church was uninvolved, but rather, that it participated in the mission through financial support, prayer, social integration, public worship and centripetal ethical-apologetic witness. If there is a role, it is through specifically commissioned evangelistis or co-workers and not the church in general. On the whole, proponents of this view argue that Paul gives little indication of any desire for his congregations to engage in centrifugal proactive proclamatory evangelistic mission to their regions.

The second view accepts that Paul did want his churches to be involved in the mission of the Pauline team and other itinerants through the dimensions listed above. However, they also maintain that Paul did envisage his churches continuing the mission within their context through their own people resources. This debate raises a number of questions that I will address in this work with particular reference to Philippians.

i. Is there evidence of Pauline churches involved in evangelism and a desire for them to continue to do so?

ii. Does Paul's notion of imitation include evangelism?

iii. What was Paul's response to situations where his presence catalysed others into evangelistic endeavour?

iv. Is there a clear line between itinerant missionaries and the workers in local churches?

v. Does Paul's understanding of pneumatology include evangelism?

Methodology

The above discussion leads to the question of how best to answer the problems posed above. While undertaking research for this analysis, several methodologies were considered. First, consideration was given to focussing the discussion on a comparative study along the lines of Ware and Dickson. For example, comparing Paul's approach to that of Judaism, Graeco-Roman religious and philosophical sects, or the Patristic Fathers. Obviously this work is extremely useful in helping us to understand the world of Paul, the mode of religious expansion and a range of possible answers to the questions. However, I considered that this was not an appropriate line of reasoning for a number of reasons.

Positively, such a study would give background to the world Paul and the Pauline churches existed in. It could also open up the range of possibilities. However such a study does do not tell us what Paul himself desired from his churches. Only Paul can tell us this.[256] In terms of comparative studies it must also be shown that there is a clear and unaffected connection between these groups, Paul and the Pauline churches. These links can only be found in the Pauline epistles themselves which brings me back the problem of comparative studies in regard to my question: I do not see clear evidence that such links emerge clearly enough to enable me to answer the question at hand. Hence, I consider that a comparative study in this regard would not ultimately answer the question of what Paul wanted from his congregations.

Secondly, the manner in which Paul is understood greatly influences the way in which comparative studies are applied. In terms of influences for example, Palestinian Judaism, Diaspora Judaism, and Graeco-Roman societal, religious and philosophical models affected Paul to some degree. If so, how that influence was manifested is highly contentious and unclear. Did Paul base his approach on that of Diaspora Judaism? If Paul was influenced, was he positively or negatively influenced? If so, was the influence on his thought and practice consistent? From the perspective of critical realism such studies are essential to forming a clear understanding of Paul, they do not in the end specifically answer the question. Within a critical realism framework, I prefer an emic approach as primary in this case as the question I am addressing is what did *Paul* want from his congregations.[257] Ultimately only he can answer this.

I consider then, that basing an answer to the question of the role of the church in proactive evangelism through models drawn from these contexts, is contentious. Paul was also quite capable of dynamic individual thought drawn from his Damascus Road experience. This capability is recognised by Bowers

---

[256] Hence my primary source for this study will be Paul's letters themselves rather than the Paul of Acts in that I accept that on the whole one should allow Paul to tell us what Paul believed on a certain issue. I consider Acts sound historically and so provides important contextual and chronological information concerning Paul and especially the 'we' accounts (Acts 16:10-17; 20:5-21:18; 27:1-28:16). Further see J.D.G. Dunn, *The Acts of the Apostles*. EC (Peterborough: Epworth, 1996), x; F.F. Bruce, *The Book of the Acts*. NICNT (Grand Rapids: Eerdmans, 1988), 7; H.J. Cadbury, "'We' and 'I' Passages in Luke-Acts,' *NTS* 3 (1956-57), 128-132); J.A. Fitzmyer, *The Acts of the Apostles*. ABC (New York: Doubleday, 1998), 103; J. Stott, *The Message of Acts*. BST (Leicester: IVP, 1990), 23-24; D.F. Williams, *Acts*. NBC (Peabody: Hendrickson, 1990), 3-10, 17; W.J. Larkin Jr, *Acts*. IVPNTCS (Leicester: IVP, 1995), 17, 22-23; C.K. Barrett, *Acts*. ICC (Vol II. Edinburgh: T&T. Clark, 1998), xxiv-xxx who covers the different views succinctly; A. Campbell, 'Do the Work of an Evangelist', *EQ* 64:2 (1992): 117-129, 118); I.H. Marshall, *Acts*. TNTC (Grand Rapids: Eerdmans, 1980), 34-44; W.H. Willimon, *Acts*. IBC (Atlanta: John Knox, 1988), 6-8. For a less positive but reasonable assessment see Fitzmyer, *Acts*, 124-127; Dunn, *Acts*, xv-xix.

[257] For a discussion of critical realism in regards to other epistemological approaches see P.G. Hiebert, *Missiological Implications of Epistemological Shifts; Affirming Truth in a Modern/Postmodern World* (Harrisburg: Trinity Press, 1999).

himself who rightly argues that Paul's mode of intentional geographical extension appears to have been 'largely unparalleled' in Paul's day.[258]

I would contend that the relationship of Paul to the practice of the early church found in the Gospel-Acts tradition is of more consequence. However, establishing the connections here is also highly contentious. Accordingly, I consider that to adequately answer the question requires exegetical work that looks at what Paul himself says about an issue and which takes account of any available literature that informs the question at hand.

Finally, the research gap that stands out most prominently to me is the failure to exegete Paul thoroughly in regards to the question at hand. My work is born of my concern that none of the works reviewed above adequately discusses the exegetical issues at hand in the passages cited. Of the works assessed only O'Brien, Dickson and Plummer discuss the issue in any real depth.

Where O'Brien is concerned, I consider his work understates the importance of congregational evangelism in regard to the theme of imitation and the Philippian and Thessalonian correspondence. In addition, he writes at a level suitable to undergraduates and thus his work does not address the complex exegetical issues related to his conclusions.[259] Dickson, in many cases, does discuss in some depth the exegetical issues at hand, but his work is weakened by the imposition of an external grid derived from his assessment of the Jewish background, which I consider tends to dominate his conclusions. Plummer's work, like Dickson's, discusses all the major texts in question; however, in that it does this within the space of short monograph, the work by necessity does not discuss in real depth the exegetical issues in relationship to rhetorical strategy and context. The other major proponents evaluated discuss the issue in either an essay, or a chapter of a book, neither of which allow a scholar to thoroughly canvass the intricate exegetical nuances of the issues at hand.

Further, Bowers and others take certain interpretative lines that are weakly supported and/or are not held by many contemporary scholars. I think that a sound exegetical base can be laid for the contention that Paul wanted his congregations as congregations to continue the mission of proclaiming the gospel in their regions.

A second approach considered but rejected was to come at the question thematically. Hence I considered writing a series of essays researching such questions as 'imitation and proclamation',[260] 'the implicit imperative of the

---

[258] Bowers, 'Propaganda': 323 notes this after comparing Paul's approach to Judaism and Hellenistic wandering preachers.

[259] Similarly see the review of his work by P. Oakes, *EQ* 70:1 (1998): 83-84. I note however, that much of the exegetical work is available elsewhere in O'Brien's impressive commentary work.

[260] Considering whether Paul's appeals for imitation included an appeal for proclamation.

gospel',[261] along with exegetical analysis of the key texts. However I found this inadequate for several reasons.

First, each text provided exegetical and contextual issues that needed serious treatment and rendered the thematic approach cumbersome. Secondly, to establish sufficient exegetical support for my argument was a very involved task, since texts were taken from all over the Paulines. To adequately analyse Paul's position requires careful and thorough exegesis of each verse involved in context. To deal with each text with a cursory paragraph citing a small selection of the views cited by exegetes I feel is not adequate.

Accordingly, I have approached the question with an exegetical study. Ideally this work would be a multi-volume work examining each Pauline epistle chronologically in order to search for clues to answering the question of whether or not there is a general imperative to evangelise in Paul.[262] This approach would ensure that I dealt with my question thoroughly. This present work is one aspect of a full analysis of all Paul's letters in this regard.

My approach then is a microcosm of the major exegetical analysis required. My focus is on tackling the question from the undisputed letter that I consider presents a substantial amount of data on the question, Philippians. This approach ensures that each text is thoroughly analysed in context. Furthermore, I choose Philippians because, as will be made evident through the exegetical analysis below, there are a substantial number of scholars who contend that, in Philippians, there is evidence of a church involved in local evangelism (Phil 1:5, 27; 2:15-16; 4:2-3 cf. 1 Thess 1:6-8; Eph 6:15, 17).

Secondly, in Philippians, Paul asks a church to emulate his example, raising the possibility that the appeal potentially may include evangelism (Phil 4:9 cf. 3:15-17; 1:15-18a; 2:5-11, 19-30; 1 Cor 4:6; 11:1; 1 Thess 1:6-8; 2:14-16; 5:1-2). Furthermore, the presentation of other Christian models within the rhetoric of Philippians needs to be examined to see whether there is an evangelistic edge to his appeal in the letter (cf. Roman proclaimers [1:14-18a]; Christ [2:5-11], Timothy and Epaphroditus [2:19-30]; Judaisers [3:1-20]; Euodia and Syntyche [4:2-3]).

Thirdly, in Philippians Paul clearly states his total positivity to a situation where his own presence has inspired the proclamation of the gospel despite wrong motives (Phil 1:14-18a). Hence, this passage must be explored to see if, in its context, it suggests that this desire extends beyond the point of his incarceration. Although *charismata* is not emphasised in the letter, the use of χάρις (cf. χαρίσματα) (1:7) and the attribution of ἀπόστολος to Epaphroditus (1:25) and to other co-workers brings into view the question of the role of the Spirit and spiritual gifts in evangelism.

---

[261] Considering how Paul's understanding of salvation and the gospel implies an imperative for all to proclaim the gospel.

[262] In a manner similar to G.D. Fee, *God's Empowering Presence* (Peabody: Hendrickson, 1994).

Structurally, I begin by briefly summarising my essential preliminary questions of background to the epistle, something I consider essential for all exegetical study. In particular I seek to emphasise the prominent place of 'gospel' and 'evangelism' throughout the letter and the manner in which they intersect with other key themes in the epistle. To do so I will examine in some depth those passages, which to some extent or another, potentially highlight congregational evangelism through the body of the epistle 1:14-18a; 1:27-30; 2:14-16a, 19-30; 4:2-3. In light of my findings concerning these passages I will explore 1:5-7 from the thanksgiving, which anticipates the content of the letter. Finally, I will examine 4:9, which to a certain extent summarises the appeal of the letter to this point.

There are certain sections of the letter which I will not discuss in any depth because of their limited importance in terms of the matter of general evangelism and the limits of space. In this regard, I will not discuss Phil 1:1-2; 4:10-23 which lack anything of significance for my discussion.[263] Similarly, 2:1-4 is concerned, in the main, with unity.[264] The Christ-example in 2:5-11 is discussed in Appendix 3 ('The Evangelistic Nuances to the Christ-Hymn'). The passage 3:1-21 is also of limited value to my discussion. My main concern here is with the content of imitation (3:17). However, I will not discuss this as evangelism is not explicit and I will discuss imitation in some depth in regards to 4:9. Neither will I discuss in detail the sections 1:9-11, 12-13, 27a,b; 2:12-13 which are general statements for Christian living and do not directly mention evangelism.[265]

My purpose is to demonstrate that the material discussed can be understood coherently in the manner presented. Due to the paucity of direct material, this question will continue to be understood in different ways, depending on the manner in which people interpret texts and the connections they believe are important. Hence this work is one contribution to the ongoing discussion of the involvement of the congregations in Paul's mission.

---

[263] In terms of evangelistic mission, the only matters or any interest are Timothy (1:1 cf. 2:19-23) and material support for the Pauline mission (Phil 4:10-19). The mention of ἐπισκόποις καὶ διακόνοις does not define this group as the recipients of the letter who are 'all' (πᾶσιν). Rather, the recipients are the whole church, the 'overseers and deacons' singled out because 'they have special responsibility' for 'tackling the issues the letter raises' (See further O'Brien, 50).

[264] I would consider that the issue of unity connects with evangelism through continuity from 1:27 (see Chapter 3) but is only relevant in terms of setting the context for the contention between Euodia and Syntyche (cf. 2:14-16; 4:2-3).

[265] In the case of 1:9 and 1:11 the general appeals for 'love' and 'the fruit of righteousness' may include evangelism due to their context (cf. 1:5-7, 12-18a), but this is not certain. In the case of 1:27a,b and 2:12-13, the content of the initial imperatives 'to live as citizens worthy of the gospel of Christ' and 'work out your salvation with fear and trembling' is determined by what follows. Comments will be made concerning these imperatives in the discussions of 1:27c-30 and 2:14-16a.

With Bowers then, I note that my view is my own and thus is open to critique.[266] I come at the text from within evangelical and charismatic traditions with evangelistic assumptions. This suggests I may be guilty of reading the text in a certain way and this may be the case. However, even if I merely succeed in presenting an alternative way of reading the text, I hope that this will be provocative and ensure the continuation of dialogue concerning evangelistic and mission theology. More importantly I hope it will lead others to take up the challenge of communicating the gospel of salvation.

Assumptions

Throughout this study I will assume the *Pauline authorship* of all thirteen letters attributed to Paul in the New Testament. I do not accept that Ephesians, Colossians, 2 Thessalonians and the Pastorals are sufficiently different in theological, personal or linguistic terms to be from different authors. What differences there are I suggest can be adequately explained by variations in occasion,[267] the shared production of Paul's letters,[268] that, in my view, the similarities between the epistles outweigh the differences, and that the undoubted brilliance and literary adaptiveness of Paul should be taken into account.[269]

Accepting the essential coherence of Paul and Luke's accounts, I will assume a traditional *chronology* for Paul's letters.[270] My primary *source* is the

---

[266] Bowers, 'Church ': 108.

[267] Three specific variable factors: 1) *The issues the recipients are encountering* which Paul addresses; 2) *Paul's situation* that impacts the manner of his response (e.g. the collection cf. 1 Cor 16:3; Spain cf. Rom 15:24; 3) *The general situation* Paul finds himself in. Further on the authorship of Ephesians see P.T. O'Brien, *The Letter to the Ephesians*. PNTC (Grand Rapids: Eerdmans, 1999), 4-47; Colossians see P.T. O'Brien, *Colossians, Philemon*. WBC 44 (Dallas: Word, 1982), xli-xlix; 2 Thessalonians see C.J. Wanamaker, *The Epistles to the Thessalonians*. NIGTC (Grand Rapids: Eerdmans, 1990), 17-21; Pastorals see G.D. Fee, *1 and 2 Timothy, Titus*. NIBC (Peabody: Hendrickson, 1984, 88), 23-26.

[268] Specifically I note the uncertainty of role concerning co-authors/senders and secretaries (Tertius [Rom 16:22], Sosthenes [1 Cor 1:1], Timothy [2 Cor 1:1, Phil 1:1; Col 1:1; 1 Thess 1:1; 2 Thess 1:1]; Tychicus [Eph 6:21]; Silas [1 Thess 1:1; 2 Thess 1:1]). The references in some of the post-scripts also suggest that Paul did not pen these letters (1 Cor 16:21; Gal 6:11; Col 4:18; 2 Thess 3:17); see G.J. Barr, 'Paul and Letter Writing in the Fifth Century', *CBQ* 28 (1966): 465-477, 477. He suggests that, in that we do not know how Paul used his secretarial assistance, we should exercise caution.

[269] I consider that a mind able to produce the theological complexity of the undisputed letter to the Romans is easily capable of adapting his vocabulary, expression, theology and style in relation to context (cf. 1 Cor 9:19-22).

[270] F.F. Bruce, *Apostle of the Heart Set Free* (Grand Rapids: Eerdmans, 1977), 474; L.C.A. Alexander, 'Chronology of Paul', in *DPL*, 115-123. Key dates assumed include: Galatians *c.* 48-50 cf. R. N. Longenecker, *Galatians*. WBC 41 (Dallas: Word, 1990),

letters of Paul in that I am seeking to determine how Paul *himself* envisaged his congregations being involved in evangelism. As Luke appears to have been with Paul in the initial evangelisation of Macedonia (Acts 16:10-40),[271] I will refer to Acts and especially the account of the evangelisation of Philippi (16:11-40) as a reliable, if incomplete account.

I also begin my study with the working assumption that the primary passion of Paul's life was proclamation of the gospel for the purpose of bringing people into relationship with God and into Christian community.[272] Clearly for Paul, this purpose was the continuation of the ministry of Christ to save a world trapped under the dominion of sin, wrath and destined for judgement (Rom 2:16; 14:10-12; 2 Cor 5:10) and, unless saved, eternal destruction (Rom 1:18-3:23; Gal 3:22-23; 2 Thess 1:6-10; 1 Tim 2:4-6). Central to Paul's passion was his Damascus Road Experience and his personal transformation from the zealous, Jewish, Pharisee, persecuting Christians to zealous Christian Apostle preaching the gospel (1 Cor 15:8; Gal 1:13-17; Phil 3:5-6; 1 Tim 1:15-16), in particular to 'the Gentiles' (Rom 1:5, 13; 11:13; 15:16, 18; Gal 1:16; 2:2, 8-9; 3:1, 6, 8; 1 Tim 2:7; 2 Tim 4:17). Apart from the salvation of the lost, the ultimate goal for Paul's mission was the establishment of congregations in the major urban areas (Rom 15:19a). His proclamation then concerned the conversion of individuals upon the hearing of the message and their integration into the local church. This priority is not at question; rather, I am seeking to assess how the converts in the churches he planted were to be involved in evangelistic mission.

Definitions

In this study *mission* extends beyond verbal proclamation of the gospel to the whole manner in which believers seek to act and speak with the intention of

---

lxxii-lxxxviii; the evangelisation of Macedonia (*c.* 49-50); 1 and 2 Thessalonians (*c.* 50 cf. F.F. Bruce, *1 & 2 Thessalonians* (Waco: Word, 1982), xxxiv-xxxv; 1 Corinthians *c.* 53-55 cf. G.D. Fee, *The First Epistle to the Corinthians*. NICNT (Grand Rapids: Eerdmans, 1987), 15; 2 Corinthians *c.* 57 cf. P.E. Hughes, *The Second Epistle to the Corinthians*. NICNT (Grand Rapids: Eerdmans, 1962), xxxv; Romans *c.* 56-58 cf. D.J. Moo, *The Epistle to the Romans*. NICNT (Grand Rapids: Eerdmans, 1996), 2-3; Ephesians *c.* 61-62 cf. O'Brien, *Ephesians*, 57; Colossians and Philemon cf. 60-61 cf. O'Brien, *Colossians, Philemon*, liii-liv; Philippians, 60-62 (see further below Chapter 1 Date of Philippians); Pastorals *c.* 63-67 cf. G.D. Fee, *Timothy*, 3-14.

[271] See the use of the second person plural in Acts 16:11-17. After that Luke returns to the third person indicating he was probably not imprisoned and did not move on from Philippi with Paul and Silas.

[272] See Rom 1:1-17; 11:13; 15:16-24; 16:25-27; 1 Cor 1:17-18; 2:1-5; 9:16-27; 2 Cor 2:12, 17; 3:6, 17; 4:1-6, 13; 5:11-20; 10:16; Gal 1:9-12, 15-16; 2:2, 7-10; Eph 3:1-9; 6:19; Phil 1:7, 16, 22; Col 1:23, 25-29; 4:4; 1 Thess 1:5; 2:1-12; 2 Thess 3:1; 1 Tim 1:1, 12-14; 2:7; 2 Tim 1:1, 11–12; Tit 1:1-2.

drawing others into the same faith and extending the lordship of Christ.[273] By *evangelism* I mean 'the proclamation of salvation in Christ to those who do not believe in him, calling them to repentance and conversion, announcing forgiveness of sin, and inviting them to become living members of Christ's earthly community and to begin a life of service to others in the power of the Holy Spirit.'[274] Hence evangelism is primarily a verbal activity of 'gospel-sharing' involving all manner of verbal communication including 'apostolic/evangelistic preaching' (cf. Acts 17:22-34), 'prophetic evangelism' (1 Cor 14:24-25), 'relational evangelism' (cf. 1 Cor 7:16) and 'work-place evangelism' (cf. Acts 18:3; 1 Thess 2:9; 2 Thess 3:7-10).

Sometimes this will be 'apologetic evangelism' which I consider to be verbal response to unbelieving enquiry (Col 4:6 cf. 1 Pet 3:15).[275] At other times this will be 'proactive evangelism' where the believer seeks to initiate gospel sharing. I understand that 'gospel-sharing' is found in many different contexts both structured and unstructured, both prepared and spontaneous. I use evangelism and *proclamation* interchangeably, the latter referring to the verbal communication of the gospel.

By 'ethical witness' I mean 'living before unbelievers in accordance with the ethical principles of the gospel for the purpose of attracting them to faith in Christ.'[276] '*Dunamis* proclamation' I consider to be evangelisation through signs and wonders (Rom 15:19; 1 Cor 4:20).[277] The 'Church' I define as the 'gathered community of those who express faith in Jesus Christ and the gospel.'

---

[273] See the helpful discussion in Dickson, *Mission-Commitment*, 8-12.

[274] Bosch, *Transforming*, 10-11.

[275] Dickson, *Mission-Commitment*, 372 calls this 'verbal apologetic' as opposed to 'missionary proclamation.'

[276] Dickson, *Mission*-Commitment, 338 calls this 'ethical apologetic.'

[277] A neglected element in Dickson, *Mission-Commitment*; it involves the use of spiritual power in signs and wonders and in particular healing, deliverance and miracle cf. J. Wimber, *Power Evangelism. Signs and Wonders Today* (London: Hodder and Stoughton, 1985), 45-60.

CHAPTER 2

Introduction to Philippians

Initial Exegetical Issues

I have chosen to focus on Philippians because, of all the undisputed Pauline letters, it contains a number of texts that have significant bearing on the question of Paul's concern for congregational evangelism. As such, the purpose of this book is to enquire of Philippians whether there are any indications of a general impulse or imperative to proclaim the gospel in the letter. In that it is critical to set the discussion in its rightful context, I begin with an introduction to the book of Philippians giving view on background and contextual issues. In addition I will discuss different approaches to the question of evangelism in Philippians before beginning my own examination.

The Authorship of Philippians

The authorship of Philippians, apart from several disputed passages, has rarely been doubted.[1] The picture of Paul in Philippians is highly consistent with what is found elsewhere in the undisputed epistles as is its language and theology.

---

[1] The views of F.C. Baur, *Paul, the Apostle of Jesus Christ* (Vol 2. London, Williams and Norgate, 1875), 45-79 against Pauline authorship have not taken hold. See for detail and refutation J.J. Müller, *The Epistles of Paul to the Philippians and to Philemon.* NICNT (Grand Rapids: Eerdmans, 1955), 15-17; J. Gnilka, *Der Philipperbrief.* HTKNT (Freiburg: Herder, 1976), 5; F.F. Bruce, *Philippians.* NIBC (Peabody: Hendrickson, 1983, 1989), 12 and 'St Paul in Macedonia. 3. The Philippian Correspondence,' *BJRL* 63 (1980-81): 260-284, 260-262. The analysis of A.Q. Morton and J. McLeman, *Christianity in the Computer Age* (New York: Harper and Row, 1965) and *Paul, the Man and the Myth. A Study in the Authorship of Greek Prose* (New York, Harper and Row, 1966) disputing Pauline authorship has been soundly rejected by H.K. McArthur, 'Computer Criticism', *ExpTim* 76 (1965): 367-70 and '*Kai* Frequency in Greek Letters', *NTS* 15 (1969): 339-49 (where he exposes serious methodological flaws); M. Whittaker, 'A.Q. Morton and J. McLeman,' *Theology* 69 (1966): 567-68; G.F. Hawthorne, *Philippians.* WBC 43 (Waco: Word, 1983), xxvii-xxvix. See also Bruce, xxvii-xxix (subsequent references to Philippians' commentaries include only author's surname and page) and especially W. Hendriksen, *Philippians.* NTC (Edinburgh: Banner of Truth, 1962), 31-36.

Echoes in the literature of the early church confirm this view.[2] As such, few contemporary writers question Paul's authorship.[3]

The reference to Timothy (1:1) is not an indication of co-authorship as the tone and content of the letter indicates.[4] While it is possible Timothy may have been Paul's *amanuensis*,[5] it is more likely he is mentioned due to his previous relationship with the Philippians (Acts 16:1, 13; Phil 2:19-23),[6] his presence with Paul in prison[7] and more importantly, his function as a role-model and in visiting Philippi on Paul's behalf (2:19-23).[8]

The only serious doubts raised concerning the authenticity of Philippians concern Phil 2:6-11.[9] As I note in Appendix 3, I consider the passage is essential to Philippians, it is Pauline in the sense that Paul has adopted it for his

---

[2] See O'Brien, *Philippians*, 9; G.F. Hawthorne, 'Philippians, Letter to the' in *DPL*, 707-13, 709 and *Philippians*, xxviii; J.J. Müller, 15; R.P. Martin, *Philippians*. TNTC (Grand Rapids: Eerdmans, 1987), 37-38; Hendriksen, 33-36.

[3] O'Brien, 9 cf. Hawthorne, xxvii-xxvix. So also Bruce, 9-11; A. Plummer, *A Commentary on St Paul's Epistle to the Philippians* (London: Robert Scott, 1919), xi-xii; J.H. Michael, *The Epistle of Paul to the Philippians*. MNTC (London: Hodder & Stoughton, 1928), x-xi; F.W. Beare, *Philippians* (London: A.C. Black, 1959), 1; M. Silva, *Philippians*. BECNT (Grand Rapids: Baker Book House, 1992), 2; G.D. Fee, *Paul's Letter to the Philippians*. NICNT (Grand Rapids: Eerdmans, 1995), 1; M. Bockmuehl, *Philippians*. BNTC (Peabody: Hendrickson, 1998), 20; P.J. Achtemeier, J.B. Green and M.M. Thompson, *Introducing the New Testament, its Literature and Theology* (Grand Rapids: Eerdmans, 2001), 391; D.A. Carson, D.J. Moo, *An Introduction to the New Testament* (Grand Rapids: Zondervan, 2005), 317-318; W.G. Kümmel, *Introduction to the New Testament* (Trans. H.C. Kee. London: SCM, 1973), 332; R.E. Brown, *An Introduction to the New Testament* (New York: Doubleday, 1997), 484.

[4] Hendriksen, 31; Michael, 1; Bruce, 12; 'Macedonia': 260. Further on co-senders and the dominance of the first person singular in Philippians see S. Byrskog, 'Co-senders, Co-Authors and Paul's Use of the First Person Plural', *ZNTW* 87 (1996): 230-250, 246-247; Fee, 60; U.B. Müller, *Der Brief an der Philipper*. THNT 11/1 (Leipzig: Evangelische Verlagsanstalt, 1993), 34; G.F. Hawthorne, 'Philippians, Letter to the' in *DPL*, 707-13, 708 on the dominance of the singular personal pronoun.

[5] Bockmuehl, 49 rightly notes that the level of involvement is impossible to ascertain. See also Barr, 'Writing': 465-477; Bruce, 251; Fee, 61; J.J. Müller, 32; Hendriksen, 44 all suggest a secretarial role.

[6] Fee, 60-61; O'Brien, 44.

[7] Silva, 39.

[8] Hawthorne, 4. Timothy may be mentioned to make the point to the Philippians that church relationships were to be based on equality rather than authority, superiority or inferiority (δοῦλοι in 2:7 cf. 2:22-23); so Silva, 39. As E.E. Ellis, 'Co-workers, Paul and His' in *DPL*, 188 notes, this mention is not 'merely ornamental.'

[9] Some also consider 3:20-21 is a hymnic non-Pauline interpolation. See J. Reumann, 'Philippians 3:20-21 – A Hymnic Fragment', *NTS* 30 (1984): 593-609. As is the case with 2:5-11, I consider that the passage is poetic but not hymnic and Pauline in that it is integral to Paul's purposes in Philippians.

purposes.

The Integrity of Philippians

For the purposes of this discussion I will accept the integrity of Philippians despite some considering Philippians a composite letter.[10] Resolving the question of integrity is not essential to the argument of this work as the major strands of the discussion concerning general evangelism are found in Phil 1-2; 4:1-9. These passages are in the main uncontroversial in this regard, the key questions surrounding the status of 3:1-4:1 and 4:10-20. In addition, it is generally agreed that Paul authored these sections and so I am confident that I am dealing with Paul's attitude in the debated texts.

Having said this, I consider the case against integrity to be weak for the following reasons. First, the external evidence from Polycarp (ἐπιστολάς; 3:20),[11] the ancient Syriac stichometry mentioning two Philippian letters,[12]

---

[10] Different views include Letter A: 1:1-3:1a; 4:2-7, 10-23; Letter B: 3:1b-4:1, 8-9 as suggested by E.J. Goodspeed, *Introduction to the New Testament* (Chicago: University of Chicago Press, 1937), 90-96 cf. Gnilka, 5-11 cf. Bruce, 'Macedonia': 260-284; G. Freidrich, *Der Brief an die Philipper.* NTD 8 (Göttingen: Vandenhoeck & Ruprecht, 1981), 126-128; M. Jones, 'The Integrity of the Epistle to the Philippians,' *Expositor* 8 (1914): 462; J. Reumann, 'Contributions of the Philippian Community to Paul and to Earliest Christianity', *NTS* 39 (1993): 438-457; P. Perkins, 'Philippians: Theology for the Heavenly Politeuma' in J.M. Bassler (ed.), *Pauline Theology, Vol 1: Thessalonians, Philippians, Galatians, Philemon* (Minneapolis: Fortress Press, 1991), 89-104, 89. Three letter proponents consider 4:10-20/23 as Letter A; 1:1-2:30/3:1a + sections of 4:1/3-7/9 and 4:21-23 as Letter B and 3:1b-4:1/3, [8-9]) as Letter C; see J. Collange, *The Epistle of Saint Paul to the Philippians* (Trans. A.W. Heathcote. London: 1979), 8; Beare, 4, 25-29; B.D. Rahtjen, 'The Three Letters of Paul', *NTS* 6 (1959-60): 167-173, 169; J.L. Blevins, 'Introduction to Philippians', *RevExp* 77 (1980): 311-325, 315; Michael, xi-xii; W. Schmithals, *Paul and the Gnostics* (Trans. J.E. Seely. Nashville: Abingdon, 1972), 72-75. W. Schenk, *Der Philipperbriefe des Paulus. Kommentar* (Stuttgart: Verlag W. Kohlhammer, 1984), 29, 76, 242; G. Bornkamm, 'Der Philipperbrief als paulinische Briefsammlung' in W.C. van Unnik, ed. *Neotestamentica et Patrisica: Eine Freundesgabe O. Cullman zu seinem 60. Geburtstag überreicht.* NovTSup 6 (London: Brill, 1962), 192-202; H. Köster, 'The Purpose of the Polemic of a Pauline Fragment (Philippians 3)', *NTS* 8 (1961-1962): 317-332; J. Müller-Bardorff, 'Zur Frage der literarischen Einheit des Phil', *WZUJ* 7 (1957-1958): 591-604.

[11] Rahtjen, 'Letters': 168.

[12] J. Fitzmyer, 'The Letter to the Philippians' in *JBC* (Vol 2. London: Geoffrey Chapman, 1970), 248; P. Sallew, 'Laodiceans and the Philippians Fragments Hypothesis', *HTR* 87 (1994): 17-27. It is probable that the Syraic stichometry reference to two Philippian letters is probably accidental repetition as argued by A. Souter, *Text and Canon of the New Testament* (London: Duckworth, 1954), 209; D. Peterlin, *Paul's Letter to the Philippians in Light of the Disunity in the Church.* NovTSup 79 (New

Catologus Sinaiticus[13] and the mention by Georgius Syncellus of more than one epistle[14] are ambiguous at best. [15] Secondly, the variation in schema concerning the supposed letters is illustrative of the problem of seeking to establish the so-called original documents.[16] Thirdly, as the extant letter indicates, no unambiguous textual evidence of compilation exists;[17] hence, I consider it best to accept it as it is. Fourthly, in that all extant manuscripts of Philippians are in the main consistent with the canonical text and that a number of scholars have established strong thematic and linguistic parallels and connections across passages which some assign to different letters, the burden of proof remains with those seeking to establish non-integrity.[18]

Fifthly, the elements of the case against the authenticity of 3:1-4:1, while plausible, are able to be interpreted adequately from the perspective of literary integrity.[19] Similarly, there is no need to consider 4:10-20 a separate earlier

---

York: E.J. Brill, 1995), 13; B.S. MacKay, 'Further Thoughts on Philippians', *NTS* 7 (1960-61): 161-170, 161.

[13] P.A. Holloway, *Consolation in Philippians. Philosophical Sources and Rhetorical Strategy* (Cambridge: CUP, 2001), 8-11 notes the listing of Philippians twice in the *Catalogus Sinaiticus* and the mention of 'First epistle to the Philippians' in *Chronographia* by ninth century Byzantine historian Georgius Syncellus which at best point to more than one epistle.

[14] See also Rahtjen, 'Letters': 167-168 who concedes *Catalogus Sinaiticus* is of 'doubtful historical value' (p168) cf. B.S. MacKay, 'Thoughts': 161-162 who also points out the problems of reliability from Syncellus; D.K. Williams, *Enemies of the Cross of Christ. The Terminology of the Cross and Conflict in Philippians.* JSNTS 223 (Sheffield: Academic Press, 2002), 46.

[15] 'Letters' may refer to other non-extant letters cf. 3:1-2 (Bruce, 16; Peterlin, *Letter*, 13); 4:10-20 (J.H. Michael, 'The First and Second Epistles to the Philippians', *ExpTim* 34 (1922-23): 106-109); 'a letter of importance' (J.B. Lightfoot, *The Epistles of St Paul. III. The First Roman Captivity. I. Epistle to the Philippians* (London: MacMillan and Co, 1894), 140-142; J.J. Müller, 20); a collection of Paul's letters sent to all churches (C.L. Mitton, *The Formation of the Pauline Corpus of Letters* (London: Epworth, 1955), 26) or churches in the region (Martin, 11-12; MacKay, 'Further': 163).

[16] T.E. Pollard, 'The Integrity of Philippians', *NTS* 13 (1966-67): 57-66, 57; Collange, 8; Perkins, 'Philippians', 89.

[17] Silva, 14; O'Brien, 12; Hawthorne, xxxii; Martin, 39.

[18] With R.T. Fortna, 'Egocentric', 221.

[19] The change in tone is consistent with the friendship genre as Fee, 9-10 notes. Hawthorne, xxxi suggests such changes are not surprising (cf. Rom 16:16-19; 2 Thess 2:13-16) cf. Pollard, 'Integrity': 59; R.T. Fortna, 'Philippians, Paul's Most Egocentric Letter' in R.T. Fortna and B.R. Gaventa (eds), *The Conversation Continues. Studies in Paul and John in Honour of J. Louis Martyn* (Nashville: Abingdon Press, 1990), 220-234. Τὸ λοιπόν need not suggest 'finally' but may be transitional as argue many including I.H. Marshall, *The Epistle to the Philippians.* EC (London: Epworth, 1992), xxxii and 'Theology', 119; Achtemeier, *Introducing*, 404-405; V. Furnish, 'The Place and Purpose of Philippians III', *NTS* 10 (1963-64): 80-88, 80; J.T. Reed, 'Philippians

letter,[20] since Paul has referred to Philippian support and Epaphroditus earlier (1:5; 2:25-30).[21] In addition, it seems a part of Paul's rhetorical strategy in

---

3:1 and the Epistolary Hesitation Formulas: the Literary Integrity of Philippians, Again', *JBL* 115 (1996): 63-90, esp. p65. The 'major' shift of tenor noted by many at 3:2 (Goodspeed, *Introduction*, 90-96; Collange, 4, 22; Beare, 3; 72-73; Schmithals, *Paul*, 72-73; Müller-Bardorff, 'Frage': 591 and others) is in fact one strongly worded verse (so Pollard, 'Integrity': 69; O'Brien, 13-16; MacKay, 'Further': 163 who points out κύων and Βλέπετε are not always used strongly) which is focussed outside the community and leads quite naturally and rhetorically into Paul's autobiographical presentation of himself as one model among many. The strong parallels with the rest of the letter (see Fee, 285-287) and especially 2:5-11 (see D.E. Garland, 'The Composition and Unity of Philippians. Some Neglected Literary Factors,' *NovT* (27 (1985): 141-73, 157-159; Marshall, xxxii; M. Jones, *The Epistle to the Philippians*. WC (London: Methven, 1918), xlvii; Pollard, 'Integrity': 58-59) and 1:27-30 (D.F. Watson, 'A Rhetorical Analysis of Philippians and its Implications for the Unity Question', *NovT* 30 (1988): 57-88, 76) and 1:3-11 (O'Brien, 16) count against a composite letter. The sense of easy continuity from 3:1 and 4:4 particularly with reference to χαίρετε ἐν κυρίω (3:1c) and χαίρετε ἐν κυρίῳ πάντοτε· πάλιν ἐρῶ, χαίρετε (4:4) reiterates the important theme of joy and a 'framing device' for the appeal of 3:1-4:9. Similarly 'stand fast' and 'have the same mindset' reflects an *inclusio* for 1:27-4:3; so Fee, 286, and not necessarily a new letter. The argument that the eschatological climax and travelogue (2:17-18) indicate the end of a letter (so R. Funk, *Language, Hermeneutic, and Word of God: the Problem of Language in the New Testament and Contemporary Theology* (New York: Harper and Row, 1966), 248-249, 263-274) has been subject to trenchant critique (see Holloway, *Consolation*, 20-23). See also Furnish, 'Place': 81-88. Marshall, xxxii and 'Theology', 119; Martin, 41 who suggest the shift in tone is due to Philippians being written over time as a process cf. U.B. Müller, 7-16 who suggests a 'dictation-break' and new information causing 3:1f.

[20] First, there is the reticence of Paul to thank the Philippians until the close of the letter (4:10-20). Some consider that the delay in the thanksgiving is unusual and an apparent afterthought (Collange, 5-6). Secondly, some consider the break from 4:9-10 is considered rather abrupt and difficult. Thirdly, it is considered unusual that Paul would wait months to thank the Philippians for the wonderful gift brought by Epaphroditus (cf. Beare, 4). So it is surmised that 4:10-20 is a separate letter delivered to Philippi soon after Epaphroditus brought the Philippian gift to Paul (cf. Müller-Bardorff, 'Frage', 596-98). This is strengthened in that 4:10-20 can function as an ancient letter in its own right and the presence of additional notes of finality in 4:8, 19-20. I agree with Fee, 423 that its placement here is emphatic and positive. I also note allusions to the giving of the Philippians earlier (1:5; 2: 25-30) and the similarly 'late concretisation' of the unity issue (1:17; 2:1-4, 14) in Paul's 'failure' to mention Euodia and Syntyche until 4:2. Similarly 'joy' is not emphasised until 3:1; 4:4 yet is clearly relevant throughout (cf. 1:4, 18 (2x), 25; 2:2, 17, 18, 29).

[21] Peterlin, *Letter*, 12-15; W.J. Dalton, 'The Integrity of Philippians', *Bib* 60 (1979): 97-102, 101; Holloway, *Consolation*, 26 note the close parallel between 1:3-11 and 4:10-20; N.A. Dahl, 'Euodia and Syntyche and Paul's Letter to the Philippians', in L.M. White and O.L. Yarbrough (ed's), *The Social World of the First Christians: Essays in*

Philippians to leave specifics of issues to the final section of the letter as is evident by the naming of Euodia and Syntyche (4:2-3) and the reference to the collection despite allusions to these two issues in the first three chapters of the letter. Finally, I note that the argument raises innumerable new questions concerning the rationale for the arrangement and the process of redaction.[22]

As O'Brien puts it: '... as such the theory is to be regarded as a conjectural emendation. It is possible that prior to their being circulated someone brought these three letters together. But there is certainly no trace of this process...'[23] In sum then, while the arguments for Philippians as a composite letter are not without warrant, it is more likely that Philippians is to be considered as a unified whole.[24]

Date and Place of Composition

As with the integrity of Philippians, the date and context for the writing of Philippians are very much in dispute. In terms of this discussion, provenance is a very important issue in 1:12-18a where Paul is positive about the way his presence in the context of writing has stimulated the community to evangelism. Hence, whether Paul is writing from a town with a Pauline community (e.g. Ephesus, Corinth) or a non-Pauline community (e.g. Rome, Caesarea) becomes important. That is, if Paul is speaking of evangelism in a Pauline community

---

Honor of Wayne A. Meeks (Minneapolis: Fortress, 1995), 1-15, 5. I consider 4:10-20 fits the autobiographical sense of the letter (similarly O'Brien, 17-18; Dalton, 'Integrity': 102; D.A. Black, 'Structure of Philippians: A Study in Textlinguistics', *NovT* 37, 1 (Jan 1995): 16-49, 24-25; G. W. Peterman, *Paul's Gift from Philippi. Conventions of Gift Exchange and Christian Giving.* SNTSMS 92. (Cambridge: CUP, 1997), 91-93, 103). With Garland, 'Composition': 152, I agree that ἐπὶ πάσῃ τῇ μνείᾳ ὑμῶν (1:5) provides an intentional thematic *inclusio* between the prologue and epilogue and that 4:10-20 is unlikely to be an individual letter as it lacks any personal details concerning his situation (cf. on contention and joy above). I also consider 4:10-20 to be understandable rhetorically (so Watson, 'Analysis', 83; B. Witherington III, *Friendship and Finances in Philippians* (Valley Forge [Pennsylvania]: Trinity Press International, 1994), 27. Marshall, 'Theology', 120 notes Paul discusses money at the end of other letters (cf. 1 Cor 16:1-4). The case for this passage is not as strong as for 3:2-4:3; so also Bruce, 17.

22 Silva, 15. For typically detailed attempts to reconstruct the hypothetical redaction situation see Gnilka, 16 who places it in Corinth. See also Williams, *Enemies*, 49 who summarises well the problem and various views.

23 O'Brien, 12; Fee, 21-22; N. Flanagan, 'A Note on Phil 3:20-21,' *CBQ* 18 (1956): 8-9; Silva, 14; G.F. Hawthorne, 'Philippians': 709; *Philippians*, xxxi cf. Bockmuehl, 24-25; L.T. Johnson, *The Writings of the New Testament an Interpretation* (Minneapolis: Fortress Press, 1999), 370: 'the hypothesis is needlessly complex and not required.' For examples of such explanations see Collange, 7; Beare, 4; Gnilka, 11-18.

24 Williams, *Enemies*, 54.

rather than Rome, then in 1:12-18a Paul gives direct access to his own perspective for his communities of faith.

The major possibilities are Rome, Ephesus or Caesarea. While it would be beneficial to my argument to opt for Ephesus, my reading of the situation strongly prefers Rome for the following reasons.[25]

First, there are a considerable number of factors, which are used in regard to the different options, which are clearly neutral.[26] Secondly, the Roman imprisonment is the only *clearly given* option for the imprisonment despite

---

[25] Rome as the point of origin for Philippians is supported by the second century Marcionite Prologue to Philippians; Bruce, 11-14; J.J. Müller, 28; Marshall, xx; H.A. Kent Jnr, 'Philippians' in F. Gaebelein (ed), *EBC* (Vol 11/12. Grand Rapids: Zondervan, 1978), 93-159, 99; Lightfoot, 30-31; Plummer, xii; O'Brien, 26; Fee, 37; Beare, 24; Silva, 8; Bockmuehl, 32; A. Motyer, *The Message of Philippians*. BST (Leicester: IVP, 1984), 18; Peterlin, *Letter*, 11; Witherington, *Friendship*, 24; Hendriksen, 30; C.J. Hemer, *The book of Acts in the Setting of Hellenistic History*. WUNT 49 (Tübingen: Mohr (Siebeck), 1989), 275, 393 who sees it as late in his imprisonment; J. H. Houlden, *Paul's Letters From Prison* (Hamondsworth: Penguin, 1970), 44; MacKay, 'Further': 169 among many others. For the completely opposite view see Kümmel, *Introduction*, 324-332 who discounts Rome and suggests Caesarea or Ephesus; C.O. Buchanan, 'Epaphroditus' Sickness and the Letter to the Philippians', *EQ* 36 (1964): 157-166.

[26] These include: 1) That Timothy was with Paul (1:1; 2:19-23) i.e. Corinth (Acts 18:4); Ephesus (1 Cor 4:17; 16:10; 2 Cor 1:1, 19 [cf. Michael, xvi]; Caesarea (Acts 20:4); Rome (Col 1:1; Phm 1) are all possibilities; 2) That Paul refers to ἀρχῇ τοῦ εὐαγγελίου (4:15) which is inconclusive (contra-Gnilka, 101 who sees this fitting Acts 19). I suggest that the opposite may be the case, the further away Paul was from these 'early days', the more intelligible it becomes; 3) Judaisers are a problem in the Macedonian area. While this leads some to date this at the time of Galatians (cf. Michael, xvii), there is nothing to suggest that Judaisers or a variant thereof were not active at the later time. Paul's repeated warning (3:1 cf. 3:18) could refer to that earlier time, but it is generally agreed that these Judaisers are not active in the Philippian church at this time and thus, it may be that their threat had receded but remained a general problem; 4) A lack of reference to the Jerusalem Collection counts against an earlier date to some (cf. Witherington, *Friendship*, 24). This however is inconclusive (so J.A.T. Robinson, *Redating*, 59) in that the Philippian church may have already contributed positively and their support for Paul and temporal distance may have obscured the importance of the collection (so Michael, xxi). Paul intends to travel from the place of writing to Philippi; 5) Some suggest an earlier date is supported by the 'clash' between Paul's plan to visit Spain and his plan in Philippians to revisit Philippi on release (2:24) (cf. J.H. Michael, xvii; R. Jewett, 'Conflicting Movements in the Early Church as Reflected in Philippians', *NovT* 12 (1970): 362-390: 364; U.B. Müller, 19 [for Ephesus]; Hawthorne, xlii [for Caesarea]). However Paul regularly changed his travel plans depending on situations and the leading of the Spirit (cf. Rom 1:13; 15:22, 24 ['hope to visit' Rome]; 1 Cor 16:9; 2 Cor 1:16-24; 2:13; 1 Thess 2:17-18 cf. Acts 16:6-10) so Bruce, 14; D. Guthrie, *New Testament Introduction* (Downers Grove: IVP, 1990), 521; 6) That the theology and circumstances of Philippians cohere best with 2 Corinthians and an earlier/later date.

hypothetical possibilities concerning Ephesus (cf. 1 Cor 15:32; 2 Cor 11:23).[27] Thirdly, while Caesarea is plausible in terms of the existence of a praetorium (cf. Acts 23:35) and the length of the imprisonment,[28] its provincial nature count against it.[29] Similarly, the lack of an apparent life-threatening intensity during the Caesarean imprisonment leaves it as an unlikely context (cf. Phil 1:7, 13, 14, 17; cf. 1:12, 19, 20-24, 29-30; 2:8; 3:10; 4:12, 14).[30] Fourthly, while the details concerning Paul's involvement in Ephesus may indicate some form of additional imprisonment (1 Cor 15:32; 16:9; 2 Cor 1:8), in reality this is purely hypothetical.[31] Fifthly, I consider that the 'journey-problem' is often

---

[27] Luke records only two imprisonments of sufficient length i.e. Caesarea (Acts 23:33f) and Rome (Acts 28:17f). In that Luke's account of Caesarea is reasonably thorough and fails to give an adequate context suiting Philippians, this leaves only Rome where Paul is situated at the completion of Acts. Alternatively one of five imprisonments of 2 Cor 11:23 could be in Paul's mind but where these occurred is unclear. Especially when it is possible that a number of incidents in Acts could have involved short imprisonments (Psidian Antioch [Acts 13:50]; Iconium [14:2]; Lystra [14:19]; Thessalonica [17:6]; Corinth [18:12] and Ephesus [19:23]). Of the imprisonments recorded, Jerusalem (Acts 22:29-23:22) and any supposed incarceration in Ephesus (Acts 19:1-41) are too short to match Philippians. This leaves Rome as the only *concrete* option. As J.A.T. Robinson, *Redating the New Testament* (London: SCM, 1976), 58 suggests, the Ephesian captivity hypothesis 'rests on no direct evidence whatsoever.' Those who hold to an Ephesian provenance however include W. Manson, 'The Date of the Epistle to the Philippians', in *Studies in the Gospels and Epistles* (Ed. M. Black. Manchester: Manchester University, 1962), 149-67; Collange, 17-19 rather optimistically speculates that an Ephesus imprisonment is beyond dispute; Gnilka, 24; U.B. Müller, 16-23; G.S. Duncan, 'A New Setting for St. Paul's Epistle to the Philippians', *ExpTim* 43 (1931-32): 7-11, 8-9; Jewett, 'Conflicting': 365; Perkins, 'Philippians', 90 prior to Paul's deliverance from a mortal threat and after Timothy's return to Ephesus from Corinth; Michael, xiv-xxi; Brown, *Introduction*, 484; Achtemeier, *Introducing*, 402-403; C. Mearns, 'The Identity of Paul's Opponents at Philippi', *NTS* 33 (1987): 194-204, 195.

[28] Luke records a time longer than a year and half at least, easily time for the interactions involved in Philippians (Acts 24:1f, 24, 27; 25:1, 6, 13, 22; 27:1) cf. Hawthorne, xl who sees the *Praetorium* as a strong argument for Caesarea. Another holding to a Caesarean provenance include Robinson, *Redating*, 60. However other factors rule Caesarea out, especially its provincial nature.

[29] A 'political backwater' (Bruce, 13 and 'Macedonia': 264 cf. O'Brien, 24; Guthrie, *Introduction*, 527).

[30] Those who consider it plausible include L. Johnson, 'The Pauline Letters from Caesarea', *ExpTim* 68 (1957-58): 24-26; Hawthorne, xliii-xliv; Kümmel, *Introduction*, 329; Robinson, *Redating*, 61. However I agree with Carson, *Introduction*, 320; U.B. Müller, 17: 'that there is no special reference in the letter to the Philippians to Caesarea as the place of writing' (my translation); Marshall, 'Theology', 121: 'a compelling case for preferring Caesarea to Rome has not yet been offered.'

[31] I also consider that: 1) Luke's supposed silence concerning such an Ephesian imprisonment is very surprising despite being aware that his account in not complete (cf. Michael, xiv-xv); 2) Paul's Roman citizenship makes an imprisonment of such length

exaggerated both in terms of the number of journeys supposedly required for the data of Philippians (two and not five) and the time needed for the journeys to take place from Rome.[32] Sixthly, the combination of references to *praetorium* (1:13) and Christians in Caesar's household (4:22) fit best in Rome and not Caesarea or Ephesus.[33] Finally, while I agree that the heightened

---

unlikely (cf. Bockmuehl, 27-28; Hendriksen, 24-25); 3) The reference to a *praetorium* does not fit as Ephesus was a capital of a senatorial rather than imperial province (see below). It is also problematic whether Ephesus had the 'occasion or facility' to hold a prisoner for long enough as noted by Hemer, *Acts*, 273. The notion (cf. Michael, xiv-xv) that Rom 16:7 refers to Ephesian imprisonment depends on two unsupported ideas. First, that Romans 16 is connected to Ephesus (for counter arguments see Moo, *Romans*, 5-9; J.D.G. Dunn, *Romans 1-8*, WBC 38A (Word, Waco, 1988), lx-lxi; B. Byrne, *Romans*. SPS (Collegeville: Michael Glazier, 1996), 29). Secondly, that Ephesus was the point of imprisonment to which Paul refers (see Plummer, *Understanding*, xiv).

32 See Collange, 16; G.S. Duncan, *St. Paul's Ephesian Ministry: A Reconstruction* (London: Hodder and Stoughton, 1929), 80-82; S.R. Llewelyn, 'Sending Letters in the Ancient World: Paul and the Philippians', *TynB* 46.2 (1995): 337-356, 338 cf. Marshall, xviii-xx while still opting for Rome; Brown, *Introduction*, 496 sees the journeys as a 'formidable obstacle'; U.B. Müller, 18; Gnilka, 21; Achtemeier, *Introducing*, 400; Blevins, 'Introduction': 314-315; Hendriksen, 30 [prefers 4]) who suggest five trips i.e. 1) Epaphroditus delivery of the gift to Paul (4:18); 2) News of Epaphroditus' illness to Philippi (2:26); 3) News of Paul's imprisonment to Philippi; 4) News of the Philippian concern for Epaphroditus upon hearing of his illness (2:26); 5) Epaphroditus is sent back (2:25). However only journeys 1 and 4 are essential, it being possible that Epaphroditus fell ill en-route to Philippi in that he 'risked his life' to deliver the gift to Paul (2:30) (so B. Reicke, 'Caesarea, Rome and the Captivity Epistles,' in W.W. Gasque and R.P. Martin (ed's), *Apostolic History and the Gospel. Biblical and Historical Essays Presented to F.F. Bruce on his 60th Birthday* (Grand Rapids, Eerdmans, 1970), 277-86, 284 cf. Fee, 37. Silva, 7 suggests three but concedes the first is debatable; Lightfoot, 36-37 suggests two to four; Llewelyn, 'Sending': 350; Bruce, 'Macedonia': 276 reconstructs this concisely cf. Fee, 97; Lightfoot, 35-37; Silva, 15. Even if it is accepted that there are more than two journeys, the problem is removed when one analyses the distances and travel times involved, each journey taking forty to fifty days (Lightfoot, 38; Bruce, 15, 23; K. Grayston, *The Letters of Paul to the Philippians and the Thessalonians*. EPC (Cambridge: Epworth, 1967), 8; Hemer, *Acts*, 273-274; Bockmuehl, 31-32; Hawthorne, xli; Beare, 19; Witherington, 24; Silva, 14; Llewelyn, 'Sending': 338). If two journeys are involved this requires a conservative total time of four months. Even if it is accepted there were five trips, this would still only require 10 months.

33 While Caesar's household may refer to slaves and freedmen of the imperial civil service throughout the empire, the greatest concentration was found in Rome and so Rome provides the best possibility for Paul's meaning here (see Bruce, 14; Hendriksen, 24; Bockmuehl, 30-32. P.R.C. Weaver, *Familia Caesaris: A Social Study of the Emperor's Freedman and Slaves* (Cambridge: CUP, 1972), 78f suggests that 70% of *Caesaris* individuals lived in Rome, 96% in Rome, Italy and North Africa). The reference to ἐν ὅλῳ τῷ πραιτωρίῳ can refer to the governor's palace or to the emperor's troops based in Rome (*BDAG* 697; Lightfoot, 99-104). The reference

evangelistic fervour and opposition to Paul referred to in Phil 1:14-18a potentially fits Ephesus (Acts 19:10),[34] it could also fit Rome in the period post-Acts.

It seems then that Rome is the best alternative. Fee rightly contends that the references to the *praetorium* and Caesar's household fit Rome better than any other context suggested; 'whereas one must look under all kinds of "stones" to turn up evidence for their existence in Ephesus or Caesarea.'[35] Not that Rome is without its problems in this regard. Luke's report of Paul's open and friendly situation in Rome does not align with Philippians where his life appears threatened (Acts 28:30-31). The evidence of 2 Tim 4:16-18, although highly disputed, suggests though, that there was a subsequent deterioration in Paul's conditions. It is probable then, that Paul wrote the letter to the Philippians from his Roman imprisonment subsequent to the point at which Luke concludes his

---

suggests Caesarea (Acts 23:35 cf. Robinson, *Redating*, 60) to some. However Caesarea's small size and the unlikelihood that Paul would have been delighted by the whole palace in Caesarea becoming aware of the reason for Paul's imprisonment (1:13) count against it; so Fee, 35-36 cf. O'Brien, 24; Lightfoot, 30 for older commentators. The reference to *praetorium* argues against an Ephesian provenance as Ephesus was in a senatorial (not imperial) province and so there is no evidence of a governor's praetorium (cf. Bruce, 12 and 'Macedonia': 263; O'Brien, 22; Fee, 35; Marshall, xx; Plummer, *Understanding,* xiv). In addition an inscription in the vicinity of Ephesus cited in support of this (See *Corpus Inscriptionum Judaiscarum* (CIL) III, 6085, 7135, 7136) has been ruled out by Bruce, 12 and 'Macedonia: 263, n.3; O'Brien, 22. Marshall, 'Theology', 121 who note that this refers not to the presence of the praetorian guard (*praetorianus*) in Ephesus, but to a patrolling guard (*stationarius*) on a Roman road outside of the city. Ephesian proponents are forced to speculate on this point of detail, which I find inadequate (cf. Michael, xv; Collange, 16; Duncan, 'Setting': 7; Gnilka, 21). While the great number of guards stationed in Rome (9000) may be a problem, with four-hourly shifts over a two year-plus period, the power of the spoken word to spread and the eagerness of Paul to share the gospel with everyone, it is feasible that Paul was speaking in actuality *as he saw it* (cf. Fee, 112-113). The case for Rome is also enhanced by the Romanisation of Philippi; the reference to the *Praetorium* and household of 'Caesar' is certain to have had an enhanced effect on those in Philippi (cf. Bockmuehl, 28).

[34] Michael, xvi. Similarly, there is a lack of evidence of an outburst of evangelistic fervour in Caesarea. Hendriksen, 25 on this point notes that Caesarea appears too small to suit this evidence. Similarly Blevins, 'Introduction': 314 who goes further suggesting there is no evidence of Caesarean opposition to Paul during his imprisonment. His suggestion that there is no church in Caesarea is ruled out by καὶ τῶν μαθητῶν in Acts 21:16. So while Paul may be referring to the work of Philip 'the evangelist' (Acts 21:8), this does not fit 1:14-18a. The case for Ephesus here is very strong with clear evidence of evangelistic activity stimulated by Paul in Ephesus (Acts 19:20) among general believers (Acts 19:9b-10), Jews (Acts 19:13-16) and conflict (Acts 19:9a, 23f). This detail of the situation in Rome is unclear in this regard and admittedly speculative.

[35] Fee, 459.

account of the spread of the Christian message (AD 61-63). It seems that the conditions of Paul's imprisonment have taken a turn for the worse and his life is now threatened (Phil 1:18f cf. 2 Tim 4:16-18). This is certainly feasible in that Paul was sent to Rome to face Caesar. Paul's activity in Rome as Luke records it could well have led to this situation. His free proclamation of the gospel to Jews and Gentiles in all likelihood has excited persecution at the hands of the two groups in Rome as elsewhere, leading to a harsher confinement (Acts 28:17-28).[36]

Having said this, I concede the possibility of Ephesus as the point of origin for Philippians despite the elements of conjecture concerning the Praetorium and possible imprisonment in Ephesus.[37] Indeed it would be to the advantage of this analysis to see it this way in that if Ephesus was the point of origin, Paul then would be writing from one Pauline church context to another. In addition Paul would be writing earlier in his career (*c.* AD 55), which would amplify the possibility that my findings apply to his whole career.[38] Furthermore, if Ephesus is the provenance, then the evidence of evangelistic fervour in Ephesus (Acts 19:10-20) enhances the probability that Paul wanted his congregations to be engaged in evangelism.[39] If that is the case, then Ephesus is a definite example of an evangelising Pauline church. However, on the whole, the case for a Roman provenance of Philippians is stronger and this analysis will be based on this assumption.

Genre

Another area of contention concerning Philippians is the matter of genre. In recent times Philippians has been classified as epideictic rhetoric,[40] deliberative

---

[36] Particularly when some of the Jews were not convinced and this led to disagreement (28:24-25). Luke does not explore the impact of Paul's proclamation to the Gentiles but it is reasonable to suspect in a city whose life was based on the Graeco-Roman pantheon and imperial cult that it was not all received with affection.

[37] I note also a number of scholars who see it as a 50/50 decision between Rome and Ephesus including Carson, *Introduction*, 321; Motyer, 17-18; Martin, 36-37; F. Thielman, *Philippians*. NIVAC (Grand Rapids: Zondervan, 1995), 18-22.

[38] Collange, 19 argues it was written between Autumn AD 52 - Spring AD 55 or between Autumn AD 54 – Spring AD 57.

[39] That there was an outbreak of evangelistic fervour is seen in Paul's own ministry (19:8), in that 'all the Jews and Greeks' in Asia heard the message in a two year period, in the incidence of signs and wonders (19:11-16) and widespread repentance and conversion (19:17-20).

[40] G.A. Kennedy, *New Testament Interpretation through Rhetorical Criticism* (Chapel Hill: University of North Carolina Press, 1984), 77; C. Basevi and J. Chapa, 'Philippians 2:6-11: The Rhetorical Function of a Pauline "Hymn"' in C.J. Claasen, *Rhetoric and the New Testament* (Leiden: Brill, 2002), 349.

rhetoric,[41] chiasmus,[42] a family letter[43] or a friendship letter.[44] While each of these approaches sheds new insight on Philippians, I am not convinced that any of the attempts to fit Philippians into these or other schemes has fully succeeded. In this study I will take the general position that Philippians is an 'Apostolic Christian letter' from Paul to the church in Philippi.

Concerning rhetorical studies, they do highlight features of the letter, which is clearly designed to convince the Philippians with regard to their conduct. Similarly, they demonstrate the interconnectedness of the whole. However, it seems Philippians resists being reduced to one theme but rather has a multiplicity of interconnected purposes, which are difficult to weight.[45] This is

---

[41] The dominant view among rhetorical critics including Watson, 'Analysis': 59; Black, 'Structure': 16; Marshall, 'Paul's Ethical Appeal in Philippians' in Porter, *Rhetoric*, 357-374; A.H. Snyman, 'Persuasion' in Philippians 4:1-20' in Porter, *Rhetoric*, 325-337; Basevi, '2:6-11', 349; Witherington, *Friendship*, 18; L.G. Bloomquist, *The Function of Suffering in Philippians*. JSNTSS 78 (Sheffield: Sheffield Academic Press, 1993), 121; R. Brucker, *'Christushymnen' oder, ' epideiktische Passagen'? Studien zum Stilwechsel im Neuen Testament und seiner Umwelt* (FRLANT 176), Göttingen: Vandenhoeck & Ruprecht, 1997), 290-300 mentioned in U.B. Müller, 16; Williams, *Enemies*, 99.

[42] A.B. Luter and M.V. Lee, 'Philippians as Chiasmus: Key to the Structure, Unity and Theme Questions', *NTS* 41 (1995): 89-101 who see the central theme as 'partnership in the gospel' expressed throughout the epistle in a chiasmic fashion i.e. (A-A': 1:3-11/4:10-20; B-B': 1:12-26/4:6-9; C-C': 1:27-2:4/4:1-5; D-D': 2:5-16/3:1b-21; E-E': 2:17-3:1 (*Midpoint*). The approach comes close to achieving the three-fold goal they express. Positively, the approach demonstrates the thematic and linguistic interconnectedness of Philippians and points to a certain structural unity and highlights the centrality of the theme, 'gospel partnership.' However, the connections are in many cased forced (esp. 1:12-26/4:6-9) and obscure the connectedness of the themes of Philippians across all parts (e.g. suggesting that 1:3-11 is chiastically related to 4:10-20 tends to obscure the other connections to this prologue throughout the epistle such as 'fellowship in the gospel' with 1:27; 2:16; 4:2). In addition and fatally, the structure elevates Timothy and Epaphroditus as the pivot of the exemplars rather than Christ, which seems to place too much emphasis on this passage.

[43] L. Alexander, 'Hellenistic Letter-Forms and the Structure of Philippians,' *JSNT* 37 (1989): 87-101.

[44] Fee, 2-7 cf. Johnson, *Writings*, 372-373; Brown, 483; P. Marshall, *Enmity in Corinth. Social Conventions in Paul's Relations with the Corinthians.* WUNT 2:23 (Tübingen: Mohr (Siebeck), 1987), 158-63; S.K. Stowers, 'Friends and Enemies in the Politics of Heaven. Reading Theology in Philippians' in Bassler, *Theology*, 105-121, esp. 107 n6; U.B. Müller, 34.

[45] J.T. Reed, 'Using Ancient Rhetorical Categories to Interpret Paul's Letters: A Question of Genre' in Porter, *Rhetoric*, 292-324 and C.J. Claasen, 'St Paul's Epistles and Ancient Greek and Roman Rhetoric', in Porter, *Rhetoric*, 319 rightly note a number of themes stand out in Philippians and the epistle continually resists being focalised into one issue. As Claasen puts it: 'more probably, there is no one theme in Philippians; instead Paul's discourse moves from topic to topic, with recognisable cohesive ties

reinforced by the wide variation in understandings of both the structure and the main theme of Philippians among those who understand it rhetorically.[46] Furthermore, I note that the connection between epistolography and formal rhetoric is still being formulated, making the whole enterprise rather tentative.[47] In addition, in that deviation from these models was a key feature of the writings of the Graeco-Roman period, assuming that all ancient writings were based on common rhetorical types is tenuous.[48] Fee rightly notes that adoption of the forms suggested tends to dominate interpretation without sufficient regard for their essential epistolary nature.[49] As U.B. Müller rightly notes it is not appropriate 'to press the whole letter into a uniform rhetorical pattern.'[50]

In light of this, while accepting that Paul had a rhetorical purpose in the letter, and that each section functions within that purpose, it is best not to impose a formal external rhetorical category upon the text. So for example, Bloomquist argues that the opponents in 3:1f are the same as in 1:15-18a on the basis that he has designated 3:1-16 as *reprehensio* which 'develops the *partitio* of 1:15-18a.'[51] This assignation allows the methodological macrostructure to obscure clear indications in the text that the opponents are different.[52] This

---

between micro-structures and macro-structures but no one overarching rhetorical macro-structure' (319).

[46] I note differing views of whether Philippians should be understood as epideictic or deliberative rhetoric (see above); whether the main theme is 'living worthy of the gospel' (Watson, Snyman, Basevi and Chapa, Black, Brucker) and if so, which dimension of this wide concept is most prominent whether 'suffering' (Bloomquist), 'friendship and finances' (Witherington) or ethical appeal (Marshall)? I note great variation in understanding of the functions of portions of the letter (esp. 1:15-18a, 18-26, 27-30; 3:1-16; 4:1-9) in terms of the different analyses.

[47] S.E. Porter, 'The Theoretical Justification for the Application of Rhetorical Categories to Pauline Epistolary Literature' in S.E. Porter and T.H. Olbricht (ed's), *Rhetoric and the New Testament. Essays from the 1992 Heidelberg Conference.* JSNTS 90 (Sheffield: Sheffield Academic Press, 1993), 99-122 esp.110, 115-116, 122: J.T. Reed, 'Categories' and C.J. Claasen, 'St Paul's Epistles and Ancient Greek and Roman Rhetoric' in Porter and Olbricht, *Rhetoric*, 286-322; S. Byrskog, 'Epistolography, Rhetoric and Letter Prescript: Romans 1.1-7 as a test case', *JSNT* 65 (1997): 27-46. However, that is not to say Paul does not use rhetorical strategies at a number of levels in a general sense. It is the application of classical rhetorical categories as the *primary* interpretative matrix to an epistle that I am wary of.

[48] Fee, 15; Bockmuehl, 23.

[49] Fee, 16.

[50] U.B. Müller, 16 (my translation).

[51] Bloomquist, *Function*, 121. The wild variance in the way rhetorical analysists interpret the text is highlighted in the exegesis that will follow. In every instance there is astonishing variation in terms of assigning the text of Philippians to rhetorical categories.

[52] See below Chapter 2 on 1:15-18a and later in this Chapter on 'opponents.'

example illustrates the danger of utilising an external structure drawn from the culture to interpret the letter.

Hence, I would agree with I.H. Marshall who suggests that such structures are simply 'too neat.'[53] It would appear then that the application of the tri-fold rhetorical models (forensic, epideictic, deliberative) from ancient rhetorical handbooks to Paul's letters is not completely justified. Similarly, the attempt to interpret Philippians as a macro-chiasmus, although recognising some of the connections within the text, fails to convince at every points and limits the potential interconnectedness of many portions of the letter.

Having said this, concerning rhetorical analysis, I agree with the application of rhetorical criticism in general terms to the Pauline epistles. After all, Paul was a proclaimer and his letters did serve in some sense as read or proclaimed documents in the place of person-to-person dialogue. They are rhetorical then in the sense that they seek to persuade. They contain rhetorical devices. In addition, it is clear that the various aspects of the letter intersect and overlap throughout. Hence, I maintain that there is rhetorical impact and import to all aspects of Philippians and this will feature in my analysis.

More promising, yet still not fully convincing, is attempts to understand Philippians in terms of epistolographical categories and especially Philippians as a letter of friendship. Loveday Alexander considers that Philippians coheres with the '*Verbindungsbrief*', a Hellenistic seven-element 'family' letter.[54] Hence, the real focus of the letter is answered in that Philippians is 'adapted and expanded by Paul and employed with the primary purpose of strengthening the "family" links between the apostle and the Christian congregation in Philippi.'[55] While few have taken up this approach, others have found the 'letter of friendship genre' more appealing, suggesting Philippians has the 'formal character' of a 'friendly letter' whereas the content of the letter 'carries on the conversation at a much deeper level of friendship.'[56]

Fee argues that Philippians contains the Graeco-Roman notion of 'true friendship' involving virtue, affection, social reciprocity in terms of giving[57] and 'agonistic' (competitive) references to enemies.[58] Philippians then is based on a friendship partnership seen in their 'partnership in the gospel',

---

[53] Marshall, xxix.

[54] See Alexander, 'Letter-forms': 90-94 for the seven elements. On 'family letters' see further J.L. White, 'Ancient Greek Letters' in D.E. Aune, *Graeco-Roman Literature and the New Testament* (Atlanta: Scholars Press, 1988), 85-106, 91-93; J.L. White, 'Introductory Formulae in the Body of the Pauline Letter', *JBL* 90 (1971), 1-97; *Light from Ancient Letters* (Philadelphia: Fortress Press, 1986), 202-213.

[55] Alexander, 'Letter-forms': 95 notes the central business of the letter is 1:12 whilst Phil 3-4 is not out of keeping with Hellenistic letters of this type and represents a 'sermon-at-a-distance' (96-100).

[56] Fee, 3 cf. Stowers, 'Friends', 110; Johnson, *Writings*, 372.

[57] Stowers, 'Friends', 110.

[58] Fee, *Philippians*, 6; Stowers, 'Friends', 113.

'benefactions to Paul', mutual suffering (1:29-30; 2:17) and mutual 'deep affection' (1:7; 4:1),[59] mutuality and reciprocity in Paul's concern for 'progress', mutual prayer (1:4, 19) and material gifts (4:10-20). The 'agonistic' element of ancient friendship is seen in the reference to 'opposition' (1:15-17, 28; 2:21; 3:2, 17-19) and a concern for the 'same mindset' (2:2-5; 4:2-3).[60] Fee sums up by stating that 'many aspects of letters of friendship are clearly evident in Philippians, not only in some of the "formal" matters, but even more so at key points along the way of the body of the letter.'[61] He suggests that the many exhortations in the letter are 'related primarily to his concern over some "posturing" within the community which, if left unchecked, will surely impede the cause of the gospel.'[62] Fee highlights the importance of moral exhortation in hortatory terms, the larger part of the letter appealing on the basis of friendship for right behaviour (1:27-2:18; 3:1-4:3). This is seen especially through the use of 'exemplary paradigms' throughout Philippians,[63] including Timothy (2:19-23) and Epaphroditus (2:25-30) 'because both exemplify the gospel',[64] and in particular Christ (2:6-11) and Paul (3:4-14).

Fee concludes that Philippians is a 'hortatory letter of friendship' sent in Paul's own stead. Thus two themes, mutual friendship and exhortation dominate.[65] Most significantly for this discussion, Fee notes the centrality of the gospel to Philippians. 'Paul and their friendship is predicated on their mutual "participation/partnership *in the gospel*".'[66] Consequently Fee sees it in terms of a three-way bond between Paul, the Philippians and Christ.

This epistolographic approach is to be preferred in that it treats the letter in terms of its primary genre as a letter rather than merely as a speech. However, I consider that neither the family or friendship approach accounts sufficiently for the material. Alexander for example, admits that Paul varies the pattern of the 'family letter' substantially (Phil 3-4). In addition the absence of 'familial language' in the opening greetings calls the 'family letter' hypothesis into question.[67] Similarly, while Fee's analysis illustrates the 'friendship' dimension of Philippians and applies to it an appropriate category, there are problems with his approach. Bockmuehl notes the absence of *philia* and *phileō* language and the social equality typical of 'letters of friendship.'[68] Furthermore he notes

---

[59] Stowers, 'Friends', 109.

[60] Supported by a large number of *hapax* legomena related to 'friendship' and 'exhortation' and a focus on living and not doctrine (Fee, 18-21).

[61] Fee, 6-7.

[62] Fee, 10.

[63] Fee, 11.

[64] Fee, 12.

[65] Fee, 12-13.

[66] Fee, 14 (Emphasis Mine).

[67] White, 'Ancient', 92.

[68] Bockmuehl, 35 notes that social equality typical of 'friendship letters' is absent in the Paul-Philippian apostle-congregation authority relationship (esp. 3:1-12).

that Greek patristic commentators acknowledge the friendliness of Philippians but do not suggest it is a 'letter of friendship.'[69] I suggest then that the epistle can at best be said to bear some resemblance to 'family' or 'friendship letters' without necessarily implying direct dependence.[70] Philippians is familial and friendly without correlating exactly with the forms.[71]

Thus, I suggest that Philippians eludes being assigned to any one particular genre or form.[72] As Bockmuehl puts it, 'no one Graeco-Roman social convention adequately captures what is undeniably a new and distinctive social phenomenon: a Jewish Apostle teaching Gentiles about faith in a Jewish Messiah, with the vision of a church composed equally of Jews and Gentiles.'[73] Bockmuehl also warns against applying Graeco-Roman social constructs in the light of Paul's *Jewish* socio-cultural and religious background. He notes other possible modes of relationship including rabbi-pupils, prophet, official emissary/*Diaspora* congregation and/or structured leadership as in Qumran and apostolic overseer/Palestinian Jewish-Christian communities. He encourages caution in applying Graeco-Roman social convention to Philippians.[74] As Bockmuehl puts it:

> Rhetorical, epistolographic and text-linguistic arguments for unity too often remain methodologically arbitrary, inappropriately prescriptive in their use of ancient parallels and patterns, or indeed mutually contradictory. They frequently require one to conform Philippians to rigid rhetorical schemes and conventions – or to interpret it solely through the myopically 'synchronic' spectacles of a strictly internal linguistic analysis, analysing the text in splendid isolation from the historical flesh-and-blood complexities affecting the author and his readers. For all their apparent methodological sophistication, such proposals tend to tax credulity and in the end prove very little indeed.[75]

Paul's letters then are not deliberative treatises or public speeches but are personal letters intended for oral reading. Hence, the standard principles of

---

[69] Bockmuehl, 35. See also J. Reumann, 'Philippians, Especially Chapter 4, as a "Letter of Friendship": Observations on a Checkered History of Scholarship' in J.T. Fitzgerald, *Friendship, Flattery, and Frankness of Speech: Studies in Friendship in the New Testament World*. NTSup 82 (Leiden: Brill, 1996), 83-106, 35.

[70] Bockmuehl, 35.

[71] White, 'Ancient', 98. I note with Bockmuehl, 38 that a number of exegetes qualify their standard paradigms in regards to Philippians.

[72] Here is an example of Paul as *spermalogos* picking up 'scraps of knowledge from everywhere' including epistle form and rhetoric cf. T. Engberg-Pedersen, 'Stoicism in Philippians' in T. Engberg-Pedersen (ed.), *Paul in his Hellenistic Context*. SNTW (Edinburgh: T&T. Clark, 1994), 256-291, 256.

[73] Bockmuehl, 38.

[74] Bockmuehl, 38. Perhaps Hawthorne, 14 is correct is seeing in Paul's letters anticipation of later fully developed rhetorical macro-forms.

[75] Bockmuehl, 24-25 and further 39-40.

formal ancient letter writing and rhetoric are not necessarily immediately and clearly applicable.[76] His letters are oral (aural), 'dictated to be read aloud' and set in the context of the living interplay of the situations of Paul, the Philippians and God/gospel/Christ.[77] Hence, I will not seek to force Paul's letters into a rhetorical or epistolographical model.

That is not to say Paul did not use Graeco-Roman letter structure, rhetoric and rhetorical structure. Rather, with Bockmuehl, I approach the text from a historical-theological perspective considering that 'it is only a historically grounded theological exegesis which can come close to uncovering the agenda implicit in the texts themselves i.e. the central convictions they were written to communicate.'[78]

Issues at Play in Philippians

As intimated above, a number of issues are at play in the epistle to the Philippians. In light of my conclusion concerning attempts to narrow the thematic reference of Philippians to one concept, it is my contention that, when considering Philippians, a number of elements that intersect in Paul's mind must be held in tension. In this section I will briefly introduce these elements including Paul's situation, the goodness of the Philippian church, persecution – opposition – suffering, contention, joy, hope, false teaching and, supremely for this discussion, whether there is a concern for evangelism and the advance of the gospel in Philippians. In the body of this study I will examine whether evangelism in a congregational and participatory sense permeates both Paul's situation in Rome and in Philippi. My purpose is not to push this dimension forward as *the theme of the letter*; rather I will explore whether, *along with other crucial elements*, general congregational evangelism is essential to the fabric of Philippians. If so then on the basis of Philippians alone, the thesis that no such impulse is detectable within Paul will prove to be tenuous.

---

[76] The relationship between epistolography and rhetoric is not completely clear. See C.A. Wanamaker, 'Epistolary vs. Rhetorical Analysis: Is a Synthesis Possible?' in K.P. Donfried and J. Beutler, *The Thessalonians Debate; Methodological Discord or Methodological Synthesis?* (Grand Rapids: Eerdmans, 2000), 255-286; E. Krentz, '1 Thessalonians: Rhetorical Flourishes and Formal Constraints' in K.P. Donfried and J. Beutler, *The Thessalonians Debate*, 287-318; R.F. Collins, '"I Command that this Letter be Read": Writing as a Manner of Speaking' in K.P. Donfried and J. Beutler, *The Thessalonians Debate*, 319-339. See also C. Clifton, 'Keeping up with Recent Studies. XVI. Rhetorical Criticism and Biblical Interpretation', *ExpTim* 100.7 (1989): 252-258 esp, 257.

[77] Fee, 16 esp. 13.

[78] Bockmuehl, 43.

Paul's Situation

Paul's missiological context is as follows. As noted above, the primary passion of Paul's life was the proclamation of the gospel for the purpose of bringing people into relationship with God and into Christian community. The particular sphere for this call is 'the Gentiles.'[79] The ultimate goal for Paul was the establishment of congregations in the major urban areas. His proclamation concerns the conversion of individuals upon the hearing of the message and their integration into the church.

At the time of Philippians, he is in Rome, a fulfilment of an earlier expressed dream and long-held desire (Rom 1:11-15; 15:24, 28). He considers that he has completed his work of establishing churches in the key centres of the regions along the northeastern rim of the Mediterranean (Rom 15:19, 23). His initial plan appears to have been to travel to Rome for a variety of reasons. First, he wants to pastorally and charismatically encourage the Roman church and to himself be encouraged by the Romans (Rom 1:11-12). Secondly, he desires to come to Rome to evangelise unbelievers (Rom 1:13-15). Thirdly, he hopes to be materially provisioned (Rom 15:24)[80] for what is his first priority; an evangelistic mission to the virgin territory of Spain in the west (Rom 15:20, 24, 28).[81]

However, according to Luke, his trip to Rome came about not by his own planning, but through appeal to Caesar, and thus he went to Rome as a prisoner (Acts 25:11-12). Whilst in Rome opportunities have come to proclaim the gospel first from house arrest (Acts 28:30-31) and now in closer confinement

---

[79] See Rom 1:5, 13; 11:13; 15:16, 18; Gal 1:16; 2:2, 8-9; 3:1, 6, 8; 1 Tim 2:7; 2 Tim 4:17.

[80] See J.D.G. Dunn, *Romans 9-16*. WBC 38B (Waco: Word, 1988), 872; J. Fitzmyer, *Romans: A New Translation with Introduction and Commentary*. ABC (New York: Doubleday, 1993), 717 and others who note that προπεμφθῆναι has the sense of helping one on their journey by providing material support, letters of introduction, transport and company on the way. In the early church it was a technical term for missionary support (Acts 15:2; 20:38; 21:5; 1 Cor 16:6, 11; 2 Cor 1:16; Tit 3:13; 3 Jn 6). R. Jewett, 'Paul, Phoebe, and the Spanish Mission', in J. Neusner et al, *The Social World of Formative Judaism and Christianity: Essays in Tribute to Howard Clark Kee* (Philadelphia: Fortress Press, 1988): 144-164, 161 suggests Phoebe was going to act as patron for this mission.

[81] It is probable Paul here is referring to the absence of Jewish and Christian communities in the west (so W.P. Bowers, 'Jewish Communities in Spain in the Time of Paul the Apostle', *JTS* (1975): 395-402; Jewett, 'Spanish': 144-147, see n6 for a list of those who assumed Jewish communities in Spain; O.F.A. Meindardus, 'Paul's Missionary Journey to Spain: Tradition and Folklore', *BA* 41 (1978): 61-63). Another possibility is that that Spain was the eschatological completion of 'the ends of the earth' ushering in the *Parousia* (cf. 'Tarshish'; Is 66 [so Aus, 'Paul's travel plans': 242-246; P. Stuhlmacher, *Paul's Letter to the Romans* (Trans. S.J. Hafemann. Louiseville: Westminster Press, 1994), 240; Dunn, *Romans 9-16*, 871.

among the guards (Phil 1:12-13), an unexpected fulfilment of his desire to proclaim the gospel. It would appear that in the intervening period, Paul has changed his plan to go to Spain immediately, rather expressing a desire to travel to Philippi soon (Phil 2:24). Opinion is divided on whether Paul did leave Rome and travel to Philippi, or indeed, to Spain.

Whilst in Rome Paul has encountered two kinds of opposition. First, there are his captors who can be defined as unbelieving Roman opponents of the Christian message at whose hands Paul faces possible death (1:19-20).[82] Significantly, there is a specific link between their treatment of Paul and evangelistic activity. This is seen first in that the gospel has advanced (1:12), the guard have been evangelised, the word has spread into the city (1:13) and the heightened Roman fervour is, in part, aimed at increasing his suffering (1:17). Paul's suffering at the hands of these Romans is mentioned again in 1:30 where Paul draws a parallel between the Philippian suffering and his own both in previous visits to Philippi and currently in Rome. The Philippians are having the same struggle (ἀγῶνα) which they have heard he is having now in Rome (νῦν ἀκούετε ἐν ἐμοί). This *potentially* suggests that there are residents in the Philippi community opposed to the Christian message that the members of the church are proclaiming. As I will seek to show in the discussion below, these are probably pagan Gentiles and not Jews since there were few Jews in Philippi.[83]

Secondly, in 1:15-18a Paul refers to Roman Christians who preach Christ falsely out of envy, rivalry and selfish ambition.[84] These negative attitudes come together in some way with a motivation to cause Paul suffering. It is certain they are Christians as they preach Christ, there being nothing in the context to suggest Paul finds them heretics such as Judaisers (1:15, 17, 18 cf. 3:2). Indeed Paul is delighted that they are preaching.

As I suggest below in my exegesis, these are probably falsely motivated authentic Christians with a Jewish (and perhaps Petrine) mindset in regard to the law who oppose Paul's law-free gospel.[85] Again evangelism lies at the heart of this opposition, Paul's opponents being evangelistically active Roman Christians seeking to increase Paul's suffering and enhance their own status and strength in the church. In Paul's report of his situation in Rome then opposition, persecution, contention, suffering and evangelism intersect at the same point. I

---

[82] Collange, 11 suggests that these are Judeo-Christian itinerant preachers who give themselves as models to be emulated in contrast to the wretched state of Paul. This is hardly likely for two reasons. First, Paul's Roman opponents are Christians who proclaim Christ. Secondly, in that the problem in Philippi is likened to Paul's situation (1:29-30), this more likely indicates persecution from Gentiles.

[83] See further below.

[84] The choice of Rome rules out the 'divine-man' Christian missionaries advocated by Jewett, 'Conflicting': 362-390. It is also debatable that the divine-man idea is established cf. Hawthorne, xliv.

[85] As Hawthorne, xlv seems to favour; see further below in discussion of the passage.

will discuss in this enquiry whether or not there is a similar interplay in the Philippian context. If so, Paul's report then should be understood not merely as general news, but rhetorically in terms of speaking into the situation at Philippi.

The Situation in Philippi

THE RECIPIENTS

It is not important to fully examine the details of the history of Philippi, the planting of the Philippian church *c.* AD 49 (see Acts 16:11-40) or subsequent Pauline visits.[86] However certain basic features of the church and city are important to this discussion. First, there is a particular prominence of women including Lydia (Acts 16:14-15, 40) and the two co-workers, Euodia and Syntyche.[87] Secondly, the generosity of the church to the Jerusalem Collection (2 Cor 8:1-5) and to Paul throughout his missionary career is markedly noteworthy (Phil 2:25-30; 4:14-19). Thirdly, the city of Philippi was highly romanised after Antony made it a Roman colony with Roman law and leadership and it having twice been settled with Roman military veterans (42 B.C; 31 B.C).[88] Fourthly, there were few Jews in the city as evidenced by the

---

[86] On date see M.J. Suggs, 'Concerning the Date of Paul's Macedonian Ministry', *NovT* 4 (1960-61): 60-68; Gnilka, 3. However Luke's account is supported in 1 Thess 2:2 and Phil 4:15. Blevins, 'Introduction': 312 suggests AD 52 which seems late. Paul revisited Philippi twice (so Collange, 2; Fee, 28; Beare, 13) or three times (so Bockmuehl, 26; Lightfoot, 60 cf. O'Brien, 8 tentatively (see also 1 Cor 16:5 cf. 2 Cor 1:16; Acts 20:2, 3, 6).

[87] In particular, I note the patronage of Lydia and the involvement of Euodia and Syntyche in mission. In addition two of the three conversion accounts in Acts were women and two of the four people mentioned by name in the letter are women. For the more prominent role of Macedonian women in public life and the question in general see especially W.W. Tarn and G.T. Griffith, *Hellenistic Civilisation* (Cleveland, E. Arnold, 1952), 98-99 cf. W.D. Thomas, 'The Place of Women in the Church at Philippi', *ExpTim* 83 (1971-72): 117-20; F.X. Malinowski, 'The Brave Women of Philippi', *BTB* 15 (1985): 60-64; V. Abrahamsen, 'Women at Philippi: The Pagan and Christian Evidence,' *JFSR* 3 (1987): 17-20; E. Barnes, 'Women in Ministry: a Matter of Discipleship' *FM* 4 (1987) 63-69; F.M. Gillman, 'Early Christian Women at Philippi', *JGWR* 1 (1990): 59-79; K.J. Torjeson, *When Women were Priests* (San Francisco: Harper, 1993), 53-109; Bockmuehl, 8, 18; O'Brien, 8; Lightfoot, 55-57; Witherington, *Friendship*, 107-108; A.B. Luter, 'Partnership in the Gospel: the Role of Women in the Church at Philippi', *JETS* 39/3 (1996): 411-420; V. Abrahamsen, *Women and Worship in Philippi. Diana/Artemis and Other Cults in the Early Christian Era* (Portland: Astarte Shell, 1995), 69-101, 193-195; M.R. D'Angelo, 'Women Partners in the New Testament', *JFSR* 6 (1990): 65-86.

[88] On the Romanisation of Philippi and other features see Collange, 1-2; Gnilka, 2-3; U.B. Müller, 1-5; Plummer, *Understanding,* vi; Witherington, *Friendship*, 21 who describes Philippi as 'Rome in a microcosm'; Bockmuehl, 4; J.E. Stambaugh and D.L.

absence of a synagogue on Paul's visit (Acts 16:13).[89] It is probable then that the population was mainly Roman, Thracian and Greek.[90] Its official language was probably Latin, with Greek as the language of everyday life.[91] Fifthly, its place on the Via Egnatia and near Neapolis meant that it was an important centre for trade.[92] So the church was predominately Gentile (Roman, Greek and perhaps Thracian)[93] converts out of the traditional Graeco-Roman religion of the time.[94] The church was in the main healthy as the positive tone of the letter demonstrates. Bruce notes that the quality of the church remained the same over the next half century as evidenced in the affirmative comments concerning it in the letters of Ignatius.[95]

The epistle is clearly written to every believer in the Philippian church (cf. 1:1: πᾶσιν τοῖς ἁγίοις ἐν Χριστῷ Ἰησοῦ τοῖς οὖσιν ἐν Φιλιίπποις). Unusually, Paul also addresses the letter to the overseers and deacons.[96]

Balch, *The New Testament in its Social Environment* (Philadelphia: Westminster Press, 1986), 155; Blevins, 'Introduction': 311-312. P. Oaks, *Philippians. From People to Letter*. SNTSMS 110 (Cambridge: CUP, 2001), 55-76 notes though that this does not necessarily imply a majority of Romans. He estimates 40% Roman, 60% Greek. However he notes that this probably made the Philippian church the most Romanised of the Pauline churches. For an analysis of the city itself, see Oaks, *Philippians*, 1-54. He argues that the approximate population of the city was 10,000 -15,000 with 46,000 in the general area.

[89] Bockmuehl, 8-10 who writes that there was 'a minimal Jewish presence in first-century Philippi' cf. Bruce, 45 and *Acts*, 310; Plummer, *Understanding,* vii-viii; Beare, 10-11; Stambaugh, *Social*, 156; Blevins, 'Introduction': 312; Lightfoot, 52; Bruce, *Acts*, 310-311; Marshall, *Acts*, 267; Barrett, *Acts*, II, 781-782; Dunn, *Acts*, 219; Fitzmyer, 585; Stott, *Acts*, 263; Williams, *Acts*, 282; Larkin, *Acts*, 235-236

[90] Bockmuehl, 4.

[91] Fee, 26.

[92] This is seen in the first convert, a Jewess Lydia from the Asian town of Thyatira who dealt in purple cloth.

[93] Bockmuehl, 18 notes that there is little real evidence for this as there are few named in the epistle. P. Pilhofer, *Philippi Vol 1: Die erste chrisliche Gemeinde Europas*. WUNT 87 (Tübingen: Mohr (Siebeck), 1995), 240-243 notes that are no Thracian names from the first six centuries.

[94] Bockmuehl, 6-8 who suggests that they were converts particularly from traditional Roman religion and the Emperor Cult without quite the religious syncretism assumed by some scholars (cf. Beare, 7).

[95] Bruce, 7; Lightfoot, 63-65 (see Polycarp, *To the Philippians*, 1:1, 2; 13:2 cf. Ignatius, *To Polycarp*, 8:1).

[96] Some like Guthrie, 523 see this as evidence for two distinct orders of officials in the early church. I prefer to see them more loosely as 'overseer' and 'one who serves' as does Achtemeier, *Introducing*, 393.

However the leaders are singled out as one aspect of the church and not as those over it, as emphasised in the use of σύν and not ὑπό.[97]

INTERSECTING DIMENSIONS OF THE PHILIPPIAN CHURCH

A Church Paul is Generally Pleased With

All indications are that Paul considered the Philippian church to be a church he views positively.[98] This is seen in various ways. First, there is Paul's thankfulness for their 'fellowship in the gospel from the beginning' for which he always prays with joy (1:5 cf. 1:6, 7).[99] Secondly, Paul's prayer for their 'love to abound *more*' suggests not that they were loveless, but that they were already a loving church; Paul's appeal is to go further in love. Thirdly, Paul's appeal for the Philippians to work out their salvation is based on his contention that they were a church that was in the main, obedient to their apostle (2:12-13).[100]

Fourthly, the manner in which Paul speaks of his joy concerning Philippi suggests that on the whole he is pleased with the church.[101] Most of the references to joy and rejoicing in the letter refer to Paul's joy over the church (1:4 cf. 1:7, 18b;[102] 2:17; 4:1, 10) and his hope that it will be deepened through his mission (1:25) and their response (2:2, 18).[103] Finally, Paul expects to hear good news from the visit of Timothy concerning the church, which indicates he expects an amicable resolution of any problem (2:19). Accordingly it is probable that any problems in the Philippian church were not cataclysmic and did not threaten the existence of the church.[104]

---

[97] Black, 'Structure': 23. T.C. Skeat, 'Did Paul Write to "Bishops and Deacons" at Philippi? A Note on Philippians 1:1', *NovT* 37, 1 (Jan 1995): 12-15 notes it is also possible that these words were omitted in P^{46} cf. Schenk, 78-82.

[98] So most commentators. For example Fee, 33-34, who notes that the problem has not led to 'division' or 'strife' as in Corinth (1 Cor 1:10-12) and the language is that of friendship and not of enemies; Gnilka, 4.

[99] In that this anticipates the content of the letter, we will discuss its content in Chapter 8.

[100] I take salvation here to be individual and eschatological but worked out in community so integrating the corporate dimension.

[101] While joy is a theme in the letter most references are to Paul's joy and not that of the church. The three imperatives (3:1; 4:4a, b) indicate however that Philippian joy is an issue in the letter (see below Chapter 2).

[102] That the Philippians' prayers for his deliverance will be successful leads him to rejoice.

[103] Seen in 1:18a with Paul's joy at the preaching of the gospel despite poor motivation in Rome.

[104] Gnilka, 5 among others notes the church appears to have continued to be a quality church according to the evidence of Polycarp of Smyrna.

A Church Concerned for Paul's Situation Materially and Generally

One definite feature of the letter is the Philippians' unique concern for Paul, which is seen in various ways throughout the letter.[105] First, Paul writes in large part to thank them for their recent gift from the heroic Epaphroditus through which his needs have been amply supplied (1:5; 2:25-30; 4:10-19).[106] Secondly, he writes to allay Philippian concerns for his situation and mission.[107] He explains that his imprisonment has not stopped the spread of the gospel but has facilitated its advance through his own ministry and that of the Roman Christians despite false motives from some (1:12-18a). Thirdly, he encourages them with the news that he is in good heart despite his situation, being confident of his deliverance (1:19-24) and his release through their prayers and the Spirit (1:19, 25-26). Fourthly, he wants them to know of his deep concern for them seen in the imminent visit of Epaphroditus (2:28), Timothy (2:23) and himself (2:24). Finally, he wants them to know that his faith is alive and well (3:7-14).

A Church Experiencing Opposition

Without question the Philippians encountered external opposition. Paul writes to encourage the Philippians in the face of these opponents.[108] By my

---

[105] This generosity was a feature of the church as also evidenced by their joyful, generous contribution to the Jerusalem collection (cf. 2 Cor 8:1-5).

[106] Bruce, 19; Achtemeier, *Introducing*, 391 represent those who see it as the main reason from which all else flows. Others like Guthrie, *Introduction*, 524; O'Brien, 35; Lightfoot, 66 see it as I do, as one reason among many. Two or three letter advocates such as Gnilka, 4; Beare, 25 see this as essential to Letter A (4:10-20). Peterlin, *Letter*, 3 suggests that the placement of the section near the end of the letter implies relative unimportance. This is inadequate when one notes other references throughout the letter. In fact his contention is self-contradictory in that the specific details of Euodia and Syntyche are also placed late in the letter (pp36-38)!

[107] Marshall, xx-xxi; Bruce, 19; Guthrie, 526; Plummer, *Understanding,* xiv-xv; O'Brien, 36.

[108] E. Lohmeyer, *Der Brief an die Philipper* (Göttingen: Vandenhoeck & Ruprecht, 1928), 4 suggests disunity in Philippi came from pride that some have in the 'perfection of martyrdom.' Achtemeier, *Introducing*, 392; Plummer, *Understanding,* xv; Bloomquist, *Function*, 7-10 suggest the suffering theme runs through the whole letter; Fee, 29; Marshall, 'Theology', 123'; Oaks, *Philippians*, 77-102 sees concrete suffering along with unity as central to Philippians. N. Walter, 'Die Philipper and das Leiden. Aus den Anfäng einer heidenchristlichen Gemeinde', in R. Schnackenburg *et al.*, *Die Kirche des Anfangs: Für Heinz Schümann* (Freiburg: Herder, 1978), 417-434 notes how strange the concept and experience of suffering for God would be to Gentile converts whilst it was familiar to Jewish and Christian thought; R. Jewett, 'The Epistolary Thanksgiving and the Integrity of Philippians', *NovT* 12 (1970): 40-53, 51. See also the summary in Williams, *Enemies*, 54-60.

reckoning, there are three groups of opponents referred to in Philippians.[109] The first group, as I will discuss more fully in Chapter 3, is probably unbelieving Gentile opponents of the Philippian church in Philippi causing the Philippians suffering in a manner similar to Paul's experience in Philippi previously and in Rome at the time of writing (1:28-30) i.e. rejection, arrest, court, imprisonment, physical and psychological suffering.[110] Paul urges his recipients not to be intimidated by these people (1:28) as they stand firm in unity, contending together for the faith of the gospel. Several factors suggest Gentile persecution here. First, they are destined for destruction implying they are unbelievers (1:29). Secondly, they are not Judaisers (or Jews) as it appears few Jews lived in Philippi and the threat in Philippians 3 of Judaising or Jewish opponents seems distant and far off,[111] and Paul's opponents in Rome are not Judaisers in that they preach Christ (1:16-18 cf. 3:2). Thirdly, their experience in Philippi is the same as Paul's suffering in Philippi (1:30 cf. Acts 16:16-33) and in Rome.[112] This suggests potentially arrest, court, imprisonment and physical/psychological suffering at the hands of Gentiles.[113] In my analysis of 1:27-30 I will discuss whether or not there is an *evangelistic dimension* to 'contending for the faith of the gospel' and suffering in the Philippian situation.

The second set of opponents are most likely Judaisers (3:2-3); that is, Jews who saw themselves as Christian preachers who proclaimed Christ in addition

---

[109] It is not my intention here to develop a full argument concerning this claim, merely to state them in straightforward terms. I will develop this more fully in my exegesis below.

[110] Gnilka, 8; U.B. Müller, 7.

[111] Some see here suffering from opponents i.e. Judaisers (Silva, 81); 'divine-man Jewish missionaries' (Collange, 71-72. For an extensive critique see Oaks, *Philippians*, 85-87); 'Jewish missionaries' (Houlden, 34, 65; Hawthorne, xlvi); 'Gnostics' (Schmithals, *Paul*, 65-122).

[112] Oaks, *Philippians*, 79 notes that while the Philippians are not in a Roman prison they are 'undergoing harsh treatment for the sake of the Gospel, as he did.' This need not rule out the idea of Gnilka, 101; O'Brien, 162; Houlden, 65; J.S. Pobee, *Persecution and Martyrdom in the Theology of Paul.* JSNTS 6 (Sheffield: JSOT Press, 1985), 108 who argue here the parallel is theological and not actual and related to suffering ὑπὲρ Χριστοῦ. I suggest that the rhetoric of Phil 1 suggests that the parallels between the experiences of Paul and the Philippians involve the actual dynamics of their situations i.e. persecution from unbelievers due to their mission endeavours (see further Chapter 3).

[113] Perkins, 'Philippians', 90; Marshall, xxii whose suggestion that organised persecution of the church by the government was not a factor at the time does not preclude sporadic contextual outbreaks as Luke reports consistently through Acts (Acts 13:50; 14:5; 16:19-40 [in Philippi]; 17:6-9; 18:12-17; 19:23-20:1); so R. Jewett, *The Thessalonian Correspondance: Pauline Rhetoric and Millenarian Piety. Foundations and Facets* (Philadelphia: Fortress, 1986), 93-94; G. Lüdemann, *Opposition to Paul in Jewish Christianity* (Trans. M.E. Boring; Minneapolis: Fortress Press, 1989), 106-109; Fee, 31-32.

to adherence to the law of Moses and especially male-circumcision.[114] Paul's language suggests they are a real, external and potential threat the Philippians are to 'watch out' for.[115] Using these people as his point of reference, Paul expounds his own renunciation of the flesh and his deeply christological orientation (3:4-17). In the face of these and other opponents, Paul appeals for the Philippians to have nothing to do with these people but to imitate him and his concerns (3:17). Significantly these people are false evangelists ('evil workers') and so potentially are negative models of evangelism.

The third set of opponents referred to are the 'enemies of the cross' (3:18). I do not accept that these opponents are necessarily the same as the 'dogs' of 3:2.[116] Rather, I suggest that τοὺς ἐχθροὺς τοῦ σταυροῦ τοῦ Χριστου ('enemies of the cross') is a general epithet for all who oppose the Christian message. These include in particular the Gentile and Judaising opponents referred to earlier (1:28-30; 3:2) and potentially others known in the Pauline/Philippians context.

I suggest this for several reasons. First, the phrase 'enemies of the cross' is general rather than specific. Secondly, πολλοί ('many') suggests a wider frame of reference than the specific group in 3:2. Thirdly, in a letter to a virtually non-Jewish church in a predominately Gentile city it would be strange to include only Judaisers (or other Jewish opposition). Fourthly, I suggest that scholars have shown over time that the details can apply equally well to a variety of opponents potential in the setting of Philippi such as Judaisers, Jews, libertines, 'divine-man' missionaries and so on, suggesting that Paul is speaking generally and not specifically here. In addition, these notions can apply equally well to

---

[114] Marshall, xxxiii-xxxiv; Jewett, 'Conflicting': 31; O'Brien, 33; Bockmuehl, 183-184; Fee, 293-294; Silva, 9-10; Motyer, 19-21; Plummer, *Understanding,* xv; O'Brien, 36; Marshall, 'Theology', 123 among many others. Two and three letter proponents see this as central to Letter B (3:1-4:?) cf. Beare, 24-25. Some such as A.F.J. Klijn, 'Paul's opponents in Philippi iii', *NovT* 7 (1965): 278-284; Pollard, 'Integrity': 61 and Hawthorne, xlv-xlvii see these as the same as the 'enemies of the cross' (3:18). They argue they are Jewish missionaries perhaps from Thessalonica. H. Köster, 'Purpose': 331 argues they are Jewish Christian missionaries combining Gnosticism with 'perfectionist doctrine of the law.' See O'Brien, 27-30 for a solid critique. For a list of those who see them as Judaisers see Jewett, 'Conflicting': 363 esp. n1.

[115] Rather than 'consider' as held by G.D. Kilpatrick, 'ΒΛΕΠΕΤΕ, Phil 3:2' in M. Black and G. Fohrer (ed's), *In Memoriam Paul Kahle* (Berlin: De Gruyter, 1968), 146-148; Garland, 'Composition': 166 who argue that Paul is holding up these Judaisers not as real opponents but as an admonitory example. The three-fold use of βλέπετε suggests a strong warning cf. O'Brien, 33.

[116] Perkins, 'Philippians', 90; Witherington, *Friendship*, 29; O'Brien, 33-35; J.J. Müller, 130; Silva, 208-211; U.B. Müller, 7, 15. With a slight twist Müller-Bardorff, 'Frage': 591-604 speculates that they are spiritualists promoting a Judaizing and libertinising message.

Gentile unbelievers.[117] Hence, I suggest that in 3:18 Paul moves from the specific (Judaisers) to the general to call for gospel-worthy conduct in the face of any opposition to the essence of the Christian faith.

A Church Experiencing a Degree of Internal Contention

As I have indicated, in general Paul views the Philippian church positively. However, it remains evident that Paul wrote to deal with some conflict in the Philippian church.[118] This discord focussed around two co-workers, Euodia and Syntyche (4:2).[119] In 4:2 Paul addresses directly two female co-workers who have assisted him in his mission but who have now fallen out. The manner in which the conflict permeates the whole epistle renders the idea that it is merely a personal dispute between two women as unlikely; 'The dispute is clearly one that affects the community or the Pauline mission; it is not just private animosity.'[120]

In light of this direct reference it is possible to discern the issue throughout the epistle. First, the thematic and linguistic links between 4:1-3 and 1:27 including 'stand firm' (1:27; 4:1) and 'contending for/in the (faith of the) gospel' (1:27; 4:2) suggest some kind of thematic *inclusio*. Secondly, the problem of disunity permeates 1:27-2:18 as seen in the references to the ideal of oneness in the congregation (ψυχη - 1:27; 2:2; 4:2) and Paul's direct appeal for the renunciation of relationally sinful behaviour (2:1-4 cf. 2:20-21, 26, 30). Thirdly, the trouble is implicit in the appeal for emulation of the attitude of Christ who embodied humble servanthood rather than self-aggrandisement (2:6-8). Fourthly, Paul's exhortation to the Philippians to live without complaint and argument as is unbefitting for the people of God (2:14). Fifthly, it is seen in Paul's presentation of positive and negative examples to the Philippians of those who demonstrate right/wrong attitudes. While relational issues appeared at hand, Paul encourages an attitudinal response based on right

---

[117] O'Brien, 452.

[118] Peterlin, *Letter*, 217-228 sees this as the central theme of the epistle as does Bruce, 19; Pollard, 'Integrity':57-58 and Black, 'Structure', 16 who sees 'unity for the gospel' reflected in Phil 4:2-3 as the 'overarching framework and motif' of the epistle. Oaks, *Philippians*, 77-102 argues that suffering and unity are the two most important themes. Others including Blevins, 'Introduction': 320; D.A. Black, 'Paul and Christian Unity: a Formal Analysis of Philippians 2:1-4', *JETS* 28 (1985): 288-300; MacKay, 'Further': 168. Motyer, 18-19; Achtemeier, *Introducing*, 392; Guthrie, *Introduction*, 526; Marshall, xxvii and 'Theology', 123; Plummer, *Understanding,* xv; Fee, 29, 32; O'Brien, 36-37; Lightfoot, 67-68 also see it as important. I suggest that without the direct mention of the disagreement between Euodia and Syntyche in 4:2-3 one could easily consider the other references to problems as general and not conflict-specific.

[119] Black, 'Structure': 16.

[120] Perkins, 'Philippians', 90.

thought patterns that will lead to behavioural change (2:2, 5, 4:2).[121] Finally, after addressing the problem in Philippi directly (4:2-3) he exhorts the Philippians to right behaviour and attitude (4:4-9).

The exact nature of the issue is debated (see exegesis below). I will discuss whether or not evangelism is in the foreground of the Philippians 'contention' at various points (1:27; 2:5-11, 15-16).

A Church With a Degree of Joylessness

As I have indicated above the majority of references to joy are concerned with Paul's joy which arise from the church (1:4, 18a, 18b) which he hopes will be enhanced (2:2). However there are indications in the contexts of his references to joy that the Philippians' joy may have become rather diminished in the face of the various problems they are experiencing implicitly and explicitly.[122] Implicitly they appear concerned over Paul's situation. He would rather that they rejoice even though he is suffering in Rome. After all, the gospel is advancing despite his suffering (1:12-18a) and he is confident of his imminent release and visit to them (1:25-26; 2:24). Just as he rejoices, so should the Philippians (2:17-18). Furthermore, their concern over reports of the Epaphroditus' illness should be replaced by joy at the manner in which he risked his life for the gospel and his impending return (2:28-30). So they should rejoice (3:1a)![123]

The three explicit references to joy are found in the appeals to 'rejoice' (3:1; 4:4 [2x]). The transitional appeal for joy in 3:1a probably refers not only to joy over Epaphroditus but to concern that the Philippians are becoming anxious because of the threat of Judaising opponents (cf. 4:6-7). The two-fold repetition of χαίρετε in 4:4 is set in the immediate context of his appeal for unity in the gospel mission (4:2-3), eschatology (4:5) and anxiety over these issues, which are addressed throughout Philippians (4:6). Consequently, the issue of joy permeates all the major concerns of the letter including Paul's situation, opponents, disunity and the gospel mission.

A Church that Needs Hope: The Importance of Eschatology and Encouragement in Philippians

Eschatology and eschatological statements and references recur throughout the epistle to the Philippians.[124] First, in the thanksgiving where Paul twice refers to

---

[121] Against Perkins, 'Philippians', 90 who argues the issue is not theological but relational. However Paul's response targets 'thinking' and theology.

[122] See P.A. Holloway, *Consolation*, passim.

[123] Seeing 3:1a as transitional serving as a final appeal for joy in light of Epaphroditus' return and leading into the threat of opponents in chapter 3.

[124] It is not my purpose to discuss the specific issues related to Paul's eschatology in Philippians in regard to his whole theological construction, as it is not relevant to the overall thesis. For further discussion see Fee, 50-52 who notes the 'already-not yet'

the *Parousia* as 'the day of the Christ/Christ Jesus' (1:6; 10). Here the reference is to the point at which God will complete the work begun in and through the Philippians and at which they will be found to be pure and blameless before God. Secondly, Paul ponders the dilemma of 'choosing' between deliverance from Roman incarceration or death. Either way, Christ will be exalted as he continues his ministry, or 'gains' through death (1:19-24). Thirdly, Paul encourages the Philippians that their fearless united contention for the faith of the gospel in the face of Gentile opposition is a sign to their opponents of their inevitable destruction. Conversely their continued perseverance despite suffering is a sign to the Philippians of their salvation (1:28 cf. 4:2-3).

Fourthly, in his reflection on the example of Christ, Paul refers to the future certainty that every living human will face God in judgement and willingly or unwillingly bow before Christ, confessing his lordship (2:10-11). Fifthly, Paul hopes that the Philippians will desist from all complaint and argument so that their lives will appear faultless in pagan Philippi. It could be here that Paul is appealing for evangelism, a dimension I will discuss in Chapter 4. This is so Paul may be able to boast before Christ that his efforts have not been vain (2:14-17).

Sixthly, Paul, in his polemic against the Judaisers and other enemies of the cross, speaks of his hope of attaining resurrection to eternal life through remaining faithful in the midst of suffering as he continues his mission (3:10-14). He wants the Philippians to emulate his example in this regard (3:15-17) assuring them they will experience bodily transformation at the return of Christ unlike their enemies (3:18-20).

Seventhly, Paul notes that the names of the co-workers are written in the book of life giving them assurance of their salvation (4:3). Finally, he hopes the Philippians will continue to give materially, so that they will receive credit before God (4:19).

This consistent recurring reference to the promise of eternal salvation at the return of Christ suggests Paul feels a strong need to encourage the Philippians eschatologically. Throughout the exegesis I will note this dimension and the manner in which it intersects with other dimensions of Philippians, notably ongoing mission, suffering, joy and hope.

A Church in Need of Corrected Thinking

Another feature of Philippians is Paul's concern for faulty thinking in the congregation.[125] This is reflected in the recurrence of the verb φρονέω which

'eschatological framework' of Philippians; Johnson, *Writings*, 371; L.J. Kreitzer, Eschatology in *DPL*, 252-269.

[125] Fee, 89; O'Brien, 66-67.

concerns 'thinking' with a range of senses.[126] The term occurs ten times in Philippians (1:7; 2:2 [2x], 5; 3:15 [2x], 19; 4:2, 10 [2x]). Significantly it is in the paraenetic passages concerned for unity in Romans that a similar concentration of the term is found (cf. Rom 8:5; 11:20; 12:3 (2), 16 (2); 14:6 (2); 15:5 cf. 1 Cor 13:11; 2 Cor 13:11; Col 3:2). Paul is addressing the faulty thinking of those at the centre of dispute in Philippi (2:2; 4:2) and appealing for them to emulate the mindset of evangelistic leaders including himself (1:7; 3:15; 4:8), Christ (2:5), others who follow the Pauline pattern including Timothy, Epaphroditus and the 'good Romans' (3:15 cf. 2:19-30; 1:15-18a).[127]

The Centrality of Ethical Witness, Prayer and Financial Support for Mission in Philippians

As I have indicated, Bowers argues that Paul's conception of the involvement of the Pauline church in mission was primarily seen in ethical witness, prayer and material support. Philippians provides ample support to the importance of these three elements in mission.

First, ethical and Christian action and witness is prominent in Paul's practice and appeal for right living in Philippians. These include servanthood (1:1; 2:7, 17), peace (1:2), thanksgiving (1:3; 4:6), prayer (1:4, 9, 19; 4:6), joy (1:4, 18a, 18b, 25, 26; 2:18, 28, 29; 3:1; 4:1, 4, 9), material generosity (1:5, 7, 9, 11; 2:25-30; 4:10-20), assurance and confidence (1:6, 19, 20, 25, 2:13, 24), love (1:8, 9, 16; 2:1, 2, 26), discernment (1:10), purity (1:10 [εἰλικρινης]; 2:15 [ἄμεμπτος], blamelessness (1:10 [ἀπρόσκοποι]); 2:15 [ἀκέραιος]), holistic righteousness in general (1:11), good will (1:15), Spirit-led lifestyle (1:19; 2:2), courage (παρρησία in 1:20), hope (1:20), labour for Christ (1:22; 2:16), faith (1:25, 29; 2:17; 3:9, 10), perseverance (1:27; 3:14; 4:1), gospel-worthy living in general (1:27), unity (1:27; 2:2; 4:2), fearlessness (1:28), participation and perseverance in suffering (1:29-30; 2:17, 27, 28, 30; 3:10), encouragement (παράκλησις 2:1) comfort (2:1), fellowship (1:5; 2:2), humility (2:3, 8), others-centredness (2:4, 20, 21), Christ-likeness (2:5), obedience (2:8, 12), working out of salvation in general (2:12), fear of God (2:12), faultlessness (2:15), glowing witness in general (2:15-16), hospitality (2:29), Spirit-inspired and led worship (3:3), glorying in Christ (3:3), personal relationship with God through Christ (3:7), faith-righteousness (3:9, 10), resurrection and heaven orientated (3:10, 14, 20-21), maturity (3:15), imitation of Paul (3:17; 4:9), gentleness (4:4), peace (4:7, 9), right thinking (4:8) and contentment in poverty or provision (4:11).[128]

---

[126] *BDAG*, 1065-1066 note three: 1) 'Think, form/hold and opinion' (1:7; 2:2a, b; 3:15a, b, 16; 4:10a, b); 2) 'Set one's mind on, be intent on' (3:19); 3) Be minded/disposed' (2:5).

[127] Notably all but one of these references to 'thinking' fall outside the passages I am examining (4:2). Hence, I will not explore in great depth this issue in the thesis.

[128] To these could be added a number of other attributes referred to in the other epistles but not explicitly referred to in Philippians.

Similarly prayer, while not highlighted, does not go unmentioned. In 1:19 Paul refers to the prayer of the Philippians for his mission, prayers that have contributed to his deliverance (1:19). Secondly, in 4:6-7 Paul appeals for the Philippians to pray in a general sense, no doubt including Paul's mission (cf. Rom 15:31-32; 2 Thess 3:2; Eph 6:19-20; Col 4:3-4; 2 Thess 3:1-2).

Financial giving to mission is most important to the fabric of Philippians, as I have already established above.

The Centrality of the Gospel Mission to the Texture of Philippians?

A final reason for the writing of Philippians is a concern for the gospel in Philippi, the focus of this study. Five scholars in particular have noted the centrality of the gospel concept to Philippians, each with a slightly different perspective.[129]

First, *Georg Eichholz* who has suggested that the inner theme to which all single statements are connected in Phil 1-2 is 'Keep and confirm the Gospel.'[130] He traces the theme through these two chapters noting that in each section, evangelism and the gospel are central. First, in 1:3-11 Paul thanks God not for financial assistance (4:10ff) but for the Philippians' sharing in the gospel. He notes that this corresponds to other such thanksgivings in Paul (cf. Rom 1:8).[131] He suggests that 2:1-4 (cf. 2:14-15), which refers to the problem of disputing and boasting, should be related to this theme, as should the true/false proclaimers of 1:15-17 and Timothy (2:20). These serve as positive and negative illustrations of 2.4.[132] He suggests that the idiom 'fellowship of the gospel' relates to Paul's desire for the gospel to be greatly honoured (cf. 1 Thess 2:13; 1:4ff; 1 Cor 9:19-23). Specifically he argues Paul is speaking about the connection between 'message and witness-existence' ('*Zeugenexistenz*').[133] Accordingly, the 'participation in the Gospel' points to the manner in which the gospel has come through the world to the Philippians and that they received it with faith and are holding fast to the gospel of their salvation.[134]

The reference to love in the intercession (1:9-10) speaks of the problem in Philippi in the witness-existence of the Philippians.[135] He suggests the theme of

---

[129] It is agreed by all scholars that the mission of Paul is prominent especially in Phil 1-2. However the active involvement of the church is not always agreed. See further Chapter 2.

[130] G. Eichholz, 'Bewahren und Bewähren des Evangeliums: Der Leitfaden von Philipper 1-2' in H. Gollwitzer and H. Traub, *Hören und Handeln. Festschift für Ernst Wolf zum 60. Geburstag* (München: Chr. Kaiser Verlag, 1962), 84-105, 85. He considers only Phil 1-2, as it is an agreed unit (85-86) (translations mine).

[131] Eichholz, 'Bewahren', 85-86.

[132] Eichholz, 'Bewahren', 87-88.

[133] Eichholz, 'Bewahren', 88-89.

[134] Eichholz, 'Bewahren', 89.

[135] Eichholz, 'Bewahren', 91.

gospel also runs through 1:12-26 seen in the expansion of the gospel in the *Praetorium* and city and through the new courage for fearless proclamation of the word in the church at the place of Paul's detention. He considers that this refers to the despondent and competitive witnesses in the place of imprisonment who daringly regained their initiative and liberty to witness again despite their differences and 'pressing opposition.'[136] Eichholz intimates that this points to the manner in which Jesus Christ accelerates the witness of the church despite its tiredness and desperation. This brings from Paul great joy and thanks.[137]

This is summed up in Paul's concluding remark (1:18a) where Paul: 'is only orientated and interested in one thing, that "Christ is proclaimed."' (1:18a).'[138] He notes Paul is delighted because this new impulse to proclaim the gospel is 'important fruit of his imprisonment' despite the fact that the two groups display differing motivations.[139] Eichholz sees the theme of 'fellowship of the gospel' continuing in 1:20-26 especially in 1:22 where continued life for Paul means 'fruit of labour (In the sense of the yield of his missionary service).'[140]

Of 1:27, Eichholz rightly observes that Paul continues the theme, turning from his own situation, to the *Zeugenexistenz* of the Philippians: 'to testify to the gospel, given the environment which is contrary to the Gospel and its opposition, forced suffering on the young church.'[141] Paul then, is urging the Philippians to live out the most crucial thing (μόνον) according to the gospel reminding the hearer of 1:5 and the need to continue to live out the gospel, as it is the power of God for salvation (cf. Rom 1:16).[142]

Similarly in 2:1-4 Eichholz suggests that Paul is appealing for a uniform 'testimony' (*Zeugenschaft*) from the *whole* community (cf. πᾶς in 1:3-11). Eichholz notes that whatever the background of 2:5-11 and Käsemann's protestation against an ethical interpretation of it, it is right to understand the hymn in context with regard to its exhortation to conformity of the Christian with Christ (1:27ff cf. 2 Cor 8.9). He argues that the purpose of the hymn is to address through the example of Christ the endangerment of the witness existence of the Philippians.[143]

Finally, Eichholz notes that the internal guideline of 1:3-11 i.e. 'message and witness-existence', continues in the appeal of 2:12-13 and especially 2:15 noting again the connection between witness-existence and salvation (cf. 1:5; 1

---

[136] Eichholz, 'Bewahren', 92.
[137] Eichholz, 'Bewahren', 93.
[138] Eichholz, 'Bewahren', 93.
[139] Eichholz, 'Bewahren', 93.
[140] Eichholz, 'Bewahren', 95.
[141] Eichholz, 'Bewahren', 96.
[142] Eichholz, 'Bewahren', 96.
[143] Eichholz, 'Bewahren', 97-102.

Cor 9:19-23).[144] He notes that 'fear and trembling' are used in 1 Cor 2:3 of Paul's witness in Corinth and the function of weakness to bring strength (2 Cor 11:9 cf. Phil 4:13).[145] He suggests that the issue here is the obedience of the Philippians (2:12 cf. 2:8; 2 Cor 7:15). On the basis of these connections Eichholz sees 2:12 as essentially parallel to 1:27 and the concern to remain committed to the gospel in unity and not allow the contradictory environment to take its witness off course.[146] Finally, he argues that 2:15-16 and the appeal for the Christians to 'live as torch-bearers in the world' and 'hold fast to the word of life', speaks directly into the Philippians' witness existence.[147] Without their perseverence on the 'word that alone brings life', Paul's missionary service would have been in vain. Finally Paul endorses the Philippians interconnectedness in joy.[148]

In terms of this discussion then, Eichholz notes the importance of 'gospel' to Phil 1-2. Unfortunately he does not specify the exact content of *Zeugenexistenz* which would be helpful in terms of the current debate. It would appear that he favours an ethical-proclamation approach although it may be that he sees both proclamation and ethics as indivisible. In addition his approach takes little cognisance of the role of models and more importantly the rhetorical significance of Paul's own prison experience and those of the models.

Peter T. O'Brien has also noted the centrality of the gospel and gospel models to Philippians.[149] He examines the use of εὐαγγέλιον in Philippians. First, he notes that in the phrase 'partnership in the gospel' (1:5), κοινωνία should be understood actively and εὐαγγέλιον as a noun of agency, combining to include monetary support, suffering, intercession and proclamation (cf. Col 1:5-6; 1 Thess 1:5; 2:13; 2 Cor 10:14).[150] Secondly, he takes note of the application of 'gospel' to Paul's ministry of defence and confirmation of the gospel and its progress and defence (1:7, 12, 16). He suggests that the application in 1:7 is general and not legal. In 1:12-18a he proposes that 'gospel' is again used actively, and the progress of the gospel was of supreme importance to Paul even above his personal situation. The advance of the

---

[144] Eichholz, 'Bewahren', 102
[145] Eichholz, 'Bewahren', 103
[146] Eichholz, 'Bewahren', 104
[147] Eichholz, 'Bewahren', 105
[148] Eichholz, 'Bewahren'105.
[149] P.T. O'Brien, 'The Importance of the Gospel in Philippians' in P.T. O'Brien and D.G. Peterson (ed's), *God who is Rich in Mercy. Essays Presented to D.B. Knox* (Homebush West [NSW]: Anzea, 1986), 213-233 and 'The Gospel and Godly Models in Philippians' in M.J. Wilkins and T. Paige, *Worship, Theology and Ministry in the Early Church. Essays in Honor of Professor R.P. Martin* (Sheffield: Academic Press, 1992), 273-284.
[150] O'Brien, 'Importance', 216-218.

gospel involved observable facts and this is measured through proclamation and not conversions.[151]

Thirdly, he examines 1:27, specifically 'conduct worthy of the gospel' and 'contending for the faith of the gospel.' The former he suggests refers to behaviour consistent with the gospel and the latter, 'the spread and growth of faith' with a stress on unity.[152] He then observes that the role of Timothy is in active evangelism and is an example of one who subordinates his own interests to those of Christ (cf. 2:4, 5-11).[153] Of Euodia and Syntyche (4:3), O'Brien suggests their involvement should be understood as active and proclamatory, which made Paul's appeal urgent, as they were representatives of Christ.[154] Finally, he notes that 'the beginning of the gospel' (4:15) best refers to the early days of the Philippian acquaintance with the message i.e. the initial period of evangelisation.

O'Brien's approach differs from Eicholz in that he argues for a broad range of dimensions including proclamation in Paul's use of gospel as applied to the Philippians. He accepts the integrity of Philippians and deals with the issue of gospel thoroughly. He suggests that 1:5, 12-14, 27-30; 4:2-3 indicate congregational evangelism. He notes that there are a number of godly models in Philippians. He contends that 2:15-16 is passive in orientation.[155] He finds 1:6, 7 to be related to redemption and not mission.

Another recent writer to note the centrality of the gospel in Philippians is *Gordon Fee*. Taking Philippians as a letter of friendship (see above), Fee suggests that 'the ultimate urgency of the letter is *the gospel*',[156] which in his view takes the form of 'the advance of the gospel' in a manner very similar to O'Brien. However, Fee further emphasises congregational involvement through several additional notions. First, he notes that 'Paul's concern for the Philippians is for their own "advance/progress in the faith (= the gospel)" (1:25).'[157] Secondly, he states that Paul's '*major* concern' is that the Philippians 'get their corporate act together for the sake of the gospel in Philippi (1:27; 2:16).'[158] Notably, unlike O'Brien in his commentary, he interprets ἐπεχοντες in 2:16 actively rather than passively i.e. holding *forth* the word of life rather than holding fast to the word of life. Fee argues that unlike other Pauline epistles, the issue in Philippians is not the *content* of the gospel but rather the living out of the gospel.[159]

---

151 O'Brien, 'Importance', 218-224.

152 O'Brien, 'Importance', 223-224.

153 O'Brien, 'Importance', 226-227.

154 O'Brien, 'Importance', 227-228.

155 As noted above in the General Introduction (Chapter 1), this stands in tension with the view expressed in his monograph *Consumed*, 126-127.

156 Fee, 47 (italics his).

157 Fee, 47.

158 Fee, 47 (italics mine).

159 Fee, 47.

George W. Murray too argues that the theme of 'corporate witness' is central to Philippians.[160] He suggests that this is seen in 'the fellowship of the gospel' (1:5) which includes partnership in the work of evangelism throughout the epistle.[161] He interprets 'grace' in 1:7 as Paul's apostolic commission,[162] 'contending for the faith of the gospel' as evangelism[163] and ἐπέχοντες as 'hold forth' the gospel in 2:16a.[164] He notes the role of Timothy (2:22) and Epaphroditus (2:25-30) without recognising their function as evangelistic models.[165] He argues for an active involvement of the women in Phil 4:3.[166] Finally, he takes the 'brothers' of 4:15 as co-workers in Paul's mission.[167] He also takes account of the overall importance of unity in evangelism.[168]

Finally, as I have summarised above in Chapter 1, *J.P. Ware* in his recent work, argues that Philippians involves an appeal to proclaim the gospel particularly on the basis of the example of the Romans (Phil 1:12-14), the appeals of 1:27 and to 'hold for the word of life' (2:16).[169]

Each of the above analyses informs the discussion. My interest is in examing the verses in question to discern to what extent the concept of congregational evangelism is present and how it interconnects with the other dynamics to which I have referred in this section including material generosity, opponents, suffering, internal contention, joy, eschatology and thinking.

Conclusion

Having explained the context for this analysis, it is now time to turn to exegesis of the text. My purpose in the exegesis is not to thoroughly discuss every element of the texts in question, but to explore the dynamic of congregational evangelism throughout Philippians. In-so-doing, I will take a concentric approach; i.e. the first point of reference will be the immediate context, the second the wider context of Philippians and the thr third, Paul's other letters. As such, I will explore whether congregational evangelism is central to Phililppians and Paul, and so put the assessment of Bowers, Bosch, Dickson and others to the test i.e. that Paul had no real notion of intentional centrifugal evangelism from his congregations.

---

160 G.W. Murray, 'Paul's Corporate Witness in Philippians', *BSac* 155 (1998): 316-326.
161 G.W. Murray, 'Witness': 316-319.
162 G.W. Murray, 'Witness': 319-320.
163 G.W. Murray, 'Witness': 320-322.
164 G.W. Murray, 'Witness': 322-323.
165 G.W. Murray, 'Witness': 323-324.
166 G.W. Murray, 'Witness': 324-325.
167 G.W. Murray, 'Witness': 326-327.
168 G.W. Murray, 'Witness': 327.
169 See above.

CHAPTER 3

Paul's Delight at Others Proclaiming the Gospel in Rome (1:14-18a)

The passage 1:12-18a forms the first part of a new section (which runs from 1:12-26) that informs the Philippian brothers and sisters (ἀδελφοί)[1] of his situation.[2] In this section, Paul relates his circumstances in prison and its impact on his mission,[3] which the Philippians were so passionately concerned about.[4] In Philippians 1:18b-26 Paul goes on to express his uncertainty about the outcome of his imprisonment along with his hope of release so that he can revisit Philippi.

In 1:12 Paul shifts from his prayer of thanksgiving and intercession to make the Philippians well aware of his own predicament in Rome.[5] This is logical in that the Philippians, mindful as they were of his confinement in Rome, would have wanted news of his fate.[6] In 1:12, Paul allays any fears the Philippians may have had that the gospel mission had been adversely affected by his imprisonment.[7] He wants them to know that the gospel mission is not thwarted

---

[1] See further on ἀδελφοί in our analysis below.

[2] O'Brien, 85-86, 107; Black, 'Structure': 31; Peterman, *Gift*, 107 correctly note the *inclusio* involving προκοπή cf. 1:12, 26.

[3] G.H. Guthrie, 'Cohesion Shifts and Stitches in Philippians' in S.E. Porter and D.A. Carson, *Discourse Analysis and Other Topics in Biblical Greek*. JSNTS 113 (Sheffield: Sheffield Academic Press, 1995): 36-50, 43: 'the unit coheres around the topic of the gospel's proclamation.'

[4] J.L. White, *The Form and Function of the Body of the Greek Letter. A Study of the Letter-Body Papyri in the Non-Literary Papyri and in Paul the Apostle*. SBLDS 138 (Missoula: Scholars Press, 1972), 78; Fee, 107-108; Bockmuehl, 72; O'Brien, 85; Wiles, 279.

[5] The use of ὅτι and τὰ κατ' ἐμε (1:12) indicates a disclosure form which gives the effects rather than the details of his imprisonment. For more see O'Brien, 89 and Letters', 552; White, *Form*, 69-70; T.Y. Mullins, 'Disclosure. A Literary Form in the New Testament,' *NovT* 7 (1964): 44-50 esp. 46-50; Hawthorne, 34; Alexander, 'Letter-forms': 92, 94; J.T. Sanders, 'The Transition from Opening Epistolary Thanksgiving to Body in the Letters of the Pauline Corpus', *JBL* 81 (1982): 348-362, 349; Fee, 106.

[6] Fee, 108.

[7] B.J. Capper, 'Paul's Dispute with Philippi', *TZ* 49.3 (1993): 193-214, 208-209 suggests that the Philippians were upset that 'they had backed (financially) a bad horse'

by his restraint. Paul expresses ironically that indeed the reverse has been the case;[8] the gospel has been furthered by his detention.[9] Indeed, the gospel has advanced (προκοπή cf. 1:25; 1 Tim 4:15).[10] Paul is highly encouraged and he wants the Philippians to be brightened by these words. Paul's report indicates that the progress of the gospel is his ultimate concern.[11]

In 1:13 Paul specifies the result (ὥστε); namely, that the gospel has progressed.[12] First, it has progressed among many of the Roman guard (ἐν ὅλῳ τῷ πραιτωρίῳ).[13] Secondly, it has been extended into a significant portion of Roman citizens (τοῖς λοιποῖς πᾶσιν).[14] These people have become aware

---

in Paul and wanted reassurance their money was furthering the mission and that the 'contract was not breached.' I consider that this is without warrant and is needlessly cynical; see Fee, 436-437 for critique.

[8] Houlden, 58, 'he has acted as a Trojan horse' entering Rome with the gospel.

[9] See O'Brien, *Consumed*, 77-81; *TDNT* 2.707-737; Bowers, *Mission*, 81-103; Dickson, *Mission-Commitment*, 393-427; J. Fitzmyer, The Gospel in the Theology of Paul', *Interpretation* 33.4 (1979): 339-350; P. Stuhlmacher (ed), *Gospel and the Gospels* (Grand Rapids: Eerdmans, 1991), 149-172 for background and content of εὐαγγέλιον and associated terms. In Paul it is the 'good news concerning salvation in Christ.' It can be active in meaning ('preach the gospel') or passive ('the content of the gospel'). O'Brien, *Consumed*, 113-115 notes here that Paul is speaking 'of the gospel as a force or agency able to accomplish something, and which has a purpose towards which it moves' (cf. Col 1:6, 10; 1 Cor 9:27; 1 Thess 1:5).

[10] See *TDNT* 6.703-19; O'Brien, 90; Fee, 111; MM, 542; G.H.R. Horsley, *New Documents Illustrating Early Christianity. A Review of Greek Inscriptions and Papyri Published in 1977* (Vol 2. Macquarie: Macquarie University, 1982), 2.95; 4.36; Engberg-Pedersen, 'Stoicism', 262, 273; Hawthorne, 34; cf. Vincent, 16; Stählin, 'Prokopê', 703-719; Martin, 70; I-J. Loh and E.A. Nida, *A Translators Handbook on Paul's Letter to the Philippians* (Stuttgart: United Bible Society, 1977), 20 for the Stoic, military and travel backgrounds of προκοπή. Usually positive, it was common in everyday non-literary Greek for general progress. Here it is used in its common non-technical mode of making progress in a good sense.

[11] O'Brien, *Philippians*, 86-87.

[12] *BDAG*, 1107: O'Brien, 91; Vincent, 16 who notes that 'the explanation being regarded as a result of the notion of προκοπή;' Silva, 68.

[13] Taking τῷ πραιτωρίῳ not as a place (so Schenk, 134 cf. Mk 15:16 and par's; Lk 23:35) but the royal guard stationed in Rome cf. Loh-Nida, 20; Plummer, *Understanding*, 20; Dickson, *Mission-Commitment*, 129. The adjective ὅλῳ is probably hyperbolic, indicating 'many.' See Michael, 30; Fee, 113; Lightfoot, 101-104; Vincent, 16-17; Marshall, 21; P.M. Reasoner, 'Political Systems', in *DPL*, 718-723, 720; Winter, 'Dangers', 294 for detail on how the gospel could have spread so rapidly among the soldiers.

[14] This certainly includes those who were judicially linked to Paul's situation and perhaps a wider group. While it should not be overly interpreted (see Lightfoot, 88; Michael, 31; O'Brien, 94), and hyperbole is perhaps in view (see Beare, 58; U.B. Müller, 52), it may indicate a large enough number for him to feel as if the whole city has been impacted (cf. Motyer, 69).

(φανερός) that he is imprisoned for his commitment to Christ as Lord, the real reason for Paul's imprisonment.[15] In other words, some kind of evangelism has occurred which has given soldiers and people of the city understanding of Paul's situation and so, have heard the gospel message.[16] This probably indicates that at least some converts have been made in this group.[17]

My interest here lies in examining the reference to the impact on those at the point of Paul's imprisonment (1:14-18) to see if there are indications that this points to a concern in Paul to inspire others to evangelise.

Paul's Delight at Roman Christians Who Have Responded to His Imprisonment with Evangelism (1:14)

In 1:14-18a Paul describes to the Philippians further details as to nature of the advance of the gospel in Rome. The gospel has advanced not only through Paul and the soldiers but also through the majority (τοὺς πλείονας) of unspecified ἀδελφοί. Because of Paul's imprisonment (τοῖς δεσμοῖς μου)[18] these ἀδελφοί have become confident (πεποιθότας) in the Lord[19] to proclaim the

---

[15] With O'Brien, 92; Fee, 112; Gnilka, 56-57; Holloway, *Consolation*, 102 taking ἐν as causal i.e. his imprisonment was due to his relationship with Christ.

[16] J.D.G. Dunn, *The Theology of Paul the Apostle* (Edinburgh: T&T. Clark, 1998), 398; Hendricksen, 69 who outlines well how this may have happened; Bockmuehl, 75; Fee, 112; Kent, 110; J.J. Müller, 49; J.M. Boice, *Philippians: An Expositional Commentary* (Grand Rapids: Zondervan, 1971), 62; Moule, 18-19; Marshall, 21; Barth, 28; O'Brien, 92 and 'Gospel', 223; Motyer, 69; Witherington, 45; B.W. Winter, 'Dangers' and Difficulties for the Pauline Missions', in P. Bolt and M. Thompson (ed's), *The Gospel to the Nations. Perspectives on Paul's Mission* (Leicester: IVP, 2000), 285-296, 294. Contra Beare, 58 who writes: 'the words do not suggest that Paul is making converts among the soldiers ... lawyers ... only that he has succeeded in making them realise that his only offence is the propagation of the gospel.'

[17] So Barth, 28; Marshall, 21. I consider that O'Brien, 'Gospel', 223; Witherington, 45; Bruce, 42; Melick, 72 do not go far enough in suggesting that some degree of conversion is not in mind.

[18] Whether τοῖς δεσμοῖς μου is instrumental ('by my bonds' so) or causal ('because of my chains') as Silva, 70 points out.

[19] Taking ἐν κυρίῳ with πεποιθότας (Vincent, 17; Hawthorne, 35; Wicks, 29; Moule, 19; Bruce, 42; O'Brien, 94; Ware, *Mission*, 178-179; Fee, 115-116; Silva, 70; Bockmuehl, 76; Craddock, 25; Loh-Nida, 21) and not with αδελφοί (cf. NIV) because: 1) ἀδελφοί ἐν κυρίῳ is not found elsewhere, the saying is redundant; 2) Paul uses πείθω with ἐν κυρίω elsewhere (Rom 14:14; Phil 2:24; Gal 5:10; 2 Thess 3:4 cf. Phil 3:3f ['in the flesh']; 2 Cor 1:9); 3) The usual emphatic placement of πεποιθώς and the Lord gives the confidence to proclaim. Schenk, 135 however takes it with 'brothers' (cf. 1 Cor 4:17; 10:5; 15:6; Phm 16) pointing to 'active co-workers (*itarbeiter*) involved in 'work of the church' (*Gemeindearbeit*). On πείθω in the perfect in the sense of confidence see *BDAG*, 792.

gospel (τὸν λόγον λαλεῖν) [20] in a more fearless manner. The accumulation of terms here (περισσοτέρως τολμᾶν ἀφόβως), indicates that these Roman Christians showed immense courage in the face of real danger.[21] Περισσοτέρος suggests that this is a renewed initiative rather than a completely new impulse[22] (cf. Rom 1:8).[23]

---

[20] With Bockmuehl, 76; O'Brien, 97; Fee, 109; Beare, 59; Hawthorne, 32 (cf. 1 Thess 1:6; Gal 6:6) preferring the shorter reading in a split decision. On the case for the longer reading see 1 Cor 14:36; 2 Cor 2:17; 4:2; Col 1:5, 25; 1 Thess 2:13; 1 Tim 4:5; 2 Tim 2:9; Tit 1:3; 2:5 cf. Eph 6:17 (ῥῆμα); Col 3:16 (of Christ); 1 Thess 1:8; 2 Cor 1:18: 2 Thess 3:1 (τοῦ κυρίου) cf. B.M. Metzger, *A Textual Commentary on the Greek New Testament* (London: United Bible Society, 1971), 611; Martin, 71. Lightfoot, 88; Bruce, 45. Silva, 69 prefers to leave it open. On τὸν λόγον λαλεῖν as a synonym for 'preach the gospel' especially in Acts (cf. P.T. O'Brien, Philippians, 96), the range of ὁ λόγος see *BDAG*, 599-601; Louw-Nida, *Lexicon*, 33.98, 33.99, 33.51, 33.100, 57.228, 89.18, 13.115, 30,13. 56.17 and 33.260 who note that here it indicates 'the content of what is preached about Christ or about the good news' cf. Fee, 116. See also absolute use in 1 Cor 15:2; Phil 1:14; Col 4:3; 1 Thess 1:6; 2 Tim 4:2), in a variety of genitive constructions meaning gospel ('word of God' [1 Cor 14:36; 2 Cor 2:17; 4:2; Col 1:5, 25; 1 Thess 2:13; 1 Tim 4:5; 2 Tim 2:9; Tit 1:3; 2:5], 'word of Christ' [Col 3:16], 'word of the Lord' [1 Thess 1:8; 2 Thess 3:1] and 'word of the cross' [1 Cor 1:18], 'my message' [1 Cor 2:4], 'word of reconciliation' [2 Cor 5:19 cf. 5:18], 'word of truth' [2 Cor 6:7; Eph 1:13; Col 1:5; 2 Tim 2:15] and 'word of life' [Phil 2:16]) and in other constructions (Rom 15:18; 1 Cor 2:11, 13; Col 3:17 cf. 1 Cor 12:8; 2 Cor 8:7; Col 4:6; 1 Tim 5:17. On the wide range of λαλέω see *BDAG*, 582-583; Louw-Nida, *Lexicon*, 33.70. As a verbal synonym for εὐαγγελίζομαι see 1 Cor 2:6, 7; 2 Cor 2:13, 17; 4:13; Eph 6:20; Col 4:3-4; 1 Thess 2:2, 4, 16.

[21] O'Brien, 'Gospel', 221 notes Paul 'goes out of his way to accumulate terms expressive of courage' cf. Fee, 116; Schenk, 136-137; Lightfoot, 88; O'Brien, 94; Beare, 59; Louw-Nida, *Lexicon*, 25.161 who note it implies boldness to the point of challenging possible danger, here Roman persecution and 78.31 where they note περισσοτέρως suggests 'a significant increase'; see further *BDAG*, 805. On πείθω ('trust', 'reliance', 'confidence') see *TDNT* 6.1-11. Τολμαω always has the sense of bravery and daring (Rom 5:7; 15:18; 1 Cor 6:1; 2 Cor 10:2, 12; 11:21; *TDNT* 8.184-185). On ἀφόβως ('without fear, fearlessly') see 1 Cor 16:10; Louw-Nida, *Lexicon*, 25.253.

[22] O'Brien, *Consumed*, 114-115 notes here a fresh initiative which is 'no momentary enthusiasm that quickly passed' but was continuing cf. Kent, 111; Fee, 116; Schenk, 136.

[23] Most commentators take ὅτι ἡ πίστις ὑμῶν καταγγέλλεται ἐν ὅλῳ τῷ κόσμῳ in Rom 1:8 passively referring to others speaking about the faith of the Romans (so Moo, *Romans*, 57 cf. O'Brien, *Thanksgivings*, 207-208; Byrne, *Romans*, 49; Schreiner, *Romans*, 48; Morris, *Romans* 56-57; Dunn, *Romans 1-8*, 8; Bruce, 76; A. Nygren, *Commentary on Romans*, (Trans. C.C. Rasmussen. London: SCM, 1952), 59-60; Cranfield, *Romans*, 75; K. Barth, *The Epistle to the Romans* (Trans. E.C. Hoskyns. London: Oxford, 1933), 32; C.K. Barrett, *A Commentary on the Epistle to the Romans*. HNTC (San Francisco: Harper, 1957), 24; O'Brien, 127; *Consumed*, 127; Bowers, '*Studies*', 112-118; 'Church', 99; Bosch, *Transforming*, 168. Peters, *Missions*, 133 takes

The Brothers of 1:14: General Christians or Co-Workers?

The identity of the brothers in 1:14 is disputed. While it is not critical to this discussion, it is helpful to seek to discern who the brothers are. While grammatically it is plausible that Paul here in 1:14 is referring to Philippi or to the impact his imprisonment is having on 'brothers in the Lord' generally, several factors make it rather more likely these brothers are to be found in the vicinity of Paul and his imprisonment. First, the connective καί links the evangelisation of the guard and particularly unbelieving Romans to the activity of the ἀδελφοί. Secondly, there is no indication of a shift of context in Paul's thought until 1:27.

More difficult is a question of the nature of these brothers. Some take these 'brothers' in a technical sense as co-workers and other evangelistic specialists.[24] Others take these 'brothers and sisters' as general Christians.[25]

Paul's use of the term ἀδελφός is shaded in a number of ways, several of which are vital for this discussion. Obviously the locution ἀδελφοί picks up the

---

it actively without comment. It is possible however that Rom 1:8 is to be taken actively of the Romans' own evangelisation in that: 1) Καταγγέλλεω is used almost exclusively by Paul of gospel proclamation (1 Cor 2:1; 9:14; Phil 1:17-18; Col 1:28 cf. 1 Cor 11:26); 2) The proclaimers are unspecified meaning it could be the Romans themselves; 3) Πίστις is a parallel term for gospel on occasion (Gal 1:23; 1 Thess 1:8; 1 Tim 2:7 cf. Rom 10:8; 2 Cor 4:13; 10:15; Phil 1:27; 4) Phil 1:14 indicates prior Roman evangelisation; 5) The parallel 1 Thess 1:8 which I take to be active (see later in Chapter 9); 6) The list in Rom 16 which includes a number of evangelistic workers.

[24] E.E. Ellis, 'Paul and His Co-Workers' in *Prophecy and Hermeneutic in Early Christianity. New Testament Essays* (Grand Rapids: Eerdmans, 1978), 15; Gnilka, 59; Harnack, *Mission 1*, 405; Plummer, *Understanding,* 19; Jewett, 'Conflicting': 369; Dickson, *Mission-Commitment*, 145-46.

[25] Martin, 186; Fee, 115; O'Brien, 89; Hawthorne, 35; Martin, 71; Motyer, 69-70; Moule, 19-20; Bockmuehl, 76; Loh-Nida, 21; Garland, 'Defense': 332; Craddock, 25; Silva, 78 with caution; Hendricksen, 70; Barth, 28; Houlden, 56; Bloomquist, *Function*, 149; Witherington, *Friendship*, 45; Beare, 59; T. Hawthorn, 'Philippians i.12-19.' With Special Reference to vv. 15. 16. 17', *ExpTim* 62 (1950-51): 316-317: 317; Kent, 111; Peterlin, *Letter,* 35; J.J. Müller, 50-51; Calvin, 234; Bruce, 44-45; Wicks, 30-31; Marshall, 21-22; M.A. Getty, *Philippians and Philemon.* NTM (Wilmington: Michael Glazier, 1987), 16; C. Osiek, *Philippians.* ANTC (Nashville: Abingdon, 2000), 39; Plummer, *Understanding,* 21; Caird, 111; Thielman, 60; G. R. Beasley-Murray, 'Philippians' in M. Black; H.H. Rowley (Ed's) *Peake's Commentary on the Bible* (London: Thomas Nelson and Sons, 1962): 985-990, 986; Lightfoot, 88; Vincent, 17-18; Collange, 55; Boice, 63; Thielman, 60; Synge, F.C. *Philippians and Colossians* (London: Torch Bible Commentaries, 1951), 24; Holloway, *Consolation*, 104; Peterman, *Gift*, 108; Grayston, 17; Ware, *Mission*, 181-182. So also U.B. Müller, 52; Michael, 26 of Ephesus. And so it seems Schnabel, *Mission*, 1460 several times although with a possible contradiction on p1437 where he lists them as co-workers; Plummer, *Understanding,* 73.

concept of the people of God as the family of God but more can be noted.[26]

Paul's primary use is the plural ἀδελφοί as a *general term of epistolary address*.[27] This usage is found six times in Philippians (1:12; 3:1, 13, 17; 4:1, 8).[28] It is apparent that these references should certainly be understood as inclusive of the whole congregation ('brothers and sisters') for several reasons. To start with, this inclusive epistolary-address usage is customary throughout the Paulines.[29] In addition as I have noted, the whole letter is addressed to *all* the Philippians (1:1). Furthermore, even if one exaggerates the role of the 'overseers and deacons' in the context of the letter, it is still highly likely that women are in some sense included in this group (cf. 4:2-3). This is seen in that the transitional address of 4:1 leads into a direct appeal to two women clearly indicating inclusiveness.[30]

Secondly, the term forms *the basis of many of Paul's paraenetic appeals for right behaviour* consistent with Christian brother/sisterhood (Rom 14:10, 13, 15, 21; 1 Cor 8-10). Christianity for Paul constitutes a new set of allegiances, one of which is the people of God as family. This family is to be characterised by a Christian ethic involving both a tolerance concerning *adiaphora* and a concern for the church's weaker members (so Rom 14:10, 13, 15, 23; 1 Cor 5:11; 6:5, 6, 8; 8:11, 12, 13; Gal 6:9-10 cf. 6:1; 1 Thess 4:6; 2 Thess 3:6, 14-15).

The two above usages illustrate Paul's third use of ἀδελφοί as a *general term for Christians*.[31] This over-arching motif is evidenced throughout the Pauline epistles and is seen in reference to instructions (1 Cor 7:12), in the context of the resurrection appearances (1 Cor 15:6) and of those from whom and to whom he writes his epistles (Rom 16:14; 1 Cor 16:12, 20; Gal 1:2; Eph 6:23; Phil 4:21; Col 1:2; 4:15; 1 Thess 4:10; 5:27; 1 Tim 4:6; 2 Tim 4:21).

---

[26] Similarly he uses it sparingly of his fellow-Jews (Rom 9:3).

[27] See Rom 1:13; 7:1, 4; 8:12; 10:1; 11:25; 12:1; 15:14, 30; 16:17; 1 Cor 1:10, 11, 26; 2:1; 3:1; 4:6; 7:24, 29; 10:1; 11:33; 12:1; 14:6, 20, 26, 39; 15:1, 50, 58; 16:15; 2 Cor 1:8; 8:1; 13:11; Gal 1:11; 3:15; 4:12, 28, 31; 5:11, 13; 6:1, 18; Eph 6:10; Phil 1:12; 3:1, 17; 4:1, 8; 1 Thess 1:4; 2:1, 9, 14, 17; 3:7; 4:1, 10, 13; 5:1, 12, 14, 25, 26; 2 Thess 1:3; 2:1, 13, 15; 3:1, 6, 13.

[28] The other use in 4:21 probably refers to those with Paul at the time of writing (further below).

[29] In support of this contention I note that in each of the Paulines there are clear examples of inclusive uses of 'brothers' due to contextual hints that women or 'all' are included in the content: Rom 1:13; 7:1, 4; 8:12; 10:1; 12:1; 15:30; 16:7 (cf. 11:25; 15:14). 1 Cor 1:10-11, 26; 2:1; 7:24, 29; 11:33; 12:1; 14:6, 20, 26, 39; 15:1, 50, 58; 16:15 (cf. 3:1; 4:6; 10:1); 2 Cor 1:8; 8:1; 13:11; Gal 4:31; 5:13; 6:1 (cf. 1:11; 3:15; 4:12; 4:28, 31; 5:11; 6:18); Eph 6:10; Phil 4:1 (cf. 1:12; 3:1, 17; 4:8); 1 Thess 1:4; 2:1; 2:9; 2:14, 17; 3:7; 4:1, 10, 13; 5:1, 12, 14, 25, 26; 2 Thess 1:3; 2:1, 13, 15; 3:1,6.

[30] Fee, 115; Bockmuehl, 237.

[31] Louw-Nida, *Lexicon*, 11.23 note that 'in the NT ἀδελφοί refers specifically to fellow believers in Christ.'

Essentially the term 'brother' is often an affectionate term meaning 'fellow believers in Christ' (cf. Rom 8:29).

A fourth use of ἀδελφοί is of *fellow Christian co-workers* and this is where our interest lies. Paul sometimes refers to other preachers or gospel workers as 'brothers' suggesting to some that it is a technical term for 'ministers',[32] 'co-workers',[33] 'leaders in ministry',[34] or 'recognised heralds.'[35] Ellis for example argues that 'brothers' in 1:14 refers to co-workers (cf. 2 Cor 8:3, 5, 9, 18f, 23; 11:9; 12:18; 1 Cor 16:10). He notes in particular Phil 4:21-23 where Paul refers to the 'brothers with me' in contrast to 'all the saints' who greet the Philippians (v22). He also notes other contexts where 'the brothers' are contrasted with Christians in general or whole churches (cf. 1 Cor 16:19-20; Eph 6:23-24; Col 4:15).[36] On the basis of these passages he suggests that wherever Paul refers to 'brothers' plural with the article we have with fair consistency 'a relatively limited group of workers, some of whom have the Christian mission and/or ministry as their primary occupation.' He notes that this is clear in the case of those appointed by the churches to accompany Paul (2 Cor 8:18; Phil 2:25 cf. Acts 19:29).[37]

In light of the four uses above he maintains that it is clear that the 'brothers' in 1:14 are gospel-workers and not general members of the Roman church. Several factors support seeing specialist proclaimers from the Roman context here. First, in 4:21-23 which is the only other mention of brothers in Paul's context there is a clear distinction between 'brothers' and the more general 'holy ones' or 'saints.'[38] Secondly, the singular ἀδελφός is used of Epaphroditus who is a co-worker, fellow-soldier and 'apostle' of the Philippian church (2:25). Thirdly, Ellis suggests that ἀδελφός in the plural + article as is found here indicates 'co-worker', while all other instances of the plural in Philippians lack the article except 2:25 and 4:21.

However there are problems with this view. First, as I have argued, in that the majority of references to 'brothers' in Philippians are inclusive, it has to be assumed that the readers in Philippi were clear on the distinction between the use of ἀδελφός generally (1:12) and technically (of co-worker [1:14]) at this point. It also relies on the assumption that Ellis is correct concerning the use of the plural with respect to co-workers and that this was well established in the minds of the Philippians which is questionable (see below). Particularly so when Paul has just used 'brothers' in the immediate context in addressing the

---

32 Michael, 37.

33 Ellis, 'Co-workers', 3-22 esp. 6-15; Gnilka, 59; Schenk, 135-136.

34 J.J. Müller, 50.

35 Dickson, *Mission-Commitment*, 149.

36 Ellis, 'Co-workers', 14; Lightfoot, 167.

37 Ellis, 'Co-workers', 15; so also Gnilka, 59.

38 So O'Brien, 554; Ollrog, *Paulus*, 78; Hawthorne, 214; Beare, 158; Bockmuehl, 269; Marshall, 124; Dickson, *Mission-Commitment*, 148.

whole Philippian church (1:12b).

Secondly, while Ellis correctly observes the delineation between 'saints' and 'brothers' in 4:21, his explanation is not the only possibility. For example, Martin prefers to describe 'brothers' here as 'fellow-Christians in the place of his confinement, including Timothy' and the 'saints' as the other Christians in the wider vicinity.[39] Michael suggests that the 'brothers' are those who are from the 'Pauline group' in Rome including those listed in Rom 16.[40] Hence it is unclear whether the brothers of 4:21 refers to a group of general Christians known in some sense to the Philippians or Paul, co-workers, those with him and/or his supporters. Thirdly, it is uncertain whether the use of 'brothers' in 4:21 should be the key interpretative device in 1:14.

Finally and most importantly, on closer examination, Ellis' contention that the plural αδελφοί 'the brothers' invariably refers to co-workers lacks exegetical certitude and is overly assumptive.[41] A close examination of the use of the plural with the article indicates a great degree of uncertainty concerning the identity and function of the Christians in almost every context.[42] On occasion Paul is not referring to co-workers and is almost certainly referring to Christians in general from his or other specified context (Romans 16:14;[43] 1 Cor 15:6;[44] 1 Thess 4:10a;[45] 5:25-26).[46] On other occasions Paul is referring to a

---

[39] Martin, 186.

[40] Michael, 229.

[41] Similarly Dickson, *Mission-Commitment*, 145-150 who only explores Col 4:7 (which contains no reference to συνεργός) and Phil 4:21 in any depth to reach the same conclusion.

[42] Leaving aside ἀδελφός in Rom 9:3 (fellow Israelites): 1 Cor 9:5; Gal 1:19 (literal brothers).

[43] The Christians in general from the same house church as those named (Moo, *Romans*, 926; C.E.B. Cranfield, *A Critical and Exegetical Commentary on the Epistle to the Romans*. ICC (2/2 Vols. Edinburgh, T&T. Clark, 1979), 795; T.R. Schreiner, *Romans*. BECNT (Grand Rapids: Baker, 1998), 797; Fitzmyer, *Romans*, 742; Dunn, *Romans 9-16*, 898; Fitzmyer, *Romans*, 742; Stuhlmacher, *Romans*, 251 suggests so or an unspecified 'brotherhood'; L. Morris, *The Epistle to the Romans* (Grand Rapids: Eerdmans, 1988), 537 who suggests perhaps an another unspecified group. Ware, *Mission*, 182 suggests the Christians connected with those previously named and is equivalent to those mentioned in 16:15.

[44] Fee, *Corinthians*, 730 rightly notes this is probably inclusive and unidentifiable cf. A.C. Thiselton, *The First Epistle to the Corinthians*. NIGTC (Grand Rapids: Eerdmans, 2000), 1206; R.F. Collins, *First Corinthians*. SPS (Collegeville: Liturgical, 1999), 536 see here men and women who saw the resurrected Christ.

[45] Wanamaker, *Thessalonians*, 161; E.J. Richard, *First and Second Thessalonians*. SPS (Collegeville: Liturgical Press, 1995), 210-211; E. Best, *The First and Second Epistles to the Thessalonians*. BNTC (London: Black, 1972), 173; Marshall, *Thessalonians*, 115; Bruce, *Thessalonians*, 91; L. Morris, *The First and Second Epistles to the Thessalonians*. NICNT (Grand Rapids: Eerdmans, 1959), 131; A.J. Malherbe, *The Letters to the Thessalonians*. ABC 32 (New York: Doubleday, 2000), 245; M.W.

group of unspecified Christians who have an assigned contextual role without any clear designation as co-worker (1 Cor 16:11,[47] 12,[48] 17; 2 Cor 9:3, 5[49]). Sometimes it is probable that Paul has in mind a church group rather than co-workers although the latter is not out of the question. That being the case, it is unwise to designate the οἱ ἀδελφοί concerned in these passages as co-workers on the basis of non-contextual references (Gal 1:2;[50] Eph 6:23;[51] Col 4:15;[52] 2

Holmes, *1 & 2 Thessalonians*. NIVAC (Grand Rapids: Eerdmans, 1998), 135 all agree it refers to *all the believers* throughout Macedonia cf. 1:7-8.

[46] Some including C. Masson, *Les deux Épîtres de Saint Paul aux Thessaloniciens*. CNT (Neuchâtel: Delachaux et Niestelé, 1957), 79 take it this to refer to the leaders who are to greet the other members of the church (referred to by Wanamaker, *Thessalonians*, 208). However the letter is directed to the whole church (1:1) and so most take this of the whole church (cf. 'all') including Wanamaker, *Thessalonians*, 208. Richard, *Thessalonians*, 286-287; Best, *Thessalonians*, 245; Morris, *Thessalonians*, 184; Bruce, *Thessalonians*, 134-135; Marshall, *Thessalonians*, 165 noting the oral reading context i.e. the whole gathered church.

[47] This is further complicated by grammatical ambiguity so can be understood either as the 'I, along with the brothers' (if so the same as 16:12) or as the brothers with Timothy (Barrett, *1 Corinthians*, 5, 391). Fee, *1 Corinthians*, 822 prefers the latter but notes that their identity is very unclear (perhaps Erastus [Acts 19:22] or others not mentioned by Luke or unknown Ephesians) cf. Hodge, *An Exposition of the First Epistle to the Corinthians* (Grand Rapids: Eerdmans, 1980), 368. To then designate these unknowns in terms of function (i.e. co-worker), is without warrant cf. Thiselton, *1 Corinthians*, 1331 who writes 'we simply do not know whether Paul means *friends*, *fellow Christians*, or *some specific group*' (italics his) cf. L. Morris, *1 Corinthians*. TNTC (Leicester: IVP, 1985), 236. Collins, *First Corinthians*, 597 notes ease of travel could mean any 'other Christians.'

[48] Fee, *1 Corinthians*, 824; Hodge, *1 Corinthians*, 368 note in 1 Cor 16:12 'the brothers' almost certainly refers to Stephanas, Fortunatus and Achaicus (1 Cor 16:17). Little is known of these three in reality apart from Stephanas and his household being the first converts in Achaia and being baptised by Paul (1 Cor 1:16). They brought material provision in an independent way and are thus possibly co-workers (1 Cor 16:16). However, in that 'the brothers' in 1 Cor 16:12 is not clearly linked to 1 Cor 16:17, and the specificity of the plural is clouded further by the epistolary address 'brothers' in 1 Cor 16:15; Collins, *First Corinthians*, 598 sees it as 'other Christians.'

[49] C. Kruse, *The Second Epistle of Paul to the Corinthians*. TBC (Grand Rapids: Eerdmans, 1987), 163; P.E. Hughes, *The Second Epistle to the Corinthians*. NICNT (Grand Rapids: Eerdmans, 1962), 326-327; E. Best, *2 Corinthians*. IBC (Louisville: John Knox, 1987), 84; Martin, *2 Corinthians*, 284 see here the brothers including Titus and two unnamed representatives (2 Cor 8:16-24) travelling with the collection. He notes those who argue against integrity see here a fresh delegation of unnamed leaders.

[50] It is unclear what Paul has in mind here. As Longenecker, *Galatians*, 5-6 notes, these are either those from the church in Antioch or travelling missionary companions depending on date, provenance and recipients. He prefers the former i.e. the church in Antioch. It is not clear which is in mind. J.D.G. Dunn, *The Epistle to the Galatians* (Peabody: Hendrickson, 1993), 30 argues it is unlikely in light of its antecedents in

Tim 4:6,[53] 21[54]). On occasion these unclear references have more likelihood of being co-workers but ambiguity still clouds the issue enough to suggest caution (1 Cor 16:20;[55] 2 Cor 11:9).[56] It is apparent then that the view that the plural

---

Hellenism and Judaism that it refers only to his missionary colleagues here although this would enhance the effectiveness of his appeal. My preference is for the southern Galatian theory, hence the church in Antioch; see R.Y.K. Fung, *Galatians.* NICNT (Grand Rapids: Eerdmans, 1988), 37; H. Ridderbos, *The Epistle of Paul to the Churches in Galatia* (London: Marshall, Morgan and Scott, 1953), 41; L. Morris, *Galatians: Paul's Charter of Christian Freedom* (Leicester: IVP, 1996), 34-35; F.F. Bruce, *The Epistle to the Galatians.* NIGTC (Exeter: Paternoster, 1982), 74). These thinkers refer to Phil 4:14 in support which, as I have noted above, is capable of alternative interpretations. However G.S. Duncan, *The Epistle of Paul to the Galatians.* MNTC (London: Hodder, 1934), 9-10 takes it not as the members of the church as the emphasis is on 'with me' but as those co-workers with him at the time of writing as do W. Neil, *The Letter of Paul to the Galatians.* CBC (Cambridge: CUP, 1967), 22; J.L. Martyn, *Galatians: A New Translation with Introduction and Commentary.* ABC. (New York, Doubleday, 1997), 85.

[51] Probably all believers as suggested by F. Foulkes, *Ephesians.* TBC (Leicester: IVP, 1989), 188; C.L. Mitton, *Ephesians.* NCBC (Grand Rapids: Eerdmans, 1973), 231; P.T. O'Brien, *The letter to the Ephesians.* PNTC (Grand Rapids: Eerdmans, 1999), 492 (perhaps due to the circular nature of the epistle); A.S. Wood, 'Ephesians' in *EBC* (Vol 11/12. Ed F. Gaebelein. Grand Rapids: Zondervan, 1978), 92; A.T. Lincoln, *Ephesians.* WBC 42 (Nashville: Nelson, 1990), 465; F.F. Bruce, *The Epistles to the Colossians to Philemon and to the Ephesians.* NICNT (Grand Rapids: Eerdmans, 1984), 415 who sees Ellis' view as only a possibility. R. Schnackenburg, *The Epistle to the Ephesians* (Edinburgh: T&T. Clark, 1991), 23 sees evidence of a wider unknown audience.

[52] Bruce, *Epistles*, 183 takes it to mean all the Christians (cf. N.T. Wright, *Colossians and Philemon.* TBC (Leicester: IVP, 1986), 159), the references to Nympha and the church being part of the whole. So also P.T. O'Brien, *Colossians, Philemon,* WBC (Waco: Word, 1982), 256; J.D.G. Dunn, *The Epistles to the Colossians and to Philemon.* NIGTC (Grand Rapids: Eerdmans, 1996), 48, 284-285; M.Y. MacDonald, *Colossians and Ephesians.* SPS (Collegeville: Liturgical, 2000), 15; D.E. Garland, *Colossians and Philemon.* NIVAC (Grand Rapids: Zondervan, 1998), 278) specifically against Ellis at this point. Other explanations include a church distinct but related from the Laodicean church (so H.A.W. Meyer, *Colossians*, 477); 'the brothers' are a Colossian family resident in Laodicea (J.B. Lightfoot, *Saint Paul's Epistles to the Colossians and to Philemon.* (9th ed. London: Macmillan, 1890), 241); two different churches (so M. Dibelius, *An die Kolosser, Epheser an Philemon.* HNT 12 (Revised H. Greeven. Tübingen: Mohr, 1953), 52).

[53] The whole church probably so A.T. Hanson, *The Pastoral Epistles.* NCBC (Grand Rapids: Eerdmans, 1982), 89; Fee, *Pastorals*, 102; P.H. Towner, *1-2 Timothy & Titus.* IVPVS (Downers Grove: IVP, 1994), 105-106.

[54] Fee, *Pastorals*, 302 suggest this group includes both leaders and general believers ('all').

[55] Fee, *1 Corinthians*, 836; Morris, *1 Corinthians*, 241 note the ambiguity here. Thiselton, *1 Corinthians*, 1344 suggests any other believers with links with Corinth or

plus the article usually or always refers to co-workers should be rejected and not used as a grid to define 'brothers' in 1:14 or elsewhere. Rather, the context alone should determine whether Paul means co-worker, general Christian or other designation.[57]

Consequently, I suggest that in light of the immediate contextual use of brothers and its broader use in Philippians and elsewhere, 'the brothers' in 1:14 should be taken inclusively of all Christians in the church (including co-workers) in Paul's context who were inspired into proactive evangelism by his presence in prison. Furthermore in light of this discussion, I suggest that if Paul were referring to a specific group within the Roman church, then he would have specified it to remove ambiguity. This is particularly so in the context of proclamation of the gospel in Philippi where, as I will argue, Paul goes on to appeal for evangelism (1:27 cf. 2:16) and where both female and male 'brothers' were involved in the proclamation of the gospel (Phil 4:2-3).

Moreover, if I am correct concerning the Roman context, several other factors come into play. First, Rom 16 gives reference to some in the Roman church who were involved in the work of the gospel. There is a strong likelihood that some of these had a proclamatory role including Prisca and

---

from Asia, or other believers from Ephesus or its region who did not meet in the home of Aquila and Prisca. It is either a generalising of those in 1 Cor 16:19 or Paul's various co-workers and travelling companions as suggests Ellis. If the latter only Sosthenes and perhaps Titus (2 Cor 2:13) can be named with confidence. Barrett, *1 Corinthians*, 396 suggests part of the Ephesian church outside the home of Prisca and Aquila (cf. Hodge, *1 Corinthians*, 371) or Corinthian Christians who have travelled to Ephesus. Hays, *1 Corinthians*, 291 takes it as the whole church i.e. brothers and sisters. Collins, *First Corinthians*, 610 sees it generally as 'the entire group of Christians that was with Paul.'

[56] Many including Martin, *2 Corinthians*, 346; Hughes, *2 Corinthians*, 388; L.L. Belleville, *2 Corinthians*, IVPNTCS (Leicester: IVP, 1996), 278 suggest here Timothy and Silas (Acts 18:5). On the other hand M. Thrall, *II Corinthians*. ICC (2 Vols. Edinburgh: T&T. Clark, 2000), II.686 rightly queries why Paul would not have named them. Hence it is equally feasible unnamed Philippian Christians brought gifts from Philippi to Paul (cf. Phil 4:14-16) as P. Barnett, *The Second Epistle to the Corinthians*. NICNT (Grand Rapids: Eerdmans, 1997), 517; C. Kruse, *2 Corinthians*, 188 (cf. Phil 4:14) suggest.

[57] Also when applied to the singular 'brother' including Quartus (Rom 16:23); Sosthenes (1 Cor 1:1; 2 Cor 1:1); Timothy (1 Cor 16:11; Col 1:1; 1 Thess 3:2; Phm 1); Titus (2 Cor 2:13); an unspecified famous proclaimer (2 Cor 8:18; 12:18); a zealous brother (2 Cor 8:22); other church messengers/apostles (2 Cor 8:23 cf. 2 Cor 9:3, 5; 11:9; Acts 20:4); Tychicus (Eph 6:21; Col 4:7); Epaphroditus (Phil 2:25); Onesimus (Col 4:9); Philemon (Phm 7, 20); Onesimus (Phm 16). These are people Paul feels a need to single out as a brother. Similarly Paul sometimes, if rarely, singles out women as 'sister.' Paul uses 'sister' (ἀδελφή) of Phoebe whom Paul commends to the Romans (Rom 16:1) and Nereus a sister whom Paul greets (Rom 16:15). He uses it generally of a believing woman (1 Cor 7:15 cf. ἀδελφός of a believing man; 9:5; 1 Tim 5:2 by analogy with a blood sister).

Aquila (Rom 16:3 cf. 1 Cor 16:19; 2 Tim 4:19; Acts 18:18, 26)[58] and Andronicus and Junia.[59] It is possible although speculative, that Andronicus and

---

[58] D.M. Scholer, 'Paul's Women Co-Workers in the Ministry of the Church', *AB* 23:4 (1987): 70-72; P. Trebilco, 'Women as Co-Workers and Leaders in Paul's letters', *JCBRF* 122 (1990): 27-36, 29-30; E. Schüssler-Fiorenza, 'Missionaries, Apostles, Co-Workers: Romans 16 and the Reconstruction of Women's Early Christian History', *Word and World* 6.4 (1986): 57-71, 66-69 who argues this persuasively. Against A.J. Köstenberger, 'Women in the Pauline mission' in Bolt and Thompson, *Perspectives*, 227 who limits her role. In response I note that Luke gives no indication that it was only Aquila who did the instructing; rather, he employs the plurals προσελάβοντο, ἀκριβέστερον and ἐξέθεντο indicating Prisca's active involvement in teaching ministry. In addition she is named before Aquila at times indicating some degree of prominence (Acts 18:18, 26; Rom 16:2; 2 Tim 4:19).

[59] It is almost certain that Junia is feminine as demonstrated by P. Lampe, 'The Roman Christians of Romans 16,' in K.P. Donfried, (ed) *The Romans Debate* (Second edition. Peabody: Hendrickson, 1991), 223. It is probable she was an apostle along with a large number of scholars including Barrett, *Romans*, 283-284; C.E.B. Cranfield, *Romans*, 788-789; B. Brooten, '"Junia…Outstanding Among the Apostles"' in L and A. Swidler, *Women Priests: A Catholic Commentary on the Vatican Declaration* (New York, Paulist, 1977), 141-44; Trebilco, 'Women': 31-32; Schüssler-Fiorenza, 'Missionaries': 68-69; Dunn, *Romans 9-16*, 894-895 who suggests it is almost certain and that Andronicus and Junia were 'premier apostles' with Barnabas and possibly Silvanus; Chrystostom, *Patrologia*, 60, 669f; Morris, *Romans*, 534; Fitzmyer, *Romans*, 737-739 who gives a list of others; Byrne, *Romans*, 451-453; F.F. Bruce, *The Epistle of Paul to the Romans. An Introduction and Commentary.* TBC (London: Tyndale, 1963), 272; P. Richardson, 'From Apostles to Virgins: Romans 16 and the Roles of Women in the Early Church', *TJT* 2 (1986): 232-261, esp. 238-39; Schreiner, *Romans*, 796; J. Ziesler, *Letter to the Romans.* NTC (London: SCM, 1989), 351; Green, *Evangelism*, 211, 290. Köstenberger, 'Women', 231 takes it as apostle but only because she is the wife of Andronicus which is, at best, a possibilty. Those who take 'Junia' as male (Junias) include Murray, *Romans II*, 229-230; R. Schnackenburg, 'Apostles Before and During Paul's Time' in Gasque and Martin, *Apostolic*, 293-294; K. Barth, *Romans*, 535; M. Black, *Romans.* NCBC (Grand Rapids: Eerdmans, 1973), 181; J. Cottrell, *The College Press New International Commentary on Romans.* (Vol 2/2. Joplin [Miss]: College Press, 1996), 474-475; W. Hendriksen, *Epistle to the Romans.* NTC (Vol 2/2. Grand Rapids: Baker, 1981), 504; E. Käsemann, *Commentary on Romans* (Trans G.W. Bromiley. Grand Rapids: Eerdmans, 1980), 414; C.H. Dodd, *The Epistle of Paul to the Romans* (London: Hodder and Stoughton, 1949), 237-238; R.C.H. Lenski, *The Interpretation of St Paul's Epistle to the Romans* (Columbas 15 [Ohio]: Wortburg Press, 1960), 905-906; P. Achtemeier, *Romans.* IBC (Louisville: John Knox, 1985), 239; Scholer, 'Co-workers': 71; Stuhlmacher, *Romans*, 248-249. Those who maintain Junia was female but, along was 'favoured by the apostles' rather than an apostle include W. Sanday and A.C. Headlam, *A Critical Commentary on the Epistle to the Romans.* ICC (Edinburgh: T&T. Clark, 1902), 422; Moo, *Romans*, 921-924 who still acknowledges they had a proclamation ministry without being Apostle cf. E. Best, *The Letter of Paul to the Romans.* CBC (Cambridge: CUP, 1967), 174-75.

Junia, an apostolic couple perhaps converted at Pentecost to then return home to Rome (Acts 2:10), or scattered from Jerusalem (Acts 8:4), planted the church in Rome.[60] Others such as Mary (Rom 16:6), Tryphena, Tryphosa and Persis (Rom 16:12) may well also have been involved in evangelism as indicated by the language of 'work.' The terms κοπιάω and κόπος have a variety of nuances including Paul's evangelistic mission (1 Cor 15:10; 2 Cor 11:23, 27; Gal 4:11; Phil 2:16; Col 1:29; 1 Tim 4:10), the evangelism of others (2 Cor 10:15; 1 Thess 1:3), Paul's labour inclusive of both evangelism and physical labour (1 Cor 15:10; 2 Cor 11:23, 27; Gal 4:11; 1 Tim 4:10) and 'preaching [including evangelism] and teaching' (1 Tim 5:17). While on occasions it could refer only to physical labour (1 Cor 4:12; 2 Cor 6:5; Eph 4:28; 2 Tim 2:6), generally of leadership (1 Thess 5:12), varying Christian-service (1 Cor 3:8; 15:58) and mission in general including the Jerusalem Collection, it is reasonable to posit that 'labour' here is evangelistic in sense.[61] If this is so then others named in Rom 16 may also have been evangelistically inclined including Rufus' mother (Rom 16:13), Julia, Nereus' sister (Rom 16:15) and the unmentioned women in the households and groups of Romans 16. It is also possible that Phoebe was a patron or minister/servant of the church in Cenchrea, which could well suggest she was involved in evangelism.[62]

Secondly, it is possible that such an invigorated proclamation by the Romans may have been an initial objective of Paul's earlier desire to travel to Rome. In Rom 1:11-12 Paul stated his desire not only for mutual encouragement, but to strengthen the Romans with 'some spiritual gift' (τι μεταδῶ χάρισμα ὑμῖν πνευματικὸν). It is possible that this desire to impart to the Romans some spiritual gift could include Paul's supreme gift, the gift of proclamation of the gospel which was central to his gift of apostleship (cf. Rom 1:1, 5, 9, 14-16).[63]

---

[60] If indeed they were converted at Pentecost, this could provide a link to Peter in the Roman church.

[61] A. von Harnack, 'κόπος (κοπῖαν, οἱ κοπιῶντες) im früchristlichen Sprachgebrauch', *ZNW* 27 (1928), 1-10; *TDNT* 3.827-830; Lampe, 'Romans 16', 223 see κοπιάω is a 'technical term for the labours of a missionary.' See also Scholer, 'Co-workers': 70; Byrne, Romans, 451; Trebilco, 'Women': 29-30 suggests they 'were involved in... demanding missionary and pastoral work in the church' (30). Fitzmyer, *Romans*, 737 sees it as unspecified work for the gospel cf. Morris, *Romans*, 533; Dunn, *Romans 9-16*, 894; Schreiner, *Romans*, 453. Moo, *Romans*, 921 rightly disputes that it is proven to be a technical term for missionary activity but leaves open the possibility that evangelism is involved.

[62] Trebilco, 'Women': 27-36 prefers to see her as patron. Scholer, 'Co-workers': 71; Ellis, 'Co-workers', 9 suggest a deacon with a role inclusive of evangelism.

[63] Byrne, *Romans*, 49-50 sees here something related to Paul's apostolic office but not primary evangelisation, as it is for the strengthening of the Romans. However this is a limited view of the impact of evangelism on the church since it can strengthen the evangelisers and increase the strength of the church through growth. Moo, *Romans*, 59 argues against this because of the absence of μου. He admits it is unspecified as does

This is supported by the prominence of the gospel and evangelism in the context (1:1-6, 9, 13-16) and that one clearly given reason for Romans is preparation for proclamation in Rome en-route to further mission in Spain (Rom 1:13-16; 15:24, 28). So while the manner of the achievement of this objective is not what Paul may have had in mind, Paul's enforced Roman incarceration ironically fulfilled his earlier wish.

In sum then, I agree with Fee who, in referring to the view of Ellis and others that 'the brother' are co-workers suggests: 'in view of Paul's usage elsewhere, and especially in view of his use of the vocative to addresses the entire community of believers to whom he writes (e.g. Phil 1:12; 3:1, 13, 17; 4:1), one seems hard pressed to make that work here.'[64] This being the case then, 'it is observable that he regards the work of "speaking the word" as the work not only of the ordained messengers but of all Christians.'[65] Marshall reinforces this point: 'Paul is obviously glad that the other Christians around him were taking up the task. The implication is that evangelism was not just the task of a few called Christian leaders. It was something that the majority of Christians could and did undertake.'[66]

'Αδελφοί here then should include the majority of believers *including* specialists in the context, whether evangelists, co-workers, leaders in the church or apostles. These people may have included those co-workers and associates with Paul at the time. Potentially this could include some of those referred to in Rom 16 (see above), Timothy (2:19-23; Col 1:1; Phm 1), Epaphroditus (2:25-30), Tychicus (Eph 6:21; Col 4:7; 2 Tim 4:12; Tit 3:12),[67] Aristarchus (Col 4:10; Phm 24),[68] Mark, (Col 4:10; Phm 24; 2 Tim 4:11),[69] Jesus/Justus (Col

---

Dunn, *Romans 1-8*, 13; Murray, *Romans I*, 22; Cranfield, *Romans* 1, 79 who takes it as general spiritual blessing as does Morris, *Romans*, 60; Fitzmyer, *Romans*, 248 (Rom 11:29; 15:27); Käsemann, *Romans*, 19: the blessings from preaching; Barrett, *Romans*, 25 sees this speculation as pointless. Fee, *Empowering*, 488 suggests the reference is to Paul's understanding of the gospel in Romans. I consider that this is less likely in that the apostolic/evangelistic gift is contextually more relevant.

64 Fee, 115; O'Brien, 89; Hawthorne, 35; Melick, 72; Martin, 71; Bockmuehl, 76; Craddock, 25; Silva, 78 with a degree of caution; Hendricksen, 70; Motyer, 69; Barth, 28; Houlden, 56; Caird, 111; Kent, 111; U.B. Müller, 52; Bruce, 45; Marshall, 21-22; Osiek, 39; Plummer, *Understanding,* 21; Thielman, 60; D.A. Carson, *Basics for Believers: An Exposition of Philippians* (Grand Rapids: Baker, 1996), 24; Barclay, *Philippians*, 27; H.A.W. Meyer, 35; C.J. Ellicott, *St Paul's Epistles to the Philippians, the Colossians, and Philemon* (London: Longmans, Green and Co, 1865), 16; Loh, 21.

65 Moule, 20. While acknowledging 'ordained' here is anachronistic, the point is well made.

66 Marshall, 22.

67 Although it is not clear that Tychicus is with Paul at the time of writing as Paul intends to send him to Ephesus (or other recipients) and Colossae.

68 If still in prison with Paul this would be unlikely.

69 If still in Rome as he may be travelling to Colossae.

4:11),[70] Epaphras (Col 1:7; 4:12; Phm 23),[71] Luke (Col 4:14; Phm 24; 2 Tim 4:11), Demas (Col 4:14; Phm 24; 2 Tim 4:10),[72] Phygelus (2 Tim 1:15), Hermogenes (2 Tim 1:15), Onesiphorus (2 Tim 1:16), Crescans (2 Tim 4:10), Titus (2 Tim 4:10), Eubulus (2 Tim 4:21), Pudens, Linus, Claudia, and other unspecified brothers and sisters (2 Tim 4:21), Artemas (Tit 3:12) and οἱ μετ' ἐμοῦ πάντες (Tit 3:15).[73] On the evidence of 2:20 it is unclear which of these if any were with Paul at the time of writing. However, it is probable that these or other specialists from the Roman context took the lead in the evangelistic response to Paul's imprisonment.

O'Brien, accepting that these are general Christians, notes that these brothers and sisters 'appeared to be individual Christians, rather than a church as a church, who were engaged in this praiseworthy endeavour.'[74] I question whether this conclusion is warranted in terms of Paul's ecclesiology and in particular his concept of the church as body of Christ. In Paul's thinking, the church is made up of a variety of individuals who, having become one in Christ, expressed their spiritual gifting and good works in many and varied ways with equal importance (Rom 12:4-8; 1 Cor 12:4-31; Eph 4:7-16). If this is the case it follows that when the members of the church engage in evangelism the church is engaged in evangelism unless there is a clear break between the church and/or church leaders and the individuals involved. To suggest that they were mere individuals intrudes a false dichotomy that does not exist in Paul's thought between church and individual unless it can be shown that the body disapproves of the endeavour.[75] Even if disapproval is noted, Paul's broader theology of the cosmic church indicates that where a believer evangelises, the church evangelises. As no such disavowal is evident, the believer who evangelises is a portion of the body of Christ expressing their faith. Similarly, as Plummer notes, the use of the general 'brothers' argues against a special class of Christian or individual separate from the church.[76]

Importantly here it is the majority of the church involved,[77] indicating that Paul is not talking about one or two individuals, but *a whole group of people* expressing its faith. That being the case, when the brothers and sisters of Rome

---

[70] A 'co-worker' and so involved in evangelism (see Chapter 5). If so, definitely pro-Paul unlike the other Jews.

[71] A church planter and servant of Christ and so involved in evangelism.

[72] Demas may at this point have left Paul (cf. Phil 2:20).

[73] Accepting Pauline authorship and a Roman provenance for Colossians, Ephesians and the Pastorals (see introduction).

[74] O'Brien, *Consumed*, 115.

[75] Marshall, 'Evangelists?' 259 notes that the line between individual and congregation is rather blurred.

[76] Plummer, *Understanding*, 73.

[77] Paul's use of πλείονας (πολύς) in 1:14 should be taken as a general reference to 'most' of the Romans (cf. 1 Cor 10:5; 15:6) cf. 'μᾶλλον', in *BDAG*, 848; O'Brien, 94; Bockmuehl, 76; Loh-Nida, 21; Bruce, 'Macedonia': 42.

preached the gospel, the church preached the gospel. In that the *majority* was involved, it is highly unlikely that the leadership of the church (or churches) in Rome were not supportive of their effort or that the individuals were operating distinctly from the church. Consequently, O'Brien goes beyond the evidence in suggesting that the proclaimers operated as individuals and not a church.

The above analysis is highly significant to this discussion. The weight of evidence suggests that the 'brothers' who spoke the gospel were ordinary members of the Roman congregation including women (Rom 16 cf. Phil 4:3) inspired by Paul, rather than merely specialist proclaimers. This suggests then that Paul wanted to see other 'ordinary' Christians emulate his own evangelistic zeal. As Silva puts it: '"Most of the brothers" in v. 14 cannot reasonably be restricted to ministers... Phil 1:14 leaves little doubt that Paul encouraged believers in general "to speak the word of God without fear."'[78] The use of terms of courage suggests that the proclaimers were inspired in the Lord to proclaim despite the potential for persecution and personal suffering.

If so, then the threat of persecution and suffering is for Paul, no reason to retreat from proclamation. This is more remarkable in light of the historical context in Rome. As Fee notes, Nero's lunacy was peaking at this time and the church was a target. Paul and others are preaching Jesus as Lord in the crux of an environment which understood Caesar as Lord. Bockmuehl thus writes: 'Paul's example, which Acts 28:31 also alludes to, was clearly infectious.'[79] Perhaps, as Fee suggests, this had led to a 'quietist' form of evangelism which was less overt and so less threatening to the Roman culture.[80] Whether or not this is the case, the Roman Christians have become more active in evangelism in the face of persecution, inspired by Paul's own example.[81] This delights Paul who is motivated to see the gospel spread.

Paul's Delight that the Gospel is Preached Despite False Motives (1:15-18a)

The Identity of the τινὲς ('some') of 1:15

Paul goes on in 1:15-18a to speak of two groups who are preaching the gospel, one positively motivated through love and the other negatively motivated to cause Paul suffering.[82] It must be established whether the two groups in 1:15-

[78] Silva, 69.

[79] See also Bockmuehl, 76.

[80] Fee, 116.

[81] Fee, 116; Holloway, 17; Thielman, 60.

[82] That they were preachers of the gospel is clear from: 1) Continuity with λόγον λαλεῖν in 1:14; 2) The three verb-noun combinations are parallel to 'parallel to preach the gospel' (Χριστὸν κηρύσσουσιν [1:15]; τὸν Χριστὸν καταγγέλλουσιν [1:17]; Χριστὸς καταγγέλλεται [1:18]. Χριστός emphasises the content of the message and

18a (τινὲς) are sub-groups of the ἀδελφῶν of 1:14 or are they different proclaimers from another context.

The connection between 1:12-14 and 1:15-18a is debated. The connective καί can be adversative indicating a sharp distinction between the 'brothers' of 1:14 and the proclaimers of 1:15f.[83] This position is taken by those who consider 1:15-18a to be an excursus, a self-contained unit independent of 1:12-14. If so, then the preachers are considered to be different from those in 1:14.[84] However, there is nothing in the context that suggests a shift from Paul's present situation. Rather, evangelistic and contextual connections between 1:12-14 and 1:15-18a suggest continuity in Paul's thought. Of particular note is the continuity throughout 1:12-18a of evangelism by others, evangelistic motivation, and most importantly, the interaction of these preachers with Paul's present situation (cf. 1:16-17). Thus, 'there is nothing in Paul's language... to suggest that he has enlarged the field of his vision between v14 and v15.'[85] Hence καί should be seen in its more usual sense as transitional, Paul continuing to develop his report from Rome (Ephesus) to Philippi and the preachers are those referred to in 1:14.[86] Silva for example, sees καί both as

---

the centrality of the work of Christ to the message (1:15 cf. 1 Cor 2:1-5; 15:3-11; 2 Cor 11:4). On κηρύσσω (1:15) ('announce, make known' by a herald or to 'proclaim aloud' generally cf. Joel 2:1; 4:9; Jonah 1:2; 3:2 and commonly in Synoptics/Acts) see Rom 2:21; 10:8, 14, 15; 1 Cor 1:23; 9:27; 15:11-12; 2 Cor 1:19; 4:5; 11:4; Gal 2:2; 5:11; Phil 1:15; Col 1:23; 1 Thess 2:9; 1 Tim 3:16; 2 Tim 4:2). On καταγγέλλω (1:17, 18) ('proclaim' cf. not in Gospels but often in Acts) see Rom 1:8; 1 Cor 2:1; 9:14; 11:26; Phil 1:17-18; Col 1:28. Notably all are in the present suggesting a present, continuous and sustained evangelistic effort.

[83] Vincent, 18; Ellicott, 17.

[84] Barth, 29; Peterlin, *Letter,* 35; Schmithals, *Paul*, 75; Gnilka, 60 a 'digression' (*kleinen Exkurs*); Hendricksen, 71; Vincent, 18; H.A.W. Meyer, 36; J.T. Reed, *A Discourse Analysis of Philippians. Method and Rhetoric in the Debate over Literary Integrity.* JSNTSS 136 (Sheffield: Sheffield Academic Press, 1997), 210.

[85] Michael, 37.

[86] So most including O'Brien, 98; Fee, 118-119; Michael, 37; Peterlin, 35; Martin, 73-74; Ware, *Mission*, 187; Marshall, 22; Collange, 53, 55; Vincent, 18; Witherington, *Friendship*, 45; Hawthorne, 36; A.L. Ash, *Philippians, Colossians & Philemon*, Outlines at Beginning of Each Book. CPNIVC (Joplin, Mo.: College Press, 1994), '1:15-18a' (no page numbers); Bloomquist, *Function*, 108; Bruce, 43 and 'Macedonia': 266; Silva, 71; Moule, 19; Houlden, 58; Wicks, 51; Bockmuehl, 77; Motyer, 70, 74; Beasley-Murray, 986; Kent, 111; Garland, 'Defense', 332; Melick, 73-74; Oaks, *Philippians*, 113-114; Carson, *Basics*, 24; C.K. Barrett, *Paul. An Introduction to his Thought* (London: Geoffrey Chapman, 1994), 39, 41-43; Caird, 111; Perkins, 90 who sees continuity with the context of imprisonment; C.H. Lenski, *The Interpretation of St Paul's Epistle to the Galatians, Ephesians and Philippians* (Minneapolis[Minn]: Augsburg), 1962, 727-728; Craddock, 25; Boice, 66; Hawthorn, 'i.12-19': 317; Loh-Nida, 22; Thielman, 61; Beare, 59; H.A.W. Meyer, 36; Barclay, *Philippians*, 28; J.J. Müller, 52; Synge, 24; Calvin, 235; Wicks, 31; F.B. Meyer, *The Epistle to the Philippians* (London: The Religious Tract

transitional and emphatic, linking the Roman situation to the Philippian awareness that some preach out of false motives.

There are a number of possibilities for the subject of τινὲς in verse 15.[87] It is possible first that Paul is referring to the varying motivations of *Christian preachers in general.* Central to this view is the supposed problem of reconciling the negative motivation of some of the Romans with ἐν κυρίῳ πεποιθότας and the fearlessness of 1:14.[88] However, several factors make this perspective unlikely. In the first place, there is no clear shift in context in the text. In addition, there are clear hints that these proclaimers are interacting directly with Paul's situation in the Roman prison, they being able not only to know (εἰδότες) and think (οἰόμενοι) about his situation, but also able to influence it for the worse.[89] Furthermore, the logical antecedent for τινὲς is ἀδελφῶν.[90] Finally, that these preachers preach 'Christ' accords with ἐν κυρίω in v14.

Similarly, these arguments greatly weaken the possibility that Paul is reflecting upon *a general problem or one from a specific church other than Rome (Ephesus) or Philippi.* Manson, for example suggests that Paul is reflecting on the parties in Corinth (cf. 1 Cor 1-4).[91] O'Brien is correct to note that this is far-fetched and a strange intrusion into the text.[92]

Neither is it probable that Paul is addressing a *heretical set of proclaimers known generally and to the Philippians* such as Gnostics or Judaisers.[93] Apart from this interrupting the flow of the passage, that these preachers proclaim 'Christ' removes any thought of an imperfect gospel.[94] In addition Paul's mild language and attitude stand in stark contrast to other contexts in which he is

---

Society, 1905), 37; U.B. Müller, 55; Jewett, 'Conflicting': 369 of Ephesus; Schenk, 137-138, 141-142 rejects it as an excursus noting the continuity of joy, courage, Pauline context, the double adverbial καί indicating reinforcement (Rom 5:7). He also notes a number of other German scholars who hold this view including Dibelius, Haupt, Schmithals, Baumbach.

[87] See Peterlin, *Letter*, 26-27 for a different summary.

[88] Fitzmyer, 249; Vincent, 18; Ellicott, 17; H.A.W. Meyer, 36; Michael, 34.

[89] Peterlin, *Letter*, 37.

[90] Hawthorne, 37; Michael, 37.

[91] Manson, 'Date': 149-67.

[92] O'Brien, 102.

[93] Those preferring Gnostics include Schmithals, *Paul*, 65-122 esp. 74. Those advocating Judaisers include Lightfoot, 88-89; Moule, 20; Beasley-Murray, 986; Lenski, 729; H.A.W. Meyer, 33; O. Cullmann, *Peter: Disciple, Apostle, Martyr* (Trans. F.V. Filson. London, SCM, 1953), 104-109; Ellicott, 17.

[94] Hawthorne, 37: 'the content of the message is sound'; Silva, 72-73; Beare, 59; Caird, 111; Craddock, 26; Motyer, 75; Barth, 31; Peterlin, *Letter*, 36; Witherington, *Friendship*, 45; Collange, 51, 57; Fitzmyer, 249; Hawthorn, 'i.12-19': 316-317; Kent, 111; Garland, 'Defense': 332; U.B. Müller, 53; Bruce, 46; Marshall, 23; Thielman, 62; Schenk, 141. Ash, '1:15-18' (CD).

dealing with heresy (3:2-3 cf. Gal 1:6-9; 2 Cor 11).[95] Here clearly 'the issue is not message but motive.'[96]

Another suggestion is that Paul is dealing with *itinerant Christian preachers* with a θεῖος ἀνήρ theology. In particular it is surmised that these preachers (1:14) with an over-realised and triumphalistic eschatology, considered suffering beneath a true apostle. So in this view Paul, who considered suffering the epitome of Christian experience in the already,[97] was jeopardising his mission. These preachers preferred that Paul demonstrate triumph over adversity, ecstatic visions, miracles, inspired rhetoric and a power ministry and so be an example of transcendent ministry. These preachers were supposedly in competition with Paul who is concerned that they will influence Philippi (2:20-21; 3:2-3).[98] This is unlikely for a number of reasons. First, as I have noted above, the evidence supports a Roman provenance rather than Ephesus which is usually associated with this view.[99] Secondly, this view requires that the opponents in 3:2-3 are not Judaisers but triumphalist Christians, which I consider unlikely.[100] Thirdly, the link between Rome, Corinth and Philippi is

---

[95] Bockmuehl, 81; Barth, 33 who sees a maturing of insight on the part of Paul; Bruce, 50; 'Paul in Acts and letters', in *DPL*, 679-692, 686; 'Macedonia': 266; C.H. Dodd, 'The Mind of Paul', *NTS* (March, 1953): 67-128; Osiek, 40.

[96] Craddock, 26; Martin, 76.

[97] Clearly for Paul, in the 'not yet', suffering will be defeated e.g. Rom 8:18-21.

[98] See Jewett, 'Conflicting': 362-390 for detail (quote p368). He notes the similarity of language between 2 Cor 12:20 and Phil 1:15-17. Similarly U.B. Müller, 55. Gnilka, 61-62 see them as Ephesian preachers on the basis that they knew Paul previously. However this is not necessary as Philippians was written near the end of his imprisonment, many in Rome knew Paul (Rom 16) and they had read Romans.

[99] See introduction.

[100] Most take it as Judaisers, as is most likely; see Fee, 293-294; O'Brien, 354-258; Silva, 168-169; Martin, 140; Micheal, 133; Theilman, 166; Hendriksen, 150; Lightfoot, 143; Moule, 57; Marshall, 76; J. Müller, 106; Kent 138; Barth, 92 cf. J. Müller-Bardorff, 'Zur Frage': 561-604 who sees them as Judaising libertinising spiritualists. Hence not merely Jews as argue Hawthorne, 125; A.F.J. Klijn, 'Paul's Opponents': 278-284; Beare, 100-102; Craddock, 56; Melick, 126; Robert R. Wicks and Ernest F. Scott, 'The Epistle to the Philippians', 73; Houlden, *Paul's letters*, 97; Watson, 'Analysis': 73-74; Stowers, 'Friends', 116; Black, 'Discourse Structure', 40; A. Lincoln, *Paradise Now and Not Yet. Studies in the Role of the Heavenly Dimension of Paul's thought with Special Reference to his Eschatology* (Cambridge: CUP, 1981), 89; John B. Polhill, 'Twin Obstacles in the Christian Path', *RevExp* 77 (1980): 359-371, 360; Chris Mearns, 'The Identity': 194-204. I consider the reference to circumcision and similarities to Galatians and Romans are decisive in this regard. Other views far less likely include D.J.Doughty, 'Citizens of Heaven Philippians 3.2-21', *NTS* 41 (1995): 102-122 who sees them as deutero-Pauline metaphorical general opponents; W.Schmithals, *Paul*, 85-88; H.Köster, 'The Purpose of Polemic in a Pauline Fragment', *NTS* 8 (1961-62): 317-331 who sees then as Gnostics; L. Gregory Bloomquist, *The Function*, 131-132 who sees here 'circumcision' as a rhetorical *topos* to negate his Epicurean opponents. It is

not at all clear.[101] Finally and conclusively, it is questionable in what way a suffering Paul would further inspire these already triumphalistic preachers (1:14)? Rather it would repudiate them!

Hence, it is probable that Paul has in mind *two differently motivated groups from within the Roman church.*[102] One view that can be quickly discounted is that those who support Paul come from the majority stimulated in 1:12-14, while those who oppose Paul from the not-so-excited minority.[103] This is unlikely in that there is no indication that the minority of 1:14 were engaged in evangelism at all.[104] Similarly, on the basis of 1:17 it is unlikely that the real target of these preachers was not Paul but Roman or Jewish authorities.[105]

Within the Roman context several options have been suggested. Craddock suggests some who had a triumphalistic perspective of Christianity and were not happy with Paul's imprisonment and his theology of suffering. He notes, 'if Paul were really of God, these painful and humiliating defeats would not occur.'[106] However, this view carries the same problems as Jewett's which has been critiqued above. Collange has suggested that these people were authentic

---

simpler in terms of Paul's ongoing issue with circumcision and the gospel to take it literally. J. Gnilka, 'Die Antipaulinische Mission in Philippi', *BZ* 9 (1965): 258-276; Robert Jewett, 'Conflicting Movements': 363-371; Collange, 122-123 take them as 'divine-man missionaries.' This approach rests on redating Philippians or 3:2f to the time of 2 Corinthians, on accomodating Phil 3:2 to 3:18-19 and an Ephesian provenance, rendering it unlikely. Holloway, *Consolation*, 135 sees them as merely triumphalists which does not account for circumcision adequately. Kenneth Grayston, 'The Opponents in Philippians 3', *ExpT* 97 (1986): 170-172 suggests they are Gentile propogandists who adopted circumcision. This is less likely than Jews as argued by A.F.J. Klijn, 'Paul's Opponents': 278-284 (who supposedly came to Philippi after Paul left); Gerald F. Hawthorne, *Philippians*, xliv-xlvii, 125. The argument for Jews is reasonable and Paul may be including both Jews and Judaisers i.e. adherants to the law and circumcision whether or not they named Christ and Jewish Judaistic missionaries. However, the case for Judaisers is stronger.

[101] See O'Brien, 104 for a solid critique.

[102] O'Brien, 98. Silva, 71; Hawthorne, 36 note the Philippians may be aware of those with spurious motives. Others include Moule, 19; Wicks, 51; J.J. Müller, 52-53. Hendricksen, 71 who sees them as Roman evangelists; Motyer, 70, 74; Beasley-Murray, 986; Kent, 111; Garland, 'Defense': 332.

[103] Witherington, *Friendship*, 45; Ellicott, 17; Moule, 19; H.A.W. Meyer, 36.

[104] Fee, 118 notes this would require a 'differentiating word like ἄλλος μέν'; O'Brien, 98.

[105] Hawthorn, 'i.12-19', 316-17, argues that these Roman Christians are preaching an anti-imperial gospel to provoke strife with the Roman authorities and not Paul. Synge, 24-25 suggests the target were Jews who had caused Paul's imprisonment. Both are ruled out in that Paul is the clear target (1:17).

[106] Craddock, 24-26.

proclaimers who wanted to reprimand Paul for seeking to gain his earlier release.[107] However there is no evidence of Paul taking such steps.

The Nature and Setting of the Two Groups

Having established that the preachers of 1:15-18 are most likely the Christians mentioned in 1:14, it is clear that Paul divides these Christians into two groups on the basis of their motivation. I will now enquire into the nature of these two groups.

The falsely motivated Roman proclaimers are characterised in five ways: φθόνος ('envy'), ἔρις ('strife, discord, contention'),[108] ἐριθεία ('selfishness, selfish ambition')[109] and οἰόμενοι θλῖψιν ἐγείρειν τοῖς δεσμοῖς μου ('supposing that they can raise up trouble for me in prison' [1:17]),[110] οὐχ ἁγνῶς ('impurely, insincerely')[111] and προφάσις ('whether by pretence').[112]

---

[107] Collange, 56.

[108] Φθόνος and ἔρις are often paired in vice lists and moral discourses of secular Greek and Hellenistic Judaism cf. Rom 1:29; Gal 5:21; 1 Tim 6:4 cf. Rom 13:13. See further O'Brien, 99. Often φθόνος was associated with acts of violence and murder; so Moo, *Romans*, 119. In Paul the two relate to negative relationships in the Christian community, fragmenting relationships cf. Fee, *Pastorals*, 142-43. The noun ἔρις is commonly used of the factional Corinthians (1 Cor 1:11; 3:3; 2 Cor 12:20) and in the Pastorals (1 Tim 6:4; Tit 3:9) cf. Louw-Nida, *Lexicon*, 39.22. Taking 'ἐριθεία' as 'selfishness, selfish ambition' rather than 'strife, contentiousness' (*BDAG*, 392; *TDNT* 2.660-661; O'Brien, 101 and most commentators cf. Phil 2:3; Rom 2:8; 2 Cor 12:20; Gal 5:20. Alternatively synonymous with envy and rivalry i.e. 'rivalry' (*Rivalität*); so Schenk, 139.

[109] See Louw-Nida, *Lexicon*, 746.1, 88.45 who notes it refers to: 'pertaining to purity of motives—"sincerely, out of pure motives, sincere motives".' The related noun ἁγνός ('pure, holy') has a cultic orientation, originally being understood as an attribute of 'the divinity and everything belonging to it' (2 Cor 7:11; 11:2; 1 Tim 5:22; Tit 2:5). It is found in Phil 4:8 concerning the thinking of the Philippians and so has rhetorical import cf. 4:2-3. Vincent, 21 notes its placement beside 'proclaiming Christ' emphasises the contradiction between the gospel and unethical proclamation (cf. 1:27). Further see *BDAG*, 13.

[110] Οἴομαι only here in Paul. Vincent, 21 notes it implies 'a belief or judgement based principally upon one's own feelings… it implies the supposition of something future and doubtful' cf. Louw-Nida, *Lexicon*, 31.29. Chiastically linked to 'know' (1:16), the proclaimers 'imagine' or 'suppose' that their heightened evangelistic fervour will cause an intensification of Paul's sufferings cf. O'Brien, 101-02. On θλῖψις ('pressing', 'pressure') it means oppression, affliction or tribulation generally (Rom 5:3b; 2 Cor 1:8), specifically (2 Cor 4:17), circumstantially (2 Cor 8:13), christologically (Col 1:24), mentally and spiritually (2 Cor 2:4). See further O'Brien, 102; Louw-Nida, *Lexicon*, 22.2; *BDAG*, 457. There is no need to limit the impact to spiritual suffering as do *BDAG*, 457.

[111] Schenk, 139: 'with unfair motives.'

The first three are essentially relational and suggest opposition or antipathy.[113] The final two summarise the whole motivation of these Christians. The terms accumulate to give a picture of seemingly sincere Christians who are apparently proclaiming the gospel for right motives, but in reality are operating dishonestly with the dual desires of furthering their own status in relation to others[114] while causing Paul increased suffering in prison. While the terms indicate personal gain and rivalry, the desire to cause Paul suffering also suggests an intense anti-Paul sentiment.

The well-motivated proclaimers are on the other hand characterised δι' εὐδοκίαν ('through good will') toward Paul and perhaps God,[115] ἐξ ἀγάπης ('from love') toward Paul and God,[116] εἰδότες ὅτι εἰς ἀπολογίαν τοῦ εὐαγγελίου κεῖμαι ('knowing that I have been divinely appointed to the defence of the gospel')[117] and ἀληθείᾳ ('from true motives').[118] This description suggests that these proclaimers are rightly motivated and are in some sense pro-Paul in that they *know* why he is imprisoned and his divine missionary role i.e. the 'Apostle to the Gentiles.'

Ash among others proposes that the issue was a matter of personal prestige where certain leaders aspired to positions of leadership and the associated accolades.[119] In light of Roman notion of status, rank and honour, this cannot be discounted here.[120] O'Brien prefers to leave the matter open saying 'it is

---

[112] Πρόφασις suggesting 'falsely alleged motive, pretext, excuse' (1 Thess 2:5 cf. Matt 23:14; Mk 12:40; Lk 20:47; Acts 27:30) and in contrast to ἀληθείᾳ.

[113] Peterlin, *Letter*, 36.

[114] O'Brien, 99 notes that the concern of φθόνος 'was more to deprive the other person of the desired thing than to gain it.'

[115] Taking εὐδοκία (chiastically opposite διὰ φθόνον καὶ ἔριν) in the sense of 'good will' toward Paul, his mission and God and perhaps with a touch of the 'favour, good pleasure' of God (LXX cf. Eph 1:5). See further *TDNT* 2.738-51; *BDAG*, 404.

[116] Here clearly love for Paul (so Fee, 120; Loh-Nida, 24). Perhaps it also indicates love for God i.e. to love Paul, God's appointed messenger (1:16b), is to love God in this context. Perhaps also motivated out of Christ's love (cf. 2 Cor 5:14). In that it stands chiastically opposite ἐριθεία and οὐχ ἁγνῶς it may be better to take it generally (cf. 1 Cor 13:5; Rom 15:1-3). Ash, '1:16' (CD), notes that it could also mean 'love for the lost' but this is probably, as he says, 'stretching it too far', in that Paul does not use love clearly in this regard.

[117] The participle clause develops the basis of 'love.' They *know* that Paul is in prison because of his divine appointment indicated by κεῖμαι ('reclining' or 'lying') which is used figuratively of his appointment (cf. military appointment to defend the gospel). See further *BDAG*, 537.

[118] Εἴτε ἀληθείᾳ here contrasted with pretext i.e. sincere, with no duplicity.

[119] A. L. Ash, '1:15-18'; Barth, 31; Calvin, 235 who compares it to his own experience during the Reformation. Thielman, 62 sees it merely in terms of personal rivalry.

[120] If so, then this is a warning against contemporary Christianity where pastors, churches and demoninations treat the faith in a consumeristic 'market' manner. However, what matters is that Christ is proclaimed despite this.

probably best to admit that we do not know precisely what prompted this personal rivalry.'[121] On the basis of the language utilised, status and personal rivalry are in all likelihood one aspect of the issue here. However, there may also be more at stake.

While full-blown Judaism or false teaching is out of the question, I suggest that the issue of motivation may be connected to some extent to theological differences within a profoundly Christian framework. Bockmuehl connects the two groups with the home group tensions of Romans 14:1-15:6.[122] He suggests that the 'competing interests are clearly still at work.'[123] In light of our understanding of the Roman church, this gives the most likely context for these rivalries for a number of reasons.[124] First, many today consider that Romans suggests that there are a number of home churches within the Roman context.[125] Secondly, the content of Romans especially chapters 14-15 suggests that some tension existed between these groups with regard to the OT law, dietary regulations and the place of Israel in the purposes of God.[126] This is an intra-Christian and not heretical issue as evidenced in that Paul calls these people 'brothers.' Thirdly, the historical expulsion of dominant Jews (AD 49) and their subsequent return (AD 54) in all probability caused a shift from initial Jewish dominance to Gentile dominance in the church leading to the 'gentilisation' of the leadership and resultant tension on the return of Jews.[127]

Fourthly, Paul's letter to Rome identified two groups within the church 2-6 years before his arrival.[128] His designation of some as 'weak', and he and others as 'strong' may well have led to further polarisation within these groups and

---

[121] O'Brien, 105.

[122] So also Caird, 111; Motyer, 77 who sees similarities with contemporary denominationalism; Bruce, 46 wonders if there was a 'Cephas' party in Rome cf. 1 Cor 1:12; Lenski, 727-728 but who sees them as Judaisers.

[123] Bockmuehl, 76-77; Fee, 121-22.

[124] Dunn, *Romans 1-8*, xlv. See p. xliv-liv for detail and references in support of this perspective.

[125] Schreiner, *Romans*, 797; As Dunn, *Romans*, II.891; Lampe, 'Romans 16', 797; P.S. Minear, *The Obedience of Faith. The Purpose of Paul in the Epistle to the Romans*. SBT 2/19 (Naperville (Ill): Allenson, 1971), 7; Moo, *Romans*, 5; Stuhlmacher, *Romans*, 7. See also Acts 28:15, 22 which as Fitzmyer, *Romans*, 34-35 notes, implies Paul was known to the Roman Christians.

[126] Fitzmyer, *Romans*, 33; Schreiner, *Romans*, 797; Karris, 'Romans 14:1-15:13 and the Occasion of Romans', in Donfried, *Romans*, 65-84, 79; Moo, *Romans*, 831.

[127] Moo, *Romans*, 831. By 'gentilisation' I mean the process of the primarily Jewish church becoming more Gentile in orientation.

[128] Assuming Romans was written in AD 55-58 as Schreiner, *Romans*, 3-5 suggests (cf. Cranfield, *Romans I*, 54-59; Zeisler, *Romans*, 19). Probably in AD 57 so Moo, *Romans*, 3; Bruce, *Apostle*, 475. See for options Dunn, *Romans 1-8*, xliii-xliv; Fitzmyer, *Romans*, 87, who opts for 57-58; as does Byrne, *Romans*, 9; Murray, *Romans I*, xvi; Schreiner, *Romans*, 4-5. Barrett, *Romans*, 5 opts for Jan-March 55.

fostered a pro-Paul and anti-Paul dynamic in regard to the law.[129] Finally, Paul's arrival in Rome with his law-free gospel has not been well received by all the Romans (Acts 28:24-25).[130] These tensions then were probably between anti-Paul, law and Jew-sensitive primarily Jewish 'weak' Christians and pro-Paul, law-free, primarily Gentile 'strong' Christians (cf. Rom 16).[131] This may be supported by Paul's comment in Col 4:11 where he notes that Aristarchus, Mark and Jesus/Justus are the only Jews (οἱ ὄντες ἐκ περιτομῆς) who have been a comfort (παρηγορία) to him in prison.[132]

It is possible then that the differing motivations among the Roman Christians in 1:15-18a may be set in such a context. These two groups would have reacted to Paul's arrival differently. Those positively inclined toward Paul ('goodwill' and 'love') have received him gladly and have been inspired by their knowledge of his example to proclaim the gospel. The anti-Pauline group on the other hand have received him negatively and were motivated by the supposition that in preaching the gospel, they would cause him increased suffering at the hands of the Roman authorities.

That such preaching activity would have led to an increase in suffering at the hands of the Romans is probable. First, an escalation in the public proclamation of Christ (1:14) would almost certainly have excited the interest of the authorities as the lordship of the Roman-crucified Christ would have been seen as a direct threat to the authority of Rome and the emperor (cf. Acts 17:7). Secondly, if significant numbers were responding to the message (1:13), this may have led to some social and economic instability as people renounced Roman religious beliefs and social practice (cf. Acts 16:16-40; 18:23-41; 1 Thess 2:2). Thirdly, in that it was well known among the guard and judicial authorities that Paul was in prison for promulgating the message (1:13), one

---

[129] Possibly with a Petrine-Paul twist. While the tradition that Peter or Paul founded the church can be ruled out (Moo, *Romans*, 4 cf. Rom 15:19-20) it is possible the tradition relates to their organising of disparate Roman groups (so Sanday-Headlam, xxv; Morris, *Romans*, 3-4; Dunn, *Romans* 1-8, xlviii). In addition 'Petrine' (Pentecost? Cf. Acts 2) and 'Pauline' Christians may well have established Christianity in Rome at different times with differing perspectives.

[130] Luke records that Jews were polarised by his message perhaps giving a basis for this falsely motivated group (see Acts 28:24-25: 'some were convinced by what he said, but others would not believe. They disagreed among themselves…' [NIV].

[131] This seems to be the view of F.B. Meyer, 39-41 who falls short of suggesting Judaism but sees here two groups in Rome and parallels them to denominational division in England in his time. The problem was probably not based exclusively on ethnic lines, but was theological in regard to Paul's gospel.

[132] O'Brien, *Epistles*, 251 suggests these are Jews generally. However Ellis, *Prophecy*, 116-128 followed by MacDonald, *Colossians*, 181; O'Brien, *Colossians*, 251-252; Wright, *Colossians*, 157-158 contend that they may be Jewish Christian evangelistic co-workers who supported Paul's view of the law and worked with Paul to evangelise Jews cf. Dunn, *Colossians*, 279 more cautiously.

easy way of potentially slowing the movement would have been to punish one of the key instigators, Paul (cf. Acts 12:1-4).

Finally, the increased evangelistic activity of the church may have excited a response from non-Christian Jews in Rome who sought increased action from the secular authorities against Christians including Paul (cf. Acts 13:45, 50; 14:5-6; 17:5-9, 13; 18:12-17; 25:2, 15; 1 Cor 15:32; 2 Cor 1:8-11; 1 Thess 1:1-6).

In addition, these opponents may have been motivated to proclaim the gospel to increase their own status, house groups and influence in the Roman church ('envy', 'rivalry', 'selfish ambition'). Hence, while both were inspired to proclaim the gospel by Paul, one was out of 'true' motivation and the other 'false.' Whatever the precise nature of the situation, what is important for this context is Paul's response to these falsely motivated preachers and to this I will now turn.

The Nature of Paul's Attitude, Joy that the Gospel is Proclaimed

Paul's response to these proclaimers begins with a rhetorical question: Τί γάρ (lit: 'for what?') which suggests 'what does it matter?'[133] Paul is effectively writing off the various motivations of the Romans as insignificant. The adverbial conjunction πλήν + ὅτι ('only, in any case, however, but') here indicates 'what counts' (Phil 3:16; 4:14 cf. 1 Cor 11:11; Eph 5:33). It serves to emphasise what is important i.e. not the motives of the proclaimers but rather that Christ is proclaimed.[134]

Paul's lack of concern for motive is seen in the dative phrase παντὶ τρόπῳ. Πᾶς suggests 'the totality of any object, mass, collective, or extension' i.e. 'all, every, each, whole.'[135] Here it is used with the noun τρόπος without the article. Τρόπος conveys the sense of 'manner, way, kind, guise.'[136] Together they suggest 'the totality of every way' (cf. 2 Thess 3:16; Rom 3:2). The clause εἴτε προφάσει εἴτε ἀληθείᾳ refers to the differing motivations of the groups of evangelising believers within Paul's context. Some preach Christ (Χριστὸς καταγγέλλεται) out of 'pretence', others out of 'true' motives.[137]

What does Paul mean here? The critical issue is the application of ὅτι παντὶ τρόπῳ Χριστὸς καταγγέλλεται to εἴτε προφάσει εἴτε ἀληθείᾳ. More specifically; does the motivational εἴτε ... εἴτε clause restrict the application of ὅτι παντὶ τρόπῳ Χριστὸς καταγγέλλεται to the issue of motivation

---

[133] *BDAG*, 1007, NIV, NRSV; Loh-Nida, 27 who take it transitionally. Alternatively 'what then' (KJV, ASV, NASB).

[134] Fee, 124. *BDAG*, 826 prefer that it introduces the grounds for the rhetorical question i.e. 'what does it matter? Except that ...'

[135] Louw-Nida, *Lexicon*, 59.23.

[136] *BDAG*, 1017.

[137] See above.

alone? Or, can the ὅτι clause be understood as a general statement?

Essentially then, the statement can be understood in two ways. First, in terms of immediate context alone; or secondly, it can be understood as a global statement with an immediate contextual application. If it is taken in the first sense without regard to Paul's use more widely, he relates 'every way' exclusively to evangelistic motivation. If so, then, κατά πάντα τρόπον refers specifically and wholly to the following εἴτε...καταγγέλλεται.[138] However if it is understood in the second way, Paul may be thinking not *only* of motivation which is clearly foremost in his mind, but also stating generically the importance of the gospel being proclaimed in any and every way and applying it in this context to the issue of motivation. If so, he could well have developed the statement in a number of different directions based on the essential issue; 'that the gospel of Christ is proclaimed!' This is an important exegetical decision for this discussion in that, if it is a global statement, then the issue of motivation does not limit Paul's thinking in 1:18. If it is taken generally, then here is emphatic and explicit support for the idea that Paul wanted other Christians to take up the evangelistic mission.

A close look at the construction suggests there are sound exegetical and theological reasons for adopting the second position. The core issue is Paul's use of εἴτε — εἴτε ('if - if, whether - or')[139] constructions. A close examination of Paul's use of this construction strongly suggests he uses εἴτε-introduced lists to illustrate a strong stand-alone theological statement. Almost exclusively the initial statements from which the εἴτε — εἴτε constructions flow are *general, stand-alone theological axioms* in their own right. Through the εἴτε — εἴτε construction they are then explicated in a contextually and rhetorically appropriate manner to illustrate the point Paul is making *in context.* The table below examines all Paul's uses of εἴτε — εἴτε constructions and clearly shows that Paul uses them to illustrate a strong universal statement followed up by one or more dimensions relevant to the situation at hand.

THE USE OF *εἴτε—εἴτε* CONSTRUCTIONS IN PAUL

Verse	**General Principle or statement**	**Contextual εἴτε application**	**Possible contextual and general alternative applications**
Rom 12:6-8	'Since we have different gifts according to the grace given to us'... let them be expressed.	εἴτε προφητείαν ... εἴτε διακονίαν ἐν τῇ διακονίᾳ, εἴτε ὁ διδάσκων ἐν τῇ διδασκαλίᾳ, εἴτε ὁ παρακαλῶν ἐν τῇ παρακλήσει·	The lists of 1 Cor 12, Eph 4:11 and other gifts unlisted (the lists are non-exhaustive).

[138] O'Brien, 106.

[139] See *BDAG*, 279.

1 Cor 3:21-22	'All things are yours!'	εἴτε Παῦλος εἴτε Ἀπολλῶς εἴτε Κηφᾶς, εἴτε κόσμος εἴτε ζῶὴ εἴτε θάνατος, εἴτε ἐνέτῶτα εἴτε μέλλοντα·	All people and things cf. Rom 8:17.
1 Cor 8:5	'Even if there are many so called gods.'	εἴτε ἐν οὐρανῷ εἴτε ἐπι γῆς	Under the earth cf. Phil 2:10.
1 Cor 10:31	'Do all things for the glory of God!'	εἴτε οὖν εἴτε πίνετε εἶτε τι ποιεῖτε	All activities known to humanity.
1 Cor 12:13	'For by one Spirit we were all baptised into one body and were given one Spirit to drink.'	εἴτε Ἰουδαῖοι εἴτε Ἑλλήες εἴτε δοῦλοι εἴτε ἐλεύθεροι	Male, female, Barbarian... any other such dual categories.
1 Cor 13:8	'Love never fails.'	εἴτε δὲ προφητεῖαι, καταργηθήσονται. εἴτε γλῶσσαι, παύσονται· εἴτε γνῶσις, καταργηθήσεται	Healings, interpretation, discernment and other gifts not required in eternity.
1 Cor 14:7	'Yet even lifeless things make sounds.'	εἴτε αὐλος εἴτε κιθάρα	Gong, Cymbals (1 Cor 13:1), trumpet (14:8)...any other lifeless object that produces sound.
2 Cor 5:9	'Therefore we make it our ambition to please God.'	εἴτε ἐνδημοῦντες εἴτε ἐκδημοῦντες	Whether in Corinth or Ephesus, male or female i.e. any dual category.
2 Cor 5:10	'We must all appear before the judgement seat of Christ, that each one may receive what is due him/her for things done in the body.'	εἴτε ἀγαθὸν εἴτε φαῦλον	According to the flesh/according to the Spirit; sinful/righteous, by faith/by law and any other category.'
2 Cor 12:1-3	'I know *a man* who was caught up to the third heaven.'	εἴτε ἐν σώματι οὐκ οἶδα, εἴτε ἐκτὸς τô σώματος οὐκ οἶδα	
Eph 6:8	'The Lord will reward everyone for whatever good he/she does.	εἴτε δοῦλος εἴτε ἐλεύθερος	Male, female, Jew, Greek... any other dual category.
Phil 1:18	**'What counts, is that in every way, Christ is proclaimed.'**	**εἴτε προφάσει εἴτε ἀληθείᾳ**	**Any mode of proclamation of the authentic gospel (see below).**

Phil 1:20	'Christ shall, even now, as always, be exalted in my body.'	εἴτε διὰ ζωῆς εἴτε διὰ θανάτου.	In plenty, want, chains, free, working or not ... any other life category.
Phil 1:27	'That you stand in one Spirit, contending together...'	εἴτε ἐλθὼν καὶ ἰδὼν ὑμᾶς εἴτε ἀπὼν ἀκούω τὰ περὶ ὑμῶν	Whether I am in prison, or free...
Col 1:16	'By him (Christ) all things were created.'	εἴτε θρόνοι εἴτε κυριότητες εἴτε ἀρχαὶ εἴτε ἐξουσίαι	Under the earth, humanity, animals, stars, sun, moon... any aspect of the created order.
Col 1:20	'And through him (Christ) to reconcile to himself all things.'	εἴτε τὰ ἐπὶ τῆς γῆς εἴτε τὰ ἐν τοῖς οὐρανοῖς	In all creation, in Israel...
1 Thess 5:10	'He died for us so that... we may live together with him.'	εἴτε γρηγορῶμεν εἴτε καθεύφωμεν	Jew, Gentile, male, female, slave, free...
2 Thess 2:15	'Stand firm and hold to the traditions we passed on to you.'	εἴτε διὰ λόγου εἴτε δι' ἐπιστολῆς ἡμῶν	By messenger... teaching Paul has handed down by any means.

The table illustrates that in all cases with εἴτε—εἴτε constructions, Paul begins by presenting a stand-alone statement and then develops it in a manner relevant to his contextual intention. Apart from two of these, the 'general principles' reveal a set of profound theological statements that stand, in the main, at the centre of Paul's theology. The only exceptions are 1 Cor 14:7 and 2 Cor 12:1-3. However, the first of these is a stand-alone philosophical truth statement. Paul utilises it contextually to serve his argument concerning the importance of prophecy over tongues in Corinth but could have taken it elsewhere. The latter is also an exclusive statement of fact, probably of his own experience, that he develops in terms of his uncertainty concerning the nature of his one-off visionary experience. He could well have developed it differently for a different purpose.

It is very probable then that 1:18a fits the same pattern of a general stand-alone axiomatic theological statement explicated in contextually relevant ways. If so, then the theological statement is 'what counts, is that in every way Christ is proclaimed.' Supporting the contention that this is a generic Pauline theological axiom is enhanced when one considers that the whole rubric under which he lived his life was 'to preach the gospel.' The contextually relevant issue he then develops is motivation in regard to Roman brothers and sisters. That is, Paul here notes that, compared to the cosmic imperative of preaching the gospel, motive is irrelevant.

Further thought suggests that Paul could potentially have supplied a huge range of other options using εἴτε—εἴτε constructions built on the central axiom 'what counts, is that in every way Christ is proclaimed.' A number of these possibilities can be drawn from his letters where there is suggested a variety of means by which the message can be communicated verbally or otherwise. Paul then, while concerned that the gospel spreads, was not confined to one mode or model. These different means provide possible categories which Paul could have supplied for the εἴτε—εἴτε construction.

To demonstrate these possibilities, it is interesting to explore Paul's letters to discern other categories he *could have* utilised in regard to the general theological principle here: 'what counts, is that, in *every way*, Christ is proclaimed!' While this is suppositional, it helps to indicate how the general axiom could have been directed in another context.

First, there is Paul's recognition of *the role of other proclaimers* in spreading the gospel. These include Paul himself (Rom 1:1, 5, 9, 10; 11:13; 15:19-24; 16:25-26; 1 Cor 1:17-18; 2:1-5; 9:16-27; 2 Cor 2:12, 17; 3:6; 4:1-6, 13; Gal 1:10-12, 15-16; 2:7; Eph 3:1-9; Phil 1:7; 1 Thess 2:1-9; 1 Tim 2:7; 2 Tim 1:11), Christ (Eph 2:17),[140] other apostles (Rom 1:1; 11:13; 16:7; 1 Cor 1:1; 4:9; 9:1, 2, 5; 12:28-29; 15:7, 9; 2 Cor 1:1; 8:23; 11:5, 13; 12:11, 12; Gal 1:1, 17, 19; Eph 1:1; 2:20; 3:5; 4:11; Phil 2:25; Col 1:1; 1 Thess 2:7; 1 Tim 1:1; 2:7; 2 Tim 1:1, 11; Tit 1:1), prophets (cf. Rom 12:6; 1 Cor 12:28, 29; 14:24-25; Eph 4:11), evangelists (Eph 4:11; 2 Tim 4:5), other unspecified believers (Eph 4:12; 6:15, 17; Phil 1:5, 12-14, 27-28; 2:16; 4:2-3; 1 Thess 1:8), teachers (Rom 12:7; 1 Cor 12:28, 29; Eph 4:11), others including Mary (Rom 16:6), Tryphena and Tryphosa, Persis (Rom 16:12), Epaphroditus (Phil 2:25), Euodia, Syntyche, Clement and other unnamed fellow workers (Phil 4:3), Timothy (Rom 15:21; Phil 2:22; 1 Tim 3:2), Apollos (1 Cor 2:5), believing wives/husbands (1 Cor 7:15-16) and Peter (Rom 10:14-17; Gal 2:7-8).

Secondly, there is the range of possibilities concerning *the context for Paul's evangelism*. Paul refers to evangelism set in the context of church services (1 Cor 14:24-25 [prophetic]), to unbelieving spouses and unbelievers in homes (1 Cor 7:15-16; 10:27), in the workplace (1 Cor 9:15, 18; 2 Cor 2:17; 12:14-15; 1 Thess 2:9; 2 Thess 3:6-12; Acts 18:3 cf. 1 Cor 7:17-24)[141] and in prison (Phil 1:13). Assuming the essential integrity of Acts, there is explicit reference to

---

[140] Taking the view this picks up the gist of Is 52:7 and most obviously refers to the literal incarnational (so Mitton, *Ephesians*, 109-110) and post-resurrection preaching (the 'gospel of peace' cf. Foulkes, *Ephesians*, 92) of Christ (cf. Matt 28:18-20; Acts 1:8); and *the theological implication* of *shalom* (cf. *reconciliation*) for all humanity rather than: 1) the death of Christ (so Lincoln, *Ephesians*, 148-149); 2) limited to a post-resurrection appearance; 3) Christ speaking through the Spirit to the apostles and so to the church (O'Brien, *Ephesians*, 207; Schnackenburg, *Ephesians*, 118; Bruce, *Epistles*, 310). If the latter however, here is further evidence of proclamation in the local church as there is no limitation.

[141] R. Hock, 'The Workshop as a Social Setting for Missionary Preaching', *CBQ* 41 (1979): 438-50.

Paul preaching evangelistically in synagogues (13:5, 14; 14:1; 17:2, 10, 17; 18:4; 19:8), prayer-places (17:13f), marketplaces (14:8-10, 15f; 16:16f; 17:17), places of philosophical debate i.e. the Areopagus (17:18f), prison (16:25f), homes (16:32; 18:7; 28:7f), a lecture hall i.e. Tyrannus (19:9), courts (18:12f), in political contexts (13:7; 24:10f; 26:1f; 28:7f); the Jerusalem temple (21:40f) and before the Sanhedrin (23:1f).[142] Furthermore his *Zentrumission* involved proclamation in different places and a desire to visit new ones (Rom 1:15; 15:19-20, 24, 28; 2 Cor 10:15-16). In addition Paul conceived of *proclamation to various people groups* including Gentiles (Rom 1:13; 15:16, 18; 1 Cor 9:21; Gal 1:16; 2:2; Eph 3:8), the weak (1 Cor 9:22), Jews (1 Cor 9:20; Gal 2:7), Greeks/non-Greeks (Rom 1:14), the wise/foolish (Rom 1:14) and so on.

Thirdly, I note that *Paul acknowledges other less obvious lines of proclamation*. These include creation (Rom 1:20), the proclamation of the Scriptures (Rom 3:2; see all references to the OT; 2 Tim 3:16), sacramental proclamation including the Lord's Supper (1 Cor 11:26) and baptism (Rom 6:3-4) and epistolary proclamation (see all letters and, in particular, 1 Cor 5:9; 2 Thess 2:15).

Fourthly, the role of the Spirit is acknowledged. Paul *understands all proclamation as Spirit-inspired* (1 Cor 2:4, 13; 2 Cor 3:6, 8) seen in signs and wonders and the Spirit's power (Rom 15:19; 2 Cor 12:12 cf. 1 Cor 2:4; 5:20). Paul constantly sought occasions given by the Spirit to proclaim even including opportunities provided by sickness and imprisonment, which he likened to gospel doors (1 Cor 16:9; 2 Cor 2:12; Gal 2:10; Col 4:3; Phil 1:12-14). This openness to the Spirit suggests Paul would have been open to any Spirit-led mode of evangelism that accurately communicated the gospel.

Fifthly, Paul was concerned for *lifestyle* as seen in his emphasis on various aspects of Christian living including love (Rom 12:9, 10; 13:8-10; 1 Cor 13:1-14:1; 2 Cor 5:14; Gal 5:13-14; Phil 1:9-10, 16), good works (Rom 12:9, 21; Gal 6:10; Eph 4:12; Phil 1:11; Col 1:10; 2 Tim 3:17), *koinōnia* proclamation (Rom 12:10), authentic Christian lifestyle (Rom 12:9-15:14; Eph 4:17-6:10; Phil 1:27; Col 1:10; 3:5-17; 1 Thess 4:3-7; 1 Tim 3:7) and proclamation through material giving (2 Cor 8-9; Gal 2:10; Phil 4:14-20).

Finally, there is the issue of *motivation* which is found in Phil 1:15-18a cf. Col 4:2-6; 2 Cor 5:14-20. I suggest in light of the above analysis that, while motive is unquestionably at issue in the context, Paul is making a general statement of his belief that 'what matters above all else is that in every way the gospel is proclaimed.' In terms of the verse any number of clarifying 'whether... or' statements could follow.

[142] On the basis of these explicit references it can fairly be assumed Paul preached in a great many other contexts as opportunity arose i.e. 'what counts, is that in every way, Christ is proclaimed.'

From this analysis possibilities can be drawn concerning different directions Paul could have taken the central truism, 'what counts, is that in every way, Christ is proclaimed' in the place of motivation. First, 'whether by me, or apostles, co-workers, evangelists, believing wives, believing husbands, prophets, elders, teachers, pastors, Apollos, general believers, by men or women' and so on. Secondly, 'whether in church meetings, homes, workplaces, prison, synagogues, prayer-places, marketplaces, the Areopagus, lecture halls, theatres, court, political contexts, Jerusalem temple, the Sanhedrin, in Rome, in Corinth, in Spain' and so on. Or alternatively: 'whether to Gentiles, Greeks/non-Greeks, the weak, to Jews to the wise/foolish, slave/free, male/female, rich/poor' and so on. Thirdly, 'whether through creation, the Scriptures, the Lord's Supper, baptism, letter, word of mouth, tradition, by example' and so on. Fourthly, it could read; 'whether by word, in signs and wonders, ethical witness, healings' and so on. Fifthly, 'whether by love, good works, *koinōnia*, giving' and so on. Finally, concerning motivation, aside from those in 1:15-18a one can include 'whether in "fear of the Lord"' (2 Cor 5:11) or a desire to 'please God' (Gal 1:10-11).

It is evident then that the statement 'what counts, is that in every way, Christ is proclaimed' is a banner for Paul's life and ministry. If this analysis is accurate, we have *evidence that Paul hoped for evangelism from others* without limitation, except where the central tenets of the gospel were violated (e.g. Judaisers). As Fee puts it, 'once again, Paul's focus is on evangelism – on Christ as God's good news for all, and therefore to be proclaimed to all.'[143] In this context there are questionable motives but these are minor compared with the great reality that the gospel is being proclaimed. As Marshall states, 'Paul's concern is solely with the effects of evangelism. And the fact is that one way or another people are hearing about Jesus. That is what matters to Paul.'[144]

That the centrality of the proclamation of the gospel is a general conclusive stand-alone theological principle of Paul's life and ministry is supported in other ways. First, as noted in Chapter 2, Paul's whole life was orientated toward one goal, to proclaim the gospel of Jesus Christ. Secondly, this interpretation fits the broader context. Paul's presentation in 1:12-18a suggests ironically that, rather than 'chain the gospel' by chaining Paul (Phil 1:7), the gospel has in fact been advanced due to his detention (cf. 2 Tim 2:9). Thirdly, Paul exhibits concern about others proclaiming the gospel only where the gospel message is distorted particularly with reference to the imperative of law-obedience for salvation (Rom 16:17-20; Gal 1:6-9; 6:12; 2 Cor 11:13-15; Phil 3:2-4; 1 Tim 1:3-7; Tit 1:10-11). That is not the case here. Rather, he is delighted the gospel is preached. It follows that he would be similarly impressed wherever believers took up the challenge.

---

[143] Fee, 124. Hawthorne, 38-39; Bockmuehl, 81 seem also to take it in this general manner.

[144] Marshall, 24.

In terms of the immediate context Paul is saying what matters above all else is not the character of the proclaimer or their motives, but the continual proclamation of the gospel.[145] The inadequate motives of these Christians and the probability that he will experience increased suffering because of their activity is of little consequence in comparison to his delight that the gospel is being preached. Paul's attitude is one of continuous 'rejoicing' (ἐν τούτῳ [Χριστὸς καταγγέλλεται][146]; χαίρω [present continuous]) that the gospel is proclaimed despite the false motives and the intent to cause him harm.[147] As Ash states, 'the preaching of Christ, even from wrong motives, was for him a cause of joy.'[148]

However, this analysis has shown that 'in every way Christ is proclaimed' should be taken to refer, *not only* to the issue of motivation but also to other possible 'ways' the gospel can be proclaimed. Paul is saying that what matters to him is that the gospel is being proclaimed in any and every way possible! This lays an exegetical and theological basis for all manner of possible ways of proclaiming the authentic gospel in Paul's context and beyond.[149]

The Rhetorical Impact on the Philippians

It could be that in 1:12-18a Paul is merely communicating his situation to allay the fears of the Philippians concerning his state and the mission in Rome. However, with Peterlin and others, I consider that there are a number of factors suggesting the passage was written with the situation in Philippi in mind.[150] Rhetorically, the passage functions in a manner similar to a brief *narratio*, introduced with the formula 'I wish you to know' which explains some of the

---

[145] Thielman, 62: 'the gospel is being preached. Ultimately, for Paul, this is all that matters.' See also Barth, 31; Gnilka, 64. Evidence Paul would prefer to see their motivation improved include: 1) Paul's intentional reference to these people at all suggests his displeasure; 2) The mention of these characteristics in vice lists suggests eternal consequences if they persist; 3) Paul's emphasis on Spirit fruit (Gal 5:22-25) and love (Rom 13:8-10; 1 Cor 13:1-14:1; Gal 5:14; Col 3:14; 1 Thess 3:12; 4:9-10); 4) His use of irony here; 5) Phil 1:27; 2:1-11, 14-15; 4:2-3, which suggest that he wants the Philippians to avoid a similar error.

[146] The antecedent of ἐν τούτω is Χριστὸς καταγγέλλεται.

[147] *BDAG*, 1075.

[148] Ash, '1:18' (CD). O'Brien, *Salvation*, 199 underplays this by saying Paul is not 'surprised' that the Roman Christians are preaching. Rather than not surprised, he is *overjoyed*! He clearly wants others to proclaim! (See Bruce, 50). L.L. Belleville, 'Authority', in *DPL*, 54-59, 58 writes, 'wrong motivation per se did not render someone an opponent in Paul's eyes. As long as "Christ is preached" he could "rejoice".'

[149] One thinks here that this could refer in a contemporary setting to any manner of creative proclamation including electronic, media, artistic, musical, dramatic, poetic and more; as long as the authentic gospel is being preached!

[150] Peterlin, *Letter*, 40; Ware, *Mission*, 185, 196-198.

issues that catalysed the writing of the letter.[151] So, Paul writes not only to allay the concerns of the Philippians but also to provide them with 'an example of how to behave in the face of adversities and adversaries, both of which the Philippians were facing or might soon face.'[152] This example is picked up in 1:27.[153] A number of factors support this contention.

First, the details concerning the falsely motivated Christians in Rome imply a rhetorical connection to the Philippians in the context of evangelistic mission.[154] The selfish ambition (ἐριθεία) of these false proclaimers in Rome sets a reference point for Paul's subsequent appeal to the Philippians to 'do nothing out of selfish ambition' (μηδὲν κατ' ἐριθείαν) in 2:3. As Paul develops his appeal through the letter through the examples of Christ, Timothy and Epaphroditus, they operate as models of selflessness to be emulated; set against the backdrop of the insincere Romans. Significantly, as I will seek to show, they all function in the arena of evangelism (2:5-7, 21, 30). Similarly, the reference to the different motivations of the Romans, informs the appeal to end the dispute between the female evangelistic co-workers (4:2-3). Furthermore, the reference to these poorly motivated Christians in Rome (ἁγνός) in evangelism gives background to the hearer as Paul encourages them to think about those things which are pure (ὅσα ἁγνά) in 4:8, suggesting evangelistic motivation is within the scope of his thinking here (cf. 4:2-3, 9). In addition, Paul's emphasis on joy also brings a contrast to the hearer as Paul seeks to correct the joylessness of conflict in the church (1:18; 2:2, 18, 29; 3:1; 4:4).

Secondly, this correlation of the experience of the Philippians and that of Paul suggests a rhetorical purpose. This is especially so in 1:28-30 where Paul clearly states that the Philippians are experiencing opposition, suffering and persecution in a manner not unlike that which Paul experienced on his initial visit to Philippi and is currently undergoing in Rome. It would seem straightforward that Paul presents himself and the positively inspired Roman Christians as positive examples to the Philippians.[155]

Hence, Paul is here encouraging the Philippians to continue to proclaim the

---

[151] Witherington, *Friendship*, 18-20, 42-49. Watson, 'Analysis': 57-88, 61-65 prefers to see 1:12-26 as integral to the *Exordium* (1:3-26) to gain 'attention, receptivity and goodwill' (62). He agrees that 1:12-26 provides a positive example for 1:27f. Bloomquist, *Function*, 148 sees here a *narratio* in 1:14-15 followed by a double *propositio* in chiastic form.

[152] Witherington, *Friendship*, 42.

[153] Witherington, *Friendship*, 43.

[154] Oaks, 113; Schenk, 137; Gnilka, 58f.

[155] Witherington, *Friendship*, 20, 45 notes that Paul is giving himself as an example. I agree that this should be extended to the Roman church as an example (both positive and negative) as suggests C.S. Wansink, *Chained in Christ. The Experience and Rhetoric of Paul's Imprisonments*. JSNTS 130. (Sheffield: Sheffield Academic Press, 1996), 139-140; cf. Elliott, *Liberating*, 197; Peterlin, *Letter*, 40.

message despite the persecution they are experiencing (cf. 1:27-30).[156] As Fee explains in regards to the whole of 1:12-26:

> Very likely, therefore, more is going on here than at first meets the eye, especially in light of 1:27-2:18...this passage, besides offering a reflection of his imprisonment, is probably also intended as a paradigm: how believers in Philippi should respond to such difficulties... with vv. 15-17 Paul anticipates the exhortations of 1:27-2:16 and 4:2-3.[157]

Paul is thus exhorting the Philippians to show the same kind of courage to continue to proclaim in the face of unbelieving persecution and suffering. As Oaks astutely says, 'a suffering Philippian would probably go beyond hearing good news about the gospel in Paul's situation and would take encouragement that the same could be replicated in their situation.'[158] He goes on, 'the point of Paul's story could be that he does not care if evangelism even deliberately exacts suffering. He would not want suffering to stop evangelism.'[159] Watson similarly suggests Paul's example provides the Philippians 'with a tangible model of living a life worthy of the gospel in spite of opposition, the central concern of Philippians.'[160]

His suffering has led to greater opportunities and expanded the mission among the Romans (cf. Gal 4:13). This is his hope for Philippi, as I will show in the discussion that follows. As Peterman concludes, 'Paul can rejoice in this because the gospel is being told. But in the Philippians' own case, the gospel must be told and lived for the partnership in the gospel to have its fullest fruit.'[161] Indeed Paul hopes his response will lead to defusing the quarrel between Euodia and Syntyche who were both workers for the gospel (4:2-3).[162] This suggests that Paul wants proclamation from Christians wherever they are found. I surmise from Paul's words here that even if there is no cessation of disagreements in the Philippian church, Paul still wants them to maintain their evangelistic witness. However, it is obviously better for the mission if this proclamation is accompanied by love and unity.[163]

---

[156] Peterman, *Gift*, 108.

[157] Fee, 107, 123-124. Similarly Beare, 60; Witherington, *Friendship*, 20, 45; Wansink, *Chained*, 139-140; Elliott, *Liberating*, 197; Peterlin, *Letter*, 40; Hawthorne, 38; Williams, *Enemies*, 111.

[158] Oaks, *Philippians*, 113.

[159] Oaks, *Philippians*, 114.

[160] Watson, 'Analysis': 64-65. So also Plummer, *Understanding*, 74: 'Paul then provides the paranetic example of believers in his current context.'

[161] Peterman, *Gift*, 109.

[162] Oaks, *Philippians*, 114.

[163] Witherington, *Friendship*, 20 notes that these rival Roman proclaimers are a negative example. However that they are proclaiming at all, despite poor motives, is still positive for Paul.

Conclusion to 1:14-18a

This analysis suggests that Paul was eager to inspire other Christians to preach the gospel. While he is in a Roman prison and it appears the mission is thwarted, in fact through his own efforts, the soldiers and the majority of the Christians in the Roman church, the gospel has been advanced. As argued above, it is more likely that these Romans are general believers who have been inspired to evangelise through Paul's presence rather than 'set-apart' preachers. Some of these believers are negatively motivated with a desire for personal gain and to cause Paul pain. Others are positively motivated out of love and good will toward Paul and God. It is probable that these believers may represent parties in the Roman church. On the one hand there may have been a group who, without being Judaisers, are 'weak', law-sensitive and anti-Paul. The others on the other hand, appear to be 'strong', pro-Paul and law-free in ethos.

Whoever they are, those motivated to cause him harm do not deter Paul. Rather, while he no doubt would prefer that they were well motivated, he is full of joy that the gospel is being preached. Paul's statement in 1:18a then, appears to be a clear statement of Paul's dominant missiological concern: 'that in every way, Christ is preached.'

Importantly, in 1:12-18a there is an interplay of most of the key themes in the letter including courageous general evangelism (1:14), contention (1:15-17), unbelieving opponents (1:12-14), suffering (1:12-14, 17) and joy (1:18 [2x]). While eschatological hope and assurance do not feature in the text itself, the theme flanks Paul's report (1:11, 19-23); particularly in Paul's expression of uncertainty about his own preference for life and death, eschatological assurance is prominent (esp. see 1:20-22).

If this analysis is correct then a sound argument can be made against those who argue that there is no clear evidence of a desire in Paul for churches to preach the gospel.[164] Rather, as Marshall puts it, 'here, then (Phil 1:12-18a), we seem to have a local church carrying on evangelism.'[165] While Bowers in his earlier work fails to account for this passage at all, in his more recent work, he notes Paul's positivity toward other preachers. He writes, 'and even when he is imprisoned, he can accept with equanimity the provocative attitudes of his opponents, so long as the proclamation continues' (Phil 1:15-18).[166] Furthermore, if I am accurate in understanding Paul to mean general Christians in Rome rather than specialists, Ollrog's conviction that co-workers alone were

---

[164] Bowers, *Studies*, 115-116; 'Church': 100-101. Interestingly Bowers does not deal with this passage in his earlier work. In terms of Philippians he only discusses 2:15-16 which he takes passively. Similarly Bosch, *Transforming*, 138 who fails to take account of the Philippian church discussing only 1 Thess 1:8; 2 Cor 3:2; Rom 1:8; 16:19 which he considers passive.

[165] Marshall, 'Theology', 157.

[166] Bowers, 'Mission', in *DPL*, 608-619, 617.

to carry on the mission is also under threat. 'Ordinary' Christians are preaching the gospel and Paul approves!

Consequently, I suggest that the passage and 1:18a in particular, is pivotal in terms of arguing that Paul saw the evangelistic mission as not only the work of specialists set apart for materially supported gospel proclamation, but of all Christians. In the words of Michael, 'it is worthy of note that Paul is speaking, not of officials or ministers of the church, but of the whole membership. Clearly, then, the proclamation of the word was looked upon as the duty and prerogative of each and all.'[167] Put another way, not only does the efficacy of the message not depend on the motives of the proclaimer, but also neither does it depend on the proclaimer's office![168] Again in the words of Peterman, 'simply put, Paul makes it plain that he rejoices whenever Christ is preached. It makes no difference even if the preachers seek to harm him in their preaching.'[169]

Hence, I conclude that Paul's passion was not only that he proclaim the gospel, but also to excite an evangelistic passion in other Christians in general, so that they would emulate his commitment to preaching the gospel. As Motyer puts it, 'the example of Paul shows us what can happen when one person is wholly given to the Lord; but we have yet to see what would happen if a whole church were on the march, a people of God on fire for God. Something like this began to happen in Rome during Paul's imprisonment.'[170]

---

[167] Michael, 33 of the whole passage 1:12-18a. Contra-Silva, 69 who argues that in 1:15-17 Paul has in view only 'recognised church leaders.' However he agrees that Paul sees evangelism as the responsibility of all.

[168] Craddock, 26 points out that the power is not contingent on the motives or feelings of the one preaching. Witherington, *Friendship*, 46: 'God can write straight with crooked lines;' Fitzmyer, 249.

[169] Peterman, *Gift*, 108.

[170] Motyer, 70.

CHAPTER 4

Evangelistic Aspects of Contending for the Faith of the Gospel (1:27-30)

In 1:27 Paul turns his full attention to the church in Philippi and, in particular, his hopes for them in his absence. As Hawthorne notes, 'immediately one is in the middle of a paraenetic section. Words of exhortation now control the thought.'[1]

The passage is launched by the imperative of 1:27 to 'live out your citizenship in a manner worthy of the gospel of Christ.' This exhortation stands as a headline for the section that runs from 1:27-2:18.[2] 1:27-30 forms the first part of the passage which can be broken into four: 1) An appeal for continued mission-unity and courage in the face of mission-opposition (1:27-30); 2) An exhortation for selfless humble unity (2:1-4); 3) The supreme example of the mission-humility of Jesus Christ in the face of suffering (2:5-11); 4) An appeal for continued, unified, loving, mission service leading to Paul's joy (2:12-18).[3]

While this is clearly a new section built around the injunction of 1:27, there are links to the preceding passage including 'gospel' (1:27 [2x] cf. 1:5, 7, 12, 16 cf. 'Christ' in 1:15, 17, 18; 'word of God' in 1:14, 22, 25), suffering (1:29 cf. 1:8, 13, 14, 15, 17, 19- 24)[4] and the central role of Christ (1:27, 29 cf. 1:1, 2, 6, 8, 11, 13, 15, 17, 18, 19, 20, 21, 23). These links illustrate that the passage builds rhetorically on the preceding section, which was focussed on Paul's situation in Rome. Whether the passage is the main proposition of Philippians

---

[1] Hawthorne, 54.

[2] O'Brien, 143; Fee, 155, Martin, 84; Beare, 66; Bockmuehl, 96; Silva, 89; Hawthorne, 54; Michael, 62; F. Stagg, 'The Mind in Jesus Christ Philippians 1:27-2:18', *RevExp* 77 (1980): 337-347, 337; Fitzmyer, 250; Kent, 118; Marshall, 34; Plummer, *Understanding,* 32; Collange, 72; Alexander, 'Letter-forms': 92-96; Peterlin, *Letter*, 52; Reed, *Analysis*, 210-219; Caird, 114 prefers to see 1:27-2:4 as a unit. Luter-Lee, 'Chiasmus', 92 prefers 1:27-2:4.

[3] O'Brien, 143 cf. Collange, 72; Peterlin, *Letter*, 52. Silva, 90 sees three sections: 1) 'The duties of Christian citizenship' (1:27-2:4); 2) 'A description of Christ's conduct as a model of Christian humility' (2:5-11); 3) 'Concluding exhortations to Christian obedience' (2:12-18); so also Plummer, *Understanding,* 32.

[4] Peterlin, *Letter*, 54 who notes that Paul's suffering provides an essential backdrop to the Philippian problem of suffering.

or not, the passage is pivotal and a summary of the whole letter.[5]

Similarly, the links between 1:27-30 and what is to come in the epistle are extensive: the verb πολιτεύεσθε cf. πολίτευμα (3:20); 'gospel' (2:22; 4:3); 'Christ' (2:1, 5, 11, 16, 21, 30; 3:3, 7, 8, 9, 12, 14, 18, 20: 4:7, 19, 21, 23); the hope of Paul visiting them in the light of the uncertainty of the outcome of his situation (2:12, 19, 23, 24, 25, 28); 'stand firm' (4:1); unity (2:2) in the Holy Spirit (2:1; 3:3); 'contend' (1:27; 4:3) 'as one for the faith' (2:17; 3:9) of the gospel (2:22; 4:3) undaunted by opposition. The theme of suffering recurs particularly in the example of Christ (2:5-11). The reference to salvation evidenced through their living out the gospel calls to mind Paul's appeal to 'work out your salvation' (Phil 2:12).

As Black notes, the boundaries of this paragraph are marked in three ways. First, Paul's use of the adverb μόνος shifts the sense from explanation to exhortation. Secondly, the thematic linkages of ἰδών and ἀκούω in 1:27 and εἴδετε and ἀκούετε in 1:30. Thirdly, the paragraph is a long sentence dependent on the single main verb πολιτεύεσθε.[6] The passage then, is one long sentence that builds upon itself which is characterised by battle or athletic terms (στήκω, συναθλέω, πάσχω and ἀγών)[7] and the socio-political term πολιτεύομαι.

Structurally, 1:27-30 is carefully constructed to build on the governing imperative 'live out your citizenship in a manner worthy of the gospel of Christ', which is developed in three main ways:

i. That the Philippians are standing firm in the Holy Spirit (1:27c).
ii. That the Philippians are continuing to do this by persevering in their struggle, in unity, for the 'faith of the gospel' (1:27d).
iii. That the Philippians do this without being intimidated by their opponents (1:28-30).[8]

My primary concern is with ii above μιᾷ ψυχῇ συναθλοῦντες τῇ πίστει τοῦ

---

[5] Whether informally or formally as argues Watson, 'Analysis': 65-67 who sees this as the *narratio*; Bloomquist, *Function*, 157-160 prefers *exhortatio* concluding the *confirmatio*; Witherington, *Friendship*, 18, 50; Black, 'Structure': 45, 48 the *propositio*. The rhetorical importance of the piece is confirmed by O'Brien, 143; Bockmuehl, 96. Silva, 89; Alexander, 'Letter-forms': 92, 96 who sees 1:27-2:18 as a 'request for reassurance about the recipients' in a 'family letter.' Reed, *Analysis*, 210-219 prefers that the passage is a general epistolary petition of Paul which follow a disclosure.

[6] Black, 'Structure': 33-34.

[7] Hawthorne, 54.

[8] The view that the passage holds strophic patterns is not widely acknowledged. On structure see for detail Fee, 159-160. I differ from his analysis in taking καὶ τοῦτο ἀπὸ θεοῦ, with O'Brien, 157, as governing both those being destroyed and those saved rather than just the latter as do H.A.W. Meyer, 64; Loh-Nida, 42. Lightfoot, 106; Barth, 48; Bruce, 36; Moule, 30 (who applies it to ἔνδειξις alone).

εὐαγγέλιου.[9] To fully interpret this clause also requires an analysis of 1:28-30 which gives clues to Paul's intent here. As I will now discuss, the meaning of Paul's appeal in 1:27c in the context of 1:28-30.

Corporate Evangelism in Philippi ('Contending for the Faith of the Gospel')?

The second aspect of 'living as citizens worthy of the gospel of Christ' is found in the construction συναθλοῦντες τῇ πίστει τοῦ εὐαγγέλιου. I contend that there are good reasons to consider that this refers to active Philippian evangelistic endeavour. Such a conclusion however, requires an analysis of συναθλέω and τῇ πίστει τοῦ εὐαγγέλιου.

The Meaning of συναθλέω in 1:27

The verb συναθλέω suggests 'contend or struggle along with 'someone' (τινί).[10] It is well recognised that the verb is drawn from a Greek athletic and/or military context either consciously or unconsciously. In its most basic sense Paul is likening the action of the Philippians to that of a Greek athlete from the Olympian games or a warrior; striving with all their might toward a common goal. This is not surprising as Paul utilises athletic imagery throughout his epistles.[11]

Concerning the term there are several clear points of agreement among scholars. First, here in 1:27 Paul uses the present participle, which has a continuous temporal sense i.e. 'as you continually contend together for the faith of the gospel.' The use of the participle here indicates that Paul is presuming that the Philippians are already engaged in contending for the faith of the gospel (cf. Phil 4:3) and his concern is their attitude and unity as they continue in their endeavour.

Secondly, it is generally agreed that the use of the prefix σύν along with μιᾷ ψυχῇ and ἐν ἑνὶ πνεύματι strongly emphasises corporate action, the

---

[9] The imperatival μόνον ἀξίως τοῦ εὐαγγελίου τοῦ Χριστοῦ πολιτεύεσθε, on its own, could involve all manner of Christian thought, behaviour and speech which is appropriate to the gospel. Consequently, it could include evangelism in and of itself. However, this is unclear in this context unless it can be proven to lie in the subsequent developments of Paul's argument. The first development, ὅτι στήκετε ἐν ἑνὶ πνεύματι speaks more of steadfastness or perseverance in the Spirit (or in unity) than evangelism. With Fee, 164-165; *Empowering*, 744-746; U.B. Müller, 77; Gnilka, 99 I take πνεύματι here as God's Spirit. However as Bruce, 56; Hawthorne, 56-57; Silva, 94; O'Brien, 150; Marshall, 35 point out, it can be taken in parallel with μιᾷ ψυχη.

[10] *BDAG*, 964; *EDNT*, 3.296.

[11] See Moule, 103-106 and the Appendices 1 and 2: 'The connection between evangelism and the military metaphor in Paul' and 'The connection between evangelism and the athletic metaphor in Paul.'

Philippians' contending in unity for the faith of the gospel. The expression μιᾷ ψυχη with a rich heritage in Greek thinking (Aristot. *Eth.Nic.* 9.8.1; 9.8.1168b; Iambl. *Vita Pyth.* 30.167), the LXX (1 Ch 12:38) and the early church (Acts 4:32), describe unity of purpose. 'Paul's use of a traditional phrase here is an expression of his concern for the Philippians' unity of heart and purpose in the face of persecution.'[12] As Bruce puts it, 'only so could they effectively commend the gospel by word and action.'[13] However this still leaves open the nature of this contending.[14]

Thirdly, it is generally recognised that the term is connected to another athletic term ἀγών ('contest') in 1:30. Here Paul speaks of the Philippians participating in the same 'struggle' which he had whilst among them in Philippi (εἴδετε ἐν ἐμοι) and which he has in his present incarceration (νῦν ἀκούετε ἐν ἐμοι). Some see more than an athletic concept here,[15] suggesting Paul is likening the Philippian Christians to gladiators in the arena.[16] Others suggest a military connotation, and thus Paul is employing the imagery of the Philippians as soldiers battling side by side against their enemies, further explicating the military metaphor στήκετε.[17] It would appear that the applications of συναθλέω to athletics, war and the arena are legitimate if applied metaphorically.[18] It is probably then best to leave it as 'striving, 'struggling' or

[12] See O'Brien, 151-152 (quote p152); Vincent, 33-34; *TDNT*, 9.608-660 for an analysis of ψυχή. Others who note unity at issue include Moule, 28-29; Beare, 66-67; Motyer, 94-95; Wicks, 40; R. Rainy, *Epistle to the Philippians*. EBC (London: Hodder & Stoughton, 1893), 87; J.J. Müller, 68; Silva, 92; Martin, 88-89; Hawthorne, 57; Bockmuehl, 99; Kent, 119; Houlden, 66; Marshall, 37; Hendriksen, 86; Beare, 67; U.B. Müller, 77; Gnilka, 99; Stagg, 'Mind': 338; Synge, 27; Oaks, *Philippians*, 77-102; Beasley-Murray, 986; Peterlin, *Letter*, 56-59 amongst many others.

[13] Bruce, 56.

[14] Even if unity is the issue and the contending subordinate, the contending is still *an* issue. This rules out the weak translation 'helping one another', one of the options given by Fee, 166.

[15] Generally of athletics Bockmuehl, 99; Hawthorne, 57; Kent, 119; Houlden, 66; Craddock, 33; Caird, 115, Wicks, 40; Rainy, 40. Or more specifically wrestling Moule, 29; Wicks, 30-31; Beare, 67-68; F.B. Meyer, 66.

[16] Lightfoot, 107; Michael, 66, 73; Hendricksen, 87 cf. O'Brien, 150; Martin, 88 who both note the connection.

[17] Michael, 66 who notes that the verb is used in military contexts as well. Martin, 88 who sees here the concept of the *phalanx* used by Philip of Macedon. See also Gnilka, 97 who suggests the church is a 'war-force' (*Kriegstruppe*) repelling attacks and Paul as the 'Commander' (*Befehlshaber*); U.B. Müller, 77 calls the church a 'fighting community'; J.J. Müller, 69; *EDNT*, 3.296; Fee, 166. Hawthorne, 57 sees here a shift from military ('stand') to athletic. Marshall, 37 sees a *possible* basis for 'onward Christian soldiers' here; Loh-Nida, 40 on the basis of context; Calvin, 241-242; Peterlin, *Letter*, 57; Boice, 104.

[18] V.C. Pfitzner, *Paul and the Agon Motif* (Leiden: Brill, 1967), 114-115 rejects the extremes of actual gladiatorial conflict. I find Pfitzner's criticisms on this specific point

'contending' together in a general powerful sense whilst bearing in mind its various associations.[19]

All this leaves open the nature of the contending. First, there are those who, on the basis of the clear reference to suffering in 1:28-30, suggest that Paul's meaning is to enduring suffering in the face of persecution from opponents.[20] I consider that the content of 1:28-30 make it unquestionable that this is at least one dimension of what Paul has in mind. However, to make it the whole issue is overstating its function and is reductionist, the suffering being one aspect of the entire situation Paul and the Philippians find themselves in. As I will demonstrate below, suffering in the context is connected to evangelism.[21]

Secondly, some see here 'contending' in regard to combating false teaching, with Paul combating the Judaisers who are challenging the gospel in Philippi (3:2f). Thirdly, Dickson suggests that the 'striving together' is limited only to living worthily of the gospel in terms of social relations in the face of opposition.[22] Finally, others suggest evangelistic endeavour is in mind. [23] In deciding between the above options several factors come into play including first, the context and secondly, the use of athletic or military metaphor and evangelism in Paul and Philippians and, in particular, συναθλέω. Finally, I will consider the meaning of τῇ πίστει τοῦ εὐαγγελίου.

It seems to me that the context supports an evangelistic interpretation.[24] There is no clear indication of false teaching in Philippians before 3:2f, the problem in Rome as I have discussed is not false teaching, but falsely motivated authentic Christians who proclaimed the gospel ('Christ').[25] On the other hand evangelism and gospel themes are prominent in Phil 1. In addition, in that 2:1-11, 14-15 appear to address the contention between Euodia and Syntyche, the only explicit reference to these women is alongside Clement and

---

surprising in that most commentators who apply συναθλέω to wrestling, the arena, war, running and other contests do not do so concretely but as an option and in an attempt to describe the impact of the metaphor in terms of Christian contention. As far as I can see all emphasise the concept of 'contending'/ 'struggling' which is at hand here. In fact he isolates and misrepresents those he quotes (see 114 n2). The precise application is a moot point.

[19] Silva, 92; H.A.W. Meyer, 63; Vincent, 34.

[20] In addition to those listed by Pfitzner, *Paul*, 115 note 2 see Oaks, *Philippians*, 77-89; Bloomquist, *Function*, 157-160; Walter, 'Leiden', 417-434; Jewett, 'Thanksgiving': 51; *TDNT* 1.167 cf. H.A.W. Meyer, 62.

[21] Those who see it as inclusive of proactive gospel mission in some sense include Oaks, *Philippians*, 80; Bloomquist, *Function*, 158; Rainy, 87; J.J. Müller, 68; Schenk, 169-171; Pfitzner, *Paul*, 117-118 who see it not as mere 'community fate', specifically suffering for the gospel.

[22] Dickson, *Mission-Commitment*, 105-106.

[23] See note 21 above.

[24] Fee, 166.

[25] See Chapter 3 above.

other co-workers who are ἐν τῷ εὐαγγελίῳ συνήθλησαν, which many understand evangelistically (4:2-3). Furthermore as I will discuss, evangelism also comes into play in Phil 2:15-16,[26] and also in the ministries of Timothy and Epaphroditus (2:22, 25). In addition, evangelism provides the backdrop to the suffering of Paul previously in Philippi and now in Rome (1 Thess 2:2; Acts 16:19-40; Phil 1:7, 12, 15-17, 19-25).

The issue of Paul's use of athletic and military metaphor I deal with in Appendices One and Two examining, 'The connection between evangelism and the athletic (and military) metaphor in the Pauline Epistles.' There I note the strong connection between athletic metaphor and evangelism on a number of occasions. This is seen in regard to his own ministry (1 Cor 9:24, 27; Gal 2:2; Phil 1:29; 3:12-14; Col 1:28-2:1; 1 Thess 2:2; 2 Tim 4:7-8), Timothy (1 Tim 4:7-10; 6:11,12; 2 Tim 2:5), the churches as the result of evangelistic toil (1 Thess 2:18-19 cf. Phil 2:16; 4:1)[27] and in terms of the spread of the gospel (2 Thess 3:1).

Similarly, in Paul's use of the military metaphor, evangelism is prominent on most occasions, including Paul's own mission. These include ὅπλων τῆς δικαιοσύνης in 2 Cor 6:7 set in the context of ἐν λόγῳ ἀληθείας. Secondly, in 2 Cor 10:3-5 where Paul clearly connects military imagery to his evangelistic ministry (τὰ γὰρ ὅπλα τῆς στρατείας ἡμῶν οὐ σαρκικὰ). Thirdly in 1 Cor 15:32 where Paul speaks of his ministry in terms of a specific occasion of fighting wild beasts (ἐθηριομάχησα ἐν 'Εφέσῳ). Furthermore, there are occasions where Paul applies military metaphor to others who are clearly gospel workers. These include Epaphroditus and Archippus, who are designated fellow-soldiers (συστρατιώτην μου cf. Phil 2:25; Phm 2 cf. Col 4:17). Similarly Timothy is considered a soldier of Christ (καλὸς στρατιώτης Χριστου Ιησοῦ) (2 Tim 2:3-4) who is to do the work of an evangelist (2 Tim 4:5). Others include Andronicus and Junia, Aristarchus and Epaphras (Rom 16:7; Col 4:10; Phm 23), who are all engaged in evangelistic mission. Finally, I argue that the most likely interpretation of Eph 6:15, 17 in the highly militaristic presentation of *general* Christian living (Eph 6:10-18), is evangelistic.

Importantly, in Phil 4:3 Paul uses the aorist συνήθλησαν to refer to the past struggle of Euodia, Syntyche, Clement and other co-workers (συνεργῶν) in the gospel (ἐν τῷ ευαγγέλιον). Schenk rightly notes that the verb is second person plural and is synonymous with συνεργοί.'[28] This explicit linguistic link would seem to suggest that evangelism falls within the range of 'contending' in 1:27.

On the other hand there are occasions where athletic imagery relates to contending in the faith *in the face of heresy* (Gal 5:7; Col 2:18) or generally of

[26] See also in Appendix 3 for the possibility of evangelism in terms of 2:5-11.
[27] See later discussions on 2:16 (Chapter 5); 4:1 (Chapter 7).
[28] Schenk, 168.

Christian effort toward salvation (Rom 9:16). This leaves open the possibility that this is in Paul's mind here. However, I consider that on the basis of context and the most obvious link in Philippians (4:2-3), proactive evangelism is the most likely interpretation. Before coming to a final conclusion however, the third matter noted above; namely, the meaning of τῇ πίστει τοῦ εὐαγγελίου, must be discussed.

The Meaning of τῇ πίστει τοῦ εὐαγγελίου in 1:27

In discussing this phrase, several issues are raised. First, the question of the nature of the dative construction τῇ πίστει needs to be clarified. Secondly, it is important to discuss the associated theological question concerning the meaning of 'faith' in this context. Thirdly, the meaning of the genitive τοῦ εὐαγγελίου must be considered. In that these decisions intersect, these will be discussed in turn and the findings clarified at the end of the section.

The dative is understood in different ways. Calvin took the dative as a dative of instrument ('by means of the faith') i.e. 'let the faith of the gospel unite you, more especially as it is a common armour against the same enemy.'[29] Lightfoot takes the dative with σύν in the participle and prefers a dative of association i.e. 'striving in concert *with* the faith.'[30] Hence faith is personified and is essentially a weapon with which the believers contend. Neither of these interpretations has convinced contemporary scholarship. First, personification of faith in this way is not found elsewhere.[31] Secondly, both interpretations miss the obvious concern for unity in σύν i.e. 'the necessity for cooperation with each other on the part of the Philippians' (cf. 2:1-4).[32] Accordingly most commentators agree that the dative should be understood as a dative of interest or advantage (*commodi*) translated 'for the faith' indicating advantage given to the faith or in the interests of the faith.[33]

While the nature of the dative is clear enough; the second matter, the meaning of 'faith' here, is more controversial. A number of scholars like Hawthorne take τῇ πίστει as a technical term for 'those things which the

---

[29] Calvin, 27.

[30] Lightfoot, 106; Plummer, *Understanding,* 34; Lohmeyer, 75-76. D.R. Hall, 'Fellow-workers with the Gospel', *ExpTim* 85 (1974): 119-130 on the basis of comparing Phil 1:27 with 2 Tim 1:8; 3 Jn 8. Gnilka, 98 similarly sees personified faith but 'for' the faith and not 'with'; Moule, 29. On a 'dative of association' see D.B. Wallace, *Greek Grammar Beyond the Basics* (Grand Rapids: Zondervan, 1996), 159.

[31] Michael, 66; O'Brien, 152.

[32] Michael, 67; O'Brien, 152; Fee, 166.

[33] *BDAG*, 964; Vincent, 34; Ellicott, 33; Fee, 166; Hawthorne, 57; O'Brien, 152; Pfitzner, *Paul*, 116; Collange, 74; H.A.W. Meyer, 63; Beare, 66; Gnilka, 99; U.B. Müller, 77; Loh-Nida, 40; Silva, 66-67, 94; Peterlin, *Letter*, 57; Bockmuehl, 99; Schenk, 168; Ellicott, 33. For more details see Wallace, *Grammar*, 142-144; Dickson, *Mission-Commitment*, 105.

Christian believes' foreshadowing the manner in which the concept of 'the faith' became a technical expression for the whole content of the Christian religion.[34] Some take it in a similar sense but add the dynamic of general activity rather than merely the content of faith. So Silva takes faith as 'faithfulness', which 'agrees well with the emphasis of the context on steadfastness.'[35] Witherington, while retaining the same emphasis, broadens the meaning here suggesting that 'the issue here is orthopraxy, a way of living, rather than orthodoxy.'[36] The emphasis for these perspectives is on the Philippians coming together to contend for the content of the gospel in the face of opposition who are bringing a false gospel.[37]

A number of scholars however, noting the contextual emphasis on evangelism outlined above, acknowledge evangelism here.[38] Moule in particular takes it this way noting similarities with 2 Thess 2:13 where Paul uses the phrase πίστει ἀληθείας in the sense of 'belief of the truth' in the context of Paul's evangelistic ministry. Here in 1:27 then the Philippians are 'to "strive together" to promote belief in the message of the Lord.' Thus Moule disputes that faith should be understood as Christian creed.[39] Schenk notes, 'πίστις is an active noun and stands in its normal technical missions sense for the verb in the aorist.'[40]

Similarly V.C. Pfitzner disputes that the struggle is a 'head-on frontal battle between the faith, and its enemies.' He suggests that 'the purpose of this struggle is not the conquest and defeat of the enemy as such, but the spread and

---

[34] Hawthorne, 57; Martin, 89 as the 'objective content of their testimony', the "grand deposit' of Christian truth committed to the church'; Marshall, 37; Kent, 118; Houlden, 66; Collange, 74; Wicks, 39; Lightfoot, 106 as the 'teaching of the gospel' i.e. *doctrina fidei*; Loh-Nida, 41; Hendricksen, 85-86 but also evangelism; L. Morris, 'Faith', in *DPL*, 290; J.J. Müller, 68-69; Michael, 67-68; Motyer, 96 see both this and evangelism in mind.

[35] Silva, 95; Vincent, 34 as 'the rule of life which distinctively characterises' the gospel.'

[36] Witherington, 53; As Oaks, *Philippians*, 85 puts it, 'the primary issue in 1:27-30 seems not to be the definition of the nature of the Gospel but a call to live in accordance with the Gospel.'

[37] Witherington, 53. See also Hendricksen, 85-86; J.J. Müller, 68-69.

[38] Moule, 29; Schenk, 168; Pfitzner, *Paul*, 152; O'Brien, 152, 'Gospel': 226, *Salvation*, 194, *Consumed*, 117-118; Peterlin, *Letter*, 58; Murray, 'Witness': 320-322; Green, *Evangelism*, 64 n.74; Fee, 166-174; Bloomquist, *Function*, 159; Schenk, 168; Melick, 90; *EDNT*, 3.296; Lightfoot, 58; Kent, 118: 'they must promote and protect the message of Christ'; Hendricksen, 85-86; Motyer, 96; Lohmeyer, 22-27; Houlden, 53 who writes 'the distinguishing mark of this faith as distinct from other "faiths" is the gospel – the good news of God's act in Christ for one man's salvation'; Craddock, 34; Bruce, 56 who notes they 'commend the gospel by word and action... the aim of their witness was to bring others to the same belief'; Peterman, *Gift*, 111 'they too need to stand for the defence and confirmation of the gospel in their own context.'

[39] Moule, 29.

[40] Schenk, 168.

growth of faith, the same goal which was set before all Paul's work.'[41]

Likewise, Peterlin disputes the notion that the Philippians are here contending against false teaching.[42] He points out the problem of context stating *'to this point, nothing in the text hints at a doctrinal controversy of this sort'* (italics mine),[43] nothing that refers to 'false teachers and fighting for the purity of Christian doctrine.'[44] He also recognises that the link between the suffering of the Philippians and that of Paul is set in the context of evangelism (1:30 cf. Acts 16:25-40; Phil 1:12-14). Hence the stress here is on behaviour. Peterlin agrees with Barth who insists that the fight is not against anybody including the opponents but is 'for the faith.'[45]

Following O'Brien who suggests proclamation is in mind wherever 'gospel' is mentioned in Philippians, Peterlin states 'it is indicative that Paul in Phil often links the idea of co-operation with the proclamation of the gospel' (cf. 1:5, 12-18, 27c; 2:22; 4:3).[46] Peterlin notes especially the use of συναθλέω with εὐαγγέλιον in 4:3 albeit with a slightly different construction. He then suggests that 'εὐαγγέλιον contains the meaning of proclamation but is not exhausted by it. *So proclamation is certainly part of the semantic baggage of εὐαγγέλιον here*' (italics mine).[47] He notes, 'this partly means that they are to proclaim the message co-operatively (note the divided witness of the Roman preachers from 1:15-16), but also that their witness will be strengthened if they strive corporately to live according to the standard which they profess.'[48]

That evangelism and contention in the context of pagan Philippi and not against false teachers is in mind is further enhanced by the probability that, as Bloomquist argues, the Philippian persecution referred to here is external.[49] He notes the work of Stambaugh and Baugh who provide evidence that the early Christians experienced a good deal of physical and personal persecution similar to Paul in Phil 1:15, 17 and 2 Cor 11:23-29.[50] Bloomquist suggests that 'there is no *a priori* reason why 1:27-30 cannot refer to the Philippians' experience or expectation of persecution.'[51] He argues 'Paul's suffering in bringing the gospel is now mirrored in the Philippians.'[52] Bloomquist finds support by comparing 2 Thess 1:4-5c and 1 Thess 1:3, 6. [53] However suffering is not the last word from

---

[41] Pfitzner, *Paul*, 152; O'Brien, 152 and 'Gospel': 226 cf. Ware, *Mission*, 217.
[42] Peterlin, *Letter*, 57.
[43] Peterlin, *Letter*, 57.
[44] Peterlin, *Letter*, 57.
[45] Barth, 47.
[46] Peterlin, *Letter*, 57.
[47] Peterlin, *Letter*, 57.
[48] Peterlin, *Letter*, 58.
[49] Bloomquist, *Function*, 157-158.
[50] Stambaugh, *Social*, 32-36.
[51] Bloomquist, *Function*, 158; Lightfoot, 58; Lohmeyer, 22-27; Houlden, 53.
[52] Bloomquist, *Function*, 158; Michael, 19; Lightfoot, 85; Grayston, 15; Vincent, 8.
[53] Bloomquist, *Function*, 159.

Paul to the Philippians and Thessalonians. 'In that Paul's converts are direct participants in his *causa* – not just jury, but co-defendants! – they, like Paul, experience suffering. But they are encouraged by Paul to look to the goal,'[54] 'that is, 'l'avancement de l'Evangile.'[55]

This active and evangelistic interpretation is enhanced by consideration of the gentive πίστει τοῦ εὐαγγελίου. It can be taken as an appositional genitive ('the faith, that is, the gospel' or 'the faith that is contained in the gospel') as does Fee,[56] or as an epexegetical genitive ('the faith, namely the gospel'). Few take it as an objective genitive: 'with trust in the gospel' or for 'greater reception of the gospel' both of which, as Silva points out, are unconvincing.[57] Barth and others favour taking it as a subjective genitive ('the faith brought about by the gospel').[58] This view lines up with taking 'faith' as the content of the gospel which the Philippians were to contend together to defend.

O'Brien and to a lesser extent Bockmuehl, take it as a genitive of origin ('the faith which is based on the gospel') and not as an appositional ('the faith which is the gospel') or an objective genitive ('the faith in the gospel').[59] Bockmuehl suggests that 'the distinction is in any case immaterial; since Paul's elliptical phrase probably encompasses both meanings. Christians are to contend for the gospel-based faith.'[60] As Marshall writes, 'if the previous phrase was about standing one's ground, this one is about active participation in a struggle or contest. It is probably correct to say that here the mood has shifted slightly from defence to attack, from maintaining a position to making an advance.'[61]

Weighing up the above, it is most likely then, that evangelism forms one component of 'contending for the faith of the gospel.' As O'Brien puts it, 'the Philippians were to stand united in their struggle for the cause of the faith – it's spread and growth, the same goal that was set before all of Paul's work.'[62] The content cannot be confined to suffering or financial support. Rather, it includes all manner of contending for the faith of the gospel including evangelism.[63] This is reinforced in Paul's own practice of 'contending' for the gospel, which involves both defensive and offensive concepts or 'defending and confirming the gospel' (1:7, 16). In that Paul later globally appeals for the Philippians to

---

[54] Bloomquist, *Function*, 159 cf. Caird, 108.

[55] 'The advancement of the gospel'; see Collange, 68 [French] quoted by Bloomquist, *Function*, 159.

[56] Fee, 167.

[57] Silva, 95.

[58] Barth, 47. This is a view that is theologically conditioned, as Fee, 167 points out. Others who take it subjectively include Vincent, 34. Gnilka, 99: 'granted by the gospel.'

[59] See also O'Brien, 152; 'Gospel': 226; *BDAG*, 819 cf. Bockmuehl, 99.

[60] Bockmuehl, 99.

[61] Marshall, 36 cf. Schenk, 168.

[62] O'Brien, 152.

[63] Prayer should also be understood here even if not contextually clear-cut (cf. 1:19; 4:6-7).

emulate his example one expects proactive evangelism to be clear-cut here in this appeal (4:9 [see Chapter 9]).

The Evangelistic Context for the Suffering of 1:28-30

As briefly indicated above, the suffering referred to in 1:28-30 reinforces the idea that Paul wants active evangelistic endeavour in several ways. In this passage Paul continues to develop the context (καί) for contending for the faith of the gospel i.e. 'not being intimidated *at all* (ἐν μηδενί) by those who oppose you.'[64] A number of factors suggest that τῶν ἀντικειμένων are Gentile non-Christian opponents in Philippi. First, while ἀντίκειμαι has a wide range of references, in the NT it is usually applied to unbelievers.[65] Secondly, the recurring second person plural and present πάσχειν and τὸν αὐτὸν ἀγῶνα ἔχοντες indicate that these are *current* ongoing opponents known to the Philippians. Thirdly, the apparent lack of a Jewish population in Philippi, the lack of reference to false teachers until Phil 3 and that these opponents in Phil 3 appear potential rather than actual, suggest Gentile unbelieving persecution.

Fourthly, the strength of πτυρόμενοι ('to be frightened, terrified, let oneself be intimidated') and the parallel to Paul's intense struggle in Philippi at the hands of Gentiles (1 Thess 2:2 cf. Acts 16:16-40) and in Rome at the hands of Roman soldiers (1:17, 20-23, 30) both suggest current strong Gentile persecution.[66] Fifthly, that these opponents will face eschatological destruction (ἀπωλείας),[67] whereas the Philippians will experience salvation (ὑμῶν δὲ σωτηρίας), also suggest unbelievers.[68]

---

[64] Michael, 68 suggests, 'never be scared for a second.'

[65] Marshall, 38 notes that 'opponents' is usually applied to non-believers in the NT but concedes this is not conclusive. In Paul it has a wide range including Ephesian (probably Ephesian-Jewish) opponents of Paul (1 Cor 16:9), the 'man of lawlessness' (2 Thess 2:4), false teachers (1 Tim 1:10) and widows who propagate false teaching (1 Tim 5:14).

[66] *BDAG*, 895 cf. O'Brien, 152; Lightfoot, 106; Martin, 89. Michael, 68 notes its use in Deut 31:6 [LXX]. The term is used of an 'uncontrollable stampede of startled horses.' Some see here a chariot race or a 'band of combatants, swordsmen or pugilists engaged in conflict'; as Wicks, 40 puts it.

[67] Not merely 'victory' and 'defeat' cf. Hawthorne, 59-60. Rather eternal salvation and destruction with O'Brien, 156-157; Fee, 169-170; Martin, 91; Michael, 70; Beare, 68; Silva, 95-96; Marshall, 38; Vincent, 34; Witherington, *Friendship*, 53. On most occasions as here of eschatological destruction set antithetically over against salvation (ἀπωλεία in Rom 9:22; 1 Cor 15:18; Phil 1:28; 3:19; 2 Thess 2:3, 10; 1 Tim 6:9; ἀπόλλυμι in Rom 14:15; 1 Cor 1:18; 2 Cor 2:15 cf. Rom 9:22; Phil 3:19-20).

[68] The idea of Hawthorne, 59-60; 'The Interpretation and Translation of Philippians 1:28b', *ExpTim* 95 (1983): 80-81' that ὑμῶν applies to both ἀπωλείας and σωτηρίας so referring to the possibilities of the destruction or salvation of the Philippians rather than the destruction of the opponents, is highly unlikely syntactically or in terms of Paul's usual antithetical use. See further Collange, 75. Taking ἥτις with what follows and not

Considering these factors, these people are almost certainly non-Christian persecuting opponents of the Philippian church rather than the opponents mentioned in 3:2.[69] Fee, for example, states that the alternative view that 3:2-3 gives the background to 1:28 'has nothing in its favour (except that both passages fall in the same letter) and everything against it.'[70]

The exact nature of the persecution in Philippi is unclear. Fee suggests that the emphasis on Christ as 'Lord' and 'saviour', and the loyalty of the general populace in Philippi to the imperial cult makes it likely that Roman citizens in Philippi were pressuring the Christians to renounce their allegiance to this Roman-crucified *kyrios*.[71] Martin proffers that this may have a reference to mob violence from the Philippian pagan populace (2:15) against the purity and worship of the Christian community.[72] Bockmuehl notes that there is good evidence to suggest that Christianity would have been viewed as a threat to the political stability of Philippi with its highly romanised culture. He posits that Paul's mission was interpreted in this way in Rom 16:20f and that the church would have been understood in the same way.[73] Other examples of severe persecution of Macedonian Christians emanating from pagans are seen in 2 Cor 8:2; 1 Thess 1:6; 2:14; 3:3; 2 Thess 1:4.[74]

All things considered then, evangelistic activity from the Philippians provides the *best* context for the opposition. First, the fact that such opposition exists at all suggests that progress into the Gentile community with gospel was

---

with τῇ πίστει in 1:27 (see Silva, 95; O'Brien, 154; Fee, 16; Michael, 70; Beare, 67; Moule, 30; Caird, 116; Hendricksen, 89; Motyer, 92; Bruce, 57; Houlden, 67; Barth, 48; Plummer, *Understanding,* 32; J.J. Müller, 69; Oaks, *Philippians*, 80).

[69] Hendricksen, 87; Collange, 75; Silva, 78, 92; Hawthorne, 58 sees them as Jews from Thessalonica attacking the church cf. Houlden, 34, 66. See the arguments of Oaks, *Philippians*, 81, 87-89; J.J. Müller, 69 against this. Mearns, 'Identity': 194 assumes that the 'they' (αὐτοί)/'you' (ὑμεῖς) antithesis implies outsiders which is not required. 'They' gives absolutely no clue as to their context.

[70] Those taking the view that the opponents were Philippian non-Christian pagans and possibly some Jews include Fee, 167; O'Brien, 153; Martin, 90; Michael, 69; Bockmuehl, 101-102; Bruce, 57; Schenk, 168-171; Kent, 119; H.A.W. Meyer, 59; Ellicott, 33; Peterlin, *Letter*, 59; Plummer, *Understanding,* 35; Black, 'Structure': 35. Marshall, 38 calls this 'the generally accepted interpretation' but expresses caution as does Craddock, 33; Vincent, 34. J.J. Müller, 68 sees them as such or opposing Jews.

[71] Fee, 167. In addition Oaks, *Philippians*, 80 rightly notes that at the point of hearing the Philippians would be less unlikely to reach back to 1:15-18a where Christians are causing Paul suffering but rather to 1:19-26 where Paul is suffering at the hands of Romans in prison.

[72] Martin, 90.

[73] According to Luke, Paul's mission certainly caused problems in the non-Jewish community (Acts 13:50; 14:5-6, 11-18; 16:16-24 [in Philippi itself]; 17:5-9, 13; 18:12-17; 19:23-41). Often Jewish and Gentile opposition was fused (Acts 13:50; 14:5-6; 17:5-9, 13; 18:12-17).

[74] Bockmuehl, 100 cf. 3, 6; Bloomquist, *Function*, 159 shows the verbal parallels.

sufficient to cause substantial antagonism.[75] Secondly, the previous appeal for 'contending for the faith of the gospel', which I have shown to be evangelistic, is clearly linked to the opposition. Hence the implication is that the opposition is either potentially or actually hindering the unified contention for the gospel mission.[76] Thirdly and decisively, the parallel in 1:30 between Paul's experience and that of the Philippians implies an evangelistic context. In particular Paul gives two points of reference, his previous visits to Philippi and his current situation in prison.

A brief exploration of both Roman and Philippian situations implies in both opposition leading to persecution and suffering *in the context of evangelistic mission*. First, in Paul's *previous experience* in Philippi there is primary and secondary evidence of persecution and suffering in the context of evangelisation (1 Thess 2:2; Acts 16:16-40). This is first-hand in 1 Thess 2:2 where Paul speaks of 'having previously suffered' (προπαθόντες) and 'having been insulted' (ὑβρισθέντες) *during* the initial evangelisation of Philippi. Paul then reminds the Thessalonians of his divinely inspired daring (ἐπαρρησιασάμεθα ἐν τῷ θεῷ) to proclaim the gospel to the Thessalonians (λαλῆσαι πρὸς ὑμᾶς τὸ εὐαγγέλιον τοῦ θεοῦ) despite great struggle (πολλῷ ἀγῶνι). Although Paul does not explicitly state that his suffering in Philippi was set in the context of evangelisation, in that the context includes an unambiguous reference to the evangelisation of Thessalonica, it would seem obvious the same applies to Philippi. The link to Acts 16:16-40 is accepted by most.[77]

According to Luke, in his initial visit Paul suffered persecution at various levels. First, from Gentile slave owners upset at the socio-economic loss caused

---

[75] Oaks, 89-96 rightly notes that the differentiation between mere Christian existence and proclamation is extremely blurred. This he demonstrates with a hypothetical outline of what life may be like for a converted family of bakers. His analysis is a constant interplay of Christian ethical decision-making and Christian verbal witness as their actions are interpreted in the non-Christian environment. He notes they would suffer from the 'abandonment of pagan worship, suspicion of secretive associations, suspicion of Jewish activities and *attempts at evangelism*' (p91 italics mine).

[76] So also Plummer, *Understanding*, 77.

[77] Including Morris, *Thessalonians*, 69; Best, *Thessalonians*, 90; Marshall, *Thessalonians*, 64; Wanamaker, *Thessalonians*, 93; Holmes, *Thessalonians*, 61; Malherbe, *Thessalonians*, 136; Bruce, *Thessalonians*, 24-25 see here in 1 Thess 2:2 a reference to the visit to Philippi in Acts 16. Others such as Richard, *Thessalonians*, 90 point to the socio-religious context 'within which Paul and colleagues announced the good news to the populations of the Greek mainland. Their reception by the general population is described in 2:2a as a rhetorical struggle or contest, which often resulted in verbal insult and ridicule.' Either way, this involves evangelism in the face of persecuting opponents as the context for his use of the athletic imagery found in 1:27-30.

by the deliverance (and conversion?)[78] of the demonised slave girl through evangelisation involving signs and wonders and proclamation[79] (16:16-18 cf. Acts 19:23-41; Rom 15:19; 2 Cor 12:2; Gal 3:5; Lk 8:37).[80] Secondly, from authorities (ἄρχοντες, στρατηγοῖς) before whom Paul and Silas were brought on spurious charges,[81] and who had them stripped and illegally and severely flogged and imprisoned (16:19-23 cf. 2 Cor 11:25).[82] Thirdly, through the crowd which was incited to join the attack (16:22). Fourthly, from the jailor who, after they had been thrown (ἔβαλον) into the prison, secured them in the inner cell with their feet in stocks (16:23-24).[83] This scenario shows the interplay of the various strands of first century Graeco-Roman culture in the spread of the faith including proselytism, religion, societal order, economics, tradition, law, justice and politics. Hence it is very difficult to isolate one dimension of the opposition and persecution in any particular case.

Secondly, as I have discussed in detail above, Paul gives first-hand evidence of *his experience* suffering from Gentiles in prison, in the context of evangelisation in his current situation (1:7, 12-18a).[84] These two parallels support an evangelistic reference point for the current suffering of the Philippians.

This is enhanced in several other ways. First, Paul here is not speaking of general suffering but of suffering '*for Christ*' i.e. the peculiar suffering that comes from suffering for the sake of Christ and his cause.[85] Due to the use of

---

[78] Her conversion is not certain but a reasonable assumption.

[79] That proclamation was involved and preceded the deliverance is clear from καταγγέλλουσιν ὑμῖν ὁδὸν σωτηρίας in Acts 16:17. It is reasonable also to assume the gospel was shared further after the deliverance.

[80] Bruce, *Acts*, 314.

[81] While the real matter was economic, they appealed to racial bigotry (anti-Semitism), religious prejudice and the threat to social order.

[82] For detail on the meaning and relationship of ἄρχοντες, στρατηγοῖς and the Latin *praetor*, *duumviri* see Barrett, *Acts*, 789. The intensity of their treatment is clear (πολλάς … πληγάς). The inability of the authorities to respect Paul's Roman citizenship was illegal (cf. Williams, *Acts*, 288).

[83] While the jailor's intent may have been safety (Larkin, *Acts*, 240), Marshall, *Acts*, 315; Barrett, *Acts*, II, 792 note that the multi-holed stocks involved could be an instrument of torture and would cause substantial discomfort. As Dunn, *Acts*, 222 says, 'the punishment is not merely salutary but severe.'

[84] On the connection to Phil 1:7 see Bockmuehl, 102; Fee, 171.

[85] Fee, 171; Fitzmyer, 250; Michael, 72. Fee notes rightly that Paul speaks of general suffering in Rom 8:17-30. For Paul's own experience of apostolic suffering, see Rom 7:21-24; Gal 2:11-16; 4:13; 1 Cor 15:30-32; 2 Cor 2:7-10; 4:6-13; 11:23-28; Phil 3:10; 4:12; 1 Thess 2:2; 2 Tim 2:9 cf. Acts 9:21-25; 9:29; 13:45, 50; 14:5, 19-20, 22; 15:36-41; 16:22-37; 17:5-9, 13-15; 19:23-41; 21:19, 27f; 22:22f; 23:1f. For general suffering in Paul, see Rom 8:18-23. On enduring persecution, see 1 Thess 1:6; 2:14-16; 2 Thess 1:4; 2 Tim 1:8; 2:3; 4:5. On God's providence in suffering, see Rom 5:3-5; 8:26, 28, 35,

'Christ' in place of gospel in 1:15-18, it is also possible that here ὑπὲρ Χριστοῦ could imply 'for the proclamation of the gospel' (1:15-18).[86] Whether or not this is the case, ὑπὲρ Χριστοῦ lies central to Paul's christology which involves the believer participating in the fullness of Christ's life including his mission (including proclamation), suffering (Phil 3:10), death (Rom 6:3-5; Gal 2:20), resurrection and exaltation (Eph 2:5-6). This christological dimension is explicitly picked up in 2:5-11 where Christ is the supreme example of right relationships.

As I will argue in appendix 3, evangelistic mission is one dimension of the context for Christ being given as example.[87] Fee sums up the Christological dimension of 1:29-30 suggesting that:

> They are to live 'on behalf of Christ' in the same way Christ himself lived – and died – on behalf of this fallen, broken world. The Christ in whom they have believed for their salvation effected that salvation because as God he poured himself out by taking the form of a servant and as man he humbled himself to the point of death – death for theirs and the world's sake – even death on a cross. That is why Paul can now explain that their salvation includes suffering 'on behalf of Christ,' since those who oppose them *as they proclaim the 'faith of the gospel of Christ'* are of a kind with those who crucified their Lord in the first place.[88]

Secondly, that Paul emphasises (οὐ μόνον [1:29]) suffering for Christ as a gift (ἐχαρίσθη)[89] alongside faith (cf. Eph 2:8), implies such suffering is to be expected for the Christian.[90] If the link to evangelism is accurate, it is possible that Paul considers that in fact, evangelism leading to suffering is *expected* of

37; 2 Cor 4:16-17; 12:7-12; Phil 1:15-18a. On the ultimate hope of the release from suffering, see Rom 8:18-25; 2 Cor 4:17; Phil 1:21.

[86] P. Bonnard, *L'épître de saint Paul aux Philippiens et l'épître aux Colossiens* (Neuchatel: Delachauz et Niestlé, 1950), 36 (as in O'Brien, 160). O'Brien, 160 suggest that this overplays the interchangeability of the two concepts. Perhaps ὑπὲρ Χριστου should be rendered 'for Christ and his cause.' Not as Hawthorne, 61 notes 'in Christ's stead' as Silva, 97 points out. Michael, 72 writes 'to help forward his cause and to enhance his glory in the eyes of [people].' Similarly Martin, 92 who notes 'for Christ' could be replaced by 'for the faith of the gospel.'

[87] See Appendix 3.

[88] Fee, 172 (italics mine).

[89] Silva, 97. The aorist tense indicates the once-for-all granting of both the privilege of believing and of suffering in the initial conversion of the Philippians; so Vincent, 36 cf. O'Brien, 159. On χαρίζομαι see Rom 8:32; 1 Cor 2:12; Gal 3:18; Phil 2:9; Phm 22.

[90] Silva, 97 notes the similarity with Eph 2:8 where faith is perhaps to be understood as a gift despite grammatical ambiguity (cf. J.J. Müller, 70). Here there is less ambiguity, faith is understood as a gift, as Hendriksen, 90 points out. Whether this needs to lead to hyper-Calvinism however, is disputable as it requires reading every reference to faith and human response in Paul through this lense which is exegetically tenuous.

Christians. If so, then the suffering of the Philippians should be no surprise, rather it is evidence of God's favour in that it is an extension of grace.[91] This calls to mind Phil 1:7 where Paul gives thanks for the Philippians sharing in the grace of Paul's apostolic commission, including his suffering.

Thirdly, I suggest that Paul's use of ἀγών ('struggle, fight') in 1:30 refers to their mutual struggle and indicates evangelism. 'Struggle' here 'describes Paul's conflict for the gospel of faith. It involves untiring toil and labour, an intense wrestling and struggle for the spread, growth, and strengthening of the faith as the goal of his mission.'[92] It indicates then the whole dimension of Paul's ministry including proclamation, suffering, prayer and so on. Here then, the struggle of Paul and co-workers (Col 4:12-13; 1 Thess 2:2) is extended to the 'members of an entire congregation.'[93] In that they share in the '*same* conflict' through their "fellowship in the gospel" (1:5), they are actively participating in the fullness of Paul's mission.[94]

The exact nature of the suffering is not outlined. However, in that Paul likens it to his own experience, it probably involves social marginalisation, physical and psychological suffering.[95] It potentially involved imprisonment and perhaps martyrdom.[96] In that, as I have shown above, the societal impact of the conversion of Gentiles was significant, it probably involved the general populace, religious and civil leaders in Philippi.

If I am correct, the suffering meted out to the Philippians is not merely due to 'their purity of life and consciousness of high calling in Christ Jesus (3:14), which were a constant challenge and rebuke to their pagan neighbours',[97] but also because they were active in proclamation of the gospel.[98] In other words the Philippians were suffering because they lived the full gospel lifestyle Paul desired, proclamation included. As Oaks puts it, 'for Paul to draw the Philippians into a sphere of suffering which can be categorised with his, probably means that he sees them as undergoing harsh treatment for the sake of the Gospel, as he did.'[99] In Philippians Paul is earnestly encouraging them to continue to do so.

---

[91] A 'divine passive'; so Hawthorne, 61.

[92] O'Brien, 161; cf. Pfitzner, *Paul*, 109-112, 126-129.

[93] O'Brien, 161-162.

[94] Fee, 171-172.

[95] On the reality of the Philippians' suffering see Oaks, *Philippians*, 77-84.

[96] That this has yet occurred is unlikely as Paul gives no indication of this or a theology of death. However, it could be a looming possibility if the correlation to his situation is applied rigorously (cf. 1:19-21).

[97] O'Brien, 160; Dickson, *Mission-Commitment*, 144.

[98] So Fee, 172.

[99] Oaks, *Philippians*, 80 who notes that the views of Gnilka, 101f; Houlden, 65 that the Philippians cannot be suffering in the same way as Paul as they are not in a Roman prison is inadequate. I would add that it is likely some of the Philippians were in a Roman prison albeit not in Rome.

Paul wanted the Christians of Philippi to continue to stand for Christ, presenting him in word and deed, determined not to be thwarted by opposition despite suffering.

In addition, it is possible that the conflict between the women in the church (4:2-3) may well be related to differing reactions to suffering, whether retreatism or triumphalism. Whether or not this is the case, in 1:27-30 Paul exhorts the Philippians to continue to evangelise as led by the Spirit in unity despite suffering (cf. 1:12-18a; 2:5-11). In other words, Paul is advocating ongoing proclamation of the gospel from this church notwithstanding opposition and suffering. This is certainly Paul's own experience and in all likelihood, what he hoped for from the Philippian church. This is confirmed in Paul's understanding of the suffering as a gift that accompanies belief (1:29 cf. 1:7; 3:10).

Indeed it could well be the *perseverance in proclamation* despite suffering which is the sign to unbelievers of the authenticity of faith and so their destruction (1:28). Whether or not this is the case, Paul here is reassuring the Philippians that their continual struggle will end in eternal salvation. In addition, they are assured of the ultimate destruction of their opponents. Hence here is found the interconnectedness of courageous general evangelism and eschatological hope.

In fact they are even to see their struggles in a positive light, 'a necessity and a gift.' In regard to suffering then the Philippians were to be imitators of Christ (cf. Phil 3:17; 4:9), co-participants in his ministry and suffering.[100]

Conclusion to 1:27-30

This discussion of 1:27-30 suggests that 'contending for the faith of the gospel' points in the same direction as my earlier analysis of 1:14-18a (see also later on 1:3-11). Specifically, Paul writes in part to urge his congregations to continue to be actively involved in evangelism despite opposition, persecution and suffering. Fee for example states: 'as always the gospel is the urgency. Thus it turns out that their own "progress and joy in the faith" (mutual love and unity) is directly related to their contending side by side "for the faith of the gospel" in the face of current opposition in Philippi.'[101]

The Philippians were not being challenged here merely to stand firm against threats to the gospel of grace. Rather 'the Philippians are to stand united in their struggle for the cause of the faith - its spread and growth, the same goal that

---

[100] Silva, 98 notes this without really recognising its implications for proclamation. I agree with his analysis, 'clearly, Paul's injunction to his churches to become imitators of him… entailed a great deal more than may appear on the surface.' Indeed, it is inclusive of proclamation in the face of persecution.

[101] Fee, 167.

was set before all of Paul's work.'[102] Bruce elaborates:

> [T]heir witness called for strenuous endeavour and united effort; they had to contend side by side for the faith of the gospel. They themselves had believed the gospel, and the aim of their witness was to bring others to the same belief. In the pursuit of this aim they had to reckon with powerful and unremitting opposition; hence the call for strenuous action.[103]

In-so-doing, Paul seems to be encouraging the same sort of attitude found in Acts 4:19-20, 31; 5:29, 40-42 where the Jerusalem apostles refuse to cease proclamation in the face of the persecution of the Sanhedrin.[104] Significantly, the situation in Philippi is corporate involving the whole church and not merely a few select proclaimers, although certain individuals may have played the leading and dominant role in the mission (Epaphroditus, Euodia, Syntyche, Clement and the more general 'overseers', deacons and 'co-workers').

However, this evangelistic concern does not exhaust the possible connections in regard to the appeal to contend in unity for the faith of the gospel. From the point of view of an oral hearing all the major themes of 1:1-26 would come to mind. In particular grace (1:2, 8), material support for mission (1:5), courageous united evangelism (1:5-7, 9-11, 12-18a, 22), suffering (1:7), love (1:8, 9), purity (1:10), works of righteousness (1:11), prayer (1:19), Spirit-led faith (1:19), faith (1:25), eschatological hope (1:19-25), and joy (1:3, 18, 25-27).

I note here again the interweaving of the core themes of the letter. Here courageous congregational evangelism merges with ethical witness (1:27a), unity (1:27 cf. 2:1-4), perseverance in the face of unbelieving opposition and persecution (1:27-30), suffering (1:29-30) and eschatological hope (1:28). While 'joy' is not explicitly mentioned, it flanks the pericope (1:25; 2:1). The latter passage continues and develops the theme of unity which will complete Paul's joy.

---

[102] O'Brien, 152.

[103] Bruce, 56 cf. Kent, 118: 'They are to be "contending" for it, a positive statement of their need to promote and protect the message of Christ, while at the same time implying that adversaries must be faced.' Capper, 'Dispute': 211 argues that Paul here wants the Philippians to keep their side of the contract with Paul, preaching in Philippi. Hendriksen, 87 notes 'Paul is interested not only in fending off attacks, but also and mainly in spreading God's glorious redemptive truth which centres on Jesus Christ and salvation in him.'

[104] See Hendricksen, 90; Michael, 72; Beare, 68; Silva, 97; Bruce, 58; H.A.W. Meyer, 66. Bockmuehl, 103 notes that this tradition is found into the second century of the early church. The basis for the refusal to proclaim is an appeal to obedience to a greater and supreme authority i.e. God over any human institution cf. Dan 3:16-18; Lk 20:25; Socrates (Plato, *Apology* 29D); 2 Macc 7:2; Josephus, *Ant.* 17.6.3; 158-59. Further see Fitzmyer, *Acts*, 304.

CHAPTER 5

Unified Ethical Witness and Proactive Evangelism (2:14-16a)

In this section (2:12-18) Paul, after concluding the Christ-hymn, resumes his apostolic exhortation. It continues, reaffirms and concludes the thought of 1:27; 'whatever happens, conduct yourselves in a manner worthy of the gospel of Christ.'[1] It builds on the 'Christ-example' (2:6-11) linked by ὥστε ('so then').[2] In other words, 'in light of the example of Christ, work out…'[3]

The key to the passage are the recurring imperatives including κατεργάζεσθε (['work out'] 2:12); ποιεῖτε (['do'] 2:14); χαίρετε (['rejoice'] 2:18) συγχαίρετε (['rejoice with'] 2:18). The first of these, κατεργάζεσθε, represents the 'main thought of the passage.'[4] It is their 'salvation' that they must work out in their life together in Philippi (cf. 1:28).[5] Especially important is the notion of obedience, Paul appealing to the previously obedient Philippians to continue so, ironing out any relational problems (2:12).[6] As Martin puts it, 'as he (Christ) obeyed, so should you!'[7]

There are a number of thematic links to the preceding sections of Philippians including 'obedience' (2:12 cf. 2:8), Paul's presence and absence in regard to Philippi (2:12 cf. 1:27), salvation (2:12 cf. 1:13, 19, 28), God's work in the lives of the Philippians (2:13 cf. 1:6, 28) 'boasting' (Phil 1:26), 'the day of Christ' (2:16cf. 1:6, 10), the faith of the Philippians (2:17 cf. 1:25, 27), service (2:17 cf. 2:7) and joy (2:17, 18 cf. 1:18). Some of these and others are found in the rest of the letter including 'beloved' (2:12 cf. 4:1), 'children' (2:15 cf. 2:22), 'sacrifice' ([θυσίᾳ] 2:17 cf. Phil 4:18), service ([λειτουργίᾳ] 2.17 cf. 2:30), faith (2:17 cf. 3:9) and joy (2:17, 18 cf. 3:1; 4:4, 10).

---

[1] O'Brien, 272-273; U.B. Müller, 116; Hawthorne, 97; Gnilka, 147 with most commentators.

[2] O'Brien, 273; Peterlin, *Letter*, 70; Witherington, *Friendship*, 70.

[3] Silva, 134.

[4] O'Brien, 273 cf. Fee, 230 calls it the '"theme" sentence' cf. Silva, 135 and most.

[5] Fee, 230.

[6] Silva, 134 who is expanding the insight of Vincent, 64 cf. Loh-Nida, 65; Bruce, 81; Caird, 125.

[7] Martin, 114; Gnilka, 148.

The passage is not merely exhortatory in a general way but addresses a real issue in the Philippian church.[8] Hawthorne suggests, 'at Philippi the church was being torn apart because Christians were motivated by a party spirit, selfishness, conceit, pride, arrogance, etc.'[9] While this analysis seems to overstate the problem, there is evidence of a degree of infighting seen in the reference here to 'complaining or arguing.'[10] This no doubt refers to the contention between Euodia and Syntyche. Hawthorne rightly recognises that 2:12-18 addresses the Philippians directly (cf. 2:1-4) rather than tangentially through the example of Christ (2:5-11). The passage is not a commentary on the hymn nor a new beginning or an interruption but continues to address this issue.[11] As I will discuss more fully in chapter 7, this problem is set in the context of struggling for the gospel, bringing evangelism into view.

It can be argued that the initial appeal ἑαυτῶν σωτηρίαν κατεργάζεσθε, being generic, could include evangelism.[12] However, taken alone, this is not clear.[13] Hence, while the main point of discussion is λόγον ζωῆς ἐπέχοντες in 2:16a and specifically, whether this indicates proactive evangelism or steadfastness. To discuss this fully I will explore 2:14, which sets the context for the appeal of 2:16a, and 2:15 which is also missiological.

Missiological Disunity in Philippi (2:14)

Although the section 2:14-16 is an independent sentence without conjunctions linking to the previous sentence, it clearly continues the thought of 2:12-13.[14] It

---

[8] Kent, 128.

[9] Hawthorne, 97. Similarly overstating the situation is Peterlin, *Letter*, 70 who writes, 'there is every reason to believe that murmurings and disputing can be taken as a "leading feature" of the Philippian church.' I suggest this is a 'feature', not necessarily a 'leading feature' cf. Collange, 109.

[10] Marshall, 59, who sees this as the essential point of the passage.

[11] Lohmeyer so Gnilka, 147 who sees it as 'a new beginning' (*Neuansatz*) cf. Barth, 69; J.J. Müller, 90.

[12] This requires: 1) Taking 'work out your salvation' individually and eschatologically rather than in a social corporate sense (with U.B. Müller, 118; Caird, 125; Beare, 90; O'Brien, 277-280; Fee, 235 esp. note 23; *Empowering*, 846-847, 876; *BDAG*, 986; Silva, 135; Motyer, 127; *TDNT*, 7.991; Hendriksen, 120-121; Barth, 72; Melick, 110; Marshall, 61) against Michael, 101 and '"Work Out Your Own Salvation"', *Expositor* 12 (1924): 439-450; Bruce, 81, 83; Gnilka, 149; Collange, 109; Martin, 115; Loh-Nida, 67; Hawthorne, 99; R.C. Swift, 'The Theme and Structure of Philippians', *BSac* 141 (1984): 234-254, 245; Williams, *Enemies*, 137; Getty, 37); 2) Taking the phrase as referring holistically to attitude, action and speech that is generated from the lives of those who experience God's salvation. If so, then evangelism is one component.

[13] However, if as I have argued, 'contending for the faith of the gospel' includes evangelism, then the initial general imperative 'live as citizens worthy of the gospel of Christ' should be understood as inclusive of evangelism. The same could apply here.

[14] O'Brien, 289.

adds contextual specificity to the previous general injunction to the Philippians to work out their salvation. As Fee says,

> [I]ndeed, apart from a specific focus on Christ himself (and that is very close at hand in vv. 6-11), every major motif in the letter is touched on in some way in these two sentences: their need for unity, the gospel (here, "the word of life"), evangelism, the opposition in Philippi ("crooked and depraved generation"), his and their relationship, suffering and joy.[15]

Specifically, they are to continue their mission and ministry in Philippi without internal squabbling so that their mission is in no way threatened.[16]

Paul appeals to the Philippians to do all things without 'complaining or arguing.' The verb ποιεῖτε brings to mind the imperatives 'obeying', 'working' and earlier, 'citizen yourselves.'[17] The use of πάντα in the emphatic first position indicates that the injunction is inclusive of all aspects of Christian existence.[18] Especially in light of the allusion to the dispute between the coworking women (cf. 4:2-3) and the subsequent references to ethical witness (2:15) and proclamation (2:16), this is suggestive of evangelism i.e. the Philippians are to conduct their evangelistic mission without grumbling and dispute.

The combination of γογγυσμῶν καὶ διαλογισμῶν gives insight into the problem in the Philippian church.[19] Here Paul calls to mind the complaining and arguing of the Israelites in the wilderness (Deut 32:5 cf. Deut 32:20).[20] As elsewhere, situations in the OT serve as warnings to the early Christians (cf. Rom 15:4; 1 Cor 10:1-11; 2 Tim 3:16).[21]

Common among those who take this line is the view that the problem in

---

[15] Fee, 240. To which I would add perseverance (2:12 cf. 1:27; 4:1) and eschatological assurance (2:16b).

[16] Gnilka, 151 suggests that this passage is not about mission but 'existence in the world.' However this is to create a disjunction between mission and existence that does not exist in Paul i.e. the two coalesce into one.

[17] Similarly Fee, 243.

[18] Moule, 46; Hawthorne, 101.

[19] O'Brien, 290 agrees there is a specific problem.

[20] Most commentators including: O'Brien, 290; Fee, 243 who notes the repetition of the verb in the Pentateuch (Exod 16:7-12 (6x); 17:3; Num 14:27-29 (3x); 16:41; 17:5 (2x), 10); Lightfoot, 117; Beare, 88-89, 92; Gnilka, 151; Houlden, 87-88; Caird, 126; Martin, 117; Kent, 129; Loh-Nida, 69; Bruce, 86-87, Hawthorne, 101; Silva, 143-144; Marshall, 63; Witherington, *Friendship*, 72; Synge, 37; Plummer, *Understanding,* 52; Craddock, 45-46; Michael, 101-102.

[21] J. Ernst, 81 as quoted in O'Brien, 290. I note also the use of the cognate verb γογγύζω indicating an explicit connection in Paul. Perhaps Paul saw the wilderness wanderings as a 'type' for the Christian church between ages as in Hebrews and John cf. *TDNT* 1.736; Gnilka, 151; Friedrich, 128.

Philippi was complaint against God and his promises and not internal dispute.[22] Alternatively, some see a parallel between the problems between Moses and Israel and Paul and the Philippians.[23] Others consider the problem to be centred on internal disagreement in the church.[24]

There is no real indication that Paul's own leadership is being questioned or that the congregation is complaining against God himself.[25] It would seem more likely that internal dispute is primarily in mind here, γογγυσμός indicating 'complaint, displeasure, expressed in murmuring' within the community[26] (cf. 1 Cor 10:1-13; Acts 6:1; 1 Pet 4:9; Jn 7:12).[27] Similarly διαλογισμός suggests 'thought, opinion, reasoning, design' (Rom 1:21; 1 Cor 3:20) and so here indicates 'doubt, dispute, argument' (cf. Rom 14:1; 1 Tim 2:8).[28] As I will explore in depth later and have intimated earlier, the dispute is not merely disunity and false attitudes (1:27; 2:1-4), but is connected to evangelistic mission (4:2-3).[29]

Direct Appeals for Missiological Endeavour Including Evangelism (2:15-16a)

The missiological emphasis of this passage is found in 2:15b-2:16a (τέκνα θεοῦ ἄμωμα μέσον γενεᾶς σκολιᾶς καὶ διεστραμμένης, ἐν οἷς φαίνεσθε ὡς φωστῆρες ἐν κόσμῳ, λόγον ζωῆς ἐπέχοντες). I will now examine these verses to draw out the missiological and in particular, the evangelistic dimension of the appeal.

An Appeal for Blameless Ethical Witness in Unbelieving Philippi (2:15)

In 2:15-16a Paul supplies the purpose (ἵνα) for the imperative of 2:14.[30] In 2:15 Paul desires an end to grumbling and argument *so that* the Philippians may be 'blameless and pure, children of God without fault in a crooked and depraved

---

[22] H.A.W. Meyer, 114; Lightfoot, 117; Vincent, 67; Beare, 92; J.J. Müller, 93; Gnilka, 151; Friedrich, 112; Caird, 127; Barth, 76; Ellicott, 52.

[23] Loh-Nida, 69.

[24] O'Brien, 291. See also Fee, 243; Loh-Nida, 69; Martin, 117; Michael, 104; Barth, 75; Bruce, 84-87; Collange, 111: 'Oh that the Philippians would stop arguing'; Hawthorne, 101; Silva, 143-144; Melick, 116. However it could be that the complaints in Philippi are tantamount to quarrelling against God cf. Fee, 243; Moule, 46; Craddock, 46; Melick, 112. Schmithals, *Paul*, 74 sees it as referring to false teachers, which I consider highly unlikely at this point.

[25] Gnilka, 151.

[26] *BDAG*, 204.

[27] O'Brien, 291.

[28] *BDAG*, 232-233; Fee, 244; Silva, 144.

[29] Bockmuehl, 155.

[30] O'Brien, 292.

generation' (NIV).[31] As Fee notes, 'the ultimate concerns are two: first, the gospel in Philippi, almost certainly the interest of evangelism, as throughout the preceding narrative about "his affairs" (1:12-26); and second, their own successful eschatological conclusion, expressed in terms of their being Paul's "boast" with the day of Christ in view.'[32] This eschatological connection is important linking mission and eschatological hope and assurance, with Paul wanting them to persevere in working out their ultimate salvation.

The term ἄμεμπτος indicates 'blameless, faultless' (Phil 3:6; 1 Thess 3:13).[33] Here it refers not to perfection but to living according to the gospel (1:27) with specific regard to relationships within the church (2:14), missiologically (2:15b) and eschatologically (2:12, 16b).[34] Paul's only other use of ἀκέραιος (lit. 'unmixed') is applied figuratively to being 'pure, innocent' in Christian living (cf. Rom 16:19).[35] Synonymous concepts are found elsewhere in Philippians (ἁγνός cf. 1:10; 4:8). The two combined 'signify that no one would be able to lay any accusation or blame against them because they were pure and sincere.'[36] Paul then, is concerned for the purity of the Philippians, refusing to compromise their commitment to ethical purity set in the context of relationships and mission.

The appeal is restated with the missiological component emphasised in 2:15b; namely, they are to be 'blameless children of God *in the midst of a crooked and corrupt generation.*' The term τέκνα θεοῦ (Rom 8:16; 9:8; Phil 2:15 cf. Rom 8:17; Gal 4:5-6; Eph 5:1) recalls Deut 32:5 and carries an implicit warning to the Philippians. In other words, 'do not become like the people of God at the time of Moses who fell into complaint and dispute'![37] Furthermore,

---

[31] Taking γένησθε in the sense of 'become' rather than 'prove yourselves to be'; so Lightfoot, 117; Moule, 46; Beare, 92; O'Brien, 293; Martin, 118; Hawthorne, 101; Hendriksen, 124; J.J. Müller, 93; or eschatologically. The eschatological dimension is introduced in Phil 1:9-11; 2:16b.

[32] Fee, 244.

[33] *BDAG*, 52.

[34] Fee, 244.

[35] *BDAG*, 35; Lightfoot, 117; *TDNT* 1.209; O'Brien, 293 notes that it was applied literally to 'undiluted wine or unalloyed metal.'

[36] O'Brien, 293.

[37] Silva, 144 notes that 'the use of that phrase could serve as a powerful reminder of the dangers created by a disobedient life.' See list above and Fee, 244 (cf. P.C. Craigie, *The Book of Deuteronomy*. NICOT (Grand Rapids: Eerdmans, 1976), 377) for details of the Hebrew and translation). This indicates as O'Brien, 294; Silva, *Philippians*, 145; Hawthorne, 102; Collange, 111 note that for Paul, Christians (albeit in continuity and fulfillment of Israel, a remnant and not a replacement theology) have 'replaced' 'Israel' as God's children. So Moule, 47 who writes: 'the "true Israelites" of Philippi were to be the antithesis of the ancient rebels.' Paul may here be alluding to the Judaisers (3:2) but this is certainly not his main point cf. Silva, 145. But see the comments of Bockmuehl, 156-157 who disputes this due to the problematic nature of the LXX and Hebrew texts

it anticipates Paul's commendation of his son (τέκνον) Timothy (2:22) as the ideal son committed to the interests of Christ including the gospel. This brings evangelism tangentially into the orb of this designation.

The Philippians are to be ἄμωμος which signifies being 'blameless' 'in a moral and religious sense'(Phil 1:15; Eph 1:4; 5:27; Col 1:22 cf. Jude 24; Rev 14:5).[38] The language recalls μωμητός ('blameworthy') of Deut 32:5, suggesting that the Philippians are to be blameless, unlike the recalcitrant Israelites. However, the focus here is not blamelessness *before God*, but in the midst of the unbelieving Philippian community (γενεᾶς σκολιᾶς καὶ διεστραμμένης).[39] Literally γενεά implies 'family, descent', here referring to those with whom the Philippians interacted at the time of the letter.[40] More exactly, it refers to those in and about Philippi who are causing them suffering through their persecution of the Christian community (cf. 1:28-30).[41]

The description σκολιᾶς καὶ διεστραμμένης picks up Deut 32:5, where it is applied to the rebellious Israelites. Here Paul reverses it, applying it not to the people of God but the pagan Philippians.[42] This negative view of pagan society is consistent with Paul's perspective elsewhere (Rom 1:28-30; 1 Cor 6:9-10; Eph 2:1-3; 4:18-19; Tit 3:3).[43] The description calls to mind 1:28-30 where members of this same crooked and corrupt generation are persecuting the Philippians. This brings opposition and suffering into view, connected again to mission.

The culture is 'crooked, unscrupulous, dishonest' (σκολιός cf. Acts 2:40)[44] and 'crooked, perverted' (διεστραμμένος [διαστρέφω].[45] These terms powerfully reveal Paul's negative view of pagan culture of his time. In the midst of this the Philippians are to be pure rather than seduced by the perversion and depravity of their culture.

2:15c indicates specifically the missiological sense of the previous verse. As

---

and challenges that here Paul is making such a judgement of Israel which is not found elsewhere in the NT. He also notes Paul's positive view of faithful 'Israel' including Gentiles by adoption (Rom 9:4; 11:29; Hos 1:10 [= LXX 2:1]).

[38] Used of cultic sacrificial purity and especially the 'the absence of defects in sacrificial animals' (Num 6:14; 19:2) and so Christ (1 Pet 1:19; Heb 9:14); so *BDAG*, 56. O'Brien, 295 recognises the interplay of indicative (status) and imperative in Paul. Paul is encouraging the Philippians to 'be what they are.'

[39] *BDAG*, 635 notes that, in 2:15, μέσος is used with the genitive as a (improper) preposition implying 'in the midst of a...'

[40] *BDAG*, 191: 'generation.' Used temporally for age (Eph 3:5, 21; Col 1:26). It can also mean 'all living' (cf. H.A. Kent, 129). However it cannot be limited only to the Philippian Christians as Silva, 144 suggests.

[41] Fee, 241, 245.

[42] Fee, 245.

[43] Fee, 245.

[44] *BDAG*, 930 suggest 'crooked', in a literal sense of a road.

[45] *BDAG*, 237 note it is used of misshapen pottery.

Martin puts it, 'the church's influence as a witnessing community is described.'[46] They are to relate to this culture by shining within it like lights. The ἐν οἷς finds its antecedent in the generation mentioned previously and the phrase further explicates how to behave in its midst (μέσον).[47] The verb φαίνεσθε can either suggest 'to shine' or 'to appear' (cf. 2 Cor 13:7).[48] The former is more likely in that they are to shine *as a star* (ὡς φωστῆρες).[49] Φαίνεσθε is best understood as an indicative rather than an imperative, dependent as it is on the main verb ποιεῖτε.[50] Along with the present tense, the indicative indicates that Paul is addressing a people who are already shining; he wants them to shine more and more.[51] In particular they are to do so by refining their mode of relating to one another, without complaint and controversy. The context for this shining is ἐν κόσμῳ, κόσμος here certainly referring as in philosophical usage to 'the sum total of everything here and now' i.e. the universe, and figuratively, the world.[52]

Paul's words here recall Dan 12:1-4.[53] There is predicted a time when 'those who are wise will shine like the brightness of the heavens, and those who lead many to righteousness, like the stars for ever and ever.' The LXX uses φανοῦσιν ὡς φωστῆρες which is very similar to φαίνεσθε ὡς φωστῆρες in Phil 2:15, suggesting that Paul has this in mind. Fee in particular bemoans the inability of others to note the connection between Phil 2:15 and Dan 12:3 and

---

[46] Martin, 120.

[47] *BDAG*, 635.

[48] *BDAG*, 1046-1047. O'Brien, 295 notes older commentators (e.g. Ellicott, 54; Plummer, *Understanding,* 53; Vincent, 69; Lightfoot, 117; Moule, 47 who suggests that either makes little difference) preferred 'appear' in the sense 'among whom you appear (are seen) as luminaries in the world.' He notes however that the middle or passive is well attested as 'shine, flash' (Matt 2:7; 24:27; Is 60:2) and is appropriate here with φωστῆρες cf. Silva, 146; Hendriksen, 124-125; Michael, 106; Hawthorne, 103; Loh-Nida, 71. Modern commentators who prefer 'appear' include J.J. Müller, 94.

[49] *BDAG*, 1046.

[50] Silva, 146-147 argues that the imperative was common among early Fathers and Calvin. Hendricksen, 124-125 indicates it is not of great importance either way as the net result is that they are to shine; Beare, 92; Loh-Nida, 71 take it this way. Preferring the indicative are Silva, 146-147; O'Brien, 296; Plummer, *Understanding,* 53. That is not to say that some imperatival force is not intended as is indicated through the dependency of the imperative 'do.'

[51] Contra-Hendriksen, 124-125 who argues there is no point in this. As Silva, 147 notes, theologically the believers already are the light of the world, Paul wants their light to shine more brightly cf. Kent, 129.

[52] *BDAG*, 561 (or perhaps 'sky'?); cf. O'Brien, 296; Bruce, 85. Taking it as 'the world' directly include Fee, 246; Martin, 120. Beare, 92 and Bockmuehl, 158 suggest that cosmic influence may be implied. The main point is that they are to shine in the world as lights shine in the universe, as Loh-Nida, 71 indicates.

[53] Noted by Fee, 246; O'Brien, 296; Beare, 92; Michael, 106; Martin, 120; Bockmuehl, 158; Marshall, 64; Gnilka, 153; U. Müller, 120; Schenk, 222; Ware, *Mission*, 251-256.

in particular the application of the Hebrew 'bringing many to righteousness' to evangelism in the context. Ware too, argues that Paul has adapted the Greek of the LXX indicating that for Paul, 'the promise of Daniel 12:3 are already fulfilled in the church as the eschatological diaspora of God.'[54] Significantly for the first century believer, stars were utilized for guiding the traveller.[55] It seems that a Philippian hearer/reader would naturally hear this as inclusive of Christian guiding others to salvation as is the import of Dan 12:3.[56] Fee quite rightly notes that the early Philippian Christians, 'who lived in a basically oral culture and would have heard Scripture read over and over again', would have heard evangelism here.[57]

Beare also suggests that Paul's comments may be influenced by the dominical saying: 'You are the light of the world... let your light shine before people, that they may see your good deeds and praise your Father in heaven' (Matt 5:14-16).[58] If there is some link as Beare suggests, then Paul may have the soteriological-missiological dimension in mind in his appeal.

Whether or not the link to Matt 5:16 is appropriate, it would seem clear that the construction explicitly encourages the Philippians, as a star shines in the universe giving light and direction, to stand out ethically in the midst of their generation. As Israel was called in the OT to be the light of the world (cf. Is 9:2-7; 42:6-7; 49:6; 58:8-10; Dan 12:3) and as Jesus was the light of the world leading others to salvation (Jn 1:4-5; 8:12; 9:5; 12:46),[59] so the Philippians were to be lights to their world (cf. Matt 5:14-16). They were to be blameless and pure, without fault demonstrating the lifestyle of the kingdom.

I would argue, particularly in regard to Dan 12:3, that this should not be interpreted merely as a static witness through behaviour and attitude, but as evangelistic in *motivation*. Paul is referring to *whole lives* demonstrating purity and blamelessness *including verbal communication* with the goal of leading many to righteousness. While it is surely true that Paul had in mind the church as an attractive force, drawing people into it as insects to light, it is feasible he had more in mind. As light radiates from a central point giving people points of reference, so Paul envisaged the church radiating out to the surrounding community in lifestyle *and word* (cf. 1 Thess 1:8).[60] They are to '"shine" in the world "over against its" darkness, while simultaneously they are to illumine the

---

[54] Ware, *Mission*, 255.

[55] Beare, 92.

[56] So also Marshall, 64 who says 'it seems likely... Paul is thinking of the way in which the good lives of Christians are a form of witness to the world around them.'

[57] Fee, 246.

[58] Beare, 92. See also Martin, 121 who notes the harmony between the two passages; Bockmuehl, 158; Bruce, 85.

[59] Beare, 93 notes the similar use of 'word', 'world' and 'life' in Jn 1:4-5.

[60] On 1 Thess 1:8 as referring to active evangelisation see later in my discussion of imitation and evangelism related to 4:9 in chapter 9.

darkness.'[61] That is, by their lives consisting of attitudes, behaviour and words, they are to be clearly distinguishable from and in opposition to, the world around them; while they are also to be God's messengers, bringing the word of life to the dying. As Bruce puts it, 'these luminaries do not shine for their own sake; they shine to provide light for all the world. The same should be true of Christians: they live for the sake of others. The church has been called a society that exists for the benefit of nonmembers.'[62]

A brief analysis of Paul's use of the dualistic light/darkness motif indicates that this is the case. Paul often refers to the duality of darkness and light, which is understandable as the OT, Judaism, Qumran and the NT consistently utilised this leitmotif to express the realms of good and evil.[63] God himself dwells in 'unapproachable light' (1 Tim 6:16). Paul clearly considered this world as a negative place, a place of darkness. Alternatively he refers to the world as night (1 Thess 5:5), the dawning of a new era with the gospel described as the day (Rom 13:12; 1 Thess 5:5). It is apparent he considered that the era of darkness was ending with *the coming of the gospel in Christ* (Rom 13:12). People in this world are blind and need guidance (Rom 2:19). The apocalyptic dualism of good and evil are mutually exclusive and separate (2 Cor 6:14).

Believers are those who have been delivered from darkness into the realm of light (Eph 5:8; Col 2:12). They are no longer children of darkness but of light, to which they belong (1 Thess 5:5). This is the realm of inheritance (Col 2:12). Those in the darkness are characterised by works of the flesh, by sin. Unbelievers have been blinded by Satan described as the 'god of this age' (2 Cor 4:4). He seeks to deceive humanity 'masquerading as an angel of light' (2 Cor 11:14). Consequently, unbelievers are unable to perceive the gospel, which is described in terms of 'the light of the gospel of the glory of Christ' (2 Cor 4:4).[64] The Christians are to 'put aside the deeds of darkness and put on the armour of light' (Rom 13:12), living as 'children of the light' (Eph 5:8). They are to display the 'fruit of light consisting of goodness, righteousness and truth' (Eph 5:9). They are to avoid being unequally joined to unbelievers in line with Paul's understanding that the two realms of righteousness (light) and wickedness (darkness) are mutually exclusive (2 Cor 6:14).

Judgement is that point at which all that was done in the dark will be brought to light (1 Cor 13:3 cf. Eph 5:13-14). The work of the Christian will be revealed and tested at that time ('the day') (1 Cor 13:3). Paul encourages his readers to

---

[61] Fee, 247.

[62] Bruce, 85.

[63] O'Brien, 296; Hawthorne, 103; Bockmuehl, 158.

[64] As Barnett, *2 Corinthians*, 220 notes, 'yet into the darkness of these blinded minds, light – God's own glory now manifested in Christ – shines forth from the gospel Paul proclaims.' Kruse, *2 Corinthians*, 104 sees here an 'allusion to creation' in Paul's Adamic christology and/or Wisdom of Solomon 7:26. With Martin, *2 Corinthians*, 79 I see the genitives as descriptive of the gospel.

withhold judgement and wait for the return of Christ at which time he will bring to light all that is hidden in darkness and expose human motives. At that time each will receive God's judgement (1 Cor 4:5).

The missiological dimension of Paul's understanding of light is explicit in 2 Cor 4:6.[65] Here Paul refers to creation where God declared, 'Let light shine out of darkness' (Gen 1:3; Is 9:2 [LXX]; Is 49:6).[66] He likens the coming of Christ to the coming of 'the light.' This light is 'the knowledge of the glory of God in the face of Christ.' In Christ he has made his light shine in the human heart (2 Cor 4:6). In accord I argue that *in Paul the concept of light, which is implicit in 'shining as stars' is missiological and evangelistic.*[67]

Shining as a star then is, in effect, the emulation of Christ and the ministry of Paul through which the gospel brings light in the darkness, removes the blinding effected by Satan, and delivers people into salvation. That is not to say that the ethical, defensive and attractive notion of shining through 'works of light' is absent or not dominant here. Rather, I am suggesting that both notions are found in Paul's understanding of light and darkness. As Schenk puts it,

> Mission and ethics are not strictly separated by Paul, as further the relationship of both 2 Cor 4:4-6 and Phil 1:27 (see above) shows. The order to be faithful inwards and outwards belong together. The testimony of the church is carried out directly verbally, just as it is indirectly through behaviour.[68]

Similarly, Hawthorne who notes that this is more than the Philippians merely standing out against the background of their society; 'rather his words came as a challenge to change that society. As light dispels darkness, so Christians are to dispel the darkness of evil and ignorance that is everywhere around them.'[69] The Philippians are to express the works of light including a cessation of complaint and controversy in the context of their life as a community of the people of God and in their evangelistic mission to Philippi, Macedonia and beyond.[70]

---

[65] Schenk, 222.

[66] Martin, *2 Corinthians*, 80 notes the OT connections.

[67] S.J. Hafemann, *2 Corinthians*, NIVAC (Grand Rapids: Zondervan, 2000), 180; D.E. Garland, *2 Corinthians*. NAC (Nashville: Broadman & Holman, 1999), 216 and others note also in regards to his own conversion (Acts 9:3; 22:6, 11; 26:13).

[68] Schenk, 222 (translation mine).

[69] Hawthorne, 103.

[70] Bockmuehl, 159; Craddock, 46 notes 'the people of God are not merely to survive, they are to take the initiative, shining as lights in the world.'

Hold Forth the Word of Life to this Generation (2:16a)

Critical to this analysis is 2:16a where Paul further explicates what he wanted of the Philippians as they work out their salvation according to God's will, power and pleasure i.e. λόγον ζωῆς ἐπέχοντες. Here is found the crux of the discussion of this passage. As is well rehearsed the phrase can be understood in two basic ways.[71] First, there are those who see it as a defensive ethical statement, 'holding fast to the word of life.'[72] Others take it evangelistically, 'holding forth the word of life.'[73]

Four questions need to be answered here. First, there is the manner in which the participle phrase relates to the previous sentence. Secondly, the best meaning of ἐπέχοντες (ἐπέχω) needs to be assessed. Thirdly, an assessment of the context must be given. Finally, the meaning of 'word of life' needs to be examined. The first question can be dealt with briefly; the other three require more in-depth analysis.

THE RELATIONSHIP OF THE PARTICIPLE TO THE PREVIOUS

On the first question, as O'Brien has pointed out, grammatically the clause appears at first to be dependent on the ἵνα of 2:15. Accordingly, he argues that it is derived from the main clause of 2:14, 'do all things without complaining or arguing' which is, in turn, a development of the key imperative to 'work out your salvation.' In other words, 2:16a forms another statement of how Paul expects his readers to behave as God's children in the world.[74] Hawthorne on the other hand regards the participle ἐπέχοντες as imperatival and so commencing a new sentence which runs through 2:16.[75] Meyer prefers to take

---

[71] A third possibility, 'correspond' based on the Syriac version has found little favour. See F. Field, *Notes on the Translation of the New Testament* (Cambridge: CUP, 1899), 194 cf. Silva, 149; Moule, 101-102. Another unpopular possibility is that of Barth, 77; H.A.W. Meyer, 117; Collange, 112, who take it possessively i.e. 'since you have the word of life.'

[72] O'Brien, 297; Silva, 146; Michael, 107; Martin, 120; Caird, 126; Hawthorne, 103-104; Bockmuehl, 158; Witherington, *Friendship*, 73; Calvin, 258, 'upholding the word of life'; Bruce, 85; Thielman, 140; Gnilka, 153; U.B. Müller, 121; Schenk, 223; Melick, 113; *EDNT*, 2.21; Williams, *Enemies*, 139; Bowers, *Studies*, 115-116; 'Church': 100-101.

[73] Fee, 244-248; Beare, 92; Hendriksen, 125; Ware, *Mission*, 291-301; J.J. Müller, 94; Moule, 49 who notes similar use in Homer, *Od.* Xvi. 443 as does Lightfoot, 118; Murray, 'Witness': 322; Ellicott, 54-55; Plummer, *Understanding,* 53; Vincent, 69; Synge, *Philippians*, 36; Loh -Nida, 71; Wicks, 66; Kent, 129; Caird, 126; Marshall, 64; 'Evangelists', 260; 'Theology', 157; Barclay, *Philippians*, 55; Carson, *Basics*, 63. Motyer, 133 suggests both are in mind; Grayston, 30.

[74] O'Brien, 297 cf. Bockmuehl, 159.

[75] Hawthorne, 103 argues that this is an imperatival participial cf. MM, 343; H.G. Meecham, 'The Use of the Participle for the Imperative in the New Testament,' *ExpTim*,

the participle as causal, the clause giving the reason for φαίνεσθε ὡς φωστῆρες ἐν κόσμῳ.[76] Recently Fee has argued that ἐπέχοντες is a modal qualifier in which Paul explains how the readers will shine.[77] Hence he renders it 'as you hold out the word of life.' This I find preferable because of contextual and grammatical reasons outlined below which lead me to prefer 'hold forth' rather than 'hold fast' for the participle.

THE MEANING OF ἐπέχοντες

The meaning of the present participle ἐπέχοντες is debated. According to *BDAG*, the verb ἐπέχω can have three senses.[78] First, it can carry the sense of 'stop' or 'stay' with someone for a period of time. This usage is found in Acts 19:22 where Luke records how Paul stayed on in Asia for a period (αὐτὸς ἐπέσχεν χρόνον εἰς 'Ασίαν). Secondly, it can mean to 'hold fast' to something or someone. Thirdly, it can mean to 'be mindful or especially observant i.e. in regards to mental processes, to hold toward or aim at someone.' This final usage is the primary NT usage found in Luke's writings (cf. Lk 14:7; Acts 3:5; 19:22).

A great deal of work has been done on analysing this term. Dickson, in taking it in the sense of 'hold fast to', argues that the majority use outside the NT is 'hold upon.' However his review concedes that both meanings are found in the comparative literature.[79] Other scholars including Lightfoot and more recently Ware have also demonstrated that there are a number of occasions where the verb means 'hold forth.'[80]

That ἐπέχω can have an outward focus is supported in an analysis of Josephus.' There are 80 undisputed uses of the term in Josephus.[81] Josephus

---

58 (1947): 207-209; C.K. Barrett, 'The Imperatival Participle', *ExpTim* 59 (1948): 165-167. I agree there is a sense of imperative here but not signalling a new beginning.

[76] H.A.W. Meyer, 117.

[77] Fee, 247.

[78] *BDAG*, 362 although both Lk 14:7 and Acts 19:22 can be taken transitively. So also Hendriksen, 126 who details these and notes that if 'holding fast' is in mind it is the only example in the NT. This being the case it has to be conceded that in other papyri 'holding fast' is well attested so *BDAG*, 362; O'Brien, 297; Michael, 107 who sees it as 'perhaps the more natural meaning of the verb.' Although this is the case, I give precedence to Paul and other NT usage. *BDAG*, 362 takes it in the sense of 'hold fast.'

[79] Dickson, *Mission-Commitment*, 108-110.

[80] Lightfoot, 118. See also Dickson, *Mission-Commitment*, 108 n.74 who notes that Ware, *Mission*, 269 summarises the comparative literature and 'successfully demonstrates what scholars have long accepted, namely that the verb can convey the notion of extension.' See too Plummer, *Understanding*, 75-76.

[81] A number of these are included in the Loeb text with associated variants (Jos. *War* 3:79; Jos. *Ant.* 2:53; 7:242; 11:285; 15:55; 20:145; Jos. *Life* 253). Seven others which I have not considered in this analysis are not included in the favoured text but are noted as variants (Jos. *War* 2.214, 441; Jos. *Ant.* 15.50; 17.86, 136, 221, 350).

uses ἐπέχω in the main of holding back i.e. 'restrain, hold back, prevent, repress.'[82] On occasion the term is used synonymously with ἔχω ('to have').[83] There are a number of uses of ἐπέχω that connote 'to hold.'[84] The verb is also applied to holding to the point of stopping,[85] or preventing.[86] Of relevance to this discussion favouring the meaning in Phil 2:16a of 'holding fast to the word of life' is a reference to 'keeping ([holding] ἐπέχοντες σαββάτου) the Sabbath' (Jos. *War* 2.634). Apart from this reference and the general sense of 'hold', there are no other passages in Josephus that have the sense akin to 'holding fast to the word of life.'[87]

The extensive dynamic is rare but not absent from Josephus. The notion of ἐπέχω as 'present' is seen in Jos. *War* 3.79 where 'the exterior circuit *presents* (ἐπέχει) the appearance of a wall.' In Jos. *Ant.* 8:82 Josephus records that ''in each of these spaces was a dividing strip *extending* (ἐπεῖχεν) to the sub-base.' In Jos. *Ant.* 11:285 he writes that the 'joy and light of salvation *came upon* (ἐπεῖχεν) the Jews both in the city and in the provinces.' Thus the joy and light of salvation *extends* beyond Israel to the Jews in the Diaspora. In Jos. *Ant.* 15:55 he speaks of the extension of darkness: 'But with darkness *coming* on.'

Significantly in Jos. *Ant.* 20:145 he speaks of a report *spreading* or *gaining currency* (φήμης ἐπισχούσης) suggesting the extension of a spoken message.[88] Similarly in *Life.* 132 Josephus writes that 'a rumour had *now spread* throughout Galilee' (Ἐπισχούσης δὲ θήμης ρην Γαλιλαίαν ἄπασαν).[89] These directly utilise the verb ἐπέχω of the extension of a verbal message, as in Phil 2:16. Thus in Josephus we find examples of ἐπέχω with the meaning of 'hold' (in the sense of 'keeping hold') and 'hold forth' in the sense of spreading a verbal message.

The upshot of this discussion is that the comparative extra-biblical evidence is ambiguous and the meaning of ἐπέχοντες cannot be decided on linguistic

---

[82] See Jos. *War* 1.222, 230, 645; 2.8, 16, 214; 4.120; 5.319, 363; 6.61, 117, 354; 7:58; Jos. *Ant.* 2:53; 3:22; 5:61, 103, 151, 157; 6:151, 312; 7:17, 77, 183, 208, 242, 291, 346; 8:295; 9:86; 11:103; 12:327; 15:103, 346; 17:208; 19:27; Jos. *Life* 103, 140, 307, 329, 379; Jos. *Ap.* 2:246. See also Dickson, *Mission-Commitment*, 109.

[83] See Jos. *War* 2.462; 5.344, 543.

[84] These include Jos. *War* 2.634; 4.442; 5.80, 186, 303; 6:180; 7:301; Jos. *Ant.* 2:101; 5:17; 19:109; 20:30; Jos. *Ap.* 1:202.

[85] See Jos. *Ant.* 11:30, 88, 95, 250; 12:337; 14:83, 276, 427; 16:124.

[86] See Jos. *Ant.* 13:143; 14:461.

[87] Other uses include 'to come upon' (Jos. *Ant.* 17:64); 'to cover' (Jos. *War* 3.487); 'to diminish' (Jos. *Ant.* 5:18); 'to put off' (Jos. *Ant.* 10.61, 198, 199).

[88] Specifically of Berenice having an intimate relationship with her brother leading to her marrying Polemo, king of Cilicia.

[89] The rumour was that Josephus himself intended to betray the country of Israel to the Romans.

grounds.[90] From the NT point of view, the evidence slightly supports an extensive interpretation. Furthermore, Hendriksen may also be correct in suggesting that Paul would more than likely have used κατέχω if he clearly intended to say 'holding', 'holding onto' or 'holding fast' (cf. 1 Cor 11:2; 15:2; 2 Cor 6:10; 1 Thess 5:21).[91]

Fee suggests that Dan 12:3 may hold the key to understanding the phrase.[92] The LXX renders the Hebrew 'those who lead many to righteousness' as 'those who hold strong to my words' using the verb κατισχύοντες ('to be dominant, prevail' or 'to win a victory over'). Fee proposes that Paul substituted in its place ἐπέχοντες which brings out the initial understanding of the Hebrew, which suggests evangelism. 'Word of life' in Phil 2:16 replaces 'my words' in that this is the mode in which the word of God has been manifested i.e. the gospel.[93]

While acknowledging the link to Dan 12:1-3 in the LXX, Dickson critiques this view for several reasons. First, he questions Fee's intertextual argument in which he draws from the LXX and then interprets Dan 12:3 in light of the Hebrew.[94] Secondly, he argues that the LXX strongly supports an ethical and

---

[90] In the LXX I discern four uses. First, in the sense of 'hold forth' ones mental attention to something whether it be possessions (Sir 5:1, 8), to dreams (Sir 34:2), to the Lord (Sir 34:15), to wisdom (Sir 15:4), generally in the sense of 'consider' (Job 18:2), to poor counsellors (Sir 37:11), to wanting a multitude of children (Sir 16:3) or to a concern to speak as an equal with an impressive person (Sir 13:11). It is also used of God observing the ungodly (Job 27:8). The second usage is to 'remain' or 'stay with someone' (Gen 8:10, 12; 2 Chron 18:5, 14; 1 Kgs 22:6, 15; Judges 20:28; 2 Kgs 4:24; 2 Macc 9:25). A third usage is 'to hold back' wrath (Jer 6:11) or attack (2 Mac 5:25). Finally, the sense of holding forth is found. First in Sir 35:11 where the author writes of not *offering* or *giving forth* an unrighteous sacrifice (καὶ μὴ ἐπἒχε θυσίᾳ ἀδίκῳ). This is significant in that in Phil 2:16-17 Paul utilises cultic language to speak of the Philippians' service (2:17) which perhaps indicates a cultic dynamic to holding forth here. It is possible also that Job 30:26 is intended in this way. Job states 'when I *offered* good (ἐπέχων ἀγαθοῖς), see, more days of evil came upon me.' Alternatively it could read, 'but when I looked for good.'

[91] Hendriksen, 126; Dickson, *Mission-Commitment*, 110 n76 argues for synonymy between ἐπέχω and κατέχω on the basis of 1 Cor 15:1-2. However his own earlier analysis, which argued that ἐπέχω holds both active and passive possibilities of meaning would undermine his argument for synonymy. In that κατέχω in all its nuances in the NT does not hold the active sense (see *BDAG*, 532-533), Hendriksen's point is strengthened.

[92] See also Schnabel, *Mission*, 1461.

[93] Fee, 247-248 followed by Marshall, 'Evangelists', 260.

[94] Dickson, *Mission-Commitment*, 110-112. He questions Fee's methodology. Dickson asks whether it is feasible that Paul drew on both the LXX and Hebrew in this way. However in that Paul was in all likelihood familiar with both, it must be conceded to be possible.

passive interpretation of 2:16.[95] However, Dickson's criticism is not conclusive. In light of Paul's general varied use of the OT both Hebrew and LXX,[96] and the passive and active possibilities in Dan 12:3, rather than ruling out Fee's view, at best it points to the ambiguity of interpreting Phil 2:16 against Dan 12:3 and that Fee's approach remains highly possible.[97]

THE QUESTION OF CONTEXT

The third issue is the question of context, which in light of the ambiguity concerning the meaning of ἐπέχω, must decide the issue. Here the apparent ambiguity of the clause is again highlighted. Both sides of the debate claim context in support of their view. On the one hand it can be argued that Paul is concerned here to see the Philippians stand fast to the word of life in the midst of a corrupt generation.[98] Dickson for example, argues that 'this section quite clearly concerns socio-ethical obedience' dependent as it is on the appeal of 2:12 and 1:27.[99] Certainly this emphasis on standing firm is seen in the epistle (1:27; 3:2; 4:1).[100] In addition it is held that the ἵνα clause of 2:16b points to Paul's concern that the Philippians stand firm in the faith so that they will be saved. Many of those who adopt this position admit a sense of mission but in a centripetal or attractive sense with a concern for eschatological salvation.[101]

On the other hand as I have demonstrated, evangelism is emphasised in the whole epistle to this point (1:12-18a, 22, 27-30; [see also later on 1:3-11 [Chapter 8]; cf. 2:5-11).[102] Furthermore, evangelism and not steadfastness, is primary in the example of Timothy, which immediately follows (2:19-23 cf. 25). Similarly, evangelism is potentially connected with the concepts of God's salvation, will, action and pleasure in 2:13 suggesting that conversion from death to life is consistent with the tenor of Paul's desire there. If I am accurate in my assessment of the problem in Philippi to which Paul refers in 2:14 (cf.

---

[95] He interprets the LXX purely passively. However, reading Dan 12:1-3 in light of the revelation of Christ as Paul did post-conversion, may have led to his reading evangelism and the eschatological resurrection into Daniel.

[96] See M. Silva, 'Old Testament in Paul' in *DPL*, 630-642 who lists where he notes Paul's use of the LXX, MT and points of dispute (631).

[97] Dickson, *Mission-Commitment*, 110-112.

[98] O'Brien, 297, *Consumed*, 118-119; Silva, 146; Michael, 108; Hawthorne, 104; Bockmuehl, 159; Witherington, *Friendship*, 73; Dickson, *Mission-Commitment*, 111; Bowers, 'Church': 100.

[99] Dickson, *Mission-Commitment*, 111. His interpretation depends on a lack of exploration of the potential evangelistic content of φαίνεσθε ὡς φωστῆρες ἐν κόσμῳ (see above) and assumes a passive interpretation of 1:27.

[100] O'Brien, 297.

[101] O'Brien, 297.

[102] A point conceded by O'Brien, 297 while adopting 'holding fast' for the participle. On 2:5-11 see Appendix 3.

4:2-3), then unified evangelism rather than steadfastness fits the context.[103] I argue this is the case. His purpose is that their witness would be enhanced in their context, with them standing out before the ungodly (Phil 2:15-16). The clause then, continues and qualifies the evangelistic thought of 'shining as stars' then this points in a centrifugal direction.[104]

Furthermore, the eschatological concern of 2:16b can be understood evangelistically. First, Paul being able to boast in their salvation worked out through right Christian living includes sharing the faith with others. Secondly, their salvation could have been successfully worked out through others they have brought to faith.[105] Paul would have even more grounds for 'boasting' at the end if those he led to Christ led many others to righteousness as well. This is exactly the sense of 1:14-18a where Paul is delighted to have stimulated evangelism in others. In addition Paul clearly sees his fulfilment of his mission as central to working out his own salvation (Phil 1:5-7; 3:12-14). This may well fall into the orb of global imitation (4:9).

THE MEANING OF λόγον ζωῆς

The fourth question I noted above is meaning and import of the phrase 'word of life.' The phrase λόγος ζωῆς is unique in Paul and is in effect a synonym for the gospel. It is probably a genitive of origin and extrapolates from the creative power of the word to bring life.[106] The term λόγος functions as a Pauline favourite for 'gospel' and, as such, on face value should be taken this way.[107]

Dickson rejects that λόγος here necessarily means gospel. He does so for several reasons. First, he argues that in only three of twenty anarthrous uses of λόγος does the noun indicate the gospel message.[108] Secondly, he notes that in the three other uses in Philippians, only in 1:14 does λόγος indicate 'gospel' whilst in 4:15, 17 λόγος indicates a 'matter/principle' or 'financial account.' He suggests that λόγος ζωῆς may well mean '(retaining) the "principle" or "fact" of life itself.'[109]

My own analysis of the anarthrous use of λόγος indicates that Dickson is

---

[103] As argue Fee, 244-248; Beare, 93; Hendriksen, 125; Kent, 129; Caird, 126; Marshall, 64.

[104] Witherington, *Friendship*, 73 argues that evangelism is referred to only in the context of seeking unity. However it can be reversed to say, keep unity to maintain your witness. The interplay of the two should not be subordinated one over the other i.e. keep united to maintain your effective witness or keep witnessing with unity.

[105] A point made by J.J. Müller, 95.

[106] O'Brien, 298-299.

[107] See 1 Cor 1:18; 2:4; 14:36; 15:2; 2 Cor 2:17; 4:2; 5:19; Gal 6:6; Eph 1:13; Phil 1:14; 2:16; Col 1:6, 25; 3:16; 4:3; 1 Thess 1:6, 8 ; 2:13; 2 Thess 2:17; 3:1; 2 Tim 2:9; 3:16; 4:2; Tit 1:3; 2:5 cf. Rom 15:18; 1 Cor 1:5, 17; 4:20; 2 Cor 6:7; 8:7; 10:10; 11:6; Eph 6:19; Col 3:17; 4:6.

[108] Dickson, *Mission-Commitment*, 113.

[109] Dickson, *Mission-Commitment*, 114.

correct to note that there is a great variety of meaning in the anarthrous form of λόγος.[110] However, I would argue that λόγος in anarthrous form means 'gospel proclamation' *directly* on five occasions, rather than three. First, in Rom 15:18 Paul refers to his ministry of verbal proclamation of the gospel (λόγῳ) as integral to his apostolic ministry alongside deeds (ἔργῳ), miraculous signs and wonders (ἐν δυνάμει σημείων καὶ τεράτων) and the power of the Spirit (ἐν δυνάμει πνεύματος [θεοῦ]). Secondly, in 1 Cor 15:2 λόγος is clearly synonymous with 'gospel' as it is the word which Paul preached to the Corinthians (τίνι λόγῳ εὐηγγελισάμην ὑμῖν). Thirdly, λόγος in Eph 6:19 is clearly verbal (ἐν ἀνοίξει τοῦ στόματός μου) and refers to gospel proclamation (ἐν παρρησίᾳ γνωρίσαι τὸ μυστήριον τοῦ εὐαγγελίου). Fourthly, as Dickson notes, in 1 Thess 2:13 Paul twice defines the anarthrous accusative of λόγος with τοῦ θεοῦ, making plain that the gospel is in mind. Similarly, in the Pastorals, the anarthrous λόγος also refers to the message proclaimed, whether pastoral or evangelistic (1 Tim 4:5; 5:17 cf. 2 Tim 4:14). This recurring use opens up a greater possibility than conceded by Dickson, that 'gospel' is in Paul's mind with his use of λόγος in Phil 2:16.

Furthermore, *in his other uses* of the anarthrous λόγος, *gospel proclamation may be in Paul's mind.* Clearly on occasion general speech is Paul's emphasis (1 Cor 14:9; Eph 4:9 cf. 5:6). However there are other occasions where gospel speech cannot be ruled out as forming part or all of the content of Paul's intent. First, I suggest that Paul's flattering statements concerning the completeness of the Corinthians giftedness including *all speech* (ἐν παντὶ λόγω) in 1 Cor 1:5 and 2 Cor 8:7 should be understood globally to include their gospel proclamation, especially if παντί is allowed its full import.[111] Secondly, ἐν λόγῳ ἀληθείας in 2 Cor 6:7 can be understood as truthful general speech or more specifically as 'in (proclaiming) the word of truth.' I agree that there are

---

[110] The range the anarthrous λόγος includes: 1) God's promised word (Rom 9:28); 2) Personal account before God (Rom 14:12; Phil 4:15, 17); 3) Proclamation of the gospel (Rom 15:18); 4) General speech (1 Cor 14:9; Eph 4:9 cf. 5:6) and in some instances possibly inclusive of evangelistic proclamation (1 Cor 1:5; 12:8a, b; 2 Cor 6:7; 8:7; Col 3:17; 2 Thess 2:17; 1 Tim 4:12; Tit 2:8); 5) Speech clearly set in the context of evangelism (1 Cor 1:17; 2:1 cf. 2:13; 4:20; Eph 6:19; 1 Thess 1:5; 2:5; 2:13a); 6) Gospel (Rom 15:18; 1 Cor 15:2; Eph 6:19; Phil 2:16; 1 Tim 4:5; 5:17; 2 Tim 4:14); 7) The word of God from tradition (of Israel, Christ and the early church) (Gal 5:14; 1 Thess 4:15; Tit 1:9); 8) Regulation (Col 2:23); 9) Report (2 Thess 2:2); 10) Spoken teaching (2 Thess 2:15; 2 Tim 1:13); 11) The message of letters (2 Thess 3:14).

[111] Particularly when it is noted that verbal gospel proclamation is referred to through the letter. Thiselton, *1 Corinthians*, 91 notes that this includes in 1 Cor 1:5 speaking 'in many modes' including proclamation, preaching and prophecy. Thrall, *2 Corinthians*, II. 528; Furnish, *2 Corinthians*, 403 includes 'general Christian discourse.' However Garland, *2 Corinthians*, 373 restricts 'speech' in 2 Cor 8:7 to tongues and prophecy; Martin, *2 Corinthians*, 262 suggests 'eloquence.'

sound reasons to prefer the latter.[112] Elsewhere ‘word of truth’ is used of the gospel (Eph 1:13; 2 Tim 3:16). Furthermore, this passage is referring to Paul’s own ministry, which is inclusive of such proclamation. Notably, the phrase is followed immediately with ἐν δυνάμει θεοῦ, calling to mind other occasions where Paul links proclamation and with signs and wonders (Rom 15:18; 1 Cor 4:20; 1 Thess 1:5) or with power (Rom 1:16; 1 Cor 1:17-18).

Thirdly, the dual references to λόγος - charismata in 1 Cor 12:8a,b (λόγος σοφίας... λόγος γνώσεως) could potentially refer to gospel proclamation. In particular, this is possible in the case of λόγος σοφίας; in that there is a strong link between gospel proclamation and wisdom in 1 Corinthians (1 Cor 1:17, 21 [2x], 24, 30; 2:1, 4, 6, 7, 13). Furthermore the use of λόγος + genitive in Paul almost exclusively refers to the proclamation of the gospel (see further below).[113] Moreover, the comprehensive nature (πᾶς) of the appeals of Col 3:17 (καὶ **πᾶν** ὅ τι ἐὰν ποιῆτε ἐν λόγῳ ἢ ἐν ἔργῳ) and 2 Thess 2:17 (ἐν **παντὶ** ἔργῳ καὶ λόγῳ) should be allowed to stand and so be understood to include evangelistic speech.[114] Similarly, in the Pastorals Paul’s appeal to Timothy to set an example in speech (ἐν λόγῳ) may well include evangelism (1

---

[112] See the persuasive arguments of Furnish, *2 Corinthians*, 345; Barnett, *2 Corinthians*, 329; Martin, *2 Corinthians*, 178; Kruse, *2 Corinthians*, 132; Hughes, *2 Corinthians*, 229-230; J. Lambrecht, *Second Corinthians*. SPS (Collegeville: Liturgical, 1999), 110 who make the interpretation ‘truthful speech’ (so Garland, *2 Corinthians*, 309; Best, *Second Corinthians*, 61) highly unlikely. Belleville, *2 Corinthians*, 170 prefers ‘a true message’; if so, it is the gospel.

[113] An idea picked up to some extent by some. Thiselton, *1 Corinthians*, 938-940 suggests an ‘articulate utterance’ of the wisdom of ‘God’s plan of salvation’ found in the ‘revelation of God in the cross.’ Fee, *1 Corinthians*, 592 suggests ‘the message of Christ crucified is God’s true wisdom... those who give spiritual utterances that proclaim Christ crucified.’ He suggests λόγος γνώσεως may be a parallel term, which may indicate evangelism. Barrett, *1 Corinthians*, 285 takes it as a wise word of ethical instruction or exhortation. However the OT concept of wisdom is not the sense of ‘wisdom’ in 1 Cor as D. Carson, *Showing the Spirit. A Theological Exposition of 1 Corinthians 12-14* (Homebush West, Anzea, 1988), 38 notes. He prefers ‘the fundamental message of Christianity.’

[114] For these reasons: 1) ἐν παντι suggests ‘every’ act or word involving action and speech toward Christian and unbeliever alike hence it is arbitrary to exclude evangelism. So Richard, *Thessalonians*, 361 suggests it is generic of ‘total human behaviour’ cf. Holmes, *Thessalonians*, 235. Best, *Thessalonians*, 322: ‘the phrase is comprehensive.’ Wanamaker, *Thessalonians*, 442 who notes that ‘heart’ denotes the whole person and ‘work and word’ suggests all human activity; 2) That evangelism is relevant is enhanced in that the prayer is followed by a request for prayer for Paul’s own gospel ministry (1 Thess 3:1); 3) Both the preceding reference to the apostolic preaching (1 Thess 2:13-15) and the following definition of the gospel message utilise the same noun λόγος (1 Thess 3:1); 4) The same phrase (ὁ λόγος τοῦ κυρίου) is applied to the proclamation of the Thessalonians in 1 Thess 1:8.

Tim 4:12).[115]

Thus, while it is true that the articular usage of λόγος more often clearly implies gospel,[116] the absence of the article does not rule out the connection as Dickson argues.[117]

As I have intimated above, more important than the presence or absence of the article, is the use here of a genitive to define λόγος. Notably, the vast majority of Paul's use of the singular of λόγος + genitive refers to the gospel. These include first, ten uses of 'the word of God' (τοῦ θεοῦ) and variants. These all refer to the message of God whether from the OT (Rom 9:6), prophetically (1 Cor 14:36),[118] the Christian message (2 Cor 2:17; 4:2; Col 1:25; 1 Thess 2:13 (2x); 2 Tim 2:9; Tit 2:5) or the accumulated Christian tradition (1 Tim 4:5). Secondly, four christological genitives including 'of the cross', 'of Christ' and 'of the Lord' all refer to gospel (1 Cor 1:18; Col 3:16; 1 Thess 1:8; 2 Thess 3:1). The only other such christological genitive refers to a specific injunction coming from the mouth of Jesus relevant to context (1 Thess 4:15). Similarly two of the three references including the genitive of ἀλήθεια clearly refer to gospel (Eph 1:13; 2 Tim 3:16). This reinforces the suggestion above that ἐν λόγῳ ἀληθείας in 2 Cor 6:7 most likely means 'in preaching the gospel of truth.' Clearly τὸν λόγον τῆς καταλλαγῆς in 2 Cor 5:19 refers to the 'gospel of reconciliation.'

Where personal pronouns are used in the genitive to define the λόγος, three clearly refer to the gospel (1 Cor 2:4; 2 Cor 1:18; Tit 1:3). On this basis ὁ λόγος ὑμῶν in Col 4:6, could well refer to the gospel speaking of the Colossians.[119] The other uses include the false gospel of the Ephesian false

---

[115] I consider ἐν λόγῳ here includes evangelistic speech as: 1) There is no limitation on the range of the speech; 2) Timothy does the work of an evangelist preaching the word (2 Tim 4:2, 5 cf. 1:6-8); 3) The role of the evangelist is to equip as well as preach (Eph 4:11-12 [see Chapter 5 on Epaphroditus and Apostle]); 4) The word λόγος implies 'gospel' on occasion (see 1 Tim 4:5; 5:17 (same construction applied to elders who preach); 2 Tim 2:9, 15; 4:2.

[116] See 1 Cor 1:18; 2:4; 14:36; 2 Cor 1:18; 2:17; 4:2; 5:19; Gal 6:6; Eph 1:13; Phil 1:14; Col 1:6, 25; 3:16; 4:3; 1 Thess 1:6, 8; 2:13c; 2 Thess 3:1; 1 Tim 4:6; 2 Tim 2:9; 3:16; 4:2; Tit 1:3; 2:5 cf. 2 Cor 10:10; 1 Thess 4:18.

[117] Other articular usages include: 1) The word of God general and specific from tradition (of Israel, Christ and the early church) (Rom 9:6, 9; 13:9; 1 Cor 15:54; 1 Tim 1:15; 3:1; 4:9; 2 Tim 2:11; 3:8 cf. 1 Tim 6:3); 2) General speech (1 Cor 4:19); 3) Paul's proclamation speech (2 Cor 10:10; 11:6); 4) The message of letters (2 Cor 10:11; 1 Thess 4:18); 5) General speech inclusive of evangelism or evangelistic speech (Col 4:6); 6) A human message as opposed to the word of God (1 Thess 2:13b); 7) False teaching (2 Tim 2:17).

[118] Fee, *1 Corinthians*, 710; Thiselton, *1 Corinthians*, 1161.

[119] See Garland, *Colossians*, 274: 'Paul has in mind also our public proclamation.' O'Brien, *Colossians*, 242 rightly notes that the phrase 'appears to be a deliberate echo of the apostle's preaching of the Word (λόγος) in Col 4:3 and includes both private

teachers in the Pastorals (2 Tim 2:17), the specific teachings of a letter (2 Thess 3:14) and in Phil 4:17 the 'account' of the Philippians before God (see above on 1 Cor 12:8).

In other contexts Paul utilises negative genitives contrasting with the authentic gospel. So he does not use a word of flattery (ἐν λόγῳ κολακείας) as he preaches the gospel (1 Thess 2:5).[120] Similarly he contrasts the authentic 'word of God' with a merely human message (1 Thess 2:13).[121] While the negative description of Paul's speaking ὁ λόγος ἐξουθενημένος in 2 Cor 10:10 may refer to his general speech, it is more likely that it refers to his mode of proclamation.[122] Similarly it is possible that τὸν λόγον τῶν πεφυσιωμένων in 1 Cor 4:19 refers not only to the speech of the 'puffed up' opponents in Corinth but their gospel proclamation.[123] Only in Eph 4:29 where Paul prohibits all fleshly speech (πᾶς λόγος σαπρὸς) does Paul utilise a genitive with no possible reference to proclamation.

In addition, I note the contextual and theological problem of Dickson proposing the alternative 'principle of life' in context in 2:16. In terms of the context, it is difficult to see why Paul would appeal to them to hold fast/forth to this principle. Rather, the clause grows out of the appeal of 2:12 which reiterates 1:27a involving living out the Christian life in the midst of an unbelieving community whilst suffering. In light of the above analysis, I suggest that it is reasonably obvious that λόγον ζωῆς in Phil 2:16 refers to the gospel of life.

Consequently the genitive ζωῆς emphasises the life-giving power of the word of God and in particular, the 'eternal life' the gospel generates in the believer. This perspective is enhanced by Paul's theological use of ζωή which on the whole refers to the life present and future that God brings through Christ and the Spirit and into which the believer is saved and are to live out i.e. eternal life.[124] This life is both a hope (1 Tim 6:12; 2 Tim 1:1; Tit 3:7) and a present reality (1 Cor 3:22; Col 3:3).[125] It stands in contrast to the power of death in

---

conversation and public proclamation' cf. MacDonald, *Colossians*, 173; Dickson, *Mission-Commitment*, 275-277 who interprets the gospel speech here by the final clause i.e. apologetic witness.

120 Malherbe, *Thessalonians*, 142; Bruce, *Thessalonians*, 29.

121 Wanamaker, *Thessalonians*, 111.

122 Martin, *2 Corinthians*, 312: 'rhetoric'; Lambrecht, *2 Corinthians*, 157; Furnish, *2 Corinthians*, 468: 'speech'; Barnett, *2 Corinthians*, 476: 'rhetorical skills.'

123 Thiselton, *1 Corinthians*, 376; Fee, *1 Corinthians*, 191.

124 See Rom 2:7; 5:10; 6:4; 7:10; 8:1, 6, 10; 11:15; 1 Cor 3:22; 2 Cor 2:25; 4:10, 11; Gal 6:8; Phil 4:3; 1 Tim 1:16; 6:19; 2 Tim 1:1, 10; Tit 1:2; 3:7. These are expressed in a variety of ways: 1) ζωὴν αἰώνιον (Rom 2:7; Gal 6:8; 1 Tim 1:16; 6:12; 2; Tit 1:2; 3:7); 2) ἐν τῇ ἐν τῇ ζωῇ αὐτοῦ (Rom 5:10); 3) ἐν καινότητι ζωῆς; 4) ζωὴ ἐκ᾽εκρῶν (Rom 11:15); 5) ἡ ζωὴ τοῦ 'Ιουσοῦ (2 Cor 4:10); 6) τῆς ζωῆς τοῦ θεοῦ (Eph 4:19); 7) τῆς ὄντως ζωῆς (1 Tim 6:19).

125 'Take hold of the eternal life to which you were called' (1 Tim 6:12).

which unbelievers live (2 Cor 2:15; Eph 4:19). This life itself is a power in the present, working in the believer and swallowing up all of earthly existence (2 Cor 4:12; 5:4; Col 3:3-4). Only rarely is it limited to human life (Rom 8:38; 1 Cor 15:19; Phil 1:20; 1 Tim 4:8). The concept of the 'principle of life' does not seem to exist in Paul, life being earthly existence or the life of God, present and future.

In this regard I also note that this life is intimately connected to soteriology and evangelism on occasion. First, in Rom 11:15 acceptance of the gospel is life from the dead (τίς ἡ πρόσλημψις εἰ μὴ ζωὴ ἐκ νεκρῶν). Secondly, in 2 Cor 2:15-16, the messenger of the gospel is like a sweet 'fragrance of life' rather than of death to the believer (2 Cor 2:15). Similarly the 'life of Jesus' (ἡ ζωὴ Ἰησοῦ) is revealed in the life of Paul and others who share the gospel (2 Cor 4:10, 11).

Finally, there are notable similarities between the constructions λόγον ζωῆς (2:16) and βίβλῳ ζωῆς (4:3). It is those who respond to the spoken gospel (λόγον ζωῆς) who are saved, their names written in the book of those who will inherit eternal life. As I will suggest on 4:2-3,[126] those specifically listed as being recorded in the latter book are co-workers of Paul who have been involved in the holding out the word to the lost.

That being the case, I suggest that the phrase λόγον ζωῆς recalls other uses of gospel and parallels in Philippians (Phil 1:5, 7, 12, 14, 15, 16, 17, 18, 27; 2:22; 4:3, 15). Significantly λόγος in 1:14 clearly refers to the Roman proclamation of the gospel. I agree with Fee who argues that the unique phrase is best understood as carrying 'the thrust of bringing life to others.'[127] However this evangelism is to be demonstrated 'not only as *preached* but also as *practised.*'[128] As J.J. Müller notes, 'the world hears the word from them, but also sees its light in their daily walk of life; their saintly lives testify to the power of the word of life.'[129] Similarly Bruce states of Christians, 'they are to present the gospel by the way they live as well as by the words they speak.'[130]

CONCLUSION TO 2:16A

In conclusion then, it seems best to read 2:16a as an explicit appeal for evangelism in light of: the continuity from the evangelistic emphasis of the epistle to this point (1:3-7, 12-18a, 22; 27-30 cf. 2:5-11) and in what follows (2:19-30; 3:2; 4:2-3); the evangelistic possibilities in 2:15b,c and in particular 'shining as stars'; the evangelistic gospel-synonym 'word of life'; the use of λόγος for proclamation of the gospel in 1:14; the probable dependency on Dan 12:3 and in particular the Hebrew 'leading many to righteousness'; the tradition

---

[126] See Chapter 7.
[127] Fee, 247.
[128] Hendriksen, 126.
[129] J.J. Müller, 95.
[130] Bruce, 85.

of Jesus which may have been in Paul's mind especially Matt 5:14-16 and a preference for 'holding forth' for ἐπέχοντες in the NT. As Fee concludes, 'thus, it is not some kind of defensive posture that is in view (as in, "hold fast so that the enemy does not take it away from you"), but evangelism, that they clean up their internal act so that they may thereby "hold firm" the gospel, the message that brings life to those who believe.'[131]

In addition it should be said that the alternative 'hold fast' does not preclude evangelism in the context. This is indicated by Michael, who correctly notes that 'contrast', by definition involves 'influence' (cf. Matt 5:16).[132] Similarly Martin notes that the two meanings 'happily dovetail. Only as we firmly "hold fast" to the gospel truth can we effectively 'hold it out.'[133] Likewise, if 'holding forth' is in mind, the concept still assumes 'holding fast' as Kent points out.[134] Indeed it is possible considering Paul's concern for both standing firm and evangelism in the epistle that he is being intentionally ambiguous, presenting both meanings to the Philippians.[135] Whether or not this is the case, the previous phrase 'shine like stars in the universe', particularly with reference to Dan 12:3 and the context of Philippians, most likely implies evangelism. In addition 'holding fast' to the gospel ('word of life') in-and-of itself, speaks of evangelism albeit among many other dimensions of Christian living (cf. 1:27a). Living the gospel involves the dimension of sharing its message of salvation where opportunity is afforded, it being the power of salvation (Rom 1:16), the sword of the Spirit (Eph 6:17), which brings salvation to those who hear it and believe (Rom 10:17). However, if this is a correct interpretation of 2:16a, evangelism is brought to the fore in a more explicit manner, contra-Bowers, Bosch and Dickson.

Conclusion to 2:14-16a

Traditional interpretations of this passage have tended to play down the missiological and evangelistic emphasis of this section of Philippians. Evangelism, I suggest, is in the intent of the appeal to hold forth the word of life (2:16a). If so, it forms an indispensable component of the general appeals to 'work out your salvation' and to 'do *everything*' (2:12-13 cf. 4:3 below). It is one aspect of the appeal to 'radiate light like stars in the universe' (2:15). The concern for right behaviour in the context of the pagan culture makes it likely that a concern for the quality of the Philippian witness is linked to the contention in the church. Hence I contend that Paul wants an end to all discord

---

[131] Fee, 248. Similarly Plummer, *Understanding*, 77: 'we find in Philippians 2:16 explicit instructions from Paul for the church to evangelize.'

[132] Michael, 107.

[133] Martin, 122.

[134] Kent, 129.

[135] So Motyer, 133, on the basis that it is not possible to decide between the two.

so that their witness will not be compromised. Essentially Paul is calling for refreshed relationships and renewed mission. The emphasis is then on lifestyle evangelism, inclusive of sharing the word, but exemplified by deed and right relationships.

It is notable here as elsewhere in this section, the major features of Philippians intersect. These include proactive evangelism (2:16 cf. 2:15), ethical witness (2:12, 15), joy (2:17-18), suffering (2:17), eschatological hope and assurance (2:12, 16) and unity rather than contention (2:15).

This conclusion further weakens the view that Paul understood the church's mission as merely centripetal. Certainly proponents of the view are right to emphasise community, unity and relationships as central, but these are to be understood in the context of evangelistic mission. Paul's mission strategy was inspired with the hope that wonderful communities of faith, working out their salvation, imitating the lifestyle and commitment of their author Christ, would lead many to faith.

CHAPTER 6

The Evangelistic Content of the Examples of Timothy and Epaphroditus (2:19-30)

After Paul's appeal to the Philippians to 'work out your salvation' (2:12) in unity, with specific reference to desisting from contention and complaint by ethical and proactive proclamatory witness, Paul turns to outline his own plans concerning the Philippians. The emphasis here falls on two individuals, Timothy and Epaphroditus who are with Paul in Rome, and who he wishes to send to Philippi. While the section appears to lack theological depth,[1] close examination suggests it is essential to the fabric of Philippians and in particular, has important rhetorical implications for this discussion.[2]

Some consider the section 2:19-30 as the conclusion to Paul's second letter to the Philippians.[3] As I indicated in the introduction (Chapter Two), such arguments are not conclusive. First, it is clear that Paul is quite able to insert his travel plans at different points in his letters,[4] all the more where the content of

[1] So Barth, 79: the passage contains 'no direct teaching.'

[2] Some consider this section the centre of the epistle including Wicks, 67.

[3] Funk, *Hermeneutic*, 264-274 for example, considers the content resembles other so-called 'travelogues' or apostolic parousia of Paul found near the conclusion of his letters giving travel plans and asserting authority (Rom 15:14-33; 1 Cor 4:14-21; Phil 2:19-30; 1 Thess 2:17-3:13; Phm 21, 22) cf. W.J. Doty, *Letters in Primitive Christianity* (Philadelphia: Fortress Press, 1973), 36-37, 43; T.Y. Mullins, 'Visit Talk in New Testament Letters', *CBQ* 35 (1977): 350-358; R.W. Funk, 'The Apostolic *Parousia*: Form and Significance' in W.R. Farmer, C.F.D. Moule and R.R. Niebuhr, *Christian History and Interpretation. Studies Presented to John Knox* (Cambridge: CUP, 1967), 249-268; Bruce, 91, 93-94; Swift, 'Theme': 246; R. Russell, 'Pauline Letter Structure in Philippians', *JETS* 25 (1982): 295-306; Martin, 126; Beare, 95; Collange, 115; Gnilka, 156. Michael, 112 considers that 2:19-24 may be a separate Pauline note to an unspecified context at another time when he was among 'persons who had not drunk deeply of the spirit of Christ.' In the context of Paul's situation in Rome (or Ephesus as Michael suggests) this seems totally unnecessary speculation.

[4] Mostly before the final greeting (Rom 15:19-33; 1 Cor 16:5-12; 2 Cor 13:1; Col 4:7-9). However, sometimes they are placed early in the letter (Rom 1:10, 13 cf. 2 Cor 2:15). Sometimes placed at a midpoint as here (Phil 2:19-30; 1 Thess 2:17-3:11).

the section speaks into the situation he is addressing.[5] Secondly, the so-called travelogue form is disputed and the genre of this section can be interpreted quite differently.[6] Finally, as I will demonstrate, the section makes good sense in the context of the flow of Philippians.

As most commentators suggest, the passage 2:19-30 represents a new section.[7] This is evidenced in that Paul shifts from a focus on the Philippian situation to his own concern to impact the Philippians through himself and his emissaries. However this disjunction should not be overplayed. The use of δε, the continuation of the first person and Paul's ongoing indirect concern for the Philippians in the section, indicate that this passage should be understood in continuity with the previous.[8]

Silva, while agreeing that this is a new section, suggests that Paul here resumes 1:18b-26 concerning his own situation.[9] I prefer the view of Fee who sees the section as outlining 'what's next' after relaying to the Philippians his own situation and his appeal for gospel-worthy citizenship.[10] He rightly notes that the order of 'my affairs' (1:18b-26), 'your affairs' (1:27-2:18) accounts for the placement of the news about Timothy ('my affairs') before Epaphroditus ('your affairs'). In addition, Timothy's concern for the interests of Jesus Christ builds on and reinforces the Christ example just given (2:6-11).[11]

Some find in the biographical details of the section insight into various aspects of the Philippians' situation. First, the reference to travel plans lead some to suggest Paul's point of incarceration is close to Philippi implying for many Ephesus and not Rome. As I indicated in my introduction, this is not decisive. The letter requires only two journeys between Philippi and the place of origin and hence, any of the suggested provenances for Philippians are adequate on this count.[12] Secondly, it is probable that the return of Epaphroditus was associated with the delivery of the letter.[13] Thirdly, the note of commendation of Epaphroditus need not be understood as a sign of tension

---

[5] Fee, 258; Houlden, 89; R.A. Culpepper, 'Co-Workers in Suffering. Philippians 2:19-30', *RevExp* 77 (1980): 349-358; Hawthorne, 108; O'Brien, 314; Melick, 116.

[6] Fee, 259 esp. note 1; Bockmuehl, 163 see here rather a Pauline 'letter of commendation' (1 Thess 3:2-3; 1 Cor 16:15-18; 2 Cor 8:16-24; Rom 16:1-2).

[7] Michael, 111.

[8] The conjunction δέ can be resumptive/transitional (Fee, 263; Silva, 154), adversative (Vincent, 73; H.A.W. Meyer, 125; O'Brien, 316; Hawthorne, 108) or referring to the matter of Paul's absence (Silva, 155).

[9] Silva, 153-154 who rejects the 'travelogue' and example approaches to the section.

[10] Fee, 258.

[11] Fee, 259-260.

[12] See Chapter 1. As Houlden, 91 says, 'our passage leaves the question of where Paul was imprisoned quite open.'

[13] Marshall, 67; Fee, 261. However Gnilka, 162 disputes this.

concerning him at Philippi.[14] Rather, they are to venerate 'such men' because they embody Paul's ideal of Christian discipleship, 'obedience to the point of death' in Christ's service (2:8, 12).

There are several clear purposes for this passage. First, Paul wants to express his plans concerning Timothy, himself and Epaphroditus.[15] More specifically he hopes to send Timothy as soon as his own situation in Rome is clarified so as to receive fresh news from Philippi (2:19, 23),[16] he wants to assure them of his future release and visit (2:24) and to tell them of his reasons for sending back Epaphroditus (2:25, 28).[17] Timothy will also follow up in person his appeal for a cessation of dispute in Philippi.

Secondly and importantly for this study, these two examples fit into the rhetoric of the letter.[18] Paul presents Timothy and Epaphroditus as positive examples of his hope for the Philippians expressed in the previous passage 1:27-2:18.[19] They continue the emphasis on example throughout the letter thus far i.e. Paul (1:7, 12-14, 26), the diversely motivated Romans (1:14-18a), the Philippians (1:5-7) and Christ (2:5-11). This will be followed by the negative examples of the Judaisers (3:2-4) and the 'enemies of the cross' (3:18), the positive examples of Paul along with other like minded Christians (3:4-17; 4:9) and the mixed examples of Philippians themselves (4:3, 10, 14-18).

---

[14] Some see here an apologetic concerning the 'hasty return' of Epaphroditus. So Michael, 119; White, *Form*, 145; Silva, 154.

[15] In this sense it is a 'travelogue', as Martin, 126 suggests.

[16] As Fee, 259. Hawthorne, 112 suggests that this is due to his need for Timothy in his current situation.

[17] His reasons for sending Epaphroditus immediately appear to be: 1) To relieve Epaphroditus' who 'longs' for the Philippians (2:26); 2) To relieve the Philippians who are deeply concerned for his welfare (2:26, 28); 3) To relieve his own concern for Epaphroditus and the Philippians (2:28); 4) To deliver the letter and so pass on news of Paul and his situation (2:29-30). Supremely as Beare, 96 puts it, 'to dispel any lingering anxiety over his health.'

[18] Whether informally (as I prefer) or formally in terms of a rhetorical structure; so Watson, 'Analysis': 71-72 who sees here a *digressio* in which Timothy and Epaphroditus are presented as godly models to develop the *propositio* (1:27-30). Bloomquist, *Function*, 173; Black, 'Structure': 39 see it as '*exempla*' central to Paul's *argumentatio* presenting servant models who embody the 'Christ-type.' Witherington, *Friendship*, 18-19; Williams, *Enemies*, 141 see 2:1-4:3 as *probatio* with Timothy and Epaphroditus as models.

[19] Motyer, 136: 'the Lord is the Christian model, they are model Christians'; Marshall, 67 who notes the link to 1:14-18a; O'Brien, 315 and 'Models': 278; Carson, *Basic*, 72-74 who sees 2:19-3:21 as concerning the emulation of good Christian leaders; Garland, 'Defense': 163; Bockmuehl, 164; Fee, 261; Hawthorne, 108, 114; Bloomquist, *Function*, 159 with great emphasis; Thielman, 151; Melick, 116; Perkins, 'Philippians', 115; Peterman, *Gift*, 119 who suggests that 3:17b should include Epaphroditus and Timothy (see below); Culpepper, 'Co-workers': 357; U.B. Müller, 125; R. Banks, 'Church Order and Government', in *DPL*, 133.

Further, in sending his two trusted colleagues, Paul demonstrates the selflessness that he is exhorting from the Philippians. Although it would be advantageous to keep both men with him, his passion for the mission to Philippi and the Philippians themselves outweighs his own need.[20] Most importantly, he is concerned that his message arrives in Philippi and that remedial action is taken to stop any further degeneration of relationships and mission there. Timothy's visit will reinforce and follow up the letter. This being the case, Paul continues his theme of presenting himself as a model to be emulated by the Philippians.[21]

The essence of this enquiry now is to draw out the evangelistic dimensions of Timothy and Epaphroditus as presented by Paul and consider how they fit into Paul's overall appeal and the implications for this study.

The Positive Example of the Co-Worker Timothy (2:19-23)

In 2:19-24 Paul expresses his plan in light of his own uncertain situation (2:17-18), to send Timothy to the Philippians soon (ταχέως cf. ἐξαυτῆς in 2:23).[22] While this is expressed as a hope (ἐλπίζω), it is a hope which is of christological origin (ἐν κυρίῳ 'Ιησοῦ), suggesting both divine guidance and a confidence born of trust in Christ's ultimate will.[23]

Paul expresses twin purposes for Timothy's visit. First and primarily,[24] that (ἵνα) he may be 'encouraged' or 'cheered up' (εὐψυχῶ) by the news he will receive from Timothy about the Philippians.[25] That is, specifically, a resolution to the Euodia-Syntyche problem. If so, then Paul will be 'well-souled' (εὐψυχέω) and full of joy concerning them. If the situation is not resolved then Timothy can function as a kind of trouble-shooter to help sort out the problem. He will then either return to Paul or perhaps wait in Philippi for Paul himself to

---

[20] Hendriksen, 135 notes a similar concern in 2 Tim 4:10-12 when he sends Tychicus to Ephesus, Crescens to Galatia and Titus to Dalmatia.

[21] Hendriksen, 134-135.

[22] Whether Epaphroditus was sent to Rome to facilitate this is unclear as preferred by Silva, 155 (tentatively). On ἐξαυτῆς as equivalent to ταχέως ('soon') see O'Brien, 326.

[23] O'Brien, 316 notes similarities to 1 Cor 4:19; 16:7; 2 Cor 1:17. Schenk, 228; Silva, 157 note the connection with πέποιθα (2:24) here suggesting hopeful expectation. Similarly Fee, 264; Bockmuehl, 164-165; Marshall, 68; Melick, 117; Martin, 127. Some including Vincent, 73; Michael, 113; Gnilka, 157; Bruce, 91; Collange, 116 see an issue of Timothy's authority here being enhanced by being 'in the Lord.' Hawthorne, 109 who also suggests 'hope' here may indicate less confidence of sending Timothy than 'confidence' at his own release. Bruce, 91 here suggests the sphere in which they act.

[24] So also Fee, 265; Michael, 165.

[25] Timothy's visit will carry further news about the resolution of Paul's situation in prison cf. O'Brien, 317; Hendriksen, 133; Silva, 156; Hawthorne, 109; Collange, 116.

come.[26] Hence, this gives Timothy's function an evangelistic edge as the resolution of the conflict among co-workers will enable the restoration of unified evangelistic mission. In the meantime Paul prefers to keep Timothy with him as support until his current situation is resolved (2:23).[27]

The details Paul gives concerning Timothy have been interpreted in various ways. Some see here a need to clear up a misunderstanding in Philippi that Paul no longer trusted Timothy.[28] Alternatively the Philippians were concerned that Timothy was no longer concerned for them.[29] Then again some have suggested Paul speaks in a complimentary fashion because the Philippians had negative feelings toward Timothy.[30] Collange for one sees here both evidence of a full-blown problem in Philippi threatening the Pauline mission and Timothy's spinelessness.[31] Similarly, Gnilka suggests that the details of the commendation relate to sending Timothy with 'full power and authority.'[32] This suggests some sort of need for Paul to flex his apostolic muscle, which is not apparent. These arguments are utterly unconvincing. Across the whole Pauline corpus it is clear that Timothy is Paul's most trusted and able colleague.[33] As O'Brien notes the issue is not 'whether Paul wants to send Timothy; it is, rather, that he cannot send him *now*.'[34] In addition, Fee notes that in 1 Thess 3:2-3 he commends Timothy after his visit to the Thessalonians, rendering suggestions of Timothy's weakness impotent.[35]

One of the main reasons Paul gives such details concerning Timothy appears to be rhetorical i.e. Paul is conveying more than merely travel plans or reinforcing Timothy's authority. The details Paul chooses to share concerning

---

[26] Bruce, 91; Martin, 127 assume that Timothy will return to Paul. However this is not certain, as Fee, 265 notes. Alternatively he may move onto another project, perhaps nearby Ephesus, as Hendriksen, 134; Kent, 132 suggest.

[27] Silva, 156-157 who notes Timothy may be Paul's only support after Epaphroditus departed.

[28] Referred to as a possibility by Silva, 156.

[29] Hence the strong language emphasising Timothy's genuine concern; mentioned by Silva, 156.

[30] Hawthorne, 109 who strangely suggests Timothy's role in the early mission was insignificant and negative. There is simply *nothing* here or anywhere else to support this contention!

[31] Collange, 116 who sees the spinelessness of Timothy as 'apparent' (1 Cor 16:10; 2 Tim 1:6f; 1 Tim 4:12). None of these verses need imply this about Timothy. See the positive comments of Ollrog, *Paulus*, 22-23.

[32] Gnilka, 158 cf. Bonnard, *L'Epitre*, 54 (see O'Brien, 320). Similarly Hawthorne, 110; Collange, 115.

[33] I suggest this may be reading too much into seemingly positive comments. While there may be indications of a reticence in Timothy at times (2 Tim 1:6-8 [if Paul wrote the Pastorals]), this does not necessarily imply an ongoing issue.

[34] O'Brien, 320 (italics his).

[35] Fee, 263.

Timothy speak rhetorically in a direct and specific manner into the situation in the Philippian church.[36]

First, in 1:1 Paul has mentioned Timothy as co-author/sender and more importantly as fellow 'servant' of Christ Jesus with Paul himself. He is also well known to the Philippians having helped in the foundation of the Philippian church and visiting with Paul on his other trips to Philippi (Acts 16:11-40; 19:21-22; 20:3-6; 1 Thess 2:2).[37] As a result, this sets the scene for this commendation.

Secondly, in this passage in 2:20, Paul says of Timothy 'for I have no one like-minded'; literally 'like-souled' (ἰσόψυχος).[38] By this Paul probably means that he has no one who is like-minded *with me* rather than I have no one like Timothy or like the Philippians themselves.[39] In other words, I have no one 'who shares my concerns', including concern for the Philippians and the gospel.[40]

In contrast, 'all' (πάντες [v21]) seek themselves and not the affairs of the Lord (τὰ Χριστοῦ Ἰησοῦ). What Paul has in mind is not completely clear here. If he is thinking of a specific group, he is probably speaking about those in Rome and not the Philippians, although it is the Philippians who are his rhetorical target.[41] If so, Paul is not writing off every Christian in Rome as he has already mentioned the rightly motivated members of the Roman church (1:14-18a).[42] Neither is he referring to Epaphroditus, who has demonstrated his

---

[36] O'Brien, 323 and 'Models': 278; Garland, 'Defense': 163; Fee, 263; Bockmuehl, 167. Motyer, 139: Marshall, 69; Hawthorne, 111; Bloomquist, *Function*, 173-178; Thielman, 152; Melick, 118; Watson, 'Analysis': 71-72; Black, 'Structure': 39; Witherington, *Friendship*, 18-19; Culpepper, 'Co-workers': 357.

[37] Martin, 130.

[38] A rare poetic word found only here and in LXX Ps 54:14 meaning 'of like mind and soul' and implying 'solidarity'; so *BDAG*, 481; O'Brien, 318; R. Jewett, *Paul's Anthropological Terms. A Study of their Use in Conflict Setting.* NovTSup 16 (Leiden: Brill, 1971), 349.

[39] Lightfoot, 120; Michael, 114; Melick, 117; Kent, 132; Gnilka, 158; Martin, 128; Beare, 96 who prefer the emphasis to fall on Timothy here i.e. 'I have no one like-minded like Timothy.' Hawthorne, 109-110 allows the ambiguity to stand. The impact on meaning is minimal either way. Few agree with Caird, 128, who takes it as 'in sympathy with your (the Philippians) outlook.'

[40] O'Brien, 318-319 who gives two clear reasons: 1) The following sentence fits this interpretation; 2) Father-son relationship supports it. I also feel it fits the rhetoric i.e. their unity is to be emulated by the Philippians; so also Wicks, 68; Thielman, 152; Fee, 267; Bruce, 92; H.A.W. Meyer, 127; Vincent, 74; Houlden, 92; Collange, 116-117; Loh-Nida, 78; Hawthorne, 109; Silva, 158; Melick, 117; Bockmuehl, 165.

[41] As Barth, 85; Collange, 117; Fee, 267-268 suggest.

[42] With Bruce, 92; Gnilka, 159; U.B. Müller, 126 against Jewett, 'Thanksgiving': 365; Fee, 268; Marshall, 69 who see here the falsely motivated proclaimers of 1:15-18a which is ruled out by the use of 'all' which includes the well-motivated brothers and sisters.

total commitment to the 'work of Christ' (2:30).[43] Similarly he cannot be referring to Luke, Aristarchus or Mark who appear to be no longer with him in Rome (Col 4:10, 14; Phm 24).[44] This leaves only a closer circle of those with him in his Roman imprisonment and who are available to travel to Philippi but will not do so. Perhaps he is referring to those who deserted him at his 'first defence' referring perhaps to his 'first imprisonment' (2 Tim 4:10).[45] Alternatively he possibly means, perhaps to some extent hyperbolically,[46] his close circle of co-workers or colleagues in Rome, who unlike Timothy, are not fully devoted to the work of the mission there.[47] Alternatively Paul does not want us to take the 'all' too literally perhaps speaking hyperbolically about the general problem of humanity not placing God's purposes first.

Whatever Paul means exactly, Timothy stands alone in some sense among Paul's colleagues as being of the same mind as Paul, totally concerned for the mission and the churches; above all, self-interest. He then stands with Epaphroditus as an example to be followed. Rhetorically he exemplifies the previous appeals for unity and oneness in mindset and mission. In particular he epitomises his call for the Philippians to stand firm as one person (μιᾷ ψυχη) in 1:27 and be 'like-minded' (σύμψυχοι) (cf. 1:15-18a; 2:14; 4:3).[48] In other words, 'be like Timothy!'[49] The unity of Timothy and Paul in the mission is illustrative of his desire for such oneness between the Philippian Christians and his mission. The emphasis in Philippians is not on unity with Paul but on *unity together* contending for the faith of the gospel.

Thirdly, Timothy's genuine (γνησίως)[50] interest in the welfare of the

---

[43] Silva, 157.

[44] Hendriksen, 135; O'Brien, 321. J.J. Müller, 98.

[45] Such as Demas; so Hendriksen, 135; Wicks, 68; Bockmuehl, 166.

[46] Collange, 117; Silva, 153-154; Bloomquist, *Function*, 175; Vincent, 74; Plummer, *Understanding,* 58; Michael, 115; Marshall, 69 suggest hyperbole here. This is possible but Paul could be speaking literally here (assuming Pauline authorship, see Assumptions Chapter One). Again it is unlikely the issue is enhancing Timothy's authority here (so Collange, 117) which appears redundant.

[47] Beare, 97; Michael, 116; Wicks, 68; Hendriksen, 135; J.J. Müller, 98; Moule, 51; Bruce, 92; Houlden, 92; Thielman, 152; Kent, 132; O'Brien, 321; Gnilka, 159; Ollrog, *Paulus*, 193-200. Fee, 268 rules this out on the basis of 4:21. However 4:21 is merely a greeting and lacks any detail concerning these people. If he is correct then it is unclear who Paul has in mind as Hawthorne, *Philippians*, 110-111; Vincent, 74 suggest. Martin, 129-130 may be right in suggesting that this is an aside concerning the self-centredness of the world and is not to be taken literally. Again meaning does not affect my conclusion.

[48] Bloomquist, *Function*, 173-174; Black, 'Structure': 39.

[49] Silva, 157 cf. U.B. Müller, 126.

[50] Collange, 117; Bruce, 94; Hawthorne, 110 suggest here the original meaning of 'legitimate', Timothy the legitimate child is applicable. Fee, 266 suggests this is far-

Philippians speaks rhetorically into the Philippian's situation.[51] He, unlike so many who are motivated (ζητοῦσιν) with self-interest (ἑαυτῶν), is motivated by the interests of Jesus Christ (2:20). This description of Timothy builds on the other examples in the epistle to date including the fellowship in the gospel of the selfless Philippians (1:5-7), Paul's selfless commitment to the mission (1:5-7, 12-14, 22), the selfless/selfish Roman Christians (1:15-18) and supremely the selfless Lord Jesus Christ (2:5-8).[52]

His reference to Timothy's attitude is directed to some in Philippi where the mission of the Philippians appears to have become threatened by selfish ambition, vain conceit and self-interest (2:3-4).[53] Timothy, along with Epaphroditus, in their working with Paul and others in evangelism, demonstrates the sort of unity Paul wants from the Philippians. Timothy then is another excellent example to the Philippians of the right attitude. Similarly, Paul himself has illustrated this attitude in placing the gospel above his own personal interests (1:12-18a) and in his preparedness to send Timothy and Epaphroditus back. The true Christian then should be concerned at all costs with the interests of Jesus Christ (2:21).[54] That these interests include evangelism is not only implicit here but as I will discuss below, is explicit in 2:22. Rhetorically all this implies Paul's desire for a similar interest in Philippi, reinforcing my earlier assessments.

Fourthly, and most importantly for this study, Paul reminds the Philippians that τὴν δὲ δοκιμὴν αὐτοῦ γινώσκετε, ὅτι ὡς πατρὶ τέκνον σὺν ἐμοὶ ἐδούλευσεν εἰς τὸ εὐαγγέλιον (v22). Paul here uses the verb δοκιμή which carries two senses. On the one hand, it can mean 'the quality of being approved' and so, 'character.'[55] That is, a character that has been proved in trial (Rom 5:4; 2 Cor 9:13). Alternatively, it can suggest a 'test, ordeal', which proves or shows one is approved (2 Cor 2:9; 8:2; 13:3). Here in 2:22 the first sense is found, Timothy having proved himself through the trials of serving in the gospel.[56] This brings suffering into the realm of Timothy's experience; he is proven through suffering.

---

fetched for the adverb unlike the adjective (1 Tim 1:2; Tit 1:4) cf. Michael, 115; Melick, 118.

[51] The verb μεριμάνω here is in a positive sense denoting being concerned for another's welfare (1 Cor 7:32-34; 12:25). Here in the future emphasising the aid Timothy will give when coming to Philippi (H.A.W. Meyer, 127; Bruce, 94; O'Brien, 319). While this indicates present and ongoing concern this should be understood as future as Fee, 266 suggests. There is no need to translate it in the present to keep the modern reader happy, as Silva, 158; O'Brien, 319 suggest.

[52] Silva, 157; Bloomquist, *Function*, 174.

[53] Fee, 268.

[54] Bloomquist, *Function*, 174; Black, 'Structure': 39 correctly note the connection of ἰσόψυχον to ἴσα in 2:6.

[55] *BDAG*, 256; O'Brien, 323.

[56] Fee, 268; Bockmuehl, 166.

Paul applies the term to suffering (Rom 5:4; 2 Cor 8:2), to proving oneself through material generosity (2 Cor 9:13) and to his own proclamation ministry (2 Cor 13:3).[57] Consequently, it is a term he particularly applies to mission, and especially 'proving' through the trials that mission brings. Timothy's trustworthiness in evangelistic mission is well known to the Philippians (γινώσκετε) through seeing Timothy in action (Acts 16:11-40; 18:5; 19:22), and through hearing reports of Timothy's work for the gospel from Paul and others.

The manner in which Timothy has proved himself is found in his service with Paul for the cause of the gospel (σὺν ἐμοὶ ἐδούλευσεν εἰς τὸ εὐαγγέλιον). Δουλεύω here is used figuratively of advancing the cause of the gospel.[58] Combined with Timothy's concern for seeking the good of others, here Timothy is subordinating his own interests for those of the gospel-mission.[59] Thus he is like Christ, continuing his mission in serving in the context of evangelistic mission (2:7 cf. 1:1). This service includes not only the Philippian evangelisation, but also his continuous involvement in mission since joining the Pauline team.[60]

Paul's positivity to Timothy is seen throughout Paul and Acts. According to Acts, initially Paul chose the half-Greek young man to travel with him on the basis of his obvious potential expressed by the believers in Lystra and Iconium (Acts 16:1-3 cf. 2 Tim 3:15).[61] Clearly this potential was realised as Timothy travelled with Paul from Lystra on Paul's second missionary journey (Acts 16:1-3, 16; 17:14, 15; 18:5; 19:22; 20:4; Rom 16:21; 1 Cor 4:17; 16:10; 2 Cor 1:1, 19; Phil 1:1; 2:19, 22; Col 1:1; 1 Thess 1:1; 3:2, 6; 2 Thess 1:1; 1 Tim 1:2, 18; 6:20; 2 Tim 1:2; Phm 1).

Paul's relationship with Timothy was extremely close then and he clearly held Timothy in the highest esteem. This is seen in his description of Timothy as his beloved and faithful child (1 Cor 4:17: μου τέκνον ἀγαπητὸν καὶ πιστόν ἐν κυρίῳ), as his 'true child in the faith' (1 Tim 1:1), as 'my child' (1 Tim 1:18) and as his 'dear child' (2 Tim 1:2). It is also seen in his trust in Timothy as his representative to work on his behalf (1 Thess 3:2, 6; Acts 19:22), teach on his behalf (1 Cor 4:17; 16:10; Acts 17:14; 19:22), to carry out

---

[57] The noun δοκιμήν also used of: 1) The Corinthians standing the test of obedience in terms of church discipline (2 Cor 2:9); 2) Of the Corinthians testing Paul to see if his speech is from Christ (2 Cor 13:3).

[58] O'Brien, 325. See further in his analysis on its range of applications in Paul cf. Schenk, 232.

[59] O'Brien, 'Gospel': 227.

[60] The aorist ἐδούλευσεν should not be limited as Schenk, 325; O'Brien, 325 emphasise.

[61] Hendriksen, 134. Marshall, *Acts*, 259 notes that Iconium was 31km away from Lystra. This suggests Timothy had a significant sphere of influence.

menial tasks (Acts 18:5),[62] to travel as Paul's aide (Rom 16:21; Acts 20:4), to co-send/write letters (2 Cor 1:1; 1 Thess 1:1; 2 Thess 1:1; Phil 1:1; Col 1:1; Phm 1) and prepare for Paul's visits (Acts 19:22; 20:4), to care for Paul's churches (1 Thess 3:2, 6; 1 Tim 1:1f; 2 Tim 1:1f) and to preach and evangelise (2 Cor 1:19; Acts 17:14; 19:22; 2 Tim 4:1-5). In other words he was trusted to carry out the full range of ministry in Paul's place (2 Tim 3:10-4:5). As in this case, Timothy was often sent by Paul to churches to strengthen and encourage the congregation (1 Thess 3:1-5; 1 Cor 4:17; 16:10-11).

Paul's designation of Timothy as τέκνον,[63] suggests that in God's service Paul and Timothy worked as father and son (ὡς πατρὶ τέκνον). Here Paul employs the concept of spiritual parenthood, derived from Judaism and the OT and which he utilises throughout his epistles.[64] In the OT, the concept of spiritual fatherhood is applied to Elijah by Elisha (2 Kgs 2:12). In Judaism it was customary for a rabbi to call his disciple 'my son.'[65] In the Talmud this was extended to the notion of begetting, the student being in a sense begotten by the teacher.[66] Rengstorf notes that the winning of a Jew to the Jewish faith was likened to the creative work of God and fulfilled the injunction to be fruitful and multiply.[67] In the mystery religions the *mystagogue* was considered the initiate's father.[68]

Paul takes up this idea and on occasions applies this to individuals including Timothy, Titus (Tit 1:4) and importantly his congregations (1 Cor 4:15; cf. Gal 4:19). In Timothy's case he was not Paul's convert, but the imagery applies to their deep and intimate relationship.[69] As Fee notes, the image goes further than mere relationship into the nature of the relationship. The concept picks up the notion of family life in the Graeco-Roman world.[70] As a son in Paul's world worked alongside the *paterfamilias*, learning the father's trade and doing the father's business, so Timothy worked alongside Paul in preaching the gospel,

---

[62] The language implies that Paul was able to be more completely devoted to proclamation at the coming of Timothy and Silas indicating that they fulfilled some of the other tasks, perhaps including providing an income through delivery of the Philippian gift (Phil 4:14-15 cf. 2 Cor 11:8-9) and arguably through their own work (cf. 18:3; 1 Cor 9:12, 15; 2 Cor 11:9). Dunn, *Acts*, 242 notes 'possibly the larger team allowed a greater balance between work and ministry.'

[63] Fee, *Philippians*, 268 notes τέκνον emphasises the relationship over against υἱός which emphasises the status of 'sonship' itself.

[64] O'Brien, *Philippians*, 324; B. Holmberg, *Paul and Power. The Structure of Authority in the Primitive Church as Reflected in the Pauline Epistles*. CBNT 11 (Lund: Gleerup, 1978), 79-81.

[65] O'Brien, 324.

[66] *B. Sanh.* 99b; cf. Str-B 3, 340-341. See further in *TDNT* 1.665-66.

[67] *TDNT* 1.666-667.

[68] O'Brien, 324.

[69] O'Brien, 325.

[70] Fee, 269; Caird, 129; Hawthorne, 111.

founding churches, pastoring the fledgling communities. Essentially this leads into Paul's concept of imitation (3:17; 4:9). As elsewhere imitation is linked to Paul's relationship to his churches as parent, the churches being Paul's children (1 Cor 4:16 cf. 11:1; Eph 5:1; Phil 3:17; 4:9; 1 Thess 1:6; 2:7, 14). Although the notion of his converts as Paul's children is not explicitly found in Philippians, it is sufficiently prevalent in other Pauline letters to suggest it was an idiom Paul used generally to define the lifestyle of his converts.

Timothy then is the ideal child, who has been tested in the suffering for the service of the gospel and has stood firm in the ordeal.[71] Rhetorically this speaks directly into the Philippian situation. They are also 'children' and are being tested for the very same reason, struggling for the cause of the gospel in the face of persecution from opponents in pagan Philippi (1:30 cf. 3:17; 4:9). Timothy functions as a positive example to them of what Paul expects from them, his children.

Specifically, *they are to imitate his concern for the interests of Christ (v21) and the gospel (v22).* An essential element of this is to persevere in their evangelistic mission to the pagan community in unity, lifestyle, deed and word (1:27; 2:14-16). They are to discern what really matters which are the interests of Christ including the voluntary submission of every person in their city and region to Christ (2:9-11).[72] They are to imitate Timothy's submission to Paul as Christ's emissary and obey the letter and get their lives and mission in order. Rather than slip into self-interest they are to persevere in their mission, finding unity afresh and renouncing any movement toward factionalism, retreatism or anti-Paulinism. They are to emulate the sonship of Timothy by continuing the gospel mission, realising that the suffering that has come is providential and proof of their salvation.

In light of this analysis, I consider it would be surprising if evangelism was not an element in Paul's thinking here. Certainly in each individual Christian their expression of their evangelistic attitude will be different dependent on spiritual gifts. This is indeed evidenced in the context itself by the different way in which Timothy, Epaphroditus and Paul express their ministries. However, I consider it likely that here Paul is giving an implicit rhetorical appeal for evangelism. It is precisely at this point that the Philippians were flagging; rather they are to unite and contend for the faith of the gospel in a fresh united way. Building on the previous passage (2:15-16) then, this gives grounds to dispute those arguing for a centripetal understanding of the churches role in evangelism in Paul.

The Positive Example of the 'Apostle' Epaphroditus (2:25-30)

In v23 Paul expresses his hope (ἐλπίζω) to send Timothy to Philippi once he

[71] Hendriksen, 136.

[72] See the discussion on the *hina* clause in Appendix 3.

sees how things turn out for him in Rome. After expressing his confidence that he himself will ultimately visit Philippi (2:24), Paul then turns to the second example, Epaphroditus. The passage takes the form of a commendation not uncommon at the time. It is generally felt that Epaphroditus is the bearer of the letter.[73]

The details, which appear straightforward, have raised a number of questions concerning the status of Epaphroditus.[74] Some suggest that Epaphroditus is involved in the aforementioned tensions in the community.[75] Others suggest that Paul is making an apology for Epaphroditus returning home earlier than expected instead of remaining with Paul to minister to his needs or perhaps because he failed in some way, hence Paul's apologetic in anticipation of criticism in Philippi.[76] Alternatively Rahjten suggests that 'Epaphroditus had already returned home and had been received with coolness if not with hostility.'[77]

Such views are surprising, unnecessary and unsupported. Surprising in that they reflect an overly negative interpretation of clearly positive comments in Paul concerning others.[78] Unnecessary in that Paul's words are easily explainable in regard to the content and rhetoric of the letter. That is, Paul is sending home a local hero and seeking to encourage the Philippians under pressure. Accordingly, his selection of detail concerning Epaphroditus speaks into this desire aptly. Unsupported in that there is no evidence that Epaphroditus was involved in the problem in Philippi in any sense whatsoever. Not only so, but this approach seems to badly overplay the problem at Philippi which appears not to be fully blown as such views seem to assume.[79]

Moreover there is also no evidence to support the assumption that Epaphroditus was to stay in Rome until Paul's situation was resolved.[80] Neither

---

[73] O'Brien, 330; Fee, 272-273; Bockmuehl, 169; Hawthorne, 115.

[74] Meaning 'honoured by Aphrodite', now a Christian. As most commentators suggest, not to be aligned with Epaphras (Col 1:7; 4:12). He is possibly from a family closely aligned with the cult of Aphrodite; so Schenk, 237.

[75] Silva, 160; O'Brien, 341.

[76] Michael, 118-119 who argues that bringing the gift was only part of the role of Epaphroditus, he was to stay with Paul as long as he had need of him. Similarly Marshall, 70 who sees here a change of plans cf. Thielman, 153; O'Brien, 333; Craddock, 51. Gnilka, 161; Kent, 136; Hawthorne, 119; Silva, 160-161.

[77] Rahjten, 'Letters': 169 assuming that he had already left Rome. See also C. O. Buchanan, 'Epaphroditus': 157-166. Fee, 274 however, notes that 2:29 defeats this view. The aorist ἡγησάμην should be understood as epistolary as O'Brien, 330; Fee, 274.

[78] On this see Fee, 273 where he notes the novelty of taking Paul's words at face value among contemporary scholars.

[79] Fee, 273.

[80] Interestingly if Michael, 119 is right in saying that Epaphroditus was to stay with Paul 'as long as he had need of him', then this is precisely what happened. Paul sent him back

is there substantiation in the text to suggest that Epaphroditus has failed in his mission in any way. Paul's commendation here and in 4:18 suggest to the contrary that Epaphroditus is to be admired and respected for his service. Paul here then is praising the Philippian church not apologising for any failure.[81] As Fee says, 'such approaches read far too much into very little.'[82] While Paul wants to keep Timothy with him and 'hopes' to send him later when his situation is resolved, in 2:25 Paul considered it 'necessary' (ἀναγκαῖος) to send back to Philippi Epaphroditus.[83] Paul's high regard for Epaphroditus is seen in his five-fold description of him as his 'brother', 'co-worker' and 'fellow-soldier', 'your apostle' and 'minister of my needs.'

Paul then gives his first reason for sending Epaphroditus home (2:26).[84] Namely, that he is concerned for Epaphroditus on two connected counts. First, that Epaphroditus 'longs' for his people the Philippians (ἐπιποθῶν ἦν πάντας ὑμᾶς).[85] Secondly, Paul writes that Epaphroditus is distressed (ἀδημονῶν) concerning the Philippians because they have heard that he was ill.[86] In Phil 2:27 Paul expands with details concerning the extent of Epaphroditus illness. Most importantly that he nearly died (παραπλήσιον θανάτῳ). However, God in his mercy, spared him; Epaphroditus recovering from his near-death experience.[87] In-so-doing, God was also merciful to Paul, sparing him 'sorrow upon sorrow' (ἵνα μὴ λύπην ἐπὶ λύπην σχω). As in the case of Paul himself, Timothy and Christ, here in Epaphroditus the motif of suffering is found. If it can be shown that Epaphroditus was evangelistic, then suffering is again linked to evangelistic mission, further encouraging the Philippians to persevere in the context of their own challenges.

---

when he no longer had need of him! On reflection, this unsupported assumption is given far too much credibility.

[81] Similarly Bockmuehl, 169.

[82] Fee, 273 who correctly writes 'the letter pours forth affection at every point.' See also Bockmuehl, 169.

[83] An epistolary aorist; so O'Brien, 330; Bockmuehl, 169; Hawthorne, 115; Bruce, 99; Martin, 133; Silva, 161; Lightfoot, 122 among many others. Not pointing to an apologetic but in contrast to Timothy coming later; so Fee, 274.

[84] No evidence exists to suppose that he was sent back because of persecution or as a substitute for Timothy who was delayed (Gnilka, 161). Hawthorne, 115 adds the possible reason that Paul and Timothy could not travel themselves.

[85] The insertion of ἰδεῖν after ὑμᾶς is probably secondary cf. Metzger, *Commentary*, 613-614; Fee. 271 esp. note 271.

[86] For the deep intensity of the terms see Hawthorne, 117.

[87] Whether 'naturally', or through the spiritual gift of healing as Fee, 279 suggests (1 Cor 12:9, 28, 30).

For these reasons (οὖν) Paul explains in 2:28 his second reason for sending him back: so that the Philippians may again 'rejoice' (πάλιν χαρῆτε),[88] and Paul himself may have less anxiety (ἀλυπότερος). Finally, in 2:29 he urges the Philippians to receive (προσδέχεσθε) Epaphroditus 'in the Lord with great joy' (ἐν κυρίῳ μετὰ πάσης χαρᾶς), and hold people such as Epaphroditus with honour (καὶ τοὺς τοιούτους ἐντίμους ἔχετε). The reason they should do so is expressed in 2:30: 'because (ὅτι) he almost died for the work of Christ (διὰ τὸ ἔργον Χριστου), risking his life to make up for the help you could not give me.'

As in the case of Timothy, Epaphroditus is presented as *a living example of Paul's desire that the Philippians live as citizens worthy of the gospel of Christ.*[89] He embodies what it means to serve and suffer as one holds forth the gospel. What is mentioned here is consistent with what Paul says about co-workers elsewhere and is specifically detailed to speak into the current situation.[90] As O'Brien puts it, Paul presents Epaphroditus, 'to give a further godly example of the way the Philippians should imitate Christ.'[91]

Evangelism and the Five-Fold Appellation Concerning Epaphroditus

Paul defines Epaphroditus as 'my brother' (τὸν ἀδελφὸν ...μου), 'my fellow worker' (συνεργὸν...μου), 'my fellow-soldier' (συστρατιώτην μου),[92] 'your apostle' (ἀπόστολον ὑμῶν) and 'minister of my needs sent from you' (λειτουργὸν τῆς χρείας μου, πέμψαι πρὸς ὑμᾶς).[93] As he does elsewhere, Paul piles up these terms to intensely state the depth of his love and regard for Epaphroditus (cf. 1 Thess 3:2; 1 Cor 4:17; Rom 16:1; Col 4:7; Eph 6:21).[94] Each of these epithets carries significance for this discussion.

---

[88] Or perhaps 'see him again and rejoice.' While commentators are divided it is not hugely important to this discussion. They are to welcome him 'wholeheartedly'; so Hawthorne, 119.

[89] Fee, 273-274; O'Brien, 329 and 'Models': 278; Hawthorne, 114; Bloomquist, *Function*, 175; Motyer, 143; Thielman, 155; Watson, 'Analysis': 71-72; Black, 'Structure': 39; Witherington, *Friendship*, 18-19; Culpepper, 'Co-workers': 357; Garland, 'Defense': 163.

[90] Ollrog, *Paulus*, 190-193 who notes that Paul describes his co-workers in terms of: 1) their work in Christ; 2) their esteem and honour in a specific context; 3) their close relationship to Paul; 4) their importance to the church (cf. Rom 16:3-4). Paul mentions only that which is applicable to the recipients context.

[91] O'Brien, 329.

[92] Ἀδελφόν, συνεργόν and συστρατιώτην are all governed by μου demonstrating deep attachment, as O'Brien, 330 notes.

[93] The first three nouns are used in Philemon 1-2 but not to one individual.

[94] As Fee, 275 notes, not necessarily in any sense of ascending order contra-Hendriksen, 139; Lightfoot, 123; Plummer, *Understanding*, 61. Fee also notes that the loading of terms also counts against seeing ulterior motives in this context.

BROTHER (αδελφός)

The first of these I have examined in some detail above in my discussion of the Roman 'brothers' in 1:14.[95] There I argued that the term on the whole refers to fellow-Christians adopted into the family of God as his children.[96] Therefore, it is a term of intimacy and speaks of 'Paul's close personal relation with and affection for him as a believer.'[97] Ellis and others consider that 'brother' here carries the sense of gospel co-worker.[98] However, this is not certain as it raises the question of why Paul would double up with the two parallel terms 'brother' and 'co-worker'? For that reason, it is most likely that 'brother' here is not precisely co-terminus with 'co-worker', and the emphasis may be on their closeness in Christ rather than their shared ministry.[99] If however, 'brother' is best understood in its technical sense, it supports seeing Epaphroditus as a gospel preacher.

CO-WORKER (συνεργός)

The second expression 'co-worker' (συνεργός) here and elsewhere is generally agreed to be a technical term for those who are set apart for missionary preaching and ministry.[100] It is worth pausing to assess the merits of this axiom of contemporary scholarship.

At one level, Paul speaks of co-workers in two senses. First there are those who are '*my/our* co-workers.' These include Prisca and Aquila, (Rom 16:3), Urbanus (Rom 16:9), Timothy (Rom 16:21), Titus (2 Cor 8:23), Euodia, Syntyche, Clement and another unspecified group in Philippi (Phil 4:3), Mark (Col 4:11; Phm 24), Justus (Col 4:11), Aristarchus (Col 4:11; Phm 24), Philemon (Phm 1), Demas (Phm 24), Luke (Phm 24), Epaphroditus (Phil 2:22) and possibly the Corinthian church (2 Cor 1:24 [see below]). On other occasions he speaks of *God's* co-workers. He includes in this Paul himself, Apollos, Peter (1 Cor 3:9) and Timothy (1 Thess 3:2).

Not all references clearly indicate proclamation from these people, which raises the question of whether proclamation is implied here. To decide this

---

95 See Chapter 3.

96 Hawthorne, 116; Martin, 133 take it to mean 'fellow-Christian.' It is certainly not a redundancy or merely because he is a man, as suggests Schenk, 236.

97 O'Brien, 330; Bockmuehl, 169; Kent, 134; Hendriksen, 139; Thielman, 154; U.B. Müller, 130.

98 Ellis, 'Co-Workers', 13-18; Marshall, 71 see here co-worker.

99 Fee, 275. See also O'Brien, 330; Michael, 120; *TDNT* 7.742; Collange, 119-120.

100 Ollrog, *Paulus*, 193-200; *TDNT* 7.873 in a broader sense than just preaching; *BDAG*, 969; Dickson, *Mission-Commitment*, 141; Fee, 275; O'Brien, 331; Bockmuehl, 170; Murray, 'Witness': 323; Hawthorne, 116; Kent, 134; Hendriksen, 139; Thielman, 154; Schenk, 237; U.B. Müller, 130. This has been called into question by Peterlin, *Letter*, 118-123 who argues that συνεργός has a broader range including compatibility with the diaconate and in Philippians refers to Christian leaders within the church.

requires an analysis of Paul's use of the terms συνεργός and ἔργον. I note first that there are a significant number of references to συνεργός which do indicate proclamation.

Clearly in the case of Timothy and Titus, these two are proclaimers. Timothy's involvement in the proclamation of the gospel is without doubt. In 1 Thess 3:2 his role is outlined, for it is said that he is 'our brother and God's fellow worker *in the gospel of Christ*.'[101] The Greek convert Titus is defined as 'co-worker' and a partner (κοινωνός) (2 Cor 8:23). His ministry involved travelling with or meeting up with Paul (Gal 2:1-3; 2 Cor 2:13; 7:6, 13, 14; 2 Tim 4:10) and involvement in the Jerusalem collection (2 Cor 8:6, 17; 12:18). As with Timothy, Titus is described as a 'true son' (Tit 1:4) who is involved in pastoral ministry in Crete, appointing elders (Tit 1:5), dealing with false teaching (Tit 1:11, 13), teaching sound doctrine (Tit 2:1) and reminding the Christians of right living (Tit 3:1-2). From this it is clear that Titus was involved in proclamatory ministry, both pastoral and evangelistic.

All those described as 'God's co-workers' including Timothy (1 Thess 3:6) are proclaimers. In 1 Cor 3:9 Paul refers to God's co-workers rather than his own.[102] These co-workers include from the context Paul, Apollos and Peter (3:4, 5, 22) and not directly the congregation.[103] In Phil 4:3 two women Euodia and Syntyche, Clement and another unspecified group are termed συνεργῶν μου. It is probable that Epaphroditus is to be included in this group. If so, then alongside Euodia, Clement and Syntyche, he struggled with Paul for the gospel mission.[104] As I will argue in more depth later in Chapter 7, it is most likely that this included evangelism. This is particularly due to Paul's use of the active athletic metaphor συναθλέω combined with εὐαγγέλιον. Notably εὐαγγέλιον is most often used in the active sense in Philippians (1:5, 12, 14, 15, 16, 17, 18, 27b; 2:16, 22; 4:15).

Prisca and Aquila, both Jews, are described as co-workers (Rom 16:3). It is certain that this married couple were involved in proclamation although Paul himself never clearly says so. Their 'coworking' ministry included hosting churches in their homes both in Rome and Ephesus (Rom 16:5; 1 Cor 16:19). From Acts it is clear that their ministry at least included travelling with Paul (Acts 18:18) and teaching Apollos (Acts 18:26).[105] It seems their ministry was

---

[101] See the above discussion on Timothy. On the other realistically possible textual variants see Metzger, *Commentary*, 631. As they involve διάκονος and συνεργός they all clearly refer to proclamation of the gospel. For detail see Wanamaker, *Thessalonians*, 127-128.

[102] Fee, *1 Corinthians*, 134; Thiselton, *1 Corinthians*, 304; Barrett, *1 Corinthians*, 86; Hays, *1 Corinthians*, 53 who note this is a possessive genitive '*under* God' not '*with* God.'

[103] O'Brien, 331. However, the passage implies Paul's expectation that others will build on the foundation he has laid, including proclamation.

[104] Gnilka, 156; along with the others and perhaps Syzgos.

[105] Peterlin, *Letter*, 121.

pastoral but also involved evangelistic proclamation and some degree of itinerancy.[106]

Although there is little explicit detail, evidence from Paul and Acts give insight into the ministries of Mark (Col 4:10), Philemon (Phm 1), Aristarchus, Demas and Luke. Mark's involvement in proclamation is probable on Paul's first missionary journey and with Barnabas in his home island Cyprus after the schism with Paul (Acts 13:13; 15:37-39).[107] Paul's later commendation suggests he continued to persevere in mission. Philemon was the host to a house church (Phm 1). His ministry involves 'love for all the saints' suggesting a strongly pastoral dynamic (Phm 5), generosity (Phm 6), care for Paul (Phm 7, 17, 20, 22) and other itinerant Christians (Phm 24). It would appear then that his ministry was in the main localised. Peterlin limits this to pastoral care, generosity and church leadership.[108] However, I consider it to be likely that evangelism is a further component of his ministry, particularly in the fluid context of a fledgling, growing church, which was in all likelihood open to unbelievers (cf. 1 Cor 14:23-25).

A group of co-workers are travelling companions of Paul. Aristarchus of Thessalonica accompanied Paul on his collection journey and appeared to be in prison with Paul in Rome suggesting he may have been with Paul throughout (Col 4:10 cf. Phm 24; Acts 19:29; 20:4; 27:2).[109] Demas travelled with Paul and unfortunately deserted him in Rome, returning to Thessalonica (Phm 24 cf. Col 4:14; 2 Tim 4:10). Luke travelled extensively with Paul (Acts 16:10-17; 20:6-21:18; 27:1-28:16), wrote the account of Acts,[110] remained behind in some contexts (Acts 17:1-20:5) and is found with him in his Roman incarceration (Phm 24 cf. Col 4:14; 2 Tim 4:11). It is reasonable to assume that these individuals were involved to some extent in preaching and teaching.

Then there are those who are mentioned as co-workers without detail. These include Urbanus (Rom 16:9), Justus (Col 4:11) and Epaphroditus (Phil 2:25). In 2 Cor 1:24 it is possible that the Corinthian Christians are described as co-workers.[111] However, it is probable that this falls into the 'we/you' antithesis which characterises 2 Cor 1-7, Paul speaking of he and his cohorts as co-workers (συνεργοί ἐσμεν) over against the congregation (χαρᾶς ὑμῶν...

---

[106] As Barrett, *Acts*, 877 notes, 'they travelled widely.'

[107] See especially εἰς τὸ ἔργον μὴ in Acts 15:38 which implies evangelism as Barrett, *Acts*, 755 notes.

[108] Peterlin, *Letter*, 119 suggests his only ministry was hosting the church and providing hospitality. He then jumps from here to argue that co-worker 'is not limited to one kind of ministry, which is preaching/teaching.' While he may in fact be correct, he is assuming Philemon does not preach/teach, which is unclear in the context.

[109] Dunn, *Acts*, 337.

[110] See the introduction, assumptions.

[111] Fee, 275.

ἑστήκατε).[112] Furthermore even if 'we' here is inclusive as some suggest,[113] there is little in the context to suggest Corinthian proclamation is at issue.[114]

The associated ἔργον ('work' with a variety of nuances),[115] from which συνεργός is derived, often refers to the work of proclaiming the gospel (1 Cor 9:1 [Paul]; 16:10; 2 Tim 4:5 [Timothy] cf. 1 Cor 3:13; Phil 1:6; Eph 4:12; 1 Thess 5:13). This reinforces the probability that 'co-worker' is almost a technical term for people who proclaim the gospel.

That the term συνεργός indicates proclamation here in 2:25 and elsewhere seems then a realistic assumption in light of the detail concerning the individuals concerned; proclamation was more often than not, a part of their ministry. It is significant that among these proclaimers are a wide range of people including Gentiles, Jews, males and females. On that basis it is reasonable to suggest that within each congregation there were those who worked alongside Paul in their given context and *continued to do so after he had departed* as I will argue below (on 4:2-3).[116]

Ollrog then is most likely correct to hold that these co-workers are proclaiming missionaries.[117] He goes further maintaining that the co-workers are church delegates who continue the mission of Paul regionally. Hence this suggests three dynamics. First, that the co-workers were appointed in some way by local churches to continue Paul's (and God's) mission.[118] Secondly, they were localised regionally to continue the work in a given sphere e.g. Asia, Macedonia and Achaia.[119] Thirdly, that their focus was on continuing the mission of Christ in the region after Paul had left.[120] It is worth assessing whether these *formal dimensions* are demonstrable in Paul.

In the case of Prisca and Aquila this is unsustainable. The couple were tentmaking Jewish exiles from Rome who travelled to Corinth and with whom Paul stayed and worked (Acts 18:1-4). Clearly they teamed up with Paul and worked together in Corinth and then travelled to Ephesus (Acts 18:8). There is no evidence however that they travelled as *delegates of the Corinthian church*. They remained in Ephesus when Paul left, continuing the ministry that they and Paul had begun (Acts 18:19). Luke writes 'he left them behind' (κἀκείνους

---

[112] O'Brien, 331; Furnish, *2 Corinthians*, 139; Barnett, *2 Corinthians*, 115; Thrall, *2 Corinthians*, I.161: only Paul, Silvanus and Timothy.

[113] Martin, *2 Corinthians*, 34-35; Best, *Second Corinthians*, 20-21; Kruse, *2 Corinthians*, 78; Belleville, *2 Corinthians*, 70. It is feasible that here is given another glimpse of Paul's desire for the congregation to be involved but it is not at all clear.

[114] 3 Jn 8, the only other reference in the NT, almost certainly refers to a group who were proclaimers in that they 'work together for the truth.'

[115] *BDAG*, 390-391.

[116] See Chapter 7.

[117] Ollrog, *Paulus*, 125: they exercised 'all possible missionary functions.'

[118] Ollrog, *Paulus*, 120-121.

[119] Ollrog, *Paulus*, 123-124.

[120] Ollrog, *Paulus*, 123-125.

κατέλιπεν αὐτοῦ) suggesting Paul's leadership of the mission. The suggestion is that Paul went into the synagogue to preach (Acts 18:19). It seems that the converts formed a church which met in the home Prisca and Aquila established in Ephesus (1 Cor 16:19). At the time of the writing of Romans they have returned to Rome and either established, re-established or relocated a church in their own home (Rom 16:3; 2 Tim 4:19). This suggests a certain independence from Paul. More likely then, they worked not as representatives of the church or of Paul, but as independent fellow gospel workers whom Paul recognised and teamed up with for mission in Corinth. They then travelled to Ephesus for a certain period of time.

A close look at Timothy again does not sustain Ollrog's perspective entirely. The initiative for taking him along appears to be Paul's (τοῦτον ἠθέλησεν ὁ Παῦλος [Acts 16:4]). Although he was well spoken of in the region, it is not clear that he was sent in any sense as a *formal representative* of the churches in the region. It would also seem that one dimension of his participation was educative, which Ollrog rules out.[121] His function appeared to be as a personal support for Paul and to carry out assigned missions on Paul's behalf when required. He was thus an extension of Paul's ministry.

Neither can it be proved that Apollos functioned in this manner (1 Cor 3:6). Unfortunately little detail of his conversion or call to ministry in Alexandria is given. Luke tells us that he received additional training in Christianity (τὴν ὁδὸν τοῦ κυρίου) from Prisca and Aquila in Ephesus and engaged in ministry including the synagogue.[122] However there is no evidence of *a church appointment or a geographical limitation*. Rather his ministry appears to be a Spirit-inspired proclamation ministry (Acts 18:25-26).[123] After further instruction from Prisca and Aquila (Acts 18:26) he left on mission to Corinth. His mission seems to have be self-initiated (βουλομένου δὲ αὐτοῦ διελθεῖν εἰς τὴν 'Αχαΐαν [Acts 18:27]). The role of the church ('brothers') was to encourage him to do so and supply him with commendation (cf. 2 Cor 3:1; Rom 16:1; Col 4:1) and *subsequent* authorisation. His mission to Achaia from Asia suggests a certain freedom of movement rather than a localised focus. There appears to be no direct relation to Paul in his mission although Paul accepts his work as of God, who through Apollos builds on the foundation he originally laid through Paul (1 Cor 3:6-7). The emphasis is not on Paul, church

---

[121] Ollrog, *Paulus*, 114-118.

[122] Barrett, *Acts*, 887-889. As Marshall, *Acts*, 303 notes, he may have picked up a garbled form of Christianity in Alexandria cf. Bruce, *Acts*, 359 n71; Dunn, *Acts*, 249.

[123] Taking the view that Apollos was a Christian despite the question over his theology of baptism cf. Acts 19:1-7. Taking ζέων τῷ πνεύματι as 'speaking by the fire of the Spirit' rather than 'burning zeal' (cf. *BDAG*, 426 [lit. 'hot in the Spirit']). On the possibility that Apollos had received the Spirit without water baptism see Marshall, *Acts*, 304; Bruce, *Acts*, 360 cf. Acts 10:44-48. It is likely that he was baptised by Prisca and Aquila and the detail omitted (see Barrett, *Acts*, 888-889).

appointment or geography but on God's work through Apollos and Paul; God's fellow workers. At the time of writing 1 Corinthians, Apollos is back in Ephesus refusing to respond to Paul's earnest appeal to travel with the Corinthian delegation back to Corinth (1 Cor 16:12). This points to a large degree of independence on the part of Apollos; he is his own man, led by God. This is confirmed in his reappearance in Crete in the early 60's (Tit 1:13).

Philemon appears to be localised in mission at the time of the writing of Philemon (Phm 1). He is perhaps the appointee of the church (or at least acceptable to them) in that he is its leader and patron. However, he could equally be Paul's delegate given responsibility for the church. In reality however, the manner of his appointment in regard to his co-worker status in Paul's mind is unclear as is the extent of his mission.[124]

There is no geographical limitation or church relationship specified in the case of the other mentioned co-workers including Mark, Aristarchus, Demas, Luke, Urbanus and Jesus/Justus (Rom 16:9; Col 4:11; Phm 24). It is probable that Mark originated in Jerusalem (Acts 12:12). He travelled with Paul and Barnabas briefly on the first journey (Acts 12:25; 13:5, 13), then with Barnabas to Crete after a fall out with Paul (Acts 15:37, 39) and is found in Rome at the time of Colossians (cf. 1 Pet 5:13; 2 Tim 4:11). It is difficult to identify any church appointment or geographical limitation here. Similarly Demas appears to be based in Rome in a non-Pauline church, and is designated co-worker in regard to working alongside Paul in mission (Col 4:14; Phm 24; 2 Tim 4:10).

Neither can it be shown that the co-workers of Phil 4:3 are church appointees and geographically limited in any way. Rather they are believers who have worked alongside Paul with no specifics given. This suggests some level of Pauline authorisation but beyond this it is difficult to read into their role any institutionalisation of their function.

In the case of Epaphroditus, while he is clearly authorised and appointed in some sense by the Philippian church ('your apostle and minister to my needs' [Phil 2:25]), the plural personal pronoun (ὑμῶν) is not attributed to his co-workership. Only in the Collection delegation is clear indication of church-appointed co-workers given (2 Cor 8:23). Clearly they had a specific function; namely, to deliver the collection.

In sum then, there is insufficient evidence of a formal church appointment nor regional limitation with regard to the co-workers of Paul. These people are converts of Paul who he has accepted as approved fellow workers through some undesignated process. Alternatively they are previously engaged evangelistic workers who have come into contact with Paul and have been accepted by him as legitimate workers with whom he is prepared to cooperate for the sake of the gospel. They have worked with him at varying stages of the

---

[124] The precise relationship of Philemon to the church in Colossae is also difficult to assess. He is probably from Colossae (cf. Col 4:9) where there is evidence of other churches (cf. Col 4:15 [Nympha's house]). See O'Brien, *Colossians and Philemon*, 248.

mission in different degrees and modes. Beyond this there is little evidence of an institutionalisation of the concept at all; rather the mode of their 'appointment' seems fluid and a thus a general designation of fellow workers in the mission.

In conclusion, it is likely that on the basis of this term συνεργός, that Epaphroditus was a proclaimer of the gospel from Philippi. He is probably one of the co-workers of 4:3 who toiled alongside Paul for the cause of the gospel in the initial evangelisation of Philippi.[125] As Dickson argues, he probably continued the work in Philippi.[126] Although his specified ministry is taking a gift to Paul for the Philippians as their messenger/Apostle (see below), his role should not be limited in this regard. He was probably chosen by the church because of his proven worth in gospel ministry, prior relationship of trust with Paul and the church and thus his suitability for the work. In addition, as I have suggested above, it possible that he (along with Timothy) is one of the well-motivated proclaimers in the Roman context (Phil 1:14-18a).[127]

FELLOW -SOLDIER (συστρατιώτης)

The third noun συστρατιώτης is highly appropriate to Paul's situation among the soldiers of Rome (1:13) and to Philippi as a community settled with Roman soldiers.[128] Συστρατιώτης originally designated soldiers who fought side by side.[129] A look at Paul's use of the notion indicates that it refers to an active role in mission.

The noun συστρατιώτης (Phil 2:25; Phm 2) and στρατεύω (1 Cor 9:7, 2 Cor 10:3-6; 1 Tim 1:18; 2 Tim 2:4-5) from which it is derived, always has some reference to gospel mission in Paul. Paul's liking for military metaphors includes use of στρατεύομαι, the middle of στρατεύω, which means 'carry out a (military) campaign; engage in military service, be a soldier.'[130]

On occasion it is used explicitly as a metaphor for evangelistic mission (1 Cor 9:7 cf. 2 Tim 2:4).[131] He also employs it to describe mission as war, although not in a human sense (2 Cor 10:3). Paul utilises the term when addressing Timothy, encouraging him to 'fight the good fight' i.e. to keep at the ministry he has been given by God (2 Tim 1:18). Correspondingly he is to 'endure hardship as a good soldier of Christ Jesus' without concern for 'civilian affairs.' Here Paul is encouraging him to continue to persevere in pleasing

---

[125] Hawthorne, 116 suggests he helped to plant the Philippian church; Martin, 133 possibly; O'Brien, 331; Bruce, 95 possibly; Moule, 52 possibly, Wicks, 69 possibly.
[126] Dickson, *Mission-Commitment*, 315-318.
[127] Dickson, *Mission-Commitment*, 315-318 cf. Bruce, 95 possibly.
[128] Fee, 275.
[129] O'Brien, 331; *BDAG*, 979. See for background *TDNT* 7.701-712.
[130] *EDNT*, 3:279.
[131] *BDAG*, 795: in our literature it is only only figuratively of those who devote themselves to the service of the gospel cf. D.G. Reid, 'Triumph' in *DPL*, 953.

Jesus his commanding officer despite the suffering that accompanies mission (2 Tim 2:3-4). That this involves evangelism is explicit in 2 Tim 4:1-5.

The compound συστρατιώτης ('fellow-soldier') used here of Epaphroditus is also applied to Archippus (Phm 2) who is instructed by Paul to 'pay careful attention to the ministry (διακονία) which he has received in the Lord, in order that he completes (πληρόω) it' (Col 4:17).[132] This undoubtedly refers to a specific ministry granted to Archippus by the Lord which could well be evangelism, although this is not clear.[133] Certainly the military image suggests engagement in conflict with opposition. The compound term 'fellow-soldier' implies a certain respect and admiration on Paul's part for these workers who endure hardship for the gospel. In the case of Epaphroditus, it is an honour forged in battling as a team for the cause of the gospel in Philippi in the face of persecuting opponents (4:2-3; 1:27-30).[134] Here then Epaphroditus is presented as '"a wounded comrade in arms", who is being sent home for rest.'[135]

In Appendix 1, 'The connection between evangelism and the military metaphor in Paul', I argue on the basis of Eph 6:15, 17 in connection with Eph 4:11-12, that Paul understood the leaders of the church to be in some senses akin to the military officers charged with leading the church as the 'army of Christ.' In that sense their role was to lead the war through discharging their ministry and through equipping the church for works of ministry i.e. training them to be soldiers for Christ in the widest sense and including being prepared and equipped to evangelise. Epaphroditus then, as Paul's co-soldier, probably carried the role of equipping the Philippian church to engage the unbelieving

---

[132] Διάκονος is applied to a wide range of ministries including government officials (Rom 13:4); Christ (Rom 15:8; Gal 2:17); Phoebe (Rom 16:1); Apollos, Paul and other ministers of the gospel (1 Cor 3:5; Eph 3:7); apostolic and gospel ministers (2 Cor 3:6; 6:4); false ministers of Satan (2 Cor 11:15); Christ, (not) a servant of sin (Gal 2:17); Tychicus (Eph 6:21; Col 4:7; 2 Tim 4:12). Διακονία is applied to the gospel ministry of Paul and others (Rom 11:13; 2 Cor 4:1; 5:17; 6:3; 11:8; 1 Tim 1:12; 2 Tim 4:5 cf. Acts 1:17; 12:25; 20:24; 21:19); to unspecified ministry in the Pauline church (Rom 12:7; 1 Cor 12:5; 16:5; Eph 4:12; Col 4:17); to the ministry of the Jerusalem Collection (Rom 15:31; 2 Cor 8:4; 9:1 cf. Acts 6:1; 11:29). As Barth, *Ephesians*, II.440 notes, this refers to 'the mutual assistance of church members in secular daily matters and the apostolic "service of the word" fulfilled for the benefit of believers and *unbelievers*' [italics mine]. Lincoln, *Ephesians*, 253 and others who adopt the first interpretation of 4:11 obviously take it in this sense.

[133] O'Brien, *Colossians*, 259. Garland, *Colossians*, 281 notes the similarity to 2 Tim 4:5. This is probably not connected to Onesimus or the collection (see Dunn, *Colossians*, 288). Wright, *Colossians*, 161 suggests a ministry of discipling young converts. Bruce, *Epistles*, 186 leaves it open; MacDonald, *Colossians*, 184 suggests dealing with false teaching.

[134] Michael, 120 from the perspective of Ephesus; Schenk, 237. Dickson, *Mission-Commitment*, 315 limits the term to meaning that they shared a 'common "battle".'

[135] Fee, 276. Similarly Kent, 134.

Philippian community. They were to be ready to preach and live the gospel with the sword of the Spirit, the word of God.[136]

APOSTLE (ἀπόστολος)

The fourth term 'apostle' (ἀπόστολος) is highly controversial.[137] My concern is not for its disputable origin but specifically what Paul means here.[138] There are two main possibilities.[139] First, that in using 'apostle' Paul is referring to Epaphroditus merely as one sent and as a *messenger/envoy* commissioned by the Philippians with a particular task, here delivering the gift to Paul.[140] Alternatively it can be argued that the term refers to Epaphroditus as an '*Apostle*' in some sense of carrying the recognised ministry of apostle.[141] If the latter is implied, here we have an example of a 'church-authorised' apostle ('your apostle') performing the spiritual ministry of apostleship with all that this entails.

Virtually all commentators assume the former for several reasons. First, the parallel with 2 Cor 8:23 where the Jerusalem Collection team made up of representatives of the churches are designated ἀπόστολοι ἐκκλησιῶν designating local church emissaries carrying out a specific task. Secondly, it is well known that the rendering of ἀπόστολος as 'messenger' is well attested. Thirdly, Paul may well intend ἀπόστολον καὶ λειτουργὸν τῆς χρείας μου

---

[136] See further Appendix 1, 'The connection between evangelism and the military metaphor in Paul.' Similarly of other soldiers named in Paul including Archippus (Phm 2; Col 4:17) and Timothy (2 Tim 2:3).

[137] It is generally agreed that the two personal pronouns μου and ὑμῶν are paired emphatically suggesting to some a disjunction between the way Epaphroditus was viewed by Paul and the Philippians. At the least this emphasises Paul's depth of feeling for Epaphroditus, as Hawthorne, 116 notes.

[138] See C.K. Barrett, 'Shaliah and Apostle,' in E. Bammel, C.K. Barrett and W.D. Davies (eds), *Donum Genilicium: New Testament Studies in Honour of David Daube* (Oxford: Clarendon Press, 1978), 88-102; J.A. Kirk, 'Apostleship since Rengstorf: Toward a Synthesis', *NTS* 21 (1975): 249-264; *TDNT* I. 407-447; F.H. Agnew, 'The Origin of the NT Apostle-Concept: a Review of Research', *JBL* 105/1 (1986): 75-96; P.W. Barnett, 'Apostle' in *DPL*, 45-51.

[139] Hawthorne, 116 sees here another possibility i.e. Paul emphasising equality between Paul and their 'apostle.'

[140] Most including Fee, 276; O'Brien, 332; Bockmuehl, 170; Beare, 98; Michael, 121; Bruce, 95; Martin, 133; Silva, 161; Lightfoot, 123; P.W. Barnett, 'Apostle' in *DPL*, 47; Wicks, 69; Barth, 87; *TDNT* 1.422; Collange, 120; J.J. Müller, 101; Motyer, 143; Kent, 134; Lightfoot, 123; Hendriksen, 139; Gnilka, 162; Schenk, 237.

[141] Marshall, 72 sees here a person commissioned directly by Jesus Christ and authorised by the congregation to take up missionary work. As Lightfoot, 196, 215 points out, Phil 1:1 and Polycarp rule out any likelihood of a 'Bishop' at this time in Philippi. However this does not any sense preclude the fluid charismatic ministry of '*Apostle*' functioning in the Pauline church cf. Eph 4:11.

to be understood as a hendiadys which reinforces interpreting 'apostleship' here in terms of a specific role.[142]

That being said, tentatively I posit that recognizing Epaphroditus as an Apostle in the more technical functional sense should not be ruled out for several reasons. First, as Dickson argues, the ἀπόστολοι ἐκκλησιῶν in 2 Cor 8:23 may well refer to 'authorised gospel heralds of the region of Macedonia.'[143] In support, he argues that by the writing of 2 Corinthians, ἀπόστολος was probably a technical term denoting 'one sent/commissioned' for the gospel (cf. 1 Cor 1:1; 4:9; 9:4-6; 15:7b; 12:28-29; 2 Cor 1:1 cf. 1 Thess 2:7).[144]

Secondly, the listing of 'apostle' at the head of the charismatic gift lists in 1 Cor 12:28-29 and Ephesians 4:11 may indicate that the notion of apostleship had become extended into a charismatic leadership function in the local Pauline church.[145] That is, along with the charismatically inspired roles of prophet, evangelist, pastor and teacher,[146] local 'apostles' with a foundational

---

[142] O'Brien, 331; Beare, 98; Marshall, 72; Lightfoot, 123; Caird, 129; Loh-Nida, 82; Bruce, 99; Michael, 121; Motyer, 143; Barth, 88. If so it does not affect the likelihood that 'apostle' means 'messenger.'

[143] Dickson, *Mission-Commitment*, 140. For detail see 116-121. See also C. Dorsey, 'Paul's Use of 'Αποστολος', *ResQ* 28.4 (1985-86): 193-200, 199.

[144] Dickson, *Mission-Commitment*, 139. So also Kirk, 'Apostleship': 262 who notes that 'the minimum definition of an apostle is he to whom the risen Lord has appeared to commission him for a special mission of proclamation and church planting. I have not been able to find a single passage in the entire Pauline corpus, whether among his generally accepted letters or disputed ones, where he makes a fundamental distinction between his apostleship and that of his co-workers.'

[145] The suggestion of Lightfoot, 196 (see also Fee, *1 Corinthians*, 620) that there is no parallel use of 'apostle' in this sense does not pay any regard to Eph 4:11 and assumes 2 Cor 8:23; Phil 2:25 uses suggest 'messenger' cf. Foulkes, *Ephesians*, 126 who suggests that Phil 2:25 can simply be ignored in this discussion, which I consider patently inadequate. In support of the suggestion that the apostleship has become a charismatic leadership function in the Pauline church I note: 1) The fact that apostles are included in the list at all in the context of the ministry of the local church (cf. 1 Cor 12:28-29; Eph 4:11); 2) That all the other functions are clearly localised suggesting 'apostle' probably is too; 3) The existence of 'apostles' beyond Paul and the 12; 4) That the appointee is God; 5) That no limitation is placed on the appointment of apostle except the gifting of the Spirit (cf. 1 Cor 12:3-6; Eph 4:11); 6) The mention of apostles from local churches (2 Cor 8:23; Phil 2:25). As Barth, *Ephesians*, II.437 notes, 'in 4:11 it is assumed that the church at all times needs the witness of "apostles" and "prophets". The author of this epistle did not anticipate that the inspired and enthusiastic ministry was to be absorbed by, and "disappear" into, offices and officers bare of the Holy Spirit and resentful of any reference to spiritual things.' While unprovable, this possibility should be taken much more seriously in contemporary scholarship.

[146] Alternatively, 'pastors who teach.' See further O'Brien, *Ephesians*, 297-298; Schnackenburg, *Ephesians*, 182.

role and call not unlike Paul, may have functioned in Pauline communities.[147] If so, then Epaphroditus could well be such a person.[148]

Thirdly, in that the office of apostle was clearly a controversial concept in the early church concerning Paul himself and others,[149] I find it highly unlikely that he would apply it loosely to others, opening up potential grounds for further misunderstanding. This is particularly so if he writes from Rome, as this is later in his ministry. Fourthly, the term is applied to other individuals outside the twelve and Paul[150] (Acts 14:4, 14 [Paul and Barnabas cf. 1 Cor 9:5-6];[151] Rom 16:7 [Andronicus and Junia];[152] 2 Cor 8:23; 11:5; 12:11, 12;[153] 1 Thess 2:6

---

[147] Christian prophets feature throughout the NT: see 1 Cor 12:27, 29; 14:29-32, 37; Eph 2:20; 3:5; 4:11 cf. Rom 12:6; 1 Cor 11:4-5; 12:10; 13:9; 14:1-4, 6, 24; 1 Thess 5:20; 1 Tim 1:18; 4:14; Acts 11:27; 13:1; 15:32; 21:10; Rev 11:10; 16:6; 18:20, 24; 22:6, 9. Evangelists are less prominent: see Eph 4:11; 2 Tim 4:5 cf. Acts 21:8. Similarly pastors (shepherds) are found infrequently: see Eph 4:11 cf. Matt 9:36; Mk 6:34; Jn 10:2. Teachers are mentioned more often: see Eph 4:11; 1 Cor 12:28; 1 Tim 2:7; 2 Tim 1:11; 4:3; Acts 13:1; Heb 5:12; Jas 3:1.

[148] Foulkes, *Ephesians*, 127 claim that the ministry of apostle and prophet ceased after the first generation is dubious historically, as Barth, *Ephesians*, 437 points out. While the designations may be debated, certainly the function of founding new Christian communities in virgin territory and bringing Spirit-inspired messages from God has continued, especially since the 18th century missionary movement and the 20th century Pentecostal and Charismatic movements. Lincoln, *Ephesians*, 249 maintains that the author of Ephesians sees these as past ministries with no real basis. If so, then the same applies to evangelist, pastor and teacher with the aorist tense of ἔδωκεν, which is clearly incorrect. Rather, the text concerns the present and future growth of the church.

[149] Evidence of the notion 'apostle' being controversial is inidicated in a number of texts including 1 Cor 4:9; 9:1-2; 15:9; 2 Cor 11:1-13; 12:12; Gal 1:1; Rev 2:2.

[150] Paul's apostolicity was clearly controversial suggesting there was opposition to the application to those beyond the twelve or to Paul himself (cf. 1 Cor 9:1-2).

[151] In Acts 14 the simplest explanation is that the apostles are Paul and Barnabas cf. Dorsey, 'Απόστολος', 199; Kirk, 'Apostleship': 264). If so this provides evidence of the shift from the initial eleven and Matthias (Acts 1:2, 26 = the eleven). All subsequent references in Acts refer to the twelve including Matthias (Acts 2:37-11:1; 15:2, 4, 6, 22, 23; 16:4). This shift is confirmed in that Barnabas is earlier explicitly described in contrast to the twelve (4:35-37), while here he is an apostle. I suggest he is an apostle of Christ through the Spirit and authorised/commissioned by the Antioch church (Acts 13:2-3). Similarly 1 Cor 9:5-6 so Kirk, 'Apostleship': 262. Others hold there was a wider group of apostles including Barnabas and others (cf. Marshall, *Acts*, 234). However at no point is this distinction made in the NT. Neither can it be proved Luke is using source material (cf. Bruce, *Acts*, 271 n.7).

[152] See on Junia above Chapter 3; they were probably a missionary apostolic couple.

[153] Taking τῶν ὑπερλίαν ἀποστόλων ... **τοιοῦτοι** ψευδαπόστολοι, ἐργάται δόλιοι, μετασχηματιζόμενοι εἰς ἀποστόλους Χριστοῦ as referring to the same people cf. Barnett, *2 Corinthians*, 523 who rightly argues that suggesting the 'superlative apostles' are the Jerusalem apostles while the 'false apostles' are other illegitimate preachers is artificial and unnecessary cf. Kruse, *2 Corinthians*, 48-50; Best, *2 Corinthians*, 104;

[Paul, Silas and Timothy cf. Acts 17:1-9];[154] cf. 1 Cor 4:9;[155] Gal 1:17[156]); and so applying it to Epaphroditus here is not necessarily incongruent. In addition I consider it unlikely that ἀπόστολον καὶ λειτουργὸν τῆς χρείας μου should be understood as a hendiadys.[157] Rather, I consider that 'your' (ὑμῶν) governs the two nouns.

Fourthly, it can be argued that his 'apostolicity' in this context is limited to his delivery of material support. However, it is noticeable that the NT notion of apostolicity involves a concern for the material care of others. This is seen of

---

Lambrecht, *2 Corinthians*, 175; Garland, *2 Corinthians*, 467-469; Belleville, *2 Corinthians*, 276; Furnish, *2 Corinthians*, 502-505; Thrall, *2 Corinthians*, 671-676. IF so then these are not the Jerusalem twelve but other rhetorically gifted Corinthian apostles (2 Cor 11:5-6) who are financially supported and gospel peddling rather than self-supporting (2:17; 11:7-9; 12:14-16); triumphalistic in contrast to Paul's weakness (11:21, 29; 12:7-10), Jewish (11:22-28) hyper-charismatic (12:1-4, 11-13) Corinthian 'apostles' (for a full discussion see Martin, *2 Corinthians*, 336-342 who prefers the twelve). Paul does not deny the possibility of their apostleship but critiques the content of their 'different Jesus, gospel' (11:4) which is effectively deceitful and Satanic (11:3, 13-15) which delegitimises their claim on the name cf. Rev 2:2.

[154] Leaving aside the complex ecclesiological issues related to apostolicity, the most straightforward explanation of the third person plural here is the co-senders Timothy and Silvanus from the initial evangelising team. See for this Richard, *Thessalonians*, 109; E. Best, 'Paul's apostolic authority', *JSNT* 27 (1986): 3-25, 4; Schnackenburg, 'Apostles', 294-295; Kirk, 'Apostleship': 264 n.1 cf. Best, *Thessalonians*, 100 who postulates the unlikely view that Paul's own apostolicity may not have been fully set at this point. Dorsey, 'Απόστολος', 199; Wanamaker, *Thessalonians*, 99 argues 'we' does not include Timothy but Silvanus who was probably an authentic apostle having witnessed the resurrection and, akin to Paul, had been commissioned by Christ (1 Cor 9:1, 2). Similarly Holmes, *Thessalonians*, 63 who admits this is not provable; Marshall, *Thessalonians*, 69-70 who does so to avoid admitting Timothy was an apostle! Bruce, *Thessalonians*, 31 to avoid this conclusion, softens 'apostle' to 'messenger', which is not appropriate for Paul. However, if 'apostolicity' was a disputed notion and term, Paul is decidedly lazy in his language at this point. Malherbe, *Thessalonians*, 86-89, 144 again to avoid the notion, argues 'we' is an epistolary plural. However the plural 'we' flows from the co-senders to this point (to 1 Thess 2:18) without break (εὐχαριστοῦμεν ...) and should be read as it is, just as ὑμῶν... refers to the whole Thessalonian church (τῇ ἐκκλησίᾳ Θεσσαλονικέων) and not some portion of it throughout.

[155] It is possible that Paul includes Apollos (so Kirk, 'Apostolos', 262; Fee, *1 Corinthians*, 714 n.47) and perhaps Timothy and Sosthenes among the apostles in 1 Cor 4:9 as the the most obvious reference in context to the third person plural (4:9, 17).

[156] The use of προ suggesting 'early, before' *BDAG*, 864 and opening up the possibility of more apostles 'after' Paul?

[157] Those not taking it as a hendiadys include Fee, 276; Hawthorne, 116; Kent, 134; Moule, 52; Hendriksen, 139; Thielman, 154. Consistency of interpretation would suggest that the first three should be taken in a similar manner i.e. 'my coworking warring brother', which I consider unlikely as it removes the power of the stand-alone terms which seems to be Paul's intention.

the Twelve in their ministry alongside the incarnate Christ.[158] Similarly, in the post-ascension Jerusalem church the apostles took responsibility for the distribution of material provision for those in need including widows.[159] Other traditionally 'apostolic' NT writings also continue this determination (esp. Jas 1:27-2:13; 1 Jn 3:16). Luke's Paul too, is concerned for the material needs of others as indicated by the delivery of the first collection from Antioch for the famine-stricken Jerusalem Christians (Acts 11:27-30). In Paul's letters the dominant example is the Jerusalem Collection (1 Cor 16:1-4; Rom 15:26-31; 2 Cor 8-9)[160] and Paul's appeal to Timothy to care for the widows in Ephesus (1 Tim 5).

Significant in this regard is the interpretation of Gal 2:10 ('all they asked is that I continue to remember the poor'). Most interpret this as an appeal from the Jerusalem apostles to Paul to continue to remember the 'Jerusalem poor' (cf. Rom 15:26).[161] However, I contend that the appeal should be taken in a broader

---

[158] See esp. the feeding miracles; Mk 6:30-44 esp. v37 and pars: 'you give them something to eat' cf. Mk 8:1-13 and pars. Similarly other general references make it clear that material provision of the needy is essential to Christian faith and apostolocity (see Matt 19:21; note that the rich ruler would then 'be perfect' [τέλειος] implying complete in terms of obedience to the law cf. Mk 10:21; Lk 18:22); Lk 12:33 ('Sell your possessions and give to the poor' [NIV]); Lk 14:13 ('But when you give a banquet, invite the *poor*, the crippled, the lame, the blind' [NIV] cf. Lk 14:21); Lk 19:8 (the example of Zacchaeus who gives half his possessions to the poor'); Mk 12:42-43 and pars.

[159] See Acts 2:44-45: ('All the believers were together and had everything in common. Selling their possessions and goods, they gave to anyone as he had need' [NIV]); Acts 4:32-37 and esp. v35 ('put it *at the apostles' feet* and it was distributed to anyone as he had need' cf. v37); 6:1-4. See also the example of Barnabas who cares for the poor (Acts 4:36; 11:30) and is called an 'apostle' by Luke in Acts 14:4.

[160] See also 1 Tim 5:3-10 and his concern for genuinely needy widows in the Ephesus community. Here Paul asks Timothy in terms of these widows to 'remembers the poor.'

[161] See for example Longenecker, *Galatians*, 59-61 who notes, 'All that can be said *with certainty* is that here in v 10 the Jewish Christians of Jerusalem are principally in view, as is true as well in Rom 15:26 (εἰς τοὺς πτωχοὺς τῶν ἁγίων τῶν ἐν 'Ιερουσαλήμ, 'for the poor among the saints in Jerusalem'). Probably πτωχοί here in 2:10 is a shortened form of the formula οἱ πτωχοὶ τῶν ἁγίων τῶν ἐν 'Ιερουσαλήμ as used in Rom 15:26, with the wording of that formula emanating from the Jerusalem church itself' (emphasis mine). This is far from certain for the reasons given above. See also Bruce, *Galatians*, 126; Timothy George, vol. 30, *Galatians*. NAC (Nashville: Broadman & Holman Publishers, 2001, c1994), 165; S. McKnight, 'Collection for the Saints' in *DPL*, 143; R.H. Stein, 'Jerusalem' in *DPL*, 472; Pheme Perkins, 'New Testament Ethics' in *ABD*, 2:664; J.B. Lightfoot, *St. Paul's Epistle to the Galatians. A Revised Text With Introduction, Notes, and Dissertations* (4th ed. London: Macmillan and Co., 1874), 110; D.C. Arichea and E.A. Nida, *A Handbook on Paul's Letter to the Galatians* (New York: United Bible Societies, 1993), 38; H.D.M. Spence-Jones, *The Pulpit Commentary: Galatians* (Bellingham, WA: Logos Research Systems, Inc., 2004), 78;

sense for these reasons.[162] First, there is no qualification in regards to the specifically Jerusalem poor in this context; rather 'the poor' (τῶν πτωχῶν)[163] here is general 'pertaining to being poor and destitute, implying a continuous state.'[164] Secondly, to connect it specifically to the Jerusalem poor requires defining it against τοὺς πτωχοὺς τῶν ἁγίων τῶν ἐν Ἰερουσαλήμ in Rom 15:26. This however, is exegetically assumptive; it being rather dubious to transfer a clause from Rom 15:26 written some eight to ten years subsequent![165] Even if we date Galatians later, it is tenuous to interpret 'the poor' in Galatians against Romans, a letter with a different purpose, content and setting. Certainly, Paul's Galatian readers would have been challenged to make this connection.

Thirdly, it also requires reading Acts 11:27-30 into Galatians 2:1-10. While I agree that these two visits should be seen as co-terminus and historically plausible,[166] I consider it tenuous exegesis at best to make this connection in that Paul in Galatians makes no reference to the collection. It is thus reductionist in a world in which poverty was a stark feature of everyday life to limit 2:10 to the poor in Jerusalem despite the possibility of a connection. Fifthly, it is assumptive to argue that the present tense of μνημονεύωμεν *necessarily* implies interpreting 2:10 against the 11:27-30 visit. While

---

Martyn, *Galatians*, 207, 222-228 who reconstructs the history in a highly ingenous, and may I say, speculative fashion; Schnabel, *Mission*, 998; Duncan, *Galatians*, 51; C.B. Cousar, *Galatians*. Interpretation (Atlanta: John Knox, 1982), 41; L.A. Jervis, *Galatians*. NIBC (Peabody: Hendrickson, 1999), 60; R.A. Cole, *Galatians*. TNTC (Grand Rapids: Eerdmans, 1984),70; H. Ridderbos, *Galatians*, 90-91; S.K. Williams, *Galatians*. ANTC (Nashville: Abingdon, 1997), 55; J. Ziesler, *The Epistle to the Galatians*. EC (London: Epworth, 1992), 17; G. Walter Hansen, *Galatians*. IVPNTCS (Leicester: IVP, 1994), 60-61; H.D. Betz, *Galatians. A Commentary of Paul's Letter to the Churches in Galatia*. Hermeneia (Philadelphia: Fortress, 1979), 102.

[162] See Dunn, *Galatians*, 112-113 who sees it generally but with specific reference to Gentile obligation to the poor in continuity with the covenant. See also L.A. Jervis, 'Collection for the Saints' in *ABD*, 1:1131, who cites this as one of possible interpretation without resolving the question. She wrongly states this is the view of E.W.D. Burton, *The Epistle to the Galatians*. ICC (Edinurgh: T&T. Clark, 1921), 99-100. Burton [99] takes it as the Jewish poor ('the poor among the Christians on the other side of the dividing line' i.e. Jews. T.D. Hanks, *ABD*, 5:418 notes that 'in Gal 2:10 "continuing to remember the destitute" ***(ptōchós)*** is viewed as a nonnegotiable element in Christian praxis.' L.Morris, *Galatians: Paul's Charter of Christian Freedom* (Leicester: IVP, 1996), 75-76.

[163] Dunn, *Galatians*, 112 notes that the poor are 'those lacking resources to maintain life even at subsistence level.'

[164] Louw-Nida, *Lexicon*, 1:563.

[165] As noted in 'Assumptions' in my General Introduction, I (with Longenecker, *Galatians*, lxxii-lxxxviii cf. Bruce, *Galatians*, 43-53) suggest Galatians to have been written *c.* 48-50 and Romans (with Moo, *Romans*, 2-3) *c.* 56-58. If one takes a later dating of Galatians these connections become less tenuous.

[166] See Longenecker, *Galatians*, lxii-lxxxiii esp. lxxx-lxxxiii.

continuing to remember can be to continue to specifically be concerned for the Judean or Jerusalem Christian poor, it could equally apply to Paul continuing to remember the poor in general terms with the first Jerusalem collection in Antioch as one example. Finally, that ἐσπούδασα ('I was eager') is singular in response to the plural μνημονεύωμεν suggests that it was an imperative Paul applied to himself and his own apostolic ministry.[167]

Thus, I suggest that it is better to regard this as a request that Paul continue the apostolic ministry of continuing to *remember the poor in general terms*; as indeed he has demonstrated in his bringing of the collection on this visit. The second Jerusalem collection then would be a concrete evidence of this general concern, rather than the limit of this concern. In this case it should be read akin to; 'in your apostolic ministry continue to remember the poor as you have remembered us in our time of need.'[168]

Interestingly, there is a parallel between the emphasis of this thesis (the question of a supposed 'silence' concerning congregational centrifugal evangelism) and Paul's silence on a general concern for the poor. I suggest that Gal 2:10 should be understood as pointing in the direction of a general concern for the poor in Paul. If this analysis is accurate, Epaphroditus in his concern for Paul in Rome on behalf of the Philippians is *doing the work of an apostle*, caring for the material needs of others.

Finally, I note that although the majority of commentators accept the non-technical interpretation of 'apostle' here, a number do so with a certain reserve. Schnabel for example suggests that the sum of the terms on 2:25 suggests that 'Epaphroditus was not merely a messenger who carried the Philippians' gift to Rome, but rather that he was actively involved in Paul's missionary activities. Epaphroditus was a co-worker in Paul's team of missionaries.'[169] Houlden too writes that 'it is going too far to say that in Paul's mind its use here was entirely non-technical whereas when he applied it to himself it always had, as it were, a capital 'A' and denoted a fully defined office which he shared with Peter and the rest.'[170] In my reckoning it is not clear where the technical and non-technical sense begins and ends.[171] On balance then, I suggest that Paul has the latter in mind for the above reasons. That is, 'Epaphroditus may be regarded as

---

[167] Schnabel, Mission, 988 notes that ἐσπούδασα can be taken as a pluperfect suggesting 'the very thing that I had been eager to do all along.'

[168] See also 2 Cor 8:14 where Paul gives a hint at this general concern in his hope that the Corinthians will help the Jerusalem Christians and subsequently when they are in need, will receive support from them in return if they are in need.

[169] Schnabel, *Mission*, 1434 cf. 1462.

[170] Houlden, 91; Hawthorne, 116 who suggests that Paul is emphasising equality between Paul and their 'apostle.' Fee, 276 who see here evidence that the term is functional before it became titular; Marshall, 72; Moule, 52 suggests 'more than *merely* a messenger may be implied' due to its sacredness in the early church.

[171] Houlden, 92.

an ἀπόστολος τῆς ἐν φιλίπποις ἐκκλησίας.'[172] It is possible too that he was sent from Philippi not only to provide for Paul's needs but as an apostle, to Paul in his evangelistic mission.[173]

Apostle in Ephesians 4:11-16

On the basis of Eph 4:11-16 I suggest his role as an apostle would have been two-fold.[174] First, in doing the work of an apostle i.e. through the leading and engifting of the Spirit, continuing the work of gospel ministry,[175] making converts and founding new congregations in virgin territories (Rom 15:20, 23; 2 Cor 10:15). Hence the apostle of the Philippian church would extend the ministry of the gospel beyond the Paul-founded community into Macedonia, Achaia and beyond (cf. Col 1:6-7; 1 Thess 1:8). Secondly, the apostle alongside the other functional charismatic leaders of the church would equip others for works of ministry.[176] This is explicit in Eph 4:12 where, after listing the five-fold leadership gifts of apostle, prophet, evangelist, pastor and teacher (or pastor-teacher),[177] Paul gives the purpose (πρὸς τὸν) of these ministries.[178]

---

[172] Dickson, *Mission-Commitment*, 317.

[173] Dickson, *Mission-Commitment*, 317.

[174] On authorship see introduction, assumptions.

[175] Including ethical witness (2 Cor 4:2; 7:6; 1 Thess 2:4), proclamation of the gospel (Rom 15:19; 1 Cor 1:17), signs and wonders (Rom 15:19; 2 Cor 12:12; Gal 3:5), persecution (2 Cor 11:21-29; Phil 1:28-30; 1 Thess 2:2) and social ministry where appropriate (Gal 2:10).

[176] Notably, the list includes evangelist. I agree with Schnabel, *Mission*, 1463 (contra G. Strecker, *EWNT* 2:176 [*EDNT* 2:70]) who argues that the evangelist proclaims the gospel to the lost and the found even to the point of establishing communities of believers.

[177] It can be taken as four i.e. pastors who teach. So Vooys, J. 'No Clergy or Laity: All Christians are Ministers in the body of Christ, Ephesians 4:11-13', *Direction* 20.1 (1991): 87-95.

[178] I take all five to be functions and not offices and all related to, but not limited by, the local church. The apostle (ἀπόστολος) I take as itinerants with a specific call from Christ directly or through his Spirit to found congregations through proclamation of the gospel and signs and wonders (see the previous discussion on Epaphroditus above). The prophet (προφήτης) I see as one who has an extraordinary supernatural ability to hear the dynamic living word from God and proclaim it whether as an itinerant or locally (cf. 1 Cor 12:29; 14:24-25, 29; Fee, *1 Corinthians*, 621. See also Acts 11:27-28; 13:1; 21:9-11; 15:32). The evangelist (εὐαγγελιστής), in line with its core meaning, I see as one who has an extraordinary call and gift to preach the gospel with effect either as an itinerant or locally. This is seen in the ministry of Philip in Samaria (Acts 8:4-40; 21:10). Timothy, as an apostle (1 Thess 2:6), was urged elsewhere to do the work of an evangelist i.e. preach his gospel. That is, he was not to neglect his evangelism gift for his other responsibilities (2 Tim 4:2, 5), which he may have been in danger of doing, perhaps through timidity (see 2 Tim 1:6-8). Hence not a teacher *per se* (as suggest A. Campbell, 'Do the Work of an Evangelist', *EQ* 64.2 (1992): 117-129 cf. E. Best.

The purpose can be understood in two senses depending on the interpretation of the prepositional phrases **πρὸς** τὸν καταρτισμὸν τῶν ἁγίων **εἰς** ἔργον διακονίας, **εἰς** οἰκοδομὴν τοῦ σώματος τοῦ Χριστοῦ.[179] In the first place the phrases can be taken as coordinate and dependent on Christ's giving (ἔδωκεν) of the ministries. Hence the ministries are given 'for the completion of the holy people of God', 'for the work of the ministry' and 'for the building up of the body of Christ.'[180] The role of the general believer in this scheme is retained in Eph 4:7, 16 where *each* receives a gift from Christ and does their own part in the growth of the church. The noun καταρτισμός is taken in the sense of 'completion' rather than 'equipping' and the phrase stands alone.

Alternatively, it is argued that the central purpose for the giving of the gifts is found in the first prepositional clause 'to prepare God's holy people.' The second prepositional clause is subordinate to the first i.e. 'for the work of ministry/service.' The third is dependent on the two initial phrases i.e. 'for building the body of Christ.'[181] If so, then the noun καταρτισμός is taken in the sense of 'equipping'[182] the people of God for the work of ministry.

The former interpretation is not without warrant. First, the prepositional phrases can be taken in this manner. Secondly, καταρτισμός can be

---

'Ministry in Ephesians', *IBS* 15.4 (1993): 143-166; Bowers, 'Church': 96) nor a mere herald (so Dickson, *Mission-Commitment*, 321-336) but with a proclaiming and equipping ministry related specifically to the task of evangelism and initial discipleship. Perhaps this ministry functions under the authority of an apostle; so D.Y. Hadidian, '*tous de euangelistas* in Eph 4,11', *CBQ* 28 (1966): 317-321, 317. The pastor (ποιμήν) as the one called to care for and oversee a church i.e. a shepherd (O'Brien, *Ephesians*, 300). The teacher (διδάσκαλος) I consider to be one who is equipped with an extraordinary ability to pass on the truths of the faith to others in a general sense (O'Brien, *Ephesians*, 300-301). The latter two roles are more particularly discipleship and local church orientated. Each is called to be a role model and equip others for ministry in their field.

179 Schnackenburg, *Ephesians*, 182-184; Lincoln, *Ephesians*, 253-255; T.D. Gordon, '"Equipping" Ministry in Ephesians 4?' *JETS* 37 (1994): 69-78; Campbell, 'Evangelist': 126; H.P. Hamaan, 'Church and Ministry: an Exegesis of Ephesians 4:1-6', *LTJ* 16.3 (1982): 121-128.

180 Lincoln, *Ephesians*, 253, suggests an anachronistic agenda for democratising the ministry lies behind the alternative. To which can be countered that the alternative interpretation potentially over-reads into Paul hierarchical and autocratic models of ministry. It seems rather, that it is more likely that this developed in the post-apostolic church and that the NT was more democratic than assumed.

181 O'Brien, *Ephesians*, 301; Fee, *Empowering*, 706; R.Y.K. Fung, 'The Nature of the Ministry According to Paul', *EQ* 54 (1982): 129-146 esp. 140-141; Barth, *Ephesians*, II.439; Mitton, *Ephesians*, 151; Snodgrass, *Ephesians*, 204; Wood, 'Ephesians', 58; Foulkes, *Ephesians*, 128; C.E. Arnold, Ephesians: *Power and Magic. The Concept of Power in Ephesians in Light of its Historical Setting*. SNTSMS 63 (Cambridge: CUP, 1989), 159-160; Vooys, J. 'No clergy', 91.

182 *BDAG*, 526; *TDNT* 1.476: 'the equipment of the saints for the work of the ministry.'

understood as 'completion' in the sense of maturity. However, neither of these arguments I consider conclusive. Even if καταρτισμός has the sense of completion in terms of maturity, the following phrase may supply the purpose of the completion i.e. complete so as to engage in works of ministry![183]

O'Brien is correct to note that the flow of the passage favours the second interpretation, as does Paul's wider theology for a number of reasons.[184] First, the passage is framed with reference to the ministries of all (Eph 4:7, 16) rather than a few.[185] Secondly, the wider context of Ephesians makes reference to blessing (Eph 1:3-19; 3:20) and involvement of all rather than a few in ministry (Eph 2:10; 6:10-17),[186] as does Paul generally (cf. 1 Cor 12:4-11; 15:58; Gal 6:9-10).[187]

Thirdly, as will be discussed more fully in regards to Phil 4:9,[188] Paul's imitatory model of ministry fits nicely with this methodology. The leader models Christian life and ministry intentionally so that the others will emulate them (Eph 5:2; 1 Cor 11:1; 1 Thess 1:6-8; Phil 3:14-17).

Fourthly, while the prepositional phrases may all be dependent on ἔδωκεν, this would have a stronger basis if the prepositions were the same in each case.[189] Finally and conclusively, the verses that follow are launched with 'we all' (καταντήσωμεν οἱ πάντες [Eph 4:13]... ὦμεν [4:14]... αὐξήσωμεν [4:15]... πᾶν τὸ σῶμα ... κατ' ἐνέργειαν ἐν μέτρῳ ἑνὸς ἑκάστου μέρους ... ἑαυτοῦ ἐν ἀγάπῃ [4:16]) indicating that this is inclusive of the whole

---

[183] While the noun is a hapax legomena, the associated verb καταρτίζω can go either way on the basis of its NT usage: 1) Favouring 'prepare and so equip' are Matt 4:21; Mk 1:19 (of preparing nets); Lk 6:40 (of preparing a student); Rom 9:22 of God's preparing objects of wrath for destruction; Heb 11:2 of preparing a body for sacrifice. 2) Favouring 'complete' include perhaps 2 Cor 13:11; 1 Thess 3:10 (although both may carry the sense of 'restored'). The sense of 'restore' is common but does not fit Ephesians (1 Cor 1:10; Gal 6:1; 1 Pet 5:10). Neither does the sense of 'create' fit (Heb 11:3), although it is possible that the leaders are the agents of God's creative power for the doing of works of service (cf. Eph 2:10). Heb 13:21 can either work either way and perhaps means 'complete' by 'equipping.'

[184] O'Brien, *Ephesians*, 302.

[185] O'Brien, *Ephesians*, 303.

[186] Barth, *Ephesians*, II. 439 suggests that the equipping involves the 'conditioning' of the saints in a battle or competition. See further on Eph 6:15, 17 in Appendix 1, 'The connection between evangelism and the military metaphor in Paul.'

[187] Notably each is inclusive: 1) 1 Cor 12:6: θεὸς ὁ ἐνεργῶν τὰ πάντα **ἐν πᾶσιν**; 2) 1 Cor 15:58: Uses the corporate epistolary address ἀδελφοί indicating all readers/hearers in Corinth (see discussion in Chapter 3); 3) Gal 6:7: ὃ γὰρ ἐὰν indicates inclusiveness.

[188] See Chapter 9.

[189] Fee, *Empowering*, 706. Rather the πρός clause suggests the penultimate purpose i.e. to equip believers for the ultimate purpose expressed in the two εἰς clauses i.e. for the work of ministry and the building up of the body. Bruce, *Epistles*, 349 however, sees the prepositional shift as decisive.

church, individual and corporate, rather than a few select individuals.[190] Included in these verses is the statement 'speaking the truth in love' which may well be inclusive of evangelism (Eph 4:15) (see below).

That being the case, the second function of the apostle was to equip the believers for works of ministry (εἰς ἔργον διακονίας) with the ultimate goal that the body of Christ (the church) will be built up (εἰς οἰκοδομὴν τοῦ σώματος τοῦ Χριστοῦ). The former engages two terms which carry evangelistic nuances, ἔργον in particular being almost a technical term for ministry.[191] As noted above,[192] the second διακονίας in both its masculine and feminine form has a variety of nuances including ministry. It is probable then that 'works of ministry' applies to the ministries general believers develop as they mature, through the equipping ministries of the leaders.[193]

That being the case, growth in the subsequent verses involves both qualitative or intensive growth toward individual and corporate maturity, and quantitative or extensive growth in terms of converts (cf. Col 1:6; 2:19).[194] In this regard first I suggest that even standing alone, one component of τῆς ἐπιγνώσεως τοῦ υἱοῦ τοῦ θεοῦ (Eph 4:13) would involve an understanding of the holistic knowledge of Christ including his mission and will for all humanity. That for Paul this included all people being saved goes without saying. That being the case, the clause suggests in its context an increased understanding of sharing the gospel among the body of Christ. This evangelistic dimension is confirmed in the purpose clause εἰς μέτρον ἡλικίας τοῦ πληρώματος τοῦ Χριστοῦ; whereby the whole universe is filled with the cosmic Christ. In Ephesians this involves including bringing all things including humanity, under the headship of Christ (Eph 1:10) through belief in the gospel (cf. Eph 1:13-14; 3:8; 4:10) i.e. through evangelism. Notably, the recipients of the letter are examples of this having believed when they 'heard the word of truth', the gospel of their salvation (Eph 1:13).

Similarly, the growth of the church into the headship of Christ (αὐξήσωμεν

---

190 Lincoln, *Ephesians*, 257; Schnackenburg, *Ephesians*, 185 among others, note the passage refers to corporate and not individual maturity. While this is the emphasis, the two are intimately connected i.e. corporate maturity is achieved when the full number of individuals are added and each individual finds full maturity. Hence corporate maturity demands individual maturity. Evangelism forms part of the contextual content and applies to all here but not all in the church participate in equal degree, rather 'each part does its work' as led and enabled by the Spirit and in accordance with their giftedness and call.

191 See above.

192 See note 132 in this chapter.

193 Not limited to evangelism nor meaning here 'deacon', but all manner of ministries (modes of service) according to the will of the head of the church, Christ (cf. Mitton, *Ephesians*, 152). Alternatively 'service' cf. O'Brien, *Ephesians*, 304.

194 Bowers, 'Church', 96 rejects that growth is involved with little exegetical discussion of the issues in this passage.

εἰς αὐτὸν τὰ πάντα, ὅς ἐστιν ἡ κεφαλή, Χριστός [Eph 4:15]) involves growing up into him 'in all things.'[195] This necessarily involves growing into the fullness *of Christ's mission* alongside other dimensions including his character and understanding. Several factors support this. First, the present participle ἀληθεύοντες suggests that it is 'as we speak the truth in love', that the church is built up into Christ. Hence as believers speak the word (cf. Eph 6:17) for edification and evangelism, growth of the church is generated. Secondly, the church grows up into him in all ways, suggesting the full range of Christ's ministry and life is in mind, including evangelism.

Thirdly, an analysis of Paul and the wider NT use of the verb αὐξάνω (Eph 4:15), confirms that evangelistic growth is commonly associated with it.[196] In Paul this is unambiguous in 1 Cor 3:6-7 where human agents are said to plant and water the seed of the word but God makes it grow. This explicitly includes evangelism through the agency of Paul and Apollos (1 Cor 3:6-7). For Paul then, growth of the church involved further evangelisation by himself and others. Similarly in Col 1:6 Paul speaks of the gospel 'bearing fruit and growing in all the world' (καρποφορούμενον καὶ αὐξανόμενον) just as it had in Colossae through the agency of Epaphras. The verbal parallels with Col 1:10 suggest that his prayer for fruitfulness and growth 'in all good works' should indicate that his prayer incorporates a desire for evangelistic converts (Col 1:10).[197] Finally, Eph 4:16 involves holistic growth in line with the whole range of the ministry gifts (Eph 4:11) and explicates that each member of the body participates differently, but with the same love. That is, the evangelistic ministry will be primarily, but not exclusively, conducted by those whose spiritual gifting tends that way.

That being the case, the removal of quantitative or extensive dimensions in

---

[195] Or in 'every way' as O'Brien, *Ephesians*, 312 puts it; and so, among every other dimension of Christ, evangelism!

[196] Sometimes in the Synoptics of literal growth concerning plants or people (Matt 6:28; Lk 1:80; 2:40; 12:27). In parabolic contexts of the growth of the kingdom or of Christians including increase in people paying allegiance to the king i.e. converts (Matt 13:32; Mk 4:8; Lk 13:19; Jn 3:30). In Acts once of population growth (Acts 7:17) but primarily of the growth of the gospel meaning converts (Acts 6:7 [ὁ λόγος τοῦ θεοῦ ηὔξανεν]; Acts 12:24 [Ὁ δὲ λόγος τοῦ θεοῦ ηὔξανεν καὶ ἐπληθύνετο]; Acts 19:20 [Οὕτως κατὰ κράτος τοῦ κυρίου ὁ λόγος ηὔξανεν καὶ ἴσχυεν]). See also 1 Pet 2:2: ἵνα ἐν αὐτῷ αὐξηθῆτε εἰς σωτηρίαν ; 2 Pet 3:18: αὐξάνετε δὲ ἐν χάριτι καὶ γνώσει τοῦ κυρίου ἡμῶν καὶ σωτῆρος Ἰησοῦ Χριστοῦ. Indeed, given that Paul picks up the notions of the gospel growing in Col 1:6, this must be seen to form one critical dimension of the churches growth (cf. Col 2:19).

[197] With Wright, *Colossians*, 54; Garland, *Colossians*, 49; Dunn, *Colossians*, 62 who admits both ethical and evangelistic may be in mind, as prefers Bruce, *Epistles*, 42. O'Brien, *Colossians*, 13 takes 'bear fruit' as of good deeds and 'growth' in terms of converts.

Eph 4:11-16 in favour of the qualitative is without warrant.[198] Not that these two notions of growth can really be dualistically separated. Surely, in that the apostle and evangelist engage in equipping, it is reasonable to argue that one dimension of Christian maturity in this case, is an increased understanding and ability to share the faith. Although it is not explicit, it is reasonable to suggest that the former is found primarily in the ministries of the prophets, pastors, and teachers while the latter in the ministries of the evangelists and apostles.[199]

In addition, while ἀληθεύω ('be truthful, speak the truth')[200] could include speaking the truth in an ethical sense (Eph 4:24, 25; 5:9; 6:14),[201] the verb here potentially carries the nuance of 'speaking the gospel of truth in love.'[202] In the only other use in Paul (Gal 4:16), 'truth' refers to the initial proclamation of the gospel in Galatia due to Paul's illness (4:13-14) and refers to Paul's message of truth over against the message of the Judaising false teachers.[203] Notably here the context also refers to Paul's recipients not being moved from the 'truth' by false teaching (4:14) and so, refers to spoken truth in a teaching/proclamatory sense.[204] Significantly, earlier, Paul describes the gospel, in a clear reference to evangelization, as the 'word of truth' (λόγον τῆς ἀληθείας [see Eph 1:13 cf.

---

[198] O'Brien, *Ephesians*, 305: 'this constructing has both an extensive and an intensive dimension to it' cf. Arnold, *Ephesians*, 159-160; Senior and Stuhlmueller, *Foundations*, 206-207; Marshall, 'Evangelists?' 261. Against Lincoln, *Ephesians*, 261 rather surprisingly in light of his interpretation of 'speaking the truth' and seeing the ministries of 4:12 as completed by ministers from the church (cf. 250, 263). See also P.T. O'Brien, 'The Church as a Heavenly and Eschatological Entity' in D.A. Carson (ed), *The Church in the Bible and the World* (Exeter: Paternoster, 1987), 89-117, 112-113 where O'Brien rightly notes the body is in one sense complete and the metaphor is developed in regards to itself and each other within the body. However the body is still extended through evangelism.

[199] Although not exhaustively, as the apostle also has a highly educative role (1 Cor 4:17; Eph 4:21; Col 1:28; 2:7; 2 Thess 2:15; 1 Tim 2:7; 6:1; 2 Tim 1:11; 3:10) as does the evangelist in the Pastorals (1 Tim 4:11, 13; 6:1, 2; 2 Tim 4:5). Similarly the prophet had an evangelistic function on occasion (1 Cor 14:20-25).

[200] *BDAG*, 43.

[201] However 5:9 and 6:14 may indicate goodness, righteousness and truth in a holistic sense including both dynamics. The two modes are not mutually exclusive. As Barth, *Ephesians*, II.444 notes: 'in the context of Eph 4:15 the *testimony* given *by speech* plays an outstanding role as the references to the confession, the ministers of the Word, true and false teaching, and lying show.'

[202] Schnackenburg, *Ephesians*, 187; Barth, *Ephesians*, II.444; Lincoln, *Ephesians*, 259-260; O'Brien, *Ephesians*, 310. Wood, 'Ephesians', 59; Mitton, *Ephesians*, 156; Snodgrass, *Ephesians*, 206; Bruce, *Epistles*, 352 note that the term literally is 'truthing' and so includes 'doing the truth.' See the argument in O'Brien, *Ephesians*, 311 against this. However, perhaps Paul is being holistic with both in mind.

[203] Especially when 'truth' in Galatians is exclusively applied to the gospel cf. ἡ ἀλήθεια τοῦ εὐαγγελίου (Gal 2:5, 14); [τῇ] ἀληθείᾳ (Gal 5:7).

[204] Foulkes, *Ephesians*, 15 notes the connection between Eph 4:14 and 15.

Gal 2:5, 14; Col 1:5]). Likewise he goes onto describe teaching as the 'truth that is in Christ Jesus' (Eph 4:21) i.e. the content of the gospel. In addition, 'in love' calls to mind the love of God expressed in his adoption of believers through the sacrificial death of Christ, a love the believer is to emulate (Eph 5:2). As O'Brien summarises then

> The apostle is not exhorting his readers to truthfulness in general or speaking honestly with one another, however appropriate or important this may be. Rather, he wants all of them to be members of a 'confessing' church, with the content of their testimony to be 'the word of truth, the gospel of their salvation' (1:13).[205]

If so, then Paul is referring to speech to one another and to unbelievers (cf. Eph 4:11-12; 6:15, 17), which serves to build the church up qualitatively and quantitatively.[206] As Schnackenburg puts it, 'the Christian who witnesses to the truth of the Gospel cannot use the same methods as a tempter who is pursuing evil intentions; he wants to convince humanity by a revelation of the truth and win them by love (cf. 2 Cor 4:2; 6:7).'[207]

Finally, if Eph 4:12 does refer to the ministry of the leaders, it still indicates that the local church is to be engaged in evangelism. That is, the mission of the gospel is continued through the ministry of apostles and evangelists from the local church. Either way, the suggestion that churches did not have a clear role in the continuation of Paul's mission is flawed. If the former interpretation is correct, then the mission is continued through the leaders of the church. If the latter is correct as I suspect, then it is continued through the leadership of spiritually equipped and inspired leaders and the 'general' members whom they equip.

Conclusion to Apostle

In sum then, I consider that there are good grounds for considering Epaphroditus to be an 'Apostle' of Christ approved for evangelistic foundational mission by the Philippian church and its founding 'Apostle', Paul.[208] His role was the continuation of the foundational mission involving

---

205 O'Brien, *Ephesians*, 311.

206 If so 'love' (ἀγάπη) provides the framework for this speech and proclamation i.e. in terms of evangelism, sharing the gospel in a loving manner. Or as Lincoln, *Ephesians*, 260 writes, 'at the heart of the proclamation of the truth is love, and a life of love is the embodiment of the truth.' It is possible that growth ἐν ἀγάπη (Eph 4:16) also carries over a sense of this truth speaking ἐν ἀγάπη cf. Lincoln, *Ephesians*, 264.

207 Schnackenburg, *Ephesians*, 187.

208 I consider it possible that Epaphroditus may be the unnamed apostle 'famous for preaching the gospel' sent from Macedonia to Corinth for the Collection with Titus and the other unnamed zealous apostle (Clement or one of the other co-workers?) (2 Cor 8:18, 23; Phil 4:3).

evangelising the unreached peoples of Macedonia, Achaia and perhaps further afield (cf. Phil 4:2-3). Thus, he would have travelled throughout the region preaching, ministering in signs and wonders and establishing fledgling communities of faith. Secondly along with other leaders, he would have been active in equipping other general believers for works of ministry (Eph 4:11-16). This would include evangelism (cf. Eph 6:15, 17)[209] amidst the full range of Christian ministry. His selection as the one to take the gift to Paul would be sensible in that he was a trusted leader in Philippi, proven in the mission.

MINISTER (λειτουργός) TO MY NEEDS (τῆς χρείας μου)

It is in the context of delivering the gift to Philippi that Epaphroditus has travelled to Rome to care for Paul's needs (see also above on apostle). It is with this is mind, that he is designated as a 'ministrant to my needs' sent from Philippi (καὶ λειτουργὸν τῆς χρείας μου, πέμψαι πρὸς ὑμᾶς). The term λειτουργός is sometimes understood as a cultic sacrificial metaphor.[210] Paul uses it on two occasions, once applied to civil governing authorities (Rom 13:6), and the other to his own ministry of preaching the gospel to the Gentiles (Rom 15:16). Here λειτουργός specifically refers to the ministry of bringing the gift from Philippi to Paul.[211] Similarly in 2:30, the gift is called 'a service', using λειτουργία (2:30).[212] The genitive construction τῆς χρείας μου refers to 'the necessities of life' (Phil 4:16, 19).[213] Although Paul uses λειτουργός of his own ministry there is insufficient evidence to conclude proclamation is involved in the term if standing alone.

Paul exhorts the Philippians to 'welcome (προσδέχεσθε) him in the Lord with great joy' and 'honour men like him.' Rather than see a problem with Epaphroditus in Philippi, this reveals the rhetorical import of Paul's words. Epaphroditus embodies exactly the response Paul wants from the Philippians who are suffering for the cause of the gospel in Philippi. In other words, receive him[214] and 'emulate the example of Epaphroditus!' The believers of Philippi are

---

[209] See for detail my Appendix 1, 'The connection between evangelism and the military metaphor in Paul.'

[210] Common in the LXX for מְשָׁרֵת but not always sacral. *BDAG*, 591suggests always with a sacral edge although this is not clear in Rom 13:6 as *TDNT* 4.230 point out.

[211] Fee, 276. It says nothing about staying on longer and caring for Paul's needs.

[212] The designation of the gift as a θυσία in 4:18 suggests some cultic orientation here cf. Hawthorne, 117.

[213] Fee, 276; Marshall, 72, 'probably.' Others such as Michael, 118-119 on the basis of πέμψαι πρὸς ὑμᾶς; Gnilka, 161; Martin, 333; Ollrog, *Paulus*, 99; Hawthorne, 333; O'Brien, 333; Bockmuehl, 170 argue this also involved remaining with Paul until not needed. While this is possible it is unsupported, πέμψαι πρὸς ὑμᾶς being neutral in intent.

[214] Note προσδέχεσθε is emphatic.

not just to be involved in the sense of material giving alone to Paul or others,[215] but are to generally contend for the cause of the gospel (1:27-30). Furthermore, Epaphroditus' service on behalf of Paul reveals the unity that he wishes to see restored in Philippi; therefore they are to struggle as one for the gospel!

Conclusion to Epaphroditus

It is unquestionable then, on the basis of the combination of the five designations ἀδελφὸς, συνεργὸς, συστρατιώτης, ἀπόστολος and λειτουργός, that Epaphroditus was a gospel proclaimer.[216] He was given the specific assignment of supporting Paul in his ministry by delivering a gift from Philippi to Paul and perhaps working with him in mission in Rome. While it is possible that Paul uses the terms purely because of his financial support for Paul, I consider this unlikely. Rather, as in the case of Paul himself (Gal 2:10), and the other apostles (cf. Acts 4:35), concern for the needs of others is an essential component of Epaphroditus' ministry.

If so, then his inclusion alongside Timothy further reinforces Paul's desire to set before the Philippians appropriate examples of continued *evangelistic* ministry in the face of suffering. Indeed it is suffering for the gospel that is paradigmatic. The intensity of Epaphroditus' suffering is seen in Paul's concentrated language. He writes of Epaphroditus that he was sick to the point of death (ἠσθένησεν παραπλήσιον θανάτῳ cf. 2:26-27). This calls to mind Paul's own near-death situation in Rome (1:20-24), which was set in the context of evangelistic mission (1:12-14)..

Thus Epaphroditus' example parallels that of Christ in 2:8 who became obedient to the point of death.[217] It was in the context of the 'work of Christ' (τὸ ἔργον Χριστοῦ) that he almost died (μέχρι θανάτου) cf. 'risked his life' (παραβολευσάμενος τῇ ψυχῇ).

Paul wants the Philippians to be as selfless as their own Epaphroditus who was committed to care for Paul notwithstanding great personal cost, who longed for the Philippians selflessly, who was more concerned for their grief at his illness than his own suffering and who risked his life for Paul and the mission. This emphasis is understandable in a situation where the Philippians were suffering in a similar way and experiencing a degree of disunity and so threatening the gospel mission. While Paul was delighted that the genuine gospel of Christ was preached in any situation, he greatly preferred that it be done in unity and love, whatever the trouble its proclaimers endured.

---

[215] Indeed Paul is not seeking further material support from the Philippians at this time (4:17).

[216] Marshall, 71.

[217] The phrase μέχρι θανάτου is found only in these two instances in Paul and designates a certain link between Epaphroditus as an example of Christ-like servanthood to the Philippians as Fee, 282; O'Brien, 'Models:' 278 make plain.

Conclusion to 2:19-30

It is clear then that Paul presents the examples of Timothy and Epaphroditus, not only to inform the Philippians of his plans concerning these two men of God, but as godly examples of 'living as citizens worthy of the gospel of Christ.' Paul's language emphasises that their selflessness for the mission of the gospel is inclusive of evangelism. There is a total absence of any qualifier precluding verbal proclamation, which would be required for the reader to filter verbal proclamation from their examples. Thus it is clear that proactive evangelism features within the range of Paul's desired response from the Philippians. As Fee puts it:

> Paul's chief concern, and the *ultimate* reason for this letter, is the progress of the gospel in Philippi. This is what he reminds them of in the thanksgiving; this is what he wants them to know about his own situation, that it is advancing the gospel in Rome even in the face of opposition; and this is what he wants to learn about them (1:27), that they are walking 'worthy of the gospel' in the face of opposition and suffering in Philippi (2:14-16). Timothy's reason for coming, therefore, besides encouragement (v. 20) and informing them about the outcome of 'Paul's affairs' (v. 23), is to 'cheer Paul' (v. 19) by reporting back about their situation (addressed in 1:27-2:18 and hopefully 'cured' by this letter before Timothy arrives), and to do so before Paul himself comes.[218]

In sum then, one of the functions of the descriptions of Timothy and Epaphroditus was to encourage unified perseverance in gospel mission in Philippi. Significantly in their examples, we see a number of the key intersecting motifs that recur in Philippians. Here they include courageous evangelism (2:22, 25), suffering (2:22, 26-30) and unity in mission (2:21-22, 25-30). Opposition is implied in the soldier imagery and the testing and proving of Timothy (2:20, 25). Joy is found in the flanking passages (2:18; 3:1 cf. 2:28). Only eschatological hope is not emphasised in this passage.

[218] Fee, 261.

CHAPTER 7

Evangelistic Disunity in the Philippian Church (4:1-3)

4:1-3 is best understood as transitional for several reasons.[1] First, it concludes and summarises aspects of Paul's appeal for imitation of the Pauline model in the face of various enemies of the faith. This is indicated with the inferential conjunction ὥστε ('therefore').[2] Secondly, it leads into the appeal for unity between the two women in 4:2. Although there is no grammatical connective between 4:1 and 4:2, the thematic and grammatical parallels to the earlier injunction of 1:27 suggest that 4:1 flows into 4:2. In addition the appeal to the women recalls,[3] climaxes and gives concrete context to earlier references to unity in the epistle (1:27; 2:2-3, 14-15).[4]

The passage is launched from Paul's injunction to the Philippians to follow his example. Rather than live in the manner of the enemies of the cross, whose

[1] Hawthorne, 176; Kent, 149; Hendriksen, 189, both see 4:1-9 as a concluding unit. O'Brien, 473; Silva, 217; Melick, 145 see 4:1 as the conclusion to the preceding while at the same time providing a transition to the appeals of 4:2-9; similarly D. Elzell, 'The Sufficiency of Christ: Philippians 4', *RevExp* 77 (1980): 373-381, 373. Collange, 142 prefers 4:2-7. See also Caird, 149 who argues 4:2-9 is an independent unit. Bockmuehl, 237 suggests 4:1-3 offers a 'direct application' of 'the principles of 3:2-21.' Watson, 'Analysis': 76-77 supported in the main by A.H. Snyman, 'Persuasion', 328-329 suggests 4:1-9 is *repetitio* a portion of the *peroratio* (4:1-20) indicating that Paul is 'encountering conflict from the Philippian congregation with regard to what constitutes a life worthy of the gospel.' Witherington, *Friendship*, 18 sees 4:2-3 as part of the *probatio* in which he deals with the most delicate matter of disunity; he sees the women as negative examples. Marshall, 107; Garland, 'Composition': 171 suggest this is the culmination of the argument of the letter. I agree with O'Brien, 474 that this is an overstatement. A number of others see it as part of Letter B (3:2-4:1) e.g. Beare, 141 who sees 3:1b; 4:2-9 as an independent letter (see Chapter 2 for critique). Martin, 167 sees 4:1-23 as the concluding unit. Bloomquist, *Function*, 135-136 sees 3:17-4:7 as the *exhortio*, a section of the *argumentatio* (1:18b-4:7); Luter, 'Role': 411-420 sees 4:15 chiastically related to 1:27-30.

[2] O'Brien, 474; Fee, 385 recognises this dimension considering 3:1-4:3 as a unit.

[3] It is generally agreed that these two are women despite the KJV (using the masculine Euodia*s*) and so not a missionary couple. So Lightfoot, 158; Bockmuehl, 238-239; Fee, 390; Hawthorne, 179; Michael, 188 who critiques older attempts to find men here.

[4] Fee, 386.

eternal destiny is destruction, they are to set their minds not on earthly things but on matters of heaven. Here this means to set their hearts and minds both toward the return of Christ and toward pressing on living out their heavenly citizenship in a fallen generation to ensure that they themselves are saved. This eschatological hope then sets the framework for Paul's appeal.

A Call to Steadfastness (4:1)

Paul's love of the Philippians is emphasised in the overlaying of four intimate terms: 'my brothers (and sisters') (ἀδελφοί [cf. 1:12; 3:1, 13, 17; 4:8, 21]), 'my beloved' (ἀγαπητοί [2:12]), 'my longed-for ones' (ἐπιπόθητοι)[5] and 'my joy and crown' (χαρὰ καὶ στέφανός).[6] The first three refer to his present sense of love and longing for the Philippians. The phrase χαρὰ καὶ στέφανός combines this current sense with an eschatological focus. As I have noted, this emphasis on eschatology is a feature of the letter thus far.[7] The repetition of 'beloved' particularly reinforces the friendship dimension of the conclusion.[8] Perhaps the intensity of Paul's positivity is due to what he is about to say, not wanting his exhortation that follows to suggest his love for the Philippians is diminished in any way by their dispute.

The appeal for steadfastness is not a new thought but builds on the previous appeals for imitation and heavenly concern (cf. 1:27).[9] Many suggest that οὕτως here refers to what has preceded rather than what follows; so Paul is saying to the Philippians 'stand firm in this way.'[10] This means that the way in

---

[5] Only here in the NT.

[6] Hawthorne, 177 puts it well: 'before the apostle begins his commands, he commends.' 'Joy' is a recurring feature of Philippians (1:4, 25; 2:2 cf. 1:18; 2:17, 18, 28; 3:1; 4:4, 10). Here Paul defines them as 'my joy' softening greatly what follows as Marshall, 108 notes. The ironing out of the problem will complete his joy (2:2).

[7] There is no need to decide between a present meaning; so O'Brien, 475-476; Hawthorne, 178; and an eschatological meaning (cf. Phil 3:12-21; 1 Cor 9:25; 1 Thess 2:19); so Lightfoot, 157; Barth, 117; Gnilka, 220; Collange, 141; Fee, 388; Bruce, 137; Moule, 77 (of 'crown' as both are applicable and decidedly linked as Bockmuehl, 237; Michael, 186-187 agree). Marshall, 105; Martin, 167 consider both 'joy' and 'crown' as forward-looking.

[8] Whether in a formal sense *a la* Fee, 387, or generally as I prefer.

[9] Especially Luter, 'Role': 412-414.

[10] The adverb οὕτως generally looks backward in Paul as J.J. Müller, 136; Michael, 186; Thielman, 193; Barth, 117; Houlden, 108 suggest and so take it with the previous material only. Consequently, it looks back to the previous passage as most agree and also 1:27 as Fee, 388-389; O'Brien, 475-476; Melick, 146; Holloway, *Consolation*, 147 note and so in reality looking both ways. Bockmuehl, 238 sees it as introductory. Hawthorne, 177; Marshall, 105 see it looking forward. Fee, 388-389; Silva, 217 sees it looking back to 1:27. Similarly, I consider that it looks back over the whole letter and its central issues and appeals which the more practical injunctions of 4:1-9 cover.

which they should stand firm is through resisting false teaching and living according to the gospel, which is eschatological and heavenly centred.[11] However, I consider that the language similarities between 1:27 and 4:1 *also* point to what follows through the 'backward looking' link to 1:27.[12] In particular, the parallel phrases στήκετε ἐν ἑνὶ πνεύματι and στήκετε ἐν κυρίω are notable.[13] The repeated use of ἐν κυρίῳ in 4:2 also suggests continuity from 4:1 i.e. the way Paul wants them to stand firm in the Lord is by being of one mind in the Lord. The use of the verb συναθλέω in both 1:27 and 4:3 further confirms this impression. Fee rightly points out that there are three essential elements of 1:27 found here i.e. '1) that you stand firm; 2) in the one Spirit, as one person; 3) contending for the faith of the gospel.'[14] In this section, I will explore in particular the manner in which εὐαγγέλιον and συναθλέω are developed in regard to evangelistic mission.

Paul's Appeal to Correct Mission-Disunity in Philippi (4:2-3)

In 4:2 the issue is unity and correcting the contention in the Philippian church. Paul turns to the specific problem he has alluded to intermittently and non-specifically throughout Philippians; the disagreement between two women in the congregation, Euodia and Syntyche. Obvious previous allusions to this issue include first, the focus on unity in 1:27. Secondly, the concern in 2:2-3 for oneness of love, spirit and purpose and a renunciation of selfish ambition, vain conceit and pride. The repeated language of 2:2 and 4:2 indicates thematic continuity between the two passages (τὸ αὐτὸ φρονῆτε [2:2] τὸ αὐτὸ φρονεῖν [4:2]).[15] Thirdly, the concern for right thinking (φρονέω) underlies the appeal for imitation of Christ's attitude (2:5-11).[16] Finally, there is Paul's appeal to cease all complaint and argument in 2:14.

In light of these more explicit references, a number of other passages contain indirect indications. These include the appeal for love in 1:9, the rhetorical import of the differently motivated Roman Christians (1:15-18),[17] the appeals for joy which may refer to the problem of joylessness due to contention in the church (1:4, 18, 25; 2:2, 17, 18, 28, 29; 3:1; 4:1, 4, 10) and Paul's description of Timothy's selflessness.[18] In addition, the wonderful unity of Paul, Timothy

---

[11] So O'Brien, 476.

[12] Holloway, 147.

[13] So also O'Brien, 476; Fee, 386, 388. 'In the Lord' here has a locative sense.

[14] Fee, 386.

[15] As Peterlin, *Letter*, 102 puts it: 4:2-3 'carries the whole baggage of 2:1-4, and serves to characterise the conflict' cf. Caird, 102; Holloway, 147; U.B. Müller, 194.

[16] D. Williams, *The Apostle Paul and Women in the Church* (Ventura, CA: Regal Books, 1977), 97 notes 2:1-11 backgrounds 4:2-3; D. Peterlin, *Letter*, 102.

[17] Holloway, *Consolation*, 147.

[18] Peterlin, *Letter*, 101.

and Epaphroditus rhetorically speaks into the fragmentation of the Philippians (2:19-30).

It is clear then that this conflict between the two women lies at the heart of Paul's concern for the Philippians.[19] As I have already indicated, the problem is not yet acute as the general positivity of the letter indicates.[20] However, Paul does not want it to escalate.[21]

Paul's desire is stated clearly in 4:2. He wants the two women Euodia and Syntyche to find agreement in Christ. He uses παρακαλέω, which means to 'appeal to, urge (strongly), exhort, encourage.'[22] These appeals are usually impassioned and urgent, addressing genuine specific situations, as here in 4:2.[23] Here is found the unique situation of Paul appealing *by name* for right conduct. Some see here the naming as negative; Garland for example suggesting a 'pastoral confrontation.'[24] However, it is better in the light of the general positivity of the whole letter to see this naming in positive terms. Fee for example suggests that they are named as evidence of a close friendship seen in his naming of them as 'co-workers.'[25]

The passage gives a little insight into the two women. Both of their names ('Success' = Euodia and 'Lucky' = Syntyche) suggest that they are Gentile and are probably converted from paganism.[26] In addition they were Paul's co-workers and probably leaders in the church.[27] In light of the origins of the

---

[19] Peterlin, *Letter*, 101-106.

[20] At this point I differ from Peterlin, *Letter*, 105 who writes: 'the tension in the Philippian church is *the* element which provides continuity to the subject-matter of Phil' (italics mine). I consider that this is an overstatement. I agree there is a conflict in the church but it is not *the* issue but *an* issue that Paul addresses alongside concern for the gospel, false teachers, persecution, joylessness, eschatology and general unity. These issues function together in some way and the exegete should beware of overstating one over the other. However, that they are mentioned at all indicates that they are essential to the fabric of Philippians (see Chapter 2).

[21] Peterlin, *Letter*, 105.

[22] *BDAG*, 765; O'Brien, 477. See similar uses in appeals (Rom 12:1, 15:30; 16:17; 1 Cor 1:10; 4:16; 16:12, 15; 2 Cor 2:8; 6:1; 8:6; 9:5; 10:1; 12:18; Eph 4:1; Phil 4:2; 1 Thess 4:1, 10; 5:14; 2 Thess 3:12; 1 Tim 1:3; 2:1; Phm 9, 10 cf. 2 Cor 5:20).

[23] Use of appeals to: live an authentic Christian life (Rom 12:1; Eph 4:1; 1 Thess 4:1); pray (Rom 15:30; 1 Tim 2:1); avoid division (Rom 16:17; 1 Cor 1:10); imitate Paul (1 Cor 4:16); reaffirm love (2 Cor 2:8); not receive God's grace in vain (2 Cor 6:1); urge a specific mission (1 Cor 16:12, 15; 2 Cor 8:6; 9:5; 12:18; 1 Tim 1:3); make a general appeal (2 Cor 10:1); heal a rift (Phil 4:2); love more (1 Thess 4:10); minister in a particular way (1 Thess 5:14; 2 Thess 3:12); show mercy to someone else (Phm 9,10).

[24] Garland, 'Composition': 172.

[25] Fee, *Philippians*, 389.

[26] Εὐοδία literally implies 'prosperous journey.'

[27] Some such as Hawthorne, 179; Lightfoot, 158 consider they may have been deaconesses (better 'deacons') which is entirely feasible but unproven (see Silva, 221). The term 'deaconess' is probably anachronistic anyway (see Peterlin, *Letter*, 106-111).

Philippian church among a group of Philippian women in a city without a synagogue this prominence is not surprising (Acts 16:13). It is probable that they were converted at this time or later through the ministry of the apostolic team, Lydia, the jailor or other members of the Philippian church.[28] Evidence suggests that women played a strong leadership role in the Philippian church. First, it is probable that Lydia was both patron and leader of the emerging Philippian church.[29] Secondly, evidence exists to suggest Macedonian women had a stronger role in public life than elsewhere in the Roman Empire.[30] It is probable also that they were women of some means, which enabled them to have the time to be involved in the ministry.[31] That Paul has to address them and the issue at all, supports seeing them as leaders whether formally or informally, in that the whole church is being affected.

Paul specifically addresses both parties in the dispute individually. His appeal is that they put aside their differences and find agreement in the Lord. As I have indicated, his language τὸ αὐτὸ φρονεῖν directly recalls Philippians 2:2 indicating that this provides a specific context for that general injunction (cf. 2:5). 'In the Lord' further recalls Philippians 2 and in particular the Christ-example of 2:5-11.[32] They are to renounce their squabble and emulate Christ with humility and obedience. They are to imitate Paul himself who seeks to know Christ as first-priority as he fulfils his calling and mission (3:4-14).[33] The

---

Whether or not this is so they *were* co-workers i.e. active participants in the evangelistic mission, which is my primary concern here. In addition, I consider it possible they were 'overseers', but again this is unsupportable and contentious (similarly Marshall, 108; Moule, 77). As Witherington, *Friendship*, 105; Silva, 221; Peterlin, *Letter*, 104; Caird, 149; J.J. Müller, 137; Hawthorne, 179; S. Heine, *Women and Early Christianity* (Minneapolis: Augsburg, 1988), 87; H. Köster, 'Letter to the Philippians', *IDBSup* (Nashville: Abingdon, 1976), 666; R. Scroggs, 'Women in the New Testament', *IDBSup* (Nashville: Abingdon, 1976), 610; Elzell, 'Sufficiency': 375; Trebilco, 'Women': 32 demonstrate, they were probably leaders and people of influence; contra-Köstenberger, 'Women', 233 who expresses some caution in ascribing leadership roles to the women.

[28] Most commentators including Fee, 390; Bockmuehl, 239; O'Brien, 478; Bruce, 140 suggest that attempts to identify Lydia with the two women are far-fetched and effectively baseless (cf. W. Ramsay, *The Bearing of Recent Discovery on the Trustworthiness of the New Testament* (London: Hodder & Stoughton, 1915), 309. Hawthorne, 179 sees it as a vague possibility. Similarly the Tübingen School's idea that the two names are allegories for the Jewish-Christian and Gentile-Christian factions in the church is to be roundly rejected as state Gnilka, 166; O'Brien, 478; Hawthorne, 179; J.J. Müller, 137; Michael, 188; Barth, 119.

[29] Fee, 390 and especially Acts 16:15, 40 which refers to her hosting the missionary team and the church of Philippi; O'Brien, 478; Elzell, 'Sufficiency': 375 among many others.

[30] See Chapter 2; Fee, 391.

[31] Witherington, 108.

[32] Fee, 392.

[33] Fee, 392.

recurrence of φρονέω in 3:15, 19 indicates the importance of right thinking in the epistle cf. 4:10.[34]

In 4:3 Paul appeals to a certain genuine companion (σύζυγος) to help these two women to resolve this difference of opinion. In the absence of evidence of σύζυγος as a proper name, it is probably best to understand the term in the sense 'true comrade.'[35] It is likely that this man was a co-worker of Paul,[36] Paul using such favourable language to describe him (cf. 1 Tim 1:2; Tit 1:4). This being the case, he could well be an itinerant from the Pauline team.[37] If so he may be Luke who according to the 'we-passage' evidence of Acts, is left behind after the Philippian mission (Acts 16:40) and rejoins Paul again on his return (Acts 20:6-21:18). It is likely that he has left Philippi with Paul and travelled to Rome, in that he is named in Colossians and Philemon (Col 4:14; Phm 23) and on the basis of the final 'we passage' in Acts (Acts 27:1-28:16). Since he is not named in Philippians, it is possible to speculate he travelled to Philippi again.[38] However, this cannot be proved.

Alternatively he may be one of the unnamed Philippian co-workers who worked alongside the women, Clement and the others and the recipient of the letter on behalf of the church and its overseers and deacons (1:1).[39] This makes sense on four grounds. First, the letter is specifically addressed to the church and the leaders, not to an itinerant. Secondly, while the phrase 'rest of my co-

---

[34] Fee, 391-392 who correctly notes also that the link to 3:15, 19 and 'earthly vs. heavenly mindsets' on the basis of the brevity of the letter, its oral reading and its 'friendship' context of Philippians, suggest these two verses are linked cf. O'Brien, 478.

[35] And probably not as a name (as suggest Michael, 191; U.B. Müller, 195 noting similar names; J.J. Müller, 139; Barth, 119; Hendriksen, 191; Gnilka, 167; Wicks, 108) as σύζυγος has never been found as a name; so *BDAG*, 954; Fee, 393; O'Brien, 481; Schenk, 272.

[36] The masculine gender of σύζυγος presupposes a male and so not as Clement of Alexandria, Origen and Erasmus suggest, a female spouse of Paul (Lydia?) or anyone else (see comments of Bockmuehl, 240; Bruce, 140 [who rightly calls it 'romantic fiction']; Calvin, 286).

[37] Fee, 393.

[38] Fee, 394 -395; Manson, 'Date': 138; M.Hájek, 'Comments on Philippians 4:3 – Who was "*Gnesios Syzygos*"?' *CV* 7 (1964): 261-262. Silas (Acts 16:19, 25) is another possibility as suggested by J.A. Bengel (as quoted by O'Brien, 480) and *TDNT* 7.749-750. Another option is Barnabas. Timothy, who was with Paul at the time, can be ruled out; despite Collange, 143; Schenk, 272 who strangely suggests him in light of Phil 2:20 (cf. Schmithals, *Paul*, 76-77, 252). Epaphroditus is also highly unlikely as he is the probable bearer of the letter as Plummer, *Understanding,* 90 suggests, although he is favoured by Lightfoot. 158; Moule, 90. The idea that this is a prayer introduced by ναί (Weisler, referred to by Hawthorne, 180) and so 'Christ' is very unlikely.

[39] Similarly O'Brien, 481. Surely there is no need to see this individual as the whole congregation as Houlden, 110; Hawthorne, 180 suggest. Such an application is not found elsewhere. Some speculate one of the women's husbands (Chrystostom); the chief 'overseer' of Philippi (Ellicott, 89), which are both possible, but unproveable.

workers' may refer to Paul's co-workers in general, in that the others named are in Philippi, the context suggests 'the 'true companion' and the 'others' may well be Philippians. Thirdly, there is no conclusive evidence that Luke was in Philippi. Fourthly, the existence of other co-workers and Epaphroditus suggests there may be a Philippian appointee who acted on Paul's behalf as leader of the team in Philippi. If so, he is a male co-worker and perhaps an overseer or deacon. Whoever this individual was, Paul asks for this person of 'tact and influence' to help them;[40] the middle of the verb συλλαμβάνω implying 'support, aid, help' for the women.[41]

The nature of the dispute is not entirely clear. It is possible but unproven that the issue is theological.[42] Suggestions include Gnosticism,[43] that one or other was attracted to the theology of the Judaisers, personal ambition or a petty quarrel.[44] I consider that there are sound reasons to suggest a link between the quarrel, ongoing evangelistic mission and suffering in the face of opposition in Philippi. And to this I now turn.

The Nature of the Involvement of Euodia and Syntyche in the Gospel Mission

Before examining the details of the text, there are sound reasons for *suggesting* that these women were involved in evangelism on the basis of the allusions to the dissension throughout the epistle, which are in all cases linked to evangelistic mission. This is seen first in 1:9 where the appeal for increased love flows out of a reference to evangelistic mission and suffering (1:5-7).[45] Secondly, the key appeal for unity in 2:1-4 flows out of an appeal for the continuation of the mission without intimidation from Gentile opponents (1:27-30 [see Chapter 4]). Thirdly, the link with evangelism is found in the manner in which the appeal for continued ethical and evangelistic mission in Philippi in 2:15-16 flows out of the appeal for a cessation of grumbling and argument in 2:14 (See Chapter 5). Finally, the example of Paul in Rome where he and the Romans continue their evangelistic mission in the midst of contention and suffering points in this direction (1:14-18a [see Chapter 3]).

As the details of the text are considered, this impression is further enhanced. These women have 'contended' with Paul in the gospel (ἐν τῷ εὐαγγελίῳ

---

[40] Beare, 145.

[41] *BDAG*, 955; O'Brien, 481 suggests this could imply that the two women were already trying to patch up the problem. Alternatively, Marshall, 109 suggests that they were on the edge as a result of the pressure.

[42] But see Peterlin, *Letter*, 103 who argues that there is no real connection in this regard.

[43] A highly unlikely idea promoted by Schmithals, *Paul*, 112-114. See O'Brien, 478; Bruce, 140; Gnilka, 166 for critique.

[44] Fee, 397, who rightly suggests this is an idea based on pure male chauvinism.

[45] See further below in Chapter 8.

συνήθλησαν μοι μετὰ)[46] in conjunction with Clement and the rest of Paul's co-workers (μετὰ καὶ Κλήμεντος καὶ τῶν λοιπῶν συνεργῶν μου). This clause suggests that these women along with the other co-workers were involved in active evangelism.[47] If not, then one wonders why Paul would have added these details which would surely be obvious to the Philippians.

This active role is indicated in several other ways. First, the earlier analysis of συναθλέω in 1:27 calls to mind Paul's athletic interpretation of the Christian life, which should be understood in active and evangelistic terms.[48] Secondly, as argued earlier, εὐαγγέλιον and parallels in Philippians are predominately active referring to action on behalf of the gospel (1:5, 12, 14, 15, 16, 17, 18, 27b; 2:16, 22; 4:15) rather than referring to the content of the gospel (1:27a).[49]

---

[46] With Fee, 395 I understand Paul's use of αἵτινες as qualitative in the sense of 'inasmuch' rather than as a simple relative pronoun 'who' (NIV; NASB; REB; Hawthorne, 180) or causally ('because they') as does O'Brien, 481.

[47] So O'Brien, 481 and 'Gospel': 227-228; Schenk, 271-272 whether or not the Christ-hymn originated from their evangelistic endeavour as he presupposes; Marshall, 108; Green, *Evangelism*, 211; Hawthorne, 180; Bruce, 139 and 'Macedonia': 283: 'συναθλέω ... implies no mere auxilliary role'; Witherington, *Friendship*, 105; Pfitzner, *Paul*, 119; Loh-Nida, 126; Thomas, 'Women': 119'; V.P. Furnish, *The Moral Teaching of Paul* (Nashville: Abingdon, 1979): 105; E. M. Tetlow, *Women and Ministry in the New Testament* (New York: Paulist Press, 1980), 126; E. Schüssler-Fiorenza, *In Memory of Her: A Feminist Theological Reconstruction of Christian Origins* (New York: Crossroad, 1983), 170; W.A. Meeks, *The First Urban Christians: The Social World of the Apostle Paul* (New Haven, Yale University, 1983), 57; Köstenberger, 'Women', 233; D'Angelo, 'Partners': 76-77 who argues that they were a missionary couple i.e. partners in mission; Johnson, *Writings*, 373; Dahl, 'Euodia', 7, 14; Oaks, *Philippians*, 125; Trebilco, 'Women': 32-33. As Malinowski, 'Brave': 62 concedes, this is the majority position; Motyer, 201; Ellis, 'Co-workers, Paul and his', in *DPL*, 187; C.S. Keener, 'Man and Woman', in *DPL*, 589-590; R. Banks, 'Church Order and Government', in *DPL*, 135; R.H. Finger, 'For the Sake of the Gospel: Paul and the Ministering Women', *DS* 19 (1993): 43-46, 45; Scholer, 'Co-Workers': 70, 72; Murray, 'Witness': 325.

[48] *TDNT* 1.167 who sees it in terms of labour here. It is worth noting that the appeal to 'stand' in 4:1 is also invested with the military consciousness of Paul, which is decidedly evangelistic (above on 1:27 cf. Eph 6:15, 17). It is no surprise to see the military metaphor followed by the active athletic reference to evangelistic endeavour as the latter is subsumed in the former. The view of Malinowski, 'Brave': 61 that συναθλέω is static unified resistance in the context of suffering and not ministry is inadequate in failing to account for Paul's use of athletic imagery which is dynamic and evangelistic (see Appendix 1, 'The connection between evangelism and the athletic metaphor in the Paul'). *BDAG*, 964 suggests here 'they fought at my side in (spreading) the gospel' with an emphasis on their courage in doing so. Similarly Thomas, 'Women': 119: 'the apostle had already used the same word in the first chapter...where the word suggests the side-by-side contending for the defence of the gospel in Christian witness and apologetic.'

[49] O'Brien, 481; Dickson, *Mission-Commitment*, 87.

Thirdly, in that Euodia and Syntyche contended with Clement and the τῶν λοιπῶν συνεργῶν, this suggests that the three named were also co-workers and so actively involved in the same mission. As discussed in regard to Epaphroditus, συνεργός in Paul usually indicates involvement in evangelism.[50]

O'Brien puts it this way: 'the sphere in which Euodia and Syntyche "contended" was ἐν τῷ εὐαγγελίῳ ("in the proclamation of the gospel", εὐαγγελιῳ being used as a noun of agency; cf. Rom 1:9; 1 Thess 3:2).'[51] Hawthorne likewise suggests, 'it implies a united struggle in preaching the gospel, on the one hand, and a sharing in the suffering that results from the struggle on the other.'[52] Marshall writes, 'this means that they had shared in the work of evangelism, and Paul does not distinguish them as women in any way from other helpers.'[53] Significantly, the conservative Carson similarly states: 'they have been at the forefront of evangelism.'[54] It is probable that this involved full participation in the suffering and struggles of Paul and his team in the initial evangelisation of Philippi and on subsequent visits (cf. Phil 1:30).[55]

Fiorenza perhaps a shade hyperbolically, describes Euodia and Syntyche as 'outstanding women missionaries', who held such authority that Paul feared 'that their dissension could do serious damage to the Christian mission.'[56] U.B. Müller notes that, 'the two women together with the other contending co-workers have shown themselves to be employed with the proclamation of the gospel.'[57] Witherington gets to the gist of the matter:

> They are his co-workers along with Clement and as such they did more than struggle on Paul's behalf on that one occasion when suffering was involved. In fact, the other use of this same verb is found in the *propositio* in 1:27, where we are told of those who fight side by side for the faith of the gospel, which surely implied some sort of sharing of the faith, even in the face of opposition. It is

---

[50] Bruce, 139. As Fee, 395 notes, while on its own 'contended at my side' does not 'necessarily imply leadership of some kind, it does so when used in this way in conjunction with Paul's own ministry, followed by a further notation about "the rest of my co-workers"' (see Chapter 6).

[51] O'Brien, 481: 'a noun of agency.'

[52] Hawthorne, 180.

[53] Marshall, 108.

[54] Carson, *Basics*, 100. Carson generally is moderately conservative on the matter of women in ministry; e.g. Carson, *Showing*, 121-131.

[55] Pfitzner, *Paul*, 180; H.A.W. Meyer, 196 limits it to suffering without the gospel context cf. O'Brien, 482.

[56] Schüssler-Fiorenza, *Memory*, 82. Certainly that he mentions them by name does suggest a great level of influence!

[57] U.B. Müller, *Philipper*, 196.

very likely that these women were not patronesses, but leaders and proclaimers of the word, those who struggled in the gospel with Paul.[58]

The second clause καὶ Κλήμεντος καὶ τῶν λοιπῶν συνεργῶν μου confirms this impression. Paul names Clement and his 'other co-workers' (συνεργῶν). As postulated earlier concerning Epaphroditus, the term συνεργός refers to Christian gospel workers either in itinerant ministry or local ministry (see Chapter 6).[59] While it is unclear why Paul mentions Clement[60] and 'the rest of my co-workers'[61] along with the women, it provides clear evidence that there were co-workers in Philippi who were gospel workers.[62] Here no gender distinction is made; the two women are named alongside male co-workers which gives no indication whatsoever of role designation in the context of the evangelism. If so, then an active meaning of εὐαγγέλιον is preferable.

It can be argued that an active meaning for εὐαγγέλιον is rendered obsolete because these two are women and such a role is incongruous with Paul's purported injunctions against the leadership of women in the Paulines (1 Cor 14:34-35; Eph 5:22-33; Col 3:19-20; 1 Tim 2:9-15). However none of these passages, no matter how rigorously, literally and universally they are interpreted and applied, remove the possibility that Paul wanted the women of the Pauline congregations to be involved *in evangelism* which is, in the main, an extra-church activity.[63] The injunction in 1 Cor 14:34-35 relates to order

[58] Witherington, *Friendship*, 106. Whether or not they were patronesses, I consider unimportant. The key point is that they were co-workers.

[59] Whether or not it is compatible with the diaconate as Peterlin, *Letters*, 119-123 argues is, for me, a moot point as it is not proven that the women were deacons cf. Gnilka, 166. Even if they were (or 'overseers') there need be no conflict between the evangelistic function of the co-worker and other functions including hospitality, financial provision, prayer and patronage. As in the contemporary church, ministry is rarely confined to one dimension but is a confluence of a number of functions. This would especially be so in a new growing church with limited resources.

[60] Most contemporary exegetes rule out the connection between this Clement and Clement of Rome. His name is Latin so he probably comes from the Roman populace of Philippi. He was well known in the congregation, a leader of some sort. The suggestion that he was the jailor (Acts 16:16-40) is possible but not provable. See discussion in Gnilka, 168.

[61] Fee, 395-396 suggests it is a Pauline aside perhaps because he does not want to exclude anyone. However this is unlikely as he mentions the 'rest' without naming them. It could be due to this Clement's prominent role in the church. The idea that it refers to his death (so Vincent, 132; Barth, 120; Beare, 145; J.J. Müller, 139) is weakened, in that, the 'rest of my co-workers' appears to refer to the living. In addition on other occasions 'book of life' is used of the living (cf. Lk 10:20; Rev 3:5).

[62] Hawthorne, 180; Witherington, *Friendship*, 105.

[63] Furthermore, as Trebilco, 'Women', 33-34 notes: 'we do know of individual women who were involved in fulfilling the tasks of an apostle, *in evangelism*, in preaching, in

within church meetings as the prepositional phrase ἐν ἐκκλησίᾳ explicitly makes clear. In addition, women were involved in prophetic ministry in Corinth, which Paul understood to involve an evangelistic dimension (1 Cor 11:5; 14:20-25). Expressly, Paul suggests that if an unbeliever or outsider (ἄπιστος ἢ ἰδιώτης)[64] visits the church gathering while everybody (πάντες προφητεύωσιν) is prophesying, that person will be convicted of his/her sin and respond with praise of God (1 Cor 14:25).[65] This suggests that, at the least, some form of evangelistic proclamation was permitted for women of the Pauline church.[66]

In addition, the appeals for the submission of wives to husbands says nothing about evangelism at all but relates to the relationship of wife to husband. Indeed elsewhere Paul explicitly suggests women are to be actively involved in evangelising their husbands which must have involved verbal communication of some sort or another (1 Cor 7:16).[67] 1 Tim 2:9-16 can be used to suggest that women were not to evangelise as there are limits placed on their teaching ministry. However on closer examination this *at the most* limits women's evangelistic mission to women (aside from husbands) only. In addition if this is intended to limit the role of women,[68] it is probable Paul is referring to prohibiting women from teaching men within the church only.[69]

Furthermore, as I have discussed in Chapter 3, there are a number of women

---

teaching, in leading house churches where the Lord's Supper would have been shared and in providing protection and patronage for Christians' (italics mine).

[64] On ἰδιώτης as a 'non-initiated member' or 'outsider' distinct from 'unbeliever' see *BDAG*, 468.

[65] This suggests that Paul was in all likelihood referring to a contextual problem among Corinthian women rather than to a universal injunction.

[66] Assuming the passage is not an interpolation (cf. Fee, *1 Corinthians*, 699-705) or a Corinthians slogan (D.W. Odell-Scott, 'Let the Women Speak in Church: an Egalitarian Interpretation of 1 Cor 14:33b-36', 90-93); see Thiselton, *1 Corinthians*, 1146-1162.

[67] Whether taken optimistically 'but remember, a wife may save her husband' giving a positive reason to remain in the marriage (so REB cf. J. Jeremias, 'Die missionarische Aufgabe in der Mischehe [1 Kor 7:16]); Fee, *1 Corinthians*, 305 (after noting the ambiguity); Collins, *First Corinthians*, 272; Barrett, *1 Corinthians*, 167; or pessimistically 'How do you know, wife, whether you will save your husband?' noting that remaining in the marriage will not necessarily lead to the salvation of the unbelieving spouse [NIV cf. Thiselton, *1 Corinthians*, 539; C. Blomberg, *1 Corinthians*. NIVAC (Grand Rapids: Zondervan, 1994), 135; Morris, *1 Corinthians*, 108]; or ambiguously, the text still assumes a concern for evangelising the unbelieving spouse (cf. 1 Pet 3:1).

[68] I consider that this is not Paul's intention. Rather, he is addressing a problem in the Ephesus community concerning women.

[69] The statement may well not be universal but relate to the specific problem of false teaching in the Ephesian church; see Fee, *Pastorals*, 73; Marshall, *Pastorals*, 455; Towner, *Pastorals*, 77-78. But see W.D. Mounce, *Pastoral Epistles*. WBC Vol 46 (Nashville: Thomas Nelson, 2000), 120-130 who argues for a wider application.

who were involved in proclamation ministry in the Paulines including Prisca (Rom 16:3), Junia (Rom 16:7) and possibly Mary (Rom 16:6), Tryphena and Tryphosa (Rom 16:12) and Persis (Rom 16:12).[70] Evangelism is also implied in 2 Timothy 1:5 through Timothy's mother Lois and his grandmother Eunice who passed onto him the Christian faith.[71] If so, it is evangelism in the context of the *oikos*, as in 1 Cor 7:16 (cf. 1 Pet 3:1). It is unclear whether others including Phoebe (Rom 16:1), Chloe (1 Cor 1:11) and Nympha (Col 4:15) were evangelistic at all.[72] In any case, the point is this: without doubt women were involved in evangelistic ministry in the Paulines.

It is most likely then that these two women along with Clement and Epaphroditus were active co-workers in the Pauline mission proclaiming the gospel.[73] Other suggestions limiting their role then are at best debatable.[74] Bockmuehl for example suggests leadership in the church perhaps in 'administration, hospitality, or oversight of pastoral or financial matters such as the church's allocation of moneys for the poor.'[75] Alford accepts an active solution but limits it to evangelism among women only writing: '"these two must have been among those [women] who, having believed, laboured *among their own sex* for" the spread of the gospel.'[76] Martin limits their support to that of Lydia (Acts 16:15, 40) and suggests that their assistance was 'material

---

[70] See above Chapter 3.

[71] Marshall, *Pastorals*, 695; Hanson, *Pastorals*, 120 note specifically Christian faith was passed on. Fee, *Pastorals*, 223 suggests both Jewish and Christian faith.

[72] See earlier in Chapter 3 on Phoebe. In that a church met in Nympha's house, it is possible that she was involved in evangelism. Similarly perhaps Apphia in the house church of Philemon in Colossae (Phm 1). In Acts 18:24 Luke uses plurals of the teaching of Apollos by Priscilla and Aquila suggesting active involvement in teaching by both Priscilla and Aquila.

[73] Marshall, 110; 'Theology', 157.

[74] Some opt for ambiguous general statements which may or may not include evangelism such as 'active service' (Michael, 192); 'associated ... in some efforts to advance the gospel' (Ellicott, 89); 'shared in the apostolic struggle' (Silva, 221); 'doing the gospel' (Fee, 392); 'co-operated in the interests of the gospel' (J.J. Müller, 139); 'courageous and energetic co-operation' (Beare, 145); 'the spread of the gospel' (Melick, 147); 'labour with Paul' (Kent, 152); they had 'cooperated harmoniously and enthusiastically with each other and with Paul and his companions' (Hendriksen, 190); 'they actively engaged with him in the apostolate' (Houlden, 108); 'zealous aid in the spread of the gospel... without a parallel in the Apostle's history elsewhere.' (Lightfoot, 56-57); 'earnest and energetic aid in St Paul's work at Philippi' (Moule, 78); 'they stood by Paul when his missionary task was hard' (Wicks, 108); 'contended alongside the apostle' (Collange, 143); 'fighting side by side with me' (Plummer, *Understanding,* 90); 'actively attended with danger and suffering' (Vincent, 132); 'fellow-workers' (Beasley-Murray, 988). J. Gnilka, 166 cf. Caird, 149; Melick, 147; Getty, 61.

[75] Bockmuehl, 238.

[76] Hawthorne, 180 quoting H. Alford, *The Greek Testament* (4 vols. London: Longmans, Green and Co, 1894) (without page reference [italics Hawthorne]).

help.'[77] Malinowski rejects the evangelistic interpretation preferring to define their involvement as 'staunch loyalty to Paul, for their bravery at Paul's side when persecution broke out and threatened him physically.'[78] Schenk however notes that this text indicates that these are 'co-workers in the missionary spread of the gospel' i.e. 'his former missionary team' (cf. 1:27). He refutes their being involved in 'diaconal activities', 'economic support', merely 'active participation in community life' or 'patronage-support.' Their function was active proclamation.[79]

In reality, Paul at no point limits the *evangelistic* involvement of women. I agree with Thomas who questions whether Paul would have used the strongly athletic συναθλέω if 'they had merely assisted him with material help and hospitality, while remaining in the background. The word συνήθλησάν suggests a more active participation in the work of Paul, probably even a vocal declaration of the faith.'[80] Finally, I find Malinowski's 'suffering' interpretation as overly narrow and based on weak analysis of Paul's use of both athletic and military terminology (see Appendices 1 and 2).

Moreover, there is no reason to suggest that they, Clement and the other co-workers, discontinued their evangelistic endeavour after Paul had moved on.[81] Paul's urgent concern that they patch up their differences indicates their work continued after Paul's departure,[82] as does the reference to Clement, the apostle Epaphroditus and other co-workers. In addition, the general phrase, 'the rest of my co-workers' may suggest a number too numerous to name. If so it may imply a reasonably large number of co-workers in Philippi. This indicates that since the planting of the church in Philippi a large number of co-workers have toiled along with Clement, the women, Epaphroditus and Pauline or other itinerants in Philippi.[83] It could even imply that the majority of the church has actively joined in the mission?

Finally, I restate that the link of gospel mission in every reference to contentiousness in the epistle suggests an ongoing role in the current context. The need to name the women in the letter also suggests a current issue.

---

[77] Martin, 168. Similarly Bonnard, *L'Epitre*, 63 as mentioned by Malinowski, 'Brave': 62.

[78] Malinowksi, 'Brave': 63; Michael, 192; Plummer, *Understanding,* 90; Lightfoot, 158 take this position. This is not strictly correct as they mention persecution but do not limit their involvement to this alone, speaking as well of their service i.e. non-specific ministry which could include evangelism.

[79] Schenk, 271-272.

[80] Thomas, 'Women': 119.

[81] As A.H. Snyman, 'Persuasion': 331 notes the logical syllogism behind 4:3 includes: 'Major premise: People who further the gospel must be helped. Minor premise: Euodia and Syntyche *further the gospel*. Conclusion: Euodia and Syntyche must be helped' (italics mine). Dickson, *Mission-Commitment*, 142.

[82] Marshall, 'Theology', 157.

[83] Marshall, 110; Luter, 'Role': 415.

This is not to suggest that these two women necessarily functioned as itinerants, engaged in market-place evangelism or other overt evangelistic activity.[84] Although this cannot be completely ruled out, it is more likely in a first century culture that, through means of natural relationships appropriate to the culture of Philippi, these women shared the message with others. Dahl suggests in his discussion of Euodia and Syntyche that:

> Women are hardly likely to have proclaimed the gospel on street-corners and in marketplaces, but other forms of communication have from an early time on contributed to the spread of Christianity. For women like Lydia and Prisca, trade and workshop offered ample opportunities to make contacts and bear testimony to the faith (see Acts 16:14; 18:3). So did the synagogues; Acts reports that Prisca/Priscilla gave Apollos more adequate instruction about 'the way (of God)' after she had hear him speak boldly in the synagogue.[85]

Furthermore, if the gospel was to be carried to all people including women, it stands to reason in any culture, and in particular those in which gender roles are well-defined, that the gospel would spread from women to women. While the role of female evangelists should not be limited to their own gender by assumption (e.g. 1 Cor 7:15), the importance of women in evangelising other women would seem obvious; especially in a middle-eastern culture where women engaged with other women and children primarily. Many of the named and unnamed women of the Pauline epistles would have been vital to the spread of the faith in this regard. Dahl rightly proposes of Euodia and Syntyche that 'they have continued and extended his work and also faced trials after he had left.'[86] It may well be that the existence in the church of Euodia and Syntyche themselves in the Philippian church is a result of the evangelistic ministry of the first Philippian convert, Lydia.

This active scenario concurs with the situation in Philippi. Oaks in his analysis notes that Paul focused his ministry on the town, which he considers made up one third of the people in the immediate Philippian region.[87] He also notes that inscriptional evidence suggests a number of dependent villages within the area.[88] He considers the social range included the elite (3%), slaves (20%), the poor (20%), colonist farmers (20%) and the service community (37%).[89] He suggests that Roman colonists made up 23% of the community.[90]

---

[84] Although as Dickson, *Mission-Commitment*, 141-142 notes, there is no absolute reason to rule this out.

[85] Dahl, 'Euodia', 5.

[86] Dahl, 'Euodia', 6; see also Dickson, *Mission-Commitment*, 141-142.

[87] Oaks, *Philippians*, 44-46 suggests 15,000 in the city and 46,000 in the region assuming 24 people per sq. km.

[88] Oaks, *Philippians*, 32.

[89] Oaks, *Philippians*, 46-49.

[90] Oaks, *Philippians*, 52.

He discusses the potential accessibility of these groups to Paul in his mission suggesting certain features limited accessibility. First, spatial accessibility i.e. in that most people of the region lived outside the city, many would not have come into contact with Paul and his message.[91] Secondly, social accessibility whereby certain groups were inaccessible to Paul including the elite,[92] whilst the poor, craftspeople and other small traders who lived in the town would provide Paul's main opportunities. In addition, apart from Lydia and the women (Acts 16) the apparent absence of a Jewish community further limited Paul's accessibility. Thirdly, he contends that some Roman members of the elite with strong allegiance to traditional and civic religions were the group which was least accessible to Paul's mission. On the other hand those following Judaism and other 'oriental' religions were more accessible. Again in Philippi, Paul was limited in this regard. Moreover, due to social contraints, many women would not have been accessible to Paul. Hence, the importance of female ministers of the gospel.

The overall import of this is that Paul's impact on the total region of Philippi would have been very limited and it would have required energetic effort from his co-workers during his mission and after his departure to make a significant evangelistic impact on the community. Working on the assumption in the introduction that Paul wanted all people to hear the gospel and be saved, it is highly probable that the co-workers named, Epaphroditus (their 'apostle'), other unnamed workers and travelling itinerants were active after Paul moved on. These people would have moved through the region preaching the gospel and establishing believing *oikos*-communities, as led by the Spirit, where converts were made (cf. 1 Thess 1:6-8).

If so, then here are four named members of the Philippian congregation and a number of unnamed co-workers who were evangelistically inclined. Perhaps they were apostles or evangelists in the Pauline sense (Eph 4:11; 2 Tim 4:5 cf. Acts 21:8). Whether or not this is the case, we have good support for the contention that there is evidence of ongoing evangelistic activity in and through the Pauline churches. Such activity would have been a delight to Paul (1:18a) and he is writing to urge them to keep up the God-work (1:27; 2:16). It is reasonable to postulate then that one of the reasons for Paul's imperative to restore unity is that the 'advance of the gospel' in Philippi was threatened

---

[91] Oaks, *Philippians*, 70 notes that the community was highly agricultural, more so than Corinth, Ephesus, Athens or Antioch meaning that for the gospel to reach these people, and for them to be integrated into churches, proactive evangelistic mission had to be undertaken.

[92] Oaks, *Philippians*, 57-58. That is, unless Paul had prior friendship, recommendation or client-patron relationships in Philippi. If some recipients were from the elite, 'an attempt by the client to proselytise would seem to fall outside what would be socially permissible.' Oaks also suggests (60) that this inaccessibility of the elite would conversely reduce the inaccessibility of the poor.

through their dispute. As Marshall puts it:

> They had shared in Paul's *struggles* in the gospel (italics Marshall's). The word used echoes 1:27 with its description of the Philippians as sharing together in the struggle to advance the gospel faith; that may suggest that the two women had been loyal colleagues of Paul in the early days of the mission in Philippi when it had not been easy, but that now, perhaps as a result of their quarrels, they were no longer taking their place with the other members of the church in the struggle. *The comment shows incidentally that the local people shared with Paul in the work of evangelism in their own area: they did not stand by and let Paul do all the work* (italics mine).[93]

This impression is sustained in Paul's intriguing assurance of eschatological salvation (ὧν τὰ ὀνόματα ἐν βίβλῳ ζωῆς) for these co-workers. This is another example of the close connection between evangelism and eschatology in the epistle (1:27-28; 2:10-11, 12-18 cf. 1:6, 11, 22; 3:10-14). Here these workers 'names are in the book of life',[94] with their evangelistic endeavour one evidence of their faith.[95] In the early church and broader Jewish context the book of life refers to the listed names of those who will receive salvation at the consummation (Rev 3:5; 13:8; 17:8; 20:12,15; 21:27; 22:19 cf. Lk 10:20; Heb 12:23; Exod 32:32-33; Ps 69:28 [LXX 68:29]; Dan 12:1; 1 Enoch 47:3; Herm. *Sim.* 2.9).[96] Furthermore, the genitive ζωῆς calls to mind 2:16 where Paul speaks of the Philippians 'holding forth the *word* **of** life.' In other words by 'holding forth the *word* **of** life' the evangelistic proclaimers reinforce the certainty that their names are written in the '*book* **of** life.'

Dickson rightly notes the verbal connections to Luke 10:1-7. First, he notes the similarity between συνεργοί and ἐργάται (Lk 10:2, 7). Secondly, the conceptual similarities between ὧν τὰ ὀνόματα ἐν βίβλῳ ζωῆς and χαίρετε δὲ ὅτι τὰ ὀνόματα ὑμῶν ἐγγὲραπται ἐν τοῖς οὐρανοῖς.[97] He suggests here is found a 'cliché' and ὧντὰ ὀνόματα ἐν βίβλῳ ζωῆς represents 'an honorific descriptor of preaching missionaries, among whom Paul included Euodia,

---

[93] Marshall, 110 cf. 'Theology', 155.

[94] I consider this refers to all named in context (so Fee, 396; O'Brien, 482; Gnilka, 168; U.B. Müller, 196; Loh-Nida, 127; Bruce, 139; Hawthorne, 181; Silva, *Philippians*, 222-223) rather than just 'the rest of my co-workers' (H.A.W. Meyer, 197, Vincent, 132; Hendriksen, 192).

[95] Not that they are saved through evangelising or any other work. Rather that these works demonstrate that they are slaves to righteousness whose actions reveal their faith. Evangelism is a fruit of the work of the Spirit within the believer (see Chapter 6 on Epaphroditus and spiritual gifts in Eph 4:11-16; below on Chapter 8 in regards to Paul's apostolic grace). See also here Col 1:10 where 'fruit' would contextually include converts (cf. Col 1:6).

[96] See further Fee, 39; O'Brien, 482. Hawthorne, 181; Bruce, 139; Caird, 150 note the connection to 3:20 suggesting a register of citizens of the heavenly commonwealth.

[97] Dickson, *Mission-Commitment*, 142.

Syntyche, Clement and the "rest".'[98]

Bruce suggests that Paul may be referring to more than just salvation. He suggests that the service for the gospel of Paul's co-workers is also recorded along with their names. This is possibly so in that Paul's concept of judgement appears to include the judgement of the work of the Christian on behalf of God (1 Cor 3:13-15).[99] If so, Paul gives all the more reason for the Philippians to emulate these co-workers (cf. 1:27).[100]

It could be argued that these proclaimers exhaust Paul's desire for proclamation from the Philippians. However there are several reasons to argue that this is not the case. First, the appeal in Phil 1:27 applies to the present *whole* congregation and is not gender-exclusive or limited to leaders only. Secondly, other Pauline passages that enlighten an understanding of evangelism are not exclusive either. In particular, spiritual gift lists (Rom 12:3-8; 1 Cor 12:4-11, 28-30; Eph 4:11),[101] and Eph 6:10-17 which apply to all believers (cf. Eph 2:10; 4:12).[102]

If it is correct to assess that Euodia, Syntyche, Clement and Epaphroditus were evangelistic co-workers, then their function in the Philippian church was in part, to equip others for works of service including sharing the faith (Eph 4:11-12; 6:15, 17).[103] Paul's presentation of Timothy as the ideal son in proclaiming the gospel enhances this perspective. In the Pastorals he is instructed to 'do the work of an evangelist' (2 Tim 4:5). Traditionally this is interpreted as proclamation of the gospel.[104] I suggest it goes further to include the equipping of the saints for the purposes of evangelistic mission.

The Nature of the Problem

The analysis above indicates that 'contending for the faith of the gospel' in

---

[98] Dickson, *Mission-Commitment*, 142.

[99] Interestingly the context here is the ministries of Paul and Apollos, which are clearly evangelistic, if not exclusively so (cf. 1 Cor 3:5-11). See especially verse 5 where Paul implies that some of the Corinthians were converted through Apollos as well as Paul.

[100] Bruce, 139.

[101] In Rom 12:4-8 I note πᾶς (12:3, 4), ἐκάστος (12:4), πολλύς (12:4, 5). In 1 Cor 12:4-11 τὰ πάντα ἐν πᾶσιν (12:6), ἰδίᾳ ἑκάστῳ (12:11). In 1 Cor 12:28-31 and Eph 4:11 it is clear not all have all the gifts but this is not linked to gender at all.

[102] The imperatives are inclusive as is ἡμῖν (Eph 6:12).

[103] See above my discussion of this passage concerning Epaphroditus Chapter 6.

[104] Interestingly, this is the final imperative in the body of 2 Timothy before Paul's final references to his situation and Rome, people, greetings and a final benediction. In that this is Paul's last letter, we have a fascinating parallels to Matthew and Luke-Acts where Jesus' final words relate to evangelistic mission (cf. Matt 28:18-20; Lk 24:46-49; Acts 1:8). Assuming one's final words reflect one's priorities, this suggests evangelism was a high priority for Jesus (and/or Matthew and Luke) and for Paul, their converts and the Evangelists.

loving unity without fear of suffering and persecution, is the key point here as in 1:27-30. This suggests a retreatism or quietism on the part of one or other of the women is possibly at issue. Alternatively, they may have fallen out over different responses to mission, one perhaps taking a triumphalistic approach, the other perhaps a retreatist? Whatever is going on, Paul appears to be encouraging them to renounce their differences and come together and take up the challenge to contend for the gospel in unity again.

The extent of the problem is disputed. That Paul needs to mention it at all,[105] names the women specifically,[106] refers to it throughout the letter, seeks the assistance of a co-worker to resolve it and appeals so directly to the problem, that the issue within a letter to be read out to the whole church,[107] all combine to suggest that the issue was rather more than a merely personal one.[108] It is possible that the problem is related to house-group factions.[109] It is feasible also that the Philippian church has grown from Lydia's house church into a number of home contexts.[110] If so, then the conflict may be between house groups with differing perspectives on theology or mission.[111]

There is no clear evidence that Paul is siding with either woman; rather he is appealing to them both to back down.[112] As I have repeated, the problem is not extreme; Paul here appears to be guarding against escalation.[113]

---

[105] Thomas, 'Women':118.

[106] Garland, 'Composition': 172; O'Brien, 478; Peterlin, *Letter*, 103 who perceptively and decisively notes that if there is not a significant issue he has no need to mention them specifically, as he has dealt generally with unity earlier.

[107] Peterlin, *Letter*, 103.

[108] As note Gnilka, 166; Trebilco, 'Women': 32. Those who argue this way include Bruce, 138; Martin, 168; Witherington, *Friendship*, 109.

[109] Peterlin, *Letter*, 217; Hawthorne, 179; Trebilco, 'Women': 32; Marshall, 108; Witherington, *Friendship*, 109; U.B. Müller, 194-195. A number of scholars approach this with caution including Bockmuehl, 239 who notes the language is individualistic and so personal. However, if the issue in Rome (1:15-18a) is based on house groups as I have suggested, then it may well reinforce this here. But only if the Philippians are aware of the details of the problem which Epaphroditus may convey to them.

[110] Possible evidence for this includes the conversion of the jailor's household (Acts 16:33); the suffering of the Philippian church (1:30) suggesting that the church had spread sufficiently to alienate the Philippi community; the role of women in Macedonia suggesting that these two women may represent leaders; the references to disunity in the church which suggest more than a mere problem between two women (1:27; 2:1-11, 14-15); the problem of the Judaisers who may have some sympathy in Philippi (3:2f); the rhetorical mention of factional problems in the Roman church and witness (1:15-18). In addition, see the discussion in Peterlin, *Letter*, 113-114.

[111] Possibly this brings into play the rhetorical intent of 1:15-18 i.e. poor motivation.

[112] Fee, 392; Bockmuehl, 239; O'Brien, 478. Seen in the repetition of παρακαλῶ applied to both women.

[113] Bockmuehl, 241; O'Brien, 479 rather than Garland, 'Composition': 173, who sees here a full-scale rift in the church.

The Implications of the Reference to Co-Workers

A final critical issue here is the implication of the reference to co-workers here working alongside Paul. Regardless of the role of Euodia and Syntyche we have incontrovertible evidence here that Paul worked with others. As argued above, this includes the two women Euodia and Syntyche, the male Clement and others unspecified probably including Epaphroditus (2:25) who laboured with him for the gospel. They worked in evangelization alongside Paul and continued to do so after his departure. That they did this undoubtedly implies that these co-workers were inspired and trained by Paul in the work of evangelism from his converts (see Chapter 9 below). This indicates that Paul sought to involve others, trained them and passed on the commission to preach the gospel. In-so-doing Paul was functioning in line with his apostolic ministry of equipping others for 'works of service' so that the church may be built up cf. Eph 4:11-12. The implications of this for this discussion cannot be underestimated. Paul wanted others to share the gospel. He passed on the commission to share. His understanding was not purely centred on himself but on those in the contexts he evangelized. This verse then provides a critical part of the puzzle of Paul's supposed silence on congregational evangelism; he did want at least some from his churches to share the gospel. If so, the church was a part of Paul's evangelistic strategy (Rom 15:19a).

Conclusion to 4:2-3

It would seem then that members of the Philippian church were actively involved in evangelism, the mission having been initiated by Paul and his team. These people worked with Paul while he was in Philippi and continued the work after his departure. These included at least the two women Euodia and Syntyche, a man Clement, a loyal co-worker and any number of other unnamed co-workers (4:2-3). The passage makes explicit the problem that Paul alludes to throughout the epistle; disunity in the evangelistic mission that is threatening the church and its impact on society. The language and evangelistic focus of the passage also supports taking 1:27 as inclusive of evangelism (cf. 2:16). Paul's appeal to the Philippians can be summarised as 'focus on what unites you: the gospel, the gospel, the gospel.'[114]

There is again a notable interplay of the main themes of the letter in the passage. These include proactive evangelism (4:2-3), unity and not contention (4:2), perseverance (4:1), eschatological hope (4:1, 3, 5), joy (4:4 [Χαίρετε twice repeated for emphasis) and ethical witness (4:2, 5 [(τὸ ἐπιεικὲς ὑμῶν γνωσθήτω) before all people (πᾶσιν ἀνθρώποις)].

[114] Carson, *Basics*, 103.

CHAPTER 8

Thanksgiving for the Philippian Involvement in Evangelistic Mission (1:3-7)

My purpose here is not to present a comprehensive analysis of the background[1] and structure[2] of the Pauline thanksgiving and its role in the Pauline epistles, but to discern in the thanksgiving of Philippians evidence of congregational evangelism and its importance in the context of the letter. In particular I will discuss 1:5-7 to discern whether the statements of Paul are inclusive of proclamation of the gospel.[3] In that it is well appreciated that the Pauline thanksgivings anticipate the key themes in the letter, the outcome to this question largely depends on the results of previous discussions concerning the content of Philippians.[4] Thus, I am discussing 1:3-7 after having examined in

---

[1] On similarities and differences to thanksgivings to the gods in Greek and to God in Hellenistic Judaism letter writing protocol see O'Brien, 54 and 'Letters', 552; White, 'Ancient': 97; Fee, 72; P. Arzt, 'The "Epistolary Introductory Thanksgiving" in the Papyri and Paul' *NovT* 36, 1 (1994): 29-46; J.T. Reed, 'Are Paul's Thanksgivings "Epistolary"', *JSNT* 61 (1996): 87-99; P. Schubert, *Form and Function of the Pauline Thanksgivings,* BZNTW 20 (Berlin: Töpelmann, 1939), 158-79; T.Y. Mullins, 'Formulas in New Testament Epistles', *JBL* 91 (1972): 380-390; Gnilka, 15; Bockmuehl, 57; U. B. Müller, 39-40.

[2] On the two essential forms and the structure of Paul's thanksgivings see P.T. O'Brien, 54-55; *Introductory Thanksgivings in the Letters of Paul.* NovTSup 49 (Leiden: Brill, 1977), 6-15; 'Letters', 551-52; Schubert, *Form*, 10-39, U. Müller, 39. On the rhetorical impact of the thanksgivings see Bockmuehl, 57; Witherington, *Friendship*, 18, 35-41; Bloomquist, *Function*, 121-123, 145-147; Hawthorne, 14; Black, 'Structure': 47-48; Watson, 'Analysis', 61-65 noting the caution of Fee, 73 esp. note 8. On the heightened positivity of the Philippian thanksgiving see Lightfoot, 82; O'Brien, 53; Beare, 52; Collange, 43. On the structure of the thanksgiving see O'Brien, 55 who discerns a recurring seven-feature form in Paul's thanksgivings, which is found in 1:3-11.

[3] One can also argue that the generic statements in 1:9 (ἵνα ἡ ἀγάπη ὑμῶν ἡ ἀγάπη ὑμῶν ἔτι μᾶλλον καὶ μᾶλλον περισσεύῃ ἐν ἐπιγνώσει καὶ πάσῃ αἰσθήσει) and 1:11 (πεπληρωμένοι καρπὸν δικαιοσύνης) could include evangelism within their range, but this is not clear.

[4] Bockmuehl, 57 notes that the introductory section serves to 'set the tone and to highlight the essential themes of the letter.' So also Fee, 73; Jewett, 'Thanksgiving', 53; Hawthorne, 15; G.P. Wiles, *Prayers. The Significance of the Intercessory Prayer Passages in the Letters of St Paul.* SNTSMS 24. (Cambridge: CUP, 1974), 206-207;

detail the other relevant sections of the letter which I have shown, in many instances, concern evangelism. Before proceeding, it is important to note the emphasis on πᾶς that carries through the thanksgiving and intercession. This indicates that the content of the thanksgiving and prayer applies *to the whole Philippian church's involvement* and not merely a select few.[5]

In 1:3-4 Paul expresses his thankfulness for the Philippians with a deliberately and emphatically repetitive construction emphasising the intensity of his positive feeling concerning the whole church; this is clear from the emphasis on 'all',[6] along with the uncommon reference to 'joy.'[7] This reference to joy anticipates its importance throughout the letter (1:18, 25; 2:1, 18; 3:1; 4:4).

The central concern here is the evangelistic orientation of the thanksgiving. As such the focus of the following discussion will centre on three constructions. First, ἐπὶ τῇ κοινωνίᾳ ὑμῶν εἰς τὸ εὐαγγέλιον ἀπὸ τῆς πρώτης ἡμέρας ἄχρι τοῦ νῦν. Secondly, ὑμῖν ἔργον ἀγαθὸν ἐπιτελέσει ἄχρι ἡμέρας Χριστου Ιησοῦ·. Finally, συγκοινωνούς μου τῆς χάριτος πάντας ὑμᾶς ὄντας. The issue is this: do any of these indicate active evangelism?

Garland, 'Defense': 328-332 and Witherington, *Friendship*, 36 who list the tone and themes clearly; Watson, 'Analysis': 62; Funk, *Hermeneutic*, 256-257; Schubert, *Form*, 71-82, 180; O'Brien, 19-46; Collange, 48-49; Bloomquist, *Function*, 122; Marshall, 6; Peterman, *Gift*, 91-93 who notes strong parallels to 4:10-20 in the thanksgiving.

[5] Black, 'Structure': 29; U. B. Müller, 41.

[6] Note: 1) He gives thanks 'every time' he remembers the Philippians (ἐπὶ πάσῃ τῇ μνείᾳ ὑμῶν); 2) He prays with joy 'at all times'; 3) He prays with joy in 'all his prayers' (ἐν πάσῃ δεήσει μου); 4) He prays with joy for 'all' of the Philippians (ὑπὲρ πάντων ὑμῶν).

[7] Silva, 44-45, 47-48. The reference to joy here in a Pauline thanksgiving recurs only in Phm 7. I will leave aside the minor exegetical questions: 1) Should εὐχαριστῶ be linked to ἐπί πάσῃ… or v5 ἐπί τῃ κοινωνία? I prefer the latter; 2) Should πάντοτε be construed with what precedes or what follows? This is not significant in regard to meaning; 3) Is μετὰ χαρᾶς … part of the preceding or following clause? Again this is not significant; 4) Should ἐπὶ μάσῃ τῇ μνείᾳ ὑμῶν be understood as 'for all your remembrance of me' or the traditional 'in all my remembrance of you.' I prefer the latter as in all other uses of μνεία in Paul's thanksgivings it is Paul who is doing the remembering cf. Hawthorne, 16-17 and Fee, 78. O'Brien, 58-61 and *Thanksgivings*, 23 and Jewett, 'Thanksgiving', 53 see it otherwise, as the first ground for thanksgiving. If this is the case, it supports further my thesis, as 1:5 probably refers more to the involvement of others; 5) Should τῇ κοινωνίᾳ ὑμῶν εἰς τὸ εὐαγγέλιον be taken with 'I thank' (1:3) or 'pray with joy' (1:4). R.L. Omanson, 'A note on the translation of Philippians 1:3-5', *BT* 29 (1978): 244-245 prefers the former. However, it is dependent on both the main verb and the preceding. As Silva, 44 notes however, 'all of the syntactical combinations yield the same sense.'

The Content of 'Your Fellowship in the Gospel' (1:5)

First, is there an evangelistic dimension to ἐπὶ τῇ κοινωνίᾳ ὑμῶν εἰς τὸ εὐαγγέλιον ἀπὸ τῆς πρώτης ἡμέρας ἄχρι τοῦ νῦν?

The Meaning of ἡ κοινωνία in 1:5

The first ground for Paul's thanksgiving is τῇ κοινωνίᾳ ὑμῶν εἰς τὸ εὐαγγέλιον.[8] The first task is to examine the range of meanings for ἡ κοινωνία. Of the nineteen instances of the noun κοινωνία ('community; fellowship; participation'),[9] eight of the verb κοινωνέω ('have a share; give a share; take a share; have fellowship'),[10] one of the adjective κοινωνικός ('sharing, beneficial to the community'),[11] four of the compound noun συγκοινωνός ('fellow participant, partner')[12] and three of the compound verb συγκοινονέω ('participate/take part in together')[13] in the NT, the vast majority are found Paul (Rom 11:17; 12:13; 15:26, 27; 1 Cor 1:9; 9:23; 10:16 (2x); 2 Cor 6:14; 8:4; 9:13; 13:13; Gal 2:9; 6:6; Eph 5:11; Phil 1:5, 7; 2:1; 3:10; 4:14, 15; Phm 6; 1 Tim 5:22; 6:18).

However, the broad use of κοινωνία and related terms in the wider NT (Acts 2:42; Heb 2:14; 13:16; 1 Pet 4:13; 1 Jn 1:3-7; 2 Jn 11; Rev 1:9; 18:4) also suggests it was a widely used in the early church despite its relative infrequency.[14] The term κοινωνία conveys a wide range of ideas including the intimate relationship of marriage (*pOxy.* 1473, 33; 3 Macc 4:6) and of material generosity (2 Cor 9:13).[15] Essential to its understanding is the concept of 'having *something* in common with *someone*.'[16]

---

[8] Here Paul uses ἐπὶ (cf. 1 Cor 1:4) rather than a causal participle (Col 1:4; 1 Thess 1:3; Phm 5) or ὅτι (Rom 1:8; 1 Cor 1:5; 2 Thess 1:3). Or it may be the second ground of the thanksgiving as suggest O'Brien, 58-61; Peterman, *Gift*, 100 who both see ἐπὶ πάσῃ τῇ μνείᾳ as the first ground referring to the material gifts of the Philippians to Paul. If they are correct this enhances my argument that the fellowship of the gospel refers to more than merely material gifts.

[9] *EDNT*, 2.303. See Acts 2:42; Rom 15:26; 1 Cor 1:9; 10:16; 2 Cor 6:14; 8:4; 9:13; 13:13; Gal 2:9; Phil 1:5; 2:1; 3:10; Phm 6; Heb 13:16; 1 Jn 1:3, 6, 7.

[10] *EDNT*, 2.203. See Rom 12:13; 15:27; Gal 6:6; Phil 4:15; 1 Tim 5:22; Heb 2:14; 1 Pet 4:13; 2 Jn 11.

[11] *EDNT*, 2.305. See 1 Tim 6:18.

[12] *EDNT*, 3.283. See Rom 11:17; 1 Cor 9:23; Phil 1:7; Rev 1:9.

[13] *EDNT*, 3.283. See Eph 5:11; Phil 4:14; Rev 18:4.

[14] Hawthorne, 19. His suggestion that it is a distinctively Pauline word is an overstatement.

[15] *BDAG*, 439; *TDNT* 3.789 who suggest it means '1) "participation"; 2) "impartation"; 3) "fellowship."

[16] J.Y. Campbell, 'Κοινωνία and its Cognates in the New Testament' in J.Y. Campbell, *Three New Testament Studies* (Leiden: E.J. Brill, 1965), 1-28, 5. Here in 1:5 is the only NT passage with a clear subjective genitive (19).

My analysis of κοινωνία and related terms discerns eight nuances to the notion of κοινωνία.[17] First, it is used of *the believer's intimate relationship with God, Father, Son* (1 Cor 1:9) *and Spirit* (2 Cor 13:14; Phil 2:1).[18] These references have both vertical (God-human) and horizontal (interpersonal) perspectives indicating that the fellowship includes the community of God and believing humanity (cf. Rom 11:17). Secondly, Paul applies κοινωνία to *participation in Christ's work and suffering* (Rom 11:17; Phil 3:10; 4:14 cf. Rev 1:9), which is expressed in the Lord's Supper (1 Cor 10:16). Thirdly, Paul uses κοινωνία *negatively* in appeals for holiness and the avoidance of κοινωνία with deeds of darkness (2 Cor 6:14 cf. Eph 5:11) or with sin (1 Tim 5:22 [κοινωνέω]; 2 Jn 11 ['evil deeds']). Fourthly, Paul regularly uses κοινωνία of *'fellowship' between believers* (Gal 2:9; Phm 6 cf. 2 Cor 13:13; Phil 2:1). Fifthly, Paul uses the cognate συγκοινωνός of *'fellowship' in the ultimate eschatological blessings of the gospel* (1 Cor 9:23).[19] Sixthly, in Phil 1:7 Paul uses συγκοινωνός to express the *Philippian participation in the grace of Paul's apostolic commission.*[20] Seventhly, he applies κοινωνία specifically to *the Jerusalem collection* in the sense of *concrete fellowship expressed in material contribution* (Rom 15:26; 2 Cor 8:4; 9:13 cf. Acts 2:42, 44-45; 4:32-37).[21] Finally, and connected to the seventh use above, he uses the verb κοινωνέω in the less *specific sense of Christians sharing materially with others* (Rom 12:13; 15:27 [collection]; Gal 6:6 [with teachers]); Phil 4:14, 15 [help for Paul by the Philippians]; Phm 6; 1 Tim 6:18).

Here in 1:5 is found a unique construction 'κοινωνία in the gospel.' The above analysis suggests five connections that are potentially relevant to the discussion of the meaning of the construction in Philippians. First, the Philippians involvement in believing the Christian message of Christ from the beginning. Secondly, it could apply to their participation in material support of Paul and/or others. Thirdly, it could refer to their participation in the sufferings

[17] *BDAG*, 439 note 4 meanings for κοινωνία: 1) Association, communion, fellowship, close relationship (cf. here in 1:5); 2) Generosity, fellow-feeling altruism (cf. 2 Cor 9:13); 3) Abstract for gift i.e. a concrete sign of fellowship (cf. Rom 15:26); 4) Participation, sharing something with someone (2 Cor 8:4).

[18] Cf. The notion of marriage (see above).

[19] Taking συγκοινωνὸς αὐτοῦ in this way rather than 'participation in the work of the gospel' (so J.H. Schütz, *Paul and the Anatomy of Apostolic Authority*. SNTSMS 26 (Cambridge: CUP, 1975): 51-52; R.S. Parry, *The First Epistle of Paul the Apostle to the Corinthians*. CGTSC (2d ed. Cambridge: CUP, 1926), 143 who takes it temptingly as 'that I may have others to share the Gospel with me.' This is ruled out in that Paul is already working for the gospel and so is redundant. Further see Fee, *1 Corinthians*, 432; Barrett, *1 Corinthians*, 216; Hodge, *1 Corinthians*, 167.

[20] Or the salvation-grace of God (see further below). Here suffering could be in mind cf. 1 Pet 4:13.

[21] Silva, 47 significantly with the preposition εἰς.

of Christ.[22] Fourthly, it may refer to their participation in the gospel through holiness and ethical witness. Finally, it may indicate their general involvement in Paul's mission, involving all of the above including active proclamation. In that εἰς τὸ εὐαγγέλιον defines the scope and meaning of κοινωνία this is the next focus of this discussion.

Paul's Use τὸ εὐαγγέλιον in Phil 1:5

It is generally agreed that the thanksgiving anticipates the themes of the letter. That being the case, Paul's use of gospel here is primarily conditioned by his use of εὐαγγέλιον (1:5, 7, 12, 16, 27 [2x]; 2:22; 4:3, 15) and parallels including 'word of God' (1:14), 'Christ' (1:15, 16, 18) and 'word of life' (2:16) in Philippians.[23]

On the basis of these connections I suggest then τὸ εὐαγγέλιον in 1:5 initially includes at least three obvious dimensions of involvement. First, in 4:15 in the context of 4:10-19 (cf. 2:25-30) εὐαγγέλιον indisputably refers to ongoing material support for the Pauline mission and team from the initial evangelisation of Philippi to the present. Secondly, εὐαγγέλιον, refers to general living according to the gospel including ongoing faith and ethical dimensions of Christian witness and living (1:27a cf. 2:12, 15; 4:4). Thirdly, as the results of my earlier analyses indicate, it includes active congregational evangelism from the Philippian church (1:27c; 2:16; 4:2-3). In particular, συναθλοῦντες τῇ πίστει τοῦ εὐαγγελίου (1:27c) and ἐν τῷ εὐαγγελίῳ συνήθλησαν in 4:3, points to unspecified, active, *general*, present and continuous Philippian involvement in the gospel mission.[24]

This is reinforced by the rhetorical impact of the references to the evangelisation of general Roman Christians (1:14-18a), Timothy (2:19-23), Epaphroditus (2:25) and Paul himself (1:7, 12-13; 4:9 cf. 3:17). In addition to these more explicit components of 'fellowship of the gospel', the epistle specifically indicates involvement in *prayer* for the Pauline mission even if there is no reference to 'the gospel' in this context (1:19). Similarly, suffering for the gospel recurs throughout in close connection to the references to evangelisation and so should be included in the content here (cf. 1:28-30). Consequently, 'gospel' here in 1:5 should be understood actively and inclusive of all manner of involvement in the gospel mission including specifically material support, ethical witness, proactive evangelization, prayer and suffering.

---

[22] Blevins, 'Introduction': 321-322.

[23] Dickson, *Mission-Commitment*, 124.

[24] As agrees Marshall, 'Theology', 151, 152, 155 who says 'they are involved in activity like his, for they too are persecuted and having to defend the gospel' (151); see further below.

Paul's Use of ἀπὸ τῆς πρώτης ἡμέρας ἄχρι τοῦ νῦν in 1:5

The phrase τῆς πρώτης ἡμέρας is understood in different ways. First, some take it as an emphatic beginning of a new statement i.e. 'I have been convinced from the first day until now that he who began a good work in you...' I agree with Silva who argues that this interpretation wrongly shifts the attention away from the Philippian conduct which is the main concern of the passage.[25] Alternatively some link the clause to 1:4 so 'I always pray with joy from the first day until now.' Silva correctly considers this unlikely in terms of word order and because Paul has 'moved from the *fact* of his prayer to the *reason* for it.'[26]

It is more likely then that τῆς πρώτης ἡμέρας calls to mind the initial experience of the gospel in Philippi (Acts 16:11-40). Τοῦ νῦν indicates the moment at which Paul penned the letter. Hence, Paul is referring to the whole time the Philippians have been Christians and if active involvement is in mind as is likely, is speaking of their continued participation in the gospel mission.[27] The clear parallel with ὅτι ἐν ἀρχῇ τοῦ εὐαγγελίου in 4:15 also suggests material giving including the Epaphroditus gift (2:25; 4:18). The reference to co-workers who 'contend' for the gospel suggests holistic involvement in the evangelistic mission from the beginning (2:25; 4:2-3).

Synthesis: Paul Use of τῇ κοινωνίᾳ ὑμῶν εἰς τὸ εὐαγγέλιον in 1:5

The phrase τῇ κοινωνίᾳ ὑμῶν εἰς τὸ εὐαγγέλιον then should be understood as 'your active participation in the gospel mission.' There is no reason to limit interpretation to that of Seesemann who argues that κοινωνία and the phrase under consideration is not a reference to the gift or proclamation but is equivalent to 'your faith.'[28] He argues that Paul here is speaking of their faith in Christ which the proclamation of the message produced from their conversion onwards i.e. the first day. In support Seesemann appeals to Rom 1:8; Col 1:4; 1 Thess 2:3; 2 Thess 1:3 and Phm 5-6. In addition, he understands the εἰς clause to be equivalent to a genitive on the basis that two genitives would be confusing to the hearers. This view requires Seesemann to understand

---

[25] Silva, 45.

[26] Silva, 45.

[27] Gnilka, 45 notes it is not that they were necessarily missionaries from the first instance, although this is possible (cf. 1 Thess 1:8).

[28] See H. Seesemann, *Der Begriff KOINΩNIA im Neuen Testament* (Giessen: Verlag von Alfred Toepelmann, 1933), 73-76, 79 mentioned in O'Brien, 61-62 cf. Hauck, *TDNT* 3.789-809 esp. 805 and Friedrich, 99; G. Panikulam, *Koinōnia in the New Testament: A Dynamic Expression of Christian Life*. AnBib 85 (Rome: Biblical Institute Press, 1979), 82. So also Collange, 45 but not in a restrictive manner. See O'Brien, 61-62; J.M. McDermott, 'The Biblical Doctrine of KOINΩNIA', *BZ* (1975): 64-77, 219-233, esp. 226-227 for further critique of this view.

εὐαγγέλιον in a passive sense referring to the content of the gospel.[29]

Significantly Seesemann has to find his essential support for this perspective from outside the epistle rather than from the evidence of the epistle itself. Unfortunately as indicated above, the content of Philippians suggests otherwise. In addition, Seesemann's view that the εἰς clause stands in the place of a genitive is arbitrary. It is simpler to accept that Paul used εἰς because it best said what he wanted.

Rather the context of the letter as I have established above, explicitly refers to Philippian involvement in the gospel including proclamation. In addition to the contextual argument as O'Brien has pointed out, εὐαγγέλιον is probably used here in the active sense, suggesting action for the gospel for three reasons. First, Paul's other uses in Philippians are predominately active (1:7, 12, 27c; 2:22; 4:2-3, 15 cf. 1:15-18).[30] Secondly, Paul uses 'gospel' actively in the other thanksgivings (Rom 1:9; Col 1:5-6; 1 Thess 1:5). Thirdly, O'Brien notes that 'gospel' is almost 'personified' in the epistle.[31] Furthermore, a passive interpretation ignores the link between belief in the gospel and activity in or related to the gospel. The evidence that the Philippians have believed from the beginning is seen in their active participation in mission.

That being the case, many commentators prefer the active sense in the phrase 'fellowship of the gospel.' However, the nature of this activity is disputed. A commonly held view is that Paul is referring exclusively to the financial support of Paul by the Philippians.[32] Lightfoot, for example, has written, 'the words signify not "your participation in the Gospel"'... but "your cooperation towards, in aid of the Gospel".'[33] He bases this on comparison with 2 Cor 9:13 and Rom 15:26 where κοινωνία carries the sense of 'contributions' or 'almsgiving' (see above).

As with most contemporary exegetes I accept that this forms one component of the Philippians' 'involvement in the gospel mission.'[34] As mentioned above

---

[29] Cf. *TDNT* 3.805.

[30] O'Brien, 62 notes only 1:27a is passive in terms of content. However this is explicated actively in 1:27c. The parallel 'word of life' (2:16) O'Brien takes passively, however as I have argued, there are excellent reasons to challenge this interpretation.

[31] Gnilka, 44 cf. O'Brien, 62. On thanksgivings see O'Brien, *Thanksgivings*, 144-55.

[32] Peterman, *Gift*, 99-103 seeing it as propagation of the gospel through support of Paul; Silva, 47; Plummer, *Understanding*, 19; Caird, 107; A.B. Luter, 'Gospel' in *DPL*, 370; Martin, 65; Beare, 52; Kent, 103; Witherington, *Friendship*, 37-38; Thielman, 38; Garland, 'Defence', 330; Black, 'Structure': 27; B.J. Capper, 'Paul's Dispute with Philippi', *TZ* 49.3 (1993): 193-214; Dickson, *Mission-Commitment*, 122-129 while acknowledging that 4:2-3 means proclamation cannot be ruled out.

[33] Lightfoot, 83.

[34] So Martin, 49; O'Brien, 61-63 and *Thanksgivings*, 24-25; 'Importance', 217-218; *Thanksgivings*, 23-25; 'The Fellowship Theme', 9-18; I-J. Loh-Nida, *Translators*, 11; Collange, 44-45; J.J. Müller, 41; Lightfoot, 83; Hawthorne, 19; Hendriksen, 52-53; Fee, 83-85; Bockmuehl, 60-61; Schenk, 95; Marshall, 10; 'Theology', 151-152; Moule, 13;

the evidence for their support is clear and is found in unambiguous references to repeated Philippian provision for Paul immediately after the evangelisation of Philippi in Thessalonica (4:16),[35] in his post-Macedonian mission (4:15 cf. 2 Cor 8:1-5)[36] and through Epaphroditus in Rome (2:25-30; 4:18). Other arguments in favour of an exclusively material interpretation of 1:5 include the suggestion that the preposition εἰς in papyri denotes the object in respect of which the money is paid in the items of an account,[37] the material dimension of κοινωνία with εἰς + acc (Rom 15:26; 1 Cor 9:13) and the temporal parallels ἀπὸ τῆς πρώτης ἡμέρας ἄχρι τοῦ νῦν (1:5) and ὅτι ἐν ἀρχῇ τοῦ εὐαγγελίου (4:15). The latter parallel could indicate a kind of *inclusio*, Paul alluding to the theme of the Philippian generosity and explicating it fully later. Consequently, it is obvious that this Philippian generosity provides a strong part of the content of the phrase in question. However it is unlikely due to the content of Philippians that this provides *all* that is implied in the phrase ἐπὶ τῇ κοινωνίᾳ ὑμῶν εἰς τὸ εὐαγγέλιον.

A third possibility is that Paul is referring exclusively to their fellowship in suffering for the gospel.[38] This finds support in the certainty that the Philippians were a suffering church facing opposition from non-Christian opponents in Philippi who are causing them to suffer (πάσχειν) in a manner similar to Paul's experience (1:28-30). Furthermore, it is supported by Paul's stated desire for the Philippians to emulate his own commitment to participate in the sufferings of Christ (3:10, 15-17). The use of κοινωνία in 3:10 strongly supports a link to 1:5. Rather than singling this out as the content for 'the fellowship of the gospel', suffering should be understood as one dynamic among others. Indeed this lines up with Paul's understanding of suffering and evangelism, which are often intimately linked in his own experience and thinking.[39]

Peterman, *Gift*, 100; Michael, 11; Bruce, 31; Bloomquist, *Function*, 146; Fitzmyer, 249; Schnabel, *Mission*, 1460; Plummer, *Understanding*, 73-74.

[35] This support was not fleeting but repeated (καὶ ἅπαξ καὶ δὶς) indicating more than once but not more than three times; so L. Morris, 'ΚΑΙ ΑΠΑΞ ΚΑΙ ΔΙΣ', *NovT* 1 (1956): 205-08.

[36] Fee, 445 notes Paul is probably referring to leaving the district rather than the city.

[37] MM, 186-187.

[38] Lightfoot, 83; J.J. Müller, 41; O'Brien, *Thanksgivings*, 25; Peterman, *Gift*, 100; Bloomquist, *Function*, 147 cf. Gnilka, 49.

[39] Examples include: Rom 15:31 (a link between carrying out the material collection and suffering); 1 Cor 4:9-13; 2 Cor 2:1-4 (both speaking of suffering at the hands of his converts); 1 Cor 9:19-27 (Paul's personal struggle for the sake of the gospel); 2 Cor 1:3-11 (suffering in Asia during his mission); 2 Cor 4:8-10, 16-18 (generally of suffering including the context of mission cf. 2 Cor 4:13-15); 2 Cor 6:3-4, 10; 11:23-29 (suffering due to the work of ministry [ἡ διάκονοι]); 2 Cor 7:5 (suffering in Macedonia); Phil 1:12-13, 19-24, 28-30 cf. 2:8, 25-30; 3:10; Col 1:24, 29; 1 Thess 1:6; 2:1-2 (suffering as

As a result of the content of Philippians, a significant number of contemporary commentators have argued for a broader, inclusive interpretation of ἐπὶ τῇ κοινωνίᾳ ὑμῶν εἰς τὸ εὐαγγέλιον, including proclamation.[40] Gnilka, rather more radically than this work proposes, goes as far as including only proclamation in his assessment. He writes:

> However, the "incorporation" of the community in the Gospel is not in mind here, because the phrase ἐις τὸ εὐαγγέλιον refers to an active role of the church, their participation in the gospel, their *participation in the proclamation of the Gospel* and not targeted at their shared profit in the Gospel. This latter has been referred to. The active participation the Philippians in the proclamation may have been varied in form, but above all it is a *direct joint-preaching*, a *sharing of the Gospel* having been adopted.[41]

Gnilka with his emphasis on the evangelistic content of 'your fellowship of the gospel' correctly notes that this 'work of proclamation' (*Verkünderwerk*) had gone on since the first day without 'church-work' necessarily pressing this

---

a direct result of evangelisation in Macedonia); 2:14; 3:3, 7; 2 Thess 3:2; 1 Tim 1:8, 11-12; 2:25; 3:10-13; 2 Tim 4:10 (desertion from workers cf. Phil 2:20).

[40] So Martin, 49; Silva, 47; O'Brien, 61-63, *Consumed*, 116; 'Fellowship': 11; 'Fellowship, Communion, Sharing,' in *DPL*, 294; P.T. O'Brien and A.J. Köstenberger, *Salvation to the Ends of the Earth: a Biblical Theology of Mission* NSBT 11 (Leicester: Apollos, 2001), 194; Fee, 84; Peterman, *Gift*, 100; J.J. Müller, 40-41; Michael, 62; Hawthorne, 19-20; Loh-Nida, 11; M.A. Getty, 13; C.J. Ellicott, *St Paul's Epistles to the Philippians, the Colossians, and Philemon* (London: Longmans, Green and Co, 1865), 5; Carson, *Basics*, 16-17; H.A.W. Meyer, 16; Motyer, 47: ''the furtherance of the gospel' (cf. RSV) i.e. 'those who truly possess the gospel also propogate it'; Green, *Evangelism*, 64 n.73; Murray, 'Witness', 318-319; *TDNT* 2.733: 'Similarly, when Paul speaks of the κοινωνία of the Philippians εἰς τὸ εὐαγγέλιον, he is *not thinking merely* of their personal activity in spreading the Gospel, nor of their financial support, but of their fellowship in the Gospel itself' (italics mine); Holloway, *Consolation*, 89 note 16; R.R. Melick, *Philippians, Colossians, Philemon*. NAC (Nashville: Broadman, Press, 1991), 57; Capper, 'Dispute': 206; Bockmuehl, 60-61; Houlden, 55; Hendriksen, 52-53 who sees it in its widest sense; Moule, 13; J.G. Janzen, 'Creation and New Creation in Phil 1:6', *HBT* 18:1 (June 1996): 27-54, 31; Lightfoot, 83 'cooperation in the widest sense'; U. B. Müller, 42; Schenk, 96, argues for an active interpretation but rejects the material; Gnilka, 44 limits it to the 'act of proclamation' (*Akt der Verkündigung*) without material assistance (but see below); Collange, 45; Michael, 11; Bloomquist, *Function*, 146; Barth, 16; Marshall, 10 and 'Theology', 151-152; Wiles, *Prayers*, 205; Bruce, 31. Campbell, 'Κοινωνία', 19; Panikulam, *Koinōnia*, 85; Fitzmyer, 249 but only material support and suffering and not proclamation; J. Hainz, κοινωνία, *EDNT* 2.304; Schnabel, *Mission*, 1460. Plummer, *Understanding*, 73-74. Dickson, *Mission-Commitment*, 128 concedes it as a possibility.

[41] Gnilka, 45. Although Gnilka limits it thus he goes on (49) to note that 'the grace' in 1:7 includes suffering and looks back to 1:5 and so I can assume he includes suffering for the gospel here in 1:5.

point. The Philippians certainly 'understood its obligation for the passing on of the message and putting it into practice.' This would have been a genuine comfort for Paul in prison.[42]

Schenk too sees only proclamation here. He does so first, because of the active sense of κοινωνία and εὐαγγέλιον (4:15; Rom 15:26; 2 Cor 9.13; 8.4). Secondly, the active sense is confirmed in the temporal reference to the first day until now. While he argues that Paul believes that 'Church work (*Gemeindearbeit*) is not gospel-proclamation, and Gospel proclamation is not a church work,' he concludes that their active participation is not their financial support but 'their own witnessing from the beginning'[43] Consequently Schenk, in contrast to Bowers, suggests that like Paul the Philippians 'became Christian missionaries as a matter of course, as 1:27 confirms.'[44] Enticing as it is for my argument, Gnilka and Schenk go too far in their analyses. It is indisputable that financial support is a component of the phrase. So for example U.B. Müller who argues that this refers to 'cooperation in the gospel' in a 'comprehensive sense', and is inclusive of, if not limited to 'love gifts.'[45]

Indeed, there are sound reasons to argue that the content of the letter points to a multi-faceted involvement in the gospel mission by the Philippians rather than one specific component. These include first, the broader meaning of κοινωνία; as demonstrated above, this has various shades of meaning. It cannot thus be assumed on semantic grounds that κοινωνία refers here to material generosity alone. Secondly, as I have discussed above, there is clear evidence of a variety of modes of involvement in the gospel in Philippians including financial support, active proclamation, ethical witness, prayer (1:19; 4:6-7)[46] and suffering. In terms of the function of the thanksgiving (and perhaps *exordium*) in regard to the thematic development of the letter, all these dimensions should be included.

Conclusion to 1:5

In conclusion then it is likely that in 1:5 Paul is giving thanks for the Philippians' continuous general involvement in the mission of the gospel. Specifically he is giving thanks for their material assistance, prayer, active involvement in evangelism, ethical witness especially loving unity and perseverance in suffering.[47] This suggests that here is found a Pauline church

---

[42] Gnilka, 45.
[43] Schenk, 96.
[44] Schenk, 96.
[45] U. B. Müller, 42.
[46] Schnabel, *Mission*, 1460.
[47] O'Brien, *Thanksgivings*, 25 includes proclamation, suffering and prayer. Hendriksen, 51-53 includes grace, faith, prayer and thanksgiving, love-fellowship, co-operation in the gospel work and warfare. He suggests that it refers to the lasting principle of

involved in general evangelism.

The Content of ἔργον ἀγαθὸν in 1:6

After Paul's expression of gratitude for the Philippians' involvement in the gospel, Paul continues his thanksgiving; expressing his confidence that God will bring to completion the good work he himself has begun in them until the return of Christ. O'Brien considers this the 'third and ultimate ground' for the apostle's thanksgiving and hence it is dependent directly on εὐχαριστῶ.[48] On the contrary I see it as a legitimate development of ἐπὶ τῇ κοινωνίᾳ ὑμῶν εἰς τὸ εὐαγγέλιον in 1:5, turning the attention from their own effort to the source of their strength, God (cf. 2:12-13). Rather than an expression of thanksgiving, it is an expression of confidence intimately linked to what he has just said.[49]

This is supported through the causal link to the previous sentence through πεποιθώς, the perfect participle of πείθω ('being confident') (cf. 1:14, 25; 2:24; 3:3, 4).[50] Paul is confident of this, τοῦτο referring not to the previous clause as Meyer suggests, but to what follows.[51] The ὅτι clause focuses on the work of God expressed through the good work he has begun among the Philippians, a good work which will be completed until the *Parousia.* The focus here is on the meaning of the ἔργον ἀγαθὸν to which Paul refers.

There is no debate concerning the emphasis of Paul's words. The emphasis is on the work of God. God is the agent who begins (ἐνάρχομαι) and completes (ἐπιτελέω) the good work. However the 'good work' is still unspecified.[52] This completion will be accomplished ἄχρι ἡμέρας Χριστοῦ Ἰησου i.e. until the return of the Lord.

There are two major suggestions made by scholars concerning the work to which Paul refers. First, that the 'good work' is the good work of redemption effected through the saving work of Christ. Secondly, that the the good work is another reference to the mission involvement of the Philippians further developing the 'fellowship of the gospel' in 1:5.

---

furthering of the gospel. The suggestion of McDermott, 'κοινωνια': 227 that the specific content is undetermined is inadequate in light of the content of the epistle.

[48] O'Brien, 63.

[49] Fee, 85.

[50] *BDAG*, 639: 'expressing present certainty or conviction.' Peterman, *Gift*, 104 rightly suggests the participle is causal.

[51] H.A.W. Meyer, 18 argues for an adverbial use here (cf. 2 Pet 1:5) i.e. 'being persuaded, for this very reason, that God will preserve you.' Silva, 55, suggests that this is 'plausible but not probable.' He notes that it would fit the context and finds support in Paul's use of αὐτὸ τοῦτο in 2 Cor 2:3. However, the word order and Paul's use of αὐτὸ τοῦτο in 2 Cor 7:11; Gal 2:10 where the adverbial force is not supported, leads almost all scholars to take αὐτὸ τοῦτο with what follows.

[52] J.M. Gundry-Volf, *Paul and Perseverance* (Westminster: John Knox, 1991), 33 notes ἔργον ἀγαθόν has no uniform meaning in Paul.

The Good Work of Redemption

A number of scholars reject that here is an allusion to the Philippians' participation in the gospel.[53] Rather, they suggest Paul here is referring to the salvific work of God, which was begun in the Philippians at their conversion and reception of the Spirit. Paul then, likens their salvation to a new creation by God, recalling God's activity as 'good work' in the Old Testament (Gen 2:2; Is 41:4; 44:6; 48:12).[54] As such, the verb ἐνάρχομαι then relates to the beginning of the Christian life[55] and ἐπιτελέω of Paul's expressed confidence that God will complete this work. The good work is not the involvement of the Philippians in the gospel ministry 'but clear evidence of this work of salvation.'[56] This requires interpreting ἐν ὑμῖν locatively, as 'in you, your midst' not instrumentally as 'through you' or causally as 'because of you.'[57]

Confirmation is found in the manner in which Paul refers to the time when God's grace was initiated in the lives of his readers (Gal 3:3 cf. 1 Cor 1:14; Col 1:5; 1 Thess 1:5-6; Phm 5f).[58] Michael argues similarly, connecting what Paul refers to here with τῆς χάριτος, interpreted as divine grace in 1:7.[59] Paul's use of the verbs ἐνάρχομαι and ἐπιτελέω in Gal 3:3 is seen as supportive of this view. Paul refers there to the foolishness of the Galatians (ἀνόητοι) who were being bewitched by the Judaisers. Paul critiques them because, although they began their Christian life with God's divine initiative through the Holy Spirit's work (ἐναρξάμενοι πνεύματι), they were now (νῦν) turning to complete their salvation through returning to life under the law (σαρκὶ ἐπιτελεῖσθε).[60]

Gundry-Volf notes that this is the only example of Paul attributing a 'good work' to God, a tradition in keeping with the OT-Jewish tradition, the Gospels (Matt 6:25-33; Lk 1:53; 12:22-31), 1 Clement (33:1, 2, 7, 8; 59:4) and allusions in Paul (2 Cor 8:9 cf. 9:9-10). In 2 Corinthians 8:9 salvation is likened to a good work which is an example the Corinthians should emulate in their

---

[53] Martin, 63; Bruce, 31-32; O'Brien, 64; Martin, 63; Michael, 13; Loh-Nida, 12; Carson, *Basics*, 17; H.A.A. Kennedy, 'The Epistle to the Philippians' in *Expositor's Greek Testament* Vol 3 (Grand Rapids: Eerdmans, 1976) 419; Hendriksen, 54-55; Caird, 107; Silva, 52; Moule, 14; Kent, 105-106; Beare, 53; J.J. Müller, 41-42; Marshall, 11-12; Thielman, 38-39; Peterman, *Gift*, 104; Michael, 13; Janzen, 'Creation': 34-35; Motyer, 48; Witherington, *Friendship*, 38; Gnilka, 46 who notes, 'but this time the activity of the church is not placed in the foreground as in V 4;' U. B. Müller, 43.

[54] Hawthorne, 21; O'Brien, 64.

[55] J.D.G. Dunn, *Baptism in the Holy Spirit: A Re-Examination of the New Testament Teaching on the Gift of the Spirit in Relation to Pentecostalism Today* (London: SCM, 1977), 108; J.M. Gundry-Volf, *Perseverance*, 33-47.

[56] O'Brien, 64; Bruce, 31-32; Martin, 63.

[57] Fee, 87.

[58] Martin, 63.

[59] Michael, 13.

[60] Martin, 63; Fee, 86.

giving.[61] She also argues the text in Phil 1:6 gives no compelling reason that the mover is not only God, but also the Philippians. She suggests that the lack of the connective τοῦτο suggests no link to the 'fellowship of the gospel.' In addition the temporal differences between the two speak of different phases. Thirdly, she contends that there is no clear activity of the Philippians, which satisfies the verb ἐπιτελέσει. She asserts it cannot refer to material generosity, as Paul is amply supplied (4:18) nor other activity as death ends the involvement of the Philippians.[62]

Fee similarly surmises that it is unlikely that Paul is referring to their grace of giving. He maintains that if that were the case, Paul would have said 'good work *through* you' and '*this* good work', rather than an indefinite good work.[63] Hence, he concludes that Paul is referring to 'salvation in Christ.' He says that this is 'yet another way of speaking about their 'participating in the gospel' – not so much about their sharing it, but about their experiencing it and living it out in Philippi.'[64] In this expression then, Paul anticipates 2:12-13 where he appeals to the Philippians to live out in Christian community this Christ-effected salvation because of God's work in them.[65]

The Good Work of the Philippian Involvement in the Gospel

The alternative interpretation is to suggest Paul is speaking of the Philippians' involvement in the ministry of the gospel, which is in reality God's work *through* them.[66] So ἐν ὑμῖν is taken instrumentally ('through you') rather than locatively.[67] Hence Bockmuehl writes, 'God's good work in these Christians, then, is to make them active participants in the gospel and its benefits. This participation includes, but goes far beyond, their material contribution to Paul's ministry.' He notes God as the author of 'good works' in 2 Thess 2:17; Eph

---

[61] Gundry-Volf, *Perseverance*, 34-36.
[62] Gundry-Volf, *Perseverance*, 36-42.
[63] Fee, 87.
[64] Fee, 87.
[65] O'Brien, 64.
[66] Bockmuehl, 62; Lightfoot, 84; H.A.W. Meyer, 19; Ellicott, 6; Hawthorne, 21; Silva, 52; Holloway, *Consolation*, 89-90; *BDAG*, 308 of the deeds of people i.e. action; Fitzmyer, 249 sees general works of the Philippians; Schenk, 96-100 sees ἔργον ἀγαθὸν not as '*nomen resultantum*' but as '*nomen actionis*' in which God works through human endeavour (cf. Rom 2:7; 13:3; 14:20; 15:28; 1 Cor 3:13; 9:1; 15:58; 2 Cor 7:1; 8:6, 11; 9:8; Phm 6, 14; LXX; EpArist 195, 227, 227, 239, 255). He sees 'good work' as corporate and parallel to *agape* (1:9 cf. 2 Cor 9:8; 1 Cor 15:58). He defines 'good work' not as 'passive faith' (cf. 1:5) but 'the whole Christian life in all its activities' i.e. inclusive of evangelism. Melick, 58-59 who concedes context favours the former.
[67] Hawthorne, 21.

2:10.[68] Similarly Lightfoot sees here, 'their co-operation (*sic*) him and affection for the Apostle.'[69]

Hawthorne states that the phrase ἔργον ἀγαθὸν 'cannot be shaken loose from its immediate context and be interpreted primarily in terms of "God's redeeming and renewing work".'[70] In support, Hawthorne links the creative activity of God (cf. Gen 2:2-3; 2 Esd 6:38, 43) to the word of God, which accomplishes that work (cf. 2 Esd 6:38, 43). 'So now in the new creation God will accomplish this "good work", that of advancing the gospel *by* human means, and in this instance by the Philippian church.'[71] Hence, while it was the work of the Philippians, they could take no credit for what was really the creative activity of God.[72]

As in the case of the former interpretation, support can be garnished from Paul's use of ἐνάρχομαι and ἐπιτελέω. Paul often uses ἐπιτελέω of the believer's participation in the Jerusalem collection (Rom 15:28; 2 Cor 8:6, 11). Of special importance is 2 Cor 8:6 where Paul pairs προενάρχομαι with ἐπιτελέω in the context of the Corinthians completing their material generosity in the Jerusalem Collection. In light of this use of the same verbs and in regard to the context of Philippians, the reference is crucial. Paul is here referring again, at least in part, to the material generosity of the Philippians. In addition, Holloway notes the link to 1:12-18a where, despite Paul's imprisonment, God continues and will complete his gospel mission, using his situation for the advancement of the mission. Such words encourage the Philippians in their struggle.[73]

Furthermore, there are sound reasons for taking Paul's use of ἔργον ἀγαθόν here of dual reference. First, it is noted that on all other occasions without exception ἔργον ἀγαθόν refers to the work of humans and not the work of God apart from human agency (Rom 2:7-10; 13:3-4; 2 Cor 9:8; Gal 6:10; Eph 2:10; Col 1:10; 2 Thess 2:17; 1 Tim 2:10; 5:10; 2 Tim 2:21; 3:17; Tit 1:16; 3:1).[74] Taking the dative construction ἐν ὑμῖν instrumentally allows for the work of God to be carried out through the Philippians and other believers. This accords with 2:12-13 where Paul urges the Philippians to continue to work out their salvation through the internal energising power of God (cf. Col 1:28-29).

Secondly, Paul's use of 'good works' is elsewhere linked to themes specific to Philippians including material generosity and evangelism. The former is found explicitly in 2 Cor 9:8 in the context of his appeal for giving to the Jerusalem Collection and refers to the manner in which God is able to cause the

[68] Bockmuehl, 62.
[69] Lightfoot, 84.
[70] Hawthorne, 21.
[71] Hawthorne, 21.
[72] Hawthorne, 21; see also *TDNT* 2.629-630.
[73] Holloway, *Consolation*, 90.
[74] Gundry-Volf, *Perseverance*, 34.

Corinthians to overflow materially so that they are able to abound in 'every good work' (περισσεύητε εἰς πᾶν ἔργον ἀγαθόν).[75] Further, evangelism may well be in the range of Paul's thinking in general references to good works (Rom 2:7-10; Gal 6:10; Col 1:10; 2 Thess 2:17 cf. 1 Tim 2:10; 5:10; 2 Tim 2:21; 3:17; Tit 1:16).

Important here is the reference to good works in Eph 2:10 where Paul speaks of the manner in which God has formed (created = κτίζω) believers (Eph 2:1-9) through the agency of Christ Jesus (ἐν Χριστῷ Ἰησοῦ) for the purpose (ἐπί + dat)[76] of good works (ἔργοις ἀγαθοῖς) which God had prepared in advance for them (προητοίμασεν ὁ θεός), so that (ἵνα) they may live in them (περιπατήσωμεν).[77] The wider context of Ephesians gives contextual indication that these good works include evangelism (cf. Eph 4:11-12; 6:15, 17, 19-20 cf. 3:7-8).[78]

In addition, the absence of the connective τοῦτο in Phil 1:6 is not decisive but is at best ambiguous, while the participle πεποιθὼς suggests continuity of thought. Neither are the supposed temporal differences decisive. Paul does not speak of two distinct phases but one continuous phase involving its beginning in and through the Philippians and culminating at the end. Furthermore, the argument that there is no Philippian action that fulfils ἐπιτελέσει misses the point. If Paul is referring to the mission work begun *through* the Philippians' 'fellowship in the gospel', then it is this that *God will complete* through them. Whether Paul is amply supplied (4:18) or the Philippians die, the good work of the gospel will be completed by God until the return of Christ; especially so when the emphasis here is on God acting through human agency. Furthermore in view of Paul's vulnerability at the time of writing (1:19-26) and the concurrent suffering of the Philippians (1:28-30), it is unlikely that he believes that the Philippians will all live until the return of Christ. Hence, it is feasible theologically, grammatically and from the context that Paul is referring to the way in which God will continue to bring forth in their context the good work of serving God in holistic mission in Philippi and beyond until the return of Christ.

The eschatological reference also points in the direction of the continuation of the good work of living out their faith including mission. As I have

---

[75] Gundry-Volf, *Perseverance*, 33-36.

[76] O'Brien, *Ephesians*, 179.

[77] As Bruce, *Epistles*, 291 notes, through the agency of Christ.

[78] O'Brien, *Ephesians*, 180 notes 'good works' here is 'a general and comprehensive expression for godly behaviour' without further definition. Barth, *Ephesians*, I.251 notes these are Spirit-inspired works. He suggests it is amplified in 4:17-6:20, which for O'Brien includes evangelism in Eph 6:15, 17 (see *Consumed*, 109-131; *Ephesians*, 475-479, 480-482). I also note Eph 4:12 'works of service' in this regard. For more detail see the discussion of Eph 4:11-16 in Chapter 6 and Appendix 1, 'The connection between evangelism and the military metaphor in Paul.'

indicated, throughout the letter Paul's appeals for living out the gospel include points of eschatological assurance (1:11, 19-23, 28; 2:9-11,16; 3:10-14, 19-4:1, 3-4). If they persevere to work out their salvation, bearing the fruit of righteousness including evangelism and without being intimidated by their enemies they will receive their salvation at the return of Christ. Why? Because God will ensure they do (cf. 2:13).

PARALLELISM IN THE STRUCTURE OF 1:5-7

Important to this discussion is an analysis of the structure of Philippians 1:5-7 which supports taking 'good works' here in parallel to 'fellowship in the gospel' and 'my grace' below. As the table and explanation on the next page demonstrates, there is a structural parallelism across the three verses.

PARALLELISM IN PHIL 1:5-7

	Philippians 1:5	**Philippians 1:6-7**	**Phil 1:7-8**
Statement of gospel involvement	ἐπὶ τῇ κοινωνίᾳ ὑμῶν εἰς τὸ εὐαγγέλιον[79]	ὅτι ὁ ἐναρξάμενος ἐν ὑμῖν ἔργον ἀγαθὸν[80]	(ἐν τῇ ἀπολογίᾳ καὶ βεβαιώσει τοῦ εὐαγγελίου) συγκοινωνούς μου τῆς χάριτος πάντας ὑμᾶς ὄντας[81]
Subordinate temporal contextual clause	ἀπὸ τῆς πρώτης ἡμέρας ἄχρι τοῦ νῦν,[82]	ἐπιτελέσει ἄχρι ἡμέρας Χριστοῦ Ἰησοῦ·[83]	ἔν τε τοῖς δεσμοῖς μου καὶ (ἐν τῇ ἀπολογίᾳ καὶ βεβαιώσει τοῦ εὐαγγελίου)[84]

[79] 'Because of *your partnership in the gospel.*'
[80] 'Because he who began a *good work* in you.'
[81] 'In the *defence and confirmation of the gospel*, you are all co-partners in *my grace.*'
[82] 'From the first day (past) until the present.'
[83] 'Will bring it to completion until the (future) day of Christ Jesus.'
[84] 'In my (present) chains (and in the [present] defence and confirmation of the gospel).'

Pauline expression of emotion	πεποιθὼς αὐτὸ τοῦτο,[85]	καθώς ἐστιν δίκαιον ἐμοὶ τοῦτο φρονεῖν ὑπὲρ πάντων ὑμῶν διὰ τὸ ἔχειν με ἐν τῇ καρδίᾳ ὑμᾶς,[86]	μάρτυς γάρ μου ὁ θεὸς ὡς ἐπιποθῶ πάντας ὑμᾶς ἐν σπλάγχνοις Χριστοῦ Ἰησοῦ.[87]

Each section has three elements. First, a statement is given ('statement of gospel involvement') redefining in different terms the manner of the involvement of the Philippians in the gospel mission. The first in 1:5 describes their holistic participation in the mission. In the second in 1:6 their involvement is defined as a 'good work' which God will complete. The third in 1:7 suggests their involvement is a gift from God as is Paul's commission to confirm and defend the gospel.

Secondly, there is a subordinate temporal and contextual clause which explains the setting for their involvement. The first in 1:5 emphasises the historical Philippian effort for the gospel. The second in 1:6 moves the attention to the future; God will bring this work to completion. The final clause in 1:7 speaks to the present whereby they are sharing in the same grace in the present that Paul is experiencing.

Thirdly, Paul includes an expression of emotion and longing. The first refers to his joy as he surveys the past. The second and third speak of his continual concern and longing for the Philippians. I consider that the three constructions repeat and emphasise the same essential thing; Paul is utterly delighted with the way in which the Philippians have participated in the gospel mission.[88]

Overall then, I consider it is preferable to take 'good work' here to refer to the mission of the church in Philippi and in general. If this is so, in what sense is God bringing this good work to completion? If Paul is referring to the good work of the gospel mission, he is encouraging the Philippians that despite their suffering from their Gentile non-Christian opponents, the threat of Judaisers, Paul's own incarceration and their squabbling, God will complete the work. The gospel mission is not ultimately dependent on them, hence they need to be joyful and put their hope in God through prayer and sustained and continuous effort for the gospel. They are to live as citizens of heaven worthy of the gospel, imitating Christ and other models with joy, faith and love because he

---

[85] 'Being *confident* of.'

[86] 'Just as it is right for me to think this of all of you because *I have you in my heart*.'

[87] 'For God is my witness as to how *I long for you* with the compassion of Christ Jesus.'

[88] Alternatively it could refer to completion of the good work of the church formation through the redemptive work of Christ. However if that were the case, evangelism remains a definite factor in the completion of the redemptive work of God in Philippi or any church.

will complete the work. This work of the gospel will go on through the whole world, with Paul being utterly confident that nothing can stop the spread of the word (cf. 1:12).

Finally, if the other view is to be preferred consideration of the context still brings evangelistic mission into the content.[89] If Paul here is referring to the work of redemption it is evident that the parallel structural balance gives the 'fellowship of the gospel' a significant place in the 'good work.' That is, this redemptive work *made evident in your continued and sustained involvement in the gospel mission including evangelism* is illustrative of the 'good work' God is doing in and through you. He will bring it to completion and by extension; the salvation of the Philippians will be complete. Again it is noticeable that Paul links eschatology, salvation and evangelism together, as in other contexts in the letter (1:28; 2:5-11, 12-18; 4:2-3).

On the whole then, there are good grounds for taking ἔργον ἀγαθον as referring to the specific good work of the Philippians in working for the propagation of the gospel. This involves multi-dimensional Spirit inspired mission through material support, prayer, active evangelistic mission, ethical witness, apologetic witness and more.

Conclusion to 1:6

Both the interpretations, as I have discussed, are legitimate in terms of Paul's theology and in terms of grammar. The phrase ἐν ὑμῖν can be taken locatively or instrumentally. In addition, if τῆς χάριτος in 1:7 is taken as a reference to salvific grace, then this would support the first interpretation. On the other hand if grace here is taken as referring to Paul's suffering and apostolic commission, then either perspective is applicable. Again an examination of Paul's use in other contexts of ἐνάρχομαι and ἐπιτελέω, shows that they are used both of human endeavour in regard to the collection (2 Cor 8:6) and of God's salvation (Gal 3:3). Neither does Paul's reference to the *Parousia* provide the solution to this impasse since, as I have demonstrated, Paul could equally be referring to the completion of the Philippians' salvation or their mission.

However, while it is not hugely important to my overall position,[90] the latter interpretation is to be preferred because of the demands of the immediate context. The essential reason for this is that I consider it evident that ἐπὶ τῇ κοινωνίᾳ ὑμῶν εἰς τὸ εὐαγγέλιον controls the following statements. This is suggested first in the repetition of τῇ κοινωνίᾳ (συγκοινωνούς) and τὸ εὐαγγέλιον in 1:7 which immediately suggests continuity of thought through

[89] Collange, 46.

[90] In that I have already established that 1:5 is inclusive of gospel proclamation as per 1:27 and 4:2-3; 4:9, probably 1:12-18a (rhetorically); 2:15-16 and the examples of Timothy and Epaphroditus (2:19-30).

the passage. Secondly, as I have noted above, 1:5-6 with v7 are parallel in structure.

The Content of χάρις in 1:7

In 1:7-8 Paul carries on and concludes the thanksgiving. Paul is expressing that it is quite right for him to think (φρονεῖν) so positively about the work of God in the gospel mission. The discussion here relates to the meaning of the phrase συγκοινωνούς μου τῆς χάριτος πάντας ὑμᾶς ὄντας. More specifically what does Paul mean by grace here? There are two major possibilities. On the one hand there are those that consider that Paul is referring to the grace of God's salvation in continuity with his 'good work' of redemption (1:6). On the other hand some argue that Paul has in mind another reference to the Philippian involvement in mission either in their active evangelism, suffering or in general.

Preliminary Exegetical Questions

Before turning to the exact nuance of grace here there are several other exegetical questions to be considered. First, there is the sense of καθώς. On the one hand it can be taken as the beginning of a new sentence and so causally ('because...') linking it to the previous; either 1:4, 1:6 or 1:3-6 in general.[91] Alternatively, as Fee rightly suggests, καθώς here does not start a new sentence but continues and concludes 1:3f and so should be rendered 'just as.'[92] Either way, Fee and O'Brien correctly relate τοῦτο to the whole previous expression of gratitude for the Philippian involvement in the gospel and Paul's confidence in the completion of the work of God.

Secondly, there is the sense of διὰ τὸ ἔχειν με ἐν τῇ καρδίᾳ ὑμᾶς which can be understood as 'you have me in your heart' or 'I have you in my heart'? Although the former is possible grammatically, word order, the explanatory γάρ and the appeal to God as witness that follows (Phil 1:8) support the latter.[93]

---

[91] Gnilka, 48; O'Brien, 66; Collange, 47; *BDAG*, 391 take it to refer to the whole. P. Bonnard, 17 of 1:4 only (mentioned by O'Brien). Vincent, 8, of 1:6 only.

[92] Fee, 88-89 cf. 1 Thess 1:5; 1 Cor 1:6.

[93] As do J.T. Reed, 'The Infinitive with Two Substantial Accusatives, an Ambiguous Construction?' *NovT* 33 (1991): 1-27; S.E. Porter, 'Word Order and Clause Structure in New Testament Greek. An Unexplored Area of Greek Linguistics using Philippians as a Test Case,' *FNT* 6 (1993): 177-206; Lightfoot, 84; Michael, 14; O'Brien, 68; Silva, 53, 56-57; Bockmuehl, 63; Beare, 52; Martin, 64; Fee, 90; F. Craddock, *Philippians*. IBC (Atlanta: John Knox, 1985), 18. However, I also note that: word order ultimately is not decisive; both interpretations fit in context; the uniqueness of διὰ τὸ ἔχειν; often the subject of the infinitive stands outside the prepositional phrase (see Hawthorne, 23; cf. Witherington, *Friendship*, 38); similar ambiguity in 1:3 (so Martin, 61, 64; Schubert, 71-82). The decision is not decisive for my analysis.

Hence, it is right for Paul to feel confident because he has the Philippians perpetually in his heart due to their co-fellowship in his suffering and mission.

Thirdly, it is preferable to take ἔν τε τοῖς δεσμοῖς μου καὶ ἐν τῇ ἀπολογίᾳ καὶ βεβαιώσει τοῦ εὐαγγελίου with συγκοινωνούς μου τῆς χάριτος πάντας ὑμᾶς ὄντας giving the sense that the Philippians are co-participators in grace with Paul both in his bonds and in his evangelistic ministry (or court defence)[94] rather than with the preceding διὰ τὸ ἔχειν με ἐν τῇ καρδίᾳ ὑμᾶς, indicating that Paul has the Philippians in his heart whether he is in prison or involved in his evangelistic ministry.[95] While the phrase can be taken with what precedes and makes good sense, then the phrase συγκοινωνούς μου τῆς χάριτος πάντας ὑμᾶς ὄντας is forced to stand alone and lacks meaning in context. Fee also notes that the word order is emphatic; 'in both of these ways they are participants together with him.'[96] The clause then is effectively explanatory; hence the NIV, 'for whether I am...' O'Brien rightly notes three other points in favour of taking it in this manner. First, he notes the repetition of ὑμᾶς. Secondly, the development of the thought as related to fellowship (1:4). Finally, the use of τέ makes it more likely that ἔν τε τοῖς δεσμοῖς μου καὶ ἐν τῇ ἀπολογίᾳ καὶ βεβαιώσει τοῦ εὐαγγελίου should be taken with what follows.[97]

Fourthly, while older commentators limited the context of ἔν τε τοῖς δεσμοῖς μου καὶ ἐν τῇ ἀπολογίᾳ καὶ βεβαιώσει τοῦ εὐαγγελίου to the legal technical sense of ἀπολογίᾳ καὶ βεβαιώσει[98] (i.e. Paul's judicial situation before a court in Rome [ἔν τε τοῖς δεσμοῖς μου]),[99] it is preferable to place it in the wider context of the general evangelistic ministry, speaking of the defensive and offensive dimensions of Paul's ministry.[100] The main reason for this is the language and the role of the gospel in Philippians, which transcends a mere judicial context, but has a societal reference in both Rome

---

[94] See the discussion in Lightfoot, 85. Alternatively the phrase is transitional and connects both ways which seems more natural in an oral setting.

[95] So H.A.W. Meyer, 20.

[96] Fee, 91.

[97] *BDAG*, 807 standing alone, hence in the sense of 'and.'

[98] Few find a hendiadys here although see Silva, 54 who suggests 'the defense that confirms the gospel.'

[99] A. Deissman, *Bible Studies* (Tr. A. Grive. Edinburgh: T&T. Clark, 1923), 104-06 cf. Gnilka, 49; Hawthorne, 23-24; Michael, 16; Collange, 47-48; Beare, 53; Craddock, 19; Kent, 106; Hendriksen, 57; Witherington, *Friendship*, 38. This view is not without warrant on the basis of the technical terminology (Acts 25:16; 2 Tim 4:16; cf. Acts 22:1, 13; 1 Cor 9:3), the specific reference to Paul's enchainment (ἔν τε τοῖς δεσμοῖς μου), taking καί as explicative (*BDAG*, 392), the link to Epaphroditus gift in prison (2:25-30) and the way in which Paul understands that it is the gospel that is really on trial (cf. Phil 1:16).

[100] See Lightfoot, 85; 'The two together will thus comprise all modes of preaching and extending the truth;' cf. Silva, 54; Fee, 93; Thielman, 40; O'Brien, 69.

(1:12-18a) and Philippi (1:27-28; 2:15-16; 4:3, 10-20).[101]

Fifthly and importantly, a decision needs to be made as to whether μου should be attached to συγκοινωνούς or χάριτος i.e. is Paul referring to the Philippians as 'my co-sharers of grace' or as 'co-sharers of my grace?' A strong case can be made for pairing μου with συγκοινωνούς.[102] It is argued first that the more natural reading of the pronouns would place μου with συγκοινωνούς.[103] Secondly, rather than using 'my grace' of his ministry, some suggest that Paul *always* uses the expression 'the grace given to me' (Rom 12:3; 15:15; 1 Cor 3:10; Gal 2:9; cf. 1 Cor 15:10; Eph 3:2, 7).[104] Thirdly, O'Brien notes that in Phil 1:25 and 2:30 there is a similar construction of a noun and a double genitive of person and thing indicating the grace of God that is in view. He suggests that 'the article (τῆς), before 'grace' (χάριτος) shows it is the grace of God that is in view.'[105]

A number of other scholars prefer placing μου with χάριτος for several reasons.[106] First, Paul in other contexts uses 'grace' as effectively a synonym for 'ministry.' Beare notes in particular Rom 1:5 where Paul refers to 'the grace and apostolic commission' in reference to his ministry of defending and confirming the gospel (cf. Rom 12:6; 15:15; 1 Cor 3:10; Gal 2:9; Eph 3:2).[107] Secondly, Lohmeyer and others take grace here as suffering, noting the parallel with 4:14 (cf. 1:29) where Paul uses the related verb συγκοινωνέω of the Philippians' co-participation with Paul's suffering (συγκοινωνήσαντες μου τῇ θλίψει).[108] Thirdly, Silva notes the link to 1 Cor 9:23 where Paul speaks of doing all things in order to be partakers (συνκοινωνός) in the gospel.[109]

In addition, as I have noted above, the parallelism indicates that Paul repeats his thankfulness for the Philippian involvement in the mission in three ways for emphasis. On balance then, the flow of Paul's discussion suggest that the latter view is preferable. Namely, that Paul is stating that the Philippians are co-sharers in his grace. It serves then as a sort of *inclusio* with 1:5, reiterating the concepts of fellowship and gospel. Both 1:5 and 1:7 refer to Paul and the Philippians' mission, which are intertwined. In 1:5 it is the Philippians' role that is emphasised, they being partners in the mission. In 1:6 God's role is prominent. Here in 1:7 the Philippians are full participants with Paul in the mission of God with all that it brings. Having said this, neither interpretation

---

[101] Similarly Fee, 93.

[102] O'Brien, 70; Fee, 91; Bockmuehl, 63; Lightfoot, 85; Vincent, 10; Kennedy, 420; Martin, 65; Hendriksen, 56; Michael, 16; Boice, 50.

[103] O'Brien, 70; Bockmuehl, 63.

[104] O'Brien, 70.

[105] O'Brien, 70.

[106] Beare, 53; cf. Silva, 53; Hawthorne, 23; Bruce, 34; Craddock, 19; Lohmeyer, 26-27; *BDAG*, 774; Gnilka, 49; Marshall, 15.

[107] Beare, 53 cf. Silva, 53. Or an hendiadys: 'the grace of his apostolic commission.'

[108] Lohmeyer, 22-27.

[109] Silva, 53.

defines grace although 'co-sharers in my grace' favours missional grace of ministry and 'my co-sharers in grace' favours redemptive grace.

The Nature of Grace in 1:7

Broadly speaking, Paul is certainly referring to grace in the sense of 'gift from God.'[110] It is commonly asserted that the use of grace with the article (τῆς χάριτος) suggests that it is divine grace that is in view.[111] However, this perspective does not stand up to close scrutiny. There are 52 instances of Paul using χάρις with the article. In most occasions the noun does indicate the redemptive grace of God. However, there are occasions when the articular noun does not refer to redemptive grace. In particular it can refer to the grace of the Jerusalem collection. In 1 Cor 16:3 Paul refers to τὴν χάριν ὑμῶν εἰς Ἰερουσαλήμ. Significantly then grace with the article sometimes refers to the grace of the Corinthians seen in their giving (cf. 2 Cor 8:6, 7, 19).[112]

Secondly, where Paul uses the expression ἡ χάρις, it carries a wide range of nuances including: the sphere of God's blessing for the saved, the grace of salvation, the grace of Paul's salvation, the grace of Paul's ministry, the grace of gifts given to believers and churches (i.e. specific gift grace), the general blessing of God and Jesus Christ Paul hopes for in his greetings and benedictions, the grace of the Jerusalem Collection, the grace of Jesus reflected in his self-denying incarnation, God's grace found in suffering, the grace of future eschatological blessing and possibly, the thanksgiving of believers.[113]

---

[110] *BDAG*, 878. Grace as the apportioning of gifts from God i.e. gift of grace (χάρισμα: Rom 1:11; 5:15a, 12:6 cf. different gifts according to grace [χαρίσματα κατὰ τὴν χάριν]; 1 Cor 1:7; 12:4, 9, 28, 30 [healings]; 31 [greater]; 1 Tim 4:14; 2 Tim 1:6; Rom 4:4, 16 [salvation]; 6:23 [eternal life]; 11:29 [Israel's election and privilege]; 7:7 [marriage]). The grace of Paul's ministry as a concrete example of the giving of gifts to God's people (Rom 1:5; 12:3; 15:15; Gal 2:9; 1 Cor 3:10; 15:10; Eph 3:2, 7, 8); the gift of blessing in response to prayer (2 Cor 1:11); grace as generosity in material giving with particular reference to the Jerusalem collection (1 Cor 16:3; 2 Cor 8:6, 7, 19 cf. 2 Cor 8:1,4); grace as gift exemplified in the example of Christ (2 Cor 8:6).

[111] Lightfoot, 85; O'Brien, 62; Martin, 64; Bockmuehl, 63; Michael, 16; Vincent, 10; Motyer, 48; cf. Fee, 91 who suggests that the use of the article indicates that Paul is referring to a prior mentioned 'grace' or a well-known 'grace.'

[112] The disputed article in Col 3:16 is best left out of the discussion.

[113] In detail arthrous uses of χάρις include: 1) The sphere of God's blessing for the saved (Rom 5:2); 2) The grace of salvation (realm) (Rom 5:15b, 17, 20, 21; 6:1; 11:6; 2 Cor 4:15; 6:1; Gal 2:21; 5:4; Eph 1:6, 7; 2:8, Col 1:6); 3) The grace of Paul's salvation (Gal 1:15; 1 Tim 1:14); 4) The grace of Paul's ministry (Rom 12:3; 1 Cor 3:10; Gal 2:9; Eph 3:2, 7; Rom 15:15; (διὰ τῆς χάριτος τῆς δοθείσης μοι) 15:10a (ἡ χάρις αὐτου), 10b (ἡ χάρις τοῦ θεοῦ [ἡ] σὺν ἐμοί); Gal 1:15 (καλέσας διὰ τῆς χάριτος αὐτοῦ); Eph 3:8 (ἐδόθη ἡ χάρις αὕτη); 5) The grace of gifts given to believers and churches i.e. specific grace (Rom 12:3; 1 Cor 1:4 [τὴν χάριν τὴν δοθεῖσαν ἡμῖν]; [ἡμῶν ἐδόθη ἡ χάρις] Eph 4:7; 2 Cor 8:1 (τὴν χάριν τοῦ θεοῦ τὴν δεδομένην ἐν

Effectively then, χάρις with the article reveals a similar range of meanings to the anarthrous noun (see note above giving the whole range).[114] This leaves open the nuance of the noun in Phil 1:7 despite the article. The problem then lies with the exact shade Paul has in mind. An analysis of Paul's use of grace opens up a variety of possibilities to consider.

SALVATION GRACE

First, the grace here can refer to the grace of God expressed generally in salvation.[115] That is, the Philippians are co-sharers in God's wonderful gracious gift of salvation with Paul. For O'Brien it is the use of the article that confirms this interpretation.[116] However as I have pointed out, whether the noun is arthrous or not does not determine meaning. That aside, this interpretation makes eminent sense when one considers Paul's association of salvation and grace.[117] However this sense is weakened in that Paul does not use 'grace' in Philippians in this way. He uses it of the general blessing of God in his greeting and benediction (1:2; 4:23), of the grace of suffering for Christ (Phil 1:29) and here in 1:7. Hence, while Paul regularly uses ἡ χάρις and derivatives in this way, the context prefers continuity with the active thrust of 1:5-6.

ταῖς ἐκκλησίαις τῆς Μακεδονίας) cf. 2 Cor 8:4; 2 Thess 1:12; 6) The general blessing of God and Jesus Christ Paul hopes for in his greetings and benedictions (Rom 16:20; 1 Cor 16:23; 2 Cor 13:13; Gal 6:18; Eph 6:24; Phil 4:23; Col 4:18: 2 Thess 3:18; 1 Tim 6:21; 2 Tim 2:1; 4:22; 7) The grace of the Jerusalem collection (1 Cor 16:3; 2 Cor 8:6, 7, 19; 8) The grace of Jesus reflected in his self denying incarnation (2 Cor 8:9); 9) God's grace found in suffering (2 Cor 12:9); 10) The grace of future eschatological blessing (Eph 2:7); 11) Thanksgiving of believers (Col 3:16?).

[114] There are a wide range of anarthrous nuances including: 1) The grace of Paul's commission (Rom 1:5; 1 Cor 15:10 [in parallel with two articular uses]); 2) The realm of grace (Rom 6:14, 15; 2 Cor 1:12); 3) Gracious speech (Eph 4:29; Col 4:6?); 3) The grace of salvation (Rom 3:24; 4:16; 5:15; 11:5, 6 [in parallel with articular use]; 2 Cor 6:1; Gal 1:6; Eph 2:5; Col 4:6?; 2 Tim 1:9; Tit 3:7); 4) Greetings (Rom 1:7; 1 Cor 1:3; 2 Cor 1:2; Gal 1:3; Eph 1:2; Phil 1:2; Col 1:2; 1 Thess 1:1; 2 Thess 1:2; 1 Tim 1:2; 2 Tim 1:2; Tit 1:4; Phm 3; 5) Gratitude (Rom 6:17; 7:25; 1 Cor 10:30; 15:57; 2 Cor 2:14; 8:16; 9:15; 1 Tim 1:12; 2 Tim 1:3); 6) Gift (Rom 4:4; 2 Cor 8:4); 6) General favour (2 Cor 1:15; 9:4, 8; 2 Thess 2:16). There seems no real distinction between the article being present or absent.

[115] O'Brien, 70; Martin, 64-5 cf. Vincent, 10; Motyer, 48; Barclay, *Philippians*, 21; H.A.W. Meyer, 23.

[116] O'Brien, 70.

[117] The link between salvation and grace is seen in that the believer is saved/justified/elect/called by God's/Christ's grace (Rom 1:24; 3:24; 11:5; Gal 1:15 cf. Rom 4:16; 5:15b; 2 Cor 6:1; Eph 1:6; 2:6-7; Tit 3:7; 1 Tim 1:14) and not through works (Rom 4:16; 5:17; 11:6; Eph 2:5, 8), law (Gal 2:21; 5:4). Furthermore, salvation is a gift χάρισμα (Rom 1:11; 5:15a, 16) and the message that saves is the gospel of grace (Gal 1:6; 2 Tim 1:9).

SUFFERING GRACE

Secondly, some interpret χάρις here actively but limit it to the grace of suffering.[118] So Martin defines grace here as 'divine strength in human weakness' (cf. 2 Cor 12:9).[119] Fee also takes it this way, noting the use of 'grace' in 1:29 where Paul speaks of how the Philippians have been 'graced' on behalf of Christ not only to believe in him, but also to suffer for his sake. Hence 'Paul very likely is referring to the "grace" of being "partners together in the defense and vindication of the gospel" even in the midst of present "chains".'[120] Similarly, Gnilka suggests that Paul is not referring to his appointment to his apostolic office, 'but to his current situation of suffering.'[121]

GIVING GRACE

Thirdly, in that Paul links grace with giving and specifically with human generosity, notably the grace of material giving, he could be referring to the grace of giving through which the Philippians share in Paul's ministry.[122] Lightfoot for example notes that this is sometimes interpreted as, 'joint-contributors to the gift which I have received.' Lightfoot however refutes this on the basis that, although χάρις can sometimes refer to material giving (e.g. 1 Cor 16:3; 2 Cor 8:4), such a restriction here serves to remove the clause from the context and so deflates the force of the passage.[123] I consider that in terms of the connections I have established between this passage and other references to the material support of mission in Paul and the clear linkage between material support and 'grace', it is logical that this forms one aspect of what Paul has in mind.

MISSION GRACE

Finally, it is commonly suggested that Paul is referring to the grace of his own apostolic ministry.[124] That is, the Philippians are sharing in Paul's apostolic

---

[118] Lightfoot, 85. Loh-Nida, 14 suggests 'grace' applies equally to the 'bonds', and to the 'defence and confirmation of the Gospel' cf. Fee, 91; Lohmeyer, 22-27; Gnilka, 49; Schenk, 105; J.J. Müller, 43; *TDNT* 2.733.

[119] Martin, 65.

[120] Fee, 91. See also Hawthorne, 23; Martin, 65-66; J.J. Müller, 43; Loh-Nida, 20; Hawthorne, 23.

[121] Gnilka, 48.

[122] Lightfoot, 85; Ellicott, 9-10; Peterman, *Gift*, 105-106.

[123] Lightfoot, 85.

[124] Beare, 53; Silva, 53; Hawthorne, 23; Fee, 91; Bruce, 34; Bockmuehl, 63; Collange, 47; Bloomquist, 145; Loh-Nida, 14; Murray, 'Witness': 320; Caird, 108; Ellicott, 9-10 seeing it generally of the various modes of involvement; Melick, 61; Marshall, 14; Peterman, *Gift*, 105; Thielman, 41; U.B. Müller, 45; J.J. Müller, 43 who takes it holistically of salvation, suffering and ministry cf. Fee, 91; O'Brien, 'Fellowship, communion', 294: 'perhaps.'

ministry of defending and confirming the gospel. This view finds support in that Paul speaks of the grace of his apostolic ministry as a concrete example of the giving of gifts to God's people (Rom 1:5; 12:3; 15:15; Gal 2:9; 1 Cor 3:10; 15:10; Eph 3:2, 7, 8). O'Brien points out that when Paul speaks of this commission he uses the phrase διὰ τῆς χάριτος τῆς δοθείσης μοι (Rom 12:3; 1 Cor 3:10; Gal 2:9; Eph 3:2, 7; Rom 15:15).[125] However again under examination this is not accurate as with reference to his ministry Paul uses other constructions involving χάρις including ἡ χάρις αὐτου (1 Cor 15:10a); ἡ χάρις τοῦ θεοῦ [ἡ] σὺν ἐμοί (1 Cor 15:10b): καλέσας διὰ τῆς χάριτος αὐτοῦ (Gal 1:15) ἐδόθη ἡ χάρις αὕτη (Eph 3:8).

Contextually this interpretation fits well considering Paul's previous reference to his apostolic ministry (ἐν τῇ ἀπολογίᾳ καὶ βεβαιώσει). Silva in support notes the parallel reference to Paul's gospel ministry in 1:5.[126] Structurally this phrase operates as a general summary statement after the two parallel statements preceding carrying on the theme of 'the fellowship of the gospel' and 'the good work.'

Conclusion to 1:7

In conclusion then, while it is reasonable to accept that grace here refers to 'God's saving grace',[127] in the context, God's saving grace is a strange intrusion despite the power of the term to trigger such a response. On the other hand the unambiguous contextually immediate reference to Paul's suffering and apostolic commission make it more likely that Paul has the grace of his apostolic commission (and so mission) in mind. These would include 'defence and confirmation of the gospel' and suffering which are linked in Paul.[128] In addition, in light of 1:5-6, all manner of ways in which the Philippians were involved in the mission both in Paul's context and their own should be included in 'grace.' This would include giving grace; this being confirmed through the use of συγκοινωνός which means 'participant, 'partner' and is sometimes used of business (Rom 11:17; 1 Cor 9:23 cf. Rev 1:9).[129] Silva may well be correct to

---

[125] O'Brien, 70; Schenk, 105.

[126] Silva, 53. He also notes the parallel to 1 Cor 9:23 of Paul's own ministry. However this link is tenuous as the sense of Paul's words is that he adopts the culture of his recipients in order to win as many as possible to Christ in order to be a participant (συγκοινωνός) in the blessings of the gospel. Here in Phil 1:7 Paul is referring to the joint participation of the Philippians with himself in the grace of the gospel ministry and suffering.

[127] Alternatively J.J. Müller, 43 suggests both are in mind. Perhaps this is another example of Pauline intentional ambiguity.

[128] See for example Rom 5:3-5; 7:21-24; 8:17-28; 1 Cor 15:30, 32; 2 Cor 4:6-10, 17; 11:23-28; 12:7-10; Gal 4:13; Phil 1:12-18a; 2:8; 1 Thess 1:6; 2:2, 14-16; 2 Thess 1:4; 2 Tim 1:8; 2:3.

[129] *BDAG*, 774.

see a link between συγκοινωνός and συνεργός ('fellow-worker') from 4:3 indicating that the Philippians participate with Paul through working with him for the cause of the gospel.[130]

Finally, I note that this reference to the 'grace' (χάρις) of his apostolic commission then brings into view Paul's pneumatology and in particular his theology of *charismata* (χαρίσματα). It is clear that Paul understands his own evangelistic ministry as a gift from God through the Spirit.[131] Accordingly, it could be that the answer to the question of the role of the congregation in the gospel mission lies in Paul's pneumatology. That is, he does not exhort evangelism because of his confidence that the Spirit will lead his people into evangelism.

This is supported in a number of ways. First, as I note above,[132] the strong role of the Spirit in Paul's own ministry suggests that the Spirit will do the same in others as the Spirit himself determines (1 Cor 12:4-7, 11). This is especially likely considering that in Paul's thinking the church corporate is a gathering of the same Spirit (1 Cor 6:19 cf. 12:13; 2 Cor 3:3; 13:14; Eph 2:22; 4:4; Phil 2:1). Secondly, as discussed above in regards to the apostolic ministry of Epaphroditus, the granting of gifts to continue the ministry of the body of Christ implies leadership and the equipping of others for the task of ministry including evangelism (Eph 4:11-12). Thirdly, as I discuss in my appendices, Paul encourages all believers to proactively evangelise as led by the Spirit (Eph 6:17).[133] Finally, I note that in the wider context of the early NT church the Spirit functions to lead and motivate the proclamation of the gospel.[134]

Conclusion 1:5-7

Thus it is probable that 1:5-7 should be interpreted actively and inclusive of

---

[130] Silva, 53-54.

[131] That this is so is seen in: 1) Paul seeing his ministry as ἡ διακονία τοῦ πνεύματος (2 Cor 3:6, 8); 2) Paul stating that his ministry of proclamation, signs and wonders was conducted in the power of the Spirit of God (Rom 15:19; 1 Cor 2:4; 2 Cor 6:6 [ἐν πνεύματι ἁγίῳ]); 3) Paul noting that his proclamation was through words inspired by the Spirit (1 Cor 2:13; 2 Cor 4:13; 1 Thess 1:5); 4) Paul including the ministry of apostle as a spiritual gift (1 Cor 12:28, 29; Eph 4:11) implying that his own apostolicity was a spiritual gift.

[132] See previous note.

[133] See Appendix 1, 'The connection between evangelism and the military metaphor in Paul.'

[134] This is seen in the ministry of Jesus (Matt 12:18 [cf. Is 42:1]; 12:28; Lk 4:14, 18 [cf. Is 61:1-2]; Jn 3:34; 6:63; Acts 10:38); Paul (Acts 9:17-20; 13:2, 4, 9; 16:6, 7; 20:22); the apostles (Matt 10:20; Mk 13:11; Lk 12:11-12; Jn 20:21-22; Acts 2:14-41 [Peter]; 4:8 [Peter], 31); other leaders (Acts 6:10 [Stephen]; 8:29 [Philip]) Acts 18:25 [Apollos]) and a wider circle of unspecified disciples involved in evangelism (Jn 15:26-27; Acts 1:8; 1 Pet 1:12).

evangelism. This then points to a church active in evangelism. This is particularly clear in the phrase τῇ κοινωνίᾳ ὑμῶν εἰς τὸ εὐαγγέλιον which in light of the content of Philippians, should be read as multidimensional including all manner of involvement, including evangelism. In addition the ἔργον ἀγαθὸν and συγκοινωνούς μου τῆς χάριτος due to the parallelism of the passage, arguably refer to (and so emphasise) the same. Here then is further evidence of congregational evangelism in Paul. I note that here we also see an interplay of the motifs of joy (1:4), suffering (1:7), evangelism (1:5-7 cf. 9, 11), perseverance (1:6), eschatological assurance (1:6 cf. 1:11) and unity in the context (1:9-10), pointing to a complex interplay of the themes outlined in the introduction.

CHAPTER 9

Imitation and Proclamation (Phil 4:9)

This chapter examines the appeal of Phil 4:9 to inquire as to whether evangelism falls within its range. Having examined the other key passages and the thanksgiving in light of my previous findings, I now turn to Phil 4:9 because, with 4:8, it concludes and summarises the previous set of admonitions and on close examination summarises the whole of the paraenesis of Philippians.[1] In addition, 4:9 is one of Paul's appeals for emulation of his own example and so it is an important verse in the discussion of the question of general evangelism in Paul (1 Cor 4:16; 11:1; Phil 3:17; Eph 5:1-2; 1 Thess 1:6; 2:14 cf. Phil 2:5-11; 2 Cor 8:9).[2]

There are two appeals for imitation in the book of Philippians (3:17; 4:9).[3] The first blends Paul's penchant for explicit imitation language (μιμητής) and the prefix συμ to appeal for unified Philippian imitation of his own example. The second appeal is thematic rather than strictly linguistic and sums up Paul's appeal with a global injunction to emulate Paul's own example in every way. While I consider there are sound reasons for arguing evangelism lies in the range of the appeal of 3:15-17,[4] this is not explicit or dominant in a context

---

[1] Fee, 413.

[2] These refer to: 1) Imitation of Paul (1 Cor 4:16; 11:1); 2) Imitation of the Pauline group and lifestyle (1 Cor 4:17; 1 Thess 1:6; Phil 3:17); 3) Imitation of Christ (1 Cor 11:1 cf. 2 Cor 8:9; Eph 5:2; Phil 2:5-11); 4) Imitation of God (Eph 5:1); 5) Imitation of churches (1 Thess 2:14).

[3] Only the first uses the language of μιμητής. However, *exempla* plays a significant role throughout the epistle in various ways. In addition to 3:15-17; 4:9, Fee, 364 rightly notes that 1:30; 2:18 also hint at imitation in regard to suffering for Christ (cf. 3:10).

[4] These reasons include: 1) False evangelism i.e. false content from Judaisers (κακοὺς ἐργάτας) and the more general 'enemies of the cross', as the starting point and context for the warning and appeals which follow (3:2); 2) Evangelism as the context for Paul's life and so example (1:7, 12-14, 22, 30) and so the content of ἐπεκτεινόμενος and διώκω (3:13-14); 3) The absence of any limiting qualifier; 4) The wider appeal to walk in accordance with 'what we have already attained' which may include evangelism if part of Paul's initial discipleship training (see 4:9); 5) The pluralising of the appeal to examples (3:17) which brings in the other evangelistic examples of Philippians (1:14-18a; 2:5-11, 19-30); 6) The reminder of heavenly citizenship recalling the evangelistic nuance of the appeal of 1:27 (cf. 4:2-3); 7) The use of athletic metaphor throughout

focused around the threat of opponents. Hence, I will not address it in depth in this discussion. In this section I will focus on 4:9 to assess whether evangelism falls within the range of Paul's appeal for imitation.

The passage begins the conclusion to the letter signalled by τὸ λοιπόν.[5] It is highly imitatory recalling 3:15-21.[6] The passage is a single sentence that involves a good deal of Greek figures of speech including anaphora (ὅσα [6x]), asyndeton,[7] polysyndeton (καί [6x]), homoioteleuton and synonymous parallelism.[8]

The two verses address right thinking (4:8) and right behaviour (4:9). As Gnilka 'the two imperatives λογίζεσθε – πράσσετε describe two sides of the same procedure and should not be torn apart.'[9] In the same vein Bockmuehl writes: 'and otherwise, devote your thoughts to what is excellent and your actions to my example.'[10]

---

which is most often evangelistic in orientation (see Appendix 2, 'The connection between evangelism and the athletic metaphor in Paul'); 8) The unqualified global appeal in 4:9. As U.B. Müller, 201 notes: 'With this idiom the thought is taken up that is stressed in 3:17 where Paul calls for the imitation of his theological attitude and himself.'

[5] Garland, 'Composition': 149; O'Brien, 499; Hawthorne, 185 take τὸ λοιπόν transitionally and as preface to exhortation (cf. 2 Cor 13:11; 1 Thess 4:1; 2 Thess 3:1) ('in addition') and see it as the conclusion of the admonitions of 4:1-9 indicating further what it means to 'stand firm' (4:1). I accept this partially but also consider that the content of 4:8-9 summarises and restates 1:27f; 2:5f, 12f; 3:17; 4:1f. Others see here the beginning of a separate letter (See 'Integrity' in Chapter 2 above). Bockmuehl, 249 suggests 'beyond that' focussed on the theme of peace and the preceding exhortations. J.A.D. Weima, *The Significance of the Pauline Letter Closings*. JSNTS 101 (Sheffield: Sheffield Academic Press, 1994), 191 sees here the beginning of the final section 4:8-23. J. Collange, 146 suggests 4:8-9 follows 4:1 and ends letter C.

[6] O'Brien, 499.

[7] Wallace, *Greek Grammar,* 658 notes 'occasionally, an independent clause is *not* introduced by a conjunctive word or phrase. This phenomenon is known as *asyndeton* (a construction "not bound together"). In such cases the function of the independent clause is implied from the literary context. Asyndeton is a vivid stylistic feature that occurs often for emphasis, solemnity, or rhetorical value (staccato effect), or when there is an abrupt change in topic. Thus, it is found, for example, with: 1. commands and exhortations, put forth in rapid succession (cf. Jn 5:8; Eph 4:26-29; Phil 4:4-6; 1 Thess 5:15-22).'

[8] Hawthorne, 185-190. O'Brien, 499 notes that each clause contains an adjective in the neuter plural namely, ἀληθῆ, σεμνά, δίκαια, ἁγνά, προσφιλῆ and εὔφημα. 'There is a deliberate play on the endings (homoioteleuton) of these adjectives: two end with η, four with α.' He also notes in v9 that five verbs end in –ατε or -ετε. He adds, 'These six clauses in synonymous parallelism are grammatically unconnected and as a result very emphatic.'

[9] Gnilka, 222 (translation mine).

[10] Bockmuehl, 250.

In 4:8, Paul appeals to the whole church (ἀδελφοί) to think (λογίζεσθε) in an eightfold way; which effectively amounts to a generic appeal to think in a manner appropriate to the gospel ('reckon', 'consider').[11] The emphasis here is on mind-set rather than action for the gospel; hence it does not really inform this discussion. Consequently, my interest lies in the more practical (πράσσετε) and the global appeal of 4:9.

The Evangelistic Content of the Appeal for Emulation (4:9)

The relationship between 4:8 and 4:9 is disputed. Schenk considers ἃ as independent of 4:8 and the first καί as adversative so Paul is introducing new material.[12] However, this is unlikely as καί is rarely adversative and Paul could have used the stronger adversatives δέ or ἀλλά. Most see 4:9 as subordinate with ἃ dependent on ταῦτα in 4:8 with καί as correlative.[13] I concur that καί here is correlative ('and') but question whether ἃ should be limited to the ταῦτα of 4:8. Rather, 4:9 provides the lens through which the virtues of 4:8 should be read i.e. the virtues point to the imitation of Paul and Christ (Phil 2:5-11; 1 Cor 11:1) and living worthily of the gospel (1:27).[14] Fee states correctly, 'in effect this sentence summarises, as well as concludes, the letter. Paul's concern throughout has been the gospel, its content ("doctrinal error" is not at issue), but its lived out expression in the world.'[15] Hence all of Philippians is in Paul's mind here including the recurring concern for the mission of the Philippian church.

In 4:9 the appeal shifts from the focus of their thinking in moral and behavioural terms to behavioural imitation of Paul. He writes, 'whatever you have learned or received or heard from me, or seen in me— continually put it into practice (πράσσετε).' Although the Greek μιμητής is not used in 4:9, clearly this falls in the rubric of Paul's appeals for imitation.[16]

Paul uses four aorist verbs (ἐμάθετε, παρελάβετε, ἠκούσατε and εἴδετε) referring to their past experience of Paul to describe the range of imitation here. The relationship between the four has been variously defined.[17] Some see them as consecutive and independent. Others consider the first three applying to Paul's teaching and the final term to his example. A more likely approach is to

---

[11] It suggests 'let your mind dwell' on these things. O'Brien, 500. Black, 'Structure': 24 notes that the elements of 4:4-9 are generic, linked to the issue of the Philippian's cooperation in the gospel (1:5). Similarly Ellicott, 94: 'they are general and inclusive.'
[12] Schenk, 318.
[13] Vincent, 140; O'Brien, 508; Fee, 413-414; Bockmuehl, 254.
[14] Fee, 419 who notes 'what he (Paul) intends, of course, is that "virtue" be filled with Christian content, exemplified by his own life and teaching (v.9).' As Hawthorne, 189 notes this verse holds 'what is ultimately of most importance for the church.'
[15] Fee, 421; Bockmuehl, 254.
[16] Fee, 419.
[17] See O'Brien, 508-509 for detail.

divide them into two pairs, the first pair referring to his teaching received on his visits and through letters, the latter pair to his example.[18]

The first ἐμάθετε, the second person plural aorist of μανθάνω means to 'gain knowledge or skill by instruction, *learn*.'[19] Paul uses it sixteen times of the twenty-five NT uses. As is the case elsewhere in the NT, the term denotes 'to learn', often effecting a changed behaviour.[20]

Paul uses it in a variety of ways including the things learned by Christians either through teachers (Rom 16:17),[21] through his letters (1 Cor 4:6; 1 Tim 5:4; Tit 3:14), in the church through prophets (1 Cor 14:31), in the home (1 Cor 14:35 cf. 1 Tim 2:11), through the initial evangelisation by Paul and others (Eph 4:20; Col 1:7) or in general (Tit 3:14). It is applied to things Paul has learnt or wants to learn from his recipients (Gal 3:2) or concerning God's provision (Phil 4:11). Paul also uses it of wrong learning from false teachers (1 Tim 5:13; 2 Tim 3:7) as opposed to the right learning Timothy is to persevere in (2 Tim 3:14 cf. Tit 3:14).

Here then, it should be understood as referring in general to all good teaching that has been learned from Paul by the Philippians (Phil 4:9). This necessarily includes the initial evangelisation and discipleship of the Philippians and any additional communiqué from Paul and/or his emissaries. As in the case of all four verbs, the use of the plural aorist refers to past teaching to the whole church. Unless it can be shown that Paul precluded evangelism from the teaching given to his converts, evangelism should be included in this appeal.

The second verb παρελάβετε, the second person plural aorist indicative of παραλαμβάνω, is found eleven times in Paul carrying the essential meaning of 'to receive.' In the NT the term takes on the semi-technical Rabbinic sense of transmitting and receiving 'tradition', referring to teaching received by Paul

[18] O'Brien, 508; Fee, 420; Bockmuehl, 255; Kent, 152; Michael, 206; Ellicott, 95; Plummer, *Understanding*, 97; Vincent, 140; U.B. Müller, 201. In any case as Loh-Nida, *Handbook*, 135 say, 'the underlying meaning remains the same.'

[19] *BDAG*, 615.

[20] Found quite commonly in the Synoptics/Acts referring to either cognitive learning alone (Acts 23:27) or cerebral learning that effects a change of behaviour in regard to understanding the Old Testament (Matt 9:13) or Jesus' own teaching (Matt 11:29; 24:32; Mk 13:28). In Hebrews 5:8 it is applied to Jesus who learned obedience through suffering. In John it is applied in a similar fashion to learning from God and hence, of responding positively to Jesus (Jn 6:45). The Jews are quoted as being stunned at Jesus' great learning (Jn 7:15). In Revelation it is applied to the new song learnt only by the 144,000 (Rev 14:3).

[21] Past authentic Christian learning: the authentic Christian teaching received by the Roman Christians as opposed to those who teach false doctrine and cause division and stumbling blocks (cf. Fitzmyer, *Romans*, 746; Stuhlmacher, *Romans*, 252-253) and consistent with Paul's teaching (cf. Schreiner, *Romans*, 802).

from others and passed onto his recipients (1 Cor 11:23; 15:3; Gal 1:12).[22] Paul however, also uses it more generally of the receipt of the gospel in his own evangelisation (1 Cor 15:1; Gal 1:9; 1 Thess 2:13), of receiving Jesus Christ as Lord (Col 2:6) and of an individual receiving a specific 'work in the Lord' (Col 4:17).[23] Paul uses it also of the teaching concerning the avoidance of sexual immorality (1 Thess 4:1-8) and idleness rather than providing for oneself (2 Thess 3:6), injunctions received from his team on his initial evangelisation of Macedonia.

Its range then possibly overlaps μανθάνω, referring to the initial gospel and subsequent teaching passed on to the Philippians. Alternatively, it specifically refers to early Christian tradition passed on by Paul to the Philippians. The latter is preferable in that a straightforward repetition of ἐμάθετε seems unnecessary. In other words Paul is referring in the first two verbs to all that he has taught them from his own experience and understanding (μανθάνω) and the Christian tradition that he has passed on (παραλαμβάνω).

Could this include evangelism? On reflection, there is a good basis to argue that Paul passed on evangelism as an imperative of Christian existence, to the Philippians, as one 'tradition' of the early church. First, there is clear and incontrovertible evidence that the early church considered evangelism as essential to its existence. This is seen first in the broad range of references to spoken evangelism in the early church.[24]

Secondly, it is apparent in the so-called 'Great Commission', which is found in some form or another in Matthew, Luke and John (Matt 28:18-20; Lk 24:45-49/Acts 1:8; Jn 20:21).[25] Whatever the complexities of interpretation these verses hold, they do emphasise that each of these writers to some extent or another, saw evangelism as central to the mission of the church. Within these accounts, although admittedly later than Paul, this mission was not focussed entirely on the apostles alone. In the Matthean commission the apostles are to teach the new disciples *all* (πάντα) aspects of Christ's teaching to the newly made disciples. Clearly 'all' includes the command in which it stands i.e. they were to make disciples to make further disciples indicating a democratisation and geographical extension of the mission through the Matthean church. In

---

[22] The Lord's Supper tradition (1 Cor 11:23), the death and resurrection of Christ (1 Cor 15:3 cf. Col 2:6), Paul's receipt of the gospel not through tradition but revelation (Gal 1:12 cf. 1:9; 1 Thess 2:13). Further see O'Brien, 509; Fee, 420; Hawthorne, 189.

[23] This raises questions against taking it always as a technical term; context should dictate meaning.

[24] So for example: Matt 4:18-22; 9:31; 10:1-10; 24:14; 28:18-20; Mk 1:17-18; 5:19-20; 6:12; 7:36; 13:10; Lk 9:1-6, 60-62; 10:1-12; 12:8-12; 14:13-14; 24:27; Jn 4:1; 4:35-38; 20:21; Acts 1:8; 2:14-40; 4:18-20, 29-30, 33; 5:19-21, 29-32, 42; 6:5, 8-10; 8:4-8; 13:49; 19:10, 23; 21:8; 1 Peter 3:15-16; Jude 23.

[25] Although the longer ending of Mark (Mk 16:9-20) is most likely a later addition (Metzger, *Textual*, 102-106), it does indicate that, at the point of its inclusion, a commission for evangelism was understood in the minds of the redactor.

Acts the outpouring of the Spirit at Pentecost came upon the whole church (πάντες) including women (Acts 1:14, 15; 2:1).[26] The subsequent narrative involves a wide range of people sharing the gospel.[27] Clearly then, as the early church developed, there was a strong sense of an evangelistic commission that extended beyond the apostles. Although difficult to absolutely prove, it is likely that there was a sense of this commission within the wider church at the time of Paul's conversion.

That being the case, it is likely that Paul would have come into contact with this on his visits to Jerusalem. In light of his own revelatory call to ministry on the Damascus Road it is reasonable to assume that in his fifteen day stay with Peter and James (Gal 1:18-19), some time was spent discussing evangelism and the commission as it was understood by Peter.[28] More decisively, his second visit fourteen years later was specifically concerned with evangelism and the gospel Paul preached to the Gentiles (Gal 2:1-2).[29] The outcome of the visit was the vindication of Paul's gospel and the division of the missiological task of reaching Gentile and Jew between Paul and Peter; Paul to continue to lead the mission to the Gentiles, and Peter to the Jews (Gal 2:7-10). This division indicates that the Jerusalem leaders and Paul himself believed in a 'great commission' to take the gospel to all humanity. Notably this is a holistic mission, Paul encouraged not only to preach the gospel but to be concerned for

---

[26] As Dunn, *Acts*, 24; Marshall, *Acts*, 68; Larkin, *Acts*, 49; Fitzmyer, *Acts*, 238 note πάντες in 2:1 suggests the 120 of Acts 1:15. Williams, *Acts*, 39 rightly notes other pilgrims may also have been there. Against this is the mention of τοῖς ἕνδεκα ἐπῆρεν in 2:14 and the variant οἱ ἀπόστολοι. Barrett notes that the latter reading is clearly secondary and I suggest may be included to limit just such an inclusive interpretation. See further Barrett, *Acts*, 112.

[27] Including Apostle's (Acts 2:14-40; 3:11-4:2, 4, 18-20, 29-30, 33; 5:19-21, 29-32, 42; 8:25; 9:35; 10:34-48); Paul (Acts 9:15-16, 20-22, 27-30; 13-28); Stephen (6:10, 13; 7:1-53); disciples *who were not apostles* (8:4-8; 11:19-21) including Philip (8:4-40; 21:8); unnamed disciples (9:31, 35, 42; 11:49; 19:10); Apollos (18:24-28).

[28] In that evangelism was core business for them all it would seem obvious that matters of evangelism, mission and the life of Christ would have come up despite ἱστορέω ('to visit', 'make the acquaintance' of someone and not 'receive instruction') being utilised cf. Neil, *Galatians*, 30; Fung, *Galatians*, 74; Dunn, *Galatians*, 73-74 who notes that it is hard to exclude the element of 'inquiry' from the verb; Martyn, Galatians, 171-172; Longenecker, *Galatians*, 38; Bruce, *Galatians*, 98: 'It would be an obvious purpose of such a visit to put to Peter a whole variety of questions about what Jesus had said on this or that topic which had cropped up in the course of Paul's missionary work.'

[29] Bruce, *Galatians*, 109: 'in the light of v7 we may conclude that he gave them an account of his gospel ministry to date.' Fung, *Galatians*, 98-99: 'the subject under discussion at the meeting was not the content of the gospel (cf. v.6) but the respective spheres of activity of the two parties.' However, it is likely that a number of other issues were discussed, although exactly what is speculative.

the poor.[30]

It is certain then, on the basis of Gal 2:1-10, that Paul knew some form of the commission to evangelise and it is likely that he passed it onto his churches.[31] In addition, we have the evidence of Paul teaching the Philippians to evangelise and the passing on of a commission in Philippians itself. As I have argued throughout, at the heart of the issues of Philippians is an appeal for continued fellowship in the full mission of the gospel in unity, steadfastness and in the face of persecution (1:5, 27, 2:14-16; 4:2-3). More important is the evidence of 4:2-3 where co-workers were inspired and trained by Paul to join the mission as his co-workers. This necessarily involved teaching and the passing on of the Great Commission tradition.

It is apparent then that Paul's language here includes proclamation. Not that this exhausts what Paul wanted from his recipients. The statement in 4:9 alerts us to the fact that Paul understood his mode of discipling as one of modelling Christian living. This included a huge range of attitudes and activities that are part of authentic Christian living. The point that is important for this discussion is that this includes proclamation of the gospel

Even in the context of this verse alone, there is ample evidence that Paul passed on his passion for the conversion of the lost to his recipients. Interestingly, Hawthorne supports this with his interpretation of παρελάβετε, suggesting that the term implies the Philippians are a link in the chain of tradition.[32] Conzelmann puts it this way: 'the obligation of the Philippians was not only to receive it, believe it, act upon it, but also themselves to pass it carefully on to others.'[33] In terms of the tradition of evangelism then, the Philippians learnt it from Paul, were to apply it in their context and then pass it

---

30 Most scholars take Gal 2:10 as a reference to the Jerusalem Collection. However, as noted above in Chapter 6 concerning the possible apostleship of Epaphroditus, it is a generic call to consider the poor as Paul goes about his mission; thus emulating the concern for the poor seen in Jesus' ministry, the early church in Jerusalem and Antioch.

31 The precise form is unclear. However the tradition is seen in the sending out the apostles (Matt 9:36-10:42; Lk 9:1-6); the sending of the seventy two (Lk 10:1-24); the eschatological sign of the gospel preached to all nations before the end (Matt 24:14; Mk 13:10); the 'Great Commission' (Matt 28:16-20; Lk 24:45-49; Acts 1:8 cf. Jn 20:21); the preaching of a wide range of believers in Acts including: the Apostles (2:14-40, 42; 3:12-26; 4:8-12; 5:20, 42; 8:25; 10:34-43; 11:14-17); other preachers including Stephen (6:8-13; 7:2-56; 8:1-11:30); scattered non-apostles (8:4; 11:19-21) including Philip (8:5-13; 26-40); Paul (9:15, 20-22, 27, 28-29; 13:5, 10-11, 15-41, 46-48; 14:1, 3, 7, 15-17, 21; 15:35; 16:13, 31-32; 17:2-3, 10-12, 17-31; 18:4, 11; 19:8-10; 22:1-21; 23:1-7; 24:10-21; 26:2-23; 28:31); proclaimers in the Antioch church including Barnabas (13:5, 46-48; 14:1, 3, 7, 15-17, 21; 15:35); Silas (Acts 16:31-32; 17:10-12); Apollos (18:25-28). See also 1 Peter 3:15.

32 H. Conzelmann, *1 Corinthians*. Hermeneia (Trans: J.W. Leitch. Philadelphia: Fortress, 1975), 195-196.

33 Hawthorne, 189.

onto the new disciples. The spread of the faith in the early church suggests this was the case.[34] There seems no reason to exclude evangelism from this broad appeal.

The third verb ἠκούσατε, the second person plural aorist indicative of ἀκούω, is used thirty-four times in Paul. The verb is a sensory expression meaning 'to hear' in literal terms. It is used broadly of hearing of the word of God through preaching and teaching,[35] the wonders of heavenly glory (1 Cor 2:9; 2 Cor 12:4), a specific piece of news (1 Cor 5:1; 11:18; Gal 1:13; 1:23; Eph 1:15; 3:2; Phil 1:27, 30; 2:26; Col 1:4, 9; 2 Thess 3:11; Phm 5) and other Christian's conversation (Eph 4:29). On some occasions the verb also carries the stronger sense of hearing *with understanding* (Rom 11:8; 1 Cor 14:2; Gal 4:21).[36] Paul's use here could summarise the previous two verbs,[37] relate to informal teaching, or as is preferable, pair with εἴδετε to summarise what they heard and saw as Paul ministered amongst them during their initial evangelisation, his ministry among them and in his visits.[38] If this is the case, hearing invariably involved hearing Paul evangelise (see below). The obvious implication of the appeal of 4:9 in terms of my enquiry is that they were to imitate his gospel proclamation in Philippi and wherever the Spirit of God took them.

The final verb is εἴδετε, the second person plural aorist indicative of ὁράω. It is used regularly by Paul and is another sensory term denoting 'seeing' in literal terms. Most often it implies physically seeing a person or people (Rom 1:11; 1 Cor 8:14; 16:7; Gal 1:19; Phil 1:27; 2:28; 1 Thess 2:17; 3:6; 2 Tim 1:4), heavenly wonders (1 Cor 2:9), God (1 Tim 6:16), Paul's handwriting (Gal 6:11) or a significant action or event (Gal 2:14; 1:30). As in the case of ἀκούω, it sometimes signifies a deeper seeing, involving seeing with the sense of *discerning* (Gal 2:7; 1 Tim 3:10). Paul also uses ὁράω in the sense of theological consideration (Rom 11:22). Here it refers comprehensively to all that they saw him do in his ministry among them. His appeal is: 'Listen to me!

---

[34] This conclusion effectively validates the soundness of the conclusions of Michael Green discussed in the introduction. Conversely it makes the position of Bowers, Bosch and Dickson untenable.

[35] This can be applied to the gospel (Rom 10:14, 18; Eph 1:13; Col 1:6, 23; 2 Tim 4:17), to hearing God's word in OT quotations (Rom 11:8; 15:21), to hearing general teaching from Paul (2 Cor 12:6; 2 Tim 1:13; 2:2) or Timothy (1 Tim 4:16; 2:2), hearing ethical teaching (Eph 4:21) or hearing the law (Gal 4:21) and false teaching (2 Tim 2:14).

[36] In Rom 11:8 is found a conflation of Deut 29:3; Is 29:10; Ps 69:23-24 which Paul utilises of the Jewish failure to hear the gospel with understanding and believe. In 1 Cor 14:2 of hearing and understanding messages in tongues. In Gal 4:21 of hearing and understanding the law.

[37] Marshall, 115 who rightly notes that the teaching passed on by emissaries may be in Paul's mind.

[38] Perhaps also with what they have heard of him whilst separate from them, as Plummer, *Understanding,* 98 suggests.

Look at me! Follow me! Imitate me!'[39]

So Paul's appeal to imitate here is comprehensive, covering all that he has taught them through preaching, teaching, tradition, letter, emissary and example. The Philippians are to 'continually do these things' (ταῦτα πράσσετε).[40] The verb πράσσω is used eighteen times in Paul and means 'to do, practice' and is most often applied to right or wrong behaviour in regard to God's standard (Rom 1:32; 2:1, 2, 3, 25; 7:15, 19; 9:11; 1 Cor 5:2; 2 Cor 5:10; 12:21; Gal 5:21). It is also used of the government bringing punishment on the wrongdoer (Rom 13:4), of Paul doing evangelism (1 Cor 9:17) or Paul's activity in general (Eph 6:21) and of Paul's desire that the Thessalonians 'do your own things' (1 Thess 4:11). Here in Phil 4:9 Paul uses the present imperative indicating he is exhorting them to *continually* 'do' or 'practice' these things.[41]

Does 'these things' include evangelistic proclamation? When the four verbs are considered it becomes clear that it undoubtedly does. First, there are those things heard from Paul through verbal teaching (ἐμάθετε) and tradition (παρελάβετε), which I have argued must include evangelism. Even if Paul did not pass on a 'Great Commission', the content of Philippians itself, as I have demonstrated, includes continued unified evangelisation in the face of persecution. In addition, there is little evidence that Paul did not pass on a commission to evangelise to his churches, rather all evidence points in the other direction. Secondly, there are those things seen and heard (ἠκούσατε) in Paul's ministry and life (εἴδετε) which clearly include evangelism.

The final verb εἴδετε in particular emphasises this point. Paul is reminding the Philippians of *all they have seen him do* in his previous visits to Macedonia. That this includes evangelistic proclamation is clear from Luke's account (Acts 16:12-40) of the first visit.

First, Paul preaches (ἐλαλοῦμεν) to a group of women at a place of prayer beside a river and Lydia responds with faith and is baptised (Acts 16:13-14). Secondly, he delivers an evil spirit from a demonised slave girl who refers to Paul's proclamation (καταγγέλλουσιν ὑμῖν ὁδὸν σωτηρίας [v17]) of the way to salvation indicating that she has heard he and the team preach over many days (πολλὰς ἡμέρας [v18]) (16:16-24).[42] Finally, there is the request of

---

[39] Hawthorne, 190.

[40] Present tense; so Hawthorne, 189.

[41] On the Greek present imperative as continuous action see (CD) W. Vine, 1997, c1996. *Vine's You Can Learn New Testament Greek!: Course of Self-Help for the Layman.* C1996 by W.E. Vine Copyright Ltd. of Bath, England. (electronic ed. Thomas Nelson: Nashville), Lesson 12, 'The Verb *(Continued)*, The imperative mood.' See also Wallace, *Greek Grammar*, 485 who writes 'with the *present*, the force generally is to *command the action as an ongoing process*' (italics his).

[42] There is no absolutely explicit reference to demonic deliverance in Paul. I consider that this link to Acts 16 is sufficient to establish that is should be included in Paul's signs and wonders ministry. Here is another area of silence which I assume was

the Philippian jailor, τί με δεῖ ποιεῖν ἵνα σωθῶ; (v30) indicating that he had heard a message referring to salvation. In context this may have come through the singing and praying of Silas and Paul (Acts 16:25), but probably involved some direct verbal proclamation (perhaps to the other prisoners) as well. In addition, Paul then summarised the gospel of faith in Christ for salvation (πίστευσον ἐπὶ τὸν κύριον Ἰησοῦν καὶ σωθήσῃ σὺ καὶ ὁ οἶκός σου [v31]).[43] He then preached the gospel to the whole family (καὶ ἐλάλησαν αὐτῷ τὸν λόγον τοῦ κυρίου [v32]). All this indicates Paul's evangelism ministry was seen and heard by at least some of the Philippians as recipients and observers.[44] This included at least proclamation, exorcism (charismatic expression), evangelism through public worship and prayer, followed by baptism and instruction of the new converts.

Luke also mentions other visits to Philippi. On one visit Luke records Paul travelled through 'speaking many words of encouragement to the people', which suggests primarily pastoral proclamation (Acts 20:2 cf. 20:4-5). It may be that he went west on this visit to Illyricum to preach the gospel, a mission which may have included members of the Macedonian churches including perhaps Epaphroditus, Clement, Syntyche, Euodia and others (cf. Rom 15:19).[45] In light of Paul's penchant for evangelism, it is certain that he engaged in further evangelistic proclamation on these later visits.[46]

It is also clear from the broader Pauline epistles that his recipients have seen him evangelizing. Paul's example included proclamation in that he lived to proclaim the gospel especially to the Gentiles.[47] In Philippians too, as indicated throughout this analysis, there is strong evidence that Paul evangelised along with Philippian co-workers (1:5; 4:2-3 cf. 1 Thess 2:1-2). Furthermore, the Philippians' conversions which were as a result of Paul's evangelistic ministry.

Thus it is apparent that one of the things that they have seen and heard Paul do is evangelism. Unless it can be shown that Paul's intent here is purely ethical or that there is some previous limitation on evangelistic mission directed to his recipients, it stands to reason that the appeal for imitation here includes the proclamation of the gospel.

---

practiced and encouraged by Paul on the basis of: 1) the evidence of Acts; 2) Paul's ministry of 'signs and wonders' and 'power' (cf. Rom 15:19; 2 Cor 12:12); 3) the practice of Christ and the early church.

[43] A confessional formula laden with theological and contextual meaning (cf. Rom 10:9; 1 Cor 12:3; Phil 2:11) cf. Barrett, *Acts*, 797.

[44] Not to mention any other evangelistic occurrences that Luke excludes from his selective account.

[45] For an alternative idea see below on 1 Thess 1:6-8.

[46] As may be implied by λόγῳ πολλῷ = 'much speaking/preaching' cf. Barrett, *Acts*, 946.

[47] See Rom 1:1-5, 13-17; 11:13; 15:17-22; 16:25-27; 1 Cor 1:17-18; 9:16-22; 2 Cor 3:17; 5:11-20; 10:13-16; Gal 1:6-9, 11-12; 2:7-10; Eph 3:1-13; Phil 1:7; Col 1:25-29; 1 Thess 2:6-12; 1 Tim 1:1, 12-14; 2 Tim 1:1, 11 –12; Tit 1:1-2.

The final consideration is Paul's intended recipients of this appeal. As throughout the epistle Paul uses his favoured ἀδελφοί (4:8). As I have consistently argued, this refers to the whole church rather than a select group (1:12, 14; 3:1, 13, 17; 4:1, 4, 21). The inclusivity of the appeal then indicates that the *whole church* is to engage in evangelism led by specialists including Apostles, Paul's team, co-workers and evangelists. Even if the work is in the hands of specialists, Paul's christology and pneumatology allows for the Spirit's generation of Christ's whole ministry in the context of each local church. These evangelists are not only to proclaim, but also to equip others for works which includes evangelistic mission (Eph 4:11-12).[48] This all argues strongly against the view that there is no general evangelistic mandate in Paul. When paired with 4:8, we have a neat pairing of ethical and evangelistic witness as is found in 2:15 (ethical) and 2:16 (evangelistic).

Finally, Paul grants the Philippians an assurance of the presence of God as they continue to emulate his example. Specifically that the 'God of peace will be with you' (καὶ ὁ θεὸς τῆς εἰρήνης ἔσται μεθ' ὑμῶν). This indicates that as they live out their Christian lives, thinking rightly and following the example of Paul (including evangelism), they can be assured of God's presence with them. Interestingly this is not completely dissimilar to the assurance of Christ's presence with his disciples as they carry out their commission as recorded by Matthew in the context of the Great Commission (καὶ ἰδοὺ ἐγὼ μεθ' ὑμῶν εἰμι πάσας τὰς ἡμέρας ἕως τῆς συντελείας τοῦ αἰωνος) cf. Matt 28:20.

Proclamation in Other References to Imitation in the Pauline Epistles

It is not my intention here to discuss in depth Paul's use of imitatory language nor to fully exegete these passages. Rather, I want to briefly explore the *content* of three of his other appeals for imitation to assess whether evangelism falls within the range of his appeal.[49]

1 Corinthians 11:1

In 1 Cor 11:1 Paul states, 'imitate me, as I imitate Christ.' The statement is the conclusion to the chiastic section beginning in 1 Cor 8:1 dealing with the problem of eating meat sacrificed to idols and Paul's apostolic authority and

[48] See above Chapter 6.

[49] I will not look at Eph 5:1-2 in which Paul appeals for imitation of God and which is primarily ethical in context. Neither will I explore 1 Cor 4:15-17 which is set in the context of his attempts to deal with factionalism based around favoured preachers and is not explicitly evangelistic in intent.

freedom.[50] The section immediately leading into the appeal concerns eating meat from the temple butchery.[51]

For a number of reasons I suggest that in this appeal Paul is making general statements which govern Christian behaviour which include evangelism within their range and which suggests more than merely an ethical/apologetic evangelistic mode of interaction with unbelievers.

First, the statement μηδεὶς τὸ ἑαυτοῦ ζητείτω ἀλλὰ τὸ τοῦ ἑτέρου ('let no one seek his own but the other') would appear to be a general axiom developed contextually.[52] That is, it is a stand-alone phrase, which could be applied in any number of directions.[53] Here it is specifically developed in terms of concern for others views on the eating of meat from the meat market.[54] In that, in Paul's own life such a motivation led to proclamation (see below), it would seem self-evident that seeking 'the other' would for a Christian committed to the salvation of others, include seeking the salvation of others who are not believers.

Secondly, the context specifically brings in relationships with unbelievers. While the passage does not refer specifically to evangelism on the part of the Corinthians, it certainly begs the question. In the first place we have clear evidence that Christians in Corinth were interacting with unbelievers (τῶν ἀπίστων) even to the point of table fellowship. In addition the salvation of the unbeliever is of prime concern. That is, in the context of the interaction between believer (τῇ ἐκκλησίᾳ τοῦ θεοῦ) and unbeliever ('Ιουδαίοις ... καὶ Ἕλλησιν). Unlerss it can be shown that Paul has clearly forbidden proactive evangelization, natural human discourse would include both apologetic and proactive evangelization.

Thirdly, the thrust of 1 Cor 10:31-11:1 leads in a general and inclusive direction. Verse 31 broadens Paul's thinking from the specific context concerning meat to '*whatever* you do...' (εἴτε ...ποιεῖτε) and 'do *all things*' (πάντα).[55] Here then Paul is concerned that the believer act holistically in a manner which has the best possible outcome for God (πάντα εἰς δόξαν θεοῦ ποιεῖτε).[56] In that hearing and believing the gospel in Paul is the means by someone appropriates salvation (cf. Rom 10:14-17; Eph 1:13-14), there is no

---

[50] 1 Cor 8; 10 dealing with issues related to freedom and eating meat sacrificed in idols. 1 Cor 9 dealing with Paul's use of his freedom in regards to his mission in addition to defending his apostolic authority and praxis. A chiasm revolving around ch9.

[51] Fee, *1 Corinthians*, 476-477.

[52] Thiselton, *1 Corinthians*, 782 sees it as a '"general axiom" or aphorism.' Fee, *1 Corinthians*, 479 suggests 'it is so basic to his understanding of Christian ethics that it probably had long been part of the instructions he gave to his churches.'

[53] Fee, *1 Corinthians*, 479 notes similar emphases in Rom 15:1-3; Phil 2:4 cf. 1 Cor 13:5.

[54] Thiselton, *1 Corinthians*, 782.

[55] Fee, *1 Corinthians*, 488 cf. Plummer, *Understanding*, 89.

[56] A general principle as Thiselton, *1 Corinthians*, 794 points out.

reason to limit this to social interaction and/or ethical/apologetic witness. Rather in 1 Cor 10:32 Paul is wanting the believer to be sensitive in their interaction with Christian and non-Christian alike so that no stumbling block (ἀπρόσκοπος) to their *coming to salvation* or *remaining in salvation* is placed before them.[57] While proactive evangelisation is not explicitly mentioned, there seems no reason to exclude it.[58]

Rather, 1 Cor 10:33 suggests that the behaviour of the believer is to be aimed at pleasing others (πᾶσιν ἀρέσκω). Notably Paul himself seeks to please all others in '*every way*' (πάντα). This suggests he does *all* that he can do in a given context to relate well to others, *so that they may be saved and remain saved.* It seems obvious that this would include careful Christian *speech.*

On its own, 'pleasing all others' could easily be misconstrued to suggest merely trying to keep everybody happy or living within social custom. However here pleasing others has a soteriological spin as seen in the purpose *hina* clause i.e. seek the good of others *that they may be saved* (ἵνα σωθῶσιν).[59] As Thistelton suggests, Paul here is speaking of his intention of 'placing *every factor* in relation to the progress of the gospel and the welfare of "the other".'[60] This brings clearly into focus his own concern for culture in his missiological approach (1 Cor 9:19-22) and encourages the view that this appeal for imitation summarises the whole section from 1 Cor 8:1-11:1.

The purpose clause of 1 Cor 10:33 (ἵνα σωθῶσιν) supplies the whole rubric under which the preceding verses should be read.[61] That is, Paul's purpose is that unbelievers may be saved and believers may persevere in their salvation. In one sense this is the purpose of Paul's whole life, 'that they may be saved.'[62]

Fourthly, this soteriological motication is exactly the thrust of the

---

[57] The debate as to whether the person in mind in v.28 is the host, an unbelieving guest or a fellow believer would appear redundant as 'anyone' (τις) suggests all of these possibilities. This is confirmed in the connections through the text: τὴν ἑαυτοῦ ([2x] 10:29) - Ἰουδαίοις γίνεσθε καὶ Ἕλλησιν καὶ τῇ ἐκκλησίᾳ τοῦ θεου (10:31) - πᾶσιν - τῶν πολλῶν (10:31).

[58] Fee, *1 Corinthians*, 489 notes that the categories are 'intentionally inclusive' and echo the language of 1 Cor 9:19-22.

[59] Fee, *1 Corinthians*, 489 who notes that the notion of 'pleasing others' to gain their approval in the context of evangelism is anathema to Paul.

[60] Thiselton, *1 Corinthians*, 795 (italics mine): However we would prefer 'salvation' rather than welfare here as this nuance is not utilised in Paul.

[61] Blomberg, *1 Corinthians*, 203 his 'motive is the salvation of as many as possible' cf. 9:19-23. Similarly O'Brien, *Salvation*, 181. Castelli, *Imitating*, 114 sees no specific content which totally neglects the reality of the situation and the emphasis on salvation.

[62] O'Brien, *Consumed*, 106-107. He notes that Bosch illegitimately limits this to attraction while Bowers does not pay heed to the purpose clause, 'so that they may be saved.'

contextually relevant passage 1 Cor 9:16-22 cf. 9:27.[63] While this passage says little about the evangelism of the Corinthians in direct terms, Paul's discussion about his own renunciation of his right to make his living from the gospel certainly reveals that Paul's evangelistic motivation is linked to his imitation of Christ and so also, by extension and without any expressed limitation, to Corinthian imitation.

In the first place, in 1 Cor 9:16 proclamation of the gospel is for Paul a necessity i.e. a compulsion (ἀνάγκη [Rom 1:13-15; Phil 3:12]).[64] In fact Paul considers himself to be subject to the judgement of God (οὐαὶ γάρ μοί ἐστιν) if he does not preach the gospel (cf. 9:27).[65] Furthermore, in 1 Cor 9:19 his purpose (ἵνα) in giving up his freedom in the gospel to enslave himself to all (πάντων) humanity is τοὺς πλείονας κερδήσω. The verb κερδαίνω suggests to 'gain' in the sense of win people (cf. Matt 18:15; 1 Pet 3:1).[66] 'The many' (τοὺς πλείονας) suggests 'as many as possible' from all humanity (πάντων [19a]).[67] Paul's desire then is to save (σώσω) as many Jews and proselytes ('Ιουδαῖος, τοῖς ὑπὸ νόμον),[68] Gentiles (τοῖς ἀνόμοις), the weak (τοῖς ἀσθενέσιν);[69] indeed as many people (τοῖς πᾶσιν) as possible by all possible

---

63 A link frequently noted e.g. Hays, *First Corinthians*, 179. See too Plummer, *Understanding*, 91-92.

64 *BDAG*, 81 puts it: 'I am under obligation;' Fee, *1 Corinthians*, 418: 'I am under compulsion'; Thiselton, *1 Corinthians*, 695: 'God's compulsion presses upon him' in a manner like Jeremiah (Jer 1:4-10; 20:7 cf. Gal 1:15); Collins, *First Corinthians*, 347: 'constraint presses upon me.'

65 Fee, *1 Corinthians*, 419. We note that interjection οὐαί throughout the NT without exception carries a note of judgement (see Matt 11:21 [2x]; 18:6 [2x]; Matt 23 [7x judgement is in mind as 23:23c,d, 32, 35, 26 shows cf. 24d, 25c, 26b, 27e, 28, 32; Lk 11:42-44]; 24:19; 26:24; 6:24-26 [4x]; 17:1 and parallels; Jude 11; Rev 8:13 [3x]; 9:12 [2x]; 11:14 [2x]; 12:12; 18:10, 16, 19). Hence it is likely so here against *BDAG*, 734 who see it as 'a state of intense hardship or distress'; Thiselton, *1 Corinthians*, 696 sees here personal 'agony' for Paul.

66 Thiselton, *1 Corinthians*, 701; Fee, *1 Corinthians*, 426-427 notes it is taken in this way to continue the 'pay' motif and means here 'save' cf. 9:22 (so Collins, *First Corinthians*, 356; Prior, *1 Corinthians*, 159.

67 Fee, *1 Corinthians*, 426-427; Thiselton, *1 Corinthians*, 701 prefers 'all the more.'

68 The combined impact of the terms includes Jews and Gentiles who have converted to Judaism or who associated with the synagogue cf. H.L. Ellison, 'Paul and the Law – "All Things to all Men"', in Gasque and Martin, *Apostolic*, 195-202; Thiselton, *1 Corinthians*, 702; Blomberg, *1 Corinthians*, 184. Alternatively as Fee, *1 Corinthians*, 429 suggests Paul mentions 'law' to emphasise his own decision to live by Jewish legal requirements to maximise his evangelistic effectiveness among those who live by the Jewish law. Collins, *First Corinthians*, 354 suggests 'Jewish Christians' which we consider most unlikely in light of the evangelistic language.

69 Perhaps referring to the weak of 1 Cor 8:7-13 but more likely a more generalising category (1 Cor 1:26-31). So Thiselton, *1 Corinthians*, 706 suggests 'the vulnerable in socio-political terms' cf. Fee, *1 Corinthians*, 431.

means (πάντως) as he proclaims of the gospel.[70] So much so that he is prepared to adapt his lifestyle and cultural and personal preferences while presenting the essence of the message (1 Cor 15:3-6 cf. Rom 1:1-4), according to the culture of his recipients so as to save some from among them.[71]

Returning to the Corinthians, this is the very attitude that Paul wants his recipients in Corinth to emulate.[72] That is, *the believer in any given context is to act and speak in the manner that best enables the unbeliever to be saved and the believer to persevere.* This *must* necessarily suggest evangelism in some circumstances. However, what this does not mean is insensitivity in evangelism. Rather the mode of proclamation itself must be conditioned to ensure the best results. Hence this suggests careful, sensitive, timely, strategic, culturally relevant and appropriate communication of the gospel in any given situation. On occasion it may even imply withholding the gospel for a better situation in that it is may not be the best means of sharing the message in a given context.[73] To limit the intent of Paul to merely social interaction, ethical witness and apologetic response is without warrant unless clearly indicated. The appeal for imitation is far too closely connected to soteriological motivation in direct connection to verbal proclamation in 1 Cor 8-10 to allow one to remove evangelism from its orb. To do so seems arbitrary and inconsistent with the evidence within the letter and the wider Pauline epistles.[74]

Fifthly and importantly, it is evident that throughout Corinthians the soteriological imperative led Paul (1 Cor 1:17, 23; 2:1, 4, 6, 13; 3:6, 10; 4:15; 9:16-23; 15:1-2, 11-19; 16:9)[75] and others (1 Cor 7:16, 32, 34; 12:8, 28, 29; 14:20-25; 15:11-19, 58; 16:10, 16) to proclaim. Furthermore, the categorisation Ἰουδαίοις γίνεσθε καὶ Ἕλλησιν picks up Paul's missiological mode in

---

[70] Thiselton, *1 Corinthians*, 706.

[71] As Fee, *1 Corinthians*, 432-433 notes the issue here is not accommodation of the gospel message to culture, but the social behaviour of the evangeliser concerning *adiaphora*.

[72] O'Brien, *Consumed*, 94-97, 105. See also P.V. Reid, 'Paul as a Model for Evangelisation', *Listening* 30.2 (1995): 83-93. Bowers, 'Church': 93-94; Morris, *1 Corinthians*, 148 limit its force to 'the good of others' without defining 'the good' i.e. that they be saved! Similarly Orr and Walther, *1 Corinthians*, 257: 'the advantage of many' i.e. what advantage except salvation?

[73] Such a principle is perhaps demonstrsated in Luke's account of Paul's experience of God forbidding him to proclaim the gospel in Asia and Bithynia while sending him to preach in Macedonia (cf. Acts 16:6-10). Notably the evangelisation of Asia was dynamic as Luke records in Acts 18-19 suggesting God's timing was at issue (see esp. Acts 19:10-17).

[74] For me this is a weakness of Dickson's position. As elsewhere, he views the passage primarily through the external grid of Jewish missiology which he constructs, rather than the evidence of the Paulines themselves (and in fact the rest of the NT). This enables him to limit the scope of Paul's perspective in line with the Jewish parameters.

[75] Thiselton, *1 Corinthians*, 794.

regards to culture from 1 Cor 9:19-22 (see above).[76] Without doubt, here this was proclamatory in content making it more likely that proclamation is in view here. It follows from the context that this appeal will lead others to proclamation. The appeal to the example of Christ further reinforces this, he being a preacher of salvation.[77] In that there was a 'Cephas party' in Corinth it is reasonable to assume that the Corinthians would have been fully conversant with the ministry and life of the earthly Christ through Peter (1 Cor 1:12; 3:22; 9:5; 15:5).[78] Seeing that Paul was well aware of this connection, as his references to Peter suggest, the appeal to *imitatio-Christi* would require limitation if it was not holistic. Interestingly within Philippians itself, we have a possible connection between Christ and the situation in Philippians which includes evangelism. As I argue in Appendix 3, the Christ example should not be understood in merely kerygmatic or ethical terms, but due to its contextual connection to relationships in Philippi among evangelistic co-workers (2:1-4; 4:2-3) and especially the *hina* clause of 2:10 which suggests Christ's purpose is the voluntary submission of all humanity before God, Christ's example is not merely ethical but evangelistic in emphasis (cf. Eph 2:17).[79]

Finally, there are the examples of 1 Cor 7:16 and 14:24-25 which suggest a soteriological motivation in Paul's thinking included proclamation. In the first, 1 Cor 7:16, Paul speaks directly of a soteriological motivation for the believing spouse where their unbelieving partner is concerned.[80] This would involve a believing spouse demonstrating love in their character and action (cf. 1 Cor 13) and sharing the faith winsomely through their speech. The second is 1 Cor 14:24-25 where the gathered Corinthians are to be concerned about unbelieving visitors at corporate worship gatherings.[81] This indicates that unbelievers and outsiders (ἄπιστος ἢ ἰδιώτης)[82] were invited to the Christian gatherings. In addition, this indicates that their behaviour at their gatherings

---

[76] Fee, *1 Corinthians*, 489.

[77] See Plummer, *Understanding*, 90 esp. note 69.

[78] The evidence suggests Peter had visited Corinth with his wife cf. K.P. Donfried and J. Fitzmyer, in R. Brown, K.P. Donfried and J. Reumann, *Peter in the NT* (London: Chapman, 1974), 32-36; Thiselton, *1 Corinthians*, 129; Fee, *1 Corinthians*, 57. If so the Corinthians would have had a full understanding of the earthly ministry of the Christ.

[79] See Appendix 3.

[80] Whether taken optimistically or pessimistically. As Fee, *1 Corinthians*, 306 puts it, 'in speaking of "saving ones spouse," Paul is referring to their "evangelising" or "winning" them, whether by word or deed' cf. Barrett, *1 Corinthians*, 167. See also Marshall, 'Evangelists', 260 who notes that in the NT the motive in mixed marriages 'is indubitably missionary'; Plummer, *Understanding*, 93-94: 'the evangelistic concern of unbelievers is assumed.'

[81] So too Plummer, *Understanding*, 94-96.

[82] On ἄπιστος ('unbeliever') and ἰδιώτης ('adherants') see *BDAG*, 468. Alternatively ἰδιώτη may simply mean 'unlearned' as Fee, *1 Corinthians*, 684 suggests. Perhaps the 'weak' of 1 Cor 9:22?

was to be conditioned by concern for the salvation of the unbeliever. Moreover, it is expected that through prophetic *proclamation* from members of the Corinthian community, male or female, unbelievers and outsiders will be saved.[83]

In addition to these evangelistically suggestive passages, there are other passages such as 1 Cor 5:9-10 and 7:17-24 (cf. 1 Cor 10:24-33) which indicate that Paul wanted the Corinthians to remain participants in their world without compromising the gospel. In that their motivation was to be soteriological as I have demonstrated above, it would follow that this involved speaking the gospel appropriately.

It is most likely then that the appeal to imitation of 1 Cor 11:1 μιμηταί μου γίνεσθε καθὼς κἀγὼ Χριστοῦ implies evangelism to some extent or another.[84] There is no limitation to the appeal in the text. Rather the appeal is generic and soteriological implying emulation of the evangelistic motivation of Christ, Paul, Peter, Timothy, Apollos and others. The imitation of Christ through the community then brings in the whole nature and range of Christ's mission including evangelism, healing, discipleship, Christian community, prayer, social justice, ethical witness, apologetic witness, worship and so on.

Significantly, the appeal of 1 Cor 11:1 is directed to the whole Corinthian community.[85] The second person imperative ('be') γίνεσθε is not limited in any way. The whole community is to imitate Paul and so Christ. Specifically in terms of the context the whole community is to be concerned that others are saved (1 Cor 10:33). As a community then, the Corinthian church is to be soteriologically motivated as was Paul. In chapter 12, Paul outlines the manner in which the commission is broken up through the community with each individual operating with their own gift/ministry-service/mode of operation within the corporate imitatory framework (Eph 4:11-16). It seems self-evident on this analysis, that evangelism is one dimension of this appeal.

---

[83] That conversion is involved is confirmed by the cumulative effect of conviction of sin and judgement as their inward thoughts are revealed (cf. Jn 16:8), the prostration before God in worship and the confession that 'God is among you' cf. Fee, *1 Corinthians*, 687. As Hays, *First Corinthians*, 239 puts it, 'Paul sees prophecy as a powerful tool for evangelism.' Carson, *Showing*, 116 suggests here that 'evangelistic preaching' is not in mind as the newcomer merely overhears what is said. However the text appears to speak of a God-given prophetic message that in a given context speaks directly and dynamically into the heart of the recipient. To restrict it as non-evangelistic appears overly interpretative.

[84] See also Thistelton, *1 Corinthians,* 796; O'Brien, *Consumed*, 103-104; De Boer, *Imitation*, 158, 207; A. Reinhartz, 'Imitators': 399; Schnabel, *Mission*, 1461-1462.

[85] Plummer, *Understanding*, 89 notes that the salutation of 1 Corinthians indicates a wider audience and set of concerns as well.

1 Thessalonians 1:6-8

Commonly 1 Thess 1:8, 'the word of the Lord echoed forth' is interpreted passively. That is, the message concerning the conversion of the Thessalonians has been taken out through the surrounding region by others.[86] However, there are very good reasons for arguing that this passage should be understood actively.[87] First, there is an indication in 1 Thess 1:3 and in particular the clauses τοῦ ἔργου τῆς πίστεως καὶ τοῦ κόπου τῆς ἀγάπης that the Thessalonians are active in evangelism.[88]

Secondly, the nature of the imitation Paul has in mind on close examination is the active evangelization the Thessalonians have engaged in. If we take the word order as determinative, it can be argued that the reference to imitation refers to the initial reception of the gospel of the Thessalonians in the face of persecution.[89] If so, it is this positive reception of the word in the face of persecution that has provided a model to the believers of Macedonia and Achaia.[90]

However, the view that imitation here refers to the initial reception of the gospel has several problems. In the first place it is unlikely that believers (τοῖς πιστεύουσιν) who had *already received* the gospel would have been so inspired by the Thessalonians *reception* of the word.[91] In addition, the likening of the reception of the gospel to that of the apostolic team and Jesus (ὑμεῖς μιμηταὶ ἡμῶν ἐγενήθητε καὶ τοῦ κυρίου) makes it unlikely that Paul has this in mind. Paul's own conversion occurred en-route to persecute the Church and direct revelation of Christ (Gal 1:12; Acts 9:1-19; 22:5-21; 26:12-23), *not due to the reception of the gospel under persecution.* His suffering came *subsequent* to his conversion *as he engaged in evangelistic mission.* Similarly our knowledge of the conversion of Timothy does not indicate severe

---

86 See most recently Dickson, *Mission-Commitment*, 95-103; Bowers, *Studies*, 106; 'Church': 92.

87 So Malherbe, *Thessalonians*, 117; Holmes, *Thessalonians*, 54; Green, *Evangelism*, 215 n.69; Best, *Thessalonians*, 80-81; Morris, *Thessalonians*, 60-61; Bruce, *Thessalonians*, 16-17; Marshall, *Thessalonians*, 56; Peters, *Missions*, 133; P. Richardson and J.C. Hurd, *From Jesus to Paul. Studies in honour of F.W. Beare* (Waterloo: Wilfred Laurier University, 1084), 133-135; Ware, 'Missionary Congregation': 126-131; Bosch, *Transforming*, 130: but then on p168 suggests otherwise?; Schnabel, *Mission*, 1459-1460; Plummer, *Understanding*, 61.

88 On κοπιάω; κόπος see above in my discussion of this term in terms of Rom 16 (Chapter 3). On ἔργον with an evangelistic reference see 1 Cor 9:1 [Paul]; 16:10; 2 Tim 4:5 [Timothy] cf. 1 Cor 3:13; Phil 1:6; Eph 4:12; 1 Thess 5:13. On 1 Thess 1:3 see also Plummer, *Understanding*, 62.

89 Dickson, *Mission-Commitment*, 97 along with the force of ὥστε; *TDNT* 4.670.

90 Marshall, *Thessalonians*, 54; Richard, *Thessalonians*, 49; Castilli, *Imitating*, 93; Bowers, 'Church': 98.

91 Best, *Thessalonians*, 77 also notes Paul elsewhere does not apply imitation to conversion.

persecution, although this cannot be ruled out (Acts 16:1-4; 2 Tim 1:5). Neither can we be confident of any details concerning the conversion of the Jewish Jerusalem leader Silas (Acts 15:23-40).[92] Finally, Jesus himself was not converted in this evangelistic sense of *receiving the word* of God.[93] In the case of all of those implied, persecution came later as they set about preaching the message.[94] So it would seem likely that Paul is thinking of something other than the reception of the message in terms of imitation here.

One aspect of the imitation would appear to be suffering.[95] However, in the case of Paul, Silas and Timothy, the context for the experience of suffering was the proclamation of the gospel (1 Thess 2:2, 14-16 [see below cf. Phil 1:28-30). Similarly, Christ was a proclaimer who suffered in the cause of bringing God's message to humanity.[96]

Imitation here then more likely refers to participation in mission including proclamation and suffering. As Richard puts it, 'the new converts, by casting an eye to the interests of the inhabitants of the Greek provinces, have become for them an example and a means to faith... The Thessalonians became imitators of Paul and his colleagues in the way they responded to the word they heard and to the extent *they dedicated their lives to the Lord's gospel* (italics mine).[97] As argued above in regards to 1 Cor 11:1 and Phil 4:9, here in 1 Thess 1:6 then, imitation includes proclamation. The imitation referred to here includes not the reception of the gospel but the blend of joy and evangelism in the face of suffering and proclamation.[98] Plummer similarly writes, 'the Thessalonian Christians were an example to others by virtue of their being a launching point

---

[92] An esteemed elder (πρεσβύτερος) and prophet of the Jerusalem church (Acts 15:23, 32); an emissary of the letter from the Jerusalem council (Acts 15:23); an itinerant missionary preacher and colleague of Paul (Acts 15:40; 2 Cor 1:19) on his second missionary journey (Acts 15:40-17:9; 2 Cor 1:19); he suffered in the course of that mission (Acts 16:22-40); an emissary of Paul (Acts 17:10-18:5); a co-sender of Paul's letters (1 Thess 1:1; 2 Thess 1:1); a friend of Peter (1 Pet 5:12). He could have been converted in the ministry of Christ or at any subsequent recorded or unrecorded preaching event in the period of Acts.

[93] As Richard, *Thessalonians*, 66 notes, 'it is hard to imagine what they would mean in terms of imitation of the Lord' in this schema.

[94] For Paul supremely seen in 2 Cor 11:23-29; for Christ his crucifixion (Phil 2:5-11); for Silas and Timothy see Acts 16:23-40; 17:4, 5, 10. Timothy may have been in prison in Rome with Paul at some point (Col 1:1).

[95] Best, *Thessalonians*, 77; Wanamaker, *Thessalonians*, 81 suggests joy and suffering.

[96] While Christian suffering in the early church was not necessarily evangelistically related (see for example Holmes, *Thessalonians*, 50), here in the flow of the text evangelism and suffering are linked.

[97] Richard, *Thessalonians*, 67 who acknowledges proclamation is part of imitation here as in 1 Cor 11:1.

[98] Richard, *Thessalonians*, 69 suggests the joy (1 Thess 1:7) which is the issue along with proclamation.

for the gospel.'[99]

That this is the case is enhanced in a second reference to imitation, 1 Thess 2:14-16. In these verses the suffering of the Thessalonians is local and likened to the suffering of the Judean churches.[100] Our only detailed knowledge of the Judean churches comes from Luke's account which connects the suffering of the Jerusalem church (Acts 4:1-22; 5:17-42; 7:1-8:3; 12:1-18) intimately to evangelistic mission (Acts 3:24; 4:16-17; 5:28, 40).[101] Paul's language here suggests that the parallel between the Judean churches and Thessalonica is connected not only with their mutual suffering, but with common attempts to stop evangelism. In the Jewish case this persecution is historic including the rejection of prophets, the killing of Christ and opposition to Christian proclamation. In opposing Christian proclamation, they displease God (καὶ θεῷ μὴ ἀρεσκόντων)[102] and all humanity (πᾶσιν ἀνθρώποις) by hindering the preachers (κωλυόντων ἡμᾶς)[103] from preaching the gospel and so thwarting their opportunity for salvation (λαλῆσαι ἵνα σωθῶσιν). The parallel to the Thessalonian situation would suggest that the church has continued the mission of Paul and has engaged in evangelism since his departure (1 Thess 1:7-8).[104] This has incited opposition and persecution from the Thessalonian community (ὑπὸ τῶν ἰδίων συμφυλετῶν), already stirred up by the initial visit by Paul and his team (Acts 17:5-9).[105] If so, this gives further incite into the situation in 1 Thess 1:6-8 (see the full analysis of this text below).

The dynamic of imitation in 1:6-8 extends beyond Christ, to Paul (and his team), to the Thessalonians and to other believers throughout the region. In v.7 Paul gives thanks that the Thessalonians have become a model (church) to all the believers in Macedonia and Achaia.[106] The sense of their example is drawn from both directions. First, ὥστε ('so then') refers to the previous clause in which Paul recalls the way in which the Thessalonians received the gospel with

---

[99] Plummer, *Understanding*, 62.

[100] I do not find the arguments against authenticity convincing; see the discussion of Wanamaker, *Thessalonians*, 29-33.

[101] See Wanamaker, *Thessalonians*, 113-114; Bruce, *Thessalonians*, 46 for other options.

[102] That is, impeding the mission as argues Wanamaker, *Thessalonians*, 115. On the not uncommon connection between 'pleasing God' and evangelism see also Gal 1:10; 2 Cor 5:9; 1 Thess 2:4; 2 Tim 2:4 cf. Rom 12:2; 14:18; 15:1-3; 1 Cor 7:32; Phil 4:18; Col 3:20.

[103] The parallelism of the imitation means that 'us' here is inclusive of Paul and his team and, by the parallel, the Thessalonians who were engaging in mission in the face of their opponents.

[104] Bruce, *Thessalonians*, 45.

[105] The persecution they have suffered continues this original experience cf. Marshall, *Thessalonians*, 78-79.

[106] *BDAG*, 1020 notes τύπος is an 'example, pattern' to be emulated (Phil 3:17; 2 Thess 3:9; Tit 2:7; 1 Tim 4:12 cf. 1 Pet 5:3).

great joy in the midst of great suffering. Consequently, the concepts of joy and suffering carry over.[107] The following sentence carries on the thought (γάρ) 'for from you the word…' i.e. proclamation of the gospel in the region.[108] That being the case, the intertwined dynamics of joy in suffering whilst proclaiming the gospel come into view. The Thessalonians have emulated Christ, Paul and his team, by receiving the word with joy in the midst of suffering and then engaging in intentional mission to their region.[109]

The third line of evidence is that the 'the word of the Lord' (ὁ λόγος τοῦ κυρίου) here most likely means 'the gospel.'[110] The dominant use of λόγος in Thessalonians is the proclaimed message (1 Thess 1:5, 6; 2:5, 13, 15). The specific construction 'word of the Lord' in the letters involves the proclamation of the gospel (2 Thess 3:1) and a specific teaching of Jesus (1 Tim 4:15). The references to λόγος in the immediate context are all to the proclaimed gospel for initial salvation (1 Thess 1:5, 6; 2:5, 13).[111] In addition, generally in Paul, λόγος + genitive involves the proclaimed gospel.[112] 'The Lord' (τοῦ κυρίου) here is more than certainly Jesus rather than God as is clear in that all uses in the letter are explicitly Christ either from their context or theology.[113] The

---

107 Wanamaker, *Thessalonians*, 82.

108 Bower, 'Church': 98 notes the continuity of thought but denies its force in regards to evangelism. Dickson, *Mission-Commitment*, 97 argues that proclamation cannot be the content of imitation as the result ὥστε makes the content clear. However equally the γάρ *continues* the statement extending the joyous reception of the gospel under persecution to the evangelisation that followed cf. Ware, 'Missionary congregation': 127. That is, Paul is speaking about an event involving reception, joy, suffering and evangelisation.

109 Ware, 'Missionary Congregation': 128; Richard, *Thessalonians*, 69-72; Bruce, *Thessalonians*, 15 who includes acceptance of the apostle's teaching, endured persecution and shared the gospel with others ('fearless proclamation'); Reinhartz, 'Imitators', 402; J. Brant, 'The Place of *Mimēsis* in Paul's Thought', *StudRel* 22.3 (1993): 285-300, 293.

110 Marshall, *Thessalonians*, 56. Richard, *Thessalonians*, 50; Bruce, *Thessalonians*, 17-18; Best, *Thessalonians*, 80; *TDNT* 4.114; Malherbe, *Thessalonians*, 117; Fee, *Empowering*, 258; Ware, 'Missionary Congregation': 127; Plummer, *Understanding*, 61.

111 Λόγος in 1 Thessalonians involves spoken proclamation (1 Thess 1:5, 6; 2:5, 13 [λόγον θεοῦ in contrast to λόγον ἀνθρώπων]; 4:15 [ἐν λόγῳ κυρίου of a specific word of Jesus]; cf. 4:18 [λόγοις of the words of the passage]; 2 Thess 2:2 [of a message of the return of Christ]; 2 Thess 2:15, 17 [ἐν παντὶ λόγῳ ἀγαθῷ of every good word including evangelism]; 2 Thess 3:1 [ὁ λόγος τοῦ κυρίου]; 2 Thess 3:14 [message of the letter].

112 See further above on 2:16a In Chapter 5 where I note that genitive constructions of anarthrous or articular forms refer to the gospel.

113 24x in Thessalonians and all clearly referring to Jesus (1:1, 3, 6, 8 [on the basis of preceding]; 2:15, 19; 3:8 [on the basis of 3:11, 13 and preceding], 11, 12 [on the basis of 3:11, 13], 13, 14; 4:2, 6 [on the basis of preceding and 4:2], 15 [2x], 16, 17 [2x]; 5:2, 9,

genitive construction can be either objective ('the message about Jesus') or as is more likely, subjective ('the message which comes from the Lord').[114]

That being the case, the 'word of the Lord' should not be mundanely identified as 'the news of your faith' (ἡ πίστις ὑμῶν ἡ πρὸς τὸν θεὸν) which has gone out (ἐξελήλυθεν).[115] Rather the emphasis lies on the 'word of the Lord' which has gone out in such a fashion that the people of the region and beyond have heard about the faith of the Thessalonians.[116] This could mean the content of the gospel, 'your faith' being used synonymously as 'your gospel' (Gal 1:23; 1 Thess 1:8; 1 Tim 2:7 cf. Rom 10:8; 2 Cor 4:13; 10:15; Phil 1:27).[117] On the other hand 'your faith' could include their existential experience of faith involving the story of their conversion and renunciation of idolatry. This is due to what follows in 1 Thess 1:9-10 where the testimony of the Thessalonians turning from idolatry is central to the message.[118] If so, we have evidence that the testimony of salvation formed an integral part of the proclamation of the early Christians as they took the gospel into their communities.[119] Most likely both the gospel and their story of salvation is in mind.

Fourthly, the combination of preposition, pronoun and main verb with the word as subject suggests evangelism from the Thessalonians (ἀφ' ὑμῶν γὰρ ἐξήχηται). The passive of ἐξηχέω is a hapax legomena and means 'ring out',[120] proclaim,[121] make known.[122] The related ἠχέω is found in 1 Cor 13:1 of the sound of a 'resounding gong' (χαλκὸς ἠχῶν) which is broadcast out when struck and in the LXX of the sound of musical instruments, crowds and the

---

12 [on the basis of previous], 23, 27 [on the basis of 28], 28); rather than God. See also Richard, *Thessalonians*, 72.

[114] Richard, *Thessalonians*, 71. Morris, *Thessalonians*, 61; Bruce, *Thessalonians*, 17 take it subjectively, 'the message which comes from the Lord.'

[115] So Bowers, 'Church': 98. However Marshall, 'Evangelists', 259 notes that 'word of the Lord' is not appropriate for a report of someone's conversion cf. Ware, 'Missionary Congregation': 127. If it is to be identified, as Dickson, *Mission-Commitment*, 100 argues, then 'word of the Lord' (i.e. the gospel), defines the latter and 'your faith in God' is in fact the gospel rather than the word of the Lord as their faith, which is most unusual. He fails to convince with his unsupported argument that the word of the Lord can include the report of conversion (see n.238).

[116] Malherbe, *Thessalonians*, 117.

[117] See above on Rom 1:8 in Chapter 3 in relation to Phil 1:14.

[118] Richard, *Thessalonians*, 72 similarly takes it as their coming faith.

[119] So also Marshall, *Thessalonians*, 56. See the proclamation of Paul before authorities in Acts 22, 26; his testimony was the springboard to his message in each case.

[120] *BDAG*, 350; Bruce, Thessalonians, 17: 'a loud ringing sound.'

[121] Louw-Nida, *Lexicon*, 33.322 suggest 'you caused the message about the Lord to be proclaimed' cf. Richard, *Thessalonians*, 50.

[122] H. Liddell, *A Lexicon: Abridged from Liddell and Scott's Greek-English Lexicon* (Oak Harbor, WA: Logos Research Systems, Inc, 1996) 274 suggest 'the word of the Lord was made known.'

raging sea.[123] In Philo it referred to the thunderous voice of God, crowds crying out to God, the trumpet of God, wind and thunder and armies.[124] As such it carries the sense of the gospel having radiated out from Thessalonica in every direction.[125]

The preposition and pronoun are emphatically placed and suggests that the word of the Lord has been proclaimed 'from *you*' (ἀφ' ὑμῶν) indicating that the Thessalonians *themselves* have taken the word of the Lord to the surrounds.[126] It is argued by passive interpreters that the pronoun should be understood in geographical terms as referring to Thessalonica.[127] That is, the word of the Lord has been made known by others who have travelled out from Thessalonica with the news of the conversion of the Thessalonians.[128] Certainly, if 'word of the Lord' is identified with 'your faith' then this is the case. However, as argued above, this is unlikely.

An analysis of the use of the second person pronoun in 1 Thessalonians is also helpful. It is significant that every other reference to 'you' (ὑμεις) in the thanksgiving[129] and generally in the letter[130] refers to people in the Thessalonian city or church rather than the locality itself. In addition we note that the other

---

[123] *TDNT* 2.954: Can be intransitive so '"to sound," "to ring," "to peal," "to boom"' or transitive '"to cause to sound";' *BDAG*, 441: 'sound, ring out.' In the LXX of the sounding of musical instruments especially the trumpet (Exod 19:16; 1 Kgs 1:41; Hos 5:8; Is 16:11); the noise of a crowd of people (Ruth 1:19; 1 Sam 4:5; 1 Kgs 1:45; Ps 82:3). Peoples ears resound (Ruth 3:11; 2 Kgs 21:12; Jer 19:3) and the noise of water (Ps 45:4; Is 17:12; 51:15; Jer 5:22; 27:42; 28:54 cf. Lk 21:25). Sir 40:13 associates it with thunder leading some to apply this to the context.

[124] See Dickson, *Mission-Commitment*, 101-102 for detail. As such he argues that it was a thunderous proclamation of the gospel in Thessalonica that is meant?

[125] Marshall, *Thessalonians*, 56: 'the spreading out of a sound from a central point in all directions'; Holmes, *Thessalonians*, 51 suggests the metaphor of 'stone-caused ripples on a pond.' Marshall, 'Evangelists', 259 notes the verb indicates something more dynamic than a report about behaviour.

[126] Marshall, *Thessalonians*, 56; Schnabel, *Mission*, 1459.

[127] Wanamaker, *Thessalonians*, 83; Dickson, *Mission-Commitment*, 102.

[128] Ollrog, *Paulus*, 130 n81; Bowers, 'Church': 99.

[129] Hence defined by τῇ ἐκκλησίᾳ Θεσσαλονικέων (1 Thess 1:1). So 1:1 (recipients of grace); 'all of you' as a basis for thanksgiving to God (1: 2); 'your work, labour, steadfastness' (1:3); 'you' = chosen brothers ('and sisters') (1:4); recipients of the gospel (1:5, 9); those who became imitators of Paul, his team and Christ (1:6); those who became models to the region (1:7); those whose faith became known (1:8a) i.e. those who rang the gospel out in 1:8b; those who turned from idolatry to Christ (1:9).

[130] See also 1 Thess 2:1, 2, 6, 7, 8 [2x], 9 [2x], 10 [2x], 11, 12 [3x], 13, 14 [2x], 17 [2x], 18, 19, 20; 3:2 [2x], 4 [2x], 5 [2x]; 6 [ἀφ' ὑμῶν = you believers in Thessalonica], 7 [2x], 8, 9, 10 [2x], 11, 12 [2x], 13; 4:1 [2x], 2, 3 [2x], 4, 6, 8, 9 [2x], 10, 11 [2x], 13, 15; 5:1, 4, 5, 12 [3x], 14, 18, 23 [2x], 24, 27, 28. Only 2:1, 9 [first ref], 17a, 18 could be taken that way but is further defined by those who heard the gospel in 2:2, 9 [second ref], 17a, 19, 20.

uses in Thessalonians of the specific clause ἀφ' ὑμῶν without exception refers to church in Thessalonica (1 Thess 2:6, 17; 3:6) as it does elsewhere in the Paulines.[131] That is, it is not a geographical concept but a sociological concept. As such, 'from you' here means, 'from you in the church in Thessalonica.' This makes a purely geographical interpretation very unlikely. Hence, Paul is here speaking of the way in which the gospel has sounded forth from the Thessalonian Christians into the surrounding region.[132] As Malherbe puts it, 'Paul sketches a picture of active preaching by the Thessalonians.'[133]

The regional focus of the churches proclamation ministry is 'in Macedonia, Achaia and in all places' (ἐν τῇ Μακεδονίᾳ καὶ [ἐν τῇ] 'Αχαΐᾳ, ἀλλ' ἐν παντὶ τόπῳ). Hence their focus has been their own region, in which they have emulated the original missionary team and have become a model to the churches of the region. In addition they have reached out beyond their own region with the gospel to a real extent.[134]

It is possible that Rom 15:19a is supportive of this active interpretation here.

---

[131] Any doubts are removed by the other two uses in the same verse which 'your love' (ἀγάπην ὑμῶν) and Paul's longing to see the members of the Thessalonians (ἡμεῖς ὑμᾶς). Those involving other relevant prepositions include the people of the locality not the locality itself cf. πρὸς ὑμᾶς (1:9; 2:1, 2, 18; 3:11); εἰς ὑμῶν (1:5; 2:9). Similarly in the wider epistles including: 1) Romans: 1:9; 15:22, 29, 32 (of Paul wanting to come to Rome and the people of the church and city to encourage and evangelise); 2) 1 Corinthians: 2:1 (of Paul's visit for initial evangelisation); 4:18, 19, 21; 16:5, 6, 7, 10, 12 (of people coming to the Corinthian church); 14:6 (Paul hypothetical visit to the Corinthian church); 14:36 (did the gospel originate in the Corinthian church or reach it only?); 3) 2 Corinthians: 1:12, 16; 8:17; 9:5; 11:9; 12:14, 17, 21; 13:1 (of people coming to the church in Corinth); 1:18 (gospel coming to the Corinthian converts); 2:1 (grief coming to the Corinthians); 3:1 (letters from or to the Corinthian church); 9:8 (grace abound to you); 4) Galatians: 3:2 (information from the Galatian Christians); 4:18, 20 (people coming to the Galatian church); 5) Ephesians 6:22 (people coming to the recipients); 6) Philippians: 2:25 (people coming to Philippi and the church); 7) Colossians: 1:6 (gospel coming to the converts and the city); 1:25 (reveal the gospel to the people of the church and city); 4:8, 10, 12 (people coming to or from the church in Colossae); 8) 2 Thessalonians: 2:5 (people coming to the church); 3:2 (of the gospel coming to the people of the Thessalonian church). Hence, Paul does not need to use δι' ὑμῶν or ὑφ' ὑμῶν, as Dickson, *Mission-Commitment*, 100 argues; the effect is the same. Ware, 'Missionary Congregation': 128 suggests it is geographical but the gospel by its own power radiated out. This is unnecessary as this study shows.

[132] Against Holmes, *Thessalonians*, 51 who argues it is not clear who carried the message. Malherbe, *Thessalonians*, 116 argues the preposition is used to avoid the notion that the people of Thessalonica are the source of the message.

[133] Malherbe, *Thessalonians*, 117.

[134] While this is another instance of Paul's hyperbole when speaking of evangelistic endeavour (cf. Rom 1:8; Col 1:6, 23 [cf. Marshall, *Thessalonians*, 56; Bruce, *Thessalonians*, 17; Malherbe, *Thessalonians*, 118]), it also indicates that the progress was sufficient for Paul to make this assertion i.e. a substantial spread of the message.

In this passage, Paul refers to his fulfilment of his mission from Jerusalem to Illyricum. In that there is no evidence that he reached the western point of Illyricum, it is possible that members of the Thessalonian church, on his behalf, travelled along the Via Egnatia to Illyricum and completed the preaching ministry begun by Paul. In that Paul considered the work of Epaphras in the Lycus Valley an extension of his own ministry (Col 1:6-7), then it is possible that when Paul went south to Berea he commissioned members of the church in Thessalonica to continue the ministry. Alternatively, Timothy and Silas led the mission from Thessalonica to that point,[135] having remained behind when Paul moved onto Athens (Acts 17:15).

It is also significant that no individuals are singled out (cf. Phil 1:5; Rom 1:8); rather, the emphasis is inclusive, Paul's thanksgiving given for 'all' (πάντων ὑμῶν [1 Thess 1:2]) the Thessalonian 'brothers and sisters' (ἀδελφοὶ [1 Thess 1:4])[136] as a group (ἀφ' ὑμῶν). In that it is highly unlikely that the whole church traveled around the region in this way and that it was individual proclaimers who led this mission, it is significant that Paul still addresses the church as a group and gives thanks for their corporate involvement. Thus, the mission of the individuals was the mission of the church. As such, here we have a church engaged in evangelistic mission.

One argument utilised against this interpretation is the close temporal proximity between the planting of the Thessalonian church and the writing of the letter, it being considered unlikely that there was insufficient time between intial evangelization and the writing of 1 Thessalonians for such a mission. If we accept the Lukan account a minimalist time frame would go something like this:

- A 75km trip to Berea (2-3 days+).[137]
- A mission to Berea involving proclamation in the synagogue of Berea, the Bereans examining the scriptures thoroughly, for news to get back to Thessalonica, for the Thessalonians to organise opposition come to Berea to drive Paul and his team out (1-2 weeks).[138]

---

[135] If Paul himself completed this, unless it occurred at a time not mentioned by Luke, it probably occurred during one of Paul's visits to Macedonia in 20:1-4.

[136] Marshall, *Thessalonians*, 52; Richard, *Thessalonians*, 47; Holmes, *Thessalonians*, 49.

[137] Barrett, *Acts*, II.817. Assuming they walked, L. Kreitzer, 'Travel in the Roman World' in *DPL*, 945 suggests 30km/day was a good speed meaning 2-3 days travel. J. Murphy-O'Conner, 'On the Road and on the Sea with St. Paul', *BibRev (*1985): 38-47, 40-41 notes 22m but it was unlikely that this could be maintained. Stambaugh, *Social*, 28 suggest 25-35m/day. Malherbe, *Thessalonians*, 72 assumes a week.

[138] A month is very minimalistic when one considers time was required for the gospel to be preached, for the Bereans to thoroughly examine the scriptures, for many Jews and Gentiles to become Christians, for news to get back to the Thessalonian Jewish Christians, for them to organise a response and for them to travel to Berea.

- A 222km trip from Berea to Athens to wait for Timothy and Silas cf. Acts 17:15 (14 days+).[139]
- An undisclosed period of waiting in Athens in which Paul engaged in evangelism while waiting for Timothy and Silas cf. Acts 17:16-34 (2 weeks).[140]
- Time for Timothy and Silas to travel to Athens (14 days+).[141]
- Some period of recuperation and fellowship in Athens in which Paul wanted to come to Thessalonica cf. 1 Thess 2:17-3:1 (1 month+).[142]
- Time for Timothy to return to Thessalonica (2 weeks +) (1 Thess 3:1).[143]
- Time for recuperation, fellowship and encouragement in Thessalonica (1 week+).[144]
- Time for Timothy to return to Corinth (Acts 18:5) (3 weeks +).[145]
- Time for Paul to write 1 Thessalonians and send it to Thessalonica (2 weeks +).

Using these estimates we come up with a minimum time of 4-5 months.[146] Certainly this is a short time for the kind of outreach suggested. However reflection on Paul's approach suggests there is indeed sufficient time for substantial evangelisation in such a short period.[147] If the Thessalonians emulated a Pauline approach as the mention of imitation suggests, and sent a significant number of converts in different directions to preach and establish small house churches in appropriate contexts and then moving on leaving further evangelisation to the converts, it becomes easily possible for all of a

---

[139] Barrett, *Acts*, 820. Allowing for no stops along the way which we consider unlikely as Paul may well have engaged in evangelism particularly on Sabbaths. Hence Malherbe, *Thessalonians*, 72 suggests 3 weeks.

[140] It is hard to be sure how long this was or whether Paul was alone at the time. Certainly long enough for him to familiarise himself with the city and its temples, go to the Areopagus and make some converts.

[141] Malherbe, *Thessalonians*, 72: 3 weeks.

[142] Paul's language in 1 Thess 2:17-3:1 suggests that the desire to return to Thessalonica was during Paul's time in Athens with Timothy and Silas (note 'we' in 3:1). Eventually they decided to risk sending Timothy back as they could stand it no longer.

[143] It would seem likely that he spent some time in Berea as well encouraging the church there. Malherbe, *Thessalonians*, 72 suggests 3 weeks.

[144] Time to hear news of evangelisation (1:8) and the positive state of the church.

[145] Malherbe, *Thessalonians*, 72 suggests 4 weeks. Perhaps Silas had remained in Thessalonica (cf. Barrett, *Acts*, II. 865).

[146] Similarly Malherbe, *Thessalonians*, 72 who suggests longer travel times and shorter stays. This correlates with the dating of the Corinth visit in Autumn 50 which is well set in regards to the edict of Claudius and the tenure of Gallio.

[147] According to a traditional Acts-Paul chronology means the first missionary journey occurred over a year (48), the second over two years (49-50) (cf. L.C.A. Alexander, 'Chronology' in *DPL*, 122-123) and Luke notes that the whole of Asia heard the word of God *in only a two year period* from Paul's ministry in Ephesus (Acts 19:10 cf. Col 1:6-7).

region as small as Macedonia and Achaia to be covered quickly.[148] After all, Paul succeeded in evangelising cities like Philippi itself in a very short time.

The work of Gill also supports this view. He notes that according to Pliny there were only about 150 communities in the province of Macedonia.[149] He also tells us that the cities in Achaia at the time were small and few lived in the countryside.[150] Now remembering that Paul and his team had already planted churches or evangelised Philippi, Thessalonica, Berea, Athens and Corinth, and had visited Amphipolus, Apollonia and Neapolis, a team from the Thessalonian church may have made significant progress in the remaining towns and villages in a short time.[151] Interestingly, Cenchrae also had a church at the time of Romans (Rom 16:1)[152] which could be a result of this ministry. Even though the quality of roading was poor at the time apart from the road from the Corinthian gulf to Patras and Nicopolis,[153] such movement remains entirely possible especially when one notes the speed at which Paul himself evangelized on his missionary journeys; particularly from a city lying on the Via Egnatia and with a port.[154] In addition, Paul's language here refers to a preaching ministry which could in fact indicate quick movement through the provinces rather than longer church planting ventures.[155]

Finally, it is notable that whoever the agents of the spread of the word of the Lord and the faith of the Thessalonians, the same temporal problem arises for both an active and passive interpretation of the text.[156] Both interpretations require people travelling through the region after the establishment of the

---

[148] Dickson, *Mission-Commitment*, 96 n39 suggests that an active approach using Paul's language meant the whole church literally went out. However, this is not necessarily the case anymore than 'in every place' is literal. A group representing the church would be sufficient to see Paul thank the whole church as the body metaphor implies.

[149] D.W.G. Gill, *The Book of Acts in its First-Century Setting* (Grand Rapids: Eerdmans, 1994), 2.397-417. He notes that Macedonia was composed of only 150 communities with mainly Illyrians in the west and Macedonians in the east. The eastern interior was settled with towns while the north-west was peopled by tribal peoples such as the Parthini.

[150] Gill, *Acts*, 2.437.

[151] Marshall, *Thessalonians*, 55 suggests that Paul may have passed through Amphipolus, Apollonia because there were Christian communities already there.

[152] Best, *Thessalonians*, 79-80.

[153] Gill, *Acts*, 2.433-453.

[154] Morris, *Thessalonians*, 61.

[155] However if they were emulating Paul, the goal was not merely converts but communities of faith.

[156] Wanamaker, *Thessalonians*, 223. Dickson, *Mission-Commitment*, 96 who writes 'it is difficult to imagine how evangelistic activity on such a large scale (reaching throughout Macedonia and Achaia) could have been undertaken by such an unestablished congregation in so short a period of time.' However if the report could have been taken by others through the region in such a short space of time, so could the message of salvation!

Thessalonian church, sharing the news of the Thessalonians conversion. In addition, the news of this sharing and general knowledge of the Thessalonian conversion and faith would have had to be relayed back to Paul involving a significant amount of travel. Thus in fact on examination, the extent of the expansion of the gospel is really no barrier to an active interpretation as some argue.[157] The scope of the spread is a problem either way. Hence with Malherbe I agree that the Thessalonians, as other Pauline churches, 'quickly took the message beyond the cities in which they were established.'[158]

Finally, in light of the above, it is possible that 1 Thess 1:8c 'therefore we have no need to speak about it' (ὥστε μὴ χρείαν ἔχειν ἡμᾶς λαλεῖν τι) should be taken as a reference to their evangelistic ministry. The indefinite pronoun τίς here renders Paul's intention far less certain than similar constructions in concerning love and eschatology (1 Thess 4:9; 5:1). In the passive framework τι is considered to refer to the faith of the Thessalonians i.e. ἡ πίστις ὑμῶν ἡ πρὸς τὸν θεὸν.[159] However this is a truncated view in that the faith is mentioned in regards to 'going out' i.e. evangelism. In addition τίς here is neuter whilst πίστις feminine rendering it unlikely that Paul is referring to anything in the immediate context.[160] It is thus likely that Paul is referring to the whole preceding 1:8a-b. That is, Paul does not need to say anything to the Thessalonians about the communication of the faith, as they were so active and successful in their activity.[161]

In clucision, I would argue that in this passage we clearly have an example of Paul's desire for his congregations to imitate his passion for evangelism. No specifics are given nor are individuals named,[162] simply his delight that they have imitated himself and his team. In addition he is delighted that they are modelling this to other churches that will then follow their lead. We have then a lead into the mind of Paul and his evangelistic strategy. He saw himself as a model to be emulated by his congregations.

1 Thessalonians 2:14-16

The passage in question is highly controversial. It has been argued by some that

---

[157] Wanamaker, *Thessalonians*, 83.

[158] Malherbe, *Thessalonians*, 68.

[159] So also active advocate Marshall, *Thessalonians*, 56; Bruce, *Thessalonians*, 17; Wanamaker, *Thessalonians*, 83 who suggest it means Paul did not need to speak about the faith of the Thessalonians in the region and beyond because the story was well told.

[160] The only neuter noun in the immediate context is πνεύματος a genitive dependent on the feminine χαρᾶς meaning it cannot be the antecedent to τι. Alternatively word order also rules out εἰδώλων in 1:9b.

[161] Malherbe, *Thessalonians*, 118 suggests λαλέω refers to preaching and so Paul has no need to preach about their faith any more?

[162] Ware, 'Missionary Congregation': 130.

the passage is a non-Pauline interpolation for three main reasons.[163] The first reason for this is the unusual double thanksgiving that is unique to the Thessalonians correspondence; the other being 1 Thessalonians 1:2-10. Secondly to some, the vitriol concerning 'the Jews' in the passage is considered to be out of keeping with Paul's attitude to Jews elsewhere. Finally, to some the letter reads better if 2:13-16 is excised, Paul moving from his reminder to the Thessalonians of his first mission (2:1-10) to his grief at being torn away from the Thessalonians and his desire to see and hear of them again (2:17-3:10).

However, these arguments do not warrant seeing the passage as a non-Pauline interpolation.[164] First, while the double thanksgiving is unusual there is no *a priori* reason that this should lead to a rejection of its authenticity. Secondly, the suggestion that the 'attack' on the Jews is non-Pauline is also tenuous. Paul is here not attacking *all Jews* but only *those Jews that have rejected the gospel and persecuted Jesus and his missionaries.* Finally, his comments are in continuity with those in the Johanine tradition concerning 'the Jews' who reject the gospel.[165]

In 1 Thess 2:14 Paul is giving thanks for the Thessalonians (ὑμεῖς); not for imitating himself as in 1:6, but for imitating *other churches*, from Judea. These probably comprised the original church in Jerusalem (cf. Gal 1:13; 1 Cor 15:9) now in dispersion due to persecution (Acts 8:4) and her daughter churches.[166] It may also include those in the greater Palestine region including Samaria and Galilee.[167] This indicates that Paul's understanding of imitation was not merely egocentric or even christocentric; rather, he wanted his congregations to emulate all good examples of Christian living including churches (cf. Phil 3:17c).[168] This notion of ecclesiological imitation is also anticipated in 1 Thess 1:7 where the Thessalonians are models to the 'believers in Macedonia and

---

[163] B.A. Pearson, '1 Thessalonians 2:13–16: A Deutero-Pauline Interpolation,' *HTR* 64 (1971): 79–94; M. Goguel, *Introduction au Nouveau Testament.* Four Volumes (Paris: Leroux, 1925).·305-307; H. Boers, 'The Form-Critical Study of Paul's Letters: 1 Thessalonians as a Case Study,' *NTS* 22 (1975–76): 140–158. For solid arguments against this view see Wanamaker, *1 Thessalonians*, 30-32; Jewett *Thessalonian Corresondance* 41.

[164] See Wanamaker, 1 Thessalonians, 34-37; W. Wuellner, 'Greek Rhetoric and Pauline Argumentation' in William R. Schoedel and Robert L. Wilken, *Early Christian Literature and the Classical Intellectual Tradition. In Honorem Robert M. Grant.* TH 54 (Paris: Beauchesne, 1979),· 177–188 esp. 180-188; so also Schmithals, *Paul and the Gnostics*, 123-218 who understands it as Paul's response to Gnostic opponents.

[165] So for example Jn 2:18; 5:16, 18; 6:41; 7:1; 10:31. While these post-date 1 Thess they indicate that 'the Jews' could be used in a perjorative sense in the early church.

[166] Bruce, *1 Thessalonians*, 45.

[167] Wanamaker, *1 Thessalonians*, 112.

[168] As I have argued throughout, in Philippians with Paul, the Romans, the historical Philippians including Euodia, Synthyche, Clement and other workers, Timothy, Epaphroditus and Christ (cf. 1 Cor 11:1). In Eph 5:1 Paul speaks of imitating God.

Achaia' through their imitation of the Pauline team.

I will now turn to assess whether proclamation is constitutive of imitation in the passage in question. In 1 Thess 2:13a-b Paul again expresses his gratitude that the message he and his team proclaimed to the Thessalonians was accepted as the word of God (cf. 1 Thess 1:6, 9). He adds that this same message is still clearly at work among the believing Thessalonians since he and his team moved onto Berea and beyond.[169] Immediately evangelism is introduced into the context, this referring to the initial evangelisation of Thessalonica. Furthermore, the whole epistle to this point is steeped in reference to initial evangelisation (cf. 1 Thess 1:3-2:12) as well as the Thessalonian continuation of the evangelistic mission (see above on 1 Thess 1:6-8).

This thought carries through to Paul's reference to imitation in 1 Thess 2:14a (γάρ). The word is at work 'for' (γάρ) you 'became imitators' (μιμηται ἐγενήθητε [aorist]) of the Judean Christian (ἐν Χριστῷ 'Ιησοῦ) churches. Paul then in 2:14d gives detail concerning the imitation; ('since' [ὅτι])[170] they had suffered from their own people the same things that the churches of Judea had suffered from the Jews who opposed them (cf. 1 Thess 1:7).

There are different ideas concerning the suffering faced by the Judean churches in 2:14e. Some suggest that this could refer to the persecution of Gentiles who were not circumcised (cf. Gal 6:12). Alternatively, it could refer to persecution of Jewish Christians by Jewish nationalists or zealots in the late forties and early fifties. Although these are possible, the soundest and most detailed point of reference is Luke's account of the Jerusalem Church in Acts.[171] Luke's account of the Jerusalem church in Acts points to a high degree of evangelistic zeal spearheaded by Peter and John.[172] So much so, that the

---

[169] This concurs with Paul's understanding of the word as an active agent in the Christians life bearing fruit (cf. Rom 1:16; 1 Cor 1:18).

[170] Taking ὅτι as a causal conjunction.

[171] This I base on: 1) The apparent connection between Paul and Luke (cf. the 'we-passages') suggesting a high degree of shared understanding; 2) Other strong connections to the Jerusalem Church and its history including Barnabas, pilgrims from Jerusalem in Antioch; 3) Discussions with Peter and other apostles specifically concerning the gospel and evangelism (cf. Gal 2:7-10). See also 'assumptions' in my General Introduction.

[172] This involved: 1) Preaching as in the cases of Peter in Jerusalem on the day of Pentecost (Acts 2:14-41), the apostles (4:22; 5:41); Stephen (Acts 7:2-56); Philip (Acts 8:5, 12, 26-40), Peter and John in Samaria (Acts 8:25; 9:32), Peter to the Gentiles (10:1-48) and general believers to Phoenicia, Cyprus and Antioch (8:4; 11:19-20). It is probable that the teaching of the apostles was at least in part, evangelistic (Acts 2:42, 47; 4:33); 2) Signs and wonders (Acts 2:43; 5:1-11, 12, 15-16; 8:6-7, 13; 9:32-34, 40-41) often in combination with preaching (Acts 3:1-4:12); 3) Prayer including a specific appeal for courage in the face of persecution (3:1; 4:29); 4) Persecution with the intent of stopping proclamation (Acts 4:13-20; 8:1-4; 9:1; 12:1-6, 18-19) including martydom (7:2-59; 12:2); 5) Intimate fellowship (Acts 2:42, 44; 5:12); 6) Radical generosity to

threat of persecution from the Jewish leaders was not able to thwart the determination of the leaders to proclaim (Acts 4:13-20; 5:17-40).[173] Rather, their threats served to intensify their resolve to preach the gospel despite the danger (see especially Acts 4:19-20, 29; 5:29, 41-42). Furthermore, this evangelistic zeal extended into Judea and Samaria through Philip (8:5-40) and to other areas including Cyprus, Phoenicia and Antioch through Christians *other than the Twelve* due to the Sauline persecution (Acts 8:4; 11:19-20).

If the correlation of the experience of the Thessalonians and the Judean Christians is taken seriously along with the thrust of 1 Thess 1:3-8 (above), evangelism lies at the heart of the situation at Thessalonica. The Thessalonians have proactively sought to evangelise their context. As they have done so, they have encountered serious opposition from Thessalonians (συμφυλετῶν).[174]

This in all likelihood included flogging, imprisonment and possibly death (cf. 1 Thess 4:13). While evangelism is not explicitly stated as the reason for the suffering, in light of the contextual connection between evangelism and suffering throughout the preceding and the parallel between the situations of Paul and the Thessalonians, it is probable (cf. 1 Thess 1:7; 2:2). In addition, the ongoing persecution of the Thessalonians itself suggests ongoing evangelisation in that the Christian church must have been seen as a threat to the Thessalonian community and way of life. As such, their must have been on-going conversions of locals unsettling the religious, economic and social order.

In 2:15 Paul then goes on to further explain the crimes of the recalcitrant Jews (τῶν καὶ).[175] First, they killed Jesus; indicative of the Jewish involvement in the crucifixion.[176] Again this brings evangelism into view; Jesus being killed, at least in part, for preaching a message that was a threat to the Jewish understanding of God and salvation history. Secondly, they killed the prophets. This probably refers to the historical rejection of prophets through the history of Israel; a recurring feature of the interpretation of Israel's history found in the

---

those in need (Acts 2:44-45; 4:32, 34-5:11; 6:1-7; 9:36).

[173] The Lucan account of the Judean church confirms that the Judean churches were constantly under pressure from Jewish religious leadership, the source of persecution being Jewish not Gentile (see Acts 4:1-22; 5:17-42; 7:1-8:3;12:1-18).

[174] *EDNT*, 3:290 note it means 'compatriot, fellow countryman' and is used here of 'your own *countrymen*' and so speaks of 'persecutions of the church in Thessalonica by its Macedonian fellow citizens.'

[175] That Paul is not condemning all Jews guards Paul from any charge of anti-semitism. See also W.D. Davies, 'Paul and the People of Israel,' *NTS* 24 (1977–78): 4–39, esp. 9. In fact 'the Jews' are not the point of Paul's thanksgiving. They are used comparitively with those Thessalonians/Macedonians who have opposed the Thessalonian church. Just as Paul understood some Jews to be truly Israel, so some Gentiles were truly Gentiles. If Paul is being anti-semitic he is also being anti-Thessalonian and so anti-Gentile (not to mention that Paul himself is a Jew!).

[176] Cf. Jn 5:18; 7:1; 8:59; 11:45-53; 18:14, 31; Acts 2:36; 3:13.

OT and on the mouth of Jesus and the writers of the NT.[177] This is a forerunner of the rejection of the messenger of God in the Christian era; the messengers of the gospel standing in continuity with the messengers of the word of God in the pre-Christ era. Thirdly, they drove out Paul and his team. This most probably refers to instances where Jews were involved in driving Paul and his team out of towns on his missionary journeys, including Thessalonica itself (1 Thess 2:2 cf. Acts 17:5-10, 13-15).[178] Paul indicates that such resistance brings displeasure to God (θεῷ μὴ ἀρεσκόνων)[179] and a general hostility to all people.

In 1 Thess 2:16a Paul explains what he means by this reference to general hostility.[180] The paradigmatic Jewish hostility which Paul has applied to the Thessalonian situation was expressed in their on-going hindrance of Paul and his co-workers from preaching the gospel to Gentiles for the purpose of seeing them saved (ἵνα σωθῶσιν). As such, any opposition to evangelism is to Paul, an *anathema*. To oppose the proclamation of the message is to stand in the way of the God's means of salvation; the hearing of the word which leads to belief and so salvation (cf. Rom 1:16; 10:14-17; 1 Cor 1:18; Eph 1:13-14). This is particularly so for the Jews in that they above all should have recognised their Messiah and the fulfilment of OT promises of the salvation of the Gentiles (cf. Hos 1:10; 2:23; Deut 32:21, 43; Ps 18:49; 117:1; Is 11:10).[181] For either Jew or Gentile, to oppose the preaching of the message is inherently evil in that *it denies the hearer the possibility of being saved*!

Because of this Jewish resistance to the evangelisation of the Gentiles Paul is scathing, suggesting two consequences. First, in 2:16b the result (εἰς τό) of this Jewish resistance involves the continual mounting up of their sin before God.[182] Specifically here this refers to sin as their resistance to the Gospel; the

---

[177] In the OT see 1 Kgs 19:10-14 cf. Rom 11:3; 2 Chron 36:15f. From Jesus see Matt 5:12; 23:29-37; Lk 11:47-50; 13:34; 16:31. In the remainder of the NT see Acts 7:52; Rom 11:3; Heb 11:32-38; Jas 5:10 cf. Mk 6:4 and pars.; Rev 16:6.

[178] See also Acts 9:29-30; 13:50; 14:4-6, 19-20. After Thessalonica Paul was to experience Jewish rejection in Ephesus (Acts 19:9) and Jerusalem specifically for referring to his call to the Gentiles (Acts 22:21).

[179] The notion of failing to please God is characteristic of those who live according to flesh and not Spirit (Rom 8:8). The single person has more potential to please the Lord because of freedom from marital concern (1 Cor 7:32). Paul's personal approach to life and ministry for himself (Gal 1:10; 1 Thess 2:4; 2 Tim 2:4) and his converts (1 Thess 4:1) was to please God and no human or institution except in terms of *adiaphora* for the purposes of salvation (1 Cor 10:32).

[180] The participle κωλυόντων is present suggesting first that this continues and explicates 2:15 and secondly, it points to the historical continuity of opposition to God's messengers through the history of the Jews into the Christian era among both Jew and Gentile.

[181] See Rom 9:25-29; 15:9-12.

[182] 'The continual filling up of their sins.' Best, *1 Thessalonians*, 118 notes that the notion of 'filling up their sins' is drawn from Gen 15:16 (cf. Dan 8:23; 2 Macc 6:14) and

divine word of God. This leads to the second result, judgement. This judgement has two temporal dimensions. In the first place, this judgement is being experienced in the present indicated by the aorist of φθάνω. Furthermore, eschatological judgement experienced at the consummation as suggested by εἰς τελος (cf. 'destruction' in Phil 1:28). Exactly what Paul means here is debated. Some ideas include Pearson who, while taking it as an interpolation, sees this as a reference to the fall of Jerusalem based on a literal interpretation of the aorist ἔφθασεν.[183] Bammel believes this refers to the Claudius' expulsion of Jews from Rome.[184] Jewett connects this to Josephus who reports a massacre in Jerusalem in AD49 which resulted from Jewish nationalistic violence.[185] Collins suggests however, that what we have here is not to be taken literally of a specific historical event. Rather, we have descriptive apocalyptic language and so it should be taken generally.[186] Best takes the aorist as indicative of the imminence and inevitability of divine wrath which had 'drawn near' and was thus about to happen when their sins were complete.[187] Wanamaker notes that his readers would have certainly understood as the events were unfolding.[188] Bruce takes it with 1 Thess 1:10 of the coming wrath from which God will deliver his people.[189]

The present-day dimension of this judgement I suggest refers to historical present and ultimately future rejection of Israel. They remain under the dominion of Rome and more importantly, sin and its consequences, having failed to realise that salvation lay in Christ the Messiah who has come to deliver them. Their resistance to the Gospel sees them remain under God's wrath (cf. Rom 1:18; 2:1-3:9) which will ultimately see them experience eternal destruction. This indicates consistency with OT prophetic interpretation of historical events such as the exile as God's judgement on human sin.

Returning to the thanksgiving here, it is now possible to have a clearer picture of what is going on. Paul is profoundly thankful that the Thessalonians had not desisted from active proclamation after his departure despite opposition.

As such we have a situation which parallels Phil 1:27-30 where as argued

---

'suggests a definite measure of sins which when completed will be followed by God's judgement.'

183 B.A. Pearson, '1 Thessalonians 2:13–16': 81-84.

184 E. Bammel,'Judenverfolgung und Naherwartung: Zur Eschatologie des Ersten Thessalonicherbriefs,' *ZTK* 56 (1959): 294–315, see esp. 300f.

185 Robert Jewett, 'The Agitators and the Galatian Congregation,' *NTS* 17 (1970–71): 198–212, see esp. 205. See also Jos, *War* 2.224-227.

186 John J. Collins, *The Apocalyptic Imagination: An Introduction to the Jewish Matrix of Christianity* (New York: Crossroads, 1984), 214. Similarly Wanamaker, *Thessalonians*, 117.

187 Best, *Thessalonians*, 120; Marshall, *Thessalonians*, 80-81;

188 Wanamaker, *Thessalonians*, 117.

189 Bruce, *Thessalonians*, 48.

above, Paul is appealing for continued proclamation despite the resistance of Gentile opposition. As is the case there, he refers to the danger of judgement on those who oppose the message (1:28). In a manner similar to Philippians then, Paul is delighted that the Thessalonians are not allowing themselves to be thwarted from evangelism, but have continued despite great suffering. Hence, imitation in this context involves both the standing firm under persecution and the proclamation of the Gospel in the face of the opposition and suffering.

Conclusion to Other References

The above analysis of these texts does not exhaust the exegetical questions or the content of imitation in each context. However, it is clear that there are sound reasons to argue that within the range of these texts imitation involved evangelism. This strengthens that Phil 4:9 involves all manner of Christian living, including evangelism.

Conclusion to 4:9

Overall then, Phil 4:9 indicates that Paul's concept of imitation includes proclamation. This is seen in his global appeal for imitation in Phil 4:9 including *all* that he has taught through word and deed. As J.J. Müller puts it: 'all that they had received from Paul by way of teaching and admonition, and by what they heard from his mouth and saw in his Christian example, this they had to do, they had to act accordingly.'[190]

Such a conclusion argues persuasively against the idea that no church in the Pauline epistles engaged in evangelism or that Paul's missionary thinking did not include his converts engaging in evangelism. When one places this alongside the content of Philippians throughout and Eph 6:15, 17 which indicates that the equipped Pauline Christian is evangelistically prepared and is to wield the word of God as their primary attacking weapon, one has to conclude that those arguing for a passive-witness viewpoint are inaccurate and reductionist in their assessment.[191]

Imitation then involves proclamation.[192] This is reinforced through the notion of example in Philippians. All negative and positive examples concern evangelism and there is no limitation placed on the imitation of the Philippians. To conclude otherwise requires a pre-assumed prohibition or limitation, which is exegetically unsound. Philippians 4:9 then provides us with the most comprehensive statement of Paul's exemplar manner of teaching. This impression is supported in other imitatory texts, particularly 1 Cor 11:1; 1

---

[190] J.J. Müller, 143-144.

[191] See in particular O'Brien, *Consumed*, 126-131 and Appendix 1, 'The connection between evangelism and the military metaphor in Paul.'

[192] Green, *Evangelism*, 215 n68.

Thess 1:6-8; 2:14-16. Paul wanted his converts to emulate all that they had heard from him in teaching and tradition and seen in his ministry i.e. all aspects of his ministry from his workplace evangelism, his theology, his soteriological concern and steadfastness in suffering. As an apostle he worked hard with his co-workers doing the whole range of spiritual activities essential to mission. These included church planting, evangelism, prayer, signs and wonders, care for the poor and needy, teaching and equipping, prophecy, leadership, ethical purity and more. For Paul, this is a continuation of the work of Christ (cf. 1 Cor 11:1). His hope and prayer was that the churches he had formed would continue this ministry. He saw his apostolic commission to the Gentiles not as a solo-operator or as being fulfilled through his team alone, as if he and his co-workers would save the world. Rather he hoped that his churches would continue and expand the ministry as led by the Holy Spirit.

This didactic approach of teaching, not only through word but also through demonstrated action, emulates Jesus' education of the disciples by taking them on a three-year intensive mission. In-so-doing Paul sought to democratise his mission first through co-workers and the spiritually endowed. Secondly, these 'specialists' were then to develop others in a similar way to take up the various elements of the mission. In this way, Paul understood that his churches would continue his mission after he moved on. In evangelistic terms then, this means that the church would take responsibility for their towns and regions.

This conclusion impacts on the way Paul's apostolic commission is understood. While Paul considered himself apostle to the uncircumcised, the mission was not confined to he and his team; rather, it was to be a mission achieved through Paul along with his disciples and churches who responded in imitation to Paul's own example. Paul cleverly directed his energies not to mere proclamation and church planting but to enabling the mission to be self-propagating. Hence Bowers' analysis that Paul's ultimate goal was the establishment of congregations in the major urban centres on the North Eastern Mediterranean rim is incomplete.[193] That Paul wanted churches there is not in doubt. But Paul's strategy looked further to the proclamation of the Gospel and the establishment of churches in the surrounding rural regions.

---

[193] See Bowers, 'Fulfilling', 185-198 esp.198.

Chapter 10

Conclusion and Implications

In this study I have examined in depth one of the thirteen Pauline epistles to explore his expectations concerning his congregations' involvement in evangelism. There is no question that my study has confirmed that Paul wanted his congregations to participate in his own mission through prayer, financial support, steadfastness in the face of opposition and false teaching, ethical witness, community unity and apologetic witness. The question I asked continually was, 'is there evidence in Philippians that Paul wanted his congregation to engage in proactive evangelism to their community and beyond?'

Conclusions

Congregational Evangelism in Philippians

In my introduction I considered that there was a lack of in-depth exegetical analysis of the Pauline epistles in regards to congregational involvement in evangelism. In addition, the texts in question were in many cases capable of interpretations that evacuated evangelism from their scope. I found that proponents who excluded proactive evangelistic endeavour in general terms including Bowers, Bosch, Dickson and specifically of Philippians, Eichholz, are able to come to their conclusions in a number of ways. This is seen in Philippians at various points.

First, in 1:5 'fellowship in the gospel' is understood in terms of support for the Pauline mission rather than active involvement. Secondly, 'brothers' in 1:14 are understood not as general Christians but as co-workers or ministers of the gospel. Thirdly, 'contending for the faith of the gospel' in 1:27 is taken to mean standing fast in face of opposition. Fourthly, in 2:16 λόγον ζωῆς ἐπέχοντες is taken as 'holding fast to the word of life.' Fifthly, the involvement of the women and others in 4:2-3 is either limited to non-proclamatory activity or some activity that ceased after Paul left Philippi. Sixthly, the appeals for imitation in 3:15-17 and 4:9 are considered to relate to ethics and lifestyle only, without regard for evangelism. Finally, little cognisance is given to the rhetorical impact on hearers of the letter of Paul's presentation of an array of examples to the Philippians, who are in all cases evangelistic.[1] This pattern of exegetical analysis allows the proponents of the passive model of church involvement to come to their conclusions.

However, my analysis has consistently argued that these texts are capable of alternative proactive interpretations, which I consider have stronger support. This conclusion supports those who argue for a proactive evangelistic mission for the Pauline churches involving not only proclamation specialists but 'general Christians.' These include earlier writers such as Green and those who have responded to Bosch and Bowers; notably, O'Brien, I.H. Marshall, Ware, Schnabel and Plummer. In terms of Philippians this is supported by the work of a number of Philippian specialists including Murray, Marshall, O'Brien (again), Fee, Bockmuehl, Schenck, Gnilka, U.B. Müller and Oaks. The evidence of Philippians confirms that Paul did want his congregations to engage in proactive evangelistic mission to Philippi and the surrounding regions. Throughout Philippians the concept of congregational evangelism recurs, fused to other main elements important to the letter. This conclusion is based on these findings:

PHILIPPIANS 1:14-18A

In this passage Paul expresses his delight that his presence in Rome encouraged most of the Roman 'brothers and sisters' to preach the message in Rome. I argued that it is probable that the ἀδελφοί of 1:14 were general Christians rather than other gospel preachers in Rome. On the basis of context I suggested that the differently motivated proclaimers of 1:15-18a were two subgroups from within the Roman Christians with different attitudes to Paul and his approach to the gospel. Paul's conclusion in 1:18a (τί γάρ; πλὴν ὅτι παντὶ τρόπῳ, εἴτε προφάσει εἴτε ἀληθείᾳ, Χριστὸς καταγγέλλεται, καὶ ἐν τούτῳ χαίρω) verified his joy with regard to all proclamation of the authentic gospel. I argued that Paul's words have rhetorical import; he is encouraging his readers in Philippi to continue to proclaim the gospel in their context, in unity and with right motivation. In addition I noted the interplay of key dimensions of the letter including unity in evangelism (1:15-17), proclamation in the face of opposition (1:13-14, 15-17), persecution (1:14, 17) and joy (1:18a).

PHILIPPIANS 1:27-30

Here I argued that μιᾷ ψυχῇ συναθλοῦντες τῇ πίστει τοῦ εὐαγγελίου is a rather direct exhortation to the Philippians to continue to proclaim the gospel. This is confirmed through the importance of evangelism in the context and the verbal parallelism that exists between 1:27-30 and 4:2-3. In the latter context, Paul uses the same verb συναθλέω clearly with reference to the

[1] As I have indicated, these include either directly or indirectly Paul, differently motivated Roman brothers and sisters, Christ, Timothy, Epaphroditus, Judaisers, enemies of the cross, Euodia and Syntyche.

involvement of his co-workers in evangelism. Thirdly, the evangelistic point of reference is confirmed in the parallel Paul draws with his own situation of suffering for the cause of the gospel in Rome and that of the Philippians (τὸν αὐτὸν ἀγῶνα ἔχοντες, οἷον εἴδετε ἐν ἐμοὶ καὶ νῦν ἀκούετε ἐν ἐμοί [1:30]). I noted the interplay of evangelism in this context with the issues of unity (1:27 [μιᾷ ψυχῇ]), suffering from opposition and persecution from Gentiles in Philippi (1:28-30) and eschatological hope (1:28b). Paul's appeal is for them to continue to proclaim the gospel in loving unity, despite persecution and potential suffering knowing that they will receive eternal life, whilst their opponents will receive destruction. This being the case, the more general initial injunction from which 1:27c-30 derives, 'conduct yourselves in a manner worthy of the gospel of Christ', should be understood as inclusive of evangelism.

PHILIPPIANS 2:14-16A

This appeal I argued included a concern for evangelism for a number of reasons.

First, there is here an appeal for a cessation of further conflict, which calls to mind the problem among evangelistic co-workers (2:14 cf. 4:2-3). Secondly, Paul appeals for ethical witness consistent with the gospel (cf. 1:27a) in a manner which illuminates Philippi and its region and attracts the pagan population to Christ. I suggested that while the emphasis here is ethical, the concept of radiating light is not purely static and behavioural in Paul; the mission of the gospel being the bringing of light of the gospel to a dark world (cf. 2 Cor 4:4-6). Thirdly, and most importantly, in a manner not unlike 1:27d, Paul here appeals directly for evangelistic endeavour (2:16a). In my analysis, I suggested that although a strong case can be made for interpreting the text passively ('hold fast the word of life'), the better interpretation of λόγον ζωῆς ἐπέχοντες is evangelistic ('hold forth the word of life'). There are a number of reasons for this including: the choice of language; the meaning of λόγον ζωῆς as 'gospel'; the possible connection to Dan 12:1-3 and, in particular, the context. I argued that the context is intensely evangelistic implicitly (2:1-11, 14) and explicitly (1:5-7, 22, 27-30; 2:22 [Timothy], 25 [Epaphroditus], 3:2 [Judaising false evangelists]; 4:2-3 [Philippians co-workers]). Hence, I consider that the appeal is for the Philippians to continue to 'hold forth the word of life' in the sense of evangelism.

I noted too in my exegesis the connection between this congregational evangelism and other key elements which feature throughout Philippians including internal contention (2:14), opposition (2:15b), suffering (2:16c-17a), eschatological hope (2:16) and joy (2:18).

PHILIPPIANS 2:19-30

In my analysis of these verses I noted the positive examples of Timothy and Epaphroditus were profoundly evangelistic. Timothy is commended as a selfless man who is concerned not for his own interests but the Philippians (2:20b) and the interests of Christ (2:21). Most importantly he has proved himself in the gospel mission, working with Paul as a son to a father in the gospel mission. I demonstrated that this involvement undoubtedly included evangelism as εἰς τὸ εὐαγγέλιον indicates (2:22). Epaphroditus, I argued, was a highly evangelistic local from Philippi who probably participated in the earlier mission of Paul and who continued to do so up until the time of writing. This I based on an in-depth analysis of the evangelistic nuances of the the first four terms of the five-fold attestation τὸν ἀδελφὸν καὶ συνεργὸν καὶ συστρατιώτην μου, ὑμῶν δὲ ἀπόστολον καὶ λειτουργὸν τῆς χρείας μου (2:25). The first three I argued were decidedly evangelistic, whilst the fourth potentially so. His example included tremendous suffering for the cause of the gospel (2:26-27, 29), another example of the interplay of the dynamics in Philippians.

I suggested that rather than merely give the Philippians a report on the travel plans and situation of these two men or commend them to the church, one of the main functions of presenting the examples of Timothy and Epaphroditus was rhetorical. That is, Paul commends these two as evangelistically inclined individuals for the Philippians to emulate. The appeal for imitation in 3:15-17 includes imitating people like these who 'live according to the pattern' given by Paul previously (3:17) rather than that of the Judaisers (3:2) and other enemies of the cross (3:18).[2] In this connection I noted that opposition and eschatological hope are also emphasised. Paul encourages the Philippians to live according to such a pattern so that they, unlike their opponents, will experience salvation and not destruction (3:19-21).

PHILIPPIANS 4:2-3

The appeal in 4:2-3 to Euodia and Syntyche to bury their differences brings together the issue of disunity and evangelism. The setting for their conflict is clearly work for the gospel (αἵτινες ἐν τῷ εὐαγγελίῳ συνήθλησάν μοι). I suggested that this appeal brings together a number of allusions to their conflict throughout the epistle (1:27; 2:1-4, 14-15). In addition, I consider that this potentially gives an evangelistic dynamic to the appeals of 2:1-4 and the Christ-example (2:5-11).[3] I discussed the nature of their involvement in the mission and concluded that the active athletic language and in particular, the reference to Clement and the other co-workers in the same breath, strongly suggests that their involvement was active evangelism. I suggested that to be consistent in

[2] See Chapter 9 for evangelistic nuances relevant to this discussion.

[3] See Appendix 3.

interpretation, to limit their involvement would require a limitation of the involvement of the other co-workers, which I consider unlikely. That being the case, here are two examples of women actively involved in evangelistic mission from the earliest days of the gospel. I also noted the reference to eschatological hope here; these co-workers assured by Paul that their names are written in the 'book of life.' Consequently, they should rejoice in the Lord (4:4) at this assurance, bringing joy into the mix. While it could be argued on the basis of 4:2-3 alone that co-workers are the only ones involved in the evangelistic mission, the reiteration of the synonymous concept of 'contending for the faith of the gospel' (1:27) applied to the whole congregation makes this unlikely. More likely, Paul mentions these people as the women, Clement and others led the congregation in general involvement in evangelism. This indicates a primary but not exclusive role from these people.

PHILIPPIANS 1:5-7

In that the thanksgivings of Paul anticipate the content of the letter in many cases, I then looked back at 1:5-7 from Paul's thanksgiving in light of the exegetical analysis of the texts above. I discussed the concept of the κοινωνίᾳ ὑμῶν εἰς τὸ εὐαγγέλιον in 1:5 arguing that this should be interpreted to include the full range of involvement in the mission of the gospel found in the body of the letter. My analysis established more than a strong possibility that evangelism should be included alongside other aspects of mission mentioned in the letter including suffering, prayer, unity, financial support and ethical witness. Somewhat more tentatively, I also suggested that the 'good work' (ἔργον ἀγαθὸν) in 1:6 and their joint participation in Paul's 'grace' (χάριτος) in 1:7 refer to the same involvement, noting that they flow out of the initial statement concerning the 'fellowship in the gospel', the structural parallelism in the text and that both terms are capable of such an interpretation linguistically.

PHILIPPIANS 4:9

I then discussed Paul's appeal that the Philippians emulate all that they had 'learned or received or heard from me, or seen in me' from 4:9. I considered that this was a holistic appeal for Philippian emulation of all that they had heard and seen from Paul in his example, letters, personal teaching and through his emissaries. I suggested that the appeal was in effect a summary of the letter to this point, which as I have argued, includes evangelism (1:27; 2:16; 4:2-3). I claimed that Paul had passed onto them a commission to evangelise that he had gleaned from his interaction with the Jerusalem Apostles over matters relating to the gospel (παρελάβετε) (cf. Gal 2:1-10). I demonstrated from my analysis of the letter and previous visits to Philippi that one of the things they had 'seen' from Paul was evangelism (cf. Acts 16:11-40) and so I argued that the phrase ἃ καὶ ἐμάθετε καὶ παρελάβετε καὶ ἠκούσατε καὶ εἴδετε ἐν ἐμοί, ταῦτα πράσσετε cannot be evacuated of evangelism. I noted that unless some previous prohibition on evangelism existed in the minds of the Philippians, this appeal would necessarily lead them to include evangelism in light of the content of the letter and Paul's practice. I also observed the note of assurance at the end of God's presence with them, as they continue to do this. I also examined in some detail 1 Corinthians 11:1, 1 Thessalonians 1:6-8 and 2:14-16 and noted that these imitatory texts suggest evangelism as a component part of imitation in each case.

I concede that the strength of my argument varies to some degree. It can be argued that the claim that 2:16 should be taken proactively lacks certitude and support from the majority of contemporary exegetes. Some will also challenge my findings on the use of *apostolos* in regards to Epaphroditus. However, I consider that my case for 1:27, especially in light of 4:2-3, is very strong indeed and represents the majority position among contemporary commentators. Unless it can be shown that co-workers did not proclaim the gospel in 4:2-3, it is difficult to come to the conclusion that the appeal of 1:27 'to contend…' is not active and proclamatory. Similarly, the categorical statement of 1:18a would seem to point to a mindset in Paul that was positive to all proclamation of the authentic gospel. Furthermore, the rhetorical impact of 1:14-18a points to Paul's desire for evangelism in Philippi from the whole church. It is difficult to imagine hearers listening to his commendation of the Romans (1:14) and not wanting to get involved in the mission or not believing that Paul desired that the gospel be preached! Likewise, the use of evangelistic example and in particular, the absolute appeal of 4:9 to imitate Paul's given teaching and example strongly suggests evangelism is a portion of the appeal. After coming to these conclusions, an active interpretation of 2:16 becomes more likely, with Paul reiterating there his appeal for evangelistic endeavour.

Thus, with those scholars who argue for a proactive ecclesiological evangelistic mission in Paul (above), I conclude that essential to the fabric of Philippians is a concern for the continued involvement of the Philippian congregation in evangelistic mission. I suggest that in each of the above contexts alongside evangelism recur the themes of suffering, unity, joy, thinking and eschatological hope, suggesting that the situation of the Philippians involved an interaction of these issues. The issue of false teachers appears to be a warning of a specific potential threat and only tangentially connects to the issue. However, it is interesting that Paul places it after his commendation of the authentic proclaimers Timothy and Epaphroditus and then leads to an appeal for imitation of himself and people such as them. This suggests that the gospel and evangelism are the unifying themes here as well, although more in terms of content than praxis. As I have stated in my Introduction my intention is not to prove that congregational evangelism is *the issue* in Philippians. Rather I have sought to establish it as *an issue* among the others noted.

It is also worthwhile to take note of the addressees of the appeals referred to above. In 4:2-3 Paul addresses two women directly, appealing for a cessation of conflict. However, in the case of other appeals in the letter, no individuals are singled out (1:27; 2:16; 4:9). Furthermore in the presentation of examples, no section or individual within the congregation in singled out. Rather, it would appear that the appeals in Philippians are to the whole ('all') church including and, perhaps especially so, the leaders (1:1). This would suggest that the whole congregation was to be concerned for the continuation of the evangelistic mission, perhaps under the leadership of the 'overseers and deacons.'[4]

As I have discussed in regards to 1:7 and 2:25 in particular, it is probable that Paul envisaged that this mission was to be spearheaded by those with a spiritual gift involving proclamation of the gospel. These include the gifts of apostle, evangelist (1 Cor 12:28; 31; Eph 4:11-16; 2 Tim 4:1-5) and, to a lesser extent, prophet (1 Cor 14:24-25). The Philippians were to operate in accord with the grace given to them, as does Paul himself. However as I discussed in regard to the role of the 'evangelist' Timothy and the 'apostle' Epaphroditus, the function of these leaders, was in part, to equip other members of the congregation for works of service, which built up the body (cf. Eph 4:11-16; 6:15, 17). Hence I consider that the whole congregation is to be involved in the proclamation of the gospel.

The Broader Question: Congregational Evangelism in the Pauline Epistles?

It is at this point that analysts disagree. Bowers argues that Paul understood that he, his co-workers and other recognised co-workers would continue the mission, while the church remained supportive of their role and witnessed ethically and responsively. Ollrog suggests that appointed co-workers from the Pauline churches continued the mission in the cities and regions. Dickson argues that the church was to be proactive in evangelism through 'heralds' who continue to take the gospel to the world. He considers that the church's role was supportive of these specialists and was limited to witness socially, ethically, through public worship and apologetically. In all cases these scholars deny that there is any real sense of proactive evangelism from the church in Paul's mind.

My analysis argues that this limitation of evangelism to those with the function of co-workers, evangelists or apostle in the mission is not apparent in Paul's letters. There are examples in Philippians of such workers (Paul, Timothy, Epaphroditus, Euodia, Syntyche, Clement and other co-workers). However, at no point is there any indication that the mission was limited to these people, nor that the congregation's role is confined in any way in relation to theirs. Rather, these people, aside from Euodia and Syntyche, are commended and presented as examples to be emulated. Notably, the appeals of 1:27 and 2:16 have no limit but are addressed to all the Philippians. I conclude with Green, O'Brien, Fee, Schnabel, I.H. Marshall, Plummer and others that Paul in actual fact envisaged *all believers* involved in the proclamation of the

[4] See Introduction.

gospel as led by their call and 'commission' through the Spirit. Consequently, pneumatology and especially *charismata* become a critical component in the discussion. Hence, I would argue that while all are to be soteriologically motivated with a concern for the salvation of the lost (and the found) (cf. 1 Cor 10:33), the extent of each person's involvement would vary.

On the basis of Eph 4:11-12 in particular,[5] the role of the 'specialists' with a divine call and commission to proclaim the gospel (cf. Gal 1:15-16; 1 Cor 9:16; Rom 1:14-15); namely, the 'heralds', 'co-workers', 'evangelists', 'apostles' was two-fold. First, their task was to continue to fulfil the commission and their call of proclamation. Secondly, they were to equip others from the congregations for the task of continuing to preach the gospel. In a first century context as evidenced by Paul's imitation language, a wedge cannot be driven through these two tasks. Rather, it is primarily through the doing of evangelism with the 'specialists' that the others are equipped to do so. This is the pattern found in Jesus' training of the disciples[6] and in Paul's imitation model. Evangelism like so much of the faith is caught as much as taught.

In-so-doing I suggest that these 'specialists' would find others with a similar strong sense of call and commision to evangelistic mission and they would take them under their wing and encourage them in this (cf. Jesus - the twelve; Paul - Timothy; Paul - co-workers). Although it cannot be conclusively demonstrated, it is likely that this happened in every one of the Pauline churches. This naturally led to a two-fold mode of mission. First it led to the 'career-proclaimer' mode whereby people gave up their 'marketplace role' for the evangelistic mission; or, as in the case of Paul, while having a 'vocational call', they voluntarily renounced this right, and were to some degree or another, self-supporting. Secondly, it led to the 'marketplace-Christian' who continued in their vocation supporting the mission in prayer and financially while witnessing as able ethically, in public worship, socially, charismatically,[7] apologetically and, *where appropriate*, proactively. All modes stand within Paul's soteriological imperative (cf. 1 Cor 10:31) and involves all manner of attitude, deed and word which enhances the potential for salvation for the recipient, whether as-yet an unbeliever or a believer. Hence, this is not whole-sale proactive confrontational proclamation, but a whole life given over to seeing others drawn to the gospel and Christ.

As noted above, Paul blended the two modes, continuing as a tentmaker whilst preaching the gospel. Consequently it is self-evident that Paul did not want all believers to give up paid employment and go into missionary service.

---

[5] See also 2 Tim 4:2, 5 where Timothy is encouraged to 'do the work of an evangelist' as one component of his ministry in Ephesus.

[6] See Matt 9:36-10:15 where Jesus traveled from town to town engaging in mission and then sent the disciples out to do the same (cf. Mk 6:6b-13; Lk 9:1-6; 10:1-12).

[7] In signs and wonders and the power of the Spirit (cf. Rom 15:19; 2 Cor 12:12; 1 Thess 1:5).

Rather, it seems that Paul encouraged his believers to emulate his example of working-mission, earning a living and sharing the gospel in and through the context of work (2 Thess 3:6-10 cf. 1 Thess 4:11-12; 1 Cor 7:17-24). Where an individual received a clear call of God and where their spiritual gifting and character (cf. 1 Cor 13) was compatible with the call, it is probable that these individuals were set apart for full-time service to the gospel (2:22, 25; 4:2-3 cf. 1 Cor 3:1-9). While Paul preferred a working-model of mission, he accepted the right of others to receive a living from the gospel (1 Cor 9:1-18). These preachers of the gospel would be supported through other Christians.

Neither can it be argued on the basis of Philippians that verbal witness should be limited to mere response to enquiry (Col 4:6 cf. 1 Pet 3:15). As I have suggested, the military and athletic imagery utilised in 1:27 suggest movement forward with the 'sword of the Spirit' with 'feet fitted with the gospel of peace' presenting the gospel lovingly to the pagan environment (Eph 6:15, 17). Indeed the only 'movement' weapon in the Christian armoury is the shoes, whilst the only 'attacking' weapon is the sword; both of which I have argued are evangelistic. The image of 'holding forth' also suggests lovingly offering the gospel to unbelievers allowing them the opportunity to reject or accept the gospel (Phil 2:16).

Furthermore, this commitment to evangelism is not to recede into retreatism or quietism when the church faces opposition, persecution and even suffering. I suggest that the appeal of 1:27-30 is an encouragement to continue and live in accordance with the gospel, standing firm in the Spirit and actively proclaiming the gospel in word and lifestyle despite persecution (1:28-30 cf. 2:8). The rhetorical impact of the example of Paul himself in Rome and Philippi and of the Roman 'brothers and sisters' reiterates this commitment (1:30 cf. 1:14-18a; 22).

The Philippians were to witness both in living in accordance with the ethic of the gospel and through loving (1:9, 27; 2:15; 4:4) verbal communication of the gospel in their environment. Philippians also confirms that the evangelism of the Philippians was to be based on the high quality of the corporate life of the congregation, which was to be an attractive environment to the people of the wider community (2:15). This centipetal feature cannot be downplayed in favour of a primarily centrifugal mode of mission. Paul placed a huge emphasis on the quality of the churches *agapē* based *koinōnia* which undoubtedly is a critical component in his understanding of the churches role in mission cf. Jn 13:34-35.

That being the case, along with a number of recent writers I suggest that Fee's approach to Philippians among modern commentators is closest to my own. He notes the centrality of the gospel mission to the epistle. He pre-empts some of my conclusions including 1:25 and 2:16. However I consider that further possibilities exist concerning the notion of good works, grace (cf. charismata) and evangelism (1:6, 7); the rhetorical and general import of 1:15-18a; the examples of Timothy and Epaphroditus; the evangelistic backdrop to the false examples of Judaisers (3:2) and so the appeals for imitation (3:17) and especially the concluding final appeal for imitation (4:9). I summarise my assessment in this way:

i. Paul wanted his congregations to be involved in evangelistic mission through the *prayer and financial support of the Pauline mission* and other recognised called and spiritually endowed preachers of the gospel.

ii. Paul wanted his congregations to witness to the gospel in verbal-responsive terms, through ethical witness in accordance with the gospel and in unity.

In addition to this:

iii. Paul wanted his congregations to continue the mission of Christ through gracious proactive verbal proclamation of the gospel in their context, whether in public services, homes, workplaces or elsewhere.[8]
iv. This mission is to involve all members of the congregation in accordance with their call, spiritual gifting, context and ability.
v. Some with special endowment recognised by Paul, co-workers and/or the leadership of the local church, were set apart as ministers of the gospel to be supported by the congregation.
vi. These leaders had the responsibility of continuing the mission, modelling the mission, leading the mission endeavours and equipping others for the task of evangelisation in their social world.
vii. Paul did not expect them all to give up their mode of employment having modelled to his congregations a working-model of evangelism for them to emulate.
viii. The verbal communication was to be accompanied by witness through lifestyle in accordance with the ethics of the gospel and community unity. The overriding motivation is soteriological, living holistically in a manner that gives the greatest hope that another, whether a believer or unbeliever, may be saved.
ix. Paul expected this evangelism and living to incite resistance and persecution from opponents but encouraged his congregations to continue to witness in love in the face of persecution.

I conclude then on the basis of my analysis of Philippians that Paul is far from silent on the issue of congregational evangelism. To come to the conclusion that whole congregations were not to continue the mission of Paul into their towns or regions would require one of four alternatives.

First, a consistent exegetical approach based on an externally applied assumption, which rules out congregational evangelism in any other disputed texts and the downplaying or limiting of indications of evangelistic interaction from ordinary Christians (cf. 1 Cor 7:12) and appeals for imitation (esp. 1 Cor 11:1; Phil 4:9). In the cases of Phil 1:27 and 4:9 we have good examples. Such

[8] Paul places no limitation on context.

a limitation is in fact very difficult to argue for.

Secondly, making the *a priori* assumption that only certain Christians are to share the faith. It is apposite to note that at no point does Paul limit evangelism to certain people. This is indicated in Philippians where at no point does Paul qualify texts concerning evangelistic involvement to certain groups or people.[9] In addition, none of the general statements concerning Christian living have a caveat 'except for evangelism' (cf. 1:9, 11, 27a; 2:12). Furthermore, as I.H. Marshall notes, 'no hard and fast line can be drawn between those who worked locally and those who worked with Paul. The work of evangelism was not confined to a Pauline travelling team but was carried on locally.'[10]

Thirdly, maintaining that some form of prohibition concerning general involvement in evangelism pre-exists the letters. However there is no indication of such a prohibition in the Paulines or in Luke's account of Paul's mission. Paul only expressed concern at others preaching the gospel where they distorted the message (cf. 3:2-3). I suggest that in the case of Philippians for example, Paul's appeal for imitation in 4:9 would require an 'except for evangelism' clause, for evangelism to be ruled out of the orb of its appeal. Similarly, 1 Cor 11:1 would read something like: 'imitate me as I imitate Christ, *except in evangelism*'; especially in light of 1 Cor 9 which focuses on aspects of Paul's gospel mission. Furthermore, in that Paul appeals consistently to evangelistic role models in Philippians, it would require some such qualification for the hearer not to be motivated to evangelise through his rhetoric. In reality, the opposite of a prohibition appears to be the case at Paul's place of imprisonment. His reaction to others preaching the gospel is utterly positive despite some of the preachers doing so through shady motives (cf. Phil 1:18a).

Finally, it would require the imposition of an external model upon the Paulines that leads the exegete to interpret texts in a certain manner. This I see in the approach of Dickson who interprets Paul according to his analysis of Second Temple Judaism. As I have indicated in regard to Philippians, at times this is strained (1:5, 27; 2:16). In my introductory comments on methodology, I argue that such an approach is hazardous in that it can impose on the text an external perspective which is not completely justified. I argue that exegetical analysis in regard to the content of the letters of Paul must be the primary reference point for the discussion. If there is to be an external point of comparison to the Pauline letters themselves, the writings of the early church and particularly the Paul of Acts should be uppermost in mind. I am not aware of any point in the New Testament where evangelism is limited to a particular group. The evangelistic mission of Christ was to be continued by the church spearheaded by set apart, Spirit-inspired and equipped proclaimers who catalysed others into mission. At no point is a limitation made on who is to

---

[9] Supremely seen in the involvement of women in evangelism (4:2-3 cf. Rom 16:3, 6, 7, 12; 1 Cor 7:16;14:24-25 in the light of 11:5).

[10] Marshall, 'Theology', 156-157.

continue the mission.

I conclude then that the hearer of Paul's letters and Philippians in particular, would have been inspired by the example of Christ, by his own example, by the example of other such preachers, the desire to please God, a fear of God, Paul's appeals for imitation, Paul's missionary strategy, the impulse of the Spirit, the urgings of those charismatically equipped and called to evangelism, to share their faith to their communities.[11] In the absence of a prohibition to proclaim, believers who had experienced the loving grace of salvation in Christ could not have been stopped from sharing the gospel.

Implications for Practice

The implications for practice are significant. The church is to continue the evangelistic mission of Christ. All believers are called to be involved in supporting this mission through prayer and financial contribution. In addition all believers are called to ethical witness, *koinōnia* and verbal communication to unbelievers in accordance with their faith and spiritual gifting. Each church too has a responsibility to seek to evangelise the people with whom they come into contact with in their daily lives in the marketplace, family, social networks; in their village, city or region. As Paul strategised to complete his mission to the Gentiles through a carefully conceived strategy, so the church is to do the same in its own context.

Such a mission is to be led by the spiritually endowed who equip others for their role in the mission. I consider that the ministries of apostle and evangelist connected to local churches are one of the keys to furthering the evangelistic task. Rather than merely being isolated itinerants, these individuals should function out of, in and through local churches and/or groups of churches, leading the mission by engaging in evangelism, church planting and, most importantly, equipping others for evangelism. More attention needs to be given by Christian training institutions to producing such people with a sense of call, the necessary gifting accompanied with Christian character along with a sound theological, missiological and sociological understanding. These individuals will then be prepared to go out and take up positions in local churches or collectives of churches that can support them prayerfully and financially. In some cases they will function as 'tentmakers', modelling mission in the marketplace, as did Paul.

The church is to be a loving, attractive community of grace consistent with the ethic of the gospel and into which unbelievers, seekers and new converts are welcomed. The resistance of the unbelieving community to the churches' efforts to evangelise should not lead the churches being inhibited by any persecution. Rather, in love, and with great courage (1:14), the church is to

---

[11] I could also add theological dimensions such as the potential destruction of the lost, the love of God and desire for all to be saved, which I have not discussed in this thesis.

continue to hold forth the word of life as it witnesses in attitude, word and deed to the community.

Limitations and Future Research

At this point it is helpful to make some comments on the limitations of my approach and future research options. Having made my case I concede that I along with other analysts have brought to the text a certain bias. In my case I come as an evangelistically inclined 'evangelical - charismatic' with a penchant to sometimes read texts optimistically. However in this analysis, I have sought to critically assess and present the material to show that the conclusions are reasonable. Consequently, I am confident that this work presents one reasonable way of interpreting the data of Paul and Philippians.

My methodology represents only one way of approaching the subject. Thematic analysis of Paul's strategy, the idea of his use of imitation, 'gospel' and other themes are other ways of approaching the subject. Further analysis and comparison with religious and philosophical groups from the environment and a comparison with Paul will be helpful in establishing the parameters of the issue. My suggestion concerning the links between the other writings of the NT and Paul requires examination of the various paradigms of evangelism in the different writings to assess the role of the congregation in evangelism. The development of the evangelistic mission in the post-apostolic period can also inform this subject; giving insight into the way the early church understood the apostolic commission. In-depth analysis of the connection between the implicit evangelistic implications of Paul's theology of salvation would be another way of coming at the issue. Finally, historical analysis of evangelism and the history of the church would yield important data in terms of the way that the Spirit has continued to inspire evangelism from God's people.

In the end, however, the best approach to the question remains in-depth exegetical analysis of the Pauline epistles asking the question 'what evidence exists explicitly, implicitly and rhetorically of the role of the congregations in evangelistic mission?' Accordingly, further exegetical work is required to confirm my conclusion that Paul did want his congregations to further the evangelistic mission from their church contexts. In particular I consider in-depth examination of 1 Corinthians (esp. 1 Cor 4:15-16; 7:16; 9:24c; 10:31-11:1 [in the light of 8:1-11:1 and esp. 9:19-22]; 12:8; 14:24-25; 15:58; 16:16), Ephesians (Eph 2:10; 4:7-16; 6:15, 17), Colossians (Col 1:6-10; 3:17; 4:5-6) and 1 Thessalonians (1 Thess 1:2, 6-8) within the rhetoric and purpose of their contexts would be potentially fruitful in this regard.

I expect that analysis of these texts, many of which I have discussed to some degree or another as have other writers in this area,[12] will confirm and nuance the findings of this analysis. That is, although Paul at one level appears to be

[12] See especially Plummer and Schnabel (for detail see General Introduction).

silent on the matter of congregational evangelism; in reality, there are a number of indications that surface suggesting that submerged beneath the surface of the letters, is a passion that his converts, led by evangelists and other 'specialist proclaimers', take up the challenge of sharing the gospel to their cities and regions as they go about their everyday lives. The words of Bruce make a fitting summary to this discussion:

> Each local church might be compared to a garden planted in a wilderness, but the church's first concern was not to prevent the wilderness from encroaching on the garden, but rather to see to it that the garden took over more and more of the wilderness. The garden was not to be 'walled around'; its boundaries were to be flexible and expandable. To change the figure, each colony of heaven was to extend its territory and incorporate more and more of its neighbourhood. Every church was to be a missionary church, and the history of the expansion of early Christianity suggests that many churches realized and fulfilled this mission. Among those that did so the church of Philippi, like the other Macedonian churches, holds an honoured place.[13]

Finally, I encourage readers of this work to come together as the one people of God and to take up the clarion call of Scripture to preach the gospel through attitude, word and deed with gentleness and respect to those unbelievers we encounter. I exhort us all to remember the words of Paul in Phil 1:18a: '*The important thing is that in every way… Christ is proclaimed*!'

[13] F.F. Bruce, 'St Paul in Macedonia': 284.

APPENDIX 1

The Connection Between Evangelism and the Military Metaphor in Paul

Military Metaphor and Paul's Ministry

An analysis of Paul's use of military imagery shows that evangelism is often prominent in the context in which he uses the image. In a number of Paul's references to Christian life and ministry as warfare, evangelism is explicitly within the scope of his thinking.[1] In the case of Paul's own ministry this is explicit and dominant. In this appendix I will briefly give evidence to this claim.

In the first place, in 2 Cor 6:7 Paul speaks of his own ministry using *weapons of righteousness* (ὅπλων τῆς δικαιοσύνης).[2] Although non-specific, in light of the centrality of evangelism to Paul's life (cf. 2 Cor 5:11, 14, 18-6:3) and the connection in Paul between evangelism and hand-weaponry (Eph 6:17[3] cf. 2 Tim 3:16-4:5), it is reasonable to suggest that this alludes in some sense to evangelism (cf. Rom 1:17; 2 Cor 10:3-5).[4] This is more probable through the preceding reference to the gospel of truth and in the power of God (ἐν λόγῳ ἀληθείας, ἐν δυνάμει θεοῦ [6:7a]), which are expressed through (διά) the

---

[1] Paul also refers to military image in terms of being taken captive by the triumphant Christ (2 Cor 2:14 cf. 4:10); thus, the believer is a captive of Christ.

[2] Garland, *2 Corinthians*, 310: a subjective genitive i.e. 'the weapons provided by righteousness.'

[3] See further on Eph 6:17 below.

[4] Hughes, *2 Corinthians*, 231. Barnett, *2 Corinthians*, 330 notes δεξιῶν καὶ ἀριστερῶν suggests being 'thoroughly equipped.' While this has merit, I prefer the view of Collins, *2 Corinthians*, 110 who suggests weapons for attack ('right hand' = sword) and defence ('left hand' = shield) are indicated (cf. Belleville, *2 Corinthians*, 171). If so, evangelism is found in the right hand. Alternatively Paul's ministry of confirmation and defence may be in mind (Phil 1:7). Best, *2 Corinthians*, 62 sees Paul is prepared for 'good fortune'=right and 'ill fortune'=left which I consider less likely in light of Paul's regular use of military metaphor.

agency of these weapons (cf. Rom 15:19-20; 1 Thess 1:5).[5] Furthermore, the connection between weaponry and evangelism is explicit in 10:4.[6] It is highly possible that Paul here has in mind 'the sword of the Spirit' (6:17) and 'the shield of faith' (Eph 6:16) in his hands. Thus, it is through the weapons of righteousness, through glory and dishonour and through bad report and good report, that Paul has thus ministered. It is most likely that Paul has evangelism in mind in this construction.

Later in 2 Cor 10:3-5 Paul clearly connects military imagery to his evangelistic ministry. In 10:1-2 he issues a warning to those in Corinth who accuse Paul of walking according to the flesh in the sense of lacking 'the empowering Spirit in his ministry.'[7] In 10:3 he refutes this charge by summarising how he and his team[8] do indeed conduct their ministry with the weaponry of God and not the world.[9] While Paul concedes that he and his team are human ('walking in the flesh') his mode of engaging in mission (στρατευόμεθα) is not worldly (οὐ κατὰ σάρκα στρατευόμεθα). More specifically, in 10:4 the weapons he and his team utilises are not the weapons of the world (τὰ γὰρ ὅπλα τῆς στρατείας ἡμῶν οὐ σαρκικὰ).

Paul then describes the source and effects of the weapons he uses. That is, they have 'divine power' (δυνατὰ τῷ θεῷ) i.e. their power source is God.[10] Paul does not develop what the 'power' is, but explains how he utilises this power.[11] Namely, this divine power is exercised in his ministry to do four things. The first three are the negative demolition ('pull down') of things that oppose God including 'strongholds' (δυνατὰ τῷ θεῷ πρὸς καθαίρεσιν ὀχυρωμάτων), 'argumentation' (λογισμοὺς καθαιροῦντες) and 'every exalted obstacle raised up against the knowledge of God' (πᾶν ὕψωμα

[5] Barnett, *2 Corinthians*, 330 considers the weapons to be the status of righteousness as opposed to false ministry (2 Cor 3:9; 11:13-14).

[6] Kruse, *2 Corinthians*, 133 writes 'what we see here is the offensive weapon of gospel presentation and argumentation... whereby the power of God is released to bring about the overthrow of false arguments and folly and bring people to the obedience of faith' cf. Belleville, *2 Corinthians*, 171.

[7] Barnett, *2 Corinthians*, 462 cf. Thrall, *2 Corinthians*, 607; Martin, *2 Corinthians*, 304; Lambrecht, *2 Corinthians*, 154.

[8] The shift to the third person in 10:3-5 probably refers to the Pauline team rather than the 'royal I.'

[9] I consider that Paul has both the opposing Corinthians and his general ministry in mind (see Barnett, *2 Corinthians*, 465-469). The general reference is clear through the recurring use of πᾶς in v.5.

[10] Probably a dative of advantage i.e. 'powerful for God's cause' (so Furnish, *2 Corinthians*, 457; Thrall, *2 Corinthians*, II.609). While a semitism is possible (i.e. 'divinely powerful' [cf. Jonah 3:3 {LXX}]) it is unlikely that the Corinthians would understand it as such. Alternatively a *dat. commodi* (cf. Phil 1:27): 'God can work powerfully through these weapons' cf. Martin, *2 Corinthians*, 305.

[11] Garland, *2 Corinthians*, 345 notes Paul does not specify the weapons but emphasises their effect.

ἐπαιρόμενον κατὰ τῆς γνώσεως τοῦ θεοῦ). Finally, after storming the opposition, Paul positively 'takes captive every notion to obey Christ' (καὶ αἰχμαλωτίζοντες πᾶν νόημα εἰς τὴν ὑπακοὴν τοῦ Χριστοῦ).

The four concepts have a strongly apologetic feel, referring to patterns of thinking, which Paul encounters and challenges in his mission. The first ὀχύρωμα ('stronghold, fortress, prison') is general and implies any area of resistance to the gospel.[12] The second, λογισμός ('calculation, reasoning, reflection, thought') more specifically refers to all manner of thought that opposes the gospel including philosophy and Jewish anti-Christian notions of wisdom.[13] The third (ὕψωμα ἐπαιρόμενον) speaks of every concept, abstract or concrete, that is exalted by humanity against the gospel,[14] which finds its essence in the knowledge of God. The final concept 'every thought' refers to every mode of thinking (πᾶν νόημα) which does not concur with the revelation of Christ.[15] In the wider context Paul appears to be speaking about all manner of thinking, philosophy and false faith (cf. 2 Cor 4:4; 11:3),[16] that he encounters as he evangelises Jews (1 Cor 1:22, 24), Gentiles (1 Cor 1:20-25) and contends with false teachers (2 Cor 11:4, 13-15).[17]

All this suggests that the power he referred to initially (δυνατὰ τῷ θεῳ) is the gospel and its proclamation (1 Cor 1:17-18 cf. Rom 1:16).[18] More specifically, it is the message of the weak crucified Messiah (1 Cor 1:23; 2:2; 3:11; 15:3-5, 11-19; 2 Cor 1:19; 4:5; 11:4) who is the wisdom of God (1 Cor

---

[12] *BDAG*, 746: 'a strong military installation.' Thrall, *2 Corinthians*, 611 notes of the array of options for this (cf. Zech 9:12 [LXX]; Prov 21:22; Babel implying Sophists and a general interpretation from Graeco-Roman philosophic tradition), the latter is most likely.

[13] *BDAG*, 598; Thrall, *2 Corinthians*, 612: 'sophistries.' I think the 'reasoning' here is probably general and including the rival Jewish missionaries and Corinthians supporters.

[14] *BDAG*, 1046: 'all pride that rises against it.' Thrall, *2 Corinthians*, 613: 'every arrogant attitude raised in opposition' but limits it to the situation in Corinth. However, the adjective πᾶς rules out limiting it to Corinth, it must be general. Martin, *2 Corinthians*, 306: 'all lofty notions that oppose.'

[15] *BDAG*, 675 notes νόημα is 'thought' in general terms. Again the reference is general (as πᾶς indicates) but relevant to the opposition in Corinth.

[16] There is certainly a strong demonic dimension to Paul's understanding of this warfare seen in the work of Satan to blind the unbeliever and send corrupt teaching through false teachers in these passages i.e. Satan is the real opponent (cf. Eph 6:10-17) cf. Garland, *2 Corinthians*, 437.

[17] Barnett, *2 Corinthians*, 466: notes arguments from synagogues (1 Cor 1:20), Gentile intellectuals in the Agora (Acts 17:17-34).

[18] Garland, *2 Corinthians*, 435. 'From references elsewhere in the Corinthians correspondence, we can assume that Paul has in view the truth of the gospel, epitomised in the word of the cross (1 Cor 1:18, 23-24; 2:5; 2 Cor 6:7; see Rom 1:16), and the knowledge of God (2:14; 4:6)' cf. Furnish, *2 Corinthians*, 462; Kruse, *2 Corinthians*, 174-175 (cf. Rom 1:5). Or more generally, of the whole panoply of Eph 6:11-17 as Hughes, *2 Corinthians*, 350-351. If so, in my view, evangelism is included (see below).

2:6-8) accompanied by the power of God through the Spirit (1 Cor 2:5, 13-14; 4:20; 2 Cor 12:12). That is, Paul encounters the various philosophical and religious ideas in his world and, through the proclamation of the gospel of Christ empowered by the Spirit and revealed in signs and wonders, defeats the arguments of opponents. As Hafemann says, 'in particular, Paul's weapons are the manifold proclamation of the truth of the gospel in the power of the Spirit.'[19] Here I see the intimate connection between military imagery and evangelism in Paul.

Finally, in regards to Paul, in 1 Cor 15:32 Paul speaks of his ministry in terms of a specific occasion of fighting wild beasts (ἐθηριομάχησα ἐν 'Εφέσῳ). This is clearly metaphorical and refers to a period of intense battling in Ephesus against opponents in the context of evangelism (cf. 1 Cor 16:9 cf. Acts 19:31-40).[20]

Military Metaphor and the Gospel Ministry of Others

In militaristic allusions in Paul's references to co-workers, evangelism is prominent. Epaphroditus and Archippus are designated fellow-soldiers (συστρατιώτην μου cf. Phil 2:25 and Phm 2). As I have discussed, the four-fold appellation of Epaphroditus as 'brother', 'co-worker', 'fellow-soldier' and 'your apostle/Apostle' unequivocally indicates active involvement of evangelism.[21] It is also credible to suggest that the ministry (τὴν διακονίαν) Archippus was urged to complete was in some sense evangelistic (Col 4:17). Even more certain is evangelism in Paul's encouragement to Timothy to endure hardship as a good soldier of Christ (καλὸς στρατιώτης Χριστου Ιησοῦ) who is not concerned with 'practical matters of life' (τοῦ βίου πραγματείαις) but with pleasing his commanding officers (στρατολογήσαντι ἀρέσῃ) (2 Tim 2:3-4 cf. 1:6-8; 2:5-6; 3:14-4:5).

In addition, on three occasions he uses the term συναιχμάλωτους in the sense of 'fellow prisoner of war', applying it to the apostles Andronicus and Junia (Rom 16:7), the ministers and co-workers Aristarchus (Col 4:10) and Epaphras (Phm 23). These probably refer to fellow Christians imprisoned in the course of gospel ministry rather than merely being taken captive by Christ (cf. 2 Cor 2:14).[22] As I have discussed earlier, Andronicus and Junia were probably apostles and as such, were involved in the fullness of apostolic ministry including evangelism and church planting.[23] Aristarchus similarly was involved

---

[19] Hafemann, *2 Corinthians*, 395.

[20] Fee, *1 Corinthians*, 770-771, who notes the connection to 1 Cor 16:9; R.E. Osborne, 'Paul and the Wild Beasts', *JBL* 85 (1966): 225-230.

[21] See Chapter 6.

[22] So Hughes, *2 Corinthians*, 77-78; Furnish, *2 Corinthians*, 175; Martin, *2 Corinthians*, 46-47; Barnett, *2 Corinthians*, 150.

[23] See Chapter 3.

in ministry as Paul's travelling companion from Thessalonica in Macedonia. He was present with Paul in Ephesus and was seized with Gaius (Acts 19:29; 20:4; 27:2). It appears he was with Paul right through to his time in Rome being with Paul on his journey to Rome (Acts 27:2). He was with Paul in prison at the time of Colossians (Col 4:10) and Philemon (Phm 23). Consequently, it is reasonable to suppose he was actively involved in evangelism.

Epaphras is definitely an evangelist. Paul reminds the Colossians of his evangelistic ministry in Colossae making converts and establishing the church in Colossae (Col 1:7) and perhaps Laodicea (Col 2:1). This probably occurred during Paul's Ephesian ministry in which he gathered disciples together in the lecture hall of Tyrannus, a base from which the gospel was spread through the Asian region including the Lycus valley over a two year period (Acts 19:9-10).[24] Epaphras it seems, went to his hometown of Colossae, preached, made converts, and established the Christian community. He is with Paul in prison at the time of the writing of Colossians (Col 4:12; Phm 23). Paul's language in 4:12 suggests Epaphras was from Colossae (ὁ ἐξ ὑμῶν);[25] he is also designated a δοῦλος Χριστοῦ [Ἰησοῦ] who wrestled (ἀγωνιζόμενος) in prayer and experienced 'much pain' (πολὺν πόνον) for the Colossians and Laodiceans. Clearly Epaphras was a praying and contending evangelist/church planter who was part of the Colossian congregation and perhaps a native Colossian. Indeed he may well have been an Apostle, as is Epaphroditus (cf. Eph 4:11).

In 1 Thess 5:8 Paul appeals to the Thessalonians to put on the elements of the armour of God listing in general terms faith, love and the hope of salvation. As noted in my discussion in Chapter 9 of the 1 Thess 1:6-8; 2:14-16, evangelism was a feature of the Thessalonian context. The three elements of the armour, faith (πίστις), love (ἀγάπη) and hope (ἐλπίς) also feature in the thanksgiving (1 Thess 1:3) which precedes Paul's reference to the Thessalonican mission to spread the gospel in their region. Hence, again there is a link between the notions to evangelism.

Ephesians 6 and Evangelism

The passage Eph 6:10-18 is undoubtedly the *crux interpretum* in regard to Paul's military imagery and evangelism. Here two of the five elements of the Christian armoury are explicitly evangelistic[26] while the others are potentially

---

[24] It is possible that the Seven Churches of Rev 2-3 were planted in this period.

[25] MacDonald, *Colossians*, 181; O'Brien, *Colossians*, 252; Dunn, *Colossians*, 280; Wright, *Colossians*, 158; Bruce, *Epistles*, 181: 'the Colossians own evangelist.'

[26] Fee, *Empowering*, 730 considers prayer as the seventh element. I prefer to see it as the foundation element to the whole armour (see further below). This distinction is minor in practice, constant prayer being essential to a Christian's spiritual progress.

so.[27] Paul begins by commanding the Christian recipients of his letter (soldiers) to 'be strong in the Lord and in his mighty power' and to 'put on the full armour of God' (πανοπλίαν τοῦ θεου) so that they can take their stand (στῆναι) against the devil's schemes. He goes on to describe the nature of the battle as not merely a battle with human agency ('flesh and blood'), but a spiritual battle against demonic forces.[28] In this battle the believer is to 'put on

---

[27] One can perhaps argue that all elements of the armoury can be seen to be evangelistic in some sense although this may be stretching things a little especially if the OT picture of Yahweh the Warrior is definitive and/or if the nature of the weapon dictates meaning. First, as I have noted, in Ephesians 'truth' is directly connected to the gospel and its proclamation (cf. Eph 1:13; 4:15, 24 cf. 5:9]). Hence 'belt of truth' may well have a gospel dimension cf. Wood, 'Ephesians', 87; O'Brien, *Ephesians*, 474; Snodgrass, *Ephesians*, 342 who sees both ethical and evangelistic interpretations here. Barth, *Ephesians*, II.768; Mitton, *Ephesians*, 225 see a connection while favouring an ethical interpretation (cf. Is 11:5). Lincoln, *Ephesians*, 448; Schnackenburg, *Ephesians*, 277; Foulkes, *Ephesians*, 181 prefer the ethical. Secondly, and more tangentially, 'righteousness' is not without evangelistic connections in Pauline thinking (see Rom 1:17 [righteousness as a facet of gospel, the power of God for salvation in 1:16 cf. 3:22]); 2 Cor 3:9 ['the ministry of righteousness']; 2 Cor 11:5; 6:7 ['weapons of righteousness'; see above]). In addition, Paul uses righteousness holistically in Eph 4:24; 5:9. While in the context it is developed ethically and relationally (Eph 4:25-6:9), the passage includes an appeal for imitation of God and in particular Christ's sacrificial death for the salvation of believers (Eph 5:1-2) just as it includes a word of worship (Eph 5:5, 19-20). Lincoln, *Ephesians*, 448; Foulkes, *Ephesians*, 181-182; Wood; 'Ephesians', 87; Mitton, *Ephesians*, 225; O'Brien, *Ephesians*, 474; Snodgrass, *Ephesians*, 342 see it ethically (cf. Is 59:17; Wis 5:18). Barth, *Ephesians*, II. 769-771 prefers soteriological righteousness. Thirdly, and least likely, is the shield of 'faith.' Πίστις is sometimes used by Paul as 'gospel' (Gal 1:23; 1 Thess 1:8; 1 Tim 2:7 cf. Rom 1:8; 2 Cor 4:13; 10:15; Phil 1:27. However, in Ephesians it is not used in this way so 'believing faith', ongoing trust in God (so Mitton, *Ephesians*, 226; Lincoln, *Ephesians*, 449; Foulkes, *Ephesians*, 183) and faithfulness to God are probably in mind (Eph 1:15; 2:8; 3:12, 17; 4:5, 13; 6:23). Similarly O'Brien, *Ephesians*, 479-480. Alternatively the 'faithfulness of God' so Snodgrass, *Ephesians*, 343; Barth, *Ephesians*, II.773 who also adds 'the faithful service of the one who is anointed by God' (including evangelism? Cf. Wood, 'Ephesians', 88 who notes the active and content senses are both in mind). Finally, the helmet of salvation (σωτήριον) could involve seeking to save others. The concept of salvation is connected to evangelism on many occasions in Paul (cf. Phil 2:15-16a in light of 2:13 'work out your salvation' [see Chapter 5]). O'Brien, *Ephesians*, 481 suggests confidence in God's *present* salvation which is emphasised in Ephesians cf. Wood, 'Ephesians', 88; Mitton, *Ephesians*, 227; Lincoln, *Ephesians*, 450. He sees it in active terms and so maybe evangelism? Alternatively Barth, *Ephesians*, II. 775-776 sees it as the 'helmet of victory' i.e. the victory of God, present and future. Snodgrass, *Ephesians*, 343; Foulkes, *Ephesians*, 183 see it as assurance of protection both present and future (Is 59:17; 1 Thess 5:8).

[28] Taking the 'principalities and powers': 1) Not as *angels* (so W. Carr, *Angels and Principalities* (ed. R.M. Wilson; London: CUP, 1981); Schnackenburg, *Ephesians*, 273-

the full armour of God' so that they can stand up against the forces of evil which have invaded the world. He then develops his concept of Christian weaponry which is comprehensive and is an effective listing of concepts foundational to Paul's understanding of Christian living.

Two elements of the weaponry suggest that evangelism is explicitly part of *the general Christians* weaponry, the shoes and the sword and to these I now turn.

Your Feet Fitted with the Readiness that Comes from the Gospel of Peace (Eph 6:15)

The first τοὺς πόδας ἐν ἑτοιμασίᾳ τοῦ εὐαγγελίου τῆς εἰρήνης probably refers to the *caliga* which were a necessary part of the Roman soldiers equipment for long marches.[29] The image then is of the Christian as a soldier ready to journey to battle. The construction ἐν ἑτοιμασίᾳ is the subject of debate. The traditional view takes up the meaning of the Greek verb and renders it as 'preparedness' or 'readiness' with reference to the soldier's readiness for battle in some way.[30] This has been challenged by some including

---

274); or 2) Not as *socio-political structures* (so E.G. Rupp, *Principalities and Powers* (London: Epworth, 1952) 11-18; H. Berkhof, *Christ and the Powers* (tr. J. Yoder. Scottdale: Herald, 1977), 25) who while suggesting Paul may have conceived of the powers as personal beings, this is clearly secondary and makes little difference (similarly see G.B. Caird, *Principalities and Powers* (Oxford: Clarendon, 1956), 12-30; A.N. Wilder, *Kerygma, Eschatology and Social Ethics in the Background of Its Eschatology* (Cambridge: CUP, 1964), 509-536; J.H. Yoder, *The Politics of Jesus* (Grand Rapids: Eerdmans, 1972), 140-153; J. Ellul, *Apocalypse* (New York: Seabury, 1977)]; 3) Not as *both evil spirits as structures* (M. Barth, *Ephesians*, I.800-801; W. Wink, *Naming the Powers* (Philadelphia: Fortress, 1984); but 4) As *evil demonic spirits* who exercise their evil in a variety of ways including *through individuals and human structures* (so C.E. Arnold, *Ephesians*, 64-68, *Powers of Darkness* (Downers Grove: IVP, 1992) and 'The Exorcism of Ephesians 6:12 in Recent Research', *JSNT* 30 (1987) 73-74; R. Yates, 'The Powers of Evil in the New Testament', *EQ* 52 (1980) 99; G.E. Ladd, *A Theology of the New Testament* (Cambridge; Lutterworth, 1974), 401-402; Bruce, *Epistles*, 404-406; P.T. O'Brien, 'Principalities and Powers: Opponents of the Church' in D.A. Carson, *Biblical Interpretation and the Church* (Nashville: T. Nelson, 1984), 110-150, 111, *Consumed*, 121 and *Ephesians*, 466-470; Snodgrass, 340; M. Green, *I Believe in Satan's Downfall* (Grand Rapids: Michigan, 1981), 86-90; Fee, *Empowering*, 725; Foulkes, *Ephesians*, 179; Wood, 'Ephesians', 86; Mitton, *Ephesians*, 222; Lincoln, *Ephesians*, 444).

[29] TDNT 5.301; Schnackenburg, *Ephesians*, 278; Barth, *Ephesians*, 2.798, O'Brien, *Consumed*, 124 and *Ephesians*, 475.

[30] *BDAG*, 401 who list no alternative; *TDNT* 2.706; O'Brien, *Ephesians*, 477 who notes Ps 9:17 (LXX 9:38); *Wisdom* 13:12; *Epistle of Aristeas*, 182; Josephus, *Antiquities* 10:1.2 cf. *Consumed*, 124; Mitton, *Ephesians*, 226; Lincoln, *Ephesians*, 449; Snodgrass, *Ephesians*, 342; Schnackenburg, *Ephesians*, 178.

M. Barth, who argues ἐν ἑτοιμασίᾳ should be rendered 'steadfast.'[31] He does so for a number of reasons. First, he argues this on the basis of the LXX use where it is used for a stand or base (Ezra 2:68; 3:3; Zech 5:11).[32] Secondly, he contends that the primary purpose of shoes in Roman times was to provide solidity.[33] Thirdly, he contends that speed demanded an absence of sandals.[34] Hence, although Barth finds a link in the 'gospel of peace' to Is 52:7, he argues that there is no sense of messenger imagery here. Rather, 'Paul speaks of the equipment provided by God which makes the Christian able to "stand" and "resist".'[35]

However, I do not find these arguments at all convincing for the following reasons. First, as Lincoln notes, the term 'nowhere actually means "firm footing," and its more usual sense is "readiness, preparedness, or preparation".'[36] Secondly, as Plummer notes, the term is never used in the LXX or the New Testament in the sense of 'firm footing' or 'steadfastness.' In the examples above from the LXX, 'the *preparedness* of the position or foundation is still determinative.'[37] Thirdly, it appears arbitrary to suggest that, while the 'gospel of peace' clearly alludes to Is 52:7, there is no carry over of the sense of a messenger into the verb. This is particularly surprising in that Barth, in Eph 2:17, explicitly links Jesus' proclamation ministry to Is 52:7.[38] If indeed Is 52:7 is in the mind of Paul in 2:17 as Barth suggests, in light of his use of it elsewhere (cf. Rom 10:15), it must be considered in interpreting the verb's meaning. It is also notable that, in contrast to the helmet, shield, belt and breastplate, the shoes do suggest movement and not mere solidity, which counts against a totally static interpretation.[39] Neither is the concept of 'standing' necessarily a static affair but involves, at least in Phil 1:27, 'contending for the faith of the gospel.' As I have argued above, this most likely implies proactive movement. Similarly the notion of a soldier itself is not a totally static

---

[31] Barth, *Ephesians*, 798; Wood, 'Ephesians', 88; Dickson, *Mission-Commitment*, 118-119; Foulkes, *Ephesians*, 182.

[32] Barth, *Ephesians*, 2.770; 797-9; Dickson, *Mission-Commitment*, 118.

[33] Barth, *Ephesians*, 798.

[34] Barth, *Ephesians*, 799.

[35] Barth, *Ephesians*, 799.

[36] Lincoln, *Ephesians*, 449; O'Brien, *Ephesians*, 477; Schnabel, *Mission*, 1464.

[37] Plummer, *Understanding*, 78.

[38] Barth, *Ephesians*, II.770, 798-799 indeed notes the connection to Eph 2:17 (I.267) and to 'gospel of peace' here.

[39] Again a point Barth, *Ephesians*, 798 notes, making it rather arbitrary to exclude it here. Whether or not *speed of movement* for the proclamation of the gospel is at issue is neither here nor there. Similarly, if 'standing' was the issue here then surely the boot would have been a more likely option as they were utilised in this way in the manner of a spiked rugby boot, as Barth, *Ephesians*, II.798 himself points out. What is at stake is long sustained movement with the gospel as led by the Spirit of God cf. Arnold, *Powers*, 156-158.

conception, but implies movement as does Paul's own ministry as a soldier for Christ.[40] In fact, the idea in a ancient near eastern and Roman world or military conquest (or any other for that matter), of a soldier merely stuck to the spot seems rather strange to say the least! That being the case, I consider it is better to opt for the traditional rendering of 'readiness or preparedness.'

What is the believer to be prepared for? Some who take ἐν ἑτοιμασίᾳ adverbially as 'steadfast' take the genitive construction τοῦ εὐαγγελίου τῆς εἰρήνης in ways that reinforce this position.[41] So it can be understood as a genitive of origin implying that this 'security' derives from the gospel. Dickson takes it as a genitive of apposition, the shoes referring to the gospel that Jesus preached (2:17) itself. Hence, the believer is steadfast in the shoes, which are the gospel, suggesting fidelity and not proclamation.[42] Another possibility is to take it subjectively i.e. 'the readiness that the gospel of peace confers.' In this interpretation the believer will be fitted with the readiness that the gospel of peace gives suggesting a defensive posture and no necessary movement to proclaim.

However, it seems to me that this is ruled out by the general notion of a soldier, who in all ages is at the ready to move at the beckoning of the commanding officer (2 Tim 2:4). In addition, the sense of movement has already been supplied by the notion of the *caliga*.[43] Similarly the connection to Is 52:7 supports this notion; 'the messenger whose beautiful feet glide over the mountaintops is ready to announce good tidings in Zion.'[44] It seems then that the genitive should be understood objectively i.e. 'the readiness to proclaim the gospel of peace.'[45] Hence, as elsewhere, εὐαγγέλιον is used in its *nomen actionis* sense, implying its proclamation as is often the case in Paul.[46] Certainly εὐαγγέλιον is in Ephesians linked to proclamation in every other

---

[40] O'Brien, *Ephesians*, 477.

[41] Foulkes, *Ephesians*, 182; Barth, *Ephesians*, II.771.

[42] Dickson, *Mission-Commitment*, 120.

[43] O'Brien, *Ephesians*, 477.

[44] O'Brien, *Ephesians*, 477; Schnabel, *Mission*, 1464.

[45] O'Brien, *Ephesians*, 477; Mitton, *Ephesians*, 226; Louw-Nida, *Lexicon*, 77.1; J.A. Robinson, *St Paul's Epistle to the Ephesians* (London: Macmillan, 1904), 215; F.F. Bruce, *The Epistle to the Ephesians* (London: Pickering and Inglis, 1961), 408; Radl, *EDNT*, 2:68; L. Morris, *Expository Reflections on the Letter to the Ephesians* (Grand Rapids: Baker, 1994), 206; Arnold, *Powers*, 157, *Ephesians*, 111; Schnackenburg, 278 who takes it holistically with an emphasis on human sense i.e. 'to proclaim God's peace and spread it abroad' cf. Lincoln, *Ephesians*, 449 who takes it objectively with no proclamatory notion; Schnabel, *Mission*, 1464: 'Paul speaks of "the readiness or preparation of the outward-going movement required for the proclamation of the good news of peace".'

[46] O'Brien, *Ephesians*, 477; Schnabel, *Mission*, 1464.

setting (cf. Eph 1:13;[47] 3:6;[48] 6:19[49]); as are the other ευαγγ - terms [εὐαγγελίζω [Eph 2:17: Christ's proclamation];[50] [Eph 3:8: Paul's proclamation]; εὐαγγελιστής [evangelists proclamation; Eph 4:11]).[51] The closest and most obvious connection is Eph 6:17 where the reference is to the word of God (ῥῆμα θεοῦ), which clearly suggests the gospel (see below). Accordingly, the believer is ready to move as led by the Spirit to share the word of God to unbeliever and believer alike (see further below).

The objective sense suggests the believer is equipped with a readiness to proclaim and live the gospel of peace.[52] The link to Is 52:7 suggests that verbal proclamation is in mind. In Isaiah, the prophet describes the joy that is brought by the messenger who announces the good news of *shalom* (שָׁלוֹם), and preaches good tidings' (מְבַשֵּׂר טוֹב) of salvation (יְשׁוּעָה) to the exiles held captive by the Babylonians.[53] The prophet comes proclaiming the good news of God's salvation to a desperate people held captive to overwhelming military powers. Here in Eph 6:15 the Christian is ready to proclaim the message of God's salvation to the people held captive by the spiritual forces of evil so that they may be saved.

It should also be noted that in the context of Ephesians, this proclamation cannot be limited to verbal communication but also to living the gospel. Indeed the image of shoes calls to mind Paul's favoured περιπατέω imagery of the whole Christian life as 'walking.' The peace is primarily reconciliation (ἀποκαταλλάξῃ) between God and humanity achieved through the cross (Eph 1:2; 2:1-10, 14, 17-18 cf. Is 52:7), but also carries the nuance of human peace, which the gospel brings to all people and races (Gentile and Jew) within the

---

[47] Here the gospel is the 'word of truth' (τὸν λόγον τῆς ἀληθείας) which the recipients heard (ὑμεῖς ἀκούσαντες) and believed and which saved them (τῆς σωτηρίας ὑμῶν).

[48] Here in a comprehensive sense. That is, it is through the gospel (διὰ τοῦ εὐαγγελίου) in its content ('the unsearchable riches of Christ' [τὸ ἀνεξιχνίαστον πλοῦτος τοῦ Χριστοῦ]) proclaimed (cf. Eph 3:7, 8), heard, received and believed.

[49] Here of Paul's prayer to be more fearless in his preaching ministry to be (ἐν παρρησίᾳ γνωρίσαι τὸ μυστήριον τοῦ εὐαγγελίου).

[50] See also O'Brien, *Ephesians*, 477; Schnabel, *Mission*, 1464 who note the link cf. Col 4:6.

[51] See Chapter 6.

[52] C.E. Arnold, *Powers*, 157; O'Brien, *Ephesians*, 476.

[53] The nouns שָׁלוֹם suggesting 'completeness, soundness, welfare, peace' and translated εἰρήνης in the LXX (1022.2); יְשׁוּעָה meaning '*salvation* by God, primarily from external evils, but often with added spiritual idea' and translated σωτηρίαν in the LXX (447.1) and מְבַשֵּׂר טוֹב 'herald as glad tidings: the salvation of God, preach (142.1) and translated εὐαγγελιζόμενος ἀγαθά in the LXX so Brown, F. (2000). *Enhanced Brown-Driver-Briggs Hebrew and English Lexicon*. Strong's, TWOT, and GK references Copyright 2000 by Logos Research Systems, Inc. (280.1). Oak Harbor, WA: Logos Research Systems.

body of Christ (Eph 2:14, 15; 4:3; 6:23).[54] Hence, Paul is most probably urging his readers to be ready to proclaim the gospel of peace, which generates both peace with God and societal peace (Eph 2:14-17).[55] Critically, this is the only weapon of *spatial movement* in the armoury. Implied here is the truth that if the believer desists from engaging in evangelistic movement alongside the wielding of the word of God (the sword of the Spirit [below]) forward progress in the battle is lost.

Significantly, Paul includes all the church as soldiers of Christ who are to be ready to share the gospel with the lost. This concurs with my finding that evangelism is expected of the general believer in Eph 4:12-16, where Paul's vision of the leaders including the evangelists in the local church, equip the general believer for works of ministry/service. The leaders function in a sense as military officers who train the general soldiers for the rigours of war. In time, as they reach maturity in their profession and display the necessary giftings, some of them will move into leadership themselves. Interestingly, Epaphroditus is termed 'soldier' in Phil 2:25 suggesting his leadership role in the equipping of the Philippians for their engagement with the lost in Philippi. Similarly Archippus is termed soldier in Colossae (Phm 2; Col 4:7).

The Sword of the Spirit, Which is the Word of God (6:17)

The second reference (καὶ τὴν μάχαιραν τοῦ πνεύματος, ὅ ἐστιν ῥῆμα θεοῦ in 6:17) is even more explicit than 6:15.[56] Here Paul calls for the believer to take up the only offensive weapon in the armour, the sword. 'Sword' (μάχαιρα) here refers to the short, straight sword used by the Roman soldiers for cutting and stabbing in the context of close combat.[57] The sword was ideal for hand-to-hand defensive and aggressive warfare.[58] This element of the armoury is the only one that can be used for both attack and defence.[59] Hence,

[54] Both indicatively and imperatively. See further O'Brien, *Ephesians*, 478.

[55] O'Brien, *Ephesians*, 477; Bruce, *Epistles*, 408; J.R.W. Stott, *The Message of Ephesians: God's New Society* (Leicester: IVP, 1979), 280; Schnackenburg, *Ephesians*, 278; Mitton, *Ephesians*, 226.

[56] Accordingly, my conclusion concerning Eph 6:15 is not essential to this thesis.

[57] See Louw-Nida, *Lexicon*, 6.33; O'Brien, *Ephesians*, 481. Unlike the long sword or ῥομφαία used for both cutting and piercing (Rom 8:35; 13:4).

[58] As Schnabel, *Mission*, 1464 notes, 'a "defensive" interpretation does not make sense, the short sword was an offensive weapon.'

[59] O'Brien, *Ephesians*, 482 i.e. not just attack. So also Schnackenburg, *Ephesians*, 279; Lincoln, *Ephesians*, 451. Similarly Phil 1:7 with the 'defence and confirmation of the gospel.' However to argue the sword is merely a defensive weapon is arbitrary and reductionist (Foulkes, *Ephesians*, 184; Wood, 'Ephesians', 89 on the basis that Jesus' temptation is the most obvious connection cf. Bruce, *Epistles*, 410). However, this connection is far from obvious contextually.

the sword of the Spirit has both a strong apologetic and proactive ring to it.[60] The connection of sword and God's spiritual word is not an innovation but is found in the OT (Is 49:2), the NT (Heb 4:12-13; Rev 19:15 cf. 2 Thess 2:8; Is 11:4) and Judaism.[61]

The genitive construction μάχαιραν τοῦ πνεύματος can be rendered in different ways. It is unlikely that here is a genitive of apposition, which would read: 'the sword which is the Spirit.'[62] As this leads to an identification of the Spirit with word of God it should be ruled out. Paul's reasoning would be thus: 'take up the sword, which is the Spirit, which is the word of God.' The identification of Spirit and word 'poses almost insuperable problems.'[63] Neither does such an interpretation continue Paul's identification of one meaning to each weapon.[64]

Others understand the genitive subjectively as 'the sword that springs from the Spirit' or as a genitive of origin or authorship 'the sword given by this Spirit.'[65] Barth, following Abbott, suggests it should be read, 'the sword which the Spirit gives you.'[66] However while this thought coheres with the spiritual origin of the 'word' (cf. 2 Tim 3:16; 2 Pet 1:21), it is unlikely that this is in Paul's mind here.[67] Others suggest here a genitive of source indicating it is the Spirit that makes the sword powerful and effective (cf. Heb 4:12).[68] Alternatively as I prefer, it may simply be a possessive genitive i.e. 'the sword which the Spirit wields' through the believer.[69]

Whichever interpretation correctly gathers Paul's intent, the image is of the believer, empowered by the Spirit, picking up the gospel empowered by the

---

[60] Dickson, *Mission-Commitment*, 120-122 rules this out arguing that the emphasis is on taking up the sword without regard to offensive or defensive movement is clutching at straws. On the contrary, the metaphor implies a real opponent to be fought and the concept is not static. The application of what it means to be a soldier of Christ in Paul's mind in the widest sense includes movement in the case of himself, Timothy, Epaphroditus and others. What sort of soldier stands still with sword in hand in a real war?

[61] See Schnackenburg, *Ephesians*, 280 for references.

[62] O'Brien, *Ephesians*, 481 unlike earlier genitives 'breastplate of righteousness', 'shield of faith', 'helmet of salvation'; Mitton, *Ephesians*, 227.

[63] Barth, *Ephesians*, 2.776 cf. Schnackenburg, *Ephesians*, 279.

[64] O'Brien, *Ephesians*, 481.

[65] Mitton, *Ephesians*, 227, 'the sword which the Spirit provides' cf. the OT as given through the prophets.

[66] Barth, *Ephesians*, 2.776.

[67] Fee, *Empowering*, 728. If the genitive ῥῆμα θεοῦ is taken as a genitive of source, this concept is still retained.

[68] Fee, *Empowering*, 728; O'Brien, *Ephesians*, 482; Schnackenburg, *Ephesians*, 279; Lincoln, *Ephesians*, 451.

[69] F.W. Beare, The Epistle to the Ephesians' in IB, 597-749; Fee, *Empowering*, 728. Similarly Foulkes, *Ephesians*, 184.

Spirit. The relative pronoun ὅ can be taken either with πνεύμα or with the syntactic construction μάχαιραν τοῦ πνεύματος. As I have said, most are in agreement with the latter.[70] Hence the sword of the Spirit is identified with the word of God.

The ῥῆμα θεοῦ is the gospel message first preached by Christ (Eph 2:17) and then by Paul to his recipients (Eph 1:13) which saved them (Eph 1:4-8, 13; 2:1-10) and which Paul (Eph 3:7-8; 6:19), apostles and evangelists (Eph 2:20; 4:11) and general believers now preach (Eph 4:12, 15; 6:15, 17).[71] It is possible that ῥῆμα here emphasises the spoken 'message' at a particular point in distinction to the more content-orientated λόγος.[72] If so, the emphasis is on Spirit-led speaking of the message of Christ as an act of spiritual warfare.

As O'Brien puts it, 'Paul is ... stressing the actual speaking forth of the message, which is given its penetration and power by the Spirit.'[73] He goes on, 'in their warfare with the powers of darkness, they are to take hold of the word of God, the gospel (1:13; 6:15) and to proclaim it in the power of the Spirit... it is the faithful speaking forth of the gospel in the realm of darkness, so that men and women held by Satan might hear this liberating and life-giving word and be freed from his grasp.'[74] Similarly Lincoln notes, 'as believers take hold of and proclaim the gospel, they are enabled to overcome in battle.'[75] It is the Spirit that makes alive the word for salvation in any given moment. It is the Spirit who leads the believer in use of the sword. It is the Spirit who ultimately works through the believer to make effective the word of God. It is also the Spirit who inspires prayer for the mission and empowers it (Eph 6:18). This makes evident that for Paul, evangelism is a highly spiritual activity infused, empowered, enabled and achieved by the Spirit through human agency. This supports the notion that in part, the answer to the seeming silence on this issue lies in a full pneumatology, the Spirit will ensure that the mission of Christ continues through the people of God.

Notably, Fee writes, 'the "word of God" that is the Spirit's sword is the faithful speaking forth of the gospel in the arena of darkness, so that men and

---

[70] Lincoln, *Ephesians*, 451, M. Barth, *Ephesians*, 776, Schnackenburg, *Ephesians*, 279.

[71] Schnackenburg, *Ephesians*, 280; Lincoln, *Ephesians*, 451; Arnold, *Ephesians*, 111; Fee, *Empowering*, 729 cf. Rom 10:17. On ῥῆμα as the word of God see Rom 10:8 [τὸ ῥῆμα τῆς πίστεως ὃ κηρύσσομεν]; Rom 10:17 [ῥήματος Χριστοῦ cf. 10:18]; Eph 5:26 (cf. 2 Cor 12:4; 13:1; Matt 4:4; 26:75; 27:14; Mk 14:72; Lk 3:2; 7:1; 22:61; 24:8; Jn 3:34; 5:47; 6:63, 68; 8:20, 47; 12:47, 48; 14:10; 15:7; 17:8; Acts 5:20, 32; 10:37, 44; 11:14, 16; Heb 1:3; 6:5 [θεοῦ ῥῆμα]; 11:3 [ῥήματι θεοῦ]; 1 Pet 1:25 [ῥῆμα κυρίου... τὸ ῥῆμα τὸ εὐαγγελισθὲν εἰς ὑμᾶς]). Barth, *Ephesians*, II.777 includes here the OT and the words of Christ.

[72] Fee, *Empowering*, 729; O'Brien, *Ephesians*, 482.

[73] O'Brien, *Ephesians*, 482 cf. Fee, *Empowering*, 728-729; Lincoln, *Ephesians*, 451.

[74] O'Brien, *Ephesians*, 482.

[75] Lincoln, *Ephesians*, 451.

women might hear and be delivered from Satan's grasp.'[76] Schnabel puts it this way: 'Paul describes in Eph 6:15,17 the primary offensive action of Christians in the fight against the attacks of Satan: the active proclamation of the good news of Jesus' death on the cross, by which he defeated all evil power, and of his resurrection to life. The message is made effective and powerful by God's Spirit.'[77] Finally, Arnold posits, 'here the preaching of the gospel is depicted as the most aggressive manoeuvre against the realm of the devil and his host by the employment of the use of the sword ... the believer is admonished to take up the sword not merely for the self defence but also "to go on the attack and make new conquests in God's cause".'[78]

In Eph 6:18 Paul links the armour of God in some way to prayer ἐν πνεύματι. Fee's view that this is the continuation of the armour is unlikely as the metaphor is left behind.[79] The connective διὰ πάσης, most probably indicates that prayer underpins *all* the armour, the means by which the armour is appropriated and utilised. It is prayer then that gives the armour its effectiveness. Hence it could be rendered 'by means of.' If this is so interpreting the genitive in a possessive sense keeps the dynamic of the Spirit in prayer alive. The word is to be wielded by the believer as led by the Spirit through prayer. In a sense the believer who is filled with the Spirit (Eph 5:18), becomes akin to the incarnate Spirit fighting the spiritual forces of evil on the Spirit's behalf.

The image here portrays the Christian as a soldier thoroughly knowledgeable in the message of God, filled with and led by the Spirit, and so, equipped for war. This fullness of preparation comes through the equipping ministries of the charismatically inspired leaders including the evangelistically inclined apostles and evangelists (Eph 4:11-12). Not only are they prepared to live out the message; they are given a specific weapon to fight the spiritual powers, the word of God. This spiritual warfare also has a defensive and apologetic orientation, the believer, through the word of God, warding off false teaching. However, the 'sword of the Spirit is clearly also offensive and indicates proactive proclamation as essential to Paul's understanding of spiritual warfare.'[80] This necessarily implies a proclamatory dynamic, as I have argued. The authentic Pauline believer is to be prepared to go and proclaim the gospel as led by the Spirit of God.

---

[76] Fee, *Empowering*, 729.

[77] Schnabel, *Mission*, 1464-1465.

[78] Arnold, *Ephesians*, 121. See also Plummer, *Understanding*, 80.

[79] Fee, *Empowering*, 730.

[80] Those taking it with evangelism include O'Brien, *Consumed*, 125 and *Ephesians*, 482; Mitton, *Ephesians*, 227-228; Fee, *Empowering*, 729; Schnackenburg, *Ephesians*, 279-80; Barth, *Ephesians*, II. 777; Lincoln, *Ephesians*, 452. Snodgrass, *Ephesians*, 344 sees it as comprehensive but still inclusive of proclamation. Barth, *Ephesians*, II.777 rightly notes that taking up the word in worship, prophetic speech and prayer cannot be excluded (Eph 4:25, 29; 5:13, 18-19).

Significantly, Paul's appeal is not confined in any way to any particular group such as apostles or co-workers. The passage is part of Paul's final address (τοῦ λοιποῦ) to all those 'saints who are in Ephesus who are faithful in Christ Jesus (Eph 1:1).'[81] Hence, here is something akin to a 'Pauline Great Commission.' As O'Brien puts it, 'Ephesians 6 shows that all believers in the apostle's churches were involved in a spiritual warfare in which they were to stand firm against the onslaughts of the evil one by resistance and *proclamation*.'[82]

Conclusion

This analysis has indicated that Paul in the main applies military metaphor in an evangelistic context. Hence, the parallel appeals of Phil 1:27 (στήκετε ἐν ἑνὶ πνεύματι) and 4:1 (στήκετε ἐν κυρίῳ) should not be understood in purely defensive terms as almost all scholars do. Rather, they should be understood dynamically including the full range of Christian action against the forces of evil. On the one hand this should include defensively standing firm in unity against non-Christian opposition and persecution, false teaching and suffering. On the other hand, it involves proactive joint action and speech on behalf of the gospel in the context of the world. The personal energy for such action is God through Christ (ἐν κυρίω) by his Spirit (ἐν ἑνὶ πνεύματ) (cf. Rom 14:4; Phil 1:6; 2:13).

---

[81] Schnackenburg, *Ephesians*, 271.
[82] O'Brien, *Consumed*, 130.

APPENDIX 2

The Connection Between Evangelism and the Athletic Metaphor in Paul

An analysis of Paul use of the athletic metaphor indicates that on almost every occasion he utilises this metaphor, evangelistic ministry features prominently in the context. In this appendix I will briefly examine examples of this.

That Paul's use of athletic imagery often has an evangelistic nuance is clearest in references to Paul's own ministry. He often defines his life of evangelistic ministry as running (τρέχω) a race (Gal 2:2). His desire is to finish the race and receive the prize of eternal life (Phil 3:13-14). In Phil 1:29 Paul uses ἀγων ('contest', 'struggle') to describe his labour in the cause of proclaiming the message so that others would come to mature relationship with Christ (cf. Col 1:28-2:1). In 1 Thess 2:2 Paul refers to his commitment to proclaim the gospel to the Philippians 'with great struggle' (ἐν πολλῷ ἀγῶνι) in the face of suffering (προπαθόντες) and being publicly insulted (ὑβρισθέντες).

The athletics-evangelism connection is most developed in 1 Cor 9:24, 27 where he speaks of his ministry in terms of the Graeco-Roman Isthmian games as a stadium or race (σταδιῳ), running (τρέχω), struggling (ἀγνωνιζόμεμος), not aimlessly (ἀδήλως) but in self-control (ἐγκρατεύεται). Similarly he describes it as boxing (πυκτεύω), pummelling his body and not beating the air (ἀέρα δέρων) to receive the prize (βραβεῖον). This he does to receive the prize of an imperishable crown (ἄφθαρτον).

Significantly in 1 Cor 9:24c Paul applies this to the Corinthians. There he appeals to them to 'run so as to lay hold of the prize' (τρέχετε ἵνα καταλάβητε). As Fee argues, τρέχετε is here an imperative rather than indicative.[1] What follows develops Paul's focus in regards to the imperative; namely, that the Corinthians emulate his own example of self-control (1 Cor 7:9),[2] and so receive the incorruptible prize of eternal life.

---

[1] Fee, *1 Corinthians*, 436 rightly critiques Pfitzner, *Paul*, 88-89 on this point noting that the imperative is the more natural reading and that this imperative controls the thought of the paragraph. Similarly Collins, *First Corinthians*, 361; Barrett, *1 Corinthians*, 217; Hodge, *1 Corinthians*, 167.

[2] *BDAG*, 274: 'to keep ones emotions, impulses, or desires under control, control oneself, abstain.'

Even more importantly the immediate context for Paul's approach here is his proclamation ministry. First, in the preceding pericope he has explained how, for cultural reasons, he renounced his freedom to receive payment from the Corinthians for preaching the gospel (1 Cor 9:19-22). That is, he modified his approach depending on the needs of his recipients, without compromising the essence of the gospel message,[3] to ensure the maximum number of people would be saved. He summarises this in 1 Cor 9:23b stating that he does 'all things for the sake of the gospel, so that I may share in its blessings.'[4]

In 1 Cor 9:24-27, Paul picks up his appeal for self-control while retaining the interaction of eternal reward and proclamation. The latter is found in 1 Cor 9:27 μή πως ἄλλοις κηρύξας αὐτὸς ἀδόκιμος γένωμαι which supplies the purpose for his subjugation of his body. The phrase 'after I have preached (κηρύξας) to others (ἄλλοις)', which uses one of his customary terms for proclamation (κηρύσσω), is clearly a reference to his preaching ministry (cf. 1 Cor 9:16-22). His purpose in continuing to preach is that he won't be disqualified (ἀδόκιμος), referring metaphorically in athletic terms to the eschatological prize that awaits him.[5]

Returning to the appeal of 1 Cor 9:24b that the Corinthians run so as to lay hold of the prize in a manner similar to Paul, it is difficult to remove a passion for evangelism from the Corinthian church from Paul's view. First, it is clear that for Paul, proclamation was the context for a disciplined athletic approach to life. Secondly, the passage places no limitation on the Christian expression of the Corinthians. In fact the opposite is the case, in that no other Christian activity is referred to; if there is one clear dimension for 'running' here, it is evangelism. Thirdly, the imperative τρέχετε is second person plural indicating the whole Corinthian congregation is in mind. Paul wants the whole church to imitate his utter dedication to their faith in a manner similar to his own. It would seem arbitrary unless in some sense prohibited to remove evangelism from the appeal. Finally, I note the appeal of 1 Cor 11:1 which parallels this appeal in its appeal for imitation (see above Chapter 9). Within this appeal, there is a clear soteriological motivation based on Paul and Christ's own missiological examples and potentially implies evangelism.

Finally, in 2 Tim 4:7-8 Paul defines his ministry as he faces impending death as a 'good fight' (καλὸν ἀγῶνα) which he has fought (ἠγώνισμαι) and a race (τετέλεκα) he has completed so that he will receive the crown of

---

[3] Fee, *1 Corinthians*, 432 notes correctly this is not about modifying the message but the lifestyle of the messenger.

[4] Preferring the view that Paul here is speaking of sharing in the blessings of the gospel (so Collins, *First Corinthians*, 356) rather than its work here (cf. Fee, *1 Corinthians*, 432). It has a similar feel to Phil 3:12-14 where Paul presses on to win the eternal prize.

[5] Taking ἀδόκιμος with Fee, *1 Corinthians*, 440 as referring to eternal life rather than disqualified from preaching the gospel as does Collins, *First Corinthians*, 362; Thiselton, *1 Corinthians*, 717.

righteousness (δικαιοσύνης στέφανος).

Similarly, Paul uses athletic imagery in relation to Timothy his favoured co-worker in an invariably evangelistic connection. He encourages him to train (γύμναζε) in godliness in contrast to physical exercise and to struggle (ἀγνωνιζόμεθα) for the gospel (1 Tim 4:7-10). He exhorts him to 'fight (ἀγνίζου) the good fight (ἀγνῶνα); take a hold of eternal life to which you were called, and you made the good confession before many witnesses (πολλῶν μαρτύρων)', thus living kingdom values and renouncing idolatry and the pursuit of wealth (1 Tim 6:11-12 cf. Heb 12:1-2). He encourages Timothy to endure hardship as a good soldier of Christ living according to the command of his superiors and contending as an athlete (ἀθλῇ) according to the rules (νομίμως ἀθλήσῃ) so that he will receive the victor's crown (στεφανοῦνται) (2 Tim 2:5).

Elsewhere he speaks of the result of his evangelistic toil, his churches, as his crown (1 Thess 2:19 cf. Phil 2:16; 4:1), στέφανος referring to the 'victory wreath placed on the heads of victorious military commanders or the winners of athletic contests to signify their achievement.'[6] Another evangelistic nuance is found in 2 Thess 3:1 where Paul asks the Thessalonians to pray for his ministry so that the gospel would 'run' (τρέχω) and be glorified. The notion here is the swift spread of the gospel either in purely Hellenic athletic terms,[7] and/or the LXX.[8]

In Phil 2:16, Paul uses τρέχω of his evangelistic ministry among the Philippians ('I did not *run* or labour in vain'). In Phil 3:12-14 Paul speaks of his commitment to 'press on' in his ministry. This has the sense of 'push, drive, set in motion' and also was used of persecute (3:6) but carries the notion of 'striving hard after' a good aim (1 Thess 5:15; 1 Cor 14:1; Rom 9:30, 31; 12:13; 14:19; 1 Tim 6:11; 2 Tim 2:22). He is 'straining' i.e. 'stretching' (ἐπεκτεινόμενος) toward what is ahead i.e. the prize (βραβεῖον). Here the prize is eschatological salvation perhaps received in similarity to the 'upward

---

[6] Not with reference to the LXX (Prov 16:31; Ezek 16:12; 23:42) but the games so Wanamaker, *Thessalonians*, 93; 87-88; *Thessalonians*, 87-88; Morris, *Thessalonians*, 96; Best, *Thessalonians*, 128; Pfitzner, *Paul*, 185; Malherbe, *Thessalonians*, 185; Bruce, *Thessalonians*, 56; Marshall, *Thessalonians*, 87.

[7] Best, *Thessalonians*, 324; Wanamaker, *Thessalonians*, 274; Holmes, *Thessalonians*, 256. Marshall, *Thessalonians*, 213 is probably right in saying that there is no need to choose between Ps 147:15 and Greek athletics as the metaphor of the race is also Jewish cf. Ps 19:5.

[8] J.E. Frame, *A Critical and Exegetical Commentary on the Epistles of St. Paul to the Thessalonians*. ICC (Edinburgh: T&T. Clark, 1912), 291 who sees the link to Ps 147:15: 'his word runs swiftly' (NIV); Richard, *Thessalonians*, 369; Morris, *Thessalonians*, 244. Alternatively Malherbe, *Thessalonians*, 444 suggests a link to Matt 24:14; Mk 13:10 and concerns the swift spread of the gospel to all nations or 'run unhindered' with 'glorified' as eternal reward.

call' of the winning runner at the Pan-Hellenic games.[9] Significantly he then exhorts the Philippians to 'think like this' (3:15) and to 'be fellow-imitators of me' (3:17), giving a distinctly evangelistic edge to the metaphor. I consider that his appeal cannot be exhausted by a static defensive posture; everything in his use of athletic metaphor points to exertion, movement and so includes proactive evangelistic endeavour. Similarly, as I have discussed in relation to Phil 1:27 and 4:2, the use of the athletic συνήθλησαν should be understood evangelistically.

It is only on several occasions that the athletic references do not have a direct evangelistic reference. To the Galatians and Colossians he uses athletic metaphor of his churches remaining strong in their faith *in the face of heresy* (Gal 5:7; Col 2:18) and so not be disqualified from their eschatological prize (καταβραβεύω).[10] On one occasion Paul uses τρέχω of false human effort toward election (Rom 9:16).

This analysis shows that Paul uses athletic metaphor to speak of Christian living as a contest not unlike an athletic event.[11] Hence, there is competition and struggle involved in living the Christian life. For he and his co-worker Timothy the context was apostolic/evangelistic ministry. In the vast majority of references, evangelism is involved, creating the likelihood that references involving athletic metaphor in Philippians are at least in part, evangelistic in content (1:27; 2:16; 3:15-17; 4:2-3). In 1 Corinthians, this emphasis is not as strong, but evangelism cannot be evacuated from the use of the metaphor (cf. 1 Cor 9:19-22). This is reinforced through the contextual dominance of evangelism throughout as this study emphasizes. In Colossae and Galatia the metaphor focuses on the contextual struggle against false teaching.

---

[9] See discussion O'Brien, 431-432; Fee, 349.

[10] Bruce, *Epistles*, 117. This is the position of Malinowski, 'Brave': 62 who limits συναθλέω here statically as 'vigorous co-operative struggle of the community in the face of external attack.'

[11] If συναθλέω is more military in sense than athletic, then this does not rule out an evangelistic dimension as I suggested above on 'standing.'

APPENDIX 3

Evangelistic Nuances to the 'Christ-Hymn' (Phil 2:5-11)

The purpose of this appendix is to ask whether there are any evangelistic overtones to the Christ-hymn (Phil 2:5-11). The first thing to note is that the context includes evangelism as I have argued above (see esp. 1:27-30; 2:14-16). In that this is so, it is not unlikely that we will find some evidence of an evangelistic edge nor is it hermeneutically flawed to allow the context to influence our interpretation. My intention is not to exegete the text in detail but to discern any potential and actual evangelistic references and allusions within it.

Assumptions Concerning the Christ-Hymn

The purpose of this section is not to discuss fully the vast array of issues regarding the Christ-hymn. However before moving on to interpretation, it is important to outline my starting points.

First, along with most modern English scholars I take the position that the passage is authentic to the original letter to the Philippians and not an interpolation.

Secondly, although it may have had its origin in this form or another in another context as a stand-alone hymn or kerygmatic piece; in that Paul has placed it in the letter and does so because he accepts it, agrees with its theology and it serves his purpose, I will assume that it is *Pauline* even if did not necessarily originate from him.[1]

Thirdly, it is debated whether it is a hymn in the more formal sense or

[1] Regardless of whether Paul wrote it or adapted it for his purposes so Fee, 192-193; O'Brien, 202; Bockmuehl, 117-120, 119; Marshall, 'Theology', 129; Martin, 112; Hawthorne, 'Letter', 77-79; Beare, 2; Silva, 105; R.B. Strimple, 'Philippians 2:5-11 in Recent Studies: Some Exegetical Conclusions', *WTJ* 41 (1979): 247-268, 250-251; Caird, 104; D.A. Black, 'The Authorship of Philippians 2:6-11: Some Literary-Critical Observations', *CTR* 2 (1900): 269-289; O'Brien, 202; Fee, 193 esp. note 3; Bockmuehl, 119-120; Carson, *Introduction*, 319 among others. For discussion of background and other issues see R.P. Martin, *Carmen Christi. Philippians ii. 5-11 in Recent Interpretation and in the Setting of Early Christian Worship* (Grand Rapids: Eerdmans, 1967, 83), 285-319; Strimple, 'Recent': 247-268; Fitzmyer, 'Aramaic: 470-483; O'Brien, 186-203; Hawthorne, 71-79; Williams, *Enemies*, 68-71.

merely poetic; I will take it as the latter but it may well have been sung in the context of early church worship. I will continue to call it the Christ-hymn for want of a better term.[2]

Fourthly, it is debated whether the primary theological meaning in its context is kerygmatic or ethical.[3] The kerygmatic position tends to interpret the hymn without regard for the context and interprets it against its supposed source (whether an Aramaic original or alternative), as a stand-alone hymn of praise proclaiming who Christ is and what he has done. The ethical perspective believes that while it may have existed separately as a stand-alone kerygmatic piece or hymn, it should be interpreted primarily in regards to its ethical appeal; Christ being presented as the supreme example to the Philippians of humility, sacrifice and perseverance.

I agree that while this is a marvellous kerygmatic statement of who Christ is and movement of his mission, in its context it is framed in a clear ethical direction derived from its setting within Philippians and not its source.[4] In that regard, as Fee points out, 'Paul's primary concern is not theological as such, but illustrative… to illustrate the kind of selflessness and humility referred to in v.3.'[5]

This ethical element is established in 2:1-4. Using four conditional cascading

---

[2] Whether or not a formal hymn with uncertain strophic structure (see summary of Weiss, Lohmeyer, Dibelius, Cerfaux and Jeremias in Martin, *Carmen*, 24-41) or our preferance of exalted Pauline prose cf. Fee, 191-197; 'Exalted': 29-46; Robbins, 'Rhetorical': 73-82; Basevi, '2:6-11': 338-355; Bockmuehl, 116-117; Marshall, 'Theology', 131; M.Hooker, Philippians 2:6-11,' in E.E. Ellis and E. Grässer, *Jesus und Paulus. Festschrift für Werner Georg Kümmel zum 70. Geburstag* (Göttingen: Vandenhoeck & Ruprecht, 1978), 151-164, 158-159; Williams, *Enemies*, 64.

[3] Rather than strictly kerygmatic as suggested by Käsemann, 'Analysis'; Martin, Carmen, 84-88; Beare, 75; Silva, 107-111. As Hooker, 2:6-11,', 151-164 notes, the kerygmatic does not rule out the ethical. For justification of the ethical position see O'Brien, 253-262, 262; Fee, 196; L.W. Hurtado, 'Jesus as Lordly Example in Philippians 2:5-11' in P. Richardson and J.C. Hurd, *From Jesus to Paul: Studies in honour of Francis Wright Beare* (Waterloo: Wilfrid Laurier University Press, 1984), 133-135; Bockmuehl, 122-123; Watson, 'Analysis': 69-70; Basevi, '2:6-11', 346, 349; J.B.Webster, 'The Imitation of Christ', *TynB* 37 (1986): 95-120; S.J. Kraftchick, 'A Necessary Detour: Paul's Metaphorical Understanding of the Philippians Hymn', *HBT* 15 (1993): 1-37; I.H. Marshall, 'The Christ-Hymn in Philippians 2:5-11', *TynB* 19 (1968): 104-127, 117.

[4] This reinforced by the incredible inability to construct an adequate background for the text whether Gnosticism (E. Käsemann); Isaiah 53 (Cerfaux and Jeremias); 'the righteous sufferer of postbiblical Judaism (E. Schweitzer); Jewish wisdom (Georgi); Adamic contrast (Héring, Cullmann, Dunn) early Christianity (Hurtado, Hawthorne), Paul. For a summary see O'Brien, 193-198. Thus consider that the passages should be understand primarily in context rather than allow an extremely uncertain set of prior assumptions rule meaning.

[5] Fee, 198.

εἴ clauses Paul reminds the Philippians of what they have in the Christ and the Spirit in the way of encouragement, love, consolation, fellowship, compassion and sympathy. On this basis in 2:2 then he urges them to resolve their differences by making his joy complete by being one in the same love, spirit and thinking. He urges them to leave behind all vestiges of selfish ambition and vain conceit (cf. 1:15-18) and rather be humble and consider others above themselves, placing them first, seeking the best for others (cf. 1 Cor 10:23-11:1). He then gives Jesus explicitly as his example in 2:5; as the NRSV puts it: 'have this attitude in yourselves which was also in Christ Jesus.'

That the text should be understood in its context is seen in the number of verbal parallels with the preceding section including 'in Christ' in 2:1 and 'in Christ Jesus' in 2:5; the use of φρονέω ("think") twice in 2:2 and 2:5; ἡγέομαι ('lead', 'suppose') in 2:3 and in 2:6; κενοδοξία ('empty glory') and κενόω ('empty') in 2:4 and 2:7; ταπεινοφροσύνη ('humility') and ταπεινόω ('humble') in 2:3 and 2:8.[6]

In this regard 2:6-8 and the voluntary self-renunciation of Jesus respond directly to the issues of 'selfish ambition' and 'vain conceit' (2:3) as does his humility serve as model to the Philippians (2:3). These clearly indicates continuity of theme, Christ being set before the Philippians as the supreme example of the kind of thinking and living he is seeking of them.

Thus, Jesus Christ is set before the Philippians as the supreme example of a right attitude as the emphasis on 'thinking' illustrates with the three-fold repetition of φρονέω in 2:1-5.[7] The Philippians are to live worthy of the gospel by taking on the attitude of Jesus Christ.[8] Clearly then, while this passage has kerygmatic appeal, Paul uses it ethically to illustrate his appeal; Jesus being his example to the Philippians.

Finally, structurally I consider it should be understood in Paul's own sentence structure rather than a find an 'original' strophic pattern.[9]

The Evangelistic Framework and Dimensions of the Christ-Example

In this section I will discuss Phil 2:5-11 to see whether there are any evangelistic nuances in its appeal. That is, should the passage be understood not only as ethically and kerygmatically but in a missiological and evangelistic manner. I will also suggest that there is an eschatological and exhortatory dynamic that should be included in any reading of the Christ-hymn.

Surprisingly few scholars note the missiological thrust of the passage. However I consider that the soteriological, eschatological and ethical dynamics

---

[6] O'Brien, 166.

[7] Fee, 199 writes 'Paul's point seems plain enough.'

[8] ἐν ὑμῖν as 'among yourselves' in the sense of 'in you' as seen 'among you.' So Fee, 200.

[9] Again Fee, 194-196. Hence it is in two parts, 2:6-8, 9-11.

are all set in the context of missiology and in particular the gospel.

Interestingly the German scholar Schenk has suggested that the passage was created by the Philippian community for witness to Hellenistic Roman citizens. As such it is a 'teaching', 'revelation' or 'interpretation' (1 Cor 14:26). Its purpose he proposes is missionary witness to evangelise within the Roman culture i.e. to advance the gospel (1:5, 12, 27). He propounds that it is written then for the propagation of the faith to unbelievers in terms of Paul's teaching in their own culture.[10] While this is speculative and few are convinced, it articulates one way of noting evangelistic dimension of the passage.

Mission Dimensions of the Christ-Hymn

I suggest that the passage refers to Christ as example not in a static sense, but as set in the context of missionary endeavour i.e. Jesus was sent from God as Messiah to die and rise so as to save humanity and as such ethics are subordinate to and set in the context of mission *per se*. There are a number of reasons for this.

First, the intertextual links in Philippians between the concepts of 2:1-11 link the appeal of the Christ-hymn to the problem in Philippians which I have shown to be explicitly linked to contention between evangelists (4:1-3 cf. 1:27; 2:14-16). As such, the ethical appeal should not be divorced from the evangelistic nuance to the conflict. That is, Paul is appealing for unity in the context of mission (4:2-3; 1:27); of contending for the cause of the gospel (1:27; 4:2-3); of shining ethically in the darkness of Philippian pagan culture (2:14-15); of holding forth the word of life (2:16). As a result, there is an evangelistic edge to the ethical appeal supplied by the broader issues which lie at the centre of the letter. It is also flanked in its context by evangelism from 1:5-7, 12-18a, 22, 27-30 and 2:19-30.

Secondly, it seems obvious that the very notion of Christ as example in Paul's writings necessarily implies evangelistic ministry in a number of ways. In the first place, Christ was in Paul's eyes a preacher of reconciliation whose ministry was continued in the work of Paul and others (Rom 1:1; Eph 2:17; 1 Cor 11:1; 2 Cor 13:3). In Eph 2:17 Paul states this explicitly: 'He came and preached peace to you who were far away and peace to those who were near' (NIV).

Again in 1 Cor 11:1 Paul concludes the section in chapters 8-10 with his statement; 'imitate me as I imitate Christ.' Included in this section is an expectation of a soteriological concern from the Corinthians and a strong statement of his personal passion for salvation and the evangelisation of the lost in 9:19-22; this indicates that evangelism of the lost is one example of imitation of Christ (see above Chapter 9).

In the third place, the notion of the body of Christ with Christ as head and so

---

10. See Schenk, 173-175, 192-193, 195, 202, 209, 336; Reumann, 'Contributions': 444.

supplying the 'mind' for the body implies evangelism as one essential dimension of the purposes of Christ from his body. This is confirmed in Eph 4:11 where the functional leaders of God's people, including apostles and evangelists with a concern for proclamation, are to equip the believers to continue the ministry of the Christ through his body so that it will be built up. As argued above, I consider growth here to be both intensive (i.e. to maturity) and extensive (new converts) (See above Chapter 6).

In addition, for Paul, Christ is saviour come to save humanity on God's behalf and so the link Christ-evangelism-salvation-Paul-church is implied and so proclamation is implicit and imperative (Phil 3:20; 2 Tim 1:10, 15; 2:4; Tit 1:4; 2:13; 3:6).

Moreover, the interests of Christ emphasised in Philippians involve evangelism through the service of Timothy (1:1; 2:21-22 cf. 2:8) suggesting rhetorically the same for the Philippians.

Thirdly, rhetorically, I suggest also that the whole passage speaks into the mission situation in the Philippian church. The passage illustrates a number of aspects of aspects of Christ's example which speak directly into the mission situation of the Philippian church or into mission in general:

i. Christ's demonstration of his divinity through intentional self-sacrifice and servanthood, rather than self-aggrandisement, indicate that intentional servanthood lies at the heart of Paul's conception of mission (2:6-7a).[11] So the Philippians are to emulate Christ and put aside their selfish ambition, vain conceit, contention, selfish interests and humble themselves, taking on the nature of servants for mission (cf. 2:3-4, 14; 4:2-3). Positively, they are to emulate the positively motivated Roman preachers (1:14-18a), Paul (4:9), Timothy (1:1 cf. 2:19-23) and Epaphroditus (2:25-30) who are evangelistic examples of selflessness for the cause of Christ.

ii. Christ's choice to become human indicates that incarnation lies at the heart of Paul's understanding of mission.[12] For the Philippians this encourages them to continue to enter into the society of Philippi, Macedonia and beyond, incarnating the person of Christ among the people (cf. 2:14-16). This is also

---

[11] With O'Brien, 208-211 and taking μορφή as speaking of Christ's eternal δόξα because μορφή Θεοῦ is δόξα cf. Strimple, 'Recent': 261; H.A.W. Meyer, 80. Taking οὐχ ἁρπαγμὸν ἡγήσατο to; εἶναι ἴσα θεῷ as Jesus refusing to to use his equality with God for his own advantage as O'Brien, 215 cf. R.W. Hoover, 'The HARPAGMOS enigma: A philosophical solution', *HTR* 64 (1971), 95-119. Understanding with O'Brien, 223-224 his self-emptying as taking the form of a slave i.e. 'he did not exchange the nature or form of God for that of a slave; instead, he displayed the nature of form of a slave' cf. Bruce, 46 (cf. Jn 13:3-5).

[12] O'Brien, 225 who notes Paul is speaking here of 'Christ's full identity with the human race.' So also Collange, 103. So also Martin, 205: 'Jesus is 'truly man, but not merely man.' Taking σκῆμα as referring 'to the way in which humanity appeared'; so O'Brien, 226 cf. H.A.W. Meyer, 94.

the mission mode of Paul who chose to incarnate in appropriate cultural form (where non-essentials were concerned) to win as many as possible (1 Cor 9:19-22). As mentioned above, Paul's appeal for imitation of his own ministry approach which is based on Christ's in 1 Cor 11:1 (cf. 2 Cor 8:9) and implies that he sees his own mission in incarnational terms and wishes the same for the body of Christ. In addition, Paul intentionally chose to be a vocation missionary witnessing from the workbench and in-so-doing, drawing people to Christ and modelling incarnational mission (2 Thess 3:7-10).[13]

iii. Christ's humility involving obedience to the point of sacrificial suffering and degrading death indicates that obedience to the point of sacrificial suffering and even martydom lie at the core of mission.[14] For Paul it has been his own consistent experience (1:12-14, 17, 30; 2:17-18; 4:12). So the Philippians should realise that their present sufferings (which he considers a gift from God cf. 1:29) are consistent with the experience of Christ (1:29; 3:10), Paul, Timothy, Epaphroditus and the Roman church, by remaining obedient to their call to faith and mission. This may lead to the point of death, but as Paul says of his own situation, death is not to be feared but anticipated with joy and hope (Phil 1:19-21). Hence the Philippians are safeguarded against any sense of naïve triumphalism or fearful retreatism.

iv. Christ's exaltation indicates that resurrection, salvation and eschatological reward are the result of faithful obedient mission.[15] That is, just as Christ was raised and exalted, so those who stand the test of remaining obedient will experience heavenly glory and reward. The exaltation of Jesus in 2:9 speaks not only theologically of the ascension, session and divinity of Jesus, but also rhetorically into the mission situation of the Philippians. Christ's exaltation

---

[13] Hock, 'Workshop': 438-50

[14] O'Brien, 227: 'he humbled himself' chiastically related to 'he emptied himself' and is the main sentence, amplifying the dependent previous clause. O'Brien argues that this speaks of humanity rather than incarnation as 'he emptied himself suggests.' However, this could be seen as kenotic; he emptied himself rather indicates incarnation but fully human ruling out docetism. As Barth, 65 notes: 'a deliberate act of *self-humiliation*' (italics mine). Noting that 'death on the cross' is 'his identification with men reached the lowest rung of the ladder' as Martin, *Carmen*, 221 puts it. With Martin, 216, Plummer, *Understanding,* 47; O'Brien, 229 taking God as the object of obedience rather than 'the wishes of the people' as Hawthorne, 87 argues; this is wholly un-Pauline (cf. Gal 1:10). O'Brien, 232 suggests that it is not the saving significance of the cross that is in view here. While this is not in the forefront of Paul's mind it cannot be removed as the context for the suffering which concurs with the missional context for the Philippian suffering.

[15] Not necessarily any human merit, but faith worked out (Phil 2:12) i.e. and obedience which springs from faith (Rom 1:5). Along with O'Brien, 236 I take ὑπερύψωσεν in an elative rather than comparative sense i.e. the point is not pre-existence, but his exaltation over all creation.

implies his resurrection and points to his glorification by the Father. Having completed his mission he is rewarded by the Father with the supreme name (κύριος).[16]

v. This vindication speaks to Paul himself (1:19-23; 2:17-18) and to the Philippians of the hope of eternal reward for a faithful completion (1:6) of their Christian life and mission. If they remain obedient to the point of death before their opponents they too can await resurrection (3:10), acceptance into eternity proper (3:20), bodily transformation (3:21) and the eternal prize (3:14, 20). In fact the opposition and suffering is itself a sign of their salvation and a gift from God (1:28-29). Indeed, Christ himself will be there and they will know the power of his resurrection as Paul himself hopes to do (3:10 cf. 1:21, 23). They are to emulate Christ and Paul, remaining obedient by living as citizens of heaven in Philippi in a manner worthy of the gospel of Christ (1:27).

The ἵνα Clause of 2:10: Result and Purpose

A fifth dimension is found in the *hina* clause of 2:10. The result and goal of the exaltation of Christ is that every human being submit to the lordship of Christ, that God may be glorified. In 2:10-11 Paul tells us 'every knee will bow' which clearly speaks of universal (πᾶν) homage.[17] The ἵνα clause of 2:10 can be understood either as indicating exclusively result ('with the result that that'),[18] purpose ('in order that'),[19] or both.[20] I agree with the latter group of scholars that ἵνα here should be understood in both ways, indicating the result and the purpose of the exaltation of Christ.

The sense of result can lead in the direction of universalism or involuntary submission. We can rule universalism out easily enough due to clear indications in Paul that many will not be saved (Phil 1:27; 3:19). We can also rule out the idea that 'every knee on earth' should be limited to spirit beings as some hold.[21] To do so requires imposing on the text a form-analysis which obscures the obvious reality that 'every knee... tongue' includes volitional

---

[16] The 'name above all names' here is most likely κύριος in light of the confession which follows, 'Jesus Christ is Lord. See O'Brien, 238 who notes that κύριος is to be interpreted against the LXX of Is 45:23 and 42:8 involving universal divine lordship i.e. he was 'θεός (2:6) becomes δοῦλος (v. 7) and is exalted to be κύριος (v. 11).'

[17] On κάμπτω ('bend or bow') signifying great reverence and submission in worship (cf. Ezra 9:5, 15; Matt 26:9) see O'Brien, 240-241.

[18] Silva, 71; J.J. Müller, 88; Fee, 223.

[19] Marshall, 'Theology', 135; Hawthorne, 92, 94; Hendriksen, 115; Kent, 125; Barth, 68: *BAGD*, 475; Vincent, 62; Michael, 95; P. Lampe, *EDNT*, 2.190.

[20] O'Brien, 239; Collange, 106; Martin, Carmen, 249; Bockmuehl, 146; Melick, 107.

[21] Whether or not this includes inanimate objects or animals (so Lightfoot, 115), it clearly implies volitional humanity.

humanity.[22] Hence I suggest then that without question the submission of all humanity dead or alive is implied. But is this involuntary or voluntary submission?

The notion of a result clause leading to 'involuntary submission' is suggested in various ways. First, involuntary submission fits the context of Is 45:18-24a and Rom 14:11. In Is 45:24 those who bow and confess includes those who have 'raged against him' who 'will come to him and be put to shame' as well as 'the descendants of Israel' who 'will be found righteous and will exult.' In Rom 14:11 Paul quotes the same passage in regard to *all* standing before God in judgement and giving account of their lives. Secondly, the reference to every knee 'in heaven, on earth and under the earth' it is agreed includes spiritual forces good and bad, not all of whom will willingly submit.[23] Finally, within the context Paul appears to use ἵνα of result (2:2).

However the purposive dimension of ἵνα is also supported here. First, the usual use of ἵνα in Paul is purposive.[24] Secondly, while universal submission is in mind in Is 45:24-25 the context is an appeal for all the nations to *willingly* 'turn' to God and 'be saved.' Hence the appeal is for all people to voluntarily submit; in that all will ultimately bow.

In the wider scope of Paul's letters, God's desire is for this to be voluntary, that being the whole point of Jesus' and Paul's mission, to encourage voluntary submission to God from all humanity (1 Tim 2:4-5). I would also argue that the context of Philippians points toward purpose; Paul having expressed his own passion for proclamation, congratulates the Philippians for their involvement and challenges them to continue in mission-unity (see above). Hence here the goal of Christ's work, death and exaltation is the willing submission of all humanity to God before whom they will bow in the eschaton.

I conclude that here the evidence suggests that purpose and result are here interconnected and inseparable. The exaltation of Christ to the name that is above all names results in all creation bowing before him. In terms of

---

[22] In particular and 'enthronement drama' as suggest Lohmeyer, 97; Martin, *Carmen*, 263. This illustrates the danger of using an imposed form to interpret a text and so obscuring the most obvious point i.e. it is humans who have knees and tongues and 'all… on earth' must include all living humanity!

[23] With O'Brien, 245 who refers to O. Hofius, *Der Christushymnus Philipper 2,6-11: Untersuchungen zu Gestalt und Aussage eines urchristlichen Psalms.* WUNT 17 (Tübingen: Mohr (Siebeck), 1991), 20-40; W.R. Carr, *Angels and Principalities* (ed. R.M. Wilson; London: Cambridge University, 1981), 86-89; Bruce, 80; Loh-Nida, 62; Hawthorne, 93 taking 'in heaven' of angels and other spiritual forces in heaven' 'on earth' as volitional living humanity including the Philippians; 'under the earth' of the dead and demonic forces of Sheol. Alternatively with Fee, 224-225 taking 'in heaven' of good and evil spiritual forces, 'on earth' as those alive at the Parousia including all in Philippi and those 'under the earth' as 'the dead.' We find it highly unlikely that all three are spiritual forces as do Beare, 86; Martin, Carmen, 257-265; Gnilka, 128.

[24] See *EDNT*, 2.190: 'about 83% of Paul's use of ἵνα is final.'

humanity, the purpose of the exaltation of Christ is that all will bow willingly before him. That being the case mission, and more particularly evangelism, is brought into the context in a more explicit manner. The purpose of Christ's mission, death, resurrection and exaltation is willing submission to the lordship of Christ and so the glorification of God. This concurs with the purpose of Christ's mission expressed in the Gospels (cf. Lk 19:10). This corresponds with the purpose of Paul's mission in evangelisation.[25]

Furthermore, this purpose encourages the Philippians to see that the goal of mission is that all will come to Christ. Knowing this, how can they retreat from mission in the face of suffering? As the Roman proclaimers were inspired by Paul in Rome to be more active in mission despite personal danger and as Christ was inspired to become obedient to the point of death; so they are to continue to proclaim the gospel, showing increased works of love, bearing the fruit of righteousness among their families, friends, workmates and enemies. The imperative of the gospel is to continue in mission so that all will be saved, for it is God's will that all be saved and come to a knowledge of the truth (1 Tim 2:4).

The Evangelistic Nuance of ἐξομολογέω

Sixthly and finally, the notion of 'confession' in Paul also potentially carries an evangelistic nuance. In its simplistic sense ἐξομολογέω means 'to declare openly or confess publically.'[26] Some commentators note that ἐξομολογέω carries the nuance 'to proclaim with thanksgiving' with the notion 'to offer praise or thanksgiving' from the LXX usage.[27] As such the picture here is of universal praise and confession to Jesus.[28] This led some to connect the witness of the church to confession.

However recent scholarship has rejected this view preferring the simple neutral meaning; hence, 'recognise' or 'acknowledge' is preferred. The premise is usually that 'in heaven...earth... under the earth' refers to powers who admit that 'this is the rightful Lord of the universe because God has installed Him in the seat of uncontested authority.'[29] If this is the case, then the notion of 'confession of Christ' in any evangelistic sense is diminished.

However, I would argue that both dynamics of ἐξομολογέω are at work here. For those who accept the lordship of Christ and confess voluntarily, they will confess with thanksgiving and praise. However for those who confess involuntarily and reluctantly, theirs will be a begrudging confession.[30]

---

[25] Similarly Bosch, *Transforming*, 178.
[26] Martin, *Carmen*, 263; O'Brien, 246.
[27] Lightfoot, 115; Plummer, *Understanding*, 49. See O'Brien, 246 for LXX analysis.
[28] Hofius, *Christushymnus*, 37-40.
[29] Martin, *Carmen*, 264.
[30] Bockmuehl, 147; O'Brien, 243.

The confession 'Jesus Christ is Lord' is 'for Paul the line of demarcation between believer and nonbeliever' (1 Cor 12:3; Rom 10:9-10).[31] It implies acknowledgement of the lordship of Christ over any other concept or thing in ones life and especially in a Philippian context, Jesus and not Caesar. It suggests a lifestyle completely given over to obedience to the Lord Jesus Christ.[32] Hence confession involves speaking the confession and living the confession in a continuous rather than punctiliar sense. As such, evangelism comes to mind in a general sense.

However there are good reasons to understand 'confess' here to have more than merely an implicit evangelistic edge. First, if living humanity is in mind as is likely, then the confession of the lordship of Jesus is not limited to any private sphere. Rather, confession is a non-dualistic notion involving all manner of attitude, action and speech which expresses submission to Christ's lordship including where appropriate, proactive evangelization. There is no duality of who confesses either, all believers are to confess.

Secondly, as hinted above, the confession 'Jesus is Lord' is a highly provocative and powerful statement in the Graeco-Roman context implying standing up for the lordship of Christ in a context of many lords; not the least, the gods of the Graeco-Roman world and the emperor cult. This would call the believer in tension with the culture on a continual basis bringing about a need for verbal explanation and confession in the public context.

Thirdly, and most importantly, the link between confession and evangelism is found in other contexts in the NT and suggests that confession is not merely a static private in-church concept. In Rom 15:9 Paul quotes Ps 18:49 (cf. 2 Sam 22:50) in regard to the Gentiles turning to God: 'therefore I will *confess* you (ἐξομολογήσομαί) among the Gentiles.' Paul moves from this through to remind the Romans of his evangelistic ministry of *confessing Christ through his proclamation to the Gentiles* (Rom 15:16). Secondly, in 2 Cor 4:13-14 there is a clear link between faith and verbal communication. This is seen in 2 Cor 4:12-13 where Paul, after outlining his apostolic ministry (cf. 4:1-7) and suffering (cf. 2 Cor 4:8-12) quotes Ps 116:10: 'I believed; therefore I have spoken knowing that the one who raised the Lord Jesus from the dead will also raise us with Jesus and present us with you in his presence (cf. Rom 10:9). As Michel suggests 'confession and the word of proclamation grow out of faith.'[33]

Finally, it is notable that this evangelistic edge is explicit in the teaching of Jesus where in Matthew 10:32 in the context of his commissioning of the 12 for mission, tells the disciples that 'anyone (πᾶς οὖν) who *confesses*

---

[31] Fee, 225.

[32] O'Brien, 203 and Fee, 218 rightly prefer the aorist subjunctive in coordination with κάμψῃ. The use of the aorist suggests an all-encompassing one-off act of submission leading to a life of submission.

[33] O. Michel, *TDNT* 5, 211.

(ὁμολογήσει) me before men/women (τῶν ἀνθρώπων) I will *acknowledge* (*confess* [ὁμολογήσω]) before my Father in heaven.' Hence, while confession marked the beginning of Christian life (cf. 1 Tim 6:12), ongoing confession included a whole life set over for service to God in Christ.

Conclusion

Although mission and evangelism are not explicitly stated in the passage, evangelism is near the surface of 2:5-11 and at times even breaks through the surface. First, evangelistic mission sets the framework for the whole of Christ's ministry and the presentation of Christ-as-example cannot ever be separated from this setting. In that, in Philippians evangelism is prominent in the passages that flank 2:5-11 (1:27-2:4; 2:12-30), this first point if further enhanced. This being the case, the request for the Philippians to emulate Christ involves imitation of Christ's in the context of mission-lifestyle.

Secondly, in 2:9-11 evangelism comes to the fore in the purpose of Christ's mission, a purpose the church takes on in its proclamation of Christ, and continuation of his mission. Specifically they are to confess Christ so that others will confess willingly i.e. one dimension of their life under the lordship of Christ is the spreading of the message with a Christlike attitude. Hence Paul is calling the church back to the basics. He is calling them to look to Christ, to lay aside their differences and in particular their lovelessness, selfish ambition and vain conceit and work together in the unity of the Spirit to see the advance of the gospel in Philippi and beyond. Among a series of excellent examples, Christ is the one the Philippians are to emulate above all else (cf. 1 Cor 11:1).

In addition I would note that the Christ-hymn gives eschatological encouragement to the Philippians to persevere as did Christ, in the face of severe suffering, and so receive eschatological reward for their efforts. If they emulate the co-workers of Phil 4:2-3, their names too will be written in the book of life.

As such alongside the kerygmatic and ethical readings of the Christ-hymn frequently employed in contemporary scholarship, I would argue that the hymn should also be understood evangelistically and eschatologically. These categories should not be seen as mutually-exclusive, Paul being eminently capable of speaking with all four dimensions in mind; and this I am convinced he is doing in the Christ-hymn.

Bibliography

Abrahamsen, V. 'Women at Philippi: The Pagan and Christian Evidence,' *JFSR* 3 (1987): 17-20.

— *Women and Worship in Philippi. Diana/Artemis and Other Cults in the Early Christian Era* (Portland: Astarte Shell, 1995).

Achtemeier, P.J. *Romans*. Interpretation. (Louisville: John Knox, 1985).

Achtemeier, P.J., J.B. Green and M.M. Thompson, *Introducing the New Testament, its Literature and Theology* (Grand Rapids: Eerdmans, 2001).

Agnew, F.H. 'The Origin of the NT Apostle-Concept: a Review of Research', *JBL* 105/1 (1986): 75-96.

Alexander, L. 'Hellenistic Letter-Forms and the Structure of Philippians,' *JSNT* 37 (1989): 87-101.

Alford, H. *The Greek Testament* (4 vols. London: Longmans, Green and Co, 1894).

Arichea D.C. and E.A. Nida, *A Handbook on Paul's Letter to the Galatians* (New York: United Bible Societies, 1993).

Arnold, C.E. *Ephesians*: *Power and Magic. The Concept of Power in Ephesians in the Light of its Historical Setting.* SNTSMS 63 (Cambridge: CUP, 1989).

— *Powers of Darkness* (Downers Grove: IVP, 1992).

— 'The Exorcism of Ephesians 6:12 in Recent Research', *JSNT* 30 (1987): 73-74.

Arzt, P. 'The "Epistolary Introductory Thanksgiving" in the Papyri and Paul', *NovT* 36, 1 (1994): 29-46.

Ash, A.L. *Philippians, Colossians & Philemon, Outlines at Beginning of Each Book.* CPNIVC (Joplin: College Press, 1994).

Bammel, E. 'Judenverfolgung und Naherwartung: Zur Eschatologie des Ersten Thessalonicherbriefs,' *ZTK* 56 (1959): 294–315.

Banks, R. *Paul's Idea of Community* (Exeter: Paternoster Press, 1980).

Barclay, W. *The Letters to Philippians, Colossians, Thessalonians.* DSB (Edinburgh: The Saint Andrew Press, 1959).

Barnes, E. 'Women in Ministry: a Matter of Discipleship', *FM* 4 (1987) 63-69.

Barnett, P. *The Second Epistle to the Corinthians.* NICNT (Grand Rapids: Eerdmans, 1997).

Barr, G.J. 'Paul and Letter Writing in the Fifth Century', *CBQ* 28 (1966): 465-477.

Barrett, C.K. *A Critical and Exegetical Commentary on the Acts of the Apostles.* ICC (2 Vols. Edinburgh: T&T. Clark, 1994, 1998).

— *A Commentary on the Epistle to the Romans*. HNTC (San Francisco: Harper, 1957).

— *Paul. An Introduction to his Thought.* (London: Geoffrey Chapman, 1994).

— 'I Am not Ashamed of the Gospel', in M. Barth, *Foi et salut selon S. Paul.* AnBib 42 (Rome: Pontifical Biblical Institute, 1970), 19-41.

— *The First Epistle to the Corinthians.* BNTC (London: Black, 1971).

— 'The Imperatival Participle', *ExpTim* 59 (1948): 165-167.

— *The Second Epistle to the Corinthians.* BNTC (London: Black, 1973).

— 'Shaliah and Apostle,' in E. Bammel, C.K. Barrett and W.D. Davies (eds), *Donum Genilicium: New Testament Studies in Honour of David Daube* (Oxford: Clarendon Press, 1978), 88-102.

— *The Signs of an Apostle* (London: Epworth, 1970).

Barth, K. *Epistle to the Philippians* (Trans. J.W. Leitch. Louisville: London, 2002).

— *The Epistle to the Romans* (Trans. E.C. Hoskyns. London: Oxford University, 1960).

Barth, M. *Ephesians.* ABC (2 Vols. New York: Doubleday, 1974).

Bauer, W., W.F. Arndt, F.W. Gingrich, and F.W. Danker, *A Greek-English Lexicon of the New Testament and Other Early Christian literature (BDAG)* (Chicago: University of Chicago Press, [3rd Edn] 2000).

Baur, F.C. *Paul, the Apostle of Jesus Christ* (Vol 2. London, Williams and Norgate, 1875).

Beare, F.W. *Philippians* (London: Black, 1959).

Beasley-Murray, G.R. 'Philippians' in M. Black; H.H. Rowley (ed's) *Peake's Commentary on the Bible* (London: Thomas Nelson and Sons, 1962), 985-990.

Beekman J. and J. Callow, *Translating the Word of God* (Grand Rapids: Eerdmans, 1974).

Beet, J.A. *A Commentary on St Paul's Epistle to the Romans* (London: Hodder and Stoughton, 1883).

Beker, J.C. *Paul the Apostle: The Triumph of God in Life and Thought* (Augsburg: Fortress Press, 1980).

Belleville, L.L. *2 Corinthians*, IVPNTCS (Leicester: IVP, 1996).

Berkhof, H. *Christ and the Powers* (tr. J. Yoder. Scottdale: Herald, 1977).

Best, E. 'Bishops and Deacons: Phil 1,1', *SE* 4 (1968): 371-376.

— *Ephesians* (Sheffield: Sheffield Academic Press, 1993).

— *Paul and his Converts* (Edinburgh: T&T. Clark, 1988).

— 'Ministry in Ephesians', *IBS* 15.4 (1993): 143-166.

— 'Paul's Apostolic Authority', *JSNT* 27 (1986): 3-25.

— *The First and Second Epistles to the Thessalonians.* BNTC (London: Black, 1972).

— *The Letter of Paul to the Romans.* CBC (Cambridge: CUP, 1967).

— *2 Corinthians.* Interpretation (Louisville: John Knox, 1987).

Betz, H.D. *Galatians. A Commentary of Paul's Letter to the Churches in Galatia.* (Philadelphia: Fortress, 1979).

Black, D.A. 'Structure of Philippians: A Study in Textlinguistics', *NovT* 37, 1 (Jan 1995): 16-49.

— 'Paul and Christian Unity: a Formal Analysis of Philippians 2:1-4', *JETS* 28 (1985): 288-300.
— *Paul, Apostle of Weakness. Asthenia and its Cognates in the Pauline Literature.* American University Studies. Series Vii, theology and religion (New York: Peter Lang, 1984).
— 'The Authorship of Philippians 2:6-11: Some Literary-Critical Observations', *CTR* 2 (1988): 269-289.
Black, M. *Romans.* NCBC (Grand Rapids: Eerdmans, 1973).
Blevins, J.L. 'Introduction to Philippians', *RevExp* 77 (1980): 311-325.
Blomberg, C. *1 Corinthians.* NIVAC (Grand Rapids: Zondervan, 1994).
Bloomquist, L.G. *The Function of Suffering in Philippians.* JSNTS 78 (Sheffield: Sheffield Academic Press, 1993).
Bockmuehl, M. *Philippians.* BNTC (Peabody: Hendrickson, 1998).
Boers, H. 'The Form-Critical Study of Paul's Letters: 1 Thessalonians as a Case Study,' *NTS* 22 (1975–76): 140–158.
Boice, J.M. *Philippians: An Expositional Commentary* (Grand Rapids: Zondervan, 1971).
Bonnard, P. *L'épître de saint Paul aux Philippiens et l'épître aux Colossiens* (Neuchatel: Delachauz et Niestlé, 1950).
Bornkamm, G. *Paul* (Trans. D.M.C. Stalker. London: Hodder and Stoughton, 1971).
— 'Der Philipperbrief als paulinische Briefsammlung' in W.C. van Unnik, ed. *Neotestamentica et Patrisica: Eine Freundesgabe O. Cullman zu seinem 60. Geburtstag überreicht.* NovTSup 6 (London: Brill, 1962), 192-202.
Bosch, D. *Transforming Mission* (New York: Orbis Books, 1992).
Bowers, W.P. 'Church and Mission in Paul', *JSNT* 44 (1991): 89-111.
— 'Fulfilling the Gospel: The Scope of the Pauline Mission', *JETS* 30/2 (1987): 185-198.
— 'Jewish Communities in Spain in the Time of Paul the Apostle', *JTS* (1975), 395-402.
— 'Paul and Religious Propaganda', *NovT* 22, 4 (1980): 316-323.
— *Studies in Paul's Understanding of his Mission* (unpublished Ph.D. dissertation, Cambridge, 1976).
Boylan, M.P. *St. Paul's Epistle to the Romans* (Dublin: Gill and Son, 1947).
Brant, J. 'The Place of *Mimēsis* in Paul's Thought', *StudRel* 22.3 (1993): 285-300.
Brewer, R.R. 'The Meaning of *Politeuesthe* in Philippians 1:27', *JBL* 73 (1954): 76-83.
Brooten, B. "'Junia… Outstanding Among the Apostles'" in L and A. Swidler, *Women priests: A Catholic Commentary on the Vatican Declaration* (New York, Paulist, 1977), 141-44.
Brown, F. (2000). *Enhanced Brown-Driver-Briggs Hebrew and English Lexicon.* Strong's, TWOT, and GK references Copyright 2000 by Logos

Research Systems, Inc. (280.1). Oak Harbor, WA: Logos Research Systems.

Brown, R.E. *An Introduction to the New Testament* (New York: Doubleday, 1997).

Brown, R.E, K.P. Donfried and J. Reumann, *Peter in the New Testament* (London: Chapman, 1974).

Bruce, F.F. *Apostle of the Heart Set Free* (Grand Rapids: Eerdmans, 1977).

— *The Book of the Acts* (Grand Rapids: Eerdmans, 1988).

— *Philippians*. NIBC (Peabody: Hendrickson, 1983, 1989).

— 'St Paul in Macedonia. 3. The Philippian Correspondence,' *BJRL* 63 (1980-81): 260-284, 260-262.

— *The Epistle of Paul to the Romans. An Introduction and Commentary.* TBC (London: Tyndale, 1963).

— *The Epistles to the Colossians to Philemon and to the Ephesians.* NICNT (Grand Rapids: Eerdmans, 1984).

— *The Epistle to the Ephesians* (London: Pickering & Inglis, 1961).

— *The Epistle to the Galatians*. NIGTC (Exeter: Paternoster, 1982).

Brucker, R. *‚Christushymnen' oder ‚epideiktische Passagen'? Studien zum Stilwechsel im Neuen Testament und seiner Umwelt.* FRLANT 176 (Göttingen: Vandenhoeck & Ruprecht, 1997).

Buchanan, C.O. 'Epaphroditus' Sickness and the Letter to the Philippians', *EQ* 36 (1964): 157-166.

Burton, E.W.D. *The Epistle to the Galatians*. ICC (T& T. Clark: Edinbugh, 1921).

Byrne, B. *Romans*. SPS (Collegeville: Michael Glazier, 1996).

Byrskog, S. 'Co-Senders, Co-Authors and Paul's Use of the First Person Plural', *ZNW* 87 (1996): 230-250.

— 'Epistolography, Rhetoric and Letter Prescript: Romans 1.1-7 as a test case', *JSNT* 65 (1997): 27-46.

Caird, G.B. *Paul's Letters from Prison* (Oxford: Oxford University Press, 1979).

— *Principalities and Powers* (Oxford: Clarendon, 1956).

Calvin, J. *The Epistle of Paul the Apostle to the Romans and to the Thessalonians.* CNTC (Trans. Ross MacKenzie. Grand Rapids: Eerdmans, 1960).

— *The Epistles of Paul to the Galatians, Ephesians, Philippians and Colossians* (Trans. T.H.L. Parker. London: Oliver and Boyd, 1965).

Campbell, A. 'Do the Work of an Evangelist', *EQ* 64:2 (1992): 117-129.

Campbell, J.Y. 'Κοινωνία and its Cognates in the New Testament' in J.Y. Campbell, *Three New Testament Studies* (Leiden: E.J. Brill, 1965), 1-28.

Campbell, R.A. *Elders, Seniority within Earliest Christianity* (Edinburgh: T&T. Clark, 1994).

Capper, B.J. 'Paul's Dispute with Philippi', *TZ* 49.3 (1993): 193-214.

Carr, W. *Angels and Principalities* (ed. R.M. Wilson; London: CUP, 1981).

Carson, D.A., D.J. Moo, *An Introduction to the New Testament* (Grand Rapids: Zondervan, 2005).

— *Basics for Believers: An Exposition of Philippians* (Grand Rapids: Baker, 1996).

— *Showing the Spirit. A Theological Exposition of 1 Corinthians 12-14* (Homebush West, Anzea, 1988).

Castilli, E.A. *Imitating Paul: A Discourse of Power* (Louiseville: John Knox, 1991).

Claasen, C.J. *Rhetoric and the New Testament* (Leiden: Brill, 2002).

— 'St Paul's Epistles and Ancient Greek and Roman Rhetoric' in Porter S.E. and T.H. Olbricht (ed's), *Rhetoric and the New Testament. Essays from the 1992 Heidelberg Conference.* JSNTS 90 (Sheffield: Sheffield Academic Press, 1993).

Clifton, C. 'Keeping Up with Recent Studies. XVI. Rhetorical Criticism and Biblical Interpretation', *ExpTim* 100.7 (1989): 252-258.

Cole, R.A. *Galatians.* TNTC (Grand Rapids: Eerdmans, 1984).

Collange, J. *The Epistle of Saint Paul to the Philippians* (Trans. A.W. Heathcote. London: 1979).

Collins, J.J. *The Apocalyptic Imagination: An Introduction to the Jewish Matrix of Christianity* (New York: Crossroads, 1984).

Collins, R.F. *First Corinthians.* SPS (Collegeville: Liturgical, 1999).

— '"I Command that this Letter be Read": Writing as a Manner of Speaking' in Donfried K.P. and Beutler, J. *The Thessalonians Debate; Methodological Discord or Methodological Synthesis?* (Grand Rapids: Eerdmans, 2000), 319-339.

Conzelman, H. *1 Corinthians.* Hermeneia (Trans: J.W. Leitch. Philadelpia: Fortress, 1975).

Cottrell, J. *The College Press New International Commentary on Romans.* (Vol 2/2. Joplin [Miss]: College Press, 1996).

Cousar, C.B. *Galatians.* Interpretation (Atlanta: John Knox, 1982).

Craddock, F. *Philippians.* Interpretation (Atlanta: John Knox, 1985).

Craigie, P.C. *The book of Deuteronomy.* NICOT (Grand Rapids: Eerdmans, 1976).

Cranfield, C.E.B. *A Critical and Exegetical Commentary on the Epistle to the Romans.* ICC (2 Vol's. Edinburgh, T&T. Clark, 1975, 1979).

Cullmann, O. *Peter: Disciple, Apostle, Martyr* (Trans. F.V. Filson. London, SCM Press, 1953), 104-109.

Culpepper, R.A. 'Co-Workers in Suffering. Philippians 2:19-30', *RevExp* 77 (1980): 349-358.

Dahl, N.A. 'Euodia and Syntyche and Paul's Letter to the Philippians', 1-15 in L.M. White and O.L. Yarbrough (ed's), *The Social World of the First Christians: Essays in Honor of Wayne A. Meeks* (Minneapolis: Fortress, 1995), 1-15.

Dalton, W.J. 'The Integrity of Philippians', *Bib* 60 (1979): 97-102.

D'Angelo, M.R. 'Women Partners in the New Testament', *JFSR* 6 (1990): 65-86.

Davies, W.D. 'Paul and the People of Israel,' *NTS* 24 (1977–78): 4–39.

Davis, C.W. *Oral Biblical Criticism: The Influence of the Principles of Orality on the Literary Structure of Paul's Epistle to the Philippians.* JSNTS 172 (Sheffield: Academic Press, 1999).

De Boer, W.P. *The Imitation of Paul: An Exegetical Study* (Kampen: University of Amsterdam, 1962).

Deissman, A. *Bible Studies* (Tr. A. Grive. Edinburgh: T&T. Clark, 1923).

Dickson, J.P. *Mission-Commitment in Ancient Judaism and in the Pauline Communities.* WUNT 2 (Tübingen: J.C.B. Mohr [Paul Siebeck], 2003).

Dibelius, M. *An die Kolosser, Epheser an Philemon.* HNT 12 (Revised H. Greeven. Tübingen: Mohr, 1953).

Dodd, C.H. *The Epistle of Paul to the Romans* (London: Hodder and Stoughton, 1949).

— 'The Mind of Paul', *NTS* (1953): 67-128.

Donfried, K.P. (ed) *The Romans Debate* (Peabody: Hendrickson, 1991).

Donfried, K.P. and Beutler, J. (eds), *The Thessalonians Debate. Methodological Discord or Methodological Synthesis?* (Grand Rapids: Eerdmans, 2000).

Doohan, H. *Paul's Vision of the Church* (Wilmington: Michael Glazier, 1989).

Dorsey, C. 'Paul's Use of 'Αποστολος', *ResQ* 28.4 (1985-86): 193-200.

Doty, W.J. *Letters in Primitive Christianity* (Philadelphia: Fortress Press, 1973).

Doughty, D.J. 'Citizens of heaven Philippians 3.2-21', *NTS* 41 (1995): 102-122.

Duncan, G.S. 'A New Setting for St. Paul's Epistle to the Philippians', *ExpTim* 43 (1931-32): 7-11.

— *St. Paul's Ephesian Ministry: A Reconstruction* (London: Hodder and Stoughton, 1929).

— *The Epistle of Paul to the Galatians.* MNTC (London: Hodder, 1934).

Dunn, J.D.G. *The Acts of the Apostles.* EC (Peterborough: Epworth, 1996).

— *Baptism in the Holy Spirit: A Re-Examination of the New Testament Teaching on the Gift of the Spirit in Relation to Pentecostalism Today* (London: SCM Press Press, 1977).

— *Romans 1-8*, WBC 38A (Word, Waco, 1988).

— *Romans 9-16.* WBC 38B (Waco: Word, 1988).

— *The Epistles to the Colossians and to Philemon.* NIGTC (Grand Rapids: Eerdmans, 1996).

— *The Epistle to the Galatians.* BNTC (Peabody: Hendrickson, 1993).

— *The Theology of Paul the Apostle* (Edinburgh: T&T. Clark, 1998).

Edwards, J.R. *Romans.* NIBC (Peabody: Hendrickson, 1992).

Eichholz, G. 'Bewahren und Bewähren des Evangeliums: Der Leitfaden von Philipper 1-2' in H. Gollwitzer and H. Traub, *Hören und Handeln.*

Festschift für Ernst Wolf zum 60. Geburstag (München: Chr. Kaiser Verlag, 1962), 84-105.
Ellicott, C.J. *St Paul's Epistles to the Philippians, the Colossians, and Philemon* (London: Longmans, Green and Co, 1865).
Elliott, N. *Liberating Paul: The Justice of God and the Politics of the Apostle* (Maryknoll: Orbis, 1994).
Ellis, E.E. *Pauline Theology: Ministry and Society* (Grand Rapids: Eerdmans, 1989).
— *Prophecy and Hermeneutic in Early Christianity. New Testament Essays* (Grand Rapids: Eerdmans, 1978).
Ellul, J. *Apocalypse* (New York: Seabury, 1977).
Elzell, D. 'The Sufficiency of Christ: Philippians 4', *RevExp* 77 (1980): 373-381.
Engberg-Pedersen, T. 'Stoicism in Philippians' in T. Engberg-Pedersen (ed.), *Paul in his Hellenistic Context*. SNTW (Edinburgh: T&T. Clark, 1994), 256-291.
Frame, J.E. *A Critical and Exegetical Commentary on the Epistles of St. Paul to the Thessalonians*. ICC (Edinburgh: T&T. Clark, 1912).
Fee, G.D. *God's Empowering Presence* (Peabody: Hendrickson, 1994).
— *Paul's Letter to the Philippians*. NICNT (Grand Rapids: Eerdmans, 1995).
— 'Philippians 2:5-11: Hymn or Exalted Pauline prose', *BBR* 2 (1992): 29-46.
— *The First Epistle to the Corinthians* (Grand Rapids: Eerdmans, 1987).
— *1 & 2 Timothy, Titus* (Peabody: Hendrickson, 1984, 88).
Field, F. *Notes on the Translation of the New Testament* (Cambridge: CUP, 1899).
Finger, R.H. 'For the Sake of the Gospel: Paul and the Ministering Women', *DS* 19 (1993): 43-46.
Fitzmyer, J.A. *Romans: A New Translation with Introduction and Commentary*. ABC (New York, Doubleday, 1993).
— *The Acts of the Apostles*. ABC (New York: Doubleday, 1998).
— 'The Aramaic Background of Philippians 2:6-11', *CBQ* 50 (1988): 470-483.
— 'The Consecutive Meaning of ἐφ' ᾧ in Romans 5:12', *NTS* 39 (1993): 321-329.
— 'The Gospel in the Theology of Paul', *Interpretation* 33.4 (1979): 339-350.
— 'The Letter to the Philippians' in *JBC* (London: Geoffrey Chapman, 1970).
Flanagan, N. 'A Note on Phil 3:20-21,' *CBQ* 18 (1956): 8-9.
Fortna, R.T. 'Philippians, Paul's Most Egocentric Letter' in R.T. Fortna and B.R. Gaventa (eds), *The Conversation Continues. Studies in Paul and John in Honour of J. Louis Martyn* (Nashville: Abingdon Press, 1990), 220-234.
Foulkes, F. *Ephesians*. TBC (Leicester: IVP, 1989).
Freidrich, G. *Der Brief an die Philipper*. NTD 8 (Göttingen: Vandenhoeck & Ruprecht, 1981).
Fung, R.Y.K. 'The Nature of Ministry According to Paul', *EQ* 54 (1982): 129-146.

Funk, R.W. *Language, Hermeneutic, and Word of God: the Problem of Language in the New Testament and Contemporary Theology* (New York: Harper and Row, 1966).

— 'The Apostolic *Parousia*: Form and Significance' in W.R. Farmer, C.F.D. Moule and R.R. Niebuhr, *Christian History and Interpretation. Studies Presented to John Knox* (Cambridge: CUP, 1967), 249-268.

Furnish, V.P. *The Love Command in the New Testament* (Nashville: Abingdon, 1972).

— *The Moral Teaching of Paul* (Nashville: Abingdon, 1979).

— 'The Place and Purpose of Philippians III', *NTS* 10 (1963-64): 80-88.

— *2 Corinthians*. ABC (New York: Doubleday, 1984).

Garland, D.E. *Colossians and Philemon.* NIVAC (Grand Rapids: Zondervan, 1998).

— 'Philippians 1:1-26: The Defense and Confirmation of the Gospel' *RevExp* 77 (1980): 327-336.

— 'The Composition and Unity of Philippians. Some Neglected Literary Factors,' *NovT* (27 (1985): 141-73.

— *2 Corinthians.* NAC (Nashville: Broadman & Holman, 1999).

Gasque, W.W. and R.P. Martin (ed's), *Apostolic History and the Gospel, Biblical and Historical Essays Presented to F.F. Bruce on his 60th Birthday* (Grand Rapids: Eerdmans, 1970).

George, Timothy, *Galatians*, NAC 30 (Nashville: Broadman & Holman Publishers, 2001, c1994), 165.

Getty, M.A. *Philippians and Philemon.* NTM (Wilmington: Michael Glazier, 1987).

Gill, D.W.G. *The Book of Acts in its First-Century setting* (5 Vols. Grand Rapids: Eerdmans, 1994).

Gillman, F.M. 'Early Christian Women at Philippi', *JGWR* 1 (1990): 59-79.

Gnilka, J. *Der Philipperbrief.* HTKNT (Freiburg: Herder, 1976).

— 'Die antipaulinische Mission in Philippi', *BZ* 9 (1965): 258-276.

Godet, F.L. *Commentary on St Paul's Epistle to the Romans* (2 Vol's. Edinburgh: T&T. Clark, 1913).

Goguel, M. *Introduction au Nouveau Testament.* Four Volumes (Paris: Leroux, 1925).

Goodspeed, E.J. *Introduction to the New Testament* (Chicago: University of Chicago Press, 1937).

Gordon, T.D. '"Equipping" Ministry in Ephesians 4?' *JETS* 37 (1994): 69-78.

Grayston, K. 'The Opponents in Philippians 3', *ExpTim* 97 (1986): 170-172.

— *The Letters of Paul to the Philippians and the Thessalonians.* EPC (Cambridge: Epworth Press, 1967).

Green, M. *Evangelism in the Early Church* (Crowborough: Highland Books, 1970).

— *I Believe in Satan's Downfall* (Grand Rapids: Michigan, 1981).

Gundry-Volf, J.M. *Paul and Perseverance* (Westminster: John Knox, 1991).

Guthrie, D. *New Testament Introduction* (Downers Grove: IVP, 1990).
Guthrie, G.H. 'Cohesion Shifts and Stitches in Philippians' in S.E. Porter and D.A. Carson, *Discourse Analysis and Other Topics in Biblical Greek.* JSNTS 113 (Sheffield: Sheffield Academic Press, 1995), 36-50.
Hafemann, S.J. *2 Corinthians*, NIVAC (Grand Rapids: Zondervan, 2000).
Hahn, F. *Mission in the New Testament* (Trans. Frank Clarke; London: SCM Press, 1965).
Hàjek, M. 'Comments on Philippians 4:3 – Who was "*Gnesios Syzygos*"?' *CV* 7 (1964): 261-262.
Hall, D.R. 'Fellow-Workers with the Gospel', *ExpTim* 85 (1974): 119-130.
Hamaan, H.P. 'Church and Ministry: an Exegesis of Ephesians 4:1-6', *LTJ* 16.3 (1982): 121-128.
Hanks, T.D. 'Poor, Poverty: New Testament' in *ABD*, 5:414-424.
Hansen, G.W. *Galatians*. IVPNTCS (Leicester: IVP, 1994).
Hanson, A.T. *The Pastoral Epistles*. NCBC (Grand Rapids: Eerdmans, 1982).
Harnack, A. *The Mission and Expansion of Christianity in the First Three Centuries* (New York: Harper & Brothers, 1961).
Harris, M. *Colossians and Philemon* (Grand Rapids: Eerdmans, 1991).
Hawthorn, T. 'Philippians i.12-19.' With Special Reference to vv. 15. 16. 17', *ExpTim* 62 (1950-51): 316-317.
Hawthorne, G.F. *Philippians*. WBC 43 (Waco: Word, 1983).
— 'The Interpretation and Translation of Philippians 1:28b', *ExpTim*95 (1983): 80-81.
Hawthorne, G.F, Martin R.P, and Reid, D.G. *Dictionary of Paul and his Letters* (DPL) (Leicester: IVP, 1993).
Heine, S. *Women and Early Christianity* (Minneapolis: Augsburg, 1988).
Hemer, C.J. *The Book of Acts in the Setting of Hellenistic History*. WUNT 49 (Tübingen: Mohr (Siebeck), 1989).
Hendriksen, W. *Epistle to the Romans*. NTC (Vol 2/2. Grand Rapids: Baker, 1981).
— *Philippians*. NTC (Edinburgh: The Banner of Truth Trust, 1962).
Hiebert, P.G. *Missiological Implications of Epistemological Shifts; Affirming Truth in a Modern/Postmodern World* (Harrisburg: Trinity Press, 1999).
Hock, R. 'The Workshop as a Social Setting for Missionary Preaching', *CBQ* 41 (1979): 438-50.
Hodge, C. *Commentary on the Epistle to the Romans* (Grand Rapids: Eerdmans, 1886, 1950).
— *An Exposition of the First Epistle to the Corinthians* (Grand Rapids: Eerdmans, 1980).
Hofius, O. *Der Christushymnus Philipper 2,6-11: Untersuchungen zu Gestalt und Aussage eines urchristlichen Psalms*. WUNT 17 (Tübingen: Mohr (Siebeck), 1991).
Holloday, C.R. 'Paul's Opponents in Philippians 3', *ResQ* 12 (1969): 77-90.

Holloway, P.A. *Consolation in Philippians. Philosophical Sources and Rhetorical Strategy* (Cambridge: CUP, 2001).

Holmberg, B. *Paul and Power. The Structure of Authority in the Primitive Church as Reflected in the Pauline Epistles*. CBNT 11 (Lund: Gleerup, 1978).

Holmes, M.W. *1 & 2 Thessalonians*. NIVAC (Grand Rapids: Eerdmans, 1998).

Hooker, M. 'Philippians 2:6-11,' in E.E. Ellis and E. Grässer (ed's), *Jesus und Paulus. Festschrift für Werner Georg Kümmel zum 70. Geburstag* (Göttingen: Vandenhoeck & Ruprecht, 1987), 151-164.

Hoover, R.W. 'The HARPAGMOS Enigma: A Philological Solution', *HTR* 64 (1971): 95-119.

Horsley, G.H.R. *New Documents Illustrating Early Christianity. A Review of Greek Inscriptions and Papyri Published in 1977* (Vol 2. Macquarie: Macquarie University, 1982).

Houlden, J.H. *Paul's Letters From Prison* (Hamondsworth: Penguin, 1970).

Hughes, P.E. *The Second Epistle to the Corinthians*. NICNT (Grand Rapids: Eerdmans, 1962).

Hultgren, A.J. *Paul's Gospel and Mission* (Philadelphia: Fortress Press, 1985).

Hurtado, L.W. 'The Book of Galatians and the Jerusalem Collection,' *JSNT* 5 (1979): 46-62.

Janzen, J.G. 'Creation and New Creation in Phil 1:6', *HBT* 18:1 (June 1996): 27-54.

Jervis, L. Ann. 'Collection for the Saints' in *ABD*, 1:1131.

— *Galatians*. NIBC (Peabody: Hendrickson, 1999).

Jewett, R. 'Conflicting Movements in the Early Church as Reflected in Philippians', *NovT* 12 (1970): 362-390.

— *Paul's Anthropological Terms. A Study of their Use in Conflict Settings*. NovTSup 16 (Leiden: Brill, 1971).

— 'Paul, Phoebe, and the Spanish Mission', in J. Neusner et al, *The Social World of Formative Judaism and Christianity: Essays in Tribute to Howard Clark Kee* (Philadelphia: Fortress Press, 1988), 144-164.

— 'The Agitators and the Galatian Congregation,' *NTS* 17 (1970–71): 198–212.

— 'The Epistolary Thanksgiving and the Integrity of Philippians', *NovT* 12 (1970): 40-53.

— *The Thessalonian Correspondence: Pauline Rhetoric and Millenarian Piety. Foundations and facets* (Philadelphia: Fortress, 1986).

Johnson, L. 'The Pauline Letters from Caesarea', *ExpTim* 68 (1957-58): 24-26.

Johnson, L.T. *Reading Romans: A Literary and Theological Commentary* (New York: Crossroad, 1997).

— *The Writings of the New Testament an Interpretation* (Minneapolis: Fortress Press, 1999).

Jones, M. *The Epistle to the Philippians*. WC (London: Methven, 1918).

— 'The Integrity of the Epistle to the Philippians,' *The Expositor* 8 (1914): 462.

Josephus, F. *Josephus in Nine Volumes* (Trans. H. St. J. Thackeray. London: William Heinemann, 1928).

Käsemann, E. *Commentary on Romans* (Trans G.W. Bromiley. Grand Rapids: Eerdmans, 1980).

Kennedy, G.A. *New Testament Interpretation through Rhetorical Criticism* (Chapel Hill: University of North Carolina Press, 1984).

Kennedy, H.A.A. 'The Epistle to the Philippians' in *Expositor's Greek Testament* Vol 3 (Ed. W.R. Nicholl. Grand Rapids: Eerdmans, 1903 [1976]).

Kent Jnr, H.A. 'Philippians' in F. Gaebelein (ed) *EBC* (Vol 11/12. Grand Rapids: Zondervan, 1978), 93-159.

Kettunen, M. *Der Abfassungszweck des Römerbriefes* (Helsinki: Suomalainen Tiedeakatemin, 1979).

Kilpatrick, G.D. 'ΒΛΕΠΕΤΕ, Phil 3:2' in M. Black and G. Fohrer (ed's), *In Memoriam Paul Kahle* (Berlin: de Gruyter, 1968), 146-148.

Kirk, J.A. 'Apostleship Since Rengstorf: Toward a Synthesis', *NTS* 21 (1975): 249-264.

Klijn, A.F.J. 'Paul's Opponents in Philippi iii', *NovT* 7 (1965): 278-284.

Knox, J, 'Romans 15:14-33 and Paul's Conception of his Apostolic Mission', *JBL* 83 (1964): 3-8.

Köster, H. 'The Purpose of the Polemic of a Pauline Fragment (Philippians 3)', *NTS* 8 (1961-1962): 317-332.

— 'Letter to the Philippians', *IDBSup* (Nashville: Abingdon, 1976).

Kraftchick, S.J. 'A Necessary Detour: Paul's Metaphorical Understanding of the Philippians Hymn', *HBT* 15 (1993): 1-37.

Krentz, E. '1 Thessalonians: Rhetorical Flourishes and Formal Constraints', in Donfried K.P. and J. Beutler, *The Thessalonians Debate; Methodological Discord or Methodological Synthesis?* (Grand Rapids: Eerdmans, 2000), 287-318.

Kruse, C. *The Second Epistle of Paul to the Corinthians*. TBC (Grand Rapids: Eerdmans, 1987).

Kümmel, W.G. *Introduction to the New Testament* (Trans. Howard Clark Kee. London: SCM Press, 1973).

Larkin Jnr, W.J. *Acts*. IVPNTCS (Leicester: IVP, 1995).

Ladd, G.E. *A Theology of the New Testament* (Cambridge; Lutterworth, 1974).

Lagrange, M.J. *St Paul: Epître aux Romains*. Etudes bibliques (Paris: Gabalda, 1950).

Lambrecht, J. *Second Corinthians*. SPS (Collegeville: Liturgical, 1999).

Leenhardt, F.S. *The Epistle to the Romans: A Commentary* (London: Lutterworth, 1957).

Legrande, L. *Unity and Plurality: Mission in the Bible* (Trans. R.R. Barr. New York: Orbis, 1990).

Lenski, R.C.H. *The Interpretation of St Paul's Epistle to the Galatians, Ephesians and Philippians* (Minneapolis [Minn]: Augsburg), 1962).

— *The Interpretation of St Paul's Epistle to the Romans* (Columbas 15 [Ohio]: Wortburg Press, 1960).

Llewelyn, S.R. 'Sending Letters in the Ancient World: Paul and the Philippians', *TynB* 46.2 (1995): 337-356.

Liddell, H. *A Lexicon: Abridged from Liddell and Scott's Greek-English Lexicon* (Oak Harbor, WA: Logos Research Systems, Inc, 1996).

Lightfoot, J.B. *St. Paul's Epistle to the Galatians. A Revised Text With Introduction, Notes, and Dissertations* (4th ed. London: Macmillan and Co., 1874).

— *Saint Paul's Epistles to the Colossians and to Philemon.* (9th ed. London: Macmillan, 1890).

— *The Epistles of St Paul. III. The First Roman Captivity. I. Epistle to the Philippians* (London: MacMillan and Co, 1894).

Lincoln, A. *Ephesians*. WBC 42 (Dallas: Word, 1990).

— *Paradise Now and Not Yet. Studies in the Role of the Heavenly Dimension of Paul's Thought with Special Reference to his Eschatology*. SNTSMS 43 (Cambridge: CUP, 1981).

Loh I-J. and E.A. Nida, *A Translators Handbook on Paul's Letter to the Philippians* (Stuttgart: United bible society, 1977).

Lohmeyer, E. *Der Brief an die Philipper* (Göttingen: Vandenhoeck & Ruprecht, 1928).

Longenecker, R. N. *Galatians*. WBC 41 (Dallas: Word, 1990).

Louw, J.P. and E.A. Nida, *Lexicon of the New Testament Based on Semantic Domains on CD-ROM* (New York: United Bible Societies) 1988, 1989.

Lührmann, D. *Galatians* (Trans. O.C. Dean; Minneapolis: Fortress Press, 1992).

Lüdemann, G. *Opposition to Paul in Jewish Christianity* (Trans. M.E. Boring; Minneapolis: Fortress Press, 1989).

Luter, A.B. 'Partnership in the Gospel: the Role of Women in the Church at Philippi': *JETS* 39/3 (1996): 411-420.

Luter A.B. and M.V. Lee, 'Philippians as Chiasmus: Key to the Structure, Unity and Theme Questions', *NTS* 41 (1995): 89-101.

Luther, M, *A Commentary on St Paul's Epistle to the Galatians* (Trans. P.S. Watson. London: J. Clarke, 1953).

MacDonald, M.Y. *Colossians and Ephesians.* SPS (Collegeville: Liturgical, 2000).

MacKay, B.S. 'Further Thoughts on Philippians', *NTS* 7 (1960-61): 161-170.

McArthur, H.K. 'Computer Criticism', *ExpTim* 76 (1965): 367-70.

— '*Kai* frequency in Greek Letters,' *NTS* 15 (1969): 339-49.

McDermott, J.M. 'The Biblical Doctrine of KOINΩNIA', *BZ* (1975): 64-77, 219-233.

McKnight, S. 'Collection for the Saints' in *DPL*, 143-146.

Malinowski, F.X. 'The Brave Women of Philippi', *BTB* 15 (1985): 60-64.

Malherbe, A.J. *The Letters to the Thessalonians.* ABC 32 (New York: Doubleday, 2000).

Manson, T.W. 'St. Paul in Ephesus: The Date of the Epistle to the Philippians', *BJRL* 23 (1939): 182-200.

Marshall, I.H. *Acts*. TNTC (Leicester: IVP, 1980).

— 'The Christ-Hymn in Philippians 2:5-11', *TynB* 19 (1968): 104-127.

— *The epistle to the Philippians*. EC (London: Epworth, 1992).

— 'The Theology of Philippians' in K.P. Donfried and I.H. Marshall, *The Theology of the Shorter Pauline Letters* (Cambridge: CUP, 1993).

— 'Who Were the Evangelists?' in J. Ådna and H. Kvalbein, *The Mission of the Early Church to Jews and Gentiles*. WUNT 127 (Tübingen: Mohr (Siebeck), 2000).

— *1 and 2 Thessalonians*. NCBC (Grand Rapids: Eerdmans, 1983).

Marshall, P. *Enmity in Corinth. Social Conventions in Paul's Relations with the Corinthians.* WUNT 2:23 (Tübingen: Mohr (Siebeck), 1987).

Martin, R.P. *Carmen Christi. Philippians ii. 5-11 in Recent Interpretation and in the Setting of Early Christian Worship* (Grand Rapids: Eerdmans, 1967).

— *Philippians*. TNTC (Grand Rapids: Eerdmans, 1987).

— *2 Corinthians*. WBC 40 (Word: Waco, 1986).

Martyn, J.L. *Galatians: A New Translation with Introduction and Commentary.* ABC 33. (New York, Doubleday, 1997).

Masson, C. *Les deux Épîtres de Saint Paul aux Thessaloniciens.* CNT (Neuchâtel: Delachaux et Niestelé, 1957).

Mearns, C. 'The Identity of Paul's Opponents at Philippi', *NTS* 33 (1987): 194-204.

Meecham, H.G. 'The Use of the Participle for the Imperative in the New Testament,' *ExpTim*, 58 (1947): 207-209.

Meeks, W.A. *The First Urban Christians: The Social World of the Apostle Paul* (New Haven, Yale University, 1983).

Meindardus, O.F.A. 'Paul's Missionary Journey to Spain: Tradition and Folklore', *BA* 41 (1978): 61-63.

Melick, R.R. *Philippians, Colossians, Philemon.* NAC (Nashville: Broadman, Press, 1991).

Metzger, B.M. *A Textual Commentary on the Greek New Testament* (London: United Bible Society, 1971).

Meyer, F.B. *The Epistle to the Philippians* (London: The religious tract society, 1905).

Meyer, H.A.W. *Critical and Exegetical Handbook to the Epistles to the Philippians and Colossians* (Trans. J.C. Moore; W.P. Dickson: Edinburgh: T&T. Clark, 1875).

— *Critical and Exegetical Commentary to the Romans* (Edinburgh: T&T. Clark, 1874).

Michael, J.H. *The Epistle of Paul to the Philippians.* MNTC (London: Hodder & Stoughton, 1928).

— 'The First and Second Epistles to the Philippians', *ExpTim* 34 (1922-23): 106-109.

— '"Work out Your Own Salvation"', *The Expositor* 12 (1924): 439-450.

Miller, E.C. 'Πολιτεύσθε' in Philippians 1:27: Some Philological and Thematic Observations', *JSNT* 15 (1982): 86-96.

Minear, P.S. *The Obedience of Faith. The Purpose of Paul in the Epistle to the Romans.* SBT 2/19 (Naperville: Allenson, 1971).

Mitton, C.L. *The Formation of the Pauline Corpus of Letters* (London: Epworth, 1955).

— *Ephesians.* NCBC (Grand Rapids: Eerdmans, 1973)

Motyer, A. *The Message of Philippians*, (Leicester: IVP, 1984).

Moo, D.J. *The Epistle to the Romans.* NICNT (Grand Rapids: Eerdmans, 1996).

Morris, L. *Expository Reflections on the Letter to the Ephesians* (Grand Rapids: Baker, 1994).

— 'ΚΑΙ ΑΠΑΞ ΚΑΙ ΔΙΣ', *NovT* 1 (1956): 205-08.

— *Galatians: Paul's Charter of Christian Freedom* (Leicester: IVP, 1996).

— *The Epistle to the Romans* (Grand Rapids: Eerdmans, 1988).

— *The First and Second Epistles to the Thessalonians.* NICNT (Grand Rapids: Eerdmans, 1959).

— *The First Epistle of Paul to the Corinthians.* TNTC (Leicester: IVP, 1985).

Morton A.Q. and McLeman, J. *Christianity in the Computer Age* (New York: Harper and Row, 1965).

— *Paul, the Man and the Myth. A Study in the Authorship of Greek Prose* (New York, Harper and Row, 1966).

Moule, H.C.G. *Epistle to the Romans* (London: Pickering and Inglis, 1887).

— *The Epistle of Paul the Apostle to the Philippians* (Cambridge: CUP, 1923).

Mounce, W.D. *Pastoral Epistles.* WBC 46 (Nashville: Thomas Nelson, 2000).

Müller, J.J. *The Epistles of Paul to the Philippians and to Philemon.* NICNT (Grand Rapids: Eerdmans, 1955).

Müller-Bardorff, J. 'Zur Frage der literarischen Einheit des Phil', *WZUJ* 7 (1957-1958): 591-604.

Müller, U.B. *Der Brief an der Philipper.* THNT 11/1 (Leipzig: Evangelische Verlagsanstalt, 1993).

Mullins, T.Y. 'Disclosure. A Literary Form in the New Testament,' *NovT* 7 (1964): 44-50.

— 'Formulas in New Testament Epistles', *JBL* 91 (1972): 380-390.

— 'Visit Talk in New Testament Letters', *CBQ* 35 (1977): 350-358.

Munck, J. *Paul and the Salvation of Mankind* (London: SCM Press, 1959).

Murphy-O'Connor, J. 'On the Road and on the Sea with St. Paul', *BibRev* (1985): 38-47.

Murray, G.W. 'Paul's Corporate Witness in Philippians', *BSac* 155 (1998): 316-326.

Murray, J. *The Epistle to the Romans.* NICNT 2 Vols (Grand Rapids: Eerdmans, 1965).

Neil, W. *The Letter of Paul to the Galatians.* CBC (Cambridge, CUP, 1967).

Neugebauer, F. *In Christus, Eine Untersuchung zum Paulinishen Glaubensverständnis* (Göttingen, 1961).

Nygren, A. *Agape and Eros. Vol 1: A Study in the Christian Idea of Love* (Trans. A.G. Hebert. London: SPCK, 1932).

— *Commentary on Romans,* (Trans. Carl C. Rasmussen. London: SCM Press, 1952).

Oaks, P. *Philippians. From People to Letter.* SNTSMS 110 (Cambridge: CUP, 2001).

Oakes, P. 'Review of P.T. O'Brien, *Gospel and Mission in the Writings of St Paul*' in *EQ* 70:1 (1998): 83-84.

O'Brien, P.T. *Colossians, Philemon,* WBC (Waco: Word, 1982).

— *Consumed by Passion. Paul and the Dynamic of the Gospel* (Homebush West: Anzea, 1993).

— *Introductory Thanksgivings in the Letters of Paul.* NovTSup 49 (Leiden: Brill, 1977).

— 'Principalities and Powers: Opponents of the Church' in D.A. Carson (ed), *Biblical Interpretation and the Church* (Nashville: T. Nelson, 1984), 110-150.

— 'The Church as a Heavenly and Eschatological Entity' in D.A. Carson (ed), *The Church in the Bible and the World* (Exeter: Paternoster, 1987), 88-117.

— *The Epistle to the Philippians.* NIGTC (Grand Rapids: Eerdmans, 1991).

— 'The Gospel and Godly Models in Philippians' in M.J. Wilkins and T. Paige (ed's), *Worship, Theology and Ministry in the Early Church. Essays in Honor of Professor R.P. Martin* (Sheffield: Academic Press, 1992), 273-284.

— 'The Importance of the Gospel in Philippians' in P.T. O'Brien and D.G. Peterson. (ed's) *God Who is Rich in Mercy. Essays Presented to D.B. Knox.* (Homebush West [NSW]: Anzea, 1986), 213-233.

— *The Letter to the Ephesians.* PNTC (Grand Rapids: Eerdmans, 1999).

O'Brien P.T. and A.J. Köstenberger, *Salvation to the Ends of the Earth: A Biblical Theology of Mission* NSBT 11 (Leicester: Apollos, 2001).

Ollrog, W.-H. *Paulus und seine Mitarbeiter: Untersuchungen zu Theorie und Praxis der paulinischen Mission* (Neukirchen-Vluyn: Neukirchener Verlag, 1979).

Omanson, R.L. 'A Note on the Translation of Philippians 1:3-5', *BT* 29 (1978): 244-245.

— 'A Note on the Translation of Philippians 1:12', *BT* 29.4 (1978): 446-48.

O'Neill, J.C. *Paul's Letter to the Romans* (Harmondsworth: Penguin, 1975).

Onwu, N. 'Mimetic Hypothesis: a Key to the Understanding of Pauline Paraenesis', *AJBS* 1.2 (1986): 95-112.

Orr, W.F and J.A. Walther, *1 Corinthians.* ABC 32 (Garden City: Doubleday, 1976).

Osborne, R.E. 'Paul and the Wild Beasts', *JBL* 85 (1966): 225-230.

Osiek, C. *Philippians*. ANTC (Nashville: Abingdon, 2000).

Panikulam, G. *Koinōnia in the New Testament: A Dynamic Expression of Christian Life*. AnBib 85 (Rome: Biblical Institute Press, 1979).

Parry, R.S. *The First Epistle of Paul the Apostle to the Corinthians*. CGTSC (2d ed. Cambridge: CUP, 1926).

Pearson, B.A. '1 Thessalonians 2:13–16: A Deutero-Pauline Interpolation,' *HTR* 64 (1971): 79–94.

Perkins, P. 'New Testament Ethics' in *ABD*, 2:652-665.

— 'Philippians: Theology for the Heavenly Politeuma' in J.M. Bassler (ed.), *Pauline Theology, Vol 1: Thessalonians, Philippians, Galatians, Philemon* (Minneapolis: Fortress Press, 1991), 89-104.

Peterlin, D. *Paul's Letter to the Philippians in Light of the Disunity in the Church*. NovTSup 79 (New York: E.J. Brill, 1995).

Peterman, G.W. *Paul's Gift from Philippi. Conventions of Gift Exchange and Christian Giving*. SNTSMS 92. (Cambridge: CUP, 1997).

Peters, G.W. *A Biblical Theology of Missions* (Chicago: Moody Press, 1972).

Pfitzner, V.C. *Paul and the Agon Motif*. NovTSup16 (Leiden: Brill, 1967).

Pilhofer, P. *Philippi Vol 1: Die erste chrisliche Gemeinde Europas*. WUNT 87 (Tübingen: Mohr (Siebeck), 1995).

Plummer, A. *A Commentary on St Paul's Epistle to the Philippians* (London: Robert Scott, 1919).

Plummer, R.L. *Paul's Understanding of the Church's Mission. Did the Apostle Paul Expect the Early Christian Communities to Evangelize?* (Milton Keynes: Paternoster, 2006).

Pobee, J.S. *Persecution and Martyrdom in the Theology of Paul*. JSNTS 6 (Sheffield: JSOT Press, 1985).

Polhill, J.B. 'Twin Obstacles in the Christian Path', *RevExp* 77 (1980): 359-371.

Pollard, T.E. 'The Integrity of Philippians', *NTS* 13 (1966-67): 57-66.

Porter, S.E. 'The Theoretical Justification for the Application of Rhetorical Categories to Pauline Epistolary Literature' in Porter S.E. and T.H. Olbricht (ed's), T.H. *Rhetoric and the New Testament. Essays from the 1992 Heidelberg Conference*. JSNTS 90 (Sheffield: Sheffield Academic Press, 1993), 99-122.

— 'Word Order and Clause Structure in New Testament Greek. An Unexplored Area of Greek Linguistics using Philippians as a Test Case,' *FNT* 6 (1993): 177-206.

Porter S.E. and T.H. Olbricht (ed's), *Rhetoric and the New Testament. Essays from the 1992 Heidelberg Conference*. JSNTS 90 (Sheffield: Sheffield Academic Press, 1993).

Prior, D. *The Message of 1 Corinthians*. BST (Leicester: IVP, 1985).

Quinn, J.D. and W.C. Wacker, *The First and Second Letters to Timothy*. EEC (Grand Rapids: Eerdmans, 2000).

Rahtjen, B.D. 'The Three Letters of Paul', *NTS* 6 (1959-60): 167-173.

Rainy, R. *Epistle to the Philippians*. EBC (London: Hodder & Stoughton, 1893).

Ramsay, W.M. 'Roads and Travel (in NT),' in J. Hastings, *Hastings Dictionary of the Bible (HDB)* (Peabody: Hendrickson, 1989), 375-402.

— *The Bearing of Recent Discovery on the Trustworthiness of the New Testament* (London: Hodder and Stoughton, 1915).

Reed, J.T. 'Are Paul's Thankgivings "Epistolary"', *JSNT* 61 (1996): 87-99.

— *A Discourse Analysis of Philippians. Method and Rhetoric in the Debate over Literary Integrity*. JSNTSS 136 (Sheffield: Sheffield Academic Press, 1997).

— 'Categories,' in Porter S.E. and T.H. Olbricht (ed's), *Rhetoric and the New Testament. Essays from the 1992 Heidelberg Conference.* JSNTS 90 (Sheffield: Sheffield Academic Press, 1993).

— 'Philippians 3:1 and the Epistolary Hesitation Formulas: the Literary Integrity of Philippians, Again', JBL 115 (1996): 63-90.

— 'The Infinitive with Two Substantial Accusatives, an Ambiguous Construction?' *NovT* 33 (1991): 1-27.

Reinhartz, A. 'On the Meaning of the Pauline Exhortation: "*mimētai mou ginesthai* – Become Imitators of Me', *StudRel* 16.4 (1987): 393-403.

Reumann, J. 'Contributions of the Philippian Community to Paul and to Earliest Christianity', *NTS* 39 (1993): 438-457.

— 'Philippians 3:20-21 – A Hymnic Fragment', *NTS* 30 (1984): 593-609.

— 'Philippians, 'Especially Chapter 4, as a "Letter of Friendship": Observations on a Checkered History of Scholarship' in J.T. Fitzgerald (ed), *Friendship, Flattery, and Frankness of Speech: Studies in Friendship in the New Testament World.* NovTSup 82 (Leiden: Brill, 1996), 83-106.

Ridderbos, H. *Paul: An Outline of his Theology* (Trans. John Richard de Witt. Grand Rapids: Eerdmans, 1975).

— *The Epistle of Paul to the Churches in Galatia* (London: Marshall, Morgan and Scott, 1953).

Richard, E.J. *First and Second Thessalonians*. SPS (Collegeville: Liturgical Press, 1995).

Richardson, P. 'From Apostles to Virgins: Romans 16 and the Roles of Women in the Early Church', *TJT* 2 (1986): 232-261.

Roberts, R. 'Old Texts in Modern Translations; Philippians 1:27 (Goodspeed),' *ExpTim* 49 (1937-38): 325-328.

Robinson, D.W.B. 'We are the Circumcision', *ABR* 15 (1967): 28-35.

Robinson, J.A.T. *St Paul's Epistle to the Ephesians* (London: Macmillan, 1904).

— *Redating the New Testament* (London: SCM Press, 1976).

Robbins, C.J. 'Rhetorical Structure of Philippians 2:6-11, *CBQ* 42 (1980): 73-82.

Ropes, J.H. '"Righteousness" and "the Righteousness of God" in the Old Testament and in St Paul', *JBL* 22 (1903): 225-226.

Rupp, E.G. *Principalities and Powers* (London: Epworth, 1952).

Russell, R. 'Pauline Letter Structure in Philippians', *JETS* 25 (1982): 295-306.

Sallew, P. 'Laodiceans and the Philippians Fragments Hypothesis', *HTR* 87 (1994): 17-27.

Sanders, J.T. 'The Transition from Opening Epistolary Thanksgiving to Body in the Letters of the Pauline Corpus', *JBL* 81 (1982): 348-362.

Sanday W. and A.C. Headlam, *A Critical Commentary on the Epistle to the Romans*. ICC (Edinburgh: T&T. Clark, 1902).

Schenk, W. *Der Philipperbriefe des Paulus. Kommentar* (Stuttgart: Verlag W. Kohlhammer, 1984).

Schmithals, W. *Paul and the Gnostics* (Trans. J.E. Seely. Nashville: Abingdon, 1972).

Schnabel, Eckhard J. *Early Christian Mission. Paul and the Early Church.* Vol 2 of 2 (Trans. E.J. Schnabel. Downers Grove/Apollos: IVP/Leicester, 2004).

Schnackenburg, R. *The Epistle to the Ephesians* (Trans. Helen Heron; Edinburgh: T&T. Clark, 1991).

Scholer, D.M. 'Paul's Women Co-Workers in the Ministry of the Church', *AB* 23:4 (1987): 70-72.

Schreiner, T.R. *Romans*. BECNT (Grand Rapids: Baker, 1998).

Schubert, P. *Form and Function of the Pauline Thanksgivings,* BZNTW 20 (Berlin: Töpelmann, 1939).

Schüssler-Fiorenza, E. 'Missionaries, Apostles, Co-Workers: Romans 16 and the Reconstruction of Women's Early Christian History', *Word and World* 6.4 (1986): 57-71.

— *In Memory of Her: A Feminist Theological Reconstruction of Christian Origins* (New York: Crossroad, 1983).

Schütz, J.H. *Paul and the Anatomy of Apostolic Authority*. SNTSMS 26 (Cambridge: CUP, 1975).

Scobie, C.H.H. 'Jesus or Paul? The Origin of the Universal Mission of the Christian Church' in P. Richardson and J.C. Hurd (ed's), *From Jesus to Paul. Studies in Honour of F.W. Beare* (Waterloo: Wilfred Laurier University, 1984), 47-60.

Senior, D and Stuhlmueller, C. *The Biblical Foundations for Mission* (London: SCM Press, 1983).

Silva, M. *Philippians*. BECNT (Grand Rapids: Baker Book House, 1992).

Scroggs, R. 'Women in the New Testament', *IDBSup* (Nashville: Abingdon, 1976).

Seesemann, H. *Der Begriff KOINΩNIA im Neuen Testament* (Giessen: Verlag von Alfred Toepelmann, 1933).

Sevenster, J.N. *Paul and Seneca*. NovTSup 4 (Leiden, Brill: 1961).

Skeat, T.C. 'Did Paul Write to "Bishops and Deacons" at Philippi? A Note on Philippians 1:1', *NovT* 37 (1995): 12-15.

Smail, T. 'The Cross and the Spirit: Towards a Theology of Renewal' in T. Smail, A. Walker and N. Wright (ed's), *Charismatic Renewal* (London: SPCK, 1995), 49-52.

Souter, A. *Text and Canon of the New Testament* (London: Duckworth, 1954).

Spence-Jones, H.D.M. *The Pulpit Commentary: Galatians* (Bellingham, WA: Logos Research Systems, Inc., 2004).

Spicq, C. *Agape in the New Testament.* Vol 2 (Trans. M.A. McNamara. St Louis: Herder, 1963-64).

Stagg, F. 'The Mind in Jesus Christ, Philippians 1:27-2:18', *RevExp* 77 (1980): 337-347.

Stambaugh J.E. and D.L. Balch, *The New Testament in its Social Environment* (Philadelphia: Westminster Press, 1986).

Stein, R.H. 'Jerusalem' in *DPL*, 463-474.

Stott, J.R.W. *The Message of Romans: God's Good News to the World.* BST (Leicester: IVP, 1994).

— *The Message of Acts*. BST (Leicester: IVP, 1990).

— *The Message of Ephesians: God's New Society*. BST (Leicester: IVP, 1979).

Stowers, S.K. 'Friends and Enemies in the Politics of Heaven. Reading Theology in Philippians' in J.M. Bassler (ed), *Pauline Theology Vol 1. Thessalonians, Philippians, Galatians, Philemon* (Minneapolis : Fortress Press, 1991), 105-121.

Strimple, R.B. 'Philippians 2:5-11 in Recent Studies: Some Exegetical Conclusions', *WTJ* 41 (1979): 247-268.

Stuhlmacher, P (ed), *Gospel and the Gospels* (Grand Rapids: Eerdmans, 1991).

— *Paul's Letter to the Romans* (Trans. Scott J. Hafemann. Louiseville [Kentucky]: Westminster/John Knox Press, 1994).

Suggs, M.J. 'Concerning the Date of Paul's Macedonian Ministry', *NovT* 4 (1960-61): 60-68.

Swift, R.C. 'The Theme and Structure of Philippians', *BSac* 141 (1984): 234-254.

Synge, F.C. *Philippians and Colossians* (London: Torch Bible Commentaries, 1951).

Tarn W.W. and G.T. Griffith, *Hellenistic Civilisation* (Cleveland, E. Arnold, 1952).

Tetlow, E. M. *Women and Ministry in the New Testament* (New York: Paulist Press, 1980).

Thielman, F. *Philippians*. NIVAC (Grand Rapids: Zondervan, 1995).

Thiselton, A.C. *The First Epistle to the Corinthians.* NIGTC (Grand Rapids: Eerdmans, 2000).

Thomas, W.D. 'The Place of Women in the Church at Philippi', *ExpTim* 83 (1971-72): 117-20.

Thrall, M. *II Corinthians*. ICC (2 Vols. Edinburgh: T&T. Clark, 1994, 1999).

Torjeson, K. J. *When Women were Priests* (San Francisco: Harper, 1993).

Towner, P.H. *1-2 Timothy & Titus*. IVPNTCS (Downers Grove: IVP, 1994).

Trebilco, P. 'Women as Co-Workers and Leaders in Paul's Letters', *JCBRF* 122 (1990): 27-36.

Vincent, M.R. *The Epistles to the Philippians and to Philemon* (Edinburgh: T&T. Clark, 1897.

Von Harnack, A. κόπος (κοπῖαν, οἱ κοπιῶντες) im früchristlichen Sprachgebrauch, *ZNW* 27 (1928), 1-10.

Vooys, J. 'No Clergy or Laity: All Christians are Ministers in the Body of Christ, Ephesians 4:11-13', *Direction* 20.1 (1991): 87-95.

Wallace, D.B. *Greek Grammar Beyond the Basics* (Grand Rapids: Zondervan, 1996).

Walter, N. 'Die Philipper and das Leiden. Aus den Anfäng einer heidenchristlichen Gemeinde', in R. Schnackenburg (ed.), *Die Kirche des Anfangs: Für Heinz Schümann* (Freiburg: Herder, 1978), 417-434.

Wanamaker, C.A. 'Epistolary vs. Rhetorical Analysis: Is a Synthesis Possible?' in Donfried K.P. and Beutler, J. *The Thessalonians Debate; Methodological Discord or Methodological Synthesis?* (Grand Rapids: Eerdmans, 2000), 255-286.

Wansink, C.S. *Chained in Christ. The Experience and Rhetoric of Paul's Imprisonments*. JSNTS 130. (Sheffield: Sheffield Academic Press, 1996).

Ware, J. *The Mission of the Church in Paul's Letter to the Philippians in the Context of Ancient Judaism* (Leiden: Brill, 2005).

— 'The Thessalonians as a missionary congregation: 1Thessalonians 1,5-8', *ZNW* 83 (1992): 126-131.

Watson, D.F. 'A Rhetorical Analysis of Philippians and its Implications for the Unity Question', *NovT* 30 (1988): 57-88.

Weaver, P.R.C. *Familia Caesaris: A Social Study of the Emperor's Freedman and Slaves* (Cambridge: CUP, 1972).

Webster, J.B. 'The Imitation of Christ', *TynB* 37 (1986): 95-120.

Wedderburn, A.J.M. *The Reasons for Romans* (Edinburgh: T&T. Clark, 1988).

Weima, J.A.D. *The Significance of the Pauline Letter Closings*. JSNTS 101 (Sheffield: Sheffield Academic Press, 1994).

White, J.L. 'Ancient Greek Letters' in D.E. Aune (ed), *Graeco-Roman Literature and the New Testament* (Atlanta: Scholars Press, 1988), 85-106.

— 'Introductory Formulae in the Body of the Pauline Letter, *JBL* 90 (1971): 1-97.

— *Light from Ancient Letters* (Philadelphia: Fortress Press, 1986).

— *The Form and Function of the Body of the Greek Letter. A Study of the Letter-Body Papyri in the Non-literary Papyri and in Paul the Apostle*. SBLDS 138 (Missoula: Scholars Press, 1972).

Whittaker, M. 'A.Q. Morton and J. McLeman,' *Theology* 69 (1966): 567-68.

Wicks, R.R. and E.F. Scott, 'The Epistle to the Philippians' in *The Interpreters Bible* (Vol II. New York: Abingdon, 1955), 3-129.

Wilder, A.N. *Kerygma, Eschatology and Social Ethics in the Background of Its Eschatology* (Cambridge: CUP, 1964).

Wiles, G.P. *Prayers. The Significance of the Intercessory Prayer Passages in the Letters of St Paul*. SNTSMS 24 (Cambridge: CUP, 1974).

Williams, D.J. *Acts*. NIBC (Peabody: Hendrickson, 1990).

Williams, D.K. *Enemies of the Cross of Christ. The Terminology of the Cross and Conflict in Philippians*. JSNTS 223 (Sheffield: Academic Press, 2002).

Williams, D. *The Apostle Paul and Women in the Church* (Ventura, CA: Regal Books, 1977).

Williams, S.K. *Galatians*. ANTC (Nashville: Abingdon, 1997).

Willimon, W.H. *Acts*. IBC (Atlanta: John Knox, 1988).

Wimber, John, *Power Evangelism. Signs and Wonders Today* (London: Hodder and Stoughton, 1985).

Wink, W. *Naming the Powers* (Philadelphia: Fortress, 1984).

Winter, B.W. 'Dangers and Difficulties for the Pauline Missions', in P. Bolt and M. Thompson (ed's), *The Gospel to the Nations. Perspectives on Paul's Mission* (Leicester: IVP, 2000), 285-296.

Witherington III, B. *Friendship and Finances in Philippians* (Valley Forge [Pennsylvania]: Trinity Press International, 1994).

Wood, A.S. 'Ephesians' in Ed F. Gaebelein, EBC (Vol 11. Grand Rapids: Zondervan, 1978), 22-92.

Wright, N.T. *Colossians and Philemon*. TBC (Leicester: IVP, 1986).

Wuellner,, W. 'Greek Rhetoric and Pauline Argumentation' in William R. Schoedel and Robert L. Wilken, *Early Christian Literature and the Classical Intellectual Tradition. In Honorem Robert M. Grant*. TH 54 (Paris: Beauchesne, 1979), 177–188.

Yates, R. 'The Powers of Evil in the New Testament', *EQ* 52 (1980) 99.

Yoder, J.H. *The Politics of Jesus* (Grand Rapids: Eerdmans, 1972).

Zerwick, M. *Biblical Greek* (Rome: Pontifical Biblical Institute, 1963).

Ziesler, J. *Letter to the Romans*. NTC (London: SCM Press, 1989).

— *The Epistle to the Galatians*. EC (London: Epworth, 1992).

—*The Meaning of Righteousness in Paul. A Linguistic and Theological Enquiry*. SNTSMS 20 (Cambridge: CUP, 1972).

Scripture Index

Romans

1 Corinthians

Philippians

Modern Authors Index

Paternoster Biblical Monographs

(All titles uniform with this volume)
Dates in bold are of projected publication

Joseph Abraham
Eve: Accused or Acquitted?
A Reconsideration of Feminist Readings of the Creation Narrative Texts in Genesis 1–3

Two contrary views dominate contemporary feminist biblical scholarship. One finds in the Bible an unequivocal equality between the sexes from the very creation of humanity, whilst the other sees the biblical text as irredeemably patriarchal and androcentric. Dr Abraham enters into dialogue with both camps as well as introducing his own method of approach. An invaluable tool for any one who is interested in this contemporary debate.

2002 / 0-85364-971-5 / xxiv + 272pp

Octavian D. Baban
Mimesis and Luke's on the Road Encounters in Luke-Acts
Luke's Theology of the Way and its Literary Representation

The book argues on theological and literary (mimetic) grounds that Luke's on-the-road encounters, especially those belonging to the post-Easter period, are part of his complex theology of the Way. Jesus' teaching and that of the apostles is presented by Luke as a challenging answer to the Hellenistic reader's thirst for adventure, good literature, and existential paradigms.

2005 */ 1-84227-253-5 / approx. 374pp*

Paul Barker
The Triumph of Grace in Deuteronomy

This book is a textual and theological analysis of the interaction between the sin and faithlessness of Israel and the grace of Yahweh in response, looking especially at Deuteronomy chapters 1–3, 8–10 and 29–30. The author argues that the grace of Yahweh is determinative for the ongoing relationship between Yahweh and Israel and that Deuteronomy anticipates and fully expects Israel to be faithless.

2004 / 1-84227-226-8 / xxii + 270pp

Jonathan F. Bayes
The Weakness of the Law
God's Law and the Christian in New Testament Perspective

A study of the four New Testament books which refer to the law as weak (Acts, Romans, Galatians, Hebrews) leads to a defence of the third use in the Reformed debate about the law in the life of the believer.

2000 / 0-85364-957-X / xii + 244pp

July 2005

Mark Bonnington

The Antioch Episode of Galatians 2:11-14 in Historical and Cultural Context

The Galatians 2 'incident' in Antioch over table-fellowship suggests significant disagreement between the leading apostles. This book analyses the background to the disagreement by locating the incident within the dynamics of social interaction between Jews and Gentiles. It proposes a new way of understanding the relationship between the individuals and issues involved.

***2005** / 1-84227-050-8 / approx. 350pp*

David Bostock

A Portrayal of Trust

The Theme of Faith in the Hezekiah Narratives

This study provides detailed and sensitive readings of the Hezekiah narratives (2 Kings 18–20 and Isaiah 36–39) from a theological perspective. It concentrates on the theme of faith, using narrative criticism as its methodology. Attention is paid especially to setting, plot, point of view and characterization within the narratives. A largely positive portrayal of Hezekiah emerges that underlines the importance and relevance of scripture.

***2005** / 1-84227-314-0 / approx. 300pp*

Mark Bredin

Jesus, Revolutionary of Peace

A Non-violent Christology in the Book of Revelation

This book aims to demonstrate that the figure of Jesus in the Book of Revelation can best be understood as an active non-violent revolutionary.

2003 / 1-84227-153-9 / xviii + 262pp

Robinson Butarbutar

Paul and Conflict Resolution

An Exegetical Study of Paul's Apostolic Paradigm in 1 Corinthians 9

The author sees the apostolic paradigm in 1 Corinthians 9 as part of Paul's unified arguments in 1 Corinthians 8–10 in which he seeks to mediate in the dispute over the issue of food offered to idols. The book also sees its relevance for dispute-resolution today, taking the conflict within the author's church as an example.

***2006** / 1-84227-315-9 / approx. 280pp*

Daniel J-S Chae

Paul as Apostle to the Gentiles

His Apostolic Self-awareness and its Influence on the Soteriological Argument in Romans

Opposing 'the post-Holocaust interpretation of Romans', Daniel Chae competently demonstrates that Paul argues for the equality of Jew and Gentile in Romans. Chae's fresh exegetical interpretation is academically outstanding and spiritually encouraging.

1997 / 0-85364-829-8 / xiv + 378pp

Luke L. Cheung

The Genre, Composition and Hermeneutics of the Epistle of James

The present work examines the employment of the wisdom genre with a certain compositional structure and the interpretation of the law through the Jesus tradition of the double love command by the author of the Epistle of James to serve his purpose in promoting perfection and warning against doubleness among the eschatologically renewed people of God in the Diaspora.

2003 / 1-84227-062-1 / xvi + 372pp

Youngmo Cho

Spirit and Kingdom in the Writings of Luke and Paul

The relationship between Spirit and Kingdom is a relatively unexplored area in Lukan and Pauline studies. This book offers a fresh perspective of two biblical writers on the subject. It explores the difference between Luke's and Paul's understanding of the Spirit by examining the specific question of the relationship of the concept of the Spirit to the concept of the Kingdom of God in each writer.

***2005** / 1-84227-316-7 / approx. 270pp*

Andrew C. Clark

Parallel Lives

The Relation of Paul to the Apostles in the Lucan Perspective

This study of the Peter-Paul parallels in Acts argues that their purpose was to emphasize the themes of continuity in salvation history and the unity of the Jewish and Gentile missions. New light is shed on Luke's literary techniques, partly through a comparison with Plutarch.

2001 / 1-84227-035-4 / xviii + 386pp

Andrew D. Clarke

Secular and Christian Leadership in Corinth

A Socio-Historical and Exegetical Study of 1 Corinthians 1–6

This volume is an investigation into the leadership structures and dynamics of first-century Roman Corinth. These are compared with the practice of leadership in the Corinthian Christian community which are reflected in 1 Corinthians 1–6, and contrasted with Paul's own principles of Christian leadership.

***2005** / 1-84227-229-2 / 200pp*

Stephen Finamore

God, Order and Chaos

René Girard and the Apocalypse

Readers are often disturbed by the images of destruction in the book of Revelation and unsure why they are unleashed after the exaltation of Jesus. This book examines past approaches to these texts and uses René Girard's theories to revive some old ideas and propose some new ones.

***2005** / 1-84227-197-0 / approx. 344pp*

David G. Firth

Surrendering Retribution in the Psalms

Responses to Violence in the Individual Complaints

In *Surrendering Retribution in the Psalms*, David Firth examines the ways in which the book of Psalms inculcates a model response to violence through the repetition of standard patterns of prayer. Rather than seeking justification for retributive violence, Psalms encourages not only a surrender of the right of retribution to Yahweh, but also sets limits on the retribution that can be sought in imprecations. Arising initially from the author's experience in South Africa, the possibilities of this model to a particular context of violence is then briefly explored.

***2005** / 1-84227-337-X / xviii + 154pp*

Scott J. Hafemann

Suffering and Ministry in the Spirit

Paul's Defence of His Ministry in II Corinthians 2:14–3:3

Shedding new light on the way Paul defended his apostleship, the author offers a careful, detailed study of 2 Corinthians 2:14–3:3 linked with other key passages throughout 1 and 2 Corinthians. Demonstrating the unity and coherence of Paul's argument in this passage, the author shows that Paul's suffering served as the vehicle for revealing God's power and glory through the Spirit.

2000 / 0-85364-967-7 / xiv + 262pp

Scott J. Hafemann

Paul, Moses and the History of Israel

The Letter/Spirit Contrast and the Argument from Scripture in 2 Corinthians 3

An exegetical study of the call of Moses, the second giving of the Law (Exodus 32–34), the new covenant, and the prophetic understanding of the history of Israel in 2 Corinthians 3. Hafemann's work demonstrates Paul's contextual use of the Old Testament and the essential unity between the Law and the Gospel within the context of the distinctive ministries of Moses and Paul.

2005 / 1-84227-317-5 / xii + 498pp

Douglas S. McComiskey

Lukan Theology in the Light of the Gospel's Literary Structure

Luke's Gospel was purposefully written with theology embedded in its patterned literary structure. A critical analysis of this cyclical structure provides new windows into Luke's interpretation of the individual pericopes comprising the Gospel and illuminates several of his theological interests.

2004 / 1-84227-148-2 / xviii + 388pp

Stephen Motyer

Your Father the Devil?

A New Approach to John and 'The Jews'

Who are 'the Jews' in John's Gospel? Defending John against the charge of antisemitism, Motyer argues that, far from demonising the Jews, the Gospel seeks to present Jesus as 'Good News for Jews' in a late first century setting.

1997 / 0-85364-832-8 / xiv + 260pp

Esther Ng

Reconstructing Christian Origins?

The Feminist Theology of Elizabeth Schüssler Fiorenza: An Evaluation

In a detailed evaluation, the author challenges Elizabeth Schüssler Fiorenza's reconstruction of early Christian origins and her underlying presuppositions. The author also presents her own views on women's roles both then and now.

2002 / 1-84227-055-9 / xxiv + 468pp

Robin Parry

Old Testament Story and Christian Ethics

The Rape of Dinah as a Case Study

What is the role of story in ethics and, more particularly, what is the role of Old Testament story in Christian ethics? This book, drawing on the work of contemporary philosophers, argues that narrative is crucial in the ethical shaping of people and, drawing on the work of contemporary Old Testament scholars, that story plays a key role in Old Testament ethics. Parry then argues that when situated in canonical context Old Testament stories can be reappropriated by Christian readers in their own ethical formation. The shocking story of the rape of Dinah and the massacre of the Shechemites provides a fascinating case study for exploring the parameters within which Christian ethical appropriations of Old Testament stories can live.

2004 / 1-84227-210-1 / xx + 350pp

Ian Paul

Power to See the World Anew

The Value of Paul Ricoeur's Hermeneutic of Metaphor in Interpreting the Symbolism of Revelation 12 and 13

This book is a study of the hermeneutics of metaphor of Paul Ricoeur, one of the most important writers on hermeneutics and metaphor of the last century. It sets out the key points of his theory, important criticisms of his work, and how his approach, modified in the light of these criticisms, offers a methodological framework for reading apocalyptic texts.

***2006** / 1-84227-056-7 / approx. 350pp*

Robert L. Plummer

Paul's Understanding of the Church's Mission

Did the Apostle Paul Expect the Early Christian Communities to Evangelize?

This book engages in a careful study of Paul's letters to determine if the apostle expected the communities to which he wrote to engage in missionary activity. It helpfully summarizes the discussion on this debated issue, judiciously handling contested texts, and provides a way forward in addressing this critical question. While admitting that Paul rarely explicitly commands the communities he founded to evangelize, Plummer amasses significant incidental data to provide a convincing case that Paul did indeed expect his churches to engage in mission activity. Throughout the study, Plummer progressively builds a theological basis for the church's mission that is both distinctively Pauline and compelling.

***2006** / 1-84227-333-7 / approx. 324pp*

July 2005

David Powys

'Hell': A Hard Look at a Hard Question

The Fate of the Unrighteous in New Testament Thought

This comprehensive treatment seeks to unlock the original meaning of terms and phrases long thought to support the traditional doctrine of hell. It concludes that there is an alternative—one which is more biblical, and which can positively revive the rationale for Christian mission.

1997 / 0-85364-831-X / xxii + 478pp

Sorin Sabou

Between Horror and Hope

Paul's Metaphorical Language of Death in Romans 6.1-11

This book argues that Paul's metaphorical language of death in Romans 6.1-11 conveys two aspects: horror and hope. The 'horror' aspect is conveyed by the 'crucifixion' language, and the 'hope' aspect by 'burial' language. The life of the Christian believer is understood, as relationship with sin is concerned ('death to sin'), between these two realities: horror and hope.

***2005** / 1-84227-322-1 / approx. 224pp*

Rosalind Selby

The Comical Doctrine

The Epistemology of New Testament Hermeneutics

This book argues that the gospel breaks through postmodernity's critique of truth and the referential possibilities of textuality with its gift of grace. With a rigorous, philosophical challenge to modernist and postmodernist assumptions, Selby offers an alternative epistemology to all who would still read with faith *and* with academic credibility.

***2005** / 1-84227-212-8 / approx. 350pp*

Kiwoong Son

Zion Symbolism in Hebrews

Hebrews 12.18-24 as a Hermeneutical Key to the Epistle

This book challenges the general tendency of understanding the Epistle to the Hebrews against a Hellenistic background and suggests that the Epistle should be understood in the light of the Jewish apocalyptic tradition. The author especially argues for the importance of the theological symbolism of Sinai and Zion (Heb. 12:18-24) as it provides the Epistle's theological background as well as the rhetorical basis of the superiority motif of Jesus throughout the Epistle.

***2005** / 1-84227-368-X / approx. 280pp*

July 2005

Kevin Walton

Thou Traveller Unknown

The Presence and Absence of God in the Jacob Narrative

The author offers a fresh reading of the story of Jacob in the book of Genesis through the paradox of divine presence and absence. The work also seeks to make a contribution to Pentateuchal studies by bringing together a close reading of the final text with historical critical insights, doing justice to the text's historical depth, final form and canonical status.

2003 / 1-84227-059-1 / xvi + 238pp

George M. Wieland

The Significance of Salvation

A Study of Salvation Language in the Pastoral Epistles

The language and ideas of salvation pervade the three Pastoral Epistles. This study offers a close examination of their soteriological statements. In all three letters the idea of salvation is found to play a vital paraenetic role, but each also exhibits distinctive soteriological emphases. The results challenge common assumptions about the Pastoral Epistles as a corpus.

***2005** / 1-84227-257-8 / approx. 324pp*

Alistair Wilson

When Will These Things Happen?

A Study of Jesus as Judge in Matthew 21–25

This study seeks to allow Matthew's carefully constructed presentation of Jesus to be given full weight in the modern evaluation of Jesus' eschatology. Careful analysis of the text of Matthew 21–25 reveals Jesus to be standing firmly in the Jewish prophetic and wisdom traditions as he proclaims and enacts imminent judgement on the Jewish authorities then boldly claims the central role in the final and universal judgement.

2004 / 1-84227-146-6 / xxii + 272pp

Lindsay Wilson

Joseph Wise and Otherwise

The Intersection of Covenant and Wisdom in Genesis 37–50

This book offers a careful literary reading of Genesis 37–50 that argues that the Joseph story contains both strong covenant themes and many wisdom-like elements. The connections between the two helps to explore how covenant and wisdom might intersect in an integrated biblical theology.

2004 / 1-84227-140-7 / xvi + 340pp

July 2005

Stephen I. Wright

The Voice of Jesus

Studies in the Interpretation of Six Gospel Parables

This literary study considers how the 'voice' of Jesus has been heard in different periods of parable interpretation, and how the categories of figure and trope may help us towards a sensitive reading of the parables today.

2000 / 0-85364-975-8 / xiv + 280pp

July 2005

Paternoster Theological Monographs

(All titles uniform with this volume)

Dates in bold are of projected publication

Emil Bartos

Deification in Eastern Orthodox Theology

An Evaluation and Critique of the Theology of Dumitru Staniloae

Bartos studies a fundamental yet neglected aspect of Orthodox theology: deification. By examining the doctrines of anthropology, christology, soteriology and ecclesiology as they relate to deification, he provides an important contribution to contemporary dialogue between Eastern and Western theologians.

1999 / 0-85364-956-1 / xii + 370pp

Graham Buxton

The Trinity, Creation and Pastoral Ministry

Imaging the Perichoretic God

In this book the author proposes a three-way conversation between theology, science and pastoral ministry. His approach draws on a Trinitarian understanding of God as a relational being of love, whose life 'spills over' into all created reality, human and non-human. By locating human meaning and purpose within God's 'creation-community' this book offers the possibility of a transforming engagement between those in pastoral ministry and the scientific community.

***2005** / 1-84227-369-8 / approx. 380 pp*

Iain D. Campbell

Fixing the Indemnity

The Life and Work of George Adam Smith

When Old Testament scholar George Adam Smith (1856–1942) delivered the Lyman Beecher lectures at Yale University in 1899, he confidently declared that 'modern criticism has won its war against traditional theories. It only remains to fix the amount of the indemnity.' In this biography, Iain D. Campbell assesses Smith's critical approach to the Old Testament and evaluates its consequences, showing that Smith's life and work still raises questions about the relationship between biblical scholarship and evangelical faith.

2004 / 1-84227-228-4 / xx + 256pp

July 2005

Tim Chester

Mission and the Coming of God

Eschatology, the Trinity and Mission in the Theology of Jürgen Moltmann

This book explores the theology and missiology of the influential contemporary theologian, Jürgen Moltmann. It highlights the important contribution Moltmann has made while offering a critique of his thought from an evangelical perspective. In so doing, it touches on pertinent issues for evangelical missiology. The conclusion takes Calvin as a starting point, proposing 'an eschatology of the cross' which offers a critique of the over-realised eschatologies in liberation theology and certain forms of evangelicalism.

***2006** / 1-84227-320-5 / approx. 224pp*

Sylvia Wilkey Collinson

Making Disciples

The Significance of Jesus' Educational Strategy for Today's Church

This study examines the biblical practice of discipling, formulates a definition, and makes comparisons with modern models of education. A recommendation is made for greater attention to its practice today.

2004 / 1-84227-116-4 / xiv + 278pp

Darrell Cosden

A Theology of Work

Work and the New Creation

Through dialogue with Moltmann, Pope John Paul II and others, this book develops a genitive 'theology of work', presenting a theological definition of work and a model for a theological ethics of work that shows work's nature, value and meaning now and eschatologically. Work is shown to be a transformative activity consisting of three dynamically inter-related dimensions: the instrumental, relational and ontological.

2005 / 1-84227-332-9 / xvi + 208pp

Stephen M. Dunning

The Crisis and the Quest

A Kierkegaardian Reading of Charles Williams

Employing Kierkegaardian categories and analysis, this study investigates both the central crisis in Charles Williams's authorship between hermetism and Christianity (Kierkegaard's Religions A and B), and the quest to resolve this crisis, a quest that ultimately presses the bounds of orthodoxy.

2000 / 0-85364-985-5 / xxiv + 254pp

July 2005

Keith Ferdinando

The Triumph of Christ in African Perspective

A Study of Demonology and Redemption in the African Context

The book explores the implications of the gospel for traditional African fears of occult aggression. It analyses such traditional approaches to suffering and biblical responses to fears of demonic evil, concluding with an evaluation of African beliefs from the perspective of the gospel.

1999 / 0-85364-830-1 / xviii + 450pp

Andrew Goddard

Living the Word, Resisting the World

The Life and Thought of Jacques Ellul

This work offers a definitive study of both the life and thought of the French Reformed thinker Jacques Ellul (1912-1994). It will prove an indispensable resource for those interested in this influential theologian and sociologist and for Christian ethics and political thought generally.

2002 / 1-84227-053-2 / xxiv + 378pp

David Hilborn

The Words of our Lips

Language-Use in Free Church Worship

Studies of liturgical language have tended to focus on the written canons of Roman Catholic and Anglican communities. By contrast, David Hilborn analyses the more extemporary approach of English Nonconformity. Drawing on recent developments in linguistic pragmatics, he explores similarities and differences between 'fixed' and 'free' worship, and argues for the interdependence of each.

***2006** / 0-85364-977-4 / approx. 350pp*

Roger Hitching

The Church and Deaf People

A Study of Identity, Communication and Relationships with Special Reference to the Ecclesiology of Jürgen Moltmann

In *The Church and Deaf People* Roger Hitching sensitively examines the history and present experience of deaf people and finds similarities between aspects of sign language and Moltmann's theological method that 'open up' new ways of understanding theological concepts.

2003 / 1-84227-222-5 / xxii + 236pp

July 2005

John G. Kelly

One God, One People

The Differentiated Unity of the People of God in the Theology of Jürgen Moltmann

The author expounds and critiques Moltmann's doctrine of God and highlights the systematic connections between it and Moltmann's influential discussion of Israel. He then proposes a fresh approach to Jewish–Christian relations building on Moltmann's work using insights from Habermas and Rawls.

***2005** / 0-85346-969-3 / approx. 350pp*

Mark F.W. Lovatt

Confronting the Will-to-Power

A Reconsideration of the Theology of Reinhold Niebuhr

Confronting the Will-to-Power is an analysis of the theology of Reinhold Niebuhr, arguing that his work is an attempt to identify, and provide a practical theological answer to, the existence and nature of human evil.

2001 / 1-84227-054-0 / xviii + 216pp

Neil B. MacDonald

Karl Barth and the Strange New World within the Bible

Barth, Wittgenstein, and the Metadilemmas of the Enlightenment

Barth's discovery of the strange new world within the Bible is examined in the context of Kant, Hume, Overbeck, and, most importantly, Wittgenstein. MacDonald covers some fundamental issues in theology today: epistemology, the final form of the text and biblical truth-claims.

2000 / 0-85364-970-7 / xxvi + 374pp

Keith A. Mascord

Alvin Plantinga and Christian Apologetics

This book draws together the contributions of the philosopher Alvin Plantinga to the major contemporary challenges to Christian belief, highlighting in particular his ground-breaking work in epistemology and the problem of evil. Plantinga's theory that both theistic and Christian belief is warrantedly basic is explored and critiqued, and an assessment offered as to the significance of his work for apologetic theory and practice.

***2005** / 1-84227-256-X / approx. 304pp*

Gillian McCulloch

The Deconstruction of Dualism in Theology

With Reference to Ecofeminist Theology and New Age Spirituality

This book challenges eco-theological anti-dualism in Christian theology, arguing that dualism has a twofold function in Christian religious discourse. Firstly, it enables us to express the discontinuities and divisions that are part of the process of reality. Secondly, dualistic language allows us to express the mysteries of divine transcendence/immanence and the survival of the soul without collapsing into monism and materialism, both of which are problematic for Christian epistemology.

2002 / 1-84227-044-3 / xii + 282pp

Leslie McCurdy

Attributes and Atonement

The Holy Love of God in the Theology of P.T. Forsyth

Attributes and Atonement is an intriguing full-length study of P.T. Forsyth's doctrine of the cross as it relates particularly to God's holy love. It includes an unparalleled bibliography of both primary and secondary material relating to Forsyth.

1999 / 0-85364-833-6 / xiv + 328pp

Nozomu Miyahira

Towards a Theology of the Concord of God

A Japanese Perspective on the Trinity

This book introduces a new Japanese theology and a unique Trinitarian formula based on the Japanese intellectual climate: three betweennesses and one concord. It also presents a new interpretation of the Trinity, a co-subordinationism, which is in line with orthodox Trinitarianism; each single person of the Trinity is eternally and equally subordinate (or serviceable) to the other persons, so that they retain the mutual dynamic equality.

2000 / 0-85364-863-8 / xiv + 256pp

Eddy José Muskus

The Origins and Early Development of Liberation Theology in Latin America

With Particular Reference to Gustavo Gutiérrez

This work challenges the fundamental premise of Liberation Theology, 'opting for the poor', and its claim that Christ is found in them. It also argues that Liberation Theology emerged as a direct result of the failure of the Roman Catholic Church in Latin America.

2002 / 0-85364-974-X / xiv + 296pp

July 2005

Jim Purves

The Triune God and the Charismatic Movement

A Critical Appraisal from a Scottish Perspective

All emotion and no theology? Or a fundamental challenge to reappraise and realign our trinitarian theology in the light of Christian experience? This study of charismatic renewal as it found expression within Scotland at the end of the twentieth century evaluates the use of Patristic, Reformed and contemporary models of the Trinity in explaining the workings of the Holy Spirit.

2004 / 1-84227-321-3 / xxiv + 246pp

Anna Robbins

Methods in the Madness

Diversity in Twentieth-Century Christian Social Ethics

The author compares the ethical methods of Walter Rauschenbusch, Reinhold Niebuhr and others. She argues that unless Christians are clear about the ways that theology and philosophy are expressed practically they may lose the ability to discuss social ethics across contexts, let alone reach effective agreements.

2004 / 1-84227-211-X / xx + 294pp

Ed Rybarczyk

Beyond Salvation

Eastern Orthodoxy and Classical Pentecostalism on Becoming Like Christ

At first glance eastern Orthodoxy and classical Pentecostalism seem quite distinct. This ground-breaking study shows they share much in common, especially as it concerns the experiential elements of following Christ. Both traditions assert that authentic Christianity transcends the wooden categories of modernism.

2004 / 1-84227-144-X / xii + 356pp

Signe Sandsmark

Is World View Neutral Education Possible and Desirable?

A Christian Response to Liberal Arguments

(Published jointly with The Stapleford Centre)

This book discusses reasons for belief in world view neutrality, and argues that 'neutral' education will have a hidden, but strong world view influence. It discusses the place for Christian education in the common school.

2000 / 0-85364-973-1 / xiv + 182pp

July 2005

Hazel Sherman

Reading Zechariah

The Allegorical Tradition of Biblical Interpretation through the Commentary of Didymus the Blind and Theodore of Mopsuestia

A close reading of the commentary on Zechariah by Didymus the Blind alongside that of Theodore of Mopsuestia suggests that popular categorising of Antiochene and Alexandrian biblical exegesis as 'historical' or 'allegorical' is inadequate and misleading.

***2005** / 1-84227-213-6 / approx. 280pp*

Andrew Sloane

On Being a Christian in the Academy

Nicholas Wolterstorff and the Practice of Christian Scholarship

An exposition and critical appraisal of Nicholas Wolterstorff's epistemology in the light of the philosophy of science, and an application of his thought to the practice of Christian scholarship.

2003 / 1-84227-058-3 / xvi + 274pp

Damon W.K. So

Jesus' Revelation of His Father

A Narrative-Conceptual Study of the Trinity with Special Reference to Karl Barth

This book explores the trinitarian dynamics in the context of Jesus' revelation of his Father in his earthly ministry with references to key passages in Matthew's Gospel. It develops from the exegeses of these passages a non-linear concept of revelation which links Jesus' communion with his Father to his revelatory words and actions through a nuanced understanding of the Holy Spirit, with references to K. Barth, G.W.H. Lampe, J.D.G. Dunn and E. Irving.

***2005** / 1-84227-323-X / approx. 380pp*

Daniel Strange

The Possibility of Salvation Among the Unevangelised

An Analysis of Inclusivism in Recent Evangelical Theology

For evangelical theologians the 'fate of the unevangelised' impinges upon fundamental tenets of evangelical identity. The position known as 'inclusivism', defined by the belief that the unevangelised can be ontologically saved by Christ whilst being epistemologically unaware of him, has been defended most vigorously by the Canadian evangelical Clark H. Pinnock. Through a detailed analysis and critique of Pinnock's work, this book examines a cluster of issues surrounding the unevangelised and its implications for christology, soteriology and the doctrine of revelation.

2002 / 1-84227-047-8 / xviii + 362pp

July 2005

Scott Swain

God According to the Gospel

Biblical Narrative and the Identity of God in the Theology of Robert W. Jenson

Robert W. Jenson is one of the leading voices in contemporary Trinitarian theology. His boldest contribution in this area concerns his use of biblical narrative both to ground and explicate the Christian doctrine of God. *God According to the Gospel* critically examines Jenson's proposal and suggests an alternative way of reading the biblical portrayal of the triune God.

***2006** / 1-84227-258-6 / approx. 180pp*

Justyn Terry

The Justifying Judgement of God

A Reassessment of the Place of Judgement in the Saving Work of Christ

The argument of this book is that judgement, understood as the whole process of bringing justice, is the primary metaphor of atonement, with others, such as victory, redemption and sacrifice, subordinate to it. Judgement also provides the proper context for understanding penal substitution and the call to repentance, baptism, eucharist and holiness.

***2005** / 1-84227-370-1 / approx. 274 pp*

Graham Tomlin

The Power of the Cross

Theology and the Death of Christ in Paul, Luther and Pascal

This book explores the theology of the cross in St Paul, Luther and Pascal. It offers new perspectives on the theology of each, and some implications for the nature of power, apologetics, theology and church life in a postmodern context.

1999 / 0-85364-984-7 / xiv + 344pp

Adonis Vidu

Postliberal Theological Method

A Critical Study

The postliberal theology of Hans Frei, George Lindbeck, Ronald Thiemann, John Milbank and others is one of the more influential contemporary options. This book focuses on several aspects pertaining to its theological method, specifically its understanding of background, hermeneutics, epistemic justification, ontology, the nature of doctrine and, finally, Christological method.

***2005** / 1-84227-395-7 / approx. 324pp*

July 2005

Graham J. Watts

Revelation and the Spirit

A Comparative Study of the Relationship between the Doctrine of Revelation and Pneumatology in the Theology of Eberhard Jüngel and of Wolfhart Pannenberg

The relationship between revelation and pneumatology is relatively unexplored. This approach offers a fresh angle on two important twentieth century theologians and raises pneumatological questions which are theologically crucial and relevant to mission in a postmodern culture.

***2005** / 1-84227-104-0 / xxii + 232pp*

Nigel G. Wright

Disavowing Constantine

Mission, Church and the Social Order in the Theologies of John Howard Yoder and Jürgen Moltmann

This book is a timely restatement of a radical theology of church and state in the Anabaptist and Baptist tradition. Dr Wright constructs his argument in dialogue and debate with Yoder and Moltmann, major contributors to a free church perspective.

2000 / 0-85364-978-2 / xvi + 252pp

July 2005

www.ingramcontent.com/pod-product-compliance
Lightning Source LLC
LaVergne TN
LVHW020523100826
845148LV00010B/1318

9781606084755